Lecture Notes in Computer Science 14725

The series Lecture Notes in Computer Science (LNCS), including its subseries Lecture Notes in Artificial Intelligence (LNAI) and Lecture Notes in Bioinformatics (LNBI), has established itself as a medium for the publication of new developments in computer science and information technology research, teaching, and education.

LNCS enjoys close cooperation with the computer science R & D community, the series counts many renowned academics among its volume editors and paper authors, and collaborates with prestigious societies. Its mission is to serve this international community by providing an invaluable service, mainly focused on the publication of conference and workshop proceedings and postproceedings. LNCS commenced publication in 1973.

Qin Gao · Jia Zhou

Editors

Human Aspects of IT for the Aged Population

10th International Conference, ITAP 2024
Held as Part of the 26th HCI International Conference, HCII 2024
Washington, DC, USA, June 29 – July 4, 2024
Proceedings, Part I

 Springer

Editors
Qin Gao
Tsinghua University
Beijing, China

Jia Zhou
Chongqing University
Chongqing, China

ISSN 0302-9743   ISSN 1611-3349 (electronic)
Lecture Notes in Computer Science
ISBN 978-3-031-61542-9   ISBN 978-3-031-61543-6 (eBook)
https://doi.org/10.1007/978-3-031-61543-6

This Springer imprint is published by the registered company Springer Nature Switzerland AG
The registered company address is: Gewerbestrasse 11, 6330 Cham, Switzerland

If disposing of this product, please recycle the paper.

Foreword

This year we celebrate 40 years since the establishment of the HCI International (HCII) Conference, which has been a hub for presenting groundbreaking research and novel ideas and collaboration for people from all over the world.

The HCII conference was founded in 1984 by Prof. Gavriel Salvendy (Purdue University, USA, Tsinghua University, P.R. China, and University of Central Florida, USA) and the first event of the series, "1st USA-Japan Conference on Human-Computer Interaction", was held in Honolulu, Hawaii, USA, 18–20 August. Since then, HCI International is held jointly with several Thematic Areas and Affiliated Conferences, with each one under the auspices of a distinguished international Program Board and under one management and one registration. Twenty-six HCI International Conferences have been organized so far (every two years until 2013, and annually thereafter).

Over the years, this conference has served as a platform for scholars, researchers, industry experts and students to exchange ideas, connect, and address challenges in the ever-evolving HCI field. Throughout these 40 years, the conference has evolved itself, adapting to new technologies and emerging trends, while staying committed to its core mission of advancing knowledge and driving change.

As we celebrate this milestone anniversary, we reflect on the contributions of its founding members and appreciate the commitment of its current and past Affiliated Conference Program Board Chairs and members. We are also thankful to all past conference attendees who have shaped this community into what it is today.

The 26th International Conference on Human-Computer Interaction, HCI International 2024 (HCII 2024), was held as a 'hybrid' event at the Washington Hilton Hotel, Washington, DC, USA, during 29 June – 4 July 2024. It incorporated the 21 thematic areas and affiliated conferences listed below.

A total of 5108 individuals from academia, research institutes, industry, and government agencies from 85 countries submitted contributions, and 1271 papers and 309 posters were included in the volumes of the proceedings that were published just before the start of the conference, these are listed below. The contributions thoroughly cover the entire field of human-computer interaction, addressing major advances in knowledge and effective use of computers in a variety of application areas. These papers provide academics, researchers, engineers, scientists, practitioners and students with state-of-the-art information on the most recent advances in HCI.

The HCI International (HCII) conference also offers the option of presenting 'Late Breaking Work', and this applies both for papers and posters, with corresponding volumes of proceedings that will be published after the conference. Full papers will be included in the 'HCII 2024 - Late Breaking Papers' volumes of the proceedings to be published in the Springer LNCS series, while 'Poster Extended Abstracts' will be included as short research papers in the 'HCII 2024 - Late Breaking Posters' volumes to be published in the Springer CCIS series.

I would like to thank the Program Board Chairs and the members of the Program Boards of all thematic areas and affiliated conferences for their contribution towards the high scientific quality and overall success of the HCI International 2024 conference. Their manifold support in terms of paper reviewing (single-blind review process, with a minimum of two reviews per submission), session organization and their willingness to act as goodwill ambassadors for the conference is most highly appreciated.

This conference would not have been possible without the continuous and unwavering support and advice of Gavriel Salvendy, founder, General Chair Emeritus, and Scientific Advisor. For his outstanding efforts, I would like to express my sincere appreciation to Abbas Moallem, Communications Chair and Editor of HCI International News.

July 2024   Constantine Stephanidis

HCI International 2024 Thematic Areas
and Affiliated Conferences

- HCI: Human-Computer Interaction Thematic Area
- HIMI: Human Interface and the Management of Information Thematic Area
- EPCE: 21st International Conference on Engineering Psychology and Cognitive Ergonomics
- AC: 18th International Conference on Augmented Cognition
- UAHCI: 18th International Conference on Universal Access in Human-Computer Interaction
- CCD: 16th International Conference on Cross-Cultural Design
- SCSM: 16th International Conference on Social Computing and Social Media
- VAMR: 16th International Conference on Virtual, Augmented and Mixed Reality
- DHM: 15th International Conference on Digital Human Modeling & Applications in Health, Safety, Ergonomics & Risk Management
- DUXU: 13th International Conference on Design, User Experience and Usability
- C&C: 12th International Conference on Culture and Computing
- DAPI: 12th International Conference on Distributed, Ambient and Pervasive Interactions
- HCIBGO: 11th International Conference on HCI in Business, Government and Organizations
- LCT: 11th International Conference on Learning and Collaboration Technologies
- ITAP: 10th International Conference on Human Aspects of IT for the Aged Population
- AIS: 6th International Conference on Adaptive Instructional Systems
- HCI-CPT: 6th International Conference on HCI for Cybersecurity, Privacy and Trust
- HCI-Games: 6th International Conference on HCI in Games
- MobiTAS: 6th International Conference on HCI in Mobility, Transport and Automotive Systems
- AI-HCI: 5th International Conference on Artificial Intelligence in HCI
- MOBILE: 5th International Conference on Human-Centered Design, Operation and Evaluation of Mobile Communications

List of Conference Proceedings Volumes Appearing Before the Conference

1. LNCS 14684, Human-Computer Interaction: Part I, edited by Masaaki Kurosu and Ayako Hashizume
2. LNCS 14685, Human-Computer Interaction: Part II, edited by Masaaki Kurosu and Ayako Hashizume
3. LNCS 14686, Human-Computer Interaction: Part III, edited by Masaaki Kurosu and Ayako Hashizume
4. LNCS 14687, Human-Computer Interaction: Part IV, edited by Masaaki Kurosu and Ayako Hashizume
5. LNCS 14688, Human-Computer Interaction: Part V, edited by Masaaki Kurosu and Ayako Hashizume
6. LNCS 14689, Human Interface and the Management of Information: Part I, edited by Hirohiko Mori and Yumi Asahi
7. LNCS 14690, Human Interface and the Management of Information: Part II, edited by Hirohiko Mori and Yumi Asahi
8. LNCS 14691, Human Interface and the Management of Information: Part III, edited by Hirohiko Mori and Yumi Asahi
9. LNAI 14692, Engineering Psychology and Cognitive Ergonomics: Part I, edited by Don Harris and Wen-Chin Li
10. LNAI 14693, Engineering Psychology and Cognitive Ergonomics: Part II, edited by Don Harris and Wen-Chin Li
11. LNAI 14694, Augmented Cognition, Part I, edited by Dylan D. Schmorrow and Cali M. Fidopiastis
12. LNAI 14695, Augmented Cognition, Part II, edited by Dylan D. Schmorrow and Cali M. Fidopiastis
13. LNCS 14696, Universal Access in Human-Computer Interaction: Part I, edited by Margherita Antona and Constantine Stephanidis
14. LNCS 14697, Universal Access in Human-Computer Interaction: Part II, edited by Margherita Antona and Constantine Stephanidis
15. LNCS 14698, Universal Access in Human-Computer Interaction: Part III, edited by Margherita Antona and Constantine Stephanidis
16. LNCS 14699, Cross-Cultural Design: Part I, edited by Pei-Luen Patrick Rau
17. LNCS 14700, Cross-Cultural Design: Part II, edited by Pei-Luen Patrick Rau
18. LNCS 14701, Cross-Cultural Design: Part III, edited by Pei-Luen Patrick Rau
19. LNCS 14702, Cross-Cultural Design: Part IV, edited by Pei-Luen Patrick Rau
20. LNCS 14703, Social Computing and Social Media: Part I, edited by Adela Coman and Simona Vasilache
21. LNCS 14704, Social Computing and Social Media: Part II, edited by Adela Coman and Simona Vasilache
22. LNCS 14705, Social Computing and Social Media: Part III, edited by Adela Coman and Simona Vasilache

47. LNCS 14730, HCI in Games: Part I, edited by Xiaowen Fang
48. LNCS 14731, HCI in Games: Part II, edited by Xiaowen Fang
49. LNCS 14732, HCI in Mobility, Transport and Automotive Systems: Part I, edited by Heidi Krömker
50. LNCS 14733, HCI in Mobility, Transport and Automotive Systems: Part II, edited by Heidi Krömker
51. LNAI 14734, Artificial Intelligence in HCI: Part I, edited by Helmut Degen and Stavroula Ntoa
52. LNAI 14735, Artificial Intelligence in HCI: Part II, edited by Helmut Degen and Stavroula Ntoa
53. LNAI 14736, Artificial Intelligence in HCI: Part III, edited by Helmut Degen and Stavroula Ntoa
54. LNCS 14737, Design, Operation and Evaluation of Mobile Communications: Part I, edited by June Wei and George Margetis
55. LNCS 14738, Design, Operation and Evaluation of Mobile Communications: Part II, edited by June Wei and George Margetis
56. CCIS 2114, HCI International 2024 Posters - Part I, edited by Constantine Stephanidis, Margherita Antona, Stavroula Ntoa and Gavriel Salvendy
57. CCIS 2115, HCI International 2024 Posters - Part II, edited by Constantine Stephanidis, Margherita Antona, Stavroula Ntoa and Gavriel Salvendy
58. CCIS 2116, HCI International 2024 Posters - Part III, edited by Constantine Stephanidis, Margherita Antona, Stavroula Ntoa and Gavriel Salvendy
59. CCIS 2117, HCI International 2024 Posters - Part IV, edited by Constantine Stephanidis, Margherita Antona, Stavroula Ntoa and Gavriel Salvendy
60. CCIS 2118, HCI International 2024 Posters - Part V, edited by Constantine Stephanidis, Margherita Antona, Stavroula Ntoa and Gavriel Salvendy
61. CCIS 2119, HCI International 2024 Posters - Part VI, edited by Constantine Stephanidis, Margherita Antona, Stavroula Ntoa and Gavriel Salvendy
62. CCIS 2120, HCI International 2024 Posters - Part VII, edited by Constantine Stephanidis, Margherita Antona, Stavroula Ntoa and Gavriel Salvendy

https://2024.hci.international/proceedings

Preface

The 10th International Conference on Human Aspects of IT for the Aged Population (ITAP 2024) was part of HCI International 2024. The ITAP conference addresses the design, adaptation, and use of IT technologies targeted to older people in order to counterbalance ability changes due to age, support cognitive, physical, and social activities, and maintain independent living and quality of life.

This year's proceedings address a variety of topics. While understanding and addressing the needs and constraints of older individuals, along with designing technologies that support and empower them, remains a consistent theme, this year's discussions focus more on the challenge posed by rapidly emerging technologies. There is a notable increase in research focusing on innovative design approaches and methods aimed at integrating older adults into ongoing technological advancements. At the same time, researchers have explored more methods and strategies to help older people to acquire new digital skills in order to stay current with evolving technologies. Another emerging theme of this year is the re-examination of chatbots and AI, particularly in light of recent advancements in large language models, regarding their potential to benefit older people's quality of life and possible approaches to incorporate older adults' requirements into the design lifecycle of these technologies. These changes highlight the importance of design approaches adopting a dynamic view of the relationship between older people and digital technologies. Continuous innovation and adaptation are crucial to ensure that the needs of the aging population are integral to the ongoing evolution of technology.

Two volumes of the HCII 2024 proceedings are dedicated to this year's edition of the ITAP conference. The first focuses on topics related to Designing for Older Adults; Older Adults' User Experience; Older Adults' Digital Competences and User Behavior; and Aging and Social Media. The second focuses on topics related to Healthy Aging; Supporting Mobility and Leisure; and Aging, Chatbots and AI.

The papers of these volumes were accepted for publication after a minimum of two single-blind reviews from the members of the ITAP Program Board or, in some cases, from members of the Program Boards of other affiliated conferences. We would like to thank all of them for their invaluable contribution, support, and efforts.

July 2024

Qin Gao
Jia Zhou

10th International Conference on Human Aspects of IT for the Aged Population (ITAP 2024)

HCI International 2025 Conference

The 27th International Conference on Human-Computer Interaction, HCI International 2025, will be held jointly with the affiliated conferences at the Swedish Exhibition & Congress Centre and Gothia Towers Hotel, Gothenburg, Sweden, June 22–27, 2025. It will cover a broad spectrum of themes related to Human-Computer Interaction, including theoretical issues, methods, tools, processes, and case studies in HCI design, as well as novel interaction techniques, interfaces, and applications. The proceedings will be published by Springer. More information will become available on the conference website: https://2025.hci.international/.

General Chair
Prof. Constantine Stephanidis
University of Crete and ICS-FORTH
Heraklion, Crete, Greece
Email: general_chair@2025.hci.international

https://2025.hci.international/

Contents – Part I

Older Adults' User Experience

Older Adults' Digital Competences and User Behavior

Aging and Social Media

Contents – Part II

Supporting Mobility and Leisure

Aging, Chatbots and AI

Designing for Older Adults

Online Semi-structured Interviews to Better Capture Generational Media Actions: The Relevance of Relaxed, Participative and Reflexive Approaches

Maria José Brites[1]([⊠]) [iD], Margarida Maneta[1] [iD], Mariana S. Müller[1] [iD], and Inês Amaral[2,3] [iD]

[1] Lusófona University, CICANT, Porto, Portugal
maria.jose.brites@ulusofona.pt
[2] Faculty of Arts and Humanities, University of Coimbra, Coimbra, Portugal
[3] Centre for Social Studies, University of Coimbra, Coimbra, Portugal

Abstract. This paper presents thoughts on the use of online semi-structured interviews in a participatory format. On one hand, in the process of interviewing and on the other by using complementary methods such as media diaries and its associated online ethnography techniques. One of the challenges of audience research is the capture of the "audiencing" [1] process, in this paper we rely on two research projects to better discuss and consider forms of doing it, in arid research contexts, such as online and with a (inter)generational dimension.

Keywords: Semi-structured interviews · media diaries · participatory methods

1 Introduction

This article proposes ways to find formats and techniques to better capture audiences of different ages and considers ways to engage them. These concerns usually occur particularly in research where there is an intention to create participatory environments, even if the research design does not involve an extended presence of the research team in a given context or previous familiarity with participants. These challenges are particularly important in audience research contexts, where it is necessary to take options in a fragmented media space that is increasingly difficult to capture consistently, especially when different generations of participants are involved within the same research and there is also an interest in thinking about different generations in their multiple ways of relating to each other and to media.

These challenges are anchored around two axes that seem to be fundamental: 1 – Considering action during the process of interviewing online, finding ways of ensuring environments for semi-structured interviews more relaxed, participatory, and reflective; 2 - Thinking about possible complementarities with the use of media diaries, as a digital ethnographic technique, better able to fix and capture the moment of the audience.

© The Author(s), under exclusive license to Springer Nature Switzerland AG 2024
Q. Gao and J. Zhou (Eds.): HCII 2024, LNCS 14725, pp. 3–12, 2024.
https://doi.org/10.1007/978-3-031-61543-6_1

2 Theoretical Overview

One of the challenges of qualitative research in the field of media studies, particularly journalism, is to capture "audiencing" [1] at the moment [2–5]. Audience studies centre substantially on the use of semi-structured interviews [3]. Our reflection will focus on two data collection techniques: the semi-structured interview [6–12] and the media diaries [13–15]. Our proposals focus on what can be understood as a performative and participatory space, capable of ensuring the participants' agency. This can be significantly interesting for researchers looking to capture audiences in depth and in their multiplicities, but it may not be sufficient for capturing relaxed, non-normative environments that translate people's feelings towards media and news spaces as faithfully as possible. As research increasingly moves into digital spaces, capturing the action and involving participants becomes more difficult.

When audience research began to gain relevance in the 1980s, it centred on a more qualitative approach, capable of enabling a holistic understanding of social phenomena. Today, one of the challenges from the point of view of capturing media use choices is more challenging and means adapting to speed, multiple possible choices, and apprehending action indirectly in the interview process.

It is, therefore, necessary to question the research, its objectives, means, and possible implications, focusing on the ontology of the research [16]. In qualitative research, these questions arise in greater depth, as it may have to fulfil more validation purposes. Birgitta Höijer [16] points to the importance of knowing who the interviewees are and what they represent when they are chosen, because what the researcher is looking for is "good informants" [16]. They have previous collective experiences that facilitate the possibility of finding dialectics beyond the interview situation itself [16]. With research validation in mind, Kim Schrøder [17] points out that the researcher must constantly reflect and be able to stimulate other scientific research.

Based on these questions, one of the constant difficulties is knowing which methodological guidelines are the most appropriate. Methodology is generally understood as determining the paths and instruments used to carry out scientific research. Methodology presupposes the research design, from hypotheses creation to the enquiry techniques. The methodological orientation tells us about the researcher's choices, from the theoretical framework and contexts, through the indication of the object, to the determination of the method and techniques. It reveals the research set-up.

In a media world that is constantly changing, the semi-structured interview continues to be a prevalent technique in media studies, although the challenges associated with it are being renewed. This relationship, which must be sufficiently distant and sufficiently close, is not easy to achieve [18]. In this case, we are looking at the interview as a provider of information that gives us a sense of reception. Reception analysis establishes that texts and their recipients are complementary elements in analysing an area of research that leads us to the discursive and social aspects of communication.

3 Methodological Approach

This article aims to provide a space for reflection on the inclusion of participatory dynamics in research that does not follow longitudinal logics that end up facilitating processes of proximity between the participants and the research [18, 19]. These aspects are discussed here within the interview process itself and also in conjunction with this technique through other complementary data collection techniques, such as diaries, here assumed not only as complementary but also in the context of digital ethnography.

To better discern these dynamics, we are going to rely on the methodological research designs of two Portuguese research projects, YouNDigital - Youth, News and Digital Citizenship (PTDC/COM-OUT/0243/2021) and MyGender (PTDC/COM-CSS/5947/2020).

YouNDigital project is being conducted in Portugal and the qualitative fieldwork part of this project was initiated with 54 online semi-structured interviews (42 interviews with young people between 15 and 24 years old; 12 interviews with people aged between 14 and 60 appointed as news influencers by the 42 previous interviewees) on news and citizenship. At the end of each interview, participants were asked to nominate a person they considered to be an influencer in terms of their news consumption habits. The interviews were conducted between July and October 2023 via Zoom video call platform. Using the QSort methodological approach [20, 21] with card-sorting exercises with a think-aloud protocol, the influencers were asked to identify and classify people, themes, or subjects that played a role in their information routine, rating them as very important, indifferent, and not important at all. By assembling the pyramid and clarifying their choices, the interviewees were encouraged to compare their current information consumption with their habits from past moments in their lives. This exercise aimed to prompt reflections about how they experienced news consumption in different periods of their lives and to identify their perceptions about it.

MyGender project is the first-ever study in Portugal to explore the interactions of young adults (18–30 years old) with the technical aspects and conceptualizations of mobile applications (m-apps). This study examined how individuals integrate these applications into their daily routines, incorporating them into their habitual practices and actively (re)negotiating their gender and sexual identities through this engagement. Three studies were implemented to analyse how young adults engage with technicity and imaginaries of mobile apps: a survey, semi-structured interviews, and diary records. A semi-structured interviewing approach was employed to delve into the subjective realms of young individuals' experiences and negotiations in their everyday lives. The methodological underpinning of the research strategy pivoted on the self-reported experiences and practices of youthhood, specifically focusing on their preferred apps and discourses surrounding the rejection of others rather than exclusively concentrating on the mere utilitarian aspects of app usage. From May to October 2022, 25 in-depth semi-structured interviews were conducted with young adults residing in Portugal (16 women and nine men) who self-identified as heavier users of mobile apps. Employing online interview platforms like Skype or Zoom facilitated real-time co-presence and interactivity between interviewees and interviewers. This approach ensured the generation of more reliable interview recordings, encompassing audio and video formats while adhering to ethical standards of obtaining informed consent.

Around these challenges, anchored around two axes that seem to be fundamental: 1 - Bearing in mind action during the process of interviewing online, finding ways of ensuring environments for semi-structured interviews more relaxed, participatory, and reflective; 2 - Thinking about possible complementarities with the use of media diaries, as a digital ethnographic technique, better able to fix and capture the moment of the audience.

In the following sections, we address issues related to online interviews within specific environments and use the media diaries technique to capture media consumption qualitatively. Both sections focus on the results obtained in the YouNDigital project.

4   Online Interviewing in Relaxed, Participative, and Reflective Environments

Asking questions and getting answers is a much more complicated task than it might first appear. One of the greatest difficulties is making the questions as unambiguous as possible. One change from traditional to postmodern-informed interviewing is that the so-called detached researcher and interviewer are recast as active agents in the interview process and attempts are made to de-privilege their agency. Another shift is that the interviewee's agency is privileged and in the name of the interviewee all manner of experimentation is undertaken to make evident his or her own sense of identity and representational practices [22].

It is difficult, if not impossible, to do so, but it is one of the most widely used research techniques in disciplines such as sociology and psychology, as a means of better understanding human beings and their interactions [6]. "The interview becomes the tool and the object, the art of sociological sociability" [6] and an encounter in which the two parties behave as equals. In the interview, the other is no longer seen as a distant person who is only there to be interviewed, categorised, measured, and catalogued. By studying others, we study the self [6]. Another very important dimension of an interview is the framework of codes, signs, and language that goes far beyond the verbalisation of words. This code, which involves both the interviewer and the interviewee, is extremely important and is all the richer when more relaxed spaces are provided in which the interviewees feel more relaxed, as Berg [8] advocates in part of his 10 commandments on interviewing.

Qualitative research will give us small parcels of knowledge in a world where boundaries between our daily lives and digital contexts have collapsed [22]. Formally, the interview takes many forms and can be used for various purposes, from the unregulated modality of everyday spaces in which we talk, ask, and answer, to journalistic spaces, and in this article our focus is centered on the online interview for research purposes. We live in an interview society [22–24] and because interview repertoires are stocked with bits of informal knowledge that people can rely on and recall when asked questions about themselves or other issues, interviewee answers become problematic as truth claims. Prepackaged sound bites, however, should not impede the interviewer's task or craft. Instead the interviewer- as evidenced by those who have experimented with the content and form of interview practices-must move beyond the static nature of traditional interviewing techniques by recognising the interview as a micro-situation within a larger sociocultural context [22].

The interview can be seen as a scenic moment [7] while giving privilege to the participant [3] meaning, and we have to be aware of this, that the participant's performance has a degree of orientation on the part of the interviewee [3]. Reflexivity can occur when participants mirror their participation in the interview [3], adding as well participatory, dynamics, and performative practices to the interview process [3, 22].

Hasebrink and Domeyer [25] consider that talk about media consumption is a complex process and often unconscious. Because of that, they added visual methods in a pilot study with people aged 20–30, following the principle of an open and user-centred approach. Participants received blank cards to complete with the main elements of their media repertoires, and in a four-step activity, they had to position the cards in a circle with "me" in the centre. The main data for analysis were verbal comments and visual data was not used as data on its own. The same authors [25] consider that this approach led to a rich body of empirical observations with detailed insights about media repertoires.

In this paper we try to think about these reflections in the context of the YouNDigital project. When we started preparing the interviews - as the research team has a qualitative matrix and experience in participatory research - we were immediately concerned about bringing in a dimension that would ensure a relaxed, participatory, and reflective online interview environment, without following strategies that are not aligned with the seriousness of the moment. This isn't the place to describe in depth the importance of good interview environments, but we do know that they are decisive to better capture the contexts in which people live [3] and get better answers [8]. Our concern was also related to the need to involve participants of different ages more in the interview, making them more oblivious to the formal context of the interview. We took into account that speaking about media habits can be difficult since this process is often unconscious [25]. Here are some proposals for thinking about more relaxed, participatory, and reflective spaces: a) the option of having a QSort[1] [26, 27] right at the start of the interview, b) having questions that point to answers at the level of the generations and to real contexts in some of the cases and, finally, c) questions (inside and outside the QSort) that point to the reflectiveness of the person being interviewed.

We note that to facilitate the participatory process, a bottom-up approach, and also to leave the participant free to respond more freely, of the eleven QSort cards, we only

---

[1] Q-methodology is a quantitative/qualitative social science method [27] considered well-suited for media reception and use [26]. It allows us to analyze individuals' subjective perceptions of an area of experience and aggregate these perceptions through a factor analysis. As a result, the Q-methodology provides both qualitative and quantitative findings, creating a typological pattern of differences and similarities between the participants' perceptions [27]. Q-methodology is applied in a card-sorting activity with a think-out-loud protocol structured based on the research questions. Participants have to place and rank these cards in a pyramid according to their daily use or importance in their lives. On each card is a statement or the particular sociocultural phenomenon being investigated [27], usually defined in a previous stage of the research. This activity has a dialogical potential and allows participants to reflect on their choices during the process. "When informants have completed the card placing process, accompanied by dialogical negotiation, they have self-analyzed their subjective news consumption universe, whose internal architecture is moreover relational" argues Schrøder [27].

had 3 pre-defined ones (War, Digital Influencer, and Television Journalist) that didn't
have to be necessarily chosen, as we can see in Fig. 1 below.

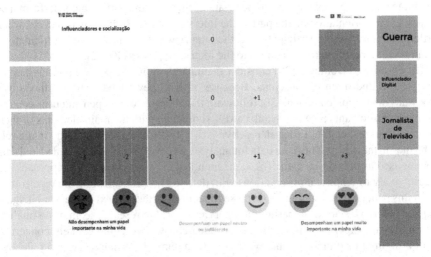

Fig. 1. The Q-Sort pyramid that was presented to the interviewees with 9 blank cards and 3
suggestions (War, Digital Influencer, and Television Journalist) that were not mandatory.

The QSort pyramid was presented as a puzzle, and the interviewers emphasized
that it was not a test, without right or wrong answers. At this point, some interviewees
expressed relief, while others referred to the activity as a "challenge". When filling in
the cards and arranging them on the pyramid, some interviewees mentioned they were
thinking about their news habits for the first time. Some reported difficulties in this
process, while others said the activity was fun.

Furthermore, focussing on the interviewee ensured that we had the flexibility to
adjust the questions to the person in front of us. In this way, we can guarantee that we
are looking at the audience through "their lens". This approach allowed the interviewees
to abstract themselves from the conditioned digital environment in which they found
themselves during the initial phase of the interview and after the open questions. In
addition, in the final part of the QSort, there was a moment for the participant to be more
reflective about their own choices, how they had felt, and whether they were sure of what
they had chosen, allowing them to change the place of the cards if they wanted. This
option allowed the participants to set the participatory and agential tone for the interview
by exploring the cards they wrote and the meanings they attributed to them within their
sphere. These more reflexive approaches were in some of the moments relevant components of the educational process that occurred with some of the interviewees during
the interviewing process [18]. At the end of the interview, more than one interviewee
said that the experience had provided relevant reflections that could be useful to other
young individuals. This happened not only because some of the subjects we mentioned
during the interview process were unclear for them in a daily basis context, but also
because in some cases they became aware for the first time about those subjects during

the interview. This clearly enhances the impact of the research on their life, alerting them to new questionings.

In addition to focusing on the personal perspective of each interviewee, and trying to capture it as accurately as possible, even if in a relaxed way, this option for a more reflective approach also made it possible to understand generational and intergenerational perspectives. Relationships with their peers, but also with other generations, shape the interviewees' relationship with the media. Dichotomously, contact with friends and colleagues or with older family members, such as parents, uncles, and grandparents, was often the basis of the reasoning developed, either through closeness, in the sense of what they are similar to and identify with, or through diversity and distancing of attitudes and practices. This point is particularly interesting if we consider, as explained above, that the current fragmentation of audiences makes it difficult to gain a more in-depth, consistent, and detailed understanding of audiences as isolated groups and in their relationship with others.

It was also possible to identify stereotypes linked to people from other generations, namely older people, which could be explored in the future. For instance, some interviewees referred to the difficulty of understanding technology or verifying online information as something inherent to older people.

4.1 Media Diaries as a Complement Capable of Capturing the Moment in Action

Traditionally utilized in anthropology and sociology, diary methods such as media diaries have become a reliable qualitative technique for longitudinal data collection [28]. In the literature, diaries have been described as a qualitative research method that, on the one hand, emphasises self-reflection [29], since it puts the participants "speaking for themselves" [30] in the first person in a moment of reasoning, subjectivity, and introspection; and, on the other hand, dispenses with the researcher's presence "as a participant observer" [30]. As a complementary method to the interview, but it can also be understood on its own, media diaries allow to "capturing life as it is narrated" [29].

Diaries are a space without the embarrassment of an interview, whether due to shyness, limited and time constraints, or technical issues, allowing us to capture the daily dimension of the interviewees [31]. This approach involves various designs to gather quantitative and qualitative data across time. Journal-type instruments, requiring narrative-style entries in response to broad questions, and log-type diary formats, employing short answer items for tracking dynamic constructs longitudinally, represent key variations [32].

Media diaries provide a comprehensive context for comprehending the determinants of consumption of media content and devices that shape individuals' lives. Therefore, researchers may examine how specific events, environments, or social interactions influence participants. This contextual insight enhances the depth of research findings, which can be further explored beyond text-based entries, allowing participants to introduce layers of their expression by integrating different types of media elements.

As part of the YouNDigital project, the diaries were based on what was said in the interview. At the end of the interview, people were asked to fill in a diary for no less than three days, but no more than five. Filling in the diary could mean writing a text or audio, or sharing links, images, or videos through WhatsApp.

The research team sent daily reminders with questions to the participants who had agreed to take part in the activity. We started with a contextual question (*What did you do today?*), moving on to questions directly linked to media consumption: *At some point during the day, was there a subject that caught your attention? (it could be in the media or conversations with friends, family…); What was that subject? (and where - TV, networks, conversation…?); Now, thinking only about the subjects that interest you most, did you see anything today that caught your attention? And did you try to find out more about it?*

The last question sought to better understand the (inter)generational dynamics that shape news consumption, based on the question: *Did you talk to anyone*? The answer to this question would allow us to understand and interpret how determining (or not) their social contexts are. And it even presupposes a performative space: the participant expresses themselves how they want, when they want, dedicating as much time as they want to fill in the diary and interconnecting various dimensions, from the personal to the social.

This data collection, considered a complementary method, depends directly on the active participation of the interviewees. While some interviewees did not adhere to the task, others started immediately after the interview. Some interviewees sent information over the weekend (which was not required) and some chose, on their own initiative, to fill in the diaries for longer than the days requested - which reveals the ability of this method to engage them.

5   Conclusions and Future Research

Adding these experiences to previous research that relied on the same concerns and methodological reflections [3], ways of avoiding the collection of data *per se*, without it involving – in addition to the collection of consumer data – the reflection of the person. This is of special value when the research aims to involve the participants in the research. In the future, we will study the interaction between diaries and semi-structured interviews in terms of validating thematic results.

Acknowledgements. This article was developed within the scope of the project "YouNDigital - Youth, News and Digital Citizenship" (PTDC/COM-OUT/0243/2021), funded by FCT — Foundation for Science and Technology, I.P. DOI https://doi.org/10.54499/PTDC/COM-OUT/0243/2021. https://youndigital.com and of the project "MyGender - Mediated young adults' practices: advancing gender justice in and across mobile apps" (PTDC/COM-CSS/5947/2020), funded by FCT — Foundation for Science and Technology, I.P. DOI https://doi.org/10.54499/PTDC/COM-CSS/5947/2020.

References

1. Fiske, J.: Audiencing: cultural practice and cultural studies. In: Denzin, K., Lincoln, Y.S. (eds.) Handbook of Qualitative Research. Norman SAGE Publications, Califórnia, Londres e Nova Deli (1994)

2. Mathieu, D., et al.: In dialogue with related fields of inquiry: the interdisciplinarity, normativity and contextuality of audience research. Participations J. Audience Reception Stud. **13**(1) (2016)
3. Mathieu, D., Brites, M.J.: Expanding the reach of the interview in audience and reception research: the performative and participatory models of interview. In: Zeller, F., Ponte, C., O'Neill, B. (eds.) Revitalising Audience Research, pp. 44–61. Routledge (2014)
4. Bird, S.E.: The Audience in Everyday Life. Routledge, Nova Iorque e Londres (2003)
5. Bird, S.E.: News practices in everyday life: beyond audience response. In: Allan, S. (ed.) The Routledge Companion to News and Journalism, pp. 417–428. Routledge, Milton Park, Abingdon, Oxon (2010)
6. Fontana, A., Frey, J.H.: Interviewing: the art of science. In: Denzin, N.K., Lincoln, Y.S. (eds.) Handbook of Qualitative Research. SAGE Publications, Califórnia, Londres e Nova Deli (1994)
7. Holstein, J.A., Gubrium, J.F.: The Active Interview. SAGE, Thousand Oaks, London and New Delhi (1995)
8. Berg, B.L.: Qualitative Research Methods for the Social Sciences. Needham Heights: A Pearson Education Company (2001)
9. Silverman, D.: Interpreting Qualitative Data: Methods for Analysing Talk, Text and Interaction. Sage Publications, London and Thousand Oaks (2001)
10. Rubin, H.J., Rubin, I.S.: Qualitative Interviewing: The Art of Hearing Data. Sage, Thousand Oaks, Londres e Nova Deli (2005)
11. Wolgemuth, J.R., et al.: Participants' experiences of the qualitative interview: considering the importance of research paradigms. Qual. Res. **15**(3), 351–372 (2015)
12. Brites, M.J.: Quando a investigação é feita com participantes ativos: Ampliar o uso das técnicas de entrevista e de grupo focal. In: Ferreira, V.S. (ed.) Pesquisar Jovens: Caminhos e desafios metodológicos, pp. 89–110. ICS, Lisbon (2017)
13. Gauntlett, D., Hill, A.: TV Living Television, culture and everyday life. British Film Institute, London e New York (2001)
14. Couldry, N., Markham, T.: Public connection through media consumption: between overso-cialization and de-socialization? Ann. Am. Acad. Pol. Soc. Sci. **608**(1), 251–269 (2006)
15. Couldry, N., Livingstone, S., Markham, T.: Media Consumption and Public Engagement: Beyond the Presumption of Attention. Palgrave, Londres (2007)
16. Höijer, B.: Ontological assumptions and generalizations in qualitative (audience) research. Eur. J. Commun. **23**(3), 275–294 (2008)
17. Schroeder, K.C.: The best of both worlds? Media audience research between rival paradigms. In: Alasuutari, P. (ed.) Rethinking the Media Audience. The New Agenda. SAGE Publications, London, Thousand Oaks, New Delhi (1999)
18. Brites, M.J.: Jovens e culturas cívicas: Por entre formas de consumo noticioso e de participação, 225 p. LabCom Books, Covilhã (2015)
19. Paus-Hasebrink, I., Kulterer, J., Sinner, P.: Social Inequality, Childhood and the Media: A Longitudinal Study of the Mediatization of Socialisation. Palgrave Macmillan, Cham (2019)
20. Peters, C., et al.: News as they know it: young adults' information repertoires in the digital media landscape. Digit. Journal. 1–24 (2021)
21. Swart, J., Broersma, M.: The trust gap: young people's tactics for assessing the reliability of political news. Int. J. Press/Politics **27**(2), 396–416 (2022)
22. Borer, M.I., Fontana, A.: Postmodern trends: expanding the horizons of interviewing practices and epistemologies. In: Gubrium, J.F., et al. (eds.) The SAGE Handbook of Interview Research: The Complexity of the Craft, pp. 45–61. SAGE, London, New Delhi and Singapore (2012)
23. Fontana, A.: Postmodern trends in interviewing. In: Gubrium, J.F., Holstein, J.A. (eds.) Postmodern Interviewing. Sage, Thousand Oaks, London and New Delhi (2003)

24. Goodin, R.E., Klingemann, H.-D.: A New Handbook of Political Science. Oxford University Press, Oxford (1998)
25. Hasebrink, U., Domeyer, H.: Media repertoires as patterns of behaviour and as meaningful practices: a multimethod approach to media use in converging media environments. Particip. J. Audience Recept. Stud. 9(2), 757–779 (2012)
26. Davis, C.H., Michelle, C.: Q methodology in audience research: bridging the qualitative/quantitative 'divide'? Particip. J. Audience Recept. Stud. 8(2), 559–593 (2011)
27. Schrøder, K.C.: Methodological pluralism as a vehicle of qualitative generalization. Particip. J. Audience Recept. Stud. 9(2), 798–825 (2012)
28. Hektner, J., Schmidt, J., Csikszentmihalyi, M.: Experience Sampling Method. Thousand Oaks, California (2007)
29. Kaun, A.: Open-ended online diaries: capturing life as it is narrated. Int J Qual Methods 9(2), 133–148 (2010)
30. Chan-Olmsted, S.M., Shay, R.: The emerging mobile media market: exploring the potential of tablets for media content consumption. Palabra Clave 17(4), 1213–1240 (2014)
31. Moe, H., Ytre-Arne, B.: The democratic significance of everyday news use: using diaries to understand public connection over time and beyond journalism. Digit. Journal. 10(1), 43–61 (2022)
32. Ma, R., Oxford, R.L.: A diary study focusing on listening and speaking: the evolving interaction of learning styles and learning strategies in a motivated, advanced ESL learner. System 43, 101–113 (2014)

Interaction Design of Elderly-Friendly Smartwatches: A Kano-AHP-QFD Theoretical Approach

Yue Cao[✉]

Nanjing Normal University, Nanjing 210019, China
yuecao97@gmail.com

Abstract. The world population is aging rapidly, and the health and care issues of the elderly are receiving increasing attention. The application of elderly smart wearable devices, represented by smartwatches, in health monitoring, is becoming more widespread. Based on the above background, a smartwatch interaction design strategy centered on elderly users is proposed to address the problem of low aging adaptability in current smartwatch design. The Kano model, hierarchical analysis method, and QFD method are integrated into the smartwatch interaction design process. Firstly, focusing on elderly users as the target, Kano was used to study user requirements, resulting in 24 user requirements classified by their attributes. Secondly, the AHP model was employed to establish the analysis matrix of the requirement indicators and determine the comprehensive weighting values of different requirement indicators. Subsequently, QFD was utilized to analyze the finalized user requirements, enabling the determination of the core design factors for smartwatch interaction design. Finally, the design scheme was conducted based on the design factors, followed by evaluation and usability testing to verify the reasonableness and feasibility of the design model and scheme.

Keywords: Smartwatch · Interaction Design · Kano Model · AHP · QFD

1 Introduction

The global demographic landscape is witnessing a rapid phenomenon of population aging, which poses the potential to surpass society's capacity to provide adequate care for the elderly [1]. Permanently entering nursing homes represents a costly means of care provision for older individuals, the majority of whom express a preference for aging in the familiarity of their own homes [2]. There is a burgeoning interest in examining the efficacy and feasibility of health monitoring and assistance delivered within the domestic sphere [3]. Several intelligent wearable devices have already integrated health monitoring functionalities, with smartwatches epitomizing aging smart wearable devices due to their convenient portability, particularly suited for elderly usage. However, smartwatches present novel concepts to elderly users, whose operational logic and design ethos significantly diverge from the functional machinery era. Factors such as limited experience, health status, income level, education, and geographic location often render elderly individuals challenged in adapting to new technologies. Moreover, they encounter difficulties stemming from the intricacy of emerging technologies and the absence of user-friendly services tailored to their needs [4].

Smartwatches have gained prominence within the Information and Communication Technology (ICT) industry owing to their multifaceted functionality and broad user appeal, yet empirical research on user perceptions and attitudes towards smartwatches remains at a nascent stage [5]. Recent strides in wearable sensor technology have unveiled substantial potential for enhancing the quality of life among the elderly [6]. Through wireless sensor networks, older adults can transmit real-time data on their physical condition to healthcare centers, thus garnering instantaneous feedback on vital signs such as heart rate and blood pressure, thereby facilitating real-time healthcare provisioning [7]. Present investigations into smartwatches for elderly users primarily concentrate on the functionalities of health monitoring and remote care, yet there exists a dearth of research on interaction design suitable for elderly users. Elderly users necessitate clearer operational cues when utilizing smartwatches, an aspect that current research inadequately addresses, with interface design failing to align with the needs of elderly users. Furthermore, elderly users constitute a minority within the user demographic of smart wearable devices, and the level of age-friendliness of smartwatches remains inadequate, lacking rigorous analysis and segmentation of user needs. Consequently, the interaction design of smartwatches for elderly users necessitates a user-centric approach, underpinned by a synthesis of qualitative and quantitative analyses of requirements to delineate specific and effective design strategies, thereby guiding subsequent design endeavors.

2   Research Methodology

In the developmental process of product design, user-oriented construction of design models involves methodologies such as the Kano model, Analytic Hierarchy Process (AHP), Quality Function Deployment (QFD), Axiomatic Design (AD), and Technique for Order of Preference by Similarity to Ideal Solution (TOPSIS). In recent years, numerous researchers have delved into systematic design methodologies, integrating these theoretical models to formulate more scientifically sound and efficient design solutions.

The collection and analysis of user requirements constitute pivotal stages in the design and development process, thereby serving as determinants of a product's success or failure. Due to the abstract, dynamic, varied, and diverse nature of user demands, deriving precise conclusions can prove challenging [8]. The Kano model, introduced by Dr. Noriaki Kano, a professor at Tokyo Institute of Technology in the 1970s, represents a user requirement analysis model [9]. The Kano model has the potential to unearth implicit or latent human needs, satisfaction of which may enhance user contentment [10]. Nonetheless, the Kano model lacks the capability to assess the relative importance among user requirements, potentially leading to a deviation in the focus of subsequent product development endeavors.

The Analytic Hierarchy Process (AHP) is well-suited for aiding decision-making in scenarios characterized by multiple interrelated factors [11]. Employing AHP facilitates the determination of weighting coefficients for user requirements identified within the

Kano model. However, neither the Kano model nor AHP provides a definitive solution for translating final user requirements into specific design parameters.

The Quality Function Deployment (QFD) theory, proposed by Japanese scholars Yoji Akao and Shigeru Mizuno, entails a multilayered deductive analysis method aimed at satisfying quality management systems, with its core essence lying in requirement transformation [12]. QFD ensures a specific method for enhancing the quality at each stage of product development [13].

This study amalgamates the product design processes of Kano, AHP, and QFD. Grounded in user requirements, this process integrates qualitative and quantitative analytical methods. By encompassing both the emotive demands users have towards products during the design process and scientifically mapping out specific parameters for design, this approach offers heightened precision in analysis and greater efficiency in decision-making compared to traditional design methodologies.

The study is delineated into three distinct phases. In the first phase, to enhance the targeted nature of the inquiry, the research focuses on the elderly population as the primary demographic of interest. Employing a combination of interview methodologies and on-site observational techniques, explicit and implicit user requirements are elicited. Through a meticulous process, the raw descriptions provided by users are translated into unambiguous user demands. Subsequently, employing the card sorting technique, demands are categorized according to experiential elements to obtain classification indices. Utilizing the Kano model, the study delineates the classification of requirements and gauges the degree of expectation associated with user demands. Concurrently, the Analytic Hierarchy Process (AHP) is employed to construct an analysis matrix for the requirement indices, thereby ascertaining the comprehensive weighting values attributed to different requirement indicators.

In the second phase, a comparative analysis is conducted between the outcomes derived from the Kano and AHP models. The results generated by the AHP model serve to refine the user demand indices selected by the Kano model. Subsequently, employing the Quality Function Deployment (QFD) methodology, a mapping analysis of the finalized user demands onto design elements is performed. This aids in the identification of core design factors pertinent to the interaction design of smartwatches.

The third phase involves the formulation of design schemes based on the identified design factors. Subsequent to the design phase, an evaluation of the proposed design schemes is conducted to analyze their rationality and feasibility. Illustrated in Fig. 1, the research framework encapsulates the investigation and proposal evaluation of elderly-friendly interaction designs for smartwatches, predicated upon the amalgamated KANO-AHP-QFD model.

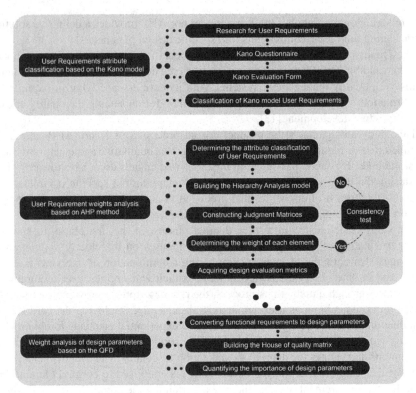

Fig. 1. KANO-AHP-QFD Hybrid Modelling Research Framework. (Self-illustrated by author.)

3 Smartwatch Interaction Design Process Based on Kano Model, AHP and QFD Methods

3.1 Kano Model-Based Requirements Extraction and Classification for Elderly Users

The observation and analysis of daily life behaviors among the elderly provide invaluable insights into their pain points and needs, thus facilitating a more nuanced understanding of their lived experiences. The target demographic for this study comprises individuals aged 60 and above, characterized by normal cognitive function and unhindered communication abilities. To ensure the relevance and specificity of the investigation, the research focuses on elderly users who have either used or been exposed to smartwatches. Adopting qualitative methodologies such as interviews and on-site observations, explicit and implicit user requirements are systematically captured. Following the collation and analysis of user research findings, a comprehensive list of 24 user demands is delineated, as presented in Table 1.

Subsequently, in adherence to the design principles outlined by the Kano questionnaire, a bifactorial approach was employed. Leveraging the elicited user requirements, a Likert 5-point scale questionnaire was meticulously crafted, as detailed in Table 1 Users were prompted to evaluate their satisfaction with each demand from both positive

Table 1. User requirements extraction.

Requirements classification	Number	Requirement Details
Functional Requirements	Q1	One-button SOS call for help
	Q2	Monitor cardiac
	Q3	Blood pressure measurement
	Q4	Medication reminder
	Q5	Monitoring of data-sharing children
	Q7	Web-based teleconsultation
	Q8	GPS positioning
	Q9	Incoming call alerts, answering calls
	Q10	Sedentary reminders
	Q11	Fall alarm
	Q12	weather alert
	Q13	Dietary records
Interaction Requirements	Q6	Simple and easy-to-understand interface
	Q20	The screen display font should be large
	Q21	The operation interface has colored ICONS
	Q22	Operation interface with animation guidance
	Q23	Can be operated by voice
	Q24	Can be operated by touch
Emotional Requirements	Q14	Beautiful appearance
Usage Requirements	Q16	Can wear on the hand
	Q17	It can be hung around your neck
	Q18	The display screen is large
	Q19	Lightweight and comfortable to wear
Economic Requirements	Q25	Moderate price (within 1000–1500 RMB)

and negative perspectives, utilizing a satisfaction scale comprising five levels: "Very Dissatisfied (1)", "Dissatisfied (2)", "Neutral (3)", "Satisfied (4)", and "Very Satisfied (5)" [14]. A total of 262 questionnaires were distributed, with the 15th question serving as an attention test item. Subsequently, 207 valid responses were obtained, which were meticulously collated and integrated. The questionnaire results were then synthesized to correspond with the Kano evaluation (see Table 1), thereby yielding insights into the relationship between user demands and product quality characteristics (Tables 2 and 3).

Taking user requirement Q1 as an illustration, 87.44% of respondents deemed the "one-key SOS emergency call" feature as a Must-be Quality (M). Consequently, this demand was categorized as a Must-be Quality (M). The Kano attributes of the other

Table 2. Kano Two-factor Fifth-order Likert questionnaire.

If available, what is your attitude?					Smartwatch requirements for designers	If not, what is your attitude?				
1	2	3	4	5		1	2	3	4	5
One-button SOS call for help										
Monitor cardiac										
Blood pressure measurement										
Medication reminder										
Monitoring of data-sharing children										
Simple and easy-to-understand interface										
……										

Table 3. Kano evaluation criteria.

Negative						
		Very Dissatisfied (1)	Dissatisfied (2)	Neutral (3)	Satisfied (4)	Very Satisfied (5)
Positive	Very Dissatisfied (1)	Q	A	A	A	O
	Dissatisfied (2)	R	I	I	I	M
	Neutral (3)	R	I	I	I	M
	Satisfied (4)	R	I	I	I	M
	Very Satisfied (5)	R	R	R	R	Q

23 user requirements were determined using the aforementioned analytical method, as depicted in Table 1.

Among the 24 user requirements delineated in Table 1, there are 6 Must-be Quality (M) attributes, 8 One-dimensional Quality (O) attributes, 4 Attractive Quality (A) attributes, and 6 Indifferent Quality (I) attributes, with no occurrences of Reverse Quality (R) or Questionable Quality (Q). Notably, GPS positioning, incoming call reminders and call answering, sedentary reminders, weather alerts, and dietary records were classified as Indifferent Quality (I). This signifies that these demands have no direct impact on enhancing user satisfaction and thus do not warrant design optimization efforts.

Must-be Quality (M) constitutes essential features of the smartwatch, where the fulfillment of such requirements does not augment user satisfaction. However, failure to meet these standards significantly diminishes user satisfaction. One-dimensional Quality

(O) represents features users expect the smartwatch to possess. Satisfaction increases when demands are met but declines relatively when they are not. Attractive Quality (A) embodies unforeseen user demands, which, if unmet, do not decrease user satisfaction; however, satisfaction experiences a substantial improvement upon fulfillment of these demands. These three Kano classifications should be duly considered throughout the smartwatch design process (Table 4).

Table 4. Kano questionnaire analysis table.

Number	Percentage (%)						Kano orientation
	A	O	M	I	R	Q	
Q1	0	0	87.44	12.56	0	0	Must-be Quality (M)
Q2	0	0	80.193	19.807	0	0	
Q3	0	0	86.957	13.043	0	0	
Q4	0	0	86.473	13.527	0	0	
Q20	0	0	79.71	20.29	0	0	
Q24	0	0	81.643	18.357	0	0	
Q5	2.899	61.353	1.932	33.816	0	0	One-dimensional Quality (O)
Q11	5.314	58.454	0.966	35.266	0	0	
Q14	1.932	54.106	12.56	31.401	0	0	
Q17	2.899	54.589	12.56	29.952	0	0	
Q19	8.213	51.208	12.077	28.502	0		
Q21	9.179	53.14	11.111	26.57	0	0	
Q23	3.382	55.556	8.696	32.367	0	0	
Q25	6.28	55.556	10.628	27.536	0	0	
Q6	82.609	0	0.966	16.425	0	0	Attractive Quality (A)
Q7	79.71	0	0	18.357	0	1.932	
Q18	78.744	0	0	21.256	0	0	
Q22	77.778	0	0	21.256	0	0.966	
Q8	4.831	0.966	0	94.203	0	0	Indifferent Quality (I)
Q9	8.696	0	0	91.304	0	0	
Q10	6.28	0.966	0	92.754	0	0	
Q12	6.28	0.966	0	92.754	0	0	
Q13	5.314	0	0	94.686	0	0	
Q16	11.111	0	0	88.889	0	0	

3.2 Calculation and Analysis of Elderly User Requirement Weights Based on AHP Method

Following the classification of user requirements for smartwatches, Kano does not provide a clear indication of the importance ranking of each demand. In order to elucidate the significance of individual requirements in the subsequent design process, a fusion of Kano and Analytic Hierarchy Process (AHP) methodologies is undertaken to compute the weights of various user demands. This amalgamation ensures precise identification of the pivotal user requirements that must be considered during the smartwatch design process.

Initially, based on the attribute analysis of user requirements for smartwatches according to Kano, a hierarchical analysis model is constructed utilizing fundamental concepts of AHP, as depicted in Fig. 2. The structural model is delineated into three hierarchical levels, aligning with the needs and design objectives of smartwatches for elderly users. These levels include: (1) the Target level, which represents the overarching objective of smartwatch interaction design; (2) the Baseline level, subdivided into Must-be attributes (M), Expected attributes (O), and Attractive attributes (A); and (3) the Sub-baseline level, further divided into specific attributes such as One-button SOS call for help (M1), Monitor cardiac (M2), Blood pressure measurement (M3), Medication reminder (M4), Large screen display font (M5), Touch-operable interface (M6), Data-sharing monitoring with children (O1), Fall alarm (O2), Beautiful appearance (O3), Necklace-wearable (O4), Lightweight and comfortable wear (O5), Colorful icon operation interface (O6), Voice-operable interface (O7), Moderate price (within 1000–1500 RMB) (O8), Simple and easy-to-understand interface (A1), Web-based teleconsultation (A2), Large display screen (A3), Animation-guided operation interface (A4), totaling 18 aspects.

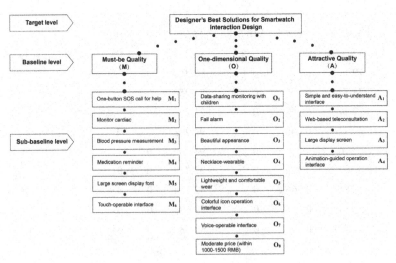

Fig. 2. Hierarchy expansion of designer demands for smartwatch. (Self-illustrated by author.)

To ensure the professionalism and applicability of the weighted results, the research opted for the AHP questionnaire design proposed by Thomas L. Saaty, employing a 9-level scale [15]. A total of 18 experts related to smartwatch interaction design were invited to fill out the matrices. This expert panel comprised 7 professionals engaged in smart wearable product design, 5 experts in the field of interaction design, 3 smartwatch interface designers, and 3 graduate students specializing in interaction design. Initially, the 18 experts were requested to evaluate the importance of each level of requirement using pairwise comparisons and ratings on a scale of 1–9. The arithmetic mean of these ratings was then computed as the basis for calculating the weights, yielding judgment matrices for each level. Subsequently, employing the geometric mean method, the weight coefficients for each level were calculated, ultimately determining the weighted values of user requirements for smartwatches. The computation process is outlined below, with results tabulated in Tables 5 and 6.

(1) Constructing a judgement matrix B:

$$B = \begin{bmatrix} a_{11} & a_{12} & \cdots & a_{1j} \\ a_{21} & a_{22} & \cdots & a_{2j} \\ \vdots & \vdots & \ddots & \vdots \\ a_{i1} & a_{i2} & \cdots & a_{ij} \end{bmatrix} \tag{1}$$

$a_{ij} \cdot a_{ji} = 1, i \neq j = 1, 2, \cdots, n.$
(2) Calculate the maximum eigenvalue (λ_{max})

$$\lambda_{max} = \frac{1}{n} \sum_{i=1}^{n} \frac{B_{w_i}}{W_i} \tag{2}$$

B_{w_i} is the i component of the vector B_w. n is the order.
(3) Consistency of results test (λ_{max})

$$I_{CI} = (\lambda_{max} - n) / (n - 1) \tag{3}$$

$$I_{CR} = I_{CI} / I_{RI} \tag{4}$$

n is the order corresponding to the evaluation scale of the judgement matrix. I_{RI} is the average stochastic consistency index. I_{CR} is the consistency ratio.
(4) Calculate the maximum eigenvalue (M_i)

$$M_i = \prod_{j=1}^{n} b_{ij}(i, j = 1, 2, \cdots, n) \tag{5}$$

b_{ij} is the demand indicator in row i, column j. n is the quantity of the demand indicator.
(5) Determine the geometric mean of the product of the scales of each layer (a_i)

$$a_i = \sqrt[n]{M_i}(i = 1, 2, \cdots, n) \tag{6}$$

(6) Calculate relative weights (W_i)

$$W_i = a_i \bigg/ \sum_{i=1}^{n} a_i \qquad (7)$$

Finally, to ensure the scientific validity of the results, a consistency test is required for the calculated results. When $I_{CR} \leq 0.1$, the consistency test is passed, and vice versa.

Table 5. Primary Indicator Weight.

Primary Indicators	M	O	A	Weight Value	I_{CR}
M	1	2	3	0.5390	0.0088
O	1/2	1	2	0.2973	
A	1/3	1/2	1	0.1638	

Table 6. Secondary Indicator Weight.

Secondary Indicators	Judgement Matrix								Partial Weight	Composite Weight	I_{CR}
M_1	1	2	2	3	3	4	×	×	0.3280	0.1768	0.0184
M_2	1/2	1	1	2	2	3	×	×	0.1918	0.1034	
M_3	1/2	1	1	2	2	3	×	×	0.1918	0.1034	
M_4	1/3	1/2	1/2	1	2	3	×	×	0.1322	0.0713	
M_5	1/3	1/2	1/2	1/2	1	2	×	×	0.0964	0.0520	
M_6	1/4	1/3	1/3	1/3	1/2	1	×	×	0.0598	0.0322	
O_1	1	1/5	2	3	1/3	1/2	1/4	2	0.0855	0.0254	0.0695
O_2	5	1	2	4	4	3	2	3	0.2800	0.0832	
O_3	1/2	1/2	1	1/2	1/2	1/3	1/3	2	0.0682	0.0202	
O_4	1/3	1/4	2	1	1	1/3	1/4	1	0.0644	0.0191	
O_5	3	1/4	2	1	1	1/2	1/3	2	0.0973	0.0289	
O_6	2	1/3	3	3	2	1	1/2	2	0.1370	0.0407	
O_7	4	1/2	3	4	3	2	1	3	0.2114	0.0628	
O_8	1/2	1/3	1/2	1	1/2	1/2	1/3	1	0.0562	0.0167	
A_1	1	5	3	2	×	×	×	×	0.4742	0.0777	0.0761
A_2	1/5	1	1/3	1/2	×	×	×	×	0.0844	0.0138	
A_3	1/3	3	1	3	×	×	×	×	0.2781	0.0456	
A_4	1/2	2	1/3	1	×	×	×	×	0.1632	0.0267	

In order to ensure the scientificity of the results, the consistency test ($I_{CR} \leq 0.1$) was carried out on the results of the judgement matrix, in which the value of the criterion layer

I_{CR} was: 0.0088, and the values of the sub-criterion layer I_{CR} were: 0.0184, 0.0695, and 0.0761 respectively, all of which were less than 0.1, and conformed to the consistency test standard.

Table 7. Relative weight calculation ranking table.

No.	Composite Weight	Number	No.	Composite Weight	Number
1	0.1768	M_1	16	0.0191	O_4
3	0.1034	M_2	12	0.0289	O_5
2	0.1034	M_3	10	0.0407	O_6
6	0.0713	M_4	7	0.0628	O_7
8	0.0520	M_5	17	0.0167	O_8
11	0.0322	M_6	5	0.0777	A_1
14	0.0254	O_1	18	0.0138	A_2
4	0.0832	O_2	9	0.0456	A_3
15	0.0202	O_3	13	0.0267	A_4

The ranked results of user requirement weights presented in Table 7 reveal that the interaction design of smartwatches for the elderly must not only meet the users' indispensable attributes, such as the One-button SOS call for help (M_1), Monitor cardiac (M_2), Blood pressure measurement (M_3), Medication reminder (M_4), Large screen display font (M_5), and Touch-operable interface (M_6), but also prioritize addressing the expectations and attractive attributes that rank high in importance. These include features like Monitoring of data-sharing with children, Fall alarm, Lightweight and comfortable wear, Voice-operable interface, Simple and easy-to-understand interface, and Operation interface with animation guidance. Once these critical requirements are met, user satisfaction with the smartwatch among the elderly demographic is poised to significantly enhance.

3.3 Design Element Analysis Based on QFD Method

Upon determining the weight values and comprehensive weights of various user requirements for smartwatches using QFD (Analytic Hierarchy Process), it becomes imperative to transform the designer's requirements for the smartwatch into product design parameters through the QFD methodology (refer to Table 8), ultimately culminating in the computation of design element weights.

Establishing the House of Quality (HOQ) serves as the cornerstone of the Quality Function Deployment (QFD) process. The HOQ illustrates the relationship between user requirements and design elements matrices, elucidating the focal points of the design team in crafting the product [16]. An expert panel (comprising five interaction designers) was convened to evaluate the correlation between user requirements for the aging-friendly smartwatch and the design elements, utilizing pairwise comparisons for

Table 8. Comparison of user requirements with design parameters.

Number	User Requirement	Design Parameter
M_1	One-button SOS call for help	Health and safety DP_1
M_2	Monitor cardiac	Health and safety DP_1
M_3	Blood pressure measurement	Health and safety DP_1
M_4	Medication reminder	Health and safety DP_1
M_5	Large screen display font	Strong recognition DP_2
M_6	Touch-operable interface	Interactive mode DP_3
O_1	Data-sharing monitoring with children	Health and safety DP_1
O_2	Fall alarm	Health and safety DP_1
O_3	Beautiful appearance	Appearance modeling DP_4
O_4	Necklace-wearable	Appearance modeling DP_4
O_5	Lightweight and comfortable to wear	Comfort level DP_5
O_6	Colorful icon operation interface	Strong recognition DP_2
O_7	Voice-operable interface	Interactive mode DP_3
O_8	Moderate price (within 1000–1500 RMB)	Price DP_6
A_1	Simple and easy-to-understand interface	Strong recognition DP_2
A_2	Web-based teleconsultation	Health and safety DP_1
A_3	Large display screen	Appearance modeling DP_4
A_4	Animation-guided operation interface	Strong recognition DP_2

scoring. As depicted in Table 9, designers rated the relevance of each of the 18 requirements for the smartwatch and the 6 design elements. Each rating was quantified, with symbols denoting strong correlation ($\bullet$), moderate correlation ($\circledcirc$), weak correlation ($\triangle$), and blank indicating no correlation. Following the quantification of correlation degrees, default values were assigned as follows: $\bullet = 5, \circledcirc = 3, \triangle = 1$, and blank space $= 0$.

The evaluation results were consolidated within the House of Quality (HOQ), where the absolute weights and relative weights of design elements' importance were computed. Subsequently, the results were imported into the HOQ's basement, and the calculation formula (8) was employed.

$$W_i = \sum_{i=1}^{q} W_i P_{ij}, \; W_k = \frac{W_j}{\sum_{i=1}^{q} X_j} \tag{8}$$

Here, W_j represents the absolute importance weight of design elements, W_i denotes the comprehensive weight of user requirements indicators, P_{ij} signifies the correlation coefficient between user requirements and design elements, and W_k represents the relative importance weight of design elements. The results of the weight calculations were then subjected to weight ranking for prioritization.

Table 9. House of Quality for design parameters in smartwatch.

UR$_x$ / DP$_x$	Composite Weight	DP$_1$	DP$_2$	DP$_3$	DP$_4$	DP$_5$	DP$_6$
M$_1$	0.1768	●					●
M$_2$	0.1034	●					●
M$_3$	0.1034	●					●
M$_4$	0.0713	●					●
M$_5$	0.0520	△	●	△			△
M$_6$	0.0322	◎	△	●		△	△
O$_1$	0.0254	◎					◎
O$_2$	0.0832	●					●
O$_3$	0.0202		△		●		◎
O$_4$	0.0191	△	◎	△	●	◎	△
O$_5$	0.0289	△			◎	●	◎
O$_6$	0.0407	△	●	△			△
O$_7$	0.0628	◎	◎	●		◎	◎
O$_8$	0.0167				△	◎	●
A$_1$	0.0777	△	●	●		●	◎
A$_2$	0.0138	◎			△		◎
A$_3$	0.0456	△	◎	◎	●	●	
A$_4$	0.0267	△	●	◎		△	
SUM (Scores)		1.2589	0.5011	0.4576	0.1925	0.4055	1.2508

Upon analysis, the relative importance weight rankings of design elements, as derived from Table 9, are as follows in descending order: DP$_1$ > DP$_6$ > DP$_2$ > DP$_3$ > DP$_5$ > DP$_4$. These findings indicate that in the context of designing smartwatches tailored for the elderly, priority should be given to health and safety, pricing, and strong identifiability. Subsequently, attention should be directed towards interaction modalities and comfort, while considerations regarding aesthetic appeal should be addressed after fulfilling the aforementioned design elements.

4   Conceptual Design of Smartwatch Based on Kano, AHP, and QFD Models

4.1   Key Functional Requirements for Smartwatch Design in Elderly Users

The foremost functional demand of smartwatches for elderly users primarily revolves around health monitoring. This encompasses monitoring vital signs such as blood pressure, heart rate, medication reminders, and fall alerts. Given the substantial physiological, psychological differences, and distinct basic needs of the elderly compared to other consumer groups, design principles for smart wearable devices targeting the elderly should emphasize lightweight and consistency [17]. Applications on the smartwatch should retain only core functionalities, with streamlined operational procedures to avoid multitasking and complex processes. Additionally, employing standardized, universally recognizable gestures or buttons (see Fig. 3) facilitates the establishment of a unified cognitive framework among elderly users. In terms of interface design, considerations must account for potential visual impairment among elderly users. Therefore, font size significantly impacts readability and the utility of health monitoring functions. Appropriately magnifying fonts enhances user experience for the elderly, ensuring greater clarity and readability. For instance, in the smartwatch interface design by aeac (see Fig. 4), prominently sized fonts enhance readability and visibility.

Fig. 3.   Apple Watch. (Source: https://osxdaily.com/2015/08/23/reduce-motion-apple-watch/)

4.2   Comfort and Affordability as Imperatives in Aging-Friendly Smartwatch Design

Comfort and pricing stand as pivotal design elements necessitating significant consideration in the design of smartwatches tailored for the elderly. Comfort is not merely confined

Fig. 4. aeac brand smartwatch. (Source: https://www.amazon.co.uk/Fitness-Monitor-Waterp roof-Counter-Smartwatch-Pink/dp/B0BXLD6CJG?th=1)

to the material and weight of the smartwatch but extends to the quality of the interactive experience. Beyond conventional gesture operations, voice control holds paramount importance for elderly users, effectively mitigating usability challenges. Light weight, ease of wear, aesthetically pleasing design, and competitive pricing are all demands from elderly users beyond the essential functionalities of smartwatches, representing crucial emotional requirements within age-appropriate design considerations.

4.3 Optimizing User Satisfaction Through Aging-Friendly Smartwatch Interaction Design

The degree of age-appropriateness in smartwatch design significantly impacts elderly user satisfaction. Age-appropriate smartwatches must accommodate the behavioral patterns and cognitive levels of elderly users. Elderly individuals often prefer to rely on their past habits and experiences, gradually diminishing curiosity and interest in learning about new things, with their learning willingness typically limited to simpler and more easily memorable matters [18]. Therefore, smartwatch interaction design should prioritize the physiological and psychological characteristics of elderly users. For instance, opting for vibrant and lively colored icons in interface design (see Fig. 5) and incorporating animated guidance (see Fig. 6) in interface design facilitates clearer operational cues for elderly users during smartwatch usage.

Fig. 5. KOSPET MAX GPS Android Smartwatch. (Source: https://www.nepal.ubuy.com/en/pro
duct/3ZQUJG4AW-kospet-optimus-2-android-smartwatch-1-6-4g-lte-phone-watch-with-blood-
oxygen-heart-rate-sleep-monitoring-13mp-rotatable-camera-and)

Fig. 6. Apple Watch animations. (Source: https://3sidedcube.com/apple-watch-animations/)

5   Conclusions

The burgeoning elderly population coupled with the perpetual evolution of societal
dynamics has engendered increasingly discerning expectations regarding quality of life
among the elderly. Smart wearable devices have emerged as facilitators of more timely,
convenient, and secure personalized services for elderly users, thereby enhancing their
overall quality of life. The user-driven smartwatch interaction design established through
the Kano-AHP-QFD methodology epitomizes a user-centric design paradigm, effectively surmounting the inertia of conventional thinking in the design process and furnish-
ing robust support for design decisions. The smartwatch interaction design framework
constructed in this study partly alleviates the limitations of singular method designs,
aiding designers in precisely identifying user requirements amidst ambiguous scenarios and facilitating informed design decisions. This framework ensures the scientific
and rational progression of product development while also presenting novel research
avenues for other user-driven product developments.

Acknowledgments. The author sends thanks to the guest editors and all anonymous reviewers for valuable comments and suggestions.

Disclosure of Interests. The author has no competing interests to declare that are relevant to the content of this article.

References

1. Bremner, J., Frost, A., Haub, C., Mather, M., Ringheim, K., Zuehlke, E.: World population highlights: key findings from PRB's 2010 world population data sheet. Popul. Bull. **65**(2), 1–12 (2010)
2. Chan, M., Estève, D., Fourniols, J.-Y., Escriba, C., Campo, E.: Smart wearable systems: current status and future challenges. Artif. Intell. Med. **56**(3), 137–156 (2012)
3. Liu, L., Stroulia, E., Nikolaidis, I., Miguel-Cruz, A., Rincon, A.R.: Smart homes and home health monitoring technologies for older adults: a systematic review. Int. J. Med. Informatics **91**, 44–59 (2016)
4. Roupa, Z., et al.: The use of technology by the elderly. Health Sci. J. **4**(2), 118 (2010)
5. Kim, K.J., Shin, D.-H.: An acceptance model for smart watches: implications for the adoption of future wearable technology. Internet Res. **25**(4), 527–541 (2015)
6. Bizjak, J., Gradišek, A., Stepančič, L., Gjoreski, H., Gams, M., Goljuf, K.: Intelligent System to Assist the Independent Living of the Elderly. IEEE (2017)
7. Li, J., Ma, Q., Chan, A.H., Man, S.: Health monitoring through wearable technologies for older adults: Smart wearables acceptance model. Appl. Ergon. **75**, 162–169 (2019)
8. Xiaowei, L.: From strategy to surface: fitness equipment design oriented by user experience. Art Des. **12**, 130–132 (2021)
9. Xu, Q., Jiao, R.J., Yang, X., Helander, M., Khalid, H.M., Opperud, A.: An analytical Kano model for customer need analysis. Des. Stud. **30**(1), 87–110 (2009)
10. Hartono, M., Chuan, T.K.: How the Kano model contributes to Kansei engineering in services. Ergonomics **54**(11), 987–1004 (2011)
11. Lee, S.: Determination of priority weights under multiattribute decision-making situations: AHP versus fuzzy AHP. J. Constr. Eng. Manag. **141**(2), 05014015 (2015)
12. Chan, L.-K., Wu, M.-L.: Quality function deployment: a literature review. Eur. J. Oper. Res. **143**(3), 463–497 (2002)
13. Kim, K.J., Kim, D.H., Min, D.K.: Robust QFD: framework and a case study. Qual. Reliab. Eng. Int. **23**(1), 31–44 (2007)
14. Matzler, K., Hinterhuber, H.H.: How to make product development projects more successful by integrating Kano's model of customer satisfaction into quality function deployment. Technovation **18**(1), 25–38 (1998)
15. Saaty, T.L.: Decision making with the analytic hierarchy process. Int. J. Serv. Sci. **1**(1), 83–98 (2008)
16. Ginting, R., Ishak, A., Malik, A.F., Satrio, M.R.: Product development with quality function deployment (QFD): a literature review. IOP Publishing (2020)

17. Haescher, M., Matthies, D.J., Srinivasan, K., Bieber, G.: Mobile assisted living: smartwatch-based fall risk assessment for elderly people (2018)
18. Sodhro, A.H., et al.: Towards wearable sensing enabled healthcare framework for elderly patients. IEEE (2020)

Human Aspects of Gerontechnology: Comprehensive Analysis of 2015–2023 ITAP Conference Papers

Shixin Fan, Yunshan Jiang, Wei Hu, and Jia Zhou[✉]

School of Management Science and Real Estate, Chongqing University, Chongqing, People's Republic of China
jiazhou@cqu.edu.cn

Abstract. As the world's population ages, designing technologies specifically tailored for older adults has become increasingly important. The International Conference on Human Aspects of IT for the Aged Population (ITAP), which focuses on the human aspects of gerontechnology, has had a profound impact on the field. This study aims to outline the development and evolution of ITAP research, providing references and inspiration for researchers exploring or preparing to study this domain. A total of 771 ITAP conference papers were retrieved from SpringerLink. Citation analysis was conducted using the HistCite application, and visualizations were created with CiteSpace software. Through visual analysis of the authors, institutions, and keywords of ITAP conference papers over the past nine years, this study reveals the research trends and characteristics of human aspects of gerontechnology within the ITAP conferences. The findings indicate that virtual reality and augmented reality have been highly researched topics since 2020. The latest burst keywords include "smartphone" and "COVID-19", highlighting some of the hottest topics over the last three years. Papers in ITAP are predominantly published by countries with ageing populations, representing over 85% of the total contributing countries. By summarizing ITAP in stages on the occasion of its 10th anniversary, this study aims to provide scholars interested in the conference with a detailed understanding of the conference and the development of human aspects of gerontechnology.

Keywords: human aspects of gerontechnology · older adults · ITAP

1 Introduction

The world's population is aging. According to the United Nations, the proportion of people aged 65 and over in the total population was 10% in 2022. It is predicted that by 2050, one in six people worldwide will be over age 65 (16%) [1]. With the population aging at an increasing rate, countries with aging populations must implement measures to accommodate the growing number of older adults. Designing technologies specifically for older adults to support them in various areas of life is an excellent way to help them stay healthy, comfortable, and safe.

Q. Gao and J. Zhou (Eds.): HCII 2024, LNCS 14725, pp. 31–42, 2024.
https://doi.org/10.1007/978-3-031-61543-6_3

Gerontechnology officially became an academic field in 1991 at the First International Congress on Gerontechnology Technology, held in Eindhoven, the Netherlands [2]. Gerontechnology, a combination of gerontology and technology, is regarded as the study of the biological, psychological, sociological, and medical aspects of aging exploiting the potential offered by technological advances [3]. The core of gerontechnology is to study the interaction between the development of older adults and technology [4]. Older adults face numerous dilemmas associated with aging, including physical and cognitive decline due to aging and disease, as well as psychological issues stemming from a lack of social contact and care. The ability of older adults to participate in everyday activities and maintain a quality of life becomes a concern in the absence of technical solutions [3]. Based on the challenges faced by older adults, Halicka & Surel [5] categorized gerontechnology into nine groups: health, education, interpersonal communication, safety, mobility, care, leisure, housing, and digital accessibility. From a technical perspective, gerontechnology offers five key ways to assist older adults: prevention, enhancement, compensation, care, and research [6]. Research has shown that the use of various gerontechnology can help older adults continue to lead healthier, more independent, and more socially engaged lives [7]. Furthermore, gerontechnology has significantly alleviated the stress on caregivers, families, and health and social care service organizations [8].

Despite the extensive research in gerontechnology, a limited number of studies genuinely focused on older adults. While the functionality of technology is important, truly meeting the actual needs and emotional experiences of the elderly is crucial. Technology should be seen as a means to an end, not the end itself. To genuinely benefit older adults, it is urgent to approach the design of gerontechnology from the human aspect. The International Conference on Human Aspects of IT for the Aged Population (ITAP), launched in 2015 as an integral part of the HCI International conference series, has addressed this need. ITAP concentrates on the abilities, requirements, attitudes, and behavioral patterns of older adults regarding IT use alongside innovative ideas, practices, and experiences related to IT applications, systems, and services for this demographic. Over the past nine years, ITAP has published more than 700 papers from more than 40 countries, drawing participation from scholars and teams at universities and institutions, including Harvard, Massachusetts Institute of Technology, RWTH Aachen University, University of Miami, et al., significantly impacting the field of human aspects of gerontechnology research. The iteration of technology has brought about change in the field of human aspects of gerontechnology. However, there is a lack of summaries of ITAP conference papers to bridge past research with future directions. Taking the 10th ITAP Conference as an opportunity, this study reviews the papers presented at ITAP over the past nine years to summarize and analyze the developmental changes and current research status in the field of gerontechnology. The purpose of this study is to elucidate the development and change of ITAP research in the field of human aspects of gerontechnology and to provide reference and inspiration for the researchers exploring the field or preparing to study the field.

2   Methods

On September 5, 2023, ITAP conference proceedings were retrieved from the Springer-Link database using the search term "Human Aspects of IT for the Aged Population". All conference papers published between 2015 and 2023 that were searchable in the database were included. The following data were extracted: year of publication, authors, author keywords, institutions, and countries. The data were exported to HistCite and CiteSpace software for citation counting and network visualization mapping.

3   Results and Discussion

3.1   The Overview of ITAP Conference Papers

Number of Papers. A total of 771 papers presented by ITAP from 2015 to 2023 can be retrieved on SpringerLink (Fig. 1). From the retrieval results, there was a decline in the number of papers published in 2021. Overall, the number of papers published each year remained relatively stable.

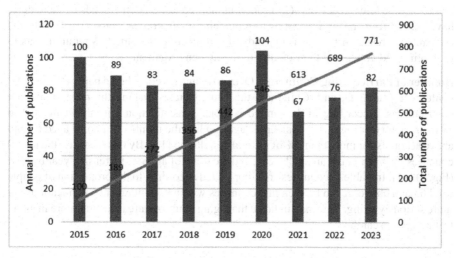

Fig. 1. Number of ITAP conference publications

The Related Topics. Each year, the organizing committee identifies and formulates the topics recommended by the ITAP conference, which, to some extent, reflect the prevailing research trends of ITAP. According to the website of the ITAP conference [9], the topics of the papers presented at the conference can be divided into three phases from 2015 to the present. The first phase, covering 2015–2020, comprised four areas: (1) older people's requirements and behavioral patterns; (2) design and evaluation of information technologies for older people; (3) technological environments for older people; (4) HCI methodological considerations. This phase was primarily classified according to user-centered design.

The second phase, covering 2021–2023, comprised ten areas: (1) health; (2) social inclusion and connectedness; (3) leisure time and entertainment; (4) home and housing; (5) e-commerce and finance; (6) mobility and transportation; (7) public IT appliances and services; (8) work; (9) interaction paradigms; (10) design methodology for older adults. This phase was mainly classified according to domain.

In the third phase, for the 2024 ITAP conference, the related topics include (1) interaction design and evaluation for older adults; (2) design methodology involving older adults; (3) promoting health among older adults; (4) strengthening social connectedness in older adults; (5) building elder-friendly environments and smart home technologies; (6) supporting mobility and transportation for older adults; (7) enhancing life quality and experience for older adults and (8) supporting social-economic well-being for older adults. This phase is also categorized by domain.

In terms of specific topics, the third phase featured a wide range of subjects related to emerging technologies such as the Internet of Things (IoT), Augmented Reality (AR), Virtual Reality (VR), and more.

The reasons for these changes may be categorized into two aspects: (1) From a technological standpoint, with an increasing number of emerging technologies being employed to assist the elderly, timely adjustments to the recommended topics of the conference become necessary. (2) From a human perspective, the needs of the elderly have shifted from basic necessities to embracing their golden years. As a result, the conference's research focus has expanded from meeting the elderly's requirements to promoting and enhancing their quality of life and environment.

Number of Participating Countries. Over 40 countries contributed papers to the ITAP conference (Table 1), with China and the United States making the most significant contributions. According to the United Nations' classification criteria established in 1956, a country or region is considered "aged" when the number of people aged 65 and above accounts for more than 7% of its total population [10]. By this measure, the top 10 countries by paper count are all "aged", and the trend of aging is increasing year by year (Fig. 2) [11]. In Table 1, countries are color-coded according to the proportion of people aged 65 and above. It can be seen that countries with a high number of publications are more seriously aging. This may indicate that aging countries are investing more in aging technology research.

3.2 Scholars and Institutions of ITAP

Academic Influence Evaluation. Various indicators were explored to ensure an objective and unbiased evaluation. Currently, there are two categories of commonly used quantitative evaluation methods to assess scholars' academic influence: (1) Evaluation indexes with a single dimension, mainly based on traditional bibliometrics, including the number of papers, total citation frequency, and average citation frequency; (2) Comprehensive evaluation indicators, such as H-index and its extension index, PageRank series indicators and Altmetrics indicators. In evaluating scholars and institutions of ITAP, the number of papers was chosen as the evaluation index due to the papers being derived from a single source and maintaining stable quality.

Table 1. Participating countries and number of papers

Rank	Country	Number	Rank	Country	Number
1	China	234	24	Australia	4
2	United States	106	25	Malaysia	4
3	Germany	74	26	Czech Republic	4
4	Japan	58	27	Mexico	4
5	Portugal	45	28	Cyprus	4
6	Canada	43	29	Saudi Arabia	4
7	United Kingdom	29	30	Chile	3
8	Italy	28	31	Greece	3
9	Sweden	27	32	Slovenia	2
10	Netherlands	22	33	New Zealand	2
11	France	18	34	Ireland	2
12	Spain	15	35	Iran	2
13	Singapore	15	36	India	2
14	Finland	11	37	Israel	1
15	Norway	11	38	Croatia	1
16	Brazil	10	39	Belgium	1
17	Switzerland	10	40	Philippines	1
18	Romania	8	41	Pakistan	1
19	Austria	7	42	United Arab Emirates	1
20	South Korea	7	43	Luxembourg	1
21	Denmark	7	44	Uruguay	1
22	Bulgaria	6	45	Poland	1
23	Iceland	5	46	Colombia	1

Color according to the proportion of people aged 65 and above.

$p \leq 7\%$	$7\% < p \leq 14\%$	$14\% < p \leq 20\%$	$p > 20\%$

Scholars and Institutions. The author information of the selected ITAP conference papers was imported into CiteSpace to obtain the Co-authorship network graph (Fig. 3). The top 10 most published scholars were from Germany, the United States, Portugal, and China. Scholars with more than 10 papers include Martina Ziefle (20), Joseph F. Coughlin (14), and Ana Isabel Veloso (10).

The institutional information of selected ITAP conference papers was imported into CiteSpace to obtain the network diagram of cooperative institutions (Fig. 4). Institutions were ranked according to the number of papers (Table 2), with twelve institutions having at least 10 articles from Germany, China, Japan, Canada, Portugal, and the United States. China had the largest number of institutions (4), followed by the United States (3). However, collaboration among the twelve institutions was weak, with only the Georgia

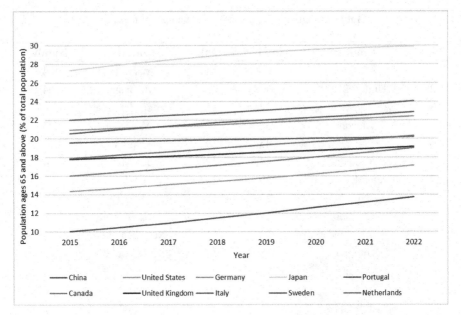

Fig. 2. Aging trends in the top 10 countries by number of papers

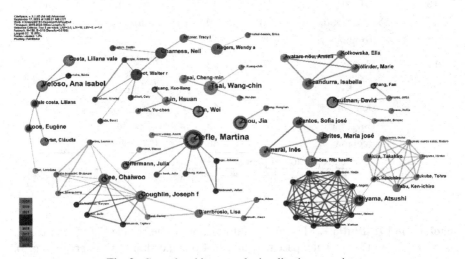

Fig. 3. Co-authorship network visualization mapping

Institute of Technology and Florida State University having collaborated. The institutions that published the most papers over the past three years were the University of Aveiro (11), followed by the University of Tokyo (10). The best papers for 2015 had the participation of the Georgia Institute of Technology. The best papers for 2016 were a collaboration between the Georgia Institute of Technology and Florida State University.

It is worth mentioning that Louisiana State University, despite publishing fewer than ten papers, won the best paper for two consecutive years in 2018 and 2019.

At RWTH Aachen University, Professor Martina Ziefle, head of the eHealth research group "Enhancing Mobility with Aging" at the Human Technology Centre, and her team have conducted extensive research on the interface between humans and technology [12]. Her projects related to the elderly include (1) GOODBROTHER, supported by COST European Cooperation in Science and Technology. It is a network of privacy-aware audio and video-based applications designed to provide daily living support for the elderly, disabled, and infirm. (2) VisuAAL, supported by Marie Skłodowska-Curie Innovative Training Networks. The project aims to bridge the gap between user requirements and the appropriate and safe use of video-based Active and Assisted Living (AAL) technologies so that older people can receive effective and supportive help [13].

Notably, all the papers published by the Massachusetts Institute of Technology were authored by Joseph F. Coughlin and his team. Joseph F. Coughlin, the Director of the MIT AgeLab, focuses his research on how longevity and service innovation will transform the business of advice [14]. The research topics at MIT AgeLab include (1) caregiving & well-being; (2) home logistics & services; (3) retirement & longevity planning; and (4) transportation & livable communities [15]. Project partners of AgeLab include Tivity Health, Inc., Monotype Imaging Inc., Touchstone Evaluations, Inc., etc.

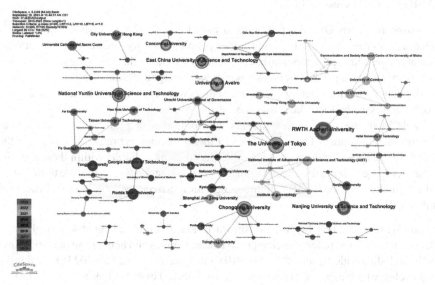

Fig. 4. Co-institution network visualization mapping

Table 2. Institutions with at least 10 papers

Rank	Institutions	Country	Number of papers
1	RWTH Aachen University	Germany	25
2	The University of Tokyo	Japan	22
3	Chongqing University	China	20
4	East China University of Science and Technology	China	17
5	Nanjing University of Science and Technology	China	16
6	National Yunlin University of Science and Technology	China	16
7	University of Aveiro	Portugal	16
8	Massachusetts Institute of Technology	USA	14
9	Concordia University	Canada	11
10	Simon Fraser University	Canada	11
11	Georgia Institute of Technology	USA	10
12	Florida State University	USA	10

3.3 Research Themes of ITAP

Keywords to Focus On. According to keyword co-occurrence analysis, nine words including older adults, elderly, aging, older people, usability, technology acceptance, dementia, age, and user experience have a frequency of more than 20. To avoid repetition in keyword clustering, synonymous keywords were merged. Terms such as elderly, older people, senior citizens, elderly people, and seniors were consolidated under the category of older adults as the secondary alias list.

Table 3 lists the top 20 high-frequency keywords after merging, along with the year of their first appearance. These keywords further refine the recommended topics of the ITAP conference and address the challenges faced by older adults within these specific domains. Figure 5 shows the clustering of keywords, generated using the title term source and log-likelihood ratio (LLR) weighting algorithm. Screen the largest nine clusters for further analysis.

Variations in Research Topics. As shown in Fig. 6, eight emergent keywords were selected, which could reflect the changes in research topics and hotspots in the field. Keywords including video games (2016–2019) and smartphone (2020–2023) have longer burst cycles, which means that research related to these keywords has had a more lasting impact on the field of human aspects of gerontechnology in ITAP. The latest burst words including smartphone and COVID-19 have been some of the hottest topics in the last three years. The emergence of research hotspots may be closely linked to technological advancements or significant social events.

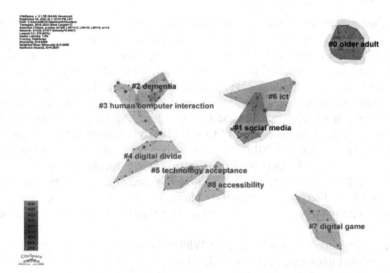

Fig. 5. The keywords cluster analysis

Table 3. Top 20 high frequency keywords

Keywords	Frequency	Year	Keywords	Frequency	Year
older adult	334	2015	virtual reality	17	2020
aging	56	2015	ICT	17	2015
usability	28	2015	assistive technology	16	2015
technology acceptance	28	2015	technology adoption	15	2016
dementia	23	2015	technology	14	2015
age	21	2015	augmented reality	13	2018
user experience	20	2015	accessibility	13	2015
social media	19	2015	ageism	12	2015
covid 19	18	2021	gamification	11	2018
human computer interaction	17	2015	smartphone	11	2016

Figure 7 illustrates the trend of keywords over time. Keywords from the same cluster are aligned on the same horizontal line, with their positions determined by the year of their first appearance. By analyzing papers that utilized these keywords, we can examine the thematic changes within each cluster.

The cluster indicated the main research objects and research contents. #0 and #2 were "older adult" and "dementia", showing the main research objects of the ITAP papers. As one of the main practitioners of elderly care, caregivers have also been included as research objects in some studies. In these two clusters, some technologies were noteworthy, including virtual reality, augmented reality, serious game, and IoT, especially virtual reality and augmented reality, which have received extensive research attention in recent years. #1, #6, and #7 were "social media", "ICT" and "digital game", among which ICT shows its strength in the context of COVID-19. Eye tracking garnered significant research interest in 2016 and 2018. However, its popularity appears to have waned in recent years, evidenced by only one article related to eye tracking being published in both 2021 and 2023. The remaining clusters 3#, 4#, 5#, and 8# dealt with the relationship between people and technology. Under the cluster of #3 human computer interaction, user-centered design research has continued, with at least two papers per year including this keyword.

Research on games continues unabated. While the cluster of #7 digital games seemed to have gone on hiatus after 2020, this didn't indicate a decline in research focused on games designed for older adults. Scholars increasingly preferred to use more specific game category names as keywords, such as mobile game, serious game, video game, etc. Therefore, the cluster of #7 digital games was not representative of the overall landscape of game research in ITAP. Other clusters also 'deal with game-related parts, such as mobile games (#0), serious game (#2), and gamification (#3).

Keywords	Year	Strength	Begin	End	2015 - 2023
design	2015	2.38	**2015**	2016	
video game	2016	2.5	**2016**	2019	
assistive technology	2015	3.86	**2017**	2019	
gamification	2018	2.74	**2018**	2020	
agesim	2015	2.78	**2019**	2021	
physical activity	2019	2.77	**2019**	2020	
smartphone	2016	2.58	**2020**	2023	
covid 19	2021	5.9	**2021**	2023	

Fig. 6. Keywords with the strongest citation burst

ICT: Information Communications Technology, IoT: Internet of Things, AI: Artificial Intelligence, HCI: Human-Computer Interaction.

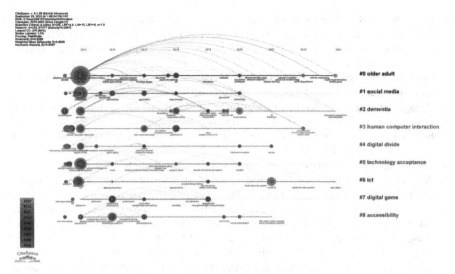

Fig. 7. The keyword timeline map

4 Conclusion

The study provides a comprehensive analysis of research on the human aspects of geron-technology in ITAP conferences. The analysis reveals that the top-ranking countries in terms of paper count were predominantly aging nations. Keywords including smartphone and COVID-19 have burst in the last three years. Emerging technologies including virtual reality and augmented reality have received extensive research attention in recent years and are expected to continue being a focal point in the future. Scholars could allocate more research efforts to the application of emerging technologies in addressing the challenges faced by older adults. Countries that are currently not experiencing aging but will undergo this demographic shift soon can also learn from the experiences of aging countries and conduct timely research on the human aspects of gerontechnology.

References

1. United Nations, Department of Economic and Social Affairs, Population Division: World Population Prospects 2022: Ten Key Messages (2022)
2. Hsu, Y.-L., Bai, D.L.: The future of gerontechnology: proposals from the new editor-in-chief. Gerontechnology **15**, 125–129 (2016). https://doi.org/10.4017/gt.2016.15.3.001.00
3. Micera, S., Bonato, P., Tamura, T.: Gerontechnology. IEEE Eng. Med. Biol. Mag. **27**, 10–14 (2008). https://doi.org/10.1109/MEMB.2008.925213
4. Bouma, H., Fozard, J.L., Bouwhuis, D.G., Taipale, V.T.: Gerontechnology in perspective. Gerontechnology **6**, 190–216 (2007). https://doi.org/10.4017/gt.2007.06.04.003.00
5. Halicka, K., Surel, D.: Gerontechnology — new opportunities in the service of older adults. Eng. Manag. Prod. Serv. **13**, 114–126 (2021). https://doi.org/10.2478/emj-2021-0025

6. Dara-Abrams, B.: Toward a model for collaborative gerontechnology: connecting elders and their caregivers. In: Sixth International Conference on Creating, Connecting and Collaborating through Computing (C5 2008), Poiters, France, pp. 109–114. IEEE (2008). https://doi.org/10.1109/C5.2008.11

7. Chen, K., Chan, A.: Use or non-use of gerontechnology—a qualitative study. IJERPH **10**, 4645–4666 (2013). https://doi.org/10.3390/ijerph10104645

8. Huang, G., Oteng, S.A.: Gerontechnology for better elderly care and life quality: a systematic literature review. Eur. J. Ageing **20**, 27 (2023). https://doi.org/10.1007/s10433-023-00776-9

9. HCI International: Home. https://www.hci.international/index.php?&MMN_position=1:1. Accessed 15 Jan 2024

10. The ageing of populations and its economic and social implications (1956)

11. Population ages 65 and above (% of total population) | Data. https://data.worldbank.org/indicator/SP.POP.65UP.TO.ZS. Accessed 15 Jan 2024

12. Univ.-Prof. Dr. Martina Ziefle - RWTH AACHEN UNIVERSITY Chair of Communication Science – English. https://www.comm.rwth-aachen.de/cms/comm/der-lehrstuhl/team/~cvsgr/martina-ziefle/?allou=1&lidx=1. Accessed 01 Feb 2024

13. Projects - RWTH AACHEN UNIVERSITY Chair of Communication Science – English. https://www.comm.rwth-aachen.de/cms/COMM/Forschung/~plff/Projekte/lidx/1/. Accessed 01 Feb 2024

14. Coughlin, J.F.: MIT AgeLab. https://agelab.mit.edu/about-us/people/joseph-f-coughlin/. Accessed 01 Feb 2024

15. About Us | MIT AgeLab. https://agelab.mit.edu/about-us/overview/. Accessed 01 Feb 2024

Development and Evaluation of Embodied Metaphors for Exergame Design: Considering Older Adults' Bodily Experiences and Individual Perceptions

Qingchuan Li[✉] and Simin Yang

School of Humanities and Social Sciences, Harbin Institute of Technology, Shenzhen, China
liqingchuan@hit.edu.cn

Abstract. Exergames are suggested to improve older adults' adherence to physical activity (PA) and thus greatly benefit their physical functions and well-being. Considering that older adults can face great challenges when mapping the input action with the exergame response, embodied metaphors have been proposed to facilitate their understanding of the gamification concept through their past bodily experiences of another activity. However, metaphorical mapping varies significantly among senior players due to individual differences and variation in technology experiences. This study therefore first carried out a focus group with four older adults to develop a variety of embodied metaphors by identifying their stereotypes of metaphorical mappings between the targeted PA movements and their past bodily experiences. Then, an online survey study was conducted among fifty-six older adults to evaluate the proposed metaphors based on their individual perceptions, including affective responses, perceived familiarity, and degrees of motion matching. This study revealed the importance of considering older adults' bodily experiences and individual preferences when designing exergames. Bodily experiences relating to every-day lives, entertainment and sports, things and animals, and childhood memories were frequently reported as embodied metaphors in the older adults' stereotypes of metaphorical mappings. The results suggest that the embodied metaphors relating to older adults' childhood games, such as rubber band skipping and shuttlecock, are the best choices to facilitate older adults' understanding of the targeted PA movements in exergame design. Furthermore, the study identified the necessity to involve older adults in the early stage of exergame development by using various user-centered research methods.

Keywords: Embodied Interaction · Exergame · Older Adults · Bodily Experience · Affective Response · Perceived Familiarity · Motion Matching

1 Introduction

Population ageing has emerged as a key global issue in recent decades. Economic and medical developments have led to a continual rise in the number and proportion of older adults aged 60 and over. In China, there are over 264 million people aged 60 and over,

Q. Gao and J. Zhou (Eds.): HCII 2024, LNCS 14725, pp. 43–58, 2024.
https://doi.org/10.1007/978-3-031-61543-6_4

with an ageing rate of 18.7% at the end of 2020. It is estimated that by 2050, the number of older adults will reach 280 million, accounting for one fifth of the total population in China [1]. This development inevitably places heavy burdens on health systems and services in China and globally [2]. Furthermore, as life expectancy increases, more and more older adults desire a better quality of life, which includes living independently and healthily as well as remaining in their own homes for as long as possible [3].

To facilitate the goals of active ageing and ageing in place, it is vital to reduce the rate of chronic disease, prevent cognitive and functional declines, and enrich the social and cultural lives of older adults. Specifically, physical activity (PA) is suggested by the World Health Organization as a promising way to limit the progression of chronic diseases and increase active life expectancy for older adults [4]. However, older adults usually face great difficulties in accepting and engaging with PA because it is repetitive and tiring. Exergames, interactive digital games that combine video games and exercise, are therefore proposed and developed for various rehabilitation and training purposes. It is suggested that exergames can improve older adults' PA adherence and further improve their physical functions, prevent cognitive decline, and enhance social communication [5].

By using sensor technologies, such as Kinect, leap motion, and Nintendo Wii, exergames can track older adults' real-time body movements and inform them about the game outcomes during PA. Nevertheless, players can face challenges when mapping their input actions with the exergame responses [6]. These un-addressed issues may be worse for older adults because this group tends to have more difficulties understanding and adopting new technologies [7, 8]. Embodied metaphors are therefore proposed to bridge this digital divide by facilitating older adults' understanding of the gamification concept (target domain) through their past bodily experiences of another (source domain) [9]. However, metaphorical mapping varies significantly among players with individual differences and experiences of technology. It is necessary to develop and identify embodied metaphors based on older adults' understandings and mental models when translating the targeted abstract metaphors into concrete concepts.

In this vein, this study aimed to determine older adults' stereotypes of metaphorical mappings through close user involvement in the early design stage of an exergame development. To fulfill the research objective, it first explored how to develop a diversity of embodied metaphors based on older adults' past bodily experiences. Second, it evaluated older adults' individual perceptions of the pro-posed embodied metaphors, including the positive affect, negative affect, perceived familiarity with each metaphor, and degree of motion matching between the proposed metaphor and targeted PA movement. The findings are expected to emphasize the importance of considering older adults' bodily experiences and individual preferences when designing exergames and show the necessity to involve older adults at an early stage of exergame development through various user-centered research methods.

2   Literature Review

Persuasive technologies have been employed to facilitate older adults' adoption of PA, including mobile and handheld devices, games and gamification platforms, and social networks [10]. Specifically, exergames, which can deliver various PA interventions in the form of games, have attracted increasing attention in recent years. By integrating an abundance of activity trackers and sensors, exergames can track players' body movements and produce corresponding stimuli to inform the game outcomes or scores. In this way, exergames create a natural and immersive way for players to interact with the systems, which have been widely applied in improving older adults' physical abilities in terms of balance [11], muscular strength [12], and flexibility [13].

However, this new design has also brought some unaddressed challenges. Due to the complexity of body movements and limitations of sensor technologies, the matching between body input and game output can be ambiguous. Although prior research has suggested that designers should encourage players to enjoy the uncertainty instead of removing the ambiguity [14], this issue can bring significant challenges for novice older adults. Specifically, due to the decline in older adults' cognitive abilities, such as working memory and processing speed, the ambiguous matching between their body inputs and game outcomes can be magnified.

Metaphor has been proposed as a means to facilitate older adults' understanding of technologies by reflecting players' mental models [15, 16]. A typical example is the graphic user interface, which utilizes users' existing knowledge and experience to help them understand the novel concepts of personal computers. In the same way, embodied metaphor, a kind of metaphor that involves people's bodily experiences of movements, manipulation of objects, or orientation in space [17], is believed to benefit users' perceptual connections between their body movement input and gaming output. As reported, embodied metaphors have been extensively applied for the purposes of computing learning and education [18]. For instance, block building is commonly used as a visual metaphor to help students understand the syntactic nature and processing of code [18]. In a Microsoft Kinect exergame of Word Out, players were asked to twist and form their bodies to match the shapes of letters in order to learn the alphabet [19, 20]. Although limited research has applied embodied metaphors in exergame designs for older adults, we believe that employing older adults' past bodily experiences of something from the source domain to support their understanding of the gamification concept in the exergame's target domain is promising as a means to reduce this group's perceived difficulties in accepting and adopting such systems.

Despite the advantages of embodied metaphor, most previous studies have mainly employed users' most familiar scenarios when designing exergames [21, 22]. For example, Zhang et al. [23] integrated four daily-life scenarios into the exergame design for upper-limb rehabilitation by closely collaborating with rehabilitation specialists. The scenarios comprised basketball playing, flying like an eagle, playing ping pong, and grabbing keys, which incurred different levels of familiarity. Their findings demonstrated that the level of familiarity was significantly and positively correlated with elderly players' satisfaction with the exergames. Nonetheless, little is known about the underlying mechanism of how users' perceived familiarity was formulated and influenced by such scenarios. Designers can only design and develop exergames for older adults by relying on the rule of thumb.

To summarize, there is a need to identify and identify older adults' stereotypes of metaphorical mappings between their past bodily experiences and the gamification concepts from exergames. Nonetheless, tackling this issue is quite challenging because the metaphorical mapping varies significantly among players. Some researchers have argued that it is necessary to develop and identify embodied metaphors based on individuals' understandings and mental models when translating the targeted abstract metaphors into concrete gamification concepts [6, 9]. Particularly, a variety of approaches has been implemented to assert the population stereotypes of metaphorical mappings, such as searching documented linguistic data, analyzing user interface patterns, direct observation, collaborating with experts, and using user-centered design processes, such as contextual interviews [24, 25].

The first two of these approaches are deemed more suitable for redesigning existing metaphorical interactions than developing new ones. When targeting the metaphorical interaction design for a totally new system, user-centered approaches are more effective to understand how user structure and reason about the targeted gamification concepts [9]. For instance, Bakker et al. employed a people-centered and iterative approach to design an embodied metaphor-based tangible learning system for children [9]. Hurtienne utilized the ethnographic method to analyze users' behaviors in a variety of healthcare settings and developed several embodied metaphors to describe the spatial relations between objects and people [26]. Manches et al. identified the representational gestures that conveyed embodied metaphors by interviewing sixteen students to determine their personal understanding of several computing concepts [18].

User-centered approaches that directly involve users in the requirements phase have gained the most attention in recent exergame research. These observations lead to the conclusion that it is important to understand older adults' stereotypes of metaphorical mappings, especially through close user involvement in the early design stage of an exergame. In detail, we argue that the metaphorical mappings should be developed and differentiated based on the voices of older adults and evaluated in terms of their affective responses, familiarity, and motion matching. Therefore, this study employed a series of user-centered approaches, namely, a focus group and questionnaire, to address the following research question: How can embodied metaphors for exergame design be developed and evaluated based on older adults' stereotypes of metaphorical mappings, with a focus on their emotional preferences, degrees of familiarity, and acceptance aspects?

3 Study 1: Development of Embodied Metaphors

3.1 Methods

Study 1 aimed to explore, through a user-centered approach, how to develop embodied metaphors by involving older adults in a focus group.

Participant Recruitment. Considering that discovering appropriate metaphorical mappings between older adults' past bodily experiences and abstract gamification concepts can be quite challenging, the participants recruited for this study were required to have used at least one kind of exercise and sporting mobile application, to engage in PA at least three time per week, and to be between 55 and 65 years old. In total, four female older adults participated in this study, with an average age of 59.0 years (age range: 56–63; SD = 3.16). Three of them indicated that they had graduated middle school, and one had graduated high school. They took PA 4.75 times per week on average (frequency range: 3–6; SD = 1.26). Regarding their physical conditions, two reported being in good physical condition, and two reported having chronic diseases, namely, shoulder and neck pain and periarthritis. All the participants had used an exercise and sporting mobile application named Tangdou (https://www.tangdou.com/), which is a video platform for teaching dances such as square dancing, exercise, and pop dance. In addition, Tik Tok (https://www.tiktok.com/) and Kuaishou (https://www.kuaishou.com/), two of the most popular online video applications, had been used by two of the participants to conduct PA. Detailed participant information is given in Table 1.

Table 1. Participant Information in Study 1.

No.	Gender	Age	Education level	Physical Conditions	Frequency of PA per week	Usage experience of exercise and sporting mobile applications
P1	Female	56	Middle school	Good	5 times	Tangdou
P2	Female	60	Middle school	Periarthritis of shoulder	6 times	Tangdou, Kuaishou
P3	Female	57	Middle school	Neck and shoulder pain	5 times	Tangdou, Tik Tok
P4	Female	63	High school	Good	3 times	Tangdou

Materials and Procedure. In order to discover as many metaphorical mappings as possible to inform the design of gamification elements in PA exergames, thirteen basic PA movements were employed as the target sources for participants to develop relevant metaphorical mappings, as shown in Fig. 1. Specifically, these movements were selected from a professional home-based PA guide for seniors published by the China Institute of Sport Science [27]. The movements covered all four categories of PA movements, namely, upper limb exercises, lower limb exercises, balance exercises, and flexibility exercises.

This focus group study was conducted in a local senior citizen center in August 2022 (see Fig. 2). Four participants were instructed to accomplish three sections of activities with the help of two researchers. First, the participants were asked to learn and conduct each PA movement by themselves. In particular, the researchers showed them illustrations of each PA movement and explained the main points of performing it. The participants then repeated the PA movement several times by themselves. Second, after understanding and mastering the PA movement, the participants were invited to discuss any possible source concepts that could enact the movement according to their past bodily experiences. Third, once a metaphor was discovered, the participants were asked to explain how they interpreted the underlying correlations between the proposed metaphor and targeted movement. A whiteboard, post-it notes, and marker pens were

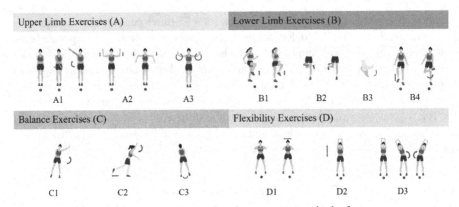

Fig. 1. Thirteen movements used as the target sources in the focus group.

provided for the participants. They were encouraged to write down their thoughts on the whiteboard at any time and, at the end, to organize all the proposed metaphors into categories based on their understanding. The focus group lasted about one hour. As a reward for participation, each participant received ¥50 (US $7.00) after finishing the focus group.

Fig. 2. The focus group conducted in Study 1.

Data Collection and Analysis. The focus group was video- and voice-recorded after the permission of the participants was obtained. All the recordings and researchers' notes were analyzed using Qualtrics. A combination of inductive and deductive approaches was used. Specifically, we analyzed in detail each of the proposed metaphors based on the dimensions of its type, category, and meaning. Then, the results were inductively supplemented with new codes coming through the data.

3.2 Results of Study 1

The results of the qualitative coding are presented in Table 2. In total, 31 metaphors were proposed for the 13 PA movements, with the number of proposed metaphors varying for each movement. It is interesting to note that although the participants were asked to suggest embodied metaphors based on their past bodily experiences to match the targeted movement concepts, they developed nine ontological metaphors as well. The ontological metaphor belongs to the strand of research in cognitive linguistics in which concepts from the target and source domains are connected through an object or substance without referring to one's bodily experience [28]. All the ontological metaphors proposed in Study 1 were based on things or animals with which the participants were familiar, such as birds, goldfish, ducks, lucky cats, clocks, spinning tops, and the alphabet. According to the participants, they suggested these metaphors because they were very familiar with such objects and could therefore easily imagine themselves as the corresponding objects moving forward like a bird or rotating clockwise.

As regards the categories involved in the proposed metaphors, four themes were summarized, 35.5% of which related to everyday lives, 29.0% to entertainment and sports, 25.8% to things and animals, and 16.1% to childhood memories. There was some overlap in the categorization of these metaphors since some belonged to more than one category. In terms of the meanings of metaphors, a majority of concepts in the source domain were aimed at changing the position or orientation of a person or object by moving, lifting, rotating, removing, extracting, jumping, raising, reaching, pulling, stretching, or kicking. Some required the current position or orientation of a person or object to be maintained. Additionally, four proposed concepts tried to connect the movements in the target domain with the concepts in the source domain through daily-life or cultural meanings, such as indicating directions, indicating time, measuring time, or money drawing.

Table 2. Results of the analysis of proposed metaphors.

PA movement	Proposed metaphors		Type	Category	Meaning
A1	1	Directing the traffic	Embodied	Everyday lives	Indicating directions
	2	Birds flying	Ontological	Things and animals	Moving forward
	3	Clockwise rotation	Ontological	Things and animals	Indicating time
A2	4	Carrying goods	Embodied	Everyday lives	Lifting things
	5	Lifting dumbbells	Embodied	Entertainment and sports	Lifting things
	6	Butterfly stroke	Embodied	Entertainment and sports	Moving forward
	7	Lucky cat waving	Ontological	Tings and animals	Bring in wealth and treasure
A3	8	Cleaning the window	Embodied	Everyday lives	Removing the dust

(*continued*)

Table 2. (*continued*)

PA movement		Proposed metaphors	Type	Category	Meaning
	9	Playing the Tai chi wheel	Embodied	Entertainment and sports	Rotating something
	10	Spinning the handkerchief	Embodied	Entertainment and sports	Rotating something
	11	Spinning top	Ontological	Things and animals	Rotating something
B1	12	Treading pickled cabbage in a barrel	Embodied	Everyday lives	Extracting liquid
	13	Stepping on the water wheel	Embodied	Everyday lives	Powering up
B2	14	The goldfish wagging its tail	Ontological	Things and animals	Moving forward
	15	Rubber band skipping	Embodied	Memories of childhood / Entertainment and sports	Jumping over obstacles
B3	16	Stepping on the gas	Embodied	Everyday lives	Speeding up
	17	Stepping on the treadle of a sewing-machine	Embodied	Everyday lives	Powering up
	18	The duck paddling its webbed feet	Ontological	Things and animals	Moving forward
B4	19	Shuttlecock kicking	Embodied	Memories of childhood	Kicking something
C1	20	Picking fruit from trees	Embodied	Everyday lives / Entertainment and sports	Reaching something
	21	Hanging lanterns	Embodied	Memories of childhood / Everyday lives	Raising something
	22	Catching flying insects	Embodied	Memories of childhood	Reaching something
	23	Half-X shaped stand	Ontological	Things and animals	Keeping still

(*continued*)

Table 2. (*continued*)

PA movement	Proposed metaphors		Type	Category	Meaning
C2	24	Skating	Embodied	Entertainment and sports	Keeping balancing
	25	Crossing a footbridge	Embodied	Memories of childhood	Keeping balancing and moving forward
C3	26	Pendulum motion	Ontological	Things and animals	Measuring time
D1	27	Pulling noodles	Embodied	Everyday lives	Changing the shape
	28	Playing the accordion	Embodied	Entertainment and sports	Producing music
D2	29	Playing volleyball	Embodied	Entertainment and sports	Reaching something
	30	Yawning while stretching	Embodied	Everyday lives	Stretching body
D3	31	Bowing	Ontological	Things and animals	Stretching body

4 Study 2: Evaluation of Embodied Metaphors

4.1 Method

Study 2 was conducted to further evaluate older adults' perceptions and preferences through the embodied metaphors proposed in Study 1. Two steps were implemented. A pilot study was employed to check the questionnaire design, and an online survey study was then carried out to evaluate the embodied metaphors.

Participant Recruitment. Ten participants aged between 55 and 65 years old were recruited in a pilot study to check whether there were any unclear or ambiguous descriptions in the questionnaire design. After revision, questionnaires were distributed online. Participants were required to be between 55 and 65 years old. Since Study 2 aimed to investigate users' perceptions of the proposed embodied metaphors among the general population of the elderly, there were no specific requirements for participants to have experience of PA or using exercise and sporting mobile applications.

In total, 56 participants, comprising 37 males and 19 females, took part in the survey study. Participants were between 55 and 65 years old, with an average age of 58.6 years and an SD of 2.36; 82.1% were between 55 and 60 years old, and 17.9% were between 61 and 65 years old. In addition, 73.2% of the participants had a college educational background while 23.2% indicated that they had graduated high school, and 3.6% reporting having graduated middle school.

Instrument Development. Study 1 aimed to evaluate the embodied metaphors covering all thirteen movements from A1 to D3. After screening, twenty embodied metaphors, numbered 1, 4, 5, 6, 8, 9, 10, 12, 13, 15, 16, 17, 19, 20, 21, 22, 25, 27, 28, and 29 in Table 2, were identified. For convenience, we renamed these embodied metaphors EM1 to EM20 correspondingly. According to the results of the pilot study, it was quite tiring and challenging for the older adults to evaluate all twenty embodied metaphors at once. Therefore, we divided the twenty embodied metaphors into four groups randomly, with each group comprising five embodied metaphors. The participants were required to evaluate only one group of embodied metaphors. In the questionnaire, a relevant picture indicating the thing or circumstance in the source domain was provided for participants to better understand the embodied metaphor. Some picture examples are shown in Fig. 3.

For each embodied metaphor, participants were first instructed to understand the concept in the source domain (e.g., directing traffic or spinning the handkerchief) by checking the picture illustrations and written descriptions in detail. Then, they were invited to report their affective responses toward the things or situations involved in this concept using an adapted version of the positive and negative affect schedule (PANAS) scales [29]. Specifically, the participants were provided with eight words that described positive affect, namely, interested, enthusiastic, proud, inspired, determined, attentive, alert, and active, and eight describing negative affect, namely, distressed, upset, scared, hostile, irritable, ashamed, nervous, and afraid, using 5-point Likert scales from 1 (totally disagree) to 5 (totally agree). After that, the participants were asked to look at the illustration for each embodied metaphor and indicate their perceptions of familiarity measured by three familiarity items adapted from Zhang et al. [30], namely, symbolic familiarity, cultural familiarity, and actionable familiarity, using a 5-point Likert scale from 1 (totally disagree) to 5 (totally agree). Lastly, the participants were provided

Fig. 3. Examples of the illustrations used in the questionnaire: (a) EM1 - Directing traffic; (b) EM16 - Catching flying insects; (c) EM8 - Treading pickled cabbage in a barrel; (d) EM11 - Spinning the handkerchief.

with the proposed embodied metaphor (see Fig. 3) and the PA movement in the source domain (see Fig. 1) one by one. They were required to demonstrate the degree of motion matching in terms of the similarity of the motion trajectory of the targeted movement and embodied metaphor using a 10-point Likert scale from 1 (not matching at all) to 10 (matching a great deal).

Data Collection and Analysis. The questionnaires were distributed in March 2023 through one of the biggest online survey panels in China, Wenjuanxing (https://www.wjx.cn/). After data cleaning, a total of 56 valid questionnaires was obtained. Descriptive analysis was utilized to explore the older adults' affective responses, perceived familiarity, and degrees of motion matching of the embodied metaphors. Specifically, the participants' positive affect was calculated by adding the scores on the eight items reporting positive feelings, and their negative affect was measured by adding the scores on the eight items reporting negative feelings [31]. Participants' perceived familiarity with the proposed metaphors was evaluated by the average scores of the three familiarity items, that is, symbolic, cultural, and actionable familiarity. Furthermore, hierarchical clustering analysis (HCA) was performed to group the proposed metaphors according to positive affect, negative affect, perceived familiarity, and degree of motion matching.

4.2   Results of Study 2

The proposed metaphors elicited average scores of 28.85 (SD = 1.93) for positive responses and 15.80 (SD = 1.86) for negative responses. These scores indicate that the metaphors proposed based on a user-centered approach achieved a medium to high level of positive affect and a relatively low level of negative affect. The results reported an average familiarity level of 3.93, with an SD of 0.26, which implies that the participants were quite familiar with the metaphors used in the target domain in terms of their symbolic, cultural, and actionable meanings. As regards the degree of motion matching, the proposed metaphors indicated an average degree of 6.94 (SD = 0.96) matching with the movements in the source domain. It seems that the degree of motion matching for the proposed metaphors varied a great deal, but all the proposed metaphors reported an acceptable degree of motion matching, in general, except EM1. The descriptive results are illustrated in Table 3.

HCA is a kind of cluster analysis with unsupervised algorithms that can group observations into groups. We used HCA to group the proposed metaphors on the basis of similarity in their positive affect, negative affect, perceived familiarity, and degree of motion matching. Table 4 presents a list of proposed metaphors divided into ranking groups according to their positive affect, negative affect, perceived familiarity, and degree of motion matching. Specifically, the group of metaphors including rubber band skipping (EM10), shuttlecock kicking (EM13), hanging lanterns (EM15), and pulling noodles (EM18) achieved the highest level of positive affect (mean = 31.64, SD = 0.36). The metaphor of playing the accordion (EM19) had the lowest level of negative affect (mean = 12.64). The group of rubber band skipping (EM10), stepping on the gas (EM11), shuttlecock kicking (EM13), and hanging lanterns (EM15) had the highest level of perceived familiarity (mean = 4.27, SD = 0.04), and the group of carrying goods (EM2), rubber

Table 3. Descriptive results of affective responses, perceived familiarity, and the degree of motion matching for the proposed metaphors.

No	Proposed Metaphor	Positive Affect	Negative Affect	Perceived Familiarity	Degree of Motion Matching
EM1	Directing the traffic	27.86	16.93	4.07	4.93
EM2	Carrying goods	27.14	15.07	3.48	7.79
EM3	Lifting dumbbells	29.50	16.43	3.98	5.64
EM4	Butterfly stroke	26.64	17.00	3.74	5.21
EM5	Cleaning the window	27.86	19.43	4.17	6.43
EM6	Playing the Tai chi wheel	28.14	14.29	4.07	6.14
EM7	Spinning the handkerchief	25.77	14.23	4.05	6.54
EM8	Treading pickled cabbage in a barrel	28.43	14.36	3.48	7.43
EM9	Stepping on the water wheel	29.86	15.36	3.50	7.50
EM10	Rubber band skipping	31.64	15.21	4.24	8.29
EM11	Stepping on the gas	25.43	16.07	4.26	8.07
EM12	Stepping on the treadle of a sewing-machine	28.43	16.00	3.88	7.43
EM13	Shuttlecock kicking	31.79	14.36	4.33	7.86
EM14	Picking fruit from trees	30.29	13.86	3.81	7.57
EM15	Hanging lanterns	32.00	16.07	4.26	5.79
EM16	Catching flying insects	28.29	15.21	3.74	7.50
EM17	Crossing a footbridge	27.79	20.79	3.83	7.29
EM18	Pulling noodles	31.14	16.50	3.79	7.14
EM19	Playing the accordion	28.79	12.64	4.05	7.07
EM20	Playing volleyball	30.29	16.14	3.95	7.21

band skip-ping (EM10), stepping on the water wheel (EM11), and shuttlecock kicking (EM13) elicited the highest degree of motion matching (mean = 8.00, SD = 0.23).

Thereafter, the second ranking group achieved mean levels of 29.98 (SD = 0.38),14.66 (SD = 0.55), 4.17, and 7.35 (SD = 0.18) in the positive affect, negative affect, perceived familiarity, and degree of motion matching, respectively. The third ranking group reported mean levels of 28.20, 16.39 (SD = 0.39), 4.03 (SD = 0.05), and 6.37 (SD = 0.20) in the positive affect, negative affect, perceived familiarity, and the degree of motion matching, respectively. In addition, the fourth ranking group indicated mean levels of 26.89 (SD = 0.35), 19.43, 3.48 (SD = 0.01), and 5.71 (SD = 0.10) in the positive affect, negative effect, perceived familiarity, and the degree of motion matching. Lastly, the fifth group elicited the lowest level of positive affect with the metaphors of spinning the handkerchief (EM7) and stepping on the water wheel (EM11) (mean = 25.60, SD = 0.24). The fifth group (EM17) achieved the highest level of negative affect (mean = 20.79) with the metaphor of crossing a footbridge. The groups of metaphors including butterfly stroke (EM4), stepping on the treadle of a sewing-machine (EM12), picking fruit from trees (EM14), catching flying insects (EM16), crossing a footbridge

Table 4. The result of ranking groups for the proposed metaphors.

Group	Positive Affect	Negative Affect*	Perceived Familiarity	The Degree of Motion Matching
1	EM10	EM19	EM10	EM2
	EM13	EM2	EM11	EM10
	EM15	EM6	EM13	EM11
	EM18	EM7	EM15	EM13
2	EM3	EM8	EM5	EM8
	EM9	EM9	EM1	EM9
	EM14	EM10	EM3	EM12
	EM20	EM13	3M6	EM14
3	EM1	EM14	EM7	EM16
	EM5	EM16	EM19	EM17
	EM6	EM1	EM20	EM18
	EM8	EM3	EM2	EM19
	EM12	EM4	EM8	EM20
	EM16	EM11	EM9	EM5
	EM17	EM12	EM4	EM6
	EM19	EM15	EM12	EM7
4	EM2	EM18	EM14	EM3
	EM4	EM20	EM16	EM15
5	EM7	EM5	EM17	EM1
	EM11	EM17	EM18	EM4

Note: *indicates the converted item.

(EM17), and pulling noodles (EM18) reported the lowest levels of perceived familiarity, and the groups of metaphors including directing the traffic (EM1) and butterfly stroke (EM4) indicated the lowest levels of motion matching. All the results of ranking groups are presented in Table 4.

Although the results of the ranked groups varied in terms of their positive affect, negative affect, perceived familiarity, and degree of motion matching, several metaphors achieved a relatively high rank across all the subjective evaluations among older adults. We recommend the metaphors related to some childhood games, such as rubber band skipping and shuttlecock, as the best choices for further PA exergames design, because these activities elicited more positive feelings and fewer negative feelings and indicated a higher level of familiarity and degree of motion matching among older adults. In contrast, the metaphors related to competitive sports or demanding activities, such as butterfly stroke and crossing a footbridge, generally elicited less positive affect, more negative feelings, less familiarity, and a lower degree of motion matching.

5 Conclusion

This study used an iterative user-centered design process to develop and identify embodied metaphors based on older adults' understanding and preferences, which can inspire co-creation in future exergame design. Based on the results, bodily experiences relating to everyday lives, entertainment and sports, things and animals, and childhood memories were frequently reported as embodied metaphors in older adults' stereotypes of metaphorical mappings. Especially, we recommend that future PA exergame designers and practitioners employ embodied metaphors related to older adults' childhood games, such as rubber band skipping and shuttlecock, to facilitate their understanding of the targeted gamification elements in exergames. Furthermore, it is argued that the metaphorical mappings should be developed and differentiated by accessing older adults' stereotypes of metaphorical mappings between their bodily experiences and the gamification elements and further evaluated in terms of their affective responses, familiarity, and motion matching.

Acknowledgments. This study was funded by the MOE (Ministry of Education in China) Liberal Arts and Social Sciences Foundation (Grant number 21YJC760040), Featured Innovation Project in Higher Education of Guangdong (Grant number 2023WTSCX169) and General Program of Stable Support Plan for Universities in Shenzhen (Grant number GXWD20231129154726002).

Disclosure of Interests. The authors have no competing interests to declare that are relevant to the content of this article.

References

1. Mao, G., Lu, F., Fan, X., Wu, D.: China's ageing population: the present situation and prospects. In: Poot, J., Roskruge, M. (eds.) Population Change and Impacts in Asia and the Pacific. NFRSAP, vol. 30, pp. 269–287. Springer, Singapore (2020). https://doi.org/10.1007/978-981-10-0230-4_12

2. Zhang, B., Zhou, R., Yang, L., Zhang, X.: Population aging and corporate innovation: evidence from China. Asia-Pac. J. Account. Econ. **30**(4), 986–1007 (2022). https://doi.org/10.1080/16081625.2022.2047741

3. Pani-Harreman, K.E., Bours, G.J.J.W., Zander, I., Kempen, G.I.J.M., Van Duren, J.M.A.: Definitions, key themes and aspects of 'ageing in place': a scoping review. Ageing Soc. **41**(9), 2026–2059 (2021). https://doi.org/10.1017/S0144686X20000094

4. Chodzko-Zajko, W.J., et al.: Exercise and physical activity for older adults. Med. Sci. Sports Exerc. **41**(7), 1510–1530 (2009). https://doi.org/10.1249/MSS.0b013e3181a0c95c

5. Kappen, D.L., Mirza-Babaei, P., Nacke, L.E.: Older adults' physical activity and exergames: a systematic review. Int. J. Hum. Comput. Interact. **35**(2), 140–167 (2019). https://doi.org/10.1080/10447318.2018.1441253

6. Maurer, B.: Embodied interaction in play: body-based and natural interaction in games. In: Dörner, R., Göbel, S., Kickmeier-Rust, M., Masuch, M., Zweig, K. (eds.) Entertainment Computing and Serious Games. LNCS, vol. 9970, pp. 378–401. Springer, Cham (2016). https://doi.org/10.1007/978-3-319-46152-6_15

7. Li, Q., Luximon, Y.: Older adults and digital technology: a study of user perception and usage behavior. In: Goonetilleke, R., Karwowski, W. (eds.) Advances in Physical Ergonomics and Human Factors. AISC, vol. 489, pp. 155–163. Springer, Cham (2016). https://doi.org/10.1007/978-3-319-41694-6_16

8. Li, Q., Luximon, Y.: Understanding older adults' post-adoption usage behavior and perceptions of mobile technology. Int. J. Des. **12**(3), 93–110 (2018)

9. Bakker, S., Antle, A.N., Van Den Hoven, E.: Embodied metaphors in tangible interaction design. Pers. Ubiquitous Comput. **16**(4), 433–449 (2012). https://doi.org/10.1007/s00779-011-0410-4

10. Aldenaini, N. Alqahtani, F., Orji, R., Sampalli, S.: Trends in persuasive technologies for physical activity and sedentary behavior: a systematic review. Front. Artif. Intell. **3**(7), 1–40 (2020). https://doi.org/10.3389/frai.2020.00007

11. Sadeghi, H., et al.: The effect of exergaming on knee proprioception in older men: a randomized controlled trial. Arch. Gerontol. Geriatr. **69**, 144–150 (2017). https://doi.org/10.1016/j.archger.2016.11.009

12. de Vries, A.W., Willaert, J., Jonkers, I., van Dieën, J.H., Verschueren, S.M.P.: Virtual reality balance games provide little muscular challenge to prevent muscle weakness in healthy older adults. Games Health J. **9**(3), 227–236 (2020). https://doi.org/10.1089/g4h.2019.0036

13. Ordnung, M., Hoff, M., Kaminski, E., Villringer, A., Ragert, P.: No overt effects of a 6-week exergame training on sensorimotor and cognitive function in older adults. A preliminary investigation. Front. Hum. Neurosci. **11**(160) (2017). https://doi.org/10.3389/fnhum.2017.00160

14. Mueller, F.F., Isbister, K.: Movement-based game guidelines. In: Proceedings of the SIGCHI Conference on Human Factors in Computing Systems (CHI 2014), pp. 2191–2200. Association for Computing Machinery. ACM, New York (2014). https://doi.org/10.1145/2556288.2557163

15. Li, Q., Luximon, Y.: The effects of 3D interface metaphor on older adults' mobile navigation performance and subjective evaluation. Int. J. Ind. Econ. **72**, 35–44 (2019). https://doi.org/10.1016/j.ergon.2019.04.001

16. Zhou, J., Chourasia, A., Vanderheiden, G.: Interface adaptation to novice older adults' mental models through concrete metaphors. Int. J. Hum.-Comput. Interact. **33**(7), 592–606 (2017). https://doi.org/10.1080/10447318.2016.1265827

17. Johnson, M.: The body in the mind: The bodily basis of meaning, imagination, and reason. University of Chicago Press, Chicago (2013)

18. Manches, A., McKenna, P.E., Rajendran, G., Robertson, J.: Identifying embodied metaphors for computing education. Comput. Hum. Behav. **105**, 105859 (2020). https://doi.org/10.1016/j.chb.2018.12.037

19. Yap, K., Zheng, C., Tay, A., Yen, C.-C., Do, E.Y.-L.: Word out! learning the alphabet through full body interactions. In: Proceedings of the 6th Augmented Human International Conference (AH 2015), pp. 101–108. Association for Computing Machinery. ACM, New York (2015). https://doi.org/10.1145/2735711.2735789

20. Paul, F.C., Goh, C., Yap, K.: Get creative with learning: word out! A full body interactive game. In: Proceedings of the 33rd Annual ACM Conference Extended Abstracts on Human Factors in Computing Systems (CHI EA 2015), pp. 81–84. Association for Computing Machinery. ACM, New York (2015). https://doi.org/10.1145/2702613.2728657

21. Konstantinidis, E.I., Billis, A.S., Mouzakidis, C.A., Zilidou, V.I., Anto-niou, P.E., Bamidis, P.D.: Design, implementation, and wide pilot deployment of FitForAll: an easy to use exergaming platform improving physical fitness and life quality of senior citizens. IEEE J. Bio-med. Health Informat. **20**(1), 189–200 (2016). https://doi.org/10.1109/JBHI.2014.2378814

22. Pirbabaei, E., Amiri, Z., Sekhavat, Y.A., Goljaryan, S.: Exergames for hand rehabilitation in elders using leap motion controller: a feasibility pilot study. Int. J. Hum.-Comput. Stud. **178**(1), 103099 (2023). https://doi.org/10.1016/j.ijhcs.2023.103099

23. Zhang, H., Wu, Q., Miao, C., Shen, Z., Leung, C.: Towards age-friendly exergame design: the role of familiarity. In: Proceedings of the Annual Symposium on Computer-Human Interaction in Play (CHI PLAY 2019). Association for Computing Machinery, pp. 45–57. ACM, New York (2019). https://doi.org/10.1145/3311350.3347191

24. Hurtienne, J., Weber, K., Blessing, L.: Prior experience and intuitive use: image schemas in user centred design. In: Langdon, P., Clarkson, J., Robinson, P. (eds.) Designing Inclusive Futures, pp. 107–116. Springer, London (2008). https://doi.org/10.1007/978-1-84800-211-1_11

25. Antle, A.N., Droumeva, M., Corness, G.: Playing with the sound maker: do embodied metaphors help children learn? In: Proceedings of the 7th International Conference on Interaction Design and Children (IDC 2008). Association for Computing Machinery, pp. 178–185. ACM, New York (2008). https://doi.org/10.1145/1463689.1463754

26. Hurtienne, J.: Primary metaphors describe standard meanings of topological arrangements. In: The Workshop Ubicomp Beyond Devices: Objects, People, Space and Meaning at the NordiCHI 2014 8th Nordic Conference on Human–Computer Interaction, Helsinki (2014)

27. Zhang, B., Xu, J.: Home-Based Exercise Guide for Seniors. Posts & Telecommunications Press, Beijing (2020)

28. Rohrer, T.: The body in space: dimensions of embodiment. In: Ziemke, T., Zlatev, J., Frank, R.M. (eds.) Body, Language and Mind, vol. 1, pp. 339–377. Mouton de Gruyter, Berlin (2007)

29. Crawford, J.R., Henry, J.D.: The positive and negative affect schedule (PANAS): construct validity, measurement properties and normative data in a large non-clinical sample. Br. J. Clin. Psychol. **43**(3), 245–265 (2004). https://doi.org/10.1348/0144665031752934

30. Zhang, H., Wang, D., Wang, Y., Chi, Y., Miao, C.: Development and validation of a practical instrument for evaluating players' familiarity with exergames. Int. J. Hum.-Comput. Stud. **145**, 102521 (2021). https://doi.org/10.1016/j.ijhcs.2020.102521

31. Watson, D., Clark, L.A., Tellegen, A.: Development and validation of brief measures of positive and negative affect: the PANAS scales. J. Pers. Soc. Psychol. **54**(6), 1063–1070 (1988). https://doi.org/10.1037/0022-3514.54.6.1063

Constructing a Multi-dimensional Social Compensation Design Scale for Older People Within the Framework of Social Media for Smart Homes

Ke Ma$^{(\boxtimes)}$ (iD), Meng Gao, and Renke He

School of Design, Hunan University, Yuelu Area, Changsha 410082, China
{make,meng_gao}@hnu.edu.cn

Abstract. Managers and designers need to understand the subtleties of social compensation design so they can make social apps that meet the psychological needs of users and keep them using them. However, there is a significant gap in the research that has already been done on creating and validating a Social Compensation Design Scale (SCDS). This study aims to fill that gap by developing and testing the SCDS, specifically for older people living alone in cities. It will be used for smart home social media and looked at through the lens of information systems design. The study used the Delphi method and two rounds of surveys to get information from older people. SPSS 25.0 and Amos 28.0 were used to analyze the data. As part of the research process, the first scale was approved by experts and then put through strict reliability and validity tests. Exploratory Factor Analysis (EFA) found four main factors, which were then improved by Confirmatory Factor Analysis (CFA). This led to a model with good fit metrics. The results show that the SCDS has four parts: quality of the user interface, quality of interactions, quality of the content, and quality of the service. These four parts are measured by 16 items. This study gives managers and designers a structured way to determine how much social compensation older users experience when using smart home social media. This will significantly assist in creating and improving social apps that improve older people's overall health and happiness.

Keywords: Social compensation design · smart home social media · older adults · subjective well-being · scale development

1 Introduction

In the 2023 World Social Report, the United Nations (2023) highlighted that the global population aged 65 and over was 761 million in 2021 and is projected to double to 1.6 billion by 2050 [1]. In China, the number of older adults living alone rose to 118 million in 2021, with expectations of surpassing 200 million by 2030 [2]. With the home-based pension model as the primary approach in China, over 90% of individuals over 60 reside in home care settings. However, a major challenge many older adults face living alone is fulfilling their social participation needs. Social participation is crucial to whether older

Q. Gao and J. Zhou (Eds.): HCII 2024, LNCS 14725, pp. 59–75, 2024.
https://doi.org/10.1007/978-3-031-61543-6_5

adults can lead independent and active lives [3]. According to the continuity theory [4], older adults' social needs do not diminish despite the decline in physiological functions or upon retirement. However, factors such as diminishing physical abilities and mobility, retirement, decreasing social circles, the impact of the post-pandemic era, and dealing with grief from widowhood or the loss of loved ones and friends [5] can lead to limited social interactions for older adults, culminating in loneliness. Loneliness is linked to depression and increases mortality risks among older people [6]. Research indicates that social interaction and participation in social activities can mitigate loneliness in older adults [7] and even reduce the risk of Alzheimer's disease [8]. Consequently, enhancing the social participation of solitary older adults is a crucial practical challenge.

Technological advancements have propelled us into an era of digitalization and intelligence, fostering intelligent innovation within the family unit system. A notable development in this landscape is the emergence of the smart home screen series, a product category that has gained prominence in recent years. Distinct from conventional household appliances, these products offer control over smart home devices and feature touchable large screens, enabling user interaction for video calls and online chats. Companies like Amazon, Alibaba, and Baidu have introduced smart home screen products, which are increasingly vital for smart aging. Intelligence and digitization play crucial roles in enhancing the lives of older adults [9]. Smart home social media is primarily characterized by users employing smart home screen products, utilizing mobile communication network technology to facilitate social interactions. Social applications are presented as information systems with a variety of social content and formats, including voice, text, graphics, and video. Studies have demonstrated that older adults engage in social media for social interaction, which positively influences their emotions, life satisfaction, and overall health. In China, the use of WeChat by solitary elderly individuals has been shown to increase their intergenerational support and social activities, thus enhancing their subjective well-being [10]. The inclusivity, recognition, and mobility satisfaction derived from social media communication provide social compensation to the elderly [11], suggesting that social media use can help older adults achieve a degree of social compensation, improving their subjective well-being. However, the extent to which smart home social media can further enhance social compensation for older adults remains an open question. A key aspect of social compensation is computer-mediated communication (CMC), with its inherent attributes that can help users address their psychosocial vulnerabilities [12]. Psychological barriers and health challenges are among the primary reasons why older adults cease using the internet [13], hindering their access to the benefits of new technologies and products. Consequently, this raises a research question: does smart home social media, as a form of information system, possess attributes that can address the psychosocial vulnerabilities of older adults?

This study aims to develop and validate a scale for social compensation design specifically tailored for urban older users within the smart home social media context, approached from the perspective of information systems design. The theoretical impetus for adopting a design-focused perspective is anchored in the work of Gregor (2002) [14], who highlighted the critical importance and necessity of design science research as a pivotal theoretical branch within information systems. Echoing this sentiment, Hooker (2004) [15] emphasized the inherently practical nature of design, advocating for its research to integrate theories from various disciplines. This interdisciplinary approach enriches the design studies paradigm, enabling the creation of theories within design science. For example, the application of social psychology theories in design practice has the potential to evolve into design science theories, demonstrating identifiable patterns. The practical rationale behind developing this scale is driven by the growing emphasis on understanding and fostering the acceptance behavior of older adults towards smart home social media applications. This focus aims to cultivate differentiated marketing strategies through social compensation and to design more competitive social media platforms. However, these endeavors necessitate a theoretically grounded and quantifiable tool. The objective of constructing this scale is to decipher the multi-dimensional essence of social compensation design, an essential factor for fostering robust connections between smart home social media and its older user base. The scale assesses how effectively the design features of smart home social media address the psychosocial vulnerabilities of older users, ultimately aiming to elevate their subjective well-being.

Social compensation is a multifaceted concept, influenced by a wide range of factors, some of which have not yet been identified or conceptualized by scholars. This study extends the work of Ma et al. (2023) [16], who, from an information systems design perspective, identified ten sub-dimensions influencing social compensation design. These dimensions are graphic features (GF), information architecture (IA), human-computer interaction (HCI), human interactivity (HI), intelligence (INT), socialization (SOC), shareability (SHA), user-generated content (UGC), social security (SE), and empathy (EMP). However, it's important to acknowledge that these are not the only possible factors. Different studies might suggest a variety of factors that influence social compensation, aiming to address the psychosocial vulnerabilities of older users in computer-mediated communication (CMC), such as different levels of technological literacy or cultural variations among the elderly. Research incorporating diverse perspectives is essential for the advancement of this field. Building on the research of Ma et al. (2023) [16] and guided by the scale development methodology of Limayem et al. (2007) [17], this study has developed a practical, multi-dimensional scale for social compensation design. This scale is specifically tailored for older users of smart home social media, addressing the unique needs and challenges of this demographic.

2 Literature Review

2.1 Social Compensation

Tracing back to the origins of social compensation, Davis and Kraus (1989) [18] initially proposed the compensation hypothesis in the 1980s while investigating the relationship between social behavior, loneliness, and mass media usage. At that time, the hypothesis suggested that media usage compensated for the absence of social connections. During this era, the prevalence of telephones and mobile phones was limited, and the Internet was even less widespread. Consequently, their research predominantly focused on more traditional media such as telephones, television, movies, books, and newspapers. The utilization of these mass media forms was theorized to counteract psychological loneliness stemming from a dearth of real-life social interactions. As the Internet evolved and gained widespread popularity, the focus shifted from traditional mass media to emerging mediums, primarily encompassing smartphones, computers, and smart homes. In these new contexts, social media has become increasingly prominent. Social media encompasses the tools and platforms utilized for sharing information, experiences, and opinions via the Internet, offering social services and facilitating online social activities. McKenna and Barge (2000) [19] were among the pioneers to propose that the Internet might offer greater benefits to certain individuals than others. They contended that individuals experiencing high levels of anxiety in face-to-face interactions might find online socialization easier. They also posited that lonely individuals, lacking robust offline social networks, might resort to the Internet to rekindle relationships. These early theories have since evolved into broader predictions that form the basis of the social compensation hypothesis, exploring the dynamic interplay between technology and social behavior.

In summary, medium compensation encompasses a wide array of media types, including television, movies, music, phone calls, text messages, and even non-internet accessible mediums like tapes, which all play a compensatory role [20]. In contrast, social compensation primarily differentiates between face-to-face communication and online-mediated communication. It mainly refers to the use of emerging media equipped with social media to compensate for loneliness arising from a lack of social relationships among various groups [12, 21]. Social compensation implies that people who struggle with offline face-to-face interactions use online means to make up for these offline deficits [22, 23]. Sometimes referred to as the "poor-get-richer" hypothesis [24], social compensation suggests that online networks can make up for insufficient offline networks. Building on previous research, Ma et al. (2023) [16] proposed that social compensation examines the process of substitution and psychological compensation by media carrying social media within a system for different groups lacking sufficient social or interpersonal relationships. This process ultimately leads to equilibrium, strengthening social connections and enhancing subjective well-being. Social compensation focuses on how computer-mediated communication (CMC) can offer relational benefits to individuals who face challenges in face-to-face interactions due to social skill deficits or low sense of well-being [25]. The main hypothesis of social compensation posits that CMC possesses unique attributes that enable users to address their psychosocial vulnerabilities [12]. For example, due to the inherent characteristics of computers that facilitate message control or anonymity, online communication might be more comfortable for some than face-to-face interactions; it also makes it easier for users to find and connect with like-minded individuals. Consequently, individuals with social psychological vulnerabilities are often more inclined towards engaging in the online environment.

2.2 Two Key Elements of Social Compensation

Social compensation is predicated on the characteristics of online social interactions as opposed to offline, face-to-face communication. Consequently, individuals who are unable or find it challenging to engage in face-to-face interactions are more likely to resort to computer-mediated communication (CMC) for their social needs. A key element of social compensation is its emphasis on the specific attributes of the medium used for communication. Wang and Shi (2021) [21] highlighted that these medium attributes, integral to social compensation, can be analyzed across dimensions such as interactivity, temporality, accessibility, replicability, storage capacity, content permanence, retrievability, portability, social cues, and information capacity. Another fundamental aspect of social compensation pertains to the varying groups involved. The mechanisms of social compensation differ due to group differences and the distinct functionalities of the medium. These mechanisms are shaped by the unique physiological and psychological characteristics, needs, usage behaviors, and socio-cultural contexts of the different groups, in conjunction with the technical characteristics, functionalities, and affordances of the medium, which unleash their compensatory potentials in diverse ways. Therefore, understanding the mechanism of social compensation necessitates a comprehensive consideration of multiple factors, encompassing both the attributes of the communication medium and the specificities of the user groups.

Social Compensation for Different Groups. The current research stage on social compensation for different groups focuses on adolescents, college students, adults, and older adults. Studies on older adult groups support social compensation. For example, Ma et al. (2023) [16] investigated the determinants of social compensation design among 24 older adults who engaged in online socialization through smart home social media, approaching the topic from an information systems design perspective. Their qualitative research findings revealed that factors influencing social compensation design encompassed graphic features (GF), information architecture (IA), human-computer interaction (HCI), human interactivity (HI), intelligence (INT), socialization (SOC), shareability (SHA), user-generated content (UGC), social security (SE), and empathy (EMP). Kong and Lee (2017) [11] conducted a random survey of 392 older adults and discovered that social media usage could facilitate social compensation for this age group.

In summary, while research on social compensation has been conducted for various groups, there's a notable gap in studies focusing on older adults. Considering the global aging population's rapid growth, it's crucial to emphasize social compensation research for this demographic to promote active aging. Therefore, this study develops and validates the Social Compensation Design Scale (SCDS) from an information system design perspective, aiming to enhance future research on social compensation among older adults.

Social Compensation for Different Medium. The unique attributes of media platforms allow users to transcend the barriers of time and space, offering remedies for challenges unattainable in offline contexts. It is crucial, however, to acknowledge the distinct characteristics and roles of various media. Consequently, the extent of social compensation hinges on the choice of media; different platforms yield varying degrees of social compensation, influenced by their inherent features. Notwithstanding, current research focusing on elderly social media users predominantly omits the consideration of other smart technologies, such as intelligent home screen devices. These innovations are a testament to the digital and intelligent evolution of home systems.

In this context, the necessity for further investigation into the social compensation of older users in smart home social media becomes evident. To date, there has been a lack of research efforts aimed at characterizing and quantifying social compensation from a process-oriented approach. Consequently, this study zeroes in on the realm of smart home social media. Through the lens of information systems design, it endeavors to devise and corroborate a scale specifically for social compensation design catering to older users. This effort is intended to lay a foundational groundwork for future empirical research in this area.

3 Framework

This study was structured in three distinct phases the development (Phase 1), exploration (Phase 2), and validation (Phase 3) of the Social Compensation Design Scale (SCDS). Phase 1 primarily focused on defining and constructing the initial scale through an analysis of pertinent literature on social compensation design influences. This phase also involved expert evaluations for content validity of the initial scale, leading to the elimination of ineffective items. In Phase 2, effective questionnaires were collected from 340 urban older users, and reliability and validity tests were performed using SPSS 25.0 software. An Exploratory Factor Analysis (EFA) was then executed via Principal Component Analysis (PCA) to investigate the scale's construct validity. This process extracted four principal components, deleted 12 subpar items, retaining 29 items. Phase 3 amassed a total of 357 valid questionnaires. Confirmatory Factor Analysis (CFA) was conducted using Amos 28.0 software to affirm the scale's structural rationality. Metrics such as reliability, convergent validity, discriminant validity, and model fit were evaluated. The study reported factor loadings, CR, and AVE for each measurement model, along with CMIN/DF, RMSEA, SRMR, CFI, AGFI, and TLI for the combined model. With the removal of 13 poor measurement items, all the aforementioned indices demonstrated statistical excellence. The study ultimately proposed a measurable and validated multi-dimensional SCDS comprising four dimensions and 16 measurement items.

3.1 Participants

In this study, two distinct participant groups were involved. The first group comprised four experts in human-computer interaction design who participated in the scale development phase. The second group consisted of urban older users in China, who engaged online in two phases of data collection – the exploratory and the validation phases.

As per the regulations of the State Council of China (1978) [26] regarding retirement age, employees in state-owned enterprises, institutions, and mass organizations who haven't been involved in physically strenuous or health-detrimental work are eligible to apply for retirement at the age of 60 for men and 50 for women, given they have a minimum of ten consecutive years of work experience. Additionally, in alignment with definitions of older adults in other nations, the American Association of Retired Persons (2024) [27] categorizes individuals aged 50 and above as older adults.

Accordingly, the target population delineated in this paper comprises urban older individuals in China, aged 50 years and above, living alone, and actively using smart home social media for social communication. This age bracket is also in line with recent studies in the field [28].

3.2 Data Collection

Online surveys offer a swift and cost-efficient method for eliciting responses from internet users [29]. This approach is particularly pertinent for this study, which investigates the behaviors of urban older users of smart home social media in China, especially under the constraints of pandemic-related restrictions. Internet-based online surveys have thus been identified as an appropriate tool for data collection. The study employed two rounds of data collection, utilizing online questionnaires developed on the Tencent Questionnaire platform. These questionnaires were distributed through the Tencent Questionnaire's Aging Group. A significant emphasis was placed on ensuring the authenticity and validity of the data gathered during this phase. Tencent Questionnaire has established a database of over 500,000 older users, representing an aging cohort that spans across 300 cities in China. This extensive group facilitates the invitation of members to participate in specific studies, aligning with the criteria set forth by each research project.

The questionnaire employed in both rounds of data collection was structured into three sections: (1) An introductory part, which elucidated the aim, social significance, scope of information gathering, potential privacy concerns, and mitigations, along with an explanation of certain terminologies used in the questionnaire; (2) The multi-dimensional Social Compensation Design Scale (SCDS), comprising various measurement items; (3) Basic information about the users. Research indicates that large-scale scales exhibit markedly enhanced reliability and validity compared to small-scale ones [30]. Therefore, each item was gauged using Likert's seven-point equidistant scale, where "1" denotes strong disagreement, "2" disagreement, "3" relative disagreement, "4" neutrality, "5" relative agreement, "6" agreement, and "7" strong agreement. The final question in the questionnaire design serves as a check to ensure participant engagement and meaningful responses. It's a simple prompt (Please note that this study is important. Please check "I don't know"), where choosing responses like "I know" or "I don't care" would indicate the respondent's lack of attentiveness.

To ensure the acquisition of high-quality data, both rounds of data collection employed stringent procedures and systems to filter responses. If a respondent completed a survey question in an unusually short time (less than 80 s) or an excessively long time (over 1,000 s), if their answers exhibited a consistent pattern (such as all 1 s or all 7 s), or if they incorrectly answered the final attention check question (selecting 'I know' or 'I don't care'), their data were excluded on the grounds that these patterns signified non-credible responses. Respondents were restricted from participating in the survey more than once, and individual participation was monitored through their WeChat ID. Additionally, as an incentive, each survey participant was awarded a cash prize.

4 Development of SCDS

4.1 Items Development Process

Wang and Shi (2021) [21] posited that the characteristics of the medium, as a component of social compensation, can be dissected into dimensions such as interactivity, temporality, accessibility, replicability, storage capacity, content stability, retrievability, portability, social cues, and informational capacity. Building upon this framework, Ma et al.

(2023) [16] delved into the determinants influencing social compensation design among 24 older adults engaging with smart home social media for online socialization, through the prism of information system design. The outcomes of this qualitative inquiry revealed that the factors affecting social compensation design encompass graphic features (GF), information architecture (IA), human-computer interaction (HCI), human interactivity (HI), intelligence (INT), socialization (SOC), shareability (SHA), user-generated content (UGC), social security (SE), and empathy (EMP).

This study extends the research of Ma et al. (2023) [16], leveraging relevant literature and integrating the unique features of smart home social media with the authors' firsthand experiences with such platforms, to delineate the factors influencing social compensation design through the lens of information systems design. Building upon this foundation, the study has further developed an initial scale for assessing social compensation design among older users within the smart home social media context. This scale encompasses 10 dimensions and includes 50 measurement items.

4.2 Expert Review

The study continued to employ the Delphi method to ensure a certain level of validity for the content of the initial scale. In this phase, four experts in human-computer interaction design were invited to assess the content validity of the initial scale. Initially, their consent was obtained, followed by an introduction to the study's background, objectives, and methodology during a Tencent meeting. The experts were then provided with the 'Request for Revision of the Initial Scale of Social Compensation Design for Older Adults Based on Smart Home Social Media.' They were asked to comment on the clarity of each specific measurement item, the correlation between measurement items within each dimension, and how well the items interpreted the higher dimensions.

Feedback from the four experts was gathered, leading to a preliminary consolidation of their comments. After multiple rounds of thorough deliberation and comparison, items identified as repetitive or contentious were removed. Additionally, items that were semantically unclear or difficult to comprehend were revised for clarity. Following this expert evaluation, nine measurement items were eliminated from the initial scale, reducing the number to 41 items. The social security (SE) dimension was redefined as social privacy concerns (SPC), creating the 'Expert-Modified Initial Scale.' For the subsequent exploratory factor analysis, measurement items for the graphic features (GF) and information architecture (IA) dimensions were denoted by UIQ + numbers. The dimensions of human-computer interaction (HCI), human interactivity (HI), and intelligence (INT) were indicated by IQ + numbers. The dimensions of socialization (SOC), shareability (SHA), and user-generated content (UGC) were labeled by CQ + numbers, and finally, the dimensions of social privacy concerns (SPC) and empathy (EMP) were represented by SQ + numbers.

5   Exploration of SCDS

5.1   Participants

At this phase, the questionnaire was constructed based on the expert-revised scale. The SCDS, comprising 41 measurement items, was employed primarily to assess ten dimensions. A total of 400 questionnaires were collected in this survey, of which 60 were deemed invalid, leaving 340 valid questionnaires. Furthermore, following the guidance of Zeng et al. (2009) [31], it is advisable for the sample size in factor and regression analysis to be 5 to 10 times the number of measurement items. Hence, with the SCDS incorporating 41 items and 340 valid questionnaires collected, the sample size is approximately eightfold the number of measurement items, satisfying the criteria for factor analysis.

5.2   Reliability and Validity Analysis

Reliability Analysis. Assessing the data quality of measurement outcomes is a critical step to validate the subsequent correlation analyses. The internal consistency of each dimension is typically evaluated using the Cronbach's alpha coefficient for reliability assessment. The Cronbach's alpha coefficient ranges from 0 to 1, with higher values indicating greater reliability. A coefficient below 0.6 is considered a failure in the reliability test, necessitating a redesign of the questionnaire or a re-collection and analysis of the data. In exploratory research, a Cronbach's alpha coefficient between 0.6 and 0.7 suggests reliability is present and acceptable. Values between 0.7 and 0.8 denote moderate reliability, between 0.8 and 0.9 indicate high reliability, and values between 0.9 and 1 signify very high reliability [32].

Upon computation (Table 1), the Cronbach's alpha coefficients for all latent variables exceeded 0.7, with some surpassing 0.8, a few exceeding 0.9, and the overall Cronbach's alpha coefficient reaching 0.958. These findings demonstrate strong internal consistency and reliability across the measurement items in the survey questionnaire.

Validity Analysis. Due to the thorough assessment of the scale's content validity prior to the empirical study, all measurement items underwent verification, ensuring the scale's robust content validity. Subsequently, to ascertain the appropriateness of conducting factor analysis on the measurement items, both the Kaiser-Meyer-Olkin (KMO) test and Bartlett's sphericity test were performed. The KMO value is expected to be above 0.7 [33], and at the very least, greater than 0.6. The p-value for Bartlett's sphericity test needs to be below 0.05. The analysis utilizing SPSS 25.0 software revealed that the scale's KMO value was 0.946, and the Bartlett's Test of Sphericity was significant, with a p-value of 0.000 (Table 2). Hence, the findings suggest the presence of common factors among the questionnaire's measurement items, making them highly suitable for factor analysis.

5.3   Exploratory Factor Analysis (EFA)

This study employed Principal Component Analysis (PCA) for Exploratory Factor Analysis (EFA) to examine the structural validity of the scale. The maximum variance orthogonal rotation method was applied to rotate factors. Factors with rotated eigenvalues

Table 1. Reliability analysis

Sub-dimensions	Number	Cronbach's alpha
Graphic Features (GF)	4	0.797
Information Architecture (IA)	3	0.710
Human-Computer Interaction (HCI)	4	0.785
Human Interactivity (HI)	4	0.873
Intelligence (INT)	4	0.814
Socialization (SOC)	5	0.919
Shareability (SHA)	5	0.912
User Generated Content (UGC)	4	0.879
Social Privacy Concerns (SPC)	4	0.876
Empathy (EMP)	4	0.889
Total	41	0.958

Table 2. KMO and Bartlett's sphericity test

KMO		0.946
Bartlett's sphericity test	Approximate chi-square	9756.557
	Degrees of freedom	820.000
	Significance	0.000

exceeding one were selected to retain common factors. Subsequent steps involved testing whether the factor structure achieved optimal status and whether each item could be attributed to a distinct latent variable, thereby establishing a logical factor structure [34]. If the factor structure appeared unreasonable, item deletion was considered necessary to reach the ideal configuration. According to Tabachnick et al. (2013) [35], a factor loading greater than 0.55 signifies that it can account for 30% of the variance in the measured items, denoting a favorable scenario. When the factor loading exceeds 0.71, it indicates that the variance of 50% of the measured items can be explained, representing an ideal situation.

In this investigation, SPSS 25.0 was deployed to conduct Exploratory Factor Analysis (EFA) on the evaluative items, culminating in the identification of four primary components. Only those items exhibiting factor loadings above 0.55 were earmarked as representatives for these components. Subsequently, items with loadings below this threshold, specifically UIQ5, IQ10, IQ12, IQ13, IQ14, IQ15, IQ18, IQ19, SQ38, SQ39, SQ40, and SQ41, were excluded. Notably, the first principal component encompassed all items from the domains of socialization (SOC), shareability (SHA), and user-generated content (UGC), signaling a profound semantic linkage among them. This necessitates a further evaluation of residual independence in the Confirmatory Factor Analysis (CFA) phase and the removal of items with significantly overlapping meanings.

The EFA process led to the exclusion of 12 items, leaving a refined set of 29. These items encapsulate key elements from pertinent literature and interviews, each demonstrating factor loadings above 0.55. There are no instances of multiple loadings among the 29 items, and collectively, they explain 61.788% of the variance across the four factors. Additionally, given the potential for multicollinearity inherent to survey methodologies, Harman's single factor test revealed that a singular factor accounted for only 29% of the total variance, substantially below the 50% benchmark. This outcome suggests that the scale possesses a suitable factor structure and robust validity, having met the criteria for the validity assessment. The study subsequently designated the first principal component as content quality (CQ), the second as user interface quality (UIQ), the third as service quality (SQ), and the fourth as interaction quality (IQ).

6 Validation of SCDS

6.1 Participants

At this stage, a questionnaire was developed utilizing the 29 chosen measurement items. Out of 421 questionnaires collected, 64 were deemed invalid, leaving 357 valid responses. Concerning sample size for structural equation modeling (SEM)—a method necessitating large-sample analysis—Hair (2009) [36] recommended that the sample size be generally 10–15 times the quantity of measurement items. With the scale comprising 29 items and 357 valid questionnaires returned, the sample size was approximately 12 times the number of measurement items, falling within the optimal range yet remaining below 500. This count suffices for the requirements of factor analysis.

6.2 Confirmatory Factor Analysis (CFA)

The four principal components identified through Exploratory Factor Analysis (EFA), along with their associated measurement items, served as the basis for the measurement models in this study. Confirmatory Factor Analysis (CFA) was conducted using Amos 28.0 software to further substantiate the validity of these measurement items. Adhering to the convergent validity criteria set forth by Hair (2009) [36] and Fornell & Larcker (1981) [32], the study ensured that: (1) Standardized factor loadings for each measurement item were greater than 0.5, indicating significant contributions of items to their respective factors; (2) Composite Reliability (CR) for each dimension exceeded 0.6, affirming the reliability of the constructs; and (3) Average Variance Extracted (AVE) for each dimension surpassed 0.5, demonstrating a satisfactory level of explained variance by the constructs.

In this analysis, the measurement models for User Interface Quality (UIQ), Interaction Quality (IQ), Content Quality (CQ), and Service Quality (SQ) were rigorously evaluated through Confirmatory Factor Analysis (CFA) to ensure their reliability and convergent validity.

For the UIQ measurement model, standardized factor loadings varied between 0.578 and 0.722, with a Composite Reliability (CR) of 0.813. Initially, the Average Variance Extracted (AVE) was 0.422, falling short of the 0.5 threshold. Upon the removal of UIQ3, UIQ4, and UIQ6, as advised for enhancing model validity, the AVE improved to 0.518, indicating the model's reliability and acceptable convergent validity.

The IQ measurement model exhibited factor loadings ranging from 0.475 to 0.802, with a CR of 0.811 and an AVE of 0.469. The loading of IQ9 stood at 0.475, below the acceptable limit of 0.5, leading to its exclusion. This adjustment raised the CR to 0.818 and the AVE to 0.533, affirming the model's reliability and its strong convergent validity.

For the CQ measurement model, factor loadings spanned from 0.665 to 0.809, accompanied by a CR of 0.946 and an AVE of 0.558. These figures underscore the model's high reliability and its solid convergent validity.

Lastly, the SQ measurement model's factor loadings ranged from 0.723 to 0.874, with a CR of 0.875 and an AVE of 0.637. This model too demonstrated reliability and robust convergent validity.

In the assessment of model fit, a CMIN/DF ratio of 3.296 was observed, falling within the acceptable range. Conversely, the RMSEA index stood at 0.08, exceeding the threshold of acceptability. The SRMR value was commendable at 0.06, while the CFI index, at 0.885, did not meet the acceptable criteria. These findings underscore the necessity for model refinement. Examination of the Modification Indices (MI) revealed a pronounced discrepancy between the measurement items IQ10 and IQ11, with an MI value peaking at 53.630. This discrepancy suggests the presence of residual non-independence, contravening the principle of residual independence. Consequently, IQ11 was excluded due to its comparatively higher standardized factor loading relative to IQ10. Similarly, an MI value of 52.171 between CQ15 and CQ16 highlighted residual non-independence, breaching the same principle. Given identical standardized factor loadings for CQ15 and CQ16, both were omitted from the model. This rigorous analytical approach was consistently applied, leading to the removal of additional measurement items: CQ13, CQ14, CQ18, CQ22, CQ24, and CQ25.

In Table 3, you can see the results of the changed model fit. All nine indicators met the level of excellence. It means that the model that was made for this study fits well.

Table 3. Indicators of model fit

Model fit	Value	Criteria	Result
CMIN	199.166	The smaller, the better	
DF	98	The bigger, the better	

(continued)

Table 3. (*continued*)

Model fit	Value	Criteria	Result
CMIN/DF	2.032	Between 1 and 3 is excellent	excellent
RMSEA	0.054	<0.06	excellent
SRMR	0.060	<0.08	excellent
CFI	0.963	>0.95	excellent
GFI	0.936	>0.9	excellent
AGFI	0.912	>0.9	excellent
TLI	0.955	>0.9	excellent

In Table 4, you can see the modified model's reliability and convergent validity. All of the indicators meet Hair's suggested criteria, which means the measurement items are reliable.

Table 4. Reliability and convergent validity of the combined model

Construct	Item	Unstd.	S.E.	Z	P	STD.	CR	AVE
UIQ	UIQ1	1				0.781	0.762	0.518
	UIQ2	0.899	0.08	11.284	***	0.734		
	UIQ5	0.906	0.088	10.335	***	0.637		
IQ	IQ7	1				0.846	0.807	0.589
	IQ8	0.966	0.064	15.176	***	0.848		
	IQ10	0.658	0.061	10.768	***	0.577		
CQ	CQ12	1				0.658	0.891	0.578
	CQ17	1.138	0.09	12.612	***	0.772		
	CQ19	1.398	0.103	13.577	***	0.849		
	CQ20	1.323	0.098	13.472	***	0.84		
	CQ21	1.211	0.095	12.704	***	0.779		
	CQ23	0.879	0.082	10.718	***	0.637		
SQ	SQ26	1				0.724	0.875	0.637
	SQ27	1.055	0.075	14.069	***	0.792		
	SQ28	1.18	0.077	15.227	***	0.874		
	SQ29	1.082	0.077	14.128	***	0.795		

Note: * p < 0.050, ** p < 0.010, *** p < 0.001

The bolded diagonal entries in Table 5 show the square root of the Average Variance Extracted (AVE). The values in the lower triangle, on the other hand, show Pearson's correlation coefficients between the constructs. The results are in line with the established rule that says the square root of the AVE should be higher than the Pearson's correlation coefficients for each construct. This alignment shows that the model has strong discriminant validity between the constructs.

Table 5. Discriminant validity of the combined model

	CR	AVE	UIQ	IQ	CQ	SQ
UIQ	0.762	0.518	**0.72**			
IQ	0.807	0.589	0.546***	**0.768**		
CQ	0.891	0.578	0.458***	0.530***	**0.761**	
SQ	0.875	0.637	0.228***	0.179**	0.210***	**0.798**

Note: * $p < 0.050$, ** $p < 0.010$, *** $p < 0.001$

Based on the above analysis, Table 6 shows that this paper finally got the SCDS. There are 4 dimensions and 16 measuring units on the scale. One set of three items measures user interface quality (UIQ). Another set of three items measures interaction quality (IQ). Six items measure content quality (CQ), and four items measure service quality (SQ).

Table 6. Social Compensation Design Scale (SCDS)

Construct	Measurement items
UIQ	UIQ-1. I feel that the text features, icon features, image features, and colors of the smart home social media interfaces meet my needs during my use
	UIQ-2. I pay attention to the text features, icon features, image features, and colors of smart home social media interfaces
	UIQ-5. I think the rationality of the functional layout, hierarchical structure, and spacing of the smart home social media interfaces affects my usage experience (such as being happier)
IQ	IQ-7. I find it natural and easy to wake up to smart home social media, and it responds to me in a timely manner
	IQ-8. I think the voice interaction of smart home social media can meet my needs, and it is natural and responsive
	IQ-10. I think the operation of smart home social media is very simple, and it is not easy to make mistakes
CQ	CQ-12. I think using smart home social media can help me better integrate into the group
	CQ-17. I feel that smart home social media can help me share information with others, which is what I need

(*continued*)

Table 6. (*continued*)

Construct	Measurement items
	CQ-19. I think using the smart home social media feature for sharing information makes me happy
	CQ-20. I feel more satisfaction from using smart home social media to share information
	CQ-21. I think I would like to use the sharing information function of smart home social media
	CQ-23. I think using smart home social media can easily generate shareable content
SQ	SQ-26. I am concerned that smart home social media may leak my personal privacy information
	SQ-27. I am concerned about the security of my chat on smart home social media
	SQ-28. I am concerned that others may steal my private information on smart home social media
	SQ-29. I'm concerned that the personal information I display on smart home social media will have a negative impact on me

7 Conclusion

Standardized rules and procedures were strictly followed during the development and validation of the SCDS. A formal measurement scale with four dimensions was made after the initial scale's content was checked for validity and two more rounds of field research. This scale was found to be reliable and valid. After EFA, it was clear that the theoretical structure of the scale matched the data very well. When it comes to smart home social media, older users' social compensation traits mostly show up in user interface quality (UIQ), interaction quality (IQ), content quality (CQ), and service quality (SQ) (SQ). The EFA results also showed that the four parts of the scale were very different in terms of what they measured and how they were put together. This shows that social compensation design is made up of four parts. The results of the CFA showed that the modified model had good indicators and a good level of fitting. The AVE was also greater than 0.5, and the CR for all four dimensions was greater than 0.7. To use the scale for quantitative measurements, this means that it is internally consistent and that its structure is stable and reliable. As a result, the process of making the scale is scientific and thorough, and the measurement is valid in terms of what it measures. To sum up, the SCDS that was created in this study is reliable and valid, and it can be used as a starting point for future quantitative research on social compensation.

Acknowledgement. This research was supported by Hunan Provincial Innovation Foundation for Postgraduate (No. CX20200425).

References

1. United Nations: New UN report calls for concrete measures to support an ageing world (2023). https://www.un.org/en/desa/new-un-report-calls-concrete-measures-support-an-ageing-world. Accessed 3 Feb 2023
2. National Bureau of Statistics of China: Interpretation of the bulletin of the seventh national population census (2021). http://www.stats.gov.cn/xxgk/jd/sjjd2020/202105/t20210512_181 7342.html. Accessed 3 Oct 2022
3. Lee, S., Choi, H.: Impact of older adults' mobility and social participation on life satisfaction in South Korea. Asian Soc. Work Policy Rev. **14**, 4 (2020). https://doi.org/10.1111/aswp. 12187
4. Atchley, R.C.: Continuity and Adaptation in Aging: Creating Positive Experiences. Johns Hopkins University Press, Baltimore (1999)
5. Bondevik, M., Skogstad, A.: The oldest old, ADL, social network, and loneliness. West. J. Nurs. Res. **20**, 325–343 (1998). https://doi.org/10.1177/019394599802000305
6. Perissinotto, C.M., Stijacic Cenzer, I., Covinsky, K.E.: Loneliness in older persons: a predictor of functional decline and death. Arch. Intern. Med. **172**, 1078–1084 (2012)
7. Cattan, M., White, M., Bond, J., Learmouth, A.: Preventing social isolation and loneliness among older people: a systematic review of health promotion interventions. Ageing Soc. **25**, 41–67 (2005). https://doi.org/10.1017/S0144686X04002594
8. Bennett, D.A., Schneider, J.A., Tang, Y., et al.: The effect of social networks on the relation between Alzheimer's disease pathology and level of cognitive function in old people: a longitudinal cohort study. Lancet Neurol. **5**, 406–412 (2006). https://doi.org/10.1016/S1474-442 2(06)70417-3
9. Gatti, F.M., Brivio, E., Galimberti, C.: "The future is ours too": a training process to enable the learning perception and increase self-efficacy in the use of tablets in the elderly. Educ. Gerontol. **43**, 209–224 (2017)
10. Song, L., Ge, Y., Zhang, X.: The relationship between wechat use by chinese urban older adults living alone and their subjective well-being: the mediation role of intergenerational support and social activity. Psychol. Res. Behav. Manag. **14**, 1543–1554 (2021). https://doi. org/10.2147/PRBM.S330827
11. Kong, J.F., Lee, G.: Elderly's uses and gratifications of social media: key to improving social compensation and social pressure. Int. J. Cyber Behav. Psychol. Learn. (IJCBPL) **7**, 23–36 (2017). https://doi.org/10.4018/IJCBPL.2017070103
12. Toma, C.L.: Online dating and psychological wellbeing: a social compensation perspective. Curr. Opin. Psychol. **46**, 101331 (2022). https://doi.org/10.1016/j.copsyc.2022.101331
13. Chiu, C.-J., Liu, C.-W.: Understanding older adult's technology adoption and withdrawal for elderly care and education: mixed method analysis from national survey. J. Med. Internet Res. **19**, e374 (2017)
14. Gregor, S.: Design theory in information systems. Australas. J. Inf. Syst. **10**, 14–22 (2002). https://doi.org/10.3127/ajis.v10i1.439
15. Hooker, J.: Is design theory possible? J. Inf. Technol. Theory Appl. (JITTA) **6**, 8 (2004)
16. Ma, K., Gao, M., Guida, F.E., He, R.: Understanding the influencing factors and mechanism of social compensation for Chinese older adults using social media in the context of smart home: a qualitative analysis. Front. Public Health **11**, 1–20 (2023). https://doi.org/10.3389/ fpubh.2023.1174920
17. Limayem, M., Hirt, S.G., Cheung, C.M.K.: How habit limits the predictive power of intention: the case of information systems continuance. MIS Q. **31**, 705–737 (2007). https://doi.org/10. 2307/25148817

18. Davis, M.H., Kraus, L.A.: Social contact, loneliness, and mass media use: a test of two hypotheses. J. Appl. Soc. Psychol. **19**, 1100–1124 (1989). https://doi.org/10.1111/j.1559-1816.1989.tb01242.x

19. McKenna, K.Y.A., Barge, J.A.: Plan 9 from cyberspace: the implications of the internet for personality and social psychology. In: Personality and Social Psychology at the Interface, pp. 57–75. Psychology Press (2000)

20. Madianou, M., Miller, D.: Migration and New Media: Transnational Families and Polymedia. Routledge, London (2011)

21. Wang, K., Shi, M.: Media compensation: theoretical reflection and research trend. Glob. J. Media Stud. **8**, 69–84 (2021). https://doi.org/10.16602/j.gjms.20210049

22. Gross, E.F., Juvonen, J., Gable, S.L.: Internet use and well-being in adolescence. J. Soc. Issues **58**, 75–90 (2002). https://doi.org/10.1111/1540-4560.00249

23. Kraut, R., Kiesler, S., Boneva, B., et al.: Internet paradox revisited. J. Soc. Issues **58**, 49–74 (2002). https://doi.org/10.1111/1540-4560.00248

24. Zywica, J., Danowski, J.: The faces of facebookers: investigating social enhancement and social compensation hypotheses; predicting facebooktm and offline popularity from sociability and self-esteem, and mapping the meanings of popularity with semantic networks. J. Comput.-Mediat. Commun. **14**, 1–34 (2008)

25. Kovaz, D.M.: Social Compensation, Social Enhancement, and Rejection in Everyday Online Conversations. Master of Arts, College of William & Mary (2011)

26. The State Council of China: Interim Measures of the State Council on Retirement and Resignation of Workers (1978). http://www.gd.gov.cn/zwgk/wjk/zcfgk/content/post_2531473.html?ivk_sa=1024320u&wd=&eqid=85b2065d00008b57000000066487ddfc. Accessed 24 Sept 2023

27. American Association of Retired Persons (AARP): About AARP. In: AARP (2024). https://www.aarp.org/. Accessed 18 Jan 2024

28. Kim, M.J., Preis, M.W., Lee, C.-K.: The effects of helping, self-expression, and enjoyment on social capital in social media: the moderating effect of avoidance attachment in the tourism context. Behav. Inf. Technol. **38**, 760–781 (2019). https://doi.org/10.1080/0144929X.2018.1552718

29. Wright, K.B.: Researching internet-based populations: advantages and disadvantages of online survey research, online questionnaire authoring software packages, and web survey services. J. Comput.-Mediat. Commun. **10**, 00 (2005). https://doi.org/10.1111/j.1083-6101.2005.tb00259.x

30. Brown, J.D.: Likert items and scales of measurement. Statistics **15**, 10–14 (2011)

31. Zeng, L., Salvendy, G., Zhang, M.: Factor structure of web site creativity. Comput. Hum. Behav. **25**, 568–577 (2009). https://doi.org/10.1016/j.chb.2008.12.023

32. Fornell, C., Larcker, D.F.: Evaluating structural equation models with unobservable variables and measurement error. J. Mark. Res. **18**, 39–50 (1981). https://doi.org/10.1177/002224378101800104

33. Kaiser, H.F.: An index of factorial simplicity. Psychometrika **39**, 31–36 (1974). https://doi.org/10.1007/BF02291575

34. Spicer, J.: Making sense of multivariate data analysis: an intuitive approach. SAGE (2005)

35. Tabachnick, B.G., Fidell, L.S., Ullman, J.B.: Using Multivariate Statistics, 7th edn. Pearson, Boston (2013)

36. Hair, J.F.: Multivariate data analysis. Faculty Publications (2009)

It's not by Accident! It's by Design. Design Methods to Reach (Inter)generational Perspective

Andreia Pinto de Sousa[1]([⊠]) [iD] and Teresa Sofia Castro[2] [iD]

[1] Lusófona University - Porto University Center, HEI Lab: Digital Human Environment Interactions Labs, Porto, Portugal
andreia.pinto.sousa@ulusofona.pt
[2] Lusófona University - Porto University Center, CICANT: Centre for Research in Applied Communication, Culture, and New Technologies, Porto, Portugal
teresa.sofia.castro@ulusofona.pt

Abstract. This paper emphasizes the significance of employing methodological approaches rooted in participatory design to facilitate intergenerational collaboration in an age range less studied (generations X to Y) in developing a web-based newsroom for young people. The research stems from the YouNDigital project, funded by the Portuguese Foundation for Science and Technology, which seeks to explore young people's interaction with news in a digitized society. A key output of the project is the development of the YouNDigital Newsroom, a web-based platform enabling youth from diverse backgrounds to share their views of the world on issues that matter to them. Drawing upon intergenerational collaboration and knowledge transfer, this paper explores the challenges and strategies in creating a platform that reflects researchers' and users' diverse perspectives and needs.

Through co-design sessions, iterative prototyping, and usability testing, the task navigated complexities within a limited timeframe and resources to foster user engagement and ownership.

The main objective was to engage users with a web-based Newsroom to generate meaningful content that reflects their perspectives on matters of interest. The design thinking sessions and continuous collaborative work were instrumental in defining potential user profiles (personas) and delineating usage contexts for each persona. The findings underscore the importance of integrating diverse perspectives and collaborative design methodologies in addressing multifaceted challenges and creating inclusive solutions across generations. Leveraging design methodologies facilitated collaboration between researchers and users in developing the YouNDigital newsroom. By incorporating user perspectives from the outset, the project aimed to create a platform that resonates with young people and researchers from different generations' interests and fosters meaningful engagement with news content in a digital era.

Keywords: Participatory Design Methods · Intergenerational Collaboration · Knowledge Transfer

1   Introduction

Design thinking and participatory methodologies are crucial in a human-centric approach; they set the foundations for the project's evolvement, which is "built on principles of collaboration, co-creation, and empowerment of users and stakeholders" [1]. This paper discusses the importance of using methodological approaches based on design and unpacks how these were applied to reach intergenerational collaboration in a specific research task involving researchers and young people in an age range less studied. This article developed from YouNDigital - Youth, News and Digital Citizenship, a project funded by the Portuguese Foundation for Science and Technology (DOI 10.54499/PTDC/COM-OUT/0243/2021). One of the project's outputs is to build the YouNDigital Newsroom, supported by a web-based platform open to the participation of young people worldwide. The second phase was an exploratory moment in the construction of the prototype, and the third was the validation with users and the research team.

After this introduction that sets the purpose of this article, we situate the topic framed on supporting literature. Followed by the description of the decisions, benefits, and challenges of design methods applied to intergenerational collaborative research and derived inputs and feedback on uses and functionalities to be implemented in the web-based YouNDigital Newsroom. The article closes with final considerations about the research and future steps.

2   Intergenerational Cooperation and Knowledge Transfer through Design Methods

Knowledge transfer has been widely discussed [2, 3], especially in the relationship between children and older adults. Intergenerational projects aim "to bridge the gap between generations, reduce age stereotypes, and improve the participation of different generations in the community" [3].

However, issues around intergenerationality also arise in other areas, and between closer generations, intergenerational knowledge transfer in the context of organizations is still scarce [2]. The gap between Generation X and Generation Y and Z is significant in what concerns work approaches. The Xers were born between 1961 and 1979 and value work, education, and money, while the Yers (born amid 1980 and 1995) are recognized as individualists, goal-driven, and independent [4, 5] Generation Z are the most educated, children of the previous generations, and their special traits are technology, to which they are accustomed since they were babies and, the rapid communication and information consuming, and being result-oriented [15].

Intergenerational cooperation brings countless benefits due to the sharing and discussing different perspectives. However, it also brings challenges due to differences in values, behaviors, and attitudes toward work, with repercussions on aspects such as focus, behavior, approach, and communication style [5].

This article reports on the strategies adopted in a research project to create a web-based newsroom for young people. The challenges of a multidisciplinary team of different generations in a research project with a limited time frame that aims to make a scientific contribution and create a solution to be used in a real context present a high degree of complexity. YouNDigital aims to capture young people's (aged 15–24) socialization, attitudes, practices, and relationships toward news and digital citizenship. Young people are expected to participate in the YouNDigital newsroom to interact and actively produce content that shares their views of the world on topics related to the 2030 Agenda and in matters that interest them in a safe and inclusive atmosphere.

To organize the tangle of knowledge and create a product that fosters engagement for this specific task, the team adopted a design thinking paradigm focusing on the behaviors and attitudes of younger people towards news consumption and sharing. The adoption of this creative approach, which originated in the field of design, is due not only to its ability to solve complex problems but also to its collaborative and exploratory approach. According to Cross, designers tackle problems through synthesis, while scientists approach problem-solving through analysis; design activity emphasizes swiftly generating a satisfactory solution rather than engaging in prolonged problem analysis [6]. The context of the design problem is also a challenge in this project; a funded research project is strictly managed through time, resources, and expected outputs.

Developing an iterative and exploratory process in this context is a design problem. How to promote knowledge sharing among researchers from diverse fields, who are also users, and accommodate young people's expectations and needs in designing a web-based newsroom?

Participatory design entails the active involvement of users in shaping the design process for work practices. It adopts a democratic stance toward creating systems encompassing social and technological aspects within human work environments. This approach contends that users should play a pivotal role in shaping designs they will utilize, advocating for equal engagement of all stakeholders, particularly users, in interaction design [7] In essence, this perspective reframes design as an exploration rather than a quest for the optimal solution to a given problem. The creative designer views the design brief not merely as a directive for a solution but as a navigational aid through uncharted terrain [6].

Co-design sessions offer numerous advantages to the design process. They involve inviting individuals who may not typically be involved in creative endeavors to participate in the ideation stage, encouraging their contributions. This approach demystifies the process, fostering a sense of ownership among stakeholders for the ideas generated. Over time, this demystification results in improved requirements and feedback as stakeholders gain insight into our methods. With ownership of the ideas, stakeholders are more motivated to understand and internalize the rationale behind design decisions, empowering them to defend these decisions when questioned [8]. Adopting this designerly way of thinking in a project, where typically the designer plays an intermediary role, is being discussed in the design research field [9, 10]. Cross [6] identified five aspects of designerly ways of thinking: (i) Designers tackle 'ill-defined' problems; (ii) Their mode of problem-solving is 'solution-focused'; (iii) Their mode of thinking is 'constructive'; (iv) They use 'codes' that translate abstract requirements into concrete objects; (v) They use these codes to both 'read' and 'write' in 'object languages'. Interdisciplinary background and practice require agile and lateral thinking skills to equip designers to navigate uncertainty and the complexities of social, cultural, commercial, and environmental factors, fostering adaptability and potentially thriving in such contexts [9].

In the next section, we will unpack how knowledge transfer occurs in designing a newsroom, considering the intergenerational collaboration supported by participatory design methods.

3   The Case of YouNDigital Project

It is widely acknowledged that participatory design is the most effective approach to designing technologies [11], which involves integrating users into the design team. However, in the context of research projects, engaging users becomes progressively challenging despite concerted efforts. The participatory nature of design thinking does not imply continuous involvement of users; it has a holistic approach to stakeholders and systems, and it is seen as an innovative process that deals with wicked problems [12] and increases the quality of the final result in several aspects [13].

The inherent difficulties of a multidisciplinary and scientific research project and the deadlines established in funded projects often result in solutions not adapted to real-life contexts and users and problems that still need to be resolved. One of the premises of the YouNDigital project was to produce a Newsroom platform open to the participation of young people worldwide that will grow and evolve with time and user input.

During this process, the management team delivered the conduction of the process to designers that collected information, organized co-creation sessions, and, through exploration, presented some solutions to be studied and discussed by experts in the different fields covered by the project and afterward tested by young people. Therefore, to the definition of the user profiles (personas) and contexts of use centered on each Persona [14], co-creation sessions were conducted with different backgrounds and generations (X, Y or Millenials, and Z) of project researchers (divided into three teams: 1, 2, and 3), leading to scientific and empiric knowledge collection (to access to a detailed description of the co-creation sessions, [14]. In the sessions, three different profiles were defined: two primary personas (the youths Julieta and Artur) and one secondary persona (the teacher José Martins), and for each Persona, was also developed a description of one day in their life. The design of YouNDigital Newsroom also paid attention to digital rights (following the commentary 25 adopted by the United Nations in 2021[1]) of participation and protection. As a result of the co-creation sessions, a list of features was defined in Table 1, which provided different discussion sessions between researchers and users, bringing different perspectives and skills to the table.

Ultimately, the sessions helped researchers assume the newsroom user's point of view and pointed out opportunities and challenges afterward, confirmed by the young people's interviews. Thus, concurrently with this process, interviews were conducted with young people (aged 22–28) who are journalists or actively engaged in journalism activities, and from those, we were also able to gauge a set of functionalities. The interviews with young people with different socio-demographic backgrounds were conducted to validate the research team's views of the developing web-based newsroom. The interview

---

[1] https://www.ohchr.org/en/documents/general-comments-and-recommendations/general-com ment-no-25-2021-childrens-rights-relation.

Table 1. Functionalities retrieved from the co-creation sessions

---

Julieta Soares (Student, 17 Years old)
Environmental activist. Passionate about nature, she led the school newspaper, becoming the best student and reads newspapers on topics of interest

---

SCENARIO 1 _ TEAM 1
Find and Share content from the application:
　　News validation:
　　Fact-Checking;
　　Quality seals - Community data.
Concern that content control may remove interest:
　　Sense of Limitation - can cause user disinterest/demotivation.
Need to study what resources are needed to control content:
　　Sustainability plans, monetary costs, people.
Process of linking accounts from different applications:
　　E.g. Instagram w/ YND app.

SCENARIO 2 _ TEAM 3
Julieta presented as Promoter:
　　Considerations made on the evolution of digital sharing vs face-to-face sharing;
Gamification:
　　Launching challenges for diverse teams;
　　Possibility of activating timers;
　　Points awarded for completing activities.
Possibility of inserting activities created by users themselves:
　　Remove the pressure of being limited to those suggested by the app;
　　Relieve problems related to inhibition or unhealthy competition.
New sharing suggestions:
　　E.g., family/team/group albums;

Artur Guedes (Student, 15 Years old)
Passionate about sports since age 6, he uses digital media exclusively for sports content. He chose Professional Tourism due to career prospects, but he dislikes studying.

SCENARIO 1 _ TEAM 2
Introduction of the Imported News feature/concept;
Introduction of Gamification Principles:
　　Attraction mechanism:
　　Task Assignment;
　　Competition by adding up points when completing a particular stage.
Possibility of exploring different profiles:

(continued)

Table 1. (*continued*)

Social Network concept
Suggestion to look at frustrations and include them in the scenarios:
Understand how we can make Artur a promoter, e.g., he does not like writing, but his. friend does, so - invite him;

Scenario 1 _ TEAM 1
Suggestion of the app as a dissemination tool in the school context:
Developing competitions
Question asked:
Who creates the contest?
Will any user be able to?
Possibility of creating posts or importing links/posts.
Possibility for the user to import/export certain content from other sources:
The same question of content validation arises;
The problem of being from any source;
Limitation to certain verified sources;
Question of Fact Checking:
Content and Verification:
Think about the flow of content validation:
Combination of automatic mechanism + human validation:
Automatic mechanism - responsible for generalized, primary filtering;
Human layer - responsible for pending content, subsequently validated.
Done collaboratively:
Possibility of using the community as a regulatory mechanism;
Based on the Rules of the Editorial Statute.
Suggestion to create Watertight Zones:
Controlled - constituted and regulated by fact-checking, human layer, and community;
Social network option - less intervention, greater individual responsibility, individual culpability.
Concept of Redaction:
Immediate: database of official/controlled/official links;
Medium: posts written by the user.

José Martins (Teacher, 35 Years old)
Dedicated teacher for 9 years, thrives on instructing older students and guiding them in skill discovery. Recognizes declining student interest and the impact of technology, he actively seeks innovative strategies, aspiring to create a productive environment by harmonizing fun and learning.

Introduction of two different scenarios - both based on the assumption of technological generation:
Classroom - derived from 1 frustration - Scenario 1;

(*continued*)

Table 1. (*continued*)

Journalism Club - derived from 1 motivation - Scenario 2.
Web-app concept:
  Scenario 1 - Students all have access to a computer - perfect conditions;
  Scenario 2 - Pairs or the possibility of working on a cell phone.
Avatar concept and personalization:
  Addresses issues of privacy and data protection, especially in the case of minors;
  Question of anonymity and its inherent possibilities (greater creative freedom and/or
  freedom from judgment.
Addresses the issue of filtering themes/topics:
  Suggestion to eliminate default filtering; manual filtering is intended, where the user
  decides what they want to see.
Writing issue:
  Sharing content written by users;
  Question of Public Sharing and the control of offensive content - how it will be mod-
  erated.

SCENARIO 2 _ TEAM 2
Creation of challenges, e.g., Journalism Olympics:
  Practical character;
  Possibility of personalization;
  Creation of tools to save news and interact with it.
Creation of Idea Rooms:
  Collaborative rooms for users to carry out specific tasks;
  Possibility of creating an interactive newspaper;
Authorship issue safeguarded through signature with avatar;
Suggestion to introduce the idea of feedback:
  Use voting mechanisms to determine a winner.

script was built to uncover expectations, features and affordances, interaction, newsroom experiences, and suggestions to reach young people effectively. From the interviews, we highlight some takeaways considered central aspects to be at the core of the newsroom: aspects related to multimedia, interaction, and engagement (Table 2) were covered by all interviewees. Moreover, the newsroom should be an inclusive space to talk about less mainstream topics (Female, 24 years old), able to reach young people from different geographies and backgrounds (Female, 22 years old), a space to share hard news in a light and easy-to-understand manner and to offer different angles on news (Male, 28 years old); settled in the promotion of freedom of speech and offer content with quality (Male, 24 years old).

Table 2. Functionalities retrieved from the interviews with young people.

Technical requirements (F = female; M = Male)	F 24 years, Degree in Communication	F 22 years, Student of Communication	M 28 years, Journal director	M 24 years, Journalist in Angola
Multimedia	Video and audio; Streaming; Inclusive features (nationality, ethnicity, disability)	Video, image, and audio; Conferencing and podcast tools	Video and audio; Podcast tools	Text (primary), video, and audio
Interaction and Engagement	Communication tools; Collaborative tools	Communication tools; Collaborative tools	Communication tools; Collaborative tools	Fact-checking
Save and Share	Create bookmark; Share across social media; Storage of data for later publishing	Share across social media		
Navigation	Responsive to various devices	Search tools within the Newsroom		Search tools within the Newsroom

The design process applied to this project phase allowed us to gather information from the research team and potential users and combine them in a multidimensional perspective, having an intergenerational continuous conversation. The structuring functions of a solution of this nature, such as creating and sharing content, required the team to reflect on the need to validate the content shared through fact-checking and given credit strategies (pedagogical and technical) for photographs and sources, the attribution of quality seals by the community, and activation of privacy and data protection - a topic we aim to explore in a future article.

This reflection raised questions about content curation before publishing due to the nature of the project and how this constraint to immediate publication could cause user disinterest/demotivation, in addition to the need for a sustainability plan for the project, taking into account monetary and personnel costs for this activity.

The awareness of the research team concerning the issues of the sharing of online information highlighted a challenge to the project: how to create a solution for young people reflecting their current practices in similar platforms and accommodate the best practices in the field or even find solutions to problems that are still being studied? Crossing these intergenerational perspectives among team members and users allowed us to create a solid set of requirements and principles aligned with the project objectives. This phase and the techniques applied [14] to gather information to inform the solution allowed the design team to develop a meaningful connection with users and stakeholders, manage the project expectations, and create a collaborative and creative environment.

After the conclusion of the definition phase, we started the ideation through prototyping to explore different approaches. The initial versions of the prototypes were developed using a collaborative tool (Figma)[2], allowing the core team of researchers to follow and comment on the prototype's evolution. This phase was crucial to materializing the specifications discussed before. Developed through different stages of fidelity (Fig. 1), it allowed us to explore information architecture and interaction. This process led to the definition of the main interactions and, consequently, the structure of the first pages, disseminating and giving shape to the knowledge gathered.

Simultaneously with the development of the prototype, research into supporting technologies for implementing digital writing began. This investigation was led by a young programmer who worked under a grant from the project. Senior researchers supervised this research, and several members decided on the tool for the research team. The team could develop something from scratch or start from a pre-existing framework; the decision fell on the latter.

This moment has highlighted the different backgrounds and experiences of the team members. The designers responsible for leading the process understood that the context in which this design problem arises, a research project with strict deadlines and resources, would be a challenge and a requirement to be considered. The exploration phase during the prototyping allowed us to define what should be the core functionalities and dictate the tone for the final solution; however, due to the specificities of the platform where the Newsroom is built (WordPress[3] - the same used on the project website) and, again, the project already mentioned constraints, the process took another path from what was initially defined.

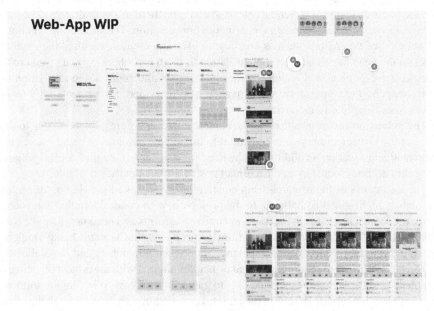

Fig. 1. Prototype development in Figma.

---

[2] Figma: https://www.figma.com/.
[3] WordPress: https://wordpress.com.

A list of functionalities organized by activities was created, which allowed a search for pre-existing solutions. This was a very demanding phase in which we had to make several adaptations due to the restrictions of the solution adopted. Different technical research was conducted to find the best way to articulate the different technical solutions. The solution found was presented to the task's core team, and based on all the work previously developed, the necessary customizations were defined. Questions about all the pre-existing solutions' functionalities were raised in these work sessions. However, the work previously developed proved to be a guide for this decision-making.

During these review and analysis sessions, the different approaches to the elements involved were evident; on the one hand, the technical perspective concerned with the solution's effective functioning, the designers who questioned the relationship between the solution and the users, and the experience. The objective would be to work on user engagement with the platform. Another perspective shared in these sessions was that of researchers in the area of digital literacy with concerns such as security, privacy, and involvement, and finally, managers who tried to ensure project fulfilment and the management of resources, namely time and people.

3.1 Young Users' Preliminary Feedback on the Web-Based Newsroom

After several iterations on the platform, a final version was presented to final users under formative usability test sessions followed by a User Experience Questionnaire. Considering that YouNDigital aims to capture young people's (aged 15–24) socialization, attitudes, practices, and relationships toward news and digital citizenship. Young people are expected to participate in the YouNDigital newsroom to interact and produce content on topics related to the 2030 Agenda and in matters that interest them in a safe and inclusive atmosphere. The evaluation protocol created for the usability test aimed to (i) Identify usability issues with the web app (effectiveness, efficiency, and satisfaction); (ii) Collect information about features and intention of use; (iii)Collect ideas on how to reach/involve young participants.

With the User Experience Questionnaire[4] [UEQ], we attempted to get the impressions of young people concerning several aspects of the user experience: Attractiveness, Perspecuity, Efficiency, Dependability, Stimulation, and Novelty. The first iteration of tests had six young participants, and the results informed us of substantial improvements.

The test sessions were conducted by a design team member supported by the programmer, who reported that the experience was very insightful and gave him another perspective on the project, his work, and the adjustments to be made. Several team members also tested the same version, and all the suggestions were registered and discussed among the team.

Preliminary results showed that the participants received the presented solution very well, and scales such as Attractiveness and Stimulation were well accepted and evaluated.

---

[4] User Experience Questionnaire: https://www.ueq-online.org/.

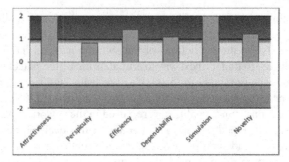

Fig. 2. Mean of User Experience Questionnaire (UEQ) scales

The scales of the UEQ can be categorized into pragmatic quality (comprising Perspicuity, Efficiency, and Dependability) and hedonic quality (including Stimulation and Originality). Pragmatic quality pertains to task-related quality aspects, while hedonic quality refers to non-task-related quality aspects. Below (Fig. 3), the mean of the three pragmatic and hedonic quality aspects is computed.

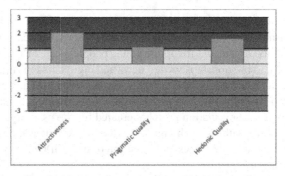

Fig. 3. Mean of the pragmatic and hedonic quality.

Scales related to visual design directly manifested in Attractiveness or even in Hedonic quality (stimulation and novelty) scale obtain high scores. However, the Pragmatic Quality related to Efficiency, Perspicuity, and Dependability must be improved to achieve a higher user evaluation. As shown in Fig. 2, Perspicuity is calculated based on the following answers (not understandable/understandable; easy to learn/not easy to learn; complicated/easy) are the lowest scale. These results reflect the team's concerns regarding the solution's ease of use, as it had to adapt to predefined structures and was not created from scratch for the problem in question. Despite this, we are not facing a negative evaluation due to the team's efforts to adapt to users' mental models and strive for the best solution for the technical constraints.

Nevertheless, YouNDigital Newsroom is available for youngsters' participation, and the design is still an ongoing process (based on feedback). The following steps are to improve the platform's functionalities and to find solutions to implement others that still need to be resolved.

4 Final Considerations

This article explored the iterative process of knowledge transfer, particularly between different generations, emphasizing intergenerational collaboration to bridge gaps and enhance community (researchers and users) participation in co-design, exploratory interviews, and feedback on user experience. Challenges arose in choosing the best approaches to foster intergenerational cooperation with a multidisciplinary background between Generation X and Y or Millenials, and Generation Z, gathering, collecting knowledge, and organizing and building from it. Another challenge was the context of the design problem, the project outputs considering strict deadlines and limited resources.

The discussion centered on describing the process, decisions, and strategies employed in a research project, YouNDigital, developing a web-based newsroom for young people, highlighting the adoption of design thinking to address complexities in a limited timeframe. Participatory design principles proved important in fostering user engagement and ownership, while co-design sessions facilitated idea generation and demystified the design process. Integrating diverse perspectives and collaborative design methodologies is essential for addressing multifaceted challenges and creating inclusive solutions across generations.

Throughout this process, the management team entrusted designers with overseeing the procedure, gathering information, facilitating co-creation sessions, and presenting potential solutions through exploration. These proposed solutions were then scrutinized and discussed by experts from various project-relevant domains before being tested by young participants. This collaboration allowed data gathering from different sources in a different context than is usual in research contexts. Besides interviews with the young people, where they identified core aspects, namely regarding multimedia, interaction, and communication tools, the team was able to participate actively in design process documentation in creating personas, requirements, wireflows, and wireframes. Through this collaborative and intergenerational process, we were able to get a list of needs and requirements, user profiles, and contexts of use to start constructing the YouNDigital Newsroom.

The human-centered approach of the design thinking process was decisive in developing a solution, considering different generations with different perspectives around creating and sharing content. Besides designing the digital platform, the designers' role in the project was to facilitate the interaction between researchers from different fields and potential users through techniques that fostered discussion around critical subjects concerning young people's news consumption and sharing. This article adds a valuable contribution to the design, media, and communication fields. This process originated an amount of data and information to be explored in future articles.

Acknowledgments. This article was developed within the scope of the project YouNDigital - Youth, News and Digital Citizenship (PTDC/COM-OUT/0243/2021/DOI 10.54499/PTDC/ COM-OUT/0243/2021) supported by national funds through FCT - Foundation for Science and Technology, I.P., under HEI-Lab R&D Unit (UIDB/05380/2020, https://doi.org/10.54499/UIDB/ 05380/2020), and CICANT - Centre for Research in Applied Communication, Culture, and New Technologies (DOI 10.54499/UIDB/05260/2020).

References

1. What is Participatory Design? | IxDF. https://www.interaction-design.org/literature/topics/par ticipatory-design#docs-internal-guid-053d91d3-7fff-c61e-a2ad-78ee0db34399. Accessed 30 Jan 2024
2. Schmidt, X., Muehlfeld, K.: 'What's so special about intergenerational knowledge transfer? Identifying challenges of intergenerational knowledge transfer. Manag. Revue **28**(4), 375–411 (2017). http://www.jstor.org/stable/26407256
3. Martins, T., et al.: Intergenerational programs review: study design and characteristics of intervention, outcomes, and effectiveness: research. J. Intergener. Relatsh. **17**(1), 93–109 (2019). https://doi.org/10.1080/15350770.2018.1500333
4. Usmani, S., Asif, M.H., Mahmood, M.Z., Khan, M.Y., Burhan, M.: Generation X and Y: impact of work attitudes and work values on employee performance. J. Manag. Res.Manag. Res. **6**(2), 51–84 (2019). https://doi.org/10.29145/jmr/62/060203
5. Rupčić, N.: Intergenerational learning and knowledge transfer – challenges and opportunities. Learn. Organ. **25**(2), 135–142 (2018). https://doi.org/10.1108/TLO-11-2017-0117
6. Cross, N.: Designerly ways of knowing. Des. Stud. **3**, 221–227 (1982)
7. Hartson, R., Pyla, P.: Background: design. In: The UX Book, pp. 397–401 (2019). https://doi. org/10.1016/B978-0-12-805342-3.00019-9
8. Hodges-Schell, M., O'Brien, J.: Living in the deliverables. In: Communicating the UX Vision, pp. 139–163 (2015). https://doi.org/10.1016/B978-0-12-420197-2.00008-4
9. Teli, M., Mcqueenie, J., Foth, M.: Intermediation in design as a practice of institutioning and commoning (2022). https://doi.org/10.1016/j.destud.2022.101132
10. Cibin, R., Robinson, S., Teli, M., Linehan, C., Maye, L., Csíkszentmihályi, C.: Shaping Social Innovation in Local Communities: The Contribution of Intermediaries, vol. 12, no. 20 (2020). https://doi.org/10.1145/3419249.3420178
11. Mannheim, I., Weiss, D., van Zaalen, Y., Wouters, E.J.M.: An "ultimate partnership": older persons' perspectives on age-stereotypes and intergenerational interaction in co-designing digital technologies. Arch. Gerontol. Geriatr.Gerontol. Geriatr. **113**, 105050 (2023). https:// doi.org/10.1016/j.archger.2023.105050
12. Bender-Salazar, R.: Design thinking as an effective method for problem-setting and needfinding for entrepreneurial teams addressing wicked problems. J. Innov. Entrep. **12**(1), 24 (2023). https://doi.org/10.1186/s13731-023-00291-2
13. Lahiri, A., Cormican, K., Sampaio, S.: Design thinking: from products to projects. Procedia Comput. Sci. **181**, 141–148 (2021). https://doi.org/10.1016/j.procs.2021.01.114
14. de Sousa, A.P., Maneta, M., Castro, T.S., Marinho, M., Brites, M.J.: YouNDigital: a multidisciplinary co-creation strategy to define audiences, users, and contexts of use of a digital newsroom. In: Mori, H., Asahi, Y., Coman, A., Vasilache, S., Rauterberg, M. (eds.) HCII 2023. LNCS, vol. 14056, pp. 326–336. Springer, Cham (2023). https://doi.org/10.1007/978-3-031-48044-7_24
15. Berkup, S.B.: Working with generations X and Y in generation Z period: management of different generations in business life. Mediterr. J. Soc. Sci.. J. Soc. Sci. **5**(19), 218 (2014). https://doi.org/10.5901/mjss.2014.v5n19p218

Accessible Interaction Design Strategies of Intelligent Products for the Elderly Based on AHP

Xinyi Wang and Yilin Wong[✉]

School of Design, Hong Kong Polytechnic University, Hong Kong 999077, China
22047408g@connect.polyu.hk, elaine-yl.wong@polyu.edu.hk

Abstract. This paper investigates the design strategies to optimize the interaction between elderly users and intelligent products. This study identifies the obstacles hindering seniors from effectively utilizing such products by employing qualitative and quantitative methodologies. The Analytic Hierarchy Process (AHP) is employed to construct an objective decision model and evaluation framework, which assesses the impact of different interaction barriers on the elderly's ability to utilize intelligent products. Based on the findings, a design strategy is formulated to enhance the accessibility and effectiveness of these products. The utilization of AHP mitigates the subjectivity inherent in the design process, particularly in addressing the diverse barriers impeding the use of intelligent products. Furthermore, it facilitates the development of an inclusive design strategy. In conclusion, this paper highlights the application of AHP in designing intelligent products for the elderly and its contribution to fostering accessible and interactive experiences, thereby offering valuable insights for future research in product design within related domains.

Keywords: AHP · elderly · intelligent products · accessibility · interaction design

1 Introduction

In the context of the evolving information and intelligence era, research has primarily focused on applying the Internet of Things (IoT) to address the challenges associated with aging. For instance, some researchers have integrated IoT technology to propose medical products tailored for the elderly, developing product service content and relevant models based on considerations of the elderly, products, and environment [1]. Fu Qiang proposed an APP-based R&D system that emphasizes establishing a comprehensive intelligent system for healthcare services within communities [2]. Moreover, scholars have also explored intelligent designs for commonly used products among the elderly, such as pill boxes, blood glucose meters, and walking aids. Some researchers [3] have designed an intelligent undergarment to enhance the mobility of the elderly, addressing issues related to limited leg mobility and the bulkiness of traditional mobility aids. Since older individuals spend considerable time at home, numerous researchers have investigated intelligent home products for the elderly to alleviate the challenges associated with learning to use such products [4]. Xu X. et al. have proposed that these products should possess simplicity, practicality, and humanization characteristics [5]. Furthermore, consideration should be given to the personality traits, psychological characteristics, and health status of the elderly [6].

Given the increasing intelligence of society and the prevalent aging phenomenon, it holds significant social importance to explore the development of intelligent information interaction products for the elderly with a focus on accessibility. Many existing products in the market suffer from complex interfaces, excessive hierarchical structures, cumbersome and intricate operations, and design solutions that neglect the physiological and psychological characteristics of the elderly, resulting in a significant discrepancy between the design outcomes and the actual needs of the target customers [7, 8]. This study examines the evolving times by considering physical and mental characteristics, identifying explicit pain points, and addressing the practical needs of the elderly. It proposes intelligent product interaction design methods suitable for older adults, offering prospective and well-grounded experience standards.

2 Research Background

2.1 Accessible Design Concept

Barrier-free design emphasizes the requirements of individuals with diverse physical disabilities and reduced functional capabilities, such as the elderly and individuals with disabilities, in planning and designing public spaces and various architectural facilities and equipment. This approach aims to create a contemporary living environment characterized by compassion and care, ensuring all individuals' safety, convenience, and comfort [9]. The notion of "accessibility" was initially introduced in the United States 1961 through the formulation of Accessibility Standards [10]. Subsequently, the United Nations put forth the concept of "barrier-free design" in 1974 [11]. In recent years, propelled by the rapid progress of society, "accessibility" has progressively emerged as a pivotal criterion for evaluating societal advancement and civilization [12].

2.2 Analytic Hierarchy Process

The Analytic Hierarchy Process (AHP) is a valuable and efficient technique for multi-criteria decision-making, which facilitates the conversion and treatment of subjective human judgments into a quantitative format [13]. By integrating qualitative textual expressions with quantitative numerical comparisons and employing mathematical models for systematic analysis, AHP effectively mitigates the inherent bias and limited perspective encountered when tackling intricate decision-making challenges [14].

3   Analysis of Interaction Barriers for Aged

3.1   User Research and Analysis of Barriers

Based on the Analytic Hierarchy Process (AHP), an examination and investigation were conducted to identify the specific interaction barriers experienced by elderly individuals. Exploring interaction barriers among the elderly when utilizing intelligent products involved a combination of quantitative research via questionnaires and qualitative research through user interviews. Detailed analysis was carried out to identify the relatively significant influencing factors. The process of user research and requirements analysis is illustrated in Fig. 1.

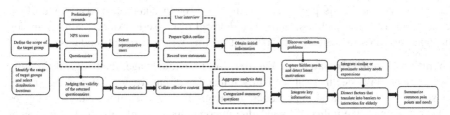

Fig. 1. Flow chart of user research and analysis of interaction barriers.

Preliminary Research. To gain insight into the satisfaction levels of the elderly and their caretakers regarding existing intelligent products for the elderly, the Net Promoter Score and questionnaires were employed. The research aimed to explore the primary expectations, presentation styles, and performance coverage of intelligent products catering to the elderly. In order to ensure relevance and accuracy, 100 questionnaires were distributed across senior communities, urban parks, and senior centers, resulting in 51, 48, and 56 valid responses, respectively.

User Interviews. Thirty representative users were selected from the elderly population involved in the initial research, and in-depth user interviews were conducted to gather comprehensive information on user needs. User statements were recorded to identify unknown issues, capture hidden needs, and unearth potential motivations. The gathered information was translated into interaction barriers through categorization, similarity analysis, and proximity evaluation.

3.2   Summary of Interaction Barriers Analysis for Older Adults

Moreover, design elements were combined to analyze potential user motivations and address ambiguous needs, providing a concrete overview of user requirements. The interaction barriers for the elderly were identified and categorized based on the senses associated with meeting each requirement. A hierarchical structure of interaction barriers was developed using KJ analysis to assess qualitative requirements for aged products and their attributes.

Physiological Decline Disorder Factors. Observations and interviews with the target group revealed a variety of barriers encountered by the elderly when using existing intelligent products. Notably, individual physiological obstacles emerged as the most prominent factors. Firstly, the elderly experience visual impairment due to age-related physiological decline. Vision loss, resulting from conditions such as cataracts and glaucoma, poses a significant obstacle to reading and information transmission, affecting older individuals' immersive viewing experience when using intelligent products. Secondly, auditory decline is also a prevalent feature, leading to reduced sound discrimination ability. Although existing hearing products in the market partially enhance the hearing experience for the elderly, numerous challenges persist. Many products require intelligent tuning mechanisms, which often result in poor interactive experiences. Users frequently encounter operational errors, potentially causing further damage to their eardrums. The decline in metabolism is primarily manifested through changes in skin posture and reduced sensitivity to tactile stimuli. The delayed response to external stimuli among the elderly creates substantial barriers to interacting with intelligent products.

Cognitive Memory Impairment Factors. As individuals age, their logical thinking and memory skills decline, subsequently impacting cognitive abilities and generating resistance to new products. In particular, the cognitive capacity of the elderly struggles to keep pace with the influx of knowledge in contemporary online society. Faced with new information, the latest advancements, and innovative technologies prevailing in an information-rich society, the elderly exhibit limited cognitive abilities for learning. Many intelligent products are prone to misunderstandings and operational errors, making it challenging for users to utilize them solely through straightforward operations. Additionally, reduced attention spans impede information gathering as older individuals need help to resist external distractions. Consequently, numerous existing products with information features exacerbate cognitive difficulties among the elderly, leading to poor user experiences when interacting with such products. Furthermore, physiological decline, such as blood vessel hardening, contributes to brain and cerebellum shrinkage, necessitating concise information display in intelligent products to facilitate recognition by the elderly.

Emotional Psychological Disorder Factors. As individuals progress through various life stages, experiencing changes in identity and roles, older individuals often encounter limited living space and reduced social interactions. Consequently, many elderly individuals face emotional challenges, including low self-esteem, anxiety, and self-imposed isolation. Firstly, low self-esteem arises from diminishing communication with the outside world and family members as social roles and interactions change over time, gradually eroding self-perception. This psychological gap engenders self-doubt and denial among the elderly, exacerbating their inferiority complex. Secondly, emotional anxiety constitutes a significant interaction barrier for older individuals, stemming from heightened psychological stress associated with declining health and diminishing personal capabilities. Anxiety manifests as irritability, depression, sensitivity, impulsiveness, and severe anxiety disorders. Therefore, designers must continuously consider and evaluate user barriers in the design process of intelligent information technology products. Failure to address the pain points of the elderly in interactive products may intensify anxiety levels, further isolating individuals, impeding communication with the outside world, disconnecting from society, and instilling fear of novelty.

3.3 Primary and Secondary Analysis of Degree of Influence of Interaction Barriers for Elderly

The Determination of Indicator Weights for the Rating Scale Assessing the Extent of Influence Posed by Interactive Barriers on Older Individuals Is as Follows. Upon analyzing the research mentioned above outcomes, it was identified that the primary indicators for achieving a "barrier-free" experience encompass physical decline barriers, cognitive memory barriers, and emotional and psychological barriers. Consequently, a hierarchical criteria structure was formulated to address the factors contributing to interaction barriers among older age groups, as depicted in Table 1.

Table 1. Table Type Styles

Types of barriers	Main impact indicators	Medium Impact Indicator
U11: Physiological decline disorder	Diminished visual senses	Auditory sensory decline
U12: Cognitive memory impairment	Decreased learning ability	Diminished memory capacity
U13:Emotional psychological disorders	Inferiority complex sensitivity	Self-isolation

The expert questionnaire method was employed to determine the weights of the indicators above. Specifically, this study presents the calculation of weights for the secondary indicators as an illustrative example. It is assumed that L experts are participating in the assessment, and a questionnaire based on the Delft method is administered to gather their opinions. The resulting ranking matrix is obtained through statistical analysis and denoted as follows:

$$A = (axi)L * M (x = 1, 2, ..., L, i = 1, 2, ..., M) \tag{1}$$

After obtaining the experts' scores, their entropy values are then calculated using entropy theory in the following steps:

1. Calculate the subjective average awareness from the affiliation function formula:

$$bxi = -\frac{\ln(h - axi)}{\ln(h - 1)}, h = M + 2 \tag{2}$$

The average awareness of all experts for indicator is:

$$bi = (b1i + b2i + ...bli)/L \tag{3}$$

2. Define recognition blindness, noted as:

$$Qi = \frac{|\max(b1i, b2i, ...bLi) - bi + \min(b1i, b2i, ...bLi) - bi|}{2} \qquad (4)$$

3. The overall awareness of experts for each indicator is denoted as:

$$ri = bi(1 - Qi) \qquad (5)$$

Then the weight of the i-th indicator in the peer group is:

$$wi = \frac{ri}{\sum_{i=1}^{M} r1}, wi > 0(i = 1, 2, ..., M) \qquad (6)$$

By the aforementioned theoretical framework, the weights assigned to each indicator were calculated utilizing the expert scoring method, specifically tailored to the elderly population under investigation in this study. Determining weights for the secondary indicators employed in this research yielded the following results (see Table 2).

Table 2. Weight of secondary indicator

Types of barriers	Main impact indicators	Medium Impact Indicator
U11: Physiological decline disorder	Diminished visual senses	Auditory sensory decline
U12: Cognitive memory impairment	Decreased learning ability	Diminished memory capacity
U13: Emotional psychological disorders	Inferiority complex sensitivity	Self-isolation

By utilizing the weighting above approach, the secondary indicators can be assigned to three distinct categories based on their level of influence, namely 'main impact indicators', 'medium impact indicators', and 'secondary impact indicators'. The detailed descriptions of these categories are outlined in Table 3.

Furthermore, Table 4 illustrates the range of scores assigned to each secondary indicator, reflecting their respective levels of importance. Higher scores indicate a greater degree of significance.

$$P = 0.6 * p1 + 0.3 * p2 + 0.1 * p3 \qquad (7)$$

$$W = 0.5 * w1 + 0.3 * w2 + 0.2 * w3 \qquad (8)$$

$$C = 0.5 * c1 + 0.3 * c2 + 0.2 * c3 \qquad (9)$$

Based on the computed final scores, the degree of influence of interaction barriers among the elderly can be ranked (see Table 5). This ranking provides valuable insights and methodological guidance for the design process.

Table 3. Interaction barriers in elderly people and their description

Tier 2 indicators	Weight
U11: Diminished visual senses	0.6
U12: Auditory sensory decline	0.3
U13: Metabolic slowdown	0.1
U21: Decreased learning ability	0.5
U22: Diminished memory capacity	0.3
U23: Concentration is easily distracted	0.2
U31: Inferiority complex sensitivity	0.5
U32: Self-isolation	0.3
U33: Emotional anxiety	0.2

Table 4. Score of each secondary indicator

Symbols	Tier 2 indicators	Score range	Final score
p1	U11: Diminished visual senses	[90, 100]	P
P2	U12: Auditory sensory decline	[80, 90]	
P3	U13: Metabolic slowdown	[0, 80]	
w1	U21: Decreased learning ability	[90, 100]	W
w2	U22:Diminished memory capacity	[80, 90]	
w3	U23: Concentration is easily distracted	[0, 80]	
c1	U31: Inferiority complex sensitivity	[90, 100]	C
c2	U32: Self-isolation	[80, 90]	
c3	U33: Emotional anxiety	[0, 80]	

Table 5. Quantified importance scale for each indicator of interaction barriers for elderly people

Risk Rating	Title	Quantification Scope
I	Most important	[80, 100]
II	Moderately important	[50, 80]
III	Least important	[0, 50]

Analysis of Barriers to Seniors Interaction and Design Elements for Intelligent Interaction Products for Seniors. Upon evaluating the calculated results, the degree of influence of interaction barriers among the elderly can be ranked as follows: physical decline barriers > cognitive memory barriers > emotional and psychological barriers.

Therefore, the design process should prioritize addressing these interaction barriers and their associated pain points. Considering the secondary weights, it is crucial to address physiological decline barriers, with visual and auditory sensory decline being primary concern, while metabolic slowdown is a secondary consideration. The presentation of audio-visual effects is critical in achieving product functionality and delivering a satisfactory user experience. Loss of sight and hearing significantly impacts the overall user experience of intelligent interactive products. Designers must explore design styles and elements that resonate with the elderly user group and adapt them to each functional aspect. It is essential to carefully consider the display of intelligent interactive products and utilize narrative color shapes that are psychologically relevant to the target group.

4   Accessible Interaction Design Strategies

In the design of products, the following factors, are considered to ensure ease of use, comprehension, and a psychologically satisfying experience for the elderly (see Table 6).

Table 6. Considerations and design strategies in the process of product design for the elderly

Factors to Consider	Design Strategy
Physiological decline disorder	Avoid absolute power-oriented products and consider the weight of products
Cognitive memory impairment	Ensure visual simplicity and clarity of interactive screens, avoiding complex functional operating systems
Emotional psychological disorders	Maintain style familiar to the user community and increase the user interaction experience

4.1   Interactive and Inclusive Design Under the Concept of Accessibility

Interactive inclusion facilitates information exchange and transfer between elderly user groups and intelligent interactive products. Typically, barriers encountered by the elderly can be categorized into three main areas: (1) physical impairments, (2) diverse physical barriers, and (3) emotional and psychological barriers. Table 7 presents a compilation of solution ideas to address these barriers effectively.

4.2   Customized Interactive Interface Design with the Concept of Accessibility

The interactive interface of intelligent products typically comprises an intricate electronic component and a virtual software interface (see Table 8). To enhance the tactile experience, selecting materials that offer a warm texture is advisable, thereby promoting favorable tactile feedback. In terms of the software interface, the application of artificial intelligence-based interaction design is actively pursued to foster increased interaction

Table 7. Existing problems and ideas

Existing Problem	Solution
Physiological Disorders	Provide diversified interaction channels and enrich interaction modes
Physiological Disorders Differentiation	Enriching the multi-channel interaction space with customized interaction methods through big data collection and artificial intelligence analysis
Emotional Psychological Disorders	Create stress-relieving design styles to soothe users' mental disorders by color, shape of products

between the product and elderly users. The underlying design concept aims to transform the product from a cold, emotionless entity into an empathetic "companion" capable of accompanying elderly users. The software's interactive graphics should embody simplicity and freshness, accompanied by soothing music and calming animations during standby periods. Furthermore, the software should be able to record comprehensive data on the daily lives of the elderly, facilitating reliable and extensive data analysis that enables caregivers to provide improved care and support.

Table 8. Ideas for customizing the interaction interface

Electronic Hard Assemblies	
Tactile	Warm textured material
Visual	Give full empathy and avoid overly abstract or flattened shapes
Virtual Software Interface	
Concept	From a product to an emotional companion
Technology Support	Based on artificial intelligence to enable product-user interaction
Sensory Style	Simple and refresh overall visuals with soothing music, healing animation effects, which combines with a multi-sensory experience

4.3 Intimate Empathy in Interactive Contexts Under the Concept of Accessibility

Based on the principle of contextual interactivity, Table 9 presents design ideas aimed at enhancing the interactive context between users and intelligent products. Two key aspects should be prioritized when creating an interactive environment for such products. Firstly, catering to user preferences, design elements such as traditional atmospheric and nostalgic retro styles and natural landscapes can be incorporated to establish a sense of familiarity between the products and users. This approach provides users with a visually rewarding experience. The interface design should emphasize the presentation of natural scenery or the creation of retro and nostalgic scenarios. For instance, implementing a virtual reality (VR) surround view effect featuring natural landscapes effectively soothes users' emotions during the waiting interface.

Moreover, the voice prompting function of the product holds great significance. Leveraging AI technology, thought-seeking and human-machine communication can be developed to facilitate user operation and engagement. Selecting an AI-generated human voice characterized by a gentle and soothing tone further enhances the creation of a warm and intimate operating guidance space, thereby augmenting the interaction's intimacy and empathy.

Table 9. Ideas for the design of intimate empathy in interactive situations

Interactive Environment Building	
Design Factors	Natural landscapes
Design Style	Traditional Atmosphere Nostalgic and vintage
Contextual Assistive Technology	
VR	Natural landscape VR effects designed for soothing
AI	Human-machine communication for user-friendly operation of product; Gentle and soothing tone of vociferates warm and intimate operating instruction space
VR	Natural landscape VR effects designed for soothing

5   Summary

This study employs the Analytic Hierarchy Process (AHP) to investigate the interaction barriers experienced by the elderly when using intelligent products. Using case studies, user research, demand analysis, and weight calculation, we systematically extract, analyze, transform, integrate, select, and address the interaction barriers faced by the elderly when using intelligent products. By doing so, we aim to mitigate the subjective biases inherent in the design process, establish clear design objectives for enhancing the accessibility of intelligent products for the elderly, and develop a comprehensive accessibility interaction design strategy. The findings suggest that the interaction between the elderly and intelligent products is complex and dynamic. To better serve the elderly population, optimizing design styles and elements based on user barrier factors is crucial while leveraging advanced technologies such as Artificial Intelligence and Virtual Reality. Furthermore, future research should also consider more intricate issues, such as the distribution of functions between intelligent interactive products and users.

References

1. Pateraki, M., et al.: Biosensors and Internet of Things in smart healthcare applications: challenges and opportunities. Wearable Implantable Med. Devices, 25–53 (2020)

2. Fu, Q.: Landscape design of suitable outdoor interaction space for the elderly. Mod. Hortic. **08**(332), 58–59 (2017)
3. Alshamrani, M.: IoT and artificial intelligence implementations for remote healthcare monitoring systems: a survey. J. King Saud Univ.-Comput. Inf. Sci. **34**(8), 4687–4701 (2022)
4. Chan, M., Campo, E., Estève, D., Fourniols, J.Y.: Smart homes—current features and future perspectives. Maturitas **64**(2), 90–97 (2009)
5. Xu, X., Tian, J.: Research on the design of barrier-free smart home products for the elderly. Design **6**, 46–47 (2013)
6. Hooker, K., Monahan, D., Shifren, K., Hutchinson, C.: Mental and physical health of spouse caregivers: the role of personality. Psychol. Aging **7**(3), 367 (1992)
7. Iancu, I., Iancu, B.: Designing mobile technology for elderly. A theoretical overview. Technol. Forecast. Soc. Change **155**, 119977 (2020)
8. Pirzada, P., Wilde, A., Doherty, G.H., Harris-Birtill, D.: Ethics and acceptance of smart homes for older adults. Inform. Health Soc. Care **47**(1), 10–37 (2022)
9. Horbliuk, S., Dehtiarova, I.: Approaches to urban revitalization policy in light of the latest concepts of sustainable urban development. Baltic J. Econ. Stud. **7**(3), 46–55 (2021)
10. Zallio, M., Clarkson, P.J.: The inclusion, diversity, equity and accessibility audit. A post-occupancy evaluation method to help design the buildings of tomorrow. Build. Environ. **217**, 109058 (2022)
11. Man, X., Yan, L.: Research on accessible design of Macau museum for disabled groups. Acad. J. Environ. Earth Sci. **5**(1), 71–79 (2023)
12. Carmel, Y.: Human societal development: is it an evolutionary transition in individuality? Philos. Trans. R. Soc. B **378**(1872), 20210409 (2023)
13. Chakraborty, S., Chatterjee, P., Das, P.P.: Multi-Criteria Decision-Making Methods in Manufacturing Environments: Models and Applications. CRC Press (2023)
14. Sahoo, S.K., Goswami, S.S.: A comprehensive review of multiple criteria decision-making (MCDM) methods: advancements, applications, and future directions. Decis. Making Adv. **1**(1), 25–48 (2023)

Catering to Seniors: Guidelines for User-Driven Perceived Aging Adaptation in User Interface Design

Zhuo Wang(✉)

The University of Edinburgh, Edinburgh EH8 9YL, UK
zhuowang210@gmail.com

Abstract. Currently, silver economy is substantial, but there is a clear supply imbalance issue. The social responsibility of companies related to aging and accessibility has gradually become a topic of concern. To design aging-friendly applications, it is necessary to have better knowledge about older adults' perceptions and experiences of mobile applications.

Given the above setting, a user-driven aging design system guide based on the perception system of the elderly has been offered as a solution to the digital divide issues created by the shortcomings in user interface design for aging adults in contemporary China. The Kano model (KANO), Analytic Hierarchy Process (AHP), and Quality Function Deployment (QFD) methods are integrated into the design of the aging design guideline. First, a quantitative study was conducted, collecting questionnaires from a total of 100 participants, including 52 individuals aged 41–50, 28 individuals aged 51–60, and 20 individuals aged 60 and above. Second, a qualitative study was carried out involving in-depth interviews with 16 participants aged 50–60. Through the research, 15 user requirements were identified and classified using KANO. Next, AHP was introduced to determine the weights of different attributes of user requirements. Finally, in order to prioritize the design elements, QFD was used to identify the design elements that needed emphasis during the design process. This study provides a basis for the perceptual information interaction of Chinese older adults within smartphone systems, offering standardized guidance for subsequent researchers in user-centered interaction design for the elderly, ultimately enhancing the well-being of the elderly.

Keywords: Aging-friendly · User-driven design · User interface · Kano model · Digital Inclusion

1 Introduction

Globally, the population is aging and the World Health Organization (WHO) predicts that, by 2050, the population aged 60 years or more will double, whilst those aged 80 years or more will number 400 million persons [1]. In 2020, the total scale of China's silver economy was about 54,000 billion yuan, accounting for 5.56% of the global silver market share. Designing for the aging population is a critical challenge that requires

© The Author(s), under exclusive license to Springer Nature Switzerland AG 2024
Q. Gao and J. Zhou (Eds.): HCII 2024, LNCS 14725, pp. 100–113, 2024.
https://doi.org/10.1007/978-3-031-61543-6_8

considering aspects of user experience, service, and technology [2]. As people age, their needs, goals, and unique issues change, and well-designed systems and technologies can help address these changes [3]. However, it is important to understand the age-related changes in cognition, movement, and behavior when designing for older adults [4]. Mobile technology has the potential to improve the health and quality of life for older adults, but previous efforts have overlooked their specific physiological differences [5].

Johnson and Finn discussed various aspects of aging, including vision, motor control, cognition, and attitude, and provided insights on working with older adults [6]. After conducting a thorough review of the literature on human-computer interaction and aging, Rot and his team created a set of user interface design guidelines centered on aging. As a case study, these guidelines were utilized to evaluate the user interface of the ActGo-Gate platform [7]. Current research has lessened some of the physical and mental stresses experienced by elderly people when using programs by addressing inclusion issues in user interface design. However, contemporary research is less user-centered, ignoring personalized user requirements and lacking a systematic framework for providing technical and design standards.

Therefore, this paper will use a research method that combines the Kano model (KANO), Analytical Hierarchy Process (AHP) and Quality Function Deployment (QFD) to study the qualitative and quantitative requirements and experiences of elder users for smartphone interface design. In the end, new ideas and guidelines for aging-friendly interface design are provided based on an elderly user-centered perspective.

2 Research Methodology

In the design research and development process, methods for constructing design models from the perspective of user needs include the KANO, QFD, AHP, The Optimal and Theory of inventive problem solving (TRIZ), Axiomatic Design (AD), and so on. In recent years, many researchers have conducted in-depth research on these model methods and integrated them into the development of design projects. KANO is used in design to analyze and classify user demand attributes, prioritize user needs, and improve user satisfaction. It has been applied in various fields such as cultural creative products [8] and outfit design [9]. By using KANO, designers can identify the key design elements that will enhance the user experience and meet the specific needs of the target users. This method allows designers to effectively extract and transform user requirements into usable data, simplifying the design process and ensuring optimal design outcomes.

AHP is used in various fields for decision-making and design evaluation purposes. It can be employed to classify and represent preferences numerically, as demonstrated in the pumping station design [11]. AHP is utilized in the design evaluation system for dining room chairs, providing quantitative analysis of user requirements and aiding designers in the early and later stages [12].

QFD is used in design research to ensure objective requirements gathering and scientific design positioning. It involves constructing a House of Quality (HOQ) to analyze the relationship between requirements, and using TRIZ to help resolve feature conflicts when designing [13]. QFD can contribute to reduce costs and time, support the decision prioritization for cloud service [14]. QFD can transform user requirements into design features. The prerequisite for completing the combination of KANO and QFD is to determine the hierarchy and priority of user needs in advance [15]. The process is user demand-driven, taking into account both user's perceptual needs in the product development process and specific design parameters in the scientific process, making analysis and decision-making more accurate and efficient than traditional design methods (Fig. 1).

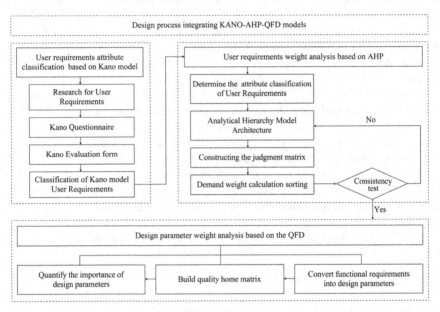

Fig. 1. Research methodology model composition diagram. Source: Author's own work.

3 Aging-Friendly User Interface Design Process Incorporating KANO, AHP and QFD Methods

3.1 Target User Requirements Extraction

This research randomly selected 100 elderly users of smartphone as target groups and conducted a questionnaire survey, including 52 individuals aged 41–50, 28 individuals aged 51–60, and 20 individuals aged 60 and above. It also extracted and analyzed the basic information of users, such as age, gender, occupation and usage frequency, and found that there are obvious individual differences in the decline of physiological characteristics in the dimensions of vision, hearing, cognition, and limb, and it is difficult to use the common physiological age (the standard of defining the elderly by physiological age in most countries is set at 60 or 65 years old and above, and anyone over 60 years old is considered an elderly person in China) to define the elderly smartphone users [16]. Therefore, this article selects the elderly group aged 50 to 60.

The characteristics of this group are aged over 50–60 years, as age increases, physical functions will gradually decline, and the following characteristics appear: unable to see or hear clearly, unable to read or understand, lose focus or memory, face cultural differences. To make the survey more targeted, this research focuses on the elderly who have a need for frequent smartphone use. They used smartphones on average no less than three times a day, with a cumulative duration of no less than one hour a day, with a high frequency of use. Interview methods and on-site observation methods are used to obtain users' explicit and implicit needs [17], as well as user journey maps and the transformation of users' original voices.

3.2 KANO-Based User Requirement Attribute Classification

Based on data integration through questionnaire surveys, in-depth interviews, and human factors research, it was found that the current applications have a high learning threshold for elderly users, with redundant functions and unclear content display. In order to solve the above problems and optimize the elderly user experience, designers need to combine user needs and product satisfaction during research and development, use KANO to conduct research and analysis, clarify user needs, and reduce the occurrence of inconsistency between the design results and users' expectations. After sorting and analyzing the user survey results, 15 user requirements were derived.

Then based on the design principles of KANO questionnaire, a 5-level Likert questionnaire was made according to the obtained user requirements, and the satisfaction was divided into five levels: like (5), necessary (4), irrelevant (3), tolerable (2) and dislike (1). The questionnaire design is shown in Table 1. Users need to evaluate whether they are satisfied with such requirements from two dimensions, positive and negative.

Table 1. Kano Two-factor Fifth-order Likert questionnaire.

If available, what is your attitude?	Aging-friendly user interface design user needs	If available, what is your attitude?
1 2 3 4 5		1 2 3 4 5
	Large font	
	Color matching	
	Loud volume	
	Typesetting	
	Font style	
	......	

KANO divides the degree to which a product satisfies user needs and preferences into five multidimensional categories: Must-be Quality (M), One-dimensional Quality (O), Attractive Quality (A), Indifferent Quality (I) and Reverse Quality (R). Table 2 shows the Kano evaluation table to determine the Kano orientation for each requirement, based on the relationship between the degree of product functional availability and user satisfaction.

Table 2. Kano evaluation.

Positive	Negative				
	Like (5)	Necessary (4)	Irrelevant (3)	Tolerable (2)	Dislike (1)
Like (5)	Q	A	A	A	O
Necessary (4)	R	I	I	I	M
Irrelevant (3)	R	I	I	I	M
Tolerable (2)	R	I	I	I	M
Dislike (1)	R	R	R	R	Q

Sorting out the KANO attributes of the 15 user requirements in Table 3, there are 6 Indifferent Quality (I), 3 Must-be Quality (M), One-dimensional Quality (O), 3 Attractive Quality (A), and there are no Reverse Quality (R). Indifferent Quality (I) include: operation feedback, operation guide, simplify setting, automatic alarm, large icon, and handwriting input method amplification. Indifferent Quality (I) have no direct impact on improving user satisfaction, so these 6 user requirements will be excluded and will not appear in the next design process; Must-be Quality (M) include: large font, loud volume, clear color. They are necessary for aging-friendly user interface design. If not met, user satisfaction will be significantly reduced, so they will also be included in the design guidelines; One-dimensional Quality (O) include: font style, color contrast, typesetting. The more these needs are taken into account in design, the higher the user satisfaction. Therefore, it is necessary to meet these needs as much as possible; Attractive Quality (A) include: font rating, volume adjustment, color matching. Optimizing the above requirements can provide users with unexpected surprises. Once satisfied, it will significantly improve user satisfaction, so it should be given special consideration in aging-friendly design.

3.3 Calculation and Analysis of User Requirement Weights Based on AHP Method

Although KANO classified the user requirements, it was not clear how important they were in the ranking. To help focus the subsequent product design, this paper used AHP to systematize user requirements, gave different levels of hierarchical decomposition, and finally obtained the weighting value through quantitative calculation.

First, based on the analysis results of user requirements in Table 3, the indicator levels of the AHP model is determined: the baseline level (Primary Indicator) is the KANO attributes M, O, and A. The sub-baseline level (Secondary Indicator) is the segmentation of user requirements. Then build an analysis model based on the basic concepts of the analytic hierarchy process (see Fig. 2).

Calculation of User Requirement Weights. In order to construct the judgement matrix and establish the weights of user requirements scientifically, and to quantify and analyze the qualitative problems, the 1–9 level proportional scaling method is used to assign scores. Create an AHP questionnaire, and invite 6 experts and scholars to compare and

Table 3. Kano statistical results.

Requirement	Percentage (%)						Kano Orientation
	A	O	M	I	R	Q	
Large font	4.0%	3.0%	60.0%	24.0%	4.0%	5.0%	M (Must-be Quality)
Operation guide	15.0%	6.0%	12.0%	43.0%	18.0%	6.0%	I (Indifferent Quality)
Large icon	8.0%	3.0%	11.0%	65.0%	13.0%	0.0%	I (Indifferent Quality)
Simplify setting	7.0%	5.0%	24.0%	56.0%	3.0%	5.0%	I (Indifferent Quality)
Font style	15.0%	41.0%	13.0%	23.0%	6.0%	2.0%	O (One-dimensional Quality)
Automatic alarm	12.0%	3.0%	12.0%	41.0%	17.0%	15.0%	I (Indifferent Quality)
Loud volume	8.0%	36.0%	37.0%	6.0%	5.0%	8.0%	M (Must-be Quality)
Handwriting input method amplification	5.0%	0.0%	11.0%	58.0%	25.0%	1.0%	I (Indifferent Quality)
Color contrast	4.0%	79.0%	14.0%	1.0%	0.0%	2.0%	O (One-dimensional Quality)
Operation feedback	22.0%	4.0%	14.0%	38.0%	18.0%	4.0%	I (Indifferent Quality)
Font rating	75.0%	17.0%	1.0%	4.0%	0.0%	3.0%	A (Attractive Quality)
Volume adjustment	34.0%	24.0%	14.0%	27.0%	1.0%	0.0%	A (Attractive Quality)
Clear color	0.0%	2.0%	84.0%	14.0%	0.0%	0.0%	M (Must-be Quality)
Typesetting	11.0%	81.0%	3.0%	4.0%	1.0%	0.0%	O (One-dimensional Quality)
Color matching	94.0%	0.0%	0.0%	5.0%	1.0%	0.0%	A (Attractive Quality)

rate the importance of each level of demand based on a 1–9 rating scale. The weight results are calculated as follows:

Taking its arithmetic mean as the basis for weight calculation, the judgment matrix at each level is obtained. In the formula, S_i and S_j $(i, j = 1, 2, ..., n)$ represent the elements, and S_{ij} represents the relative importance of S_i to S_j. Numerical value, if the result is

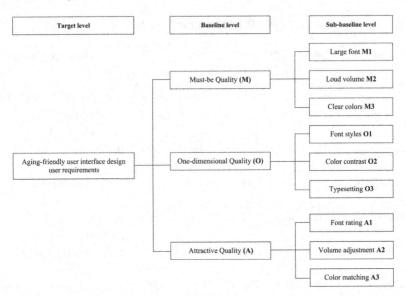

Fig. 2. Hierarchy expansion of design requirements for aging-friendly user interface. Source: Author's own work.

opposite, it is expressed as $1/S_{ij}$.

$$S = \left(S_{ij}\right)_{n \times n} = \begin{bmatrix} S11 & S12 & \cdots & S1n \\ S21 & S22 & \cdots & S2n \\ \vdots & \vdots & \ddots & \vdots \\ Sn1 & Sn2 & \cdots & Snm \end{bmatrix} \tag{1}$$

Determine the maximum eigenroot $\lambda_{\max}$ of the matrix and perform a consistency test. n is the value corresponding to the judgment moment evaluation scale; I_{RI} is the consistency index; I_{CR} is the consistency ratio.

$$I_{CI} = \frac{\lambda_{\max} - n}{n - 1}$$

$$I_{CR} = \frac{I_{CI}}{I_{RI}} \tag{2}$$

In order to ensure the scientific validity of the results, a consistency test ($I_{CR} \leq$ 0.1) is carried out on the results of the judgement matrix, in which the I_{CR} value of the Primary Indicator in Table 4 is: 0.037, and the Secondary Indicator I_{CR} values in Table 5 are: 0.062, 0.052, 0.062, respectively, which are all less than 0.1, and in line with the consistency test standard.

Calculate the total weight values of the 9 Secondary Indicator weights and sort the composite weights, see Table 6. This leads to the design features that need to be prioritized.

Table 4. Primary Indicator Weight.

Primary Indicators	M	O	A	Weight Value	I_{CR}
M	1	5	3	0.637	
O	1/5	1	1/3	0.105	0.037
A	1/3	3	1	0.258	

Table 5. Secondary Indicator Weight.

Secondary Indicators	M	O	A	Weight Value	Composite Weight	I_{CR}
M1	1	1/5	1/7	0.072	0.045	0.062
M2	5	1	1/3	0.279	0.117	
M3	7	3	1	0.649	0.413	
O1	1	2	3	0.528	0.055	0.052
O2	1/2	1	3	0.333	0.034	
O3	1/3	1/3	1	0.139	0.014	
A1	1	3	7	0.649	0.167	0.062
A2	1/3	1	5	0.279	0.071	
A3	1/7	1/5	1	0.072	0.018	

Table 6. Ranking of indicator weight.

M1	M2	M3	O1	O2	O3	A1	A2	A3
0.045	0.117	0.413	0.055	0.034	0.014	0.167	0.071	0.018
6	3	1	5	7	9	2	4	8

3.4 Design Element Analysis Based on QFD Methods

After clarifying the weight value of each user requirement in the aging-friendly user interface design through AHP and analysis by expert group, these user requirements were used to be transformed into design parameters through QFD method, as shown in Table 7.

Based on the weight values of user requirements obtained from the AHP, the quality house of the aging-friendly user interface design is established as shown in Table 8, where the different symbols are the default values of $\triangle = 1$, $\textcircled{\odot} = 1.2$, and $\bullet = 1.5$, and the sum of the products of all requirements under the function and the Composite Weight values is the final score of the function. The score will provide focused support for the design parameters development.

Table 7. Comparison of user requirements with design parameters.

Category	Number	User Requirement	Design Parameter
Font	M1	Large font	Font size, weight, line height DP_1
	O1	Font styles	Non-serif font DP_2
	O3	Typesetting	Layout and readability DP_3
	A1	Font rating	Font size and multiples DP_4
Color	M3	Clear colors	Color value DP_5
	O2	Color contrast	Text and background contrast DP_6
	A3	Color matching	Color combinations DP_7
Sound	M2	Loud volume	Sound contrast sensitivity DP_8
	A2	Volume adjustment	dB range DP_9

Table 8. House of Quality for design parameters in aging-friendly user interface.

	Composite Weight	DP_1	DP_2	DP_3	DP_4	DP_5	DP_6	DP_7	DP_8	DP_9
M1	0.045	●		●	●					
M2	0.117								●	●
M3	0.413			△		●	●	●		
O1	0.055	◎	●	△						
O2	0.034					●	●	●		
O3	0.014	●	△	●	◎					
A1	0.167	●		△	●					
A2	0.071								●	●
A3	0.018									
SUM (Scores)		0.405	0.096	0.725	0.334	0.670	0.670	0.670	0.282	0.282

4 Aging-Friendly User Interface Design Guideline

Based on the design parameters and key analysis established by the KANO-AHP-QFD method, this study conducted design research and practice on the aging-friendly user interface from three dimensions: font, color, and sound, and formed a design guideline.

4.1 Font

Non-serif Font. Users gain quick access to information via the interface's text, and the readability of the language has a direct impact on the user experience. Text that is easy to read allows consumers to recognize information more quickly. Non-serif font offer a more defined structure and more eye-catching outlines than serif fonts, which might help to avoid tiredness (see Fig. 3).

Non-serif font - OPlus Sans   Serif font-Semisun

Fig. 3. Non-serif font and Serif font comparison.

Font Size, Weight, Line Height. The font weight used improves hierarchy and distinguishes importance. Use Bold or Medium font weights for small fonts up to 18sp, and avoid using Light font weights and lower. The text is the most important element for users to understand the information, appropriate font size is the foundation to ensure the efficiency of information access. Considering the applicability of the application for the elderly, the minimum font size is not less than 16 sp, and the font size of the reading content is not less than 18 sp. It is advised that no more than 2–3 font styles be used on the same page to avoid the interference of reading information generated by too many font styles (see Fig. 4).

Default   Aging-friendly

Fig. 4. Aging-friendly reading user interface example.

Layout and Readability. In general, the page information is divided into three levels: the first level of key information, the second level of supporting information, and the third level of additional information. In order to ensure the completeness of information display and avoid difficulty in understanding due to missing text. Reduce text truncation as font size increases to guarantee comprehensive display of primary and secondary information. When text is contained in a container, such as a card, the container can be stretched appropriately to display additional text (see Fig. 5). Use responsive layout to restructure the position changes of elements and try to ensure that text is displayed in a stacked layout above secondary elements. Reading speed slows down due to aging eyesight, and moving information is more likely to distract users and reduce readability. Therefore, it is necessary to try to ensure that primary and secondary information is displayed clearly and completely without scrolling. Scrolling speed needs to be slowed down according to the length and complexity of the content.

Fig. 5. Minimizing comparisons of truncated text displays

Font Size Grades and Multiples. Users can customize the multiple size display of elements. Small, Default, Medium, Large, and Extra Large are the five sizes available. In the aging-friendly mode, the large/G4 standard is default, font and line height ratio is enlarged to 1.5 times, graphic components, buttons, spacing, etc. ratio is enlarged to 1.15 times, 30 sp and above fonts are no longer enlarged, except in particular cases (see Fig. 6).

Grading	Small	Default	Medium	Large	Extra Large
G3	0.9	1.0	1.15	1.15	1.15
G4	0.9	1.0	1.15	1.35	1.35
sp (Default)	0.9	1.0	1.15	1.35	1.6
dp (Invariant)	1.0	1.0	1.0	1.0	1.0

Fig. 6. Font size grades and multiples comparison.

4.2 Color

Color Value. As age increases, their lenses become yellow and cloudy, resulting in a decrease in their ability to distinguish colors at the blue end of the spectrum, but their ability to distinguish red and yellow areas remains relatively stable [18]. Color vision in the elderly has difficulty primarily in perceiving and discriminating colors of shorter wavelengths (see Fig. 7). Therefore, when designing for the elderly, try to avoid asking the elderly to distinguish colors with shorter wavelengths, and try to avoid using adjacent cold color combinations.

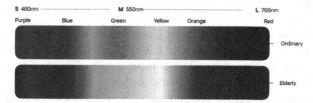

Fig. 7. Ordinary and elderly wavelengths compared.

Text and Background Contrast. As we age, the pupillary sphincter inevitably declines, eventually stabilizing around the age of 60. Elderly users' sensitivity to light, ability to distinguish similar colors, and ability to distinguish details all decrease. In order to ensure that older users can read the content clearly in both light and dark modes, it is necessary to set the text and background color values (see Fig. 8).

Fig. 8. Aging-friendly text and background color values.

4.3 Sound

Hearing is also an important source of information for us. However, as we age, the auditory center of the human brain begins to decline, leading to hearing loss and even presbycusis in the elderly, hearing sounds but not hearing the content; low-frequency sounds cannot be heard (e.g. drums), high-frequency sounds cannot be tolerated (e.g., the sound of a sharp scrape), and stereo sound becomes noise.

Therefore, it is recommended to consider the following points when designing: The notification sound can be increased in volume, the appropriate decibel for normal young people is 70 dB, and 90 dB is more recommended for the elderly, but avoid uncomfortable sound, and deal with the ambient sound, so as to make the content sound clearer; Provide subtitles for videos and guides, and text transcription for audio files, and display subtitles using static text wherever possible.

5   Conclusion

With the development of society, the elderly group occupies a more and more important position in the society, so the attention to the needs of the elderly in user interface design becomes more and more urgent. This paper aims to propose a set of guidelines for user interface design based on user-perceived aging adaptation to better meet the needs of elderly users. During the design process, it systematically consider the user's perceived aging needs by integrating the use of KANO, AHP and QFD, and incorporate them into the consideration of design decisions. Compared with the traditional design approach, proposed user-driven design model pays more attention to personalization and user experience to better adapt to the perception and usage habits of the elderly.

Ultimately, this research not only provides an innovative approach to the field of user interface design, but also fills in the gaps of existing design methods to some extent. By focusing on the requirements of the elderly, we expect that more designers will be motivated to pay attention to the elderly users in their future work and design closer to the real needs of the users, thus achieving a win-win situation between the design and the users. In practice, this study encourages designers to actively adopt the guidelines and incorporate user needs into the design process to provide more friendly and easy-to-use user interfaces for the elderly. Through continuous practice and improvement, this user-driven design concept will play an increasingly important role in future interface design.

Acknowledgments. The authors wish to express her most sincere gratitude to the OPPO Mobile Communications (Guangdong) Co., Ltd. team for their crucial support in conducting user interviews and offering valuable professional advice. Their contributions greatly enriched this article.

Disclosure of Interests.   The authors have no competing interests to declare that are relevant to the content of this article.

References

1. World Health Organization. https://www.who.int/news-room/fact-sheets/detail/ageing-and-health. Accessed 28 Jan 2024
2. People's Daily Online. http://society.people.com.cn/n1/2022/1114/c428181-32565709.html. Accessed 14 Nov 2023
3. Sheng-huang, L., Chaiwoo, L., Maria, C.Y., Joseph, F.C.: Footwear design considerations for an aging population from user experience, service, and technology aspects. Proc. Hum. Fact. Ergon. Soc. Ann. Meet. **66**(1), 1667–1672 (2022)
4. McLaughlin, A.C., Pryor, M., Feng, J.: Design the Technological Society for an Aging Population, 1st edn. Information Science Reference, Hershey, Pennsylvania, USA (2019)

5. Xu, L., Fritz, H.A., Shi, W.: User centric design for aging population: early experiences and lessons. In: 2016 IEEE First International Conference on Connected Health: Applications, Systems and Engineering Technologies (CHASE), pp. 338–339. IEEE, Washington, DC, USA (2020)
6. Jeff, J., Kate, F.: Designing user interfaces for an aging population: towards universal design. In: CHI EA 2016: Proceedings of the 2016 CHI Conference Extended Abstracts on Human Factors in Computing Systems, pp. 1011–1012. Association for Computing Machinery, New York, NY, United States (2016)
7. Artur, R., Robert, K., Wieslawa, G.: Design and assessment of user interface optimized for elderly people. A case study of Actgo-Gate platform. In: The 3rd International Conference on Information and Communication Technologies for Ageing Well and e-Health, pp. 157–163. SciTePress, Porto, Portugal (2017)
8. Wen-Hui, W.: The application of KANO model in the design of cultural creative products. Appl. Math. Nonlinear Sci. **8**(2), 1851–1858 (2023)
9. Suriati, A., Ruzy, H.H., Umi, N.T., Massila, K., Halimatun, H.: Identifying aesthetic quality attributes using Kano model: case study of Malay women's office outfit design. Int. J. Sustain. Constr. Eng. Technol. **14**(2), 168–175 (2023)
10. Berger, C.: Kano's methods for understanding customer-defined quality. Center Qual. Manag. **2**(4), 3–36 (1993)
11. Briceño-León, C.X., Sanchez-Ferrer, D.S., Iglesias-Rey, P.L., Martinez-Solano, F.J., Mora-Melia, D.: Methodology for pumping station design based on analytic hierarchy process (AHP). Water **13**(20), 2073–4441 (2021)
12. Liu, M., Zhu, X., Chen, Y., Kong, Q.: Evaluation and design of dining room chair based on analytic hierarchy process (AHP) and fuzzy AHP. BioResources **18**(2), 2574–2588 (2023)
13. Zong-Sheng, W., Baoyi, Z.: QFD/TRIZ based mechanical structure design of elderly walker. J. Phys. Conf. Ser. Bristol **2542**(1), 1742–6596 (2023)
14. Dąbrowski, M.: Implementation of the SWOT analysis and the QFD method in the design process as a key decision-making factor when implementing cloud solutions in the organization. Nat. Secur. Stud. **27**(1), 71–84 (2023)
15. Griffin, A., Hauser, J.R.: The voice of the customer. Mark. Sci. **12**(1), 1–27 (1993)
16. Shu-lian, X.: Changes in visual, auditory and psychomotor responses in the elderly and their coping. Chin. Ment. Health J. **2**(3), 136–137 (1988)
17. Mei, Y., Xue, Y.: Intelligent products design for elderly people based on the participatory design method. Packag. Eng. **39**(12), 81–85 (2018)
18. Wolff, B.E., et al.: Color vision and neuroretinal function in diabetes. Doc. Ophthalmol. **130**(2), 131–139 (2015)

Gerontechnology Design:
Navigating Pluralistic Value Conflicts

Shimeng Xiao[1,2]([envelope]) [iD] and Long Liu[1]

[1] College of Design and Innovation, Tongji University, Shanghai, China
xsm2108@126.com, liulong@tongji.edu.cn
[2] Art Institute, Jinggangshan University, Ji'an, Jiangxi, China

Abstract. This study aimed to explore the resolution strategies of multiple value conflicts in gerontological technology design, with a special focus on the integration process of self-service health screening equipment in elderly health ecosystems. By adopting the methodological framework of value-sensitive design and dilemma design, this study aims to address the conflict between autonomy, privacy, and personalization needs that older adults face when using technology products. In the literature review section, we review relevant research in the field of gerontology, with a particular focus on different ways of integrating technology into elder care. We discuss the theoretical background and practical applications of value-sensitive design, as well as methods previously used to explore and address value conflicts in technology design. For our methodology, we adopted qualitative research methods, including literature analysis and case studies. We conducted semistructured interviews and focus groups to gather the views and experiences of older people, healthcare professionals, and stakeholders. Additionally, we conducted a triangular analysis of conceptual studies, empirical studies, and technical studies to gain a comprehensive understanding of the complexities and challenges of gerontechnology design. In the findings section, we propose a value-based description model that identifies key value conflicts in gerontechnology design and provides strategies for resolving these conflicts. We carried out design practice based on the theoretical section, producing product prototypes and interfaces. Our findings indicate that integrating the perspectives and needs of different stakeholders during the design process and fully considering the values and lifestyles of older adults can effectively reconcile value conflicts, thereby increasing user acceptance and satisfaction with gerontechnology products.

Keywords: Gerontechnology · Value-sensitive Design · Dilemma-driven Design · Descriptive Model

1 Introduction

The current state of our world has been shaped by the inevitable trends of aging and technological advancement [1]. Gerontech, which combines elderly care services with smart technology, offers innovative solutions to address the shortage of labor and medical resources, as well as the limitations faced by elderly people in independent living. As

Q. Gao and J. Zhou (Eds.): HCII 2024, LNCS 14725, pp. 114–127, 2024.
https://doi.org/10.1007/978-3-031-61543-6_9

a result, gerontech has emerged as a powerful tool for promoting sustainable development in society. With the rapid development of smart technology and the diverse range of applications, the design of gerontech is characterized by diversity and uncertainty. Scholars emphasize the importance of integrating values from the early stages of technology design, recognizing the multiple values and interests involved [2]. In the design process of gerontech, conflicting values can easily arise, which can impact the interaction between the product and its stakeholders. Therefore, effectively resolving and integrating these contradictions has become an urgent issue. Particularly in the internal design process of prediction, creation, realization, and application, designers are increasingly focusing on analyzing and coordinating the contradictions and oppositions among the multiple values held by stakeholders. In the design of aged technology products, it is crucial to comprehend and balance the needs and expectations of various stakeholders. This ensures that products and services effectively fulfill the requirements of target users while generating value for other relevant entities. This accomplishment necessitates interdisciplinary collaboration, thorough user research, and ongoing iterative design.

Resolving and integrating pluralistic value conflicts in the design process of gerontechnology products has become a pressing issue. This is especially true during the intrinsic technology design processes of prediction, creation, realization, and application. Designers are now paying significant attention to analyzing and coordinating the contradictions and oppositions among stakeholders' pluralistic values. These values are considered beliefs about what is good or desirable and include human autonomy, security, sustainability, or privacy. Ethicists and philosophers of technology have developed methods such as value-sensitive design (VSD) and responsible research and innovation to incorporate these values into technology design. Inspired by the Delft University of Technology white paper on 'Value Change and Technology Design', our research aims to uncover the key components that harmonize value conflicts in the technological design and application of gerontechnology products. We aim to construct a descriptive model within gerontechnology design. The presence of dilemmas and conflicts in system design not only presents challenges but also provides insights into the interconnectedness of systems. In the field of gerontechnology, these conceptual conflicts, intergroup conflicts, and individual dilemmas are particularly evident in the multidimensional dynamic relationships between technology and users. The design and application of medical care technologies, such as self-service health screening devices, involve complex pluralistic value conflicts between autonomy, privacy, the personalized needs of elderly people, and universal design principles. This study utilizes a dilemma-driven design approach to identify and explore multilayered conflicts and dilemmas in gerontechnology product design. By using self-service health screening devices as a case study and employing the value-sensitive design (VSD) methodology, we develop a descriptive model of pluralistic values.

2   Literature Review

2.1   Literature Review on Dilemma-Driven Design in System Design

Dilemma-driven design is a conceptual approach in system design that focuses on resolving conflicts arising from competing values or requirements. This approach is particularly relevant in fields such as gerontechnology, where designers need to navigate complex value landscapes involving multiple stakeholders. Ozkaramanli and colleagues (2016) elaborate on this concept, emphasizing its usefulness in addressing conflicts within individuals. They argue that dilemma-driven design enables a nuanced understanding of user needs and preferences, especially when these needs conflict with each other or with available technological possibilities [3] (Fig. 1).

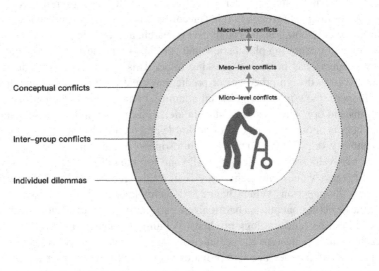

Fig. 1. Visualization based on the dilemma-driven design model.

2.2   Literature Review on Value-Sensitive Design

Value-sensitive design is a methodological system proposed by Batya Friedman, a professor at the School of Information at the University of Washington, in the 1990s. It aims to address ethical issues in the early stages of information technology design. The main focus is on incorporating the values of stakeholders into the design of information systems and making value trade-offs and guidance through specific methods. Value-sensitive design emphasizes the interpretation and maintenance of human values in a principled and comprehensive manner during the design process. It provides researchers and designers with a theoretical approach to uphold human well-being, rights, and justice in the system [4]. The article 'Value-Sensitive Design' by Friedman presents multiple cases illustrating that the criteria for evaluating systems vary depending on the project, including reliability, efficiency, correctness, etc. However, the most crucial aspect is that technical design should encompass or at least reflect the core human values. [5] Cenci and Cawthorne [6] combined value-sensitive design with the capability approach [7] proposed by Sen, which enhances the ethical democratic introduction of value-sensitive design. This combination provides an 'objective and fair' value selection procedure and guides the resolution of diverse and incommensurable issues with different priorities, values, and legitimate goals.

The lack of commitment to specific ethical theories in practical applications of VSD poses a challenge. However, this makes it suitable for applied science, particularly in the implementation of welfare-oriented technological design in specific social contexts. Jacobs proposed CSD (capability sensitive design) based on VSD and combined it with the relevant theories of the capability approach. The aim was to conduct a normative evaluation of technical design, especially in the context of health and welfare [8]. CSD provides more specific rules than VSD does, serving as a more detailed design guidance method. This approach aligns well with the common goal of technology design, which is to enhance and expand human capabilities and work [9]. CSD focuses on conversion factors and the ability of individuals to transform resources into capabilities while also helping analyze human diversity. The ultimate goal of CSD is to normatively evaluate technical designs based on their ability to extend human value [10]. Value-sensitive design allows designers to repeatedly and iteratively engage in tasks such as value input, value selection, and value trade-offs throughout the design and development process, providing valuable guidance. Methodological guidance and suggestions for medical design. Value-sensitive design is widely used in subdivided fields such as medical equipment design research, medical information design research, and medical service design research [11]. Because of its characteristics, a value-sensitive design can be used as a guiding methodology in this research design.

2.3 Research Status of Shanghai Community Self-service Sign Detection Equipment

As early as 2007, China's former Ministry of Health encouraged organizations from all walks of life to take action in building a healthy lifestyle for all people. By detecting health indicators and chronic disease risk factors early, diseases can be detected and managed in a timely manner, reducing harm and economic consequences. Since then, various community services promoting disease prevention have been launched in China. In recent years, government-led public health institutions known as health huts have emerged in communities. These health huts rely on community public spaces to provide services such as physical examinations, intervention guidance, health promotion, and knowledge acquisition. Before health huts became a business model, many organizations, groups, and individuals volunteered to provide free health services to community residents. Later, medical equipment manufacturers specialized in such projects and collaborated with governments, communities, streets, and other service providers to promote this model. Regional and standardized health cabins began to appear, and communities gradually adopted these devices for convenience [12]. Over time, a comprehensive form of equipment offering various self-service options started to appear in the health cabin project. These machines, also known as 'health all-in-one machines' or 'public health all-in-one machines', are based on cloud platform big data. Multiple instruments required for daily physical examinations are integrated, and test results are uploaded to personal health files through the ID card login system [13] (Fig. 2).

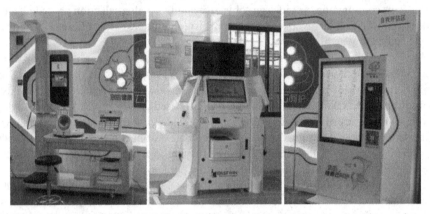

Fig. 2. Equipment in the Shanghai Health Cabin (from left to right: sign detection equipment, physical fitness detection equipment, interactive screen) (Picture source: https://www.Shxwcb. Com/318196.Html.

3 Methodology

This study is divided into four phases. First, the theoretical foundation and conceptual research stage delves into the theory of value-sensitive design through literature analysis, establishing a solid foundation for subsequent research. Moreover, this paper considers the relevant value of self-service sign detection among stakeholders and communities, preparing for empirical research (Fig. 3).

Through the use of the ternary research method of value-sensitive theory, this study aims to identify value appeals and explore value transformation. By visualizing the ternary relationship diagram based on a previous literature review, the practical trans-formation path of design as the starting point of value becomes clearer. Additionally, the study investigated the design attributes associated with cost-effectiveness, perceived use-fulness, usability, safety, and comfort. Empirical research is conducted through a recruit-ment and observation interview process involving elderly individuals in the community (Table 1).

The second phase involves empirical research, where data are collected through observation and semistructured interviews. The observations focus on older adults' inter-actions with existing equipment and their performance within the wellness hut to capture value suppression. The interviews directly gathered the opinions and value demands of stakeholders, providing inspiration and an overall perspective on product design (Fig. 4).

To explore the opinions and values of various stakeholders on self-service testing equipment, the author conducted in-depth semistructured interviews with direct stake-holders. The semistructured interview questions were designed to tap into stakehold-ers' understanding, opinions, and values of the technology. These questions typically

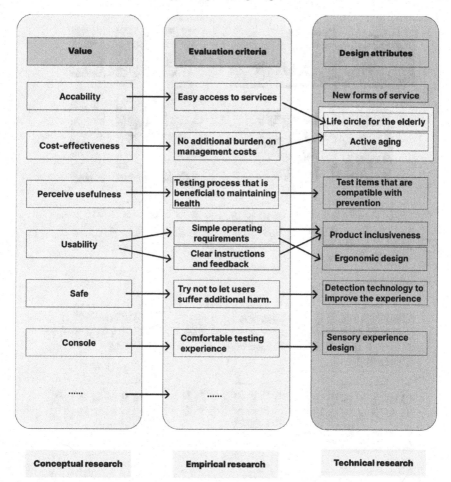

Fig. 3. The Transformation Relationship of Ternary Research.

Table 1. Self-service sign detection for direct stakeholders.

Professionals	Assigned by the service agency for operational sign testing in cooperation with the government
Community volunteers	The active force of community service, with the dual use of services and the provision of services
Elderly users	Elderly residents with various degrees of health needs

focused on the stakeholder's evaluative judgment of the technology (e.g., whether they considered it good or bad) and the reasons behind their judgment. Additionally, other considerations raised by stakeholders were also explored. To gain a better understanding of the current situation, the author also interviewed the person in charge of a community

Fig. 4. Research observation and semistructured interview pictures and affinities.

service agency. The interviews focused on the operation of health cabins by the agency and included their views on self-service testing equipment (Table 2).

Table 2. Recruitment criteria.

Recruitment criteria	
Age:	over 60 years old
Ability:	Have enough mobility, feeling and cognitive ability, and be able to complete daily activities independently
Residence:	Long-term fixed residence

Different levels of familiarity with digital interactive devices and community services can result in varying perceptions of self-service testing among users. To gain a comprehensive understanding of different residents' views on self-service health examination equipment, the author conducted interviews with elderly individuals who had different experiences with community services. Three users with varying levels of experience in self-service testing services were recruited for semistructured interviews. The involvement of service providers, including professionals and volunteers, was crucial to the study, as observed in the previous study. Health huts can be found in various locations, such as large local comprehensive senior care centers, personal health service stations, and activity centers for seniors. Additionally, smaller neighbor centers and community services are also worth investigating. The author visited these facilities and conducted offline interviews with a total of 5 service staff. It is important to note that the community volunteers visited by the author were all elderly individuals in the younger age group (Table 3).

Table 3. Summary of the overall basic information of the interviewees.

Object	Code name	Age	Surrounding environment	Medical treatment/medical experience
user	User A	68	Have a relatively complete community health service	Experienced autonomous testing equipment
	User B	70	Community health services with volunteers	
	User C	61	There is no community health service	Have not experienced autonomous testing equipment
Community volunteers	Volunteer A	63	Health Cabin (Community Cultural Activity Center)	Nonprofessional medical background, understand basic health knowledge
	Volunteer B	66	Health Cabin (Community Cultural Activity Center)	
	Volunteer C	61	Good neighborhood in the community	
Professionals	Professional A	55	Health Cabin (community is the old center)	Received professional physical examination training

(continued)

Table 3. (*continued*)

Object	Code name	Age	Surrounding environment	Medical treatment/medical experience
	Professional B	35	Health Cabin (community is the old center)	
Expert	Expert A	-	Health Cabin (Community Health Service Center)	Professional medical background

With the exception of the interview with resident C, which was conducted online, most interviews were conducted offline. Recordings and notes were taken during the offline interviews, while typewriting and audio were used to transcribe them. During the online interviews, only notes and some chat records were kept as per the interviewee's request. The online interviews focused mainly on current products and services, as well as participants' views on health maintenance. Since the topic revolves around personal health and because it is challenging to find independent users, offline interviews were primarily conducted through chatting in the health hut to create a relaxed atmosphere. In contrast, online interviews aimed to uncover the needs of potential users of such services

Fig. 5. Affinity map stage 2: Information clustering (intercepting the valid part).

by asking participants to imagine what an efficient community health screening service would look like. Subsequently, the value provided in the value-set stage was used as the initial theme for subsequent analysis interviews, and the content of the interviews was summarized and organized. The data were visualized and presented in the form of an affinity chart (Fig. 5).

4 Findings and Analysis

Data analysis employs analytical usability assessment and affinity diagrams to evaluate the usability of existing aging technology equipment and extract key insights from complex data. In the third phase, technical research translates important values into actual designs through literature research and desktop research. It defines the feasible scope of the design and outlines new service and product landscapes. Finally, in the fourth phase, service and product positioning, a new service picture is established based on the transition design perspective, and the business model of the new service system is visualized via business canvas analysis. A design backtracking approach is used to create a transformation path and identify current feasible options. The focus group further investigates users' views on solutions to value tension in retrospective design and explores user preferences and reasons in depth. This study aims to comprehensively explore different dilemmas and value-sensitive design issues in the design of aging technology products through these four stages, providing strong support for related product design. Several major value conflicts are derived from interviews and demand and focus groups: conflicts of kinglyness, privacy and personal needs.

The current service model is based on community or street settings, where each community is equipped with self-service physical sign detection equipment. However, there is a significant problem with the current service model, which is the underutilization of equipment. Upon analysis, it is clear that the current service model fails to meet the value needs of users, especially in terms of accessibility. Additionally, the scarcity of resources and the difficulty in training professionals contribute to the service provider's need for cost-effectiveness, making it challenging for the current service model to expand its role. Currently, only doctors who visit once or twice a week take the initiative to gather the surrounding residents for testing. Limited contact scenarios further restrict the ability of the equipment to be fully utilized (Fig. 6).

This paragraph discusses the concept of value and the resolution of value conflicts in design. The essay mentions the use of mechanism appeals and the identification and classification of value in empirical research. The paragraph also introduces dilemma-driven design theory, which suggests to using personal dilemmas as opportunities for design innovation. This study highlights the importance of understanding the value demands and conflicts of stakeholders and how value-sensitive methods can guide the conceptual design process. The paragraph further emphasizes the significance of interviews and focus groups in identifying needs and value retrospectives in experience design. Additionally, the analysis and iteration of technical pain points in aging technology products

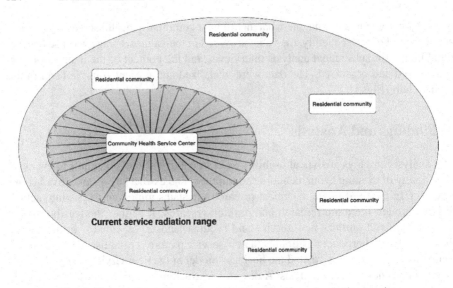

Fig. 6. Current physical radiation situation of self-service testing service.

are mentioned to obtain a final value description model. This model can be used to analyze and identify values and conflicts in the design process, providing better guidance for designers (Fig. 7).

This study uses dilemma-driven design theory as a breakthrough to identify value conflicts in the design practice stage. The observations and interviews in the empirical research look at the generation of multiple values from micro, meso and macro perspectives and make full use of the theoretical basis to excavate and identify value demands. Based on the value description model, future aging technology products were designed, and a prototype of a self-service health screening device was produced.

The positioning is designed according to the theoretical model, and the design prototype is produced. The whole set of equipment consists of a blood pressure detector; a comprehensive detector that can measure blood sugar, blood oxygen, pulse, blood lipids and heart rate; an interactive touch screen; a wireless charging base with a thermal paper printer; and a packaging box (Figs. 8 and 9).

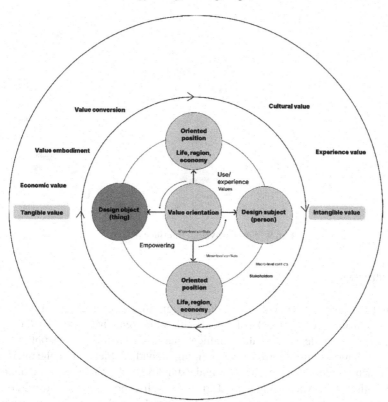

Fig. 7. Value description model.

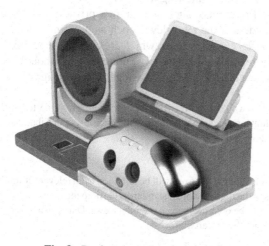

Fig. 8. Product prototype design draft.

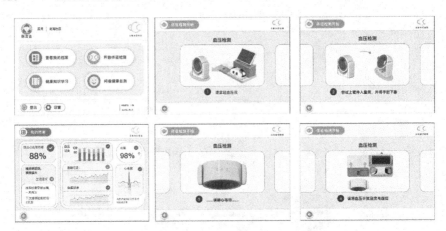

Fig. 9. Service system interface design.

5 Discussion

In the field of geriatric technology product design, this study focuses on a dilemma-driven design theoretical model combined with value-sensitive design methods. The aim is to explore in depth the value conflicts that arise when elderly people use self-service health monitoring devices. By examining individual dilemmas at the microlevel, this approach provides a comprehensive understanding of the challenges and dilemmas that older adults face when using these devices, as well as potential value conflicts. This study emphasizes the importance of using dilemma-driven theoretical approaches and value-sensitive design methods in geriatric technology design to address value conflicts related to self-service health monitoring for older adults. This study highlights the need to balance microlevel dilemmas, such as usability, privacy, and personalization, with the needs of stakeholders at the meso level, such as performance and interoperability. Additionally, macrolevel considerations, which are currently underexplored, are crucial for building a holistic technology ecosystem. Future research should focus on addressing conflicts at multiple levels to achieve inclusive gerontech designs.

Acknowledgments. We would like to express our sincere gratitude to all the elderly participants, community volunteers, and professionals who generously contributed to this study for their valuable insights and feedback.

Ethical. Considerations Ethical approval will be obtained from relevant committees to ensure that the research conforms to the highest ethical standards. Participants will be informed of the research purpose, and consent will be obtained before the interviews. Data privacy and confidentiality will be maintained throughout the research process.

References

1. Peine, A., Marshall, B.L., Martin, W., Neven, L.: Socio-Gerontechnology: Interdisciplinary Critical Studies of Aging and Technology. Routledge (2021)
2. Grunwald, A.: Technology assessment and design for values. In: van den Hoven, J., Vermaas, P.E., van de Poel, I. (eds.) Handbook of Ethics, Values, and Technological Design, pp. 67–86. Springer, Dordrecht (2015). https://doi.org/10.1007/978-94-007-6970-0_4
3. Ozkaramanli, D., Desmet, P.M., Ozcan, E.: Beyond resolving dilemmas: three design directions for addressing intrapersonal concern conflicts. Des. Issues **32**(3), 78–91 (2016)
4. Liu, R., Chen, F.: Innovative methods and ethical considerations in technological design: a review of Friedman's value sensitive design methodology. J. Northeastern Univ. (Soc. Sci.) **16**(03), 232–237 (2014)
5. Friedman, B.: Value-sensitive design. Interactions **3**(6), 16–23 (1996). https://doi.org/10.1145/242485.242493
6. Cenci, A., Cawthorne, D.: Refining value sensitive design: a (capability-based) procedural ethics approach to technological design for well-being. Sci. Eng. Ethics **26**, 2629–2662 (2020)
7. Wells, TR.: Sen's capability approach (2012)
8. Jacobs, N.: Capability sensitive design for health and wellbeing technologies. Sci. Eng. Ethics, 1–29 (2020). https://doi.org/10.1007/s11948-020-00275-5
9. Mangera, T., Kienhöfer, F., Carlson, K.J., et al.: DFMA of a paediatric prosthetic knee (2019)
10. Borning, A., Muller, M.: Next steps for value sensitive design. In: Proceedings of the SIGCHI Conference on Human Factors in Computing Systems, pp. 1125–1134 (2012). https://doi.org/10.1145/2207676.2208560
11. Davis, J., Nathan, L.P.: Value sensitive design: applications, adaptations, and critiques. In: van den Hoven, J., Vermaas, P.E., van de Poel, I. (eds.) Handbook of Ethics, Values, and Technological Design, pp. 11–40. Springer, Dordrecht (2015). https://doi.org/10.1007/978-94-007-6970-0_3
12. Gu, Y.: Health huts: easy to build and hard to walk into China's strategic emerging industries **23**, 52–53 (2015)
13. Yang, S., Zhang, A., He, G.: Research on the development path of intelligent healthy houses in Shanghai under the background of healthy city concept. China's J. Public Health Manag. **37**(5), 567–570 (2021)

Older Adults' User Experience

Activities to Encourage Older Adults' Skills in the Use of Digital Technologies on the Example of Multigenerational Houses in Germany

Dietmar Jakob⬥, Johannes Kuchler$^{(\boxtimes)}$⬥, Diane Ahrens$^{(\boxtimes)}$⬥, and Florian Wahl$^{(\boxtimes)}$⬥

Deggendorf Institute of Technology, Dieter-Görlitz-Platz 1, 94469 Deggendorf, Germany
{dietmar.jakob,johannes.kuchler,diane.ahrens,
florian.wahl}@th-deg.de

Abstract. Against the backdrop of demographic change and advancing digitalization, digital skills are indispensable for older adults. Nevertheless, using digital technologies is not a matter of course for this group. Due to their structures and regional networking, multigenerational houses (MGHs) are suitable platforms for promoting media skills for older adults.

Training programs consisting of courses and media consultation hours for older adults to strengthen their digital skills were initiated and carried out in Bavarian MGHs. The aim was to understand better the mechanisms, potential, and challenges of promoting digital skills among older adults in MGHs. To this end, expert interviews were conducted with managers of seven selected MGHs in April 2023.

The results show that older adults respond positively to the training programs and see considerable added value. Providing programs to promote media skills in MGHs can help to reduce the digital divide and enable older adults to participate better in a digitally shaped society.

Keywords: Older Adults · Digital Inclusion · Multigenerational Houses. · Promoting Digital Skills

1 Introduction

Demographic developments in industrialized societies are leading to a continuous increase in the proportion of elderly in the population. This demographic shift represents a significant challenge that affects social security systems [10, 44] and places new demands on the individual lifestyles of older adults [17]. In the course of this development, the promotion of digital skills among older adults is becoming increasingly relevant, as digital technologies not only serve as a means of social participation but also have the potential to secure the autonomy and quality of life of older people [22].

Q. Gao and J. Zhou (Eds.): HCII 2024, LNCS 14725, pp. 131–145, 2024.
https://doi.org/10.1007/978-3-031-61543-6_10

This paper promotes digital skills among older adults within multigenerational houses (MGHs). These multifunctional facilities are considered promising social structures that enable intergenerational interactions and serve as an environment where older adults are specifically strengthened in their media skills [5, 28, 33, 47].

According to Rieger-Kirnbauer, teaching media skills in adult education opens up new learning paths alongside traditional course programs [40]. Against this background, Wilhelm et al. and Jakob and Wilhelm developed a two-part learning concept specifically for older adults, consisting of training courses and supplementary media consultation hours [50], evaluated it [15, 16] and published it together with the Fraunhofer Institute as a recommendation for action for Bavarian municipalities [44], which served as a blueprint for initiating corresponding programs.

This provided the MGHs with handouts for organizing and implementing training courses to promote digital skills among older adults aged 60 and over.

The purpose of the recommendation for action was to promote target group-appropriate training programs and low-threshold contact points for dealing with digital technologies, initially in Bavarian MGHs. The aim was to comprehensively involve, advise, inform, and support older adults using digital products and services. The aim was to provide older adults with basic knowledge of digital technologies and deepen their existing knowledge in line with their needs.

Against this background, the question arises as to what extent MGHs can act as catalytic platforms to facilitate older adults' access to digital technologies, strengthen their competence, and thus promote their participation in the digital society.

To deepen this question and due to the lack of related literature, the work in Sect. 2 will build on a theoretical framework that briefly highlights aspects of the digital divide and participation as well as the importance of digital technologies for older adults on the one hand and focuses on MGHs as social contexts on the other. The aim is to consider the potential of these structures and possible barriers and challenges in promoting digital skills among older adults. Due to the unique, no related work was identified.

Section 3 presents the motivations and goals of the work. The methodology of this paper in Sect. 4 is based on a careful selection of research participants, appropriate data collection tools such as guided expert interviews, and systematic data analysis. By applying this methodology, the work aims to generate practice-relevant findings and evaluate the suitability of MGHs as a venue for teaching media skills to older adults. Section 5 presents the results of the guideline-based expert interviews and then discusses them in Sect. 6. Section 7 finishes the paper with conclusions and implications for practice.

In particular, we provide specific recommendations for practical action. Because of the rapid developments in the digital world and the changing social requirements, this work contributes to optimizing structures and opportunities that enable older adults to access and make meaningful use of digital technologies.

2 Theoretical Framework

The theoretical framework begins in Subsect. 2.1 with a distinction between the digital divide between the generations discussed in the literature and then distinguishes the concept of "digital inclusion" in Subsect. 2.2. Building on this, Subsect. 2.3 describes the importance of digital technologies for older adults. Subsection 2.4 then introduces MGHs and their structures in Germany.

2.1 Digital Divide

The digital divide concept is one aspect of promoting media skills among older adults. Hargittai describes the digital divide as the gap between those who have access to or use digital technologies and those who do not have access to or do not use digital technologies. The author understands this in binary terms and distinguishes between the "haves" and the "have nots" [11]. This occurs particularly among older adults due to various factors:

Entry Barriers. Older adults often have limited access to digital technologies. This may be due to financial constraints, lack of suitable devices, or insufficient internet access [2, 3].

Capability Gaps. A significant aspect of the digital divide is the lack of digital skills. Many older people have yet to have the opportunity to familiarise themselves with digital technologies, resulting in lower self-efficacy and inhibitions when using technology [13, 21].

Social and Cultural Factors. Negative age stereotypes and assumptions can limit the participation of older adults in the digital space. In addition, a lack of support and educational programs for older adults can make digital inclusion more complex [46].

Generational Differences. The digital divide exists not only between older and younger people but also within the group of older adults. Older people tend to use digital technologies less than younger seniors, and socioeconomic status, language skills, level of education, and digital literacy influence usage [2, 14].

In connection with the digital divide that seems to exist between younger and older people, Prensky makes a strict distinction between "digital immigrants" and "digital natives." The author refers to "digital immigrants" as a group of older people struggling to learn how to use digital technologies. In contrast, "digital natives" refers to all those people who have grown up with these technologies [37, 38]. Loos disagrees with Prensky's strict interpretation and suggests using the term "digital spectrum" instead [26]. Lenhart and Horrigan proposed this term because the conceptualization of the digital divide as a binary model that classifies individuals as either online or offline is, in the authors' opinion, an inadequate representation of internet inclusion. A more precise and nuanced perspective emerges from considering a spectrum of access that considers the varying degrees of internet use and non-use and the associated inequalities. Furthermore, according to Lenhart & Horrigan, the online population is characterized by a remarkable fluctuation reflecting dynamic and variable internet use [25].

2.2 Digital Inclusion

Digital inclusion refers to the extent to which older people can participate in the digital world. It includes access to digital technologies and the skills and knowledge to use them effectively. Digital inclusion can contribute significantly to improving the quality of life of older people by enabling access to information, services, and social networks.

Fischl et al. show that older adults in Sweden consider digital technologies helpful for their daily and community lives. These technologies can help them to live at home for longer by supporting and facilitating relevant activities [8]. During the COVID-19 pandemic in Sweden, a study found that older adults' digital social inclusion contributes significantly to maintaining their mental health. Using the internet and digital tools can mitigate the adverse psychological effects of the pandemic [10]. A Dutch study shows that digital inclusion and self-management skills are positively correlated in older adults. Email use and meeting new people online are particularly relevant [42].

Reuter et al. suggest that creating an environment that promotes the digital inclusion among older adults is crucial. Partnerships at different levels can help to improve digital skills and enable inclusive digital inclusion [39].

These studies show that digital inclusion offers many benefits for older adults, such as improving mental well-being and fostering social connections. At the same time, challenges such as overcoming technological barriers and safety concerns need to be considered. Creating age-appropriate and user-friendly digital offerings is essential.

2.3 Importance of Digital Technologies for Older Adults

The importance of digital technologies for older adults in the context of "Activities to promote the skills of older adults in using digital technologies in multigenerational houses" is diverse. Digital technologies, especially voice assistance systems such as Amazon Alexa, Google Assistant, or Siri, can play a crucial role for older adults in various areas of life.

Social Participation and Communication. Digital technologies enable older adults to communicate and interact with family members, friends, and other generations, regardless of geographical distance. Video telephony, social media, and online platforms offer opportunities for social networking and exchanging experiences [3, 7, 9, 14, 26, 30, 31, 36, 43, 45, 49].

Access to Information and Education. Access to digital technology allows older adults to access information more efficiently, whether for current news, health information, or educational purposes. Online courses and digital education platforms offer continuous personal development opportunities [7, 26, 31, 35, 43, 45].

Health Promotion. Digital technologies offer numerous applications in the health sector, from fitness apps and health monitoring to telemedicine services. Older adults can actively manage their health through digital health applications and gain access to support services [3, 7, 22–24, 35, 45].

Everyday Support. Technological solutions such as smart home applications and intelligent assistance systems can help older people to organize their everyday lives more independently. This ranges from automated lighting systems to medication reminders [1, 20, 22, 23, 35].

Cultural Participation. Digital technologies enable older adults to access cultural offerings through virtual museum visits, streaming concerts, or enjoying literature in digital form. This promotes cultural participation and mental well-being [45].

In MGHs, targeted activities can help to make it easier for older adults to access these digital opportunities and strengthen their skills in using technology. This contributes to the individual quality of life of older adults and promotes intergenerational exchange and the integration of digital technologies into the social structure of MGHs [29, 34].

2.4 Multigenerational Houses

MGHs are complex social structures that address an aging society's social and demographic challenges. In this context, "MGHs" refers to non-profit organizations offering various services and activities to promote social interaction between different age groups [4, 19, 41]. These facilities aim to create intergenerational encounters, strengthen social cohesion, and consider the individual needs of varying age groups. From a scientific perspective, MGHs can be characterized by the following features:

- **Multifunctionality.** MGHs are characterized by their versatility. They offer living space and integrate various social, cultural, health, and educational services under one roof. This multifunctionality makes it possible to cater to a wide range of needs and interests [5, 28, 33, 47].
- **Interaction and integration**. A central concern of MGHs is promoting interaction between the generations. Through joint activities, such as workshops, events, or community projects, an atmosphere is created that enables the exchange of experiences and skills between the different age groups [4, 18, 27, 32, 41, 47, 48].
- **Support for all stages of life**. MGHs see themselves as places that offer support and services for people at different stages of life. This includes the needs of older people and families, children, and young adults. This creates an integrative environment that enables a holistic view of life at different stages of life [18, 27, 28, 32, 41, 47, 48].
- **Local networking**. MGHs are usually firmly integrated into their local communities. They cooperate with regional organizations, schools, health facilities, and other social service providers to create a comprehensive network for the residents [4, 5, 27, 28, 32, 33, 41].

The scientific analysis of MGHs refers to contributions that examine the effects of these structures on social integration, quality of life, intergenerational learning, and the promotion of a sense of community. Overall, MGHs represent an innovative form of social infrastructure that aims to meet the challenges of an aging society comprehensively and sustainably.

3 Motivation and Goal-Setting

The intensive examination of the topic "Activities to promote the skills of older adults in the use of digital technologies in MGHs" includes the background of the need to develop innovative solutions for the social challenges of an aging society. The motivation for this research is anchored in various aspects:

- **Social change.** The demographic trend towards an older population is a defining factor of social change. In this context, enabling older people to participate actively in the digital society is becoming increasingly important.
- **Equal opportunities and inclusion.** Digital technologies offer opportunities to improve one's quality of life and participate in social life. Targeted promotion of the digital skills of older adults helps to overcome existing digital divides and enable the inclusive use of digital resources.
- **Innovation in MGHs.** MGHs act as hubs of social innovation. Integrating digital technologies in these structures opens up the potential for improved intergenerational interaction. It promotes creating a dynamic environment that meets the needs of different age groups.
- **Quality of life in old age.** The focus on promoting the digital skills of older adults aims to improve their quality of life in old age. Digital technologies can help reduce social isolation, facilitate access to health information, and increase autonomy in everyday life.
- **Practical relevance and recommendations for action.** Research in this area aims to generate scientific findings and derive practical recommendations for action. Concrete approaches for the design of future social interventions are to be developed by understanding the needs of older people and the potential of promoting digital technologies in MGHs.
- **Added value for society.** Addressing this topic helps to create added value for society. Promoting the digital skills of older people in MGHs can improve individual quality of life and contribute to a more inclusive and intergenerational society.
- **Digital education.** Many older adults have had little contact with digital technologies in their previous lives. As a result, they sometimes find it difficult to operate and therefore use these technologies. Promoting media skills in dealing with these technologies could reduce fear of contact by offering appropriate educational programs.

3.1 Goal Setting

This work aims to develop a deep understanding of the mechanisms, potentials, and challenges of promoting digital skills among older adults in MGHs. Specifically, the following objectives will be pursued:

- **Analyzing the needs of older adults.** Identifying the needs of older people in the context of digital technologies within MGHs to derive needs-based interventions.
- **Development of favorable framework conditions and success factors.** Derivation of practice-oriented strategy for the targeted promotion of digital skills of older adults in MGHs, taking into account their specific needs and obstacles.
- **Evaluation of carrier potential.** Analysis of the educational programs offered in MGHs to evaluate the impact of the courses and media consultation hours.
- **Evaluation of success factors and obstacles.** Analyse digital skills promotion activities in MGHs to identify success factors and potential barriers.
- **Generation of practice-relevant recommendations for action.** Derivation of recommendations for action for implementing effective digital support measures in MGHs to ensure the transfer of scientific findings into practical application.

By achieving these goals, this research should help develop concrete measures to improve the digital skills of older adults in MGHs and thus positively contribute to overcoming the social challenges in the context of demographic change.

3.2 Research Questions

This work is based on the following research questions:

RQ 1: How can the digital competencies of older adults be specifically promoted in MGHs?

RQ 2: Which structural framework conditions influence the implementation of programs to promote digital skills among older adults in MGHs?

RQ 3: What success factors and challenges are observed in providing services to promote digital skills among older people in MGHs?

These research questions are intended to help shed light on the complex aspects of promoting digital skills among older adults in MGHs and to generate scientific findings for practical application.

4 Method

The basis for the qualitative data collection was a carefully developed semi-structured interview guide [6, 12]. This guide was designed to consider relevant literature, previous studies, and theoretical models to ensure a structured exploration of the topics in the context of digital promotion of media skills in multigenerational houses.

In a brainstorming session at the beginning of planning the guidelines, the team documented all questions of interest for the research project. In the next step, the pool of questions was checked for suitability, and all irrelevant questions were deleted. All remaining questions were categorized according to subject areas and served as the basis for the subsequent text analysis. The summary of the questions resulted in the use of the interview guide.

Target Group Selection. The target group for this qualitative survey consisted of responsible representatives from seven of a total of 88 state-funded Bavarian MGHs in the seven Bavarian administrative districts. The selection was based on a quota sample with predefined criteria (see Table 1) and the willingness to participate in the interviews, intended to ensure that the interviewees represent a structurally identical image of the relevant stakeholders in this context.

The responsible representatives were explicitly selected according to predefined criteria to ensure that the structure and characteristics of the MGHs were adequately represented. This included factors such as regional location (administrative districts), the number of inhabitants of the city (or town), and the number of inhabitants of the district where an MGH is located.

The interviews were conducted from 2023-04-17 to 2023-04-21 and were related to the observation period from 2018-07-01 to 2023-06-30.

Table 1 lists the selected MGHs in detail in a structured manner.

Table 1. MGHs selected for the interviews

Selection parameters							
ID/ City	P1 Fürth	P2 Bamberg	P3 Hassfurt	P4 München	P5 Lindau	P6 Langquaid	P7 Waldmünchen
Administrative District	Middle Franconia	Upper Franconia	Lower Franconia	Upper Bavaria	Swabia	Lower Bavaria	Upper Palatinate
Inhabitants City	127,748	77,592	13,800	1,472,000	24,673	5,147	6,691
Inhabitants District	892,580	530,366	661,967	2,372407	972,558	640,027	567,305

Conducting Interviews On-Site. Two interviewers on-site at the MGHs conducted the expert interviews in person. This method enabled direct interaction with the interview participants and created an atmosphere of trust for an open exchange.

Voluntary Participation and Anonymity. Participation in the interviews was voluntary and anonymous. This was communicated transparently to the interview participants, and their consent was obtained to ensure they could express themselves freely.

Pre-test of the Interview Guide. A pre-test of the interview guide was carried out before the data collection to identify potential weaknesses or ambiguities in the guide and optimize the question structure. The pre-test was successfully tested in three selected MGHs so that these could be included in the data collection.

Data Evaluation and Analysis. The interviews were transcribed to analyze the data. The transcribed texts were then coded using the thematic text analysis method [7] and qualitative data analysis software (MaxQDA). Further subcategories were defined based on the main categories predefined in the interview guide, and the deductively developed codes were discussed and formed in the team. For this purpose, the text sections within each data element were labeled and assigned a code.

This methodological approach ensured that the data collected was accurate, reliable, and contextually relevant and allowed for an in-depth exploration of the experiences, opinions, and perspectives of MGH leaders on promoting digital skills among older adults.

5   Results

The MGHs planned, organized, and implemented low-threshold training courses and 1:1 media consultation hours to promote older adults' skills in using digital technologies.

No fees were charged to the participants for utilizing the services. Two MGHs reported receiving voluntary donations from the participants.

Recruitment of Participants. Participant recruitment in four out of seven MGHs (57%) occurred exclusively within the facilities by publicizing the offers using flyers, word-of-mouth, or posters. Three MGHs also broadcast the offers in regional and national newspapers or the university website (43%).

Participants were recruited within a local radius of fewer than 40 km from the respective MGH. All MGHs (100%) reported that the participants came from the immediate vicinity of the center. Throughout the funding periods from 2018 to 2022, only one MGH (14%) observed returning participants, while five MGHs (72%) had both returning and new participants using the services. One MGH was unable to provide any information (14%).

Staff Deployed to Implement the Programs. Two MGHs (29%) mainly used full-time teachers or counselors for the implementation, as this facility focused on professionals from the outset. Two MGHs (29%) used a mixture of full-time staff and volunteer experts. One MGH (14%) reported that volunteers and students were entrusted with the implementation due to its proximity to the university. One MGH (14%) opted to employ only volunteers for cost reasons. One MGH (14%) initially only employed full-time staff but later relied exclusively on volunteers.

P5 described the situation as follows:

"It's always easier when you have people with whom you can plan firmly, where it's clear who is employed, who is bound by instructions, who is there then and then. With volunteers, I can't rely on them being there every week; if they have something private or another job, then that always takes priority for them" (trans., P5).

Training Materials. Six MGHs (86%) provided the participants with specially created teaching materials to organize the training courses. One MGH (14%) did not use training materials, as the offerings focused on media consultation hours with 1:1 counseling.

Effects and Challenges of the Coronavirus Pandemic Throughout the Funding Period. The coronavirus pandemic significantly impacted the MGHs' ability to provide their services. Due to contact restrictions, the services could not be delivered in person, and online services had to be used. In four MGHs (57%), the services were provided as video and telephone consultations during this time. The remaining three MGHs (43%) did not offer online services, with one MGH stating that the effort involved would have needed to be lowered.

Demand for the services during the coronavirus pandemic varied. While two MGHs (29%) observed increased demand for the services - especially online services - demand collapsed at four MGHs (57%). The reasons those responsible gave were participants' fear of contagion, no demand from participants, the decision not to switch to online services, or the fact that participants no longer needed the services or had lost touch due to a greater affinity with technology.

P6 reported positive effects:

"Yes, when Corona started, it took a while, but the demand increased dramatically. It was also the case that a lot of things could no longer take place in person, and we then also offered lectures digitally, and many people said, "Phew, that won't work", but it worked; everyone somehow had a grandchild or children who then set it up on a tablet, on a computer, with a laptop and then there were real public viewing events where four or five people sat in front of a laptop and listened to the lecture" (trans., P6).

Two MGHs (29%) reported that it had taken time after the coronavirus pandemic subsided for participants to return to the center. One MGH observed that it was no longer just those who were not tech-savvy but increasingly also older adults who were already tech-savvy who used the services.

Acceptance of the Programs by Participants - Success Factors. Three MGHs (43%) rated the participants' responses to the programs very well. A further three MGHs (43%) rated the response as good (43%), while one MGH (14%) observed a low response.

According to the responsible persons at one MGH (14%), the participants cited the flexibility and individuality of the programs without using a predetermined curriculum as reasons for taking advantage of them. According to two MGHs (29%), another reason was that the programs were provided free of charge, as the established training providers charged participation fees. The fact that the programs took place as an open meeting place was also rated highly positively by one MGH (14%). Further positive feedback from the participants was received from one MGH (14%) for organizing the courses in small groups and for the low-threshold access to the classes.

Summarising the benefits of the programs from the perspective of the MGHs, six MGHs (86%) confirmed added value for their facility. From the participants' point of view, six MGHs (86%) reported a high added value for the participants. One MGH was unable to provide any information (14%).

"We have people who come every fortnight, so really a lot on call, exactly. The programs are very well received. So it's already the case that some of our consultation hours are full, that the need is definitely there, and that they are very well received" (trans., P4).

In summary, all MGHs (100%) reported that the continuous promotion of media skills among older adults within MGHs is beneficial for everyone involved.

6 Discussion

The intention in writing this paper was to analyze the extent to which MGHs appear suitable for promoting media skills among older adults using digital technologies due to their social structures. These aspects are primarily based on helping older adults to achieve more significant digital - and therefore social - equality of opportunity and digital inclusion.

Based on guided interviews with seven responsible representatives of MGHs in the German state of Bavaria, selected according to defined criteria, data was collected to generate practice-relevant findings.

Due to their multifunctionality, educational programs in MGHs are well suited to promoting older people's skills in using digital technologies. The results reflect a high degree of participant satisfaction with the programs and cover the needs and interests of older adults in this context. A partially learner-centered approach (andragogical teaching), which Neves and Mead also suggest [30], was used to implement the offers.

Intergenerational integration, a central concern of MGHs, was strengthened with the help of the educational programs, with students acting as trainers and thus implementing these programs in cooperation with the older adults. One of the main tasks of MGHs is to offer support for all phases of life. By initiating the educational programs, the MGHs are fulfilling this task, as the results show that the programs were successfully implemented and taken up by the participants. The measures offered also contributed to better networking of the MGHs in the local communities, as full-time and voluntary staff had to be found to run the programs. To this end, staff from other regional educational institutions (e.g., adult education centers) and committed staff from non-profit organizations, among others, were used. This made it possible to expand existing networks and intensify cooperation.

As summarised by the interview results, the older adults took advantage of the measures offered. They expressed considerable added value that could strengthen their digital inclusion in society.

In particular, the two-part training concept consisting of courses on the one hand and media consultation hours on the other enabled the MGHs to provide low-threshold learning opportunities for older adults.

However, challenges have also been observed for the implementation of corresponding offers. Particularly during the coronavirus pandemic, a decline in not only the number of participants but also in the number of full-time and voluntary staff at MGHs was confirmed in some cases. The latter also appears to be one of the significant challenges in recruiting sufficient staff to run the programs.

7 Conclusion, Limitations, and Further Work

MGHs can be seen as a suitable venue for promoting digital skills among older adults.

RQ1 aimed to gain insights into how the digital competencies of older adults can be specifically promoted in MGHs. RQ 1 can be answered because, ideally, these facilities should continuously provide appropriate programs tailored to the participant's needs and expanded. Due to the high demand, these programs should not be limited to conventional training courses and media counseling sessions. Still, consideration should be given to expanding the range of services beyond this. These could be presentations on specific topics (e.g., data protection and data security, voice assistants).

RQ 1 can be answered to the effect that these facilities should ideally offer suitable, extended programs tailored to the needs of the participants on an ongoing basis. The effects of the coronavirus pandemic have shown that the demand for programs to promote media skills among older adults is unbroken and that there is still a need for them.

RQ 2 should clarify which structural framework conditions influence the implementation of programs to promote digital skills among older adults in MGHs. The effectiveness and efficiency of the programs are heavily dependent on the method of participant recruitment and the staffing of the MGHs. The initiation, organization, and implementation of corresponding measures require considerable work from those responsible at the facilities and are associated with costs for providing premises, personnel resources, and technical equipment.

RQ 2 can, therefore, be answered to the effect that this supportive assistance, be it in the organization, implementation, and financing of offers to promote media skills among older adults, is required from external sources. The state or local authorities by the public sector could provide the necessary financial resources, or local companies could support such initiatives through sponsorship. It would also be possible to charge course or participation fees for older adults for utilizing the offers within an affordable framework. This would require monitoring the extent to which the participants would still accept the programs.

Which success factors and challenges are observed in providing services to promote digital skills among older people in MGHs should be determined with RQ 3.

One of the success factors in providing services to promote digital skills among older adults in MGHs is the immediate proximity of the facilities to the participants within a maximum distance of 40 km. The results on the acceptance of and satisfaction with the programs offered by the participants are evident in this regard. The challenge for the MGHs is to acquire competent staff suitable for carrying out the programs from a peda-gogical and/or andragogical point of view. Premises are available in the MGHs and play a rather subordinate role. Furthermore, those responsible for the MGHs are sometimes overstretched in planning, organization, and implementation, so consideration should be given to recruiting additional staff for these tasks. Based on these practical examples, RQ 3 can be answered to the effect that both success factors and obstacles have been identified and that practice-oriented recommendations for action for these services and their implementation can be recommended from a central, including state, perspective.

The study's limitations are that the seven MGHs selected only represent a cross-section, and results are therefore not generalizable and cannot be transferred to other facilities (e.g., educational institutions).

In addition, in one MGH, the responsible manager changed several times, which meant that, in some cases, it was impossible to provide comprehensive and clarifying answers to questions about implementing the programs. This is reflected in the interview results, which show that delivering information on various aspects was impossible. The results also demonstrate the situation in the Federal Republic of Germany, where MGHs were established as meeting places in almost every district and, in some cases, state-subsidized facilities. However, the chosen survey method was suitable for identifying positive experiences, challenges, and obstacles in implementing measures to promote media skills among older people in the MGH environment.

To summarise, it should be noted that in many respects, MGHs are well-suited as a platform for implementing programs to promote digital skills among older adults. Future research should evaluate educational programs to identify the unique needs of older adults in acquiring media skills to strengthen the digital inclusion of this group of people. In terms of reducing the digital divide, providing services in MGHs helps older adults participate more in today's digital society. The initiative presented is intended to encourage older adults to join in and prepare them for the digital future.

Acknowledgments. This work was partly funded by the Bavarian State Ministry of Labour, Family, and Social Affairs (StMAS).

References

1. Alexakis, G., Panagiotakis, S., Fragkakis, A., Markakis, E., Vassilakis, K.: Control of smart home operations using natural language processing, voice recognition and IoT technologies in a multi-tier architecture. Designs 3(3), 32 (2019). https://doi.org/10.3390/designs3030032
2. Bergström, A.: Digital equality and the uptake of digital applications among seniors of different age. Nordicom Rev. **38**(s1), 79–91 (2017). https://doi.org/10.1515/nor-2017-0398
3. Biniok, P.: Digitale teilhabe älterer menschen. konvergenz von technikoptionen und sozialgewinnen. In: Bröckerhoff, P., Kaspar, R., Hansen, S., Woopen, C. (eds.) Normenwandel in der alternden Gesellschaft, pp. 87–103. Springer, Heidelberg (2023). https://doi.org/10.1007/978-3-662-65918-2_7
4. Bohnsack, C., Wagener, S.: Alter und soziale Beziehungen: Das Mehrgenerationenhaus "Nachbarschatz" (2011)
5. Braun, S. (ed.): Gesellschaftliches Engagement von Unternehmen: Der deutsche Weg im internationalen Kontext . Wiesbaden: VS Verlag für Sozialwissenschaften (2010)
6. Döring, N.: Forschungsmethoden und Evaluation in den Sozial- und Humanwissenschaften. Berlin, Heidelberg: Springer, Heidelberg (2023). https://doi.org/10.1007/978-3-662-64762-2
7. Fischl, C., Asaba, E., Nilsson, I.: Exploring potential in participation mediated by digital technology among older adults. J. Occup. Sci. **24**(3), 314–326 (2017). https://doi.org/10.1080/14427591.2017.1340905
8. Fischl, C., Lindelöf, N., Lindgren, H., Nilsson, I.: Older adults' perceptions of contexts surrounding their social participation in a digitalized society-an exploration in rural communities in Northern Sweden. Eur. J. Ageing **17**(3), 281–290 (2020). https://doi.org/10.1007/s10433-020-00558-7
9. Francis, J., Ball, C., Kadylak, T., Cotten, S.R.: Aging in the digital age: conceptualizing technology adoption and digital inequalities. In: Neves, B.B. Vetere, F. (eds.) Ageing and Digital Technology, pp. 35–49. Springer, Singapore (2019). https://doi.org/10.1007/978-981-13-3693-5_3
10. Ghazi, S.N., Anderberg, P., Berglund, J.S., Berner, J., Dallora, A.L.: Psychological health and digital social participation of the older adults during the COVID-19 pandemic in blekinge, Sweden-an exploratory study. Int. J. Environ. Res. Public Health **19**(6) (2022). https://doi.org/10.3390/ijerph19063711
11. Hargittai, E.: The digital divide and what to do about it. In: New Economy Handbook, pp. 821–839 (2003)
12. Helfferich, C.: Die Qualität qualitativer Daten. VS Verlag für Sozialwissenschaften, Wiesbaden (2009)
13. Hill, R., Betts, L.R., Gardner, S.E.: Older adults' experiences and perceptions of digital technology: (Dis)empowerment, wellbeing, and inclusion. Comput. Hum. Behav. **48**, 415–423 (2015). https://doi.org/10.1016/j.chb.2015.01.062
14. Ivan, L., Loos, E., Bird, I.: The impact of 'technology generations' on older adults' media use: Review of previous empirical research and a seven-country comparison. Gerontechnology **19**(4), 1–19 (2020). https://doi.org/10.4017/gt.2020.19.04.387
15. Jakob, D.: Projekt "BLADL-Besser Leben im Alter mit Digitalen Lösungen" Senioren digital ertüchtigen, begeistern und unterstützen. In Smart Region: Angewandte digitale Lösungen für den ländlichen Raum: Best Practices aus den Modellprojekten „Digitales Dorf Bayern " (pp. 117–138) Springer (2023)
16. Jakob, D., Wilhelm, S.: Imparting media literacy to the elderly evaluating the efficiency and sustainability of a two-part training concept (2022)
17. Ju, Y.J., et al.: Quality of life and national pension receipt after retirement among older adults. Geriatr. Gerontol. Int. **17**(8), 1205–1213 (2017). https://doi.org/10.1111/ggi.12846

18. Jürgens, O.: Impulse im ländlichen Raum. Bielefeld: wbv Publikation (2012)
19. Köstler, U., Marks, H.: Mehrgenerationenhäuser als gelebtes genossenschaftliches Gemein-schaftsformprinzip. In: Schmale, I., Blome-Drees, J. (eds.), Genossenschaft innovativ, pp. 217–228. Springer Fachmedien Wiesbaden, Wiesbaden (2017)
20. Kowalski, J., Jaskulska, A., Skorupska, K., Abramczuk, K., Biele, C., Kopeć, W.: Older adults and voice interaction. In: Brewster, S., Fitzpatrick, G., Cox, A., Kostakos V. (eds.) CHI '19: CHI Conference on Human Factors in Computing Systems, Glasgow Scotland UK, 04 05 2019 09 05 2019, New York, NY, USA, pp. 1–6. ACM (2019). https://doi.org/10.1145/329 0607.3312973
21. Kreidenweis, H.: Digitaler Wandel in der Sozialwirtschaft : Nomos Verlagsgesellschaft mbH & Co. KG (2018)
22. Kricheldorff, C., Müller, C., Pelizäus, H., Wahl, H.-W.: Kommerziell verfügbare digitale Technik im Alltag Älterer: ein Forschungsupdate. Z. Gerontol. Geriatr. 55(5), 365–367 (2022). https://doi.org/10.1007/s00391-022-02091-x
23. Künemund, H., Fachinger, U.: Alter und Technik. Wiesbaden: Springer Fachmedien Wies-baden (2018)
24. Kunonga, T.P., Spiers, G.F., Beyer, F.R., Hanratty, B., Boulton, E., Hall, A.: Effects of digital technologies on older people's access to health and social care: umbrella review. J. Med. Internet Res. 23(11), e25887 (2021). https://doi.org/10.2196/25887
25. Lenhart, A., Horrigan, J.B.: Re-visualizing the digital divide as a digital spectrum. IT & society 1(5), 23–39 (2003)
26. Loos, E. F.: Senior citizens: Digital immigrants in their own country? Observatorio (OBS*) J. 6, 1–23 (2012)
27. Mehrgenerationenhäuser II, Aktionsprogramm Mehrgenerationenhäuser II: Schwerpunkt-thema Alter und Pflege Alter und Pflege (2012)
28. Neubart, R. (ed.): Altenselbsthilfe. Springer, Heidelberg (2018). https://doi.org/10.1007/978-3-662-55154-7
29. Neubart, R.: Gegenseitige Unterstützung zwischen den Generationen. In: Neubart, R. (ed.), Altenselbsthilfe, pp. 187–195. Springer, Heidelberg (2018). https://doi.org/10.1007/978-3-662-55154-7_11
30. Neves, B.B., Mead, G.: Digital technology and older people: towards a sociological approach to technology adoption in later life. Sociology 55(5), 888–905 (2018). https://doi.org/10.1177/0038038520975587
31. Neves, B.B., Vetere, F. (eds.): Ageing and Digital Technology. Springer, Singapore (2019)
32. Niederfranke, A.: Neue Dienstleistung für alle Lebensalter: Das Aktionsprogramm Mehrgen-erationenhäuser. Recht der Jugend und des Bildungswesens 56(2), 184–191 (2008). https://doi.org/10.5771/0034-1312-2008-2-184
33. Niederfranke, A.: Mehrgenerationenhäuser und Unternehmen: Eine starke Allianz für alle Lebensalter. In: Braun, S. (ed.), Gesellschaftliches Engagement von Unternehmen: Der deutsche Weg im internationalen Kontext, pp. 295–306. Wiesbaden: VS Verlag für Sozialwissenschaften (2010)
34. Ornig, N., Suchowitz, I., Valtin, A., Kraft, C.: Evaluation im Bundesprogramm Mehrgenera-tionenhaus (2021)
35. Peek, S.T.M., Luijkx, K.G., Rijnaard, M.D., Nieboer, M.E., van der Voort, C.S., Aarts, S.: Older adults' reasons for using technology while aging in place. Gerontology 62(2), 226–237 (2016). https://doi.org/10.1159/000430949
36. Pirhonen, J., Lolich, L., Tuominen, K., Jolanki, O., Timonen, V.: "These devices have not been made for older people's needs" – older adults' perceptions of digital technologies in Finland and Ireland. Technol. Soc. 62, 101287 (2020). https://doi.org/10.1016/j.techsoc.2020.101287
37. Prensky, M.: Digital natives, digital immigrants. Horizon 9(5), 1–6 (2001)

38. Prensky, M.: Digital natives, digital immigrants part 2: do they really think differently? Horizon **9**(6), 1–6 (2001)

39. Reuter, A., Xu, W., Iwarsson, S., Olsson, T., Schmidt, S.M.: Optimising conditions and environments for digital participation in later life: a macro-meso-micro framework of partnership-building. Front. Psychol. **14**, 1107024 (2023). https://doi.org/10.3389/fpsyg.2023.1107024

40. Rieger-Kirnbauer, A.: Ältere Menschen und neue Medien-ein Widerspruch?: intergeneratives Lernen als möglicher Weg zur Medienkompetenz/vorgelegt von Anita Rieger-Kirnbauer. Graz (2009)

41. Rott, C., Stanek, S.: Evaluation der Heidelberger Seniorenzentren 2007/2008 : Abschlussbericht: Institut für Gerontologie, Universität Heidelberg (2009)

42. Scheffer, M.M., Menting, J., Boeije, H.R.: Self-management of social well-being in a cross-sectional study among community-dwelling older adults: the added value of digital participation. BMC Geriatr. **21**(1), 539 (2021). https://doi.org/10.1186/s12877-021-02482-6

43. Schirmer, W., Geerts, N., Vercruyssen, A., Glorieux, I.: Digital skills training for older people: the importance of the 'lifeworld.' Arch. Gerontol. Geriatr. **101**, 104695 (2022). https://doi.org/10.1016/j.archger.2022.104695

44. Sczogiel, S., et al.: DIGITAL FIT IM ALTER Handlungsempfehlung für Gemeinden zu Bildungsangeboten für Senioren : Unpublished (2020)

45. Sen, K., Prybutok, G., Prybutok, V.: The use of digital technology for social wellbeing reduces social isolation in older adults: a systematic review. SSM – Popul. Health **17**, 101020 (2022). https://doi.org/10.1016/j.ssmph.2021.101020

46. Sin, F., Berger, S., Kim, I.-J., Yoon, D.: Digital social interaction in older adults during the COVID-19 pandemic. Proc. ACM Hum.-Comput. Interact. **5**(CSCW2), 1–20 (2021). https://doi.org/10.1145/3479524

47. Staats, M., Gess, C., Henkel, A.I.: Aktionsprogramm Mehrgenerationenhäuser. Lokale Infrastruktur für alle Generationen. Ergebnisse aus dem Aktionsprogramm Mehrgenerationenhäuser (2012). https://doi.org/10.25656/01:7984

48. Staats, M., Reinecke, M., Moldenhauer, A.: Intergenerationales Lernen in Mehrgenerationenhäusern. Bildung und Erziehung **65**(3), 293–308 (2012)

49. Suden, W.: Digitale teilhabe im alter: aktivierung oder diskriminierung? In: Stadelbacher, S., Schneider, W. (eds.) Lebenswirklichkeiten des Alter(n)s, pp. 267–289. Wiesbaden: Springer Fachmedien Wiesbaden (2020)

50. Wilhelm, S., Jakob, D., Dietmeier, M.: Development of a senior-friendly training concept for imparting media literacy: Gesellschaft für Informatik e.V. (2019)

Between the Present and the Past: Using Card-Sorting and Biographical Approaches to Identify News Influencers' Media Habits

Mariana S. Müller(✉) 📧, Ana Filipa Oliveira📧, Margarida Maneta📧,
and Maria José Brites📧

Lusófona University, CICANT, Porto, Portugal
mariana.muller@ulusofona.pt

Abstract. Validating news through close relationships (e.g. family and friends) is a strategy that young people use to assess the trustworthiness of news [1]. Also, some authors argue that "interactions with media are embedded within a biographical understanding of time" [2]. Considering this, this paper focuses on using semi-structured interviews with biographical features and based on the Q-Sort methodological approach [3, 4], as a qualitative strategy to map past and present news consumption habits. We reflect on this methodological approach to analyse changes in media consumption over time, emphasising social and inter-generational contexts. As part of a larger project, we conducted twelve interviews with individuals - from different ages and backgrounds - previously identified by youth (between 15–24 years old) as their news influencers. The interviews (N = 12) were conducted via Zoom video call platform between July and October 2023. Findings indicate that some strategies contribute to obtaining more thought-provoking answers from interviewees. Namely paying attention to spontaneous mentions of past periods or important events in their lives and mentions of changing media habits. Even though remembering is a complex process, Q-sort helped participants to reflect upon and talk about their media habits. Moreover, our bio-graphical approach with Q-Sort methodology revealed interesting findings with participants of distinct ages and backgrounds.

Keywords: Q-sort · Biographical Approach · Qualitative Research · Media Consumption · News Influencers

1 Introduction

This paper aims to examine the use of semi-structured interviews, with a biographical approach and based on a Q-Sort methodology, to analyse media consumption habits over time. This approach aims to capture intergenerational and social contexts related to media habits. We propose reflecting on this qualitative strategy in the context of a Portuguese project focused on young people, news and digital citizenship - YouNDigital (PTDC/COM-OUT/0243/2021).

We structured the sample for this paper (12 interviews) based on 42 previous interviews with young people who indicated other individuals that influenced their news consumption - henceforth referred to as 'news influencers'.

In the following sections, we present an overview of young people's media habits in the digital era, emphasising their strategies to validate news, which includes relying on close relationships. Our theoretical framework comprises the notion of memory and its relationship with media habits. Considering that speaking about media is a complex and often unconscious process [5], we argue that Q-sort methodology with a biographical approach is a relevant qualitative approach to map past and present media habits.

2   Who is Relevant and When? Young People and Their Particular Way of Consuming News

Young people born and raised in the digital age are immersed in distinct forms of news and information consumption [1, 6]. Multiplatform dynamics and personal preferences highlighted by algorithmic influence prevail in their consumption routines. According to Galan et al. [7], young audiences see news not just as what you "should know" but also as what is useful, interesting and fun to know.

The Digital News Report 2023 highlights a rise of TikTok and other video-led networks influenced by the younger generations. In general, they pay more attention to influencers or celebrities than to journalists [8]. In line with this, the results of the YouNDigital survey reveal that young people generally follow instagrammers and youtubers to find out what's going on in the world [9]. Moreover, and as indicated by the Digital News Report 2023, news brands' websites and apps are less connected to young generations around the globe. Younger people prefer to access news through their search, social media or mobile aggregators.

Concerning news consumption, Swart [1] highlights that family and friends play an essential role in validating the information consumed, being a widely used tactic by young people to assess the trustworthiness of news. This may disclose the possible influence of intergenerational relationships on news consumption. In addition, studies show that digital media "is transforming audiences' practices" [10], not only in the sense that younger people trust and turn to older people but the other way around. In particular, intergenerational relationships have boosted seniors' use of technology positively [11], not only because it reflects on the confidence and skills of the older people, but also because it shapes and strengthens relationships between generations. Considering this, it is relevant to analyse who are the persons who have had an influential role in youth and their news consumption habits.

The YouNDigital project aims to map who plays a role in young people's news consumption in Portugal and to identify who plays a crucial role in consumption habits. Based on 42 semi-structured interviews, young people aged between 15 and 24, identified 12 individuals who they considered their news influencers. Subsequently, these people were interviewed with the main objective of mapping their media habits, and how they relate to news in a digitalised and datafied context. In this paper, we intend to analyse how biographical interviews can be useful for mapping media habits in the context of intergenerational relationships. We argue that semi-structured interviews, with biographical characteristics, based on the Q-Sort methodological approach are a relevant qualitative strategy for mapping past and present news consumption habits.

3   A Biographical Approach that Calls for Memory and Nostalgia

Understanding the news habits of the present and the past requires memory. Erll [12] asserts that the notion of memory involves forgetting: "Remembering and forgetting are two sides – or different processes – of the same coin, that is, memory. Forgetting is the very condition for remembering". Remembering is a selective and partial process that goes beyond merely reproducing facts. It can be understood as a social process and a product.

Considering this, Cabecinhas [13] argues that aspects such as power relations, filters that operate in a given cultural context, personal experiences and trajectories should be considered in analysis that triggers memory. Moreover, memory is directly connected with social structures and individual sociocultural frameworks [12, 13]. According to Erll [12], media are in a central position in a cultural notion of memory on an individual and collective level. In the first decade of the 2000s, the author [12] already identified, in the new media (e.g. Facebook and YouTube), an acceleration of images and narratives about the past that shaped the daily experience of many people.

Aligned with this, distinct researchers [14, 15] have mapped movements that connect media and nostalgia. Expressions of nostalgia have emerged in social networks and groups and are focused on objects, media products and styles. One of the visible consequences is the creation of cultural products that exalt specific periods and reinforce expressions of nostalgia, such as the Netflix TV show The Stranger Things.

Niemeyer [14] considers that nostalgia can be a private or public return to the past and sometimes relates to an imagination of the future. The author [14] argues that this wave of nostalgia is not just fashion or a trend and it can express different ways to deal with time. The re-emergence of nostalgia can also be a reaction to fast technologies in a clear paradox since distinct movements are growing online.

Analysing oldness and newness as categories to describe media, authors [2] argue that "interactions with media are embedded within a biographical understanding of time". In the author's proposal, life histories and narratives of media are merged to provide more nuanced ways to comprehend media, its discourses, and narratives. Through the interviewee's narratives, we aim to analyse the possibilities of mapping media habits in the present and past, considering a biographical approach and a social perspective of memory.

4   Q-Sort as a Qualitative Strategy to Map Past and Present News Consumption

Analysing audience studies, Schrøder [16] points out an empirical shift in the field. An idea of "decoding" encounters with media "texts" was replaced by mapping audience participation in the wider mediascapes in a mixed-methods research design. Schrøder [3] argues that using the Q-methodological approach with qualitative and quantitative analysis allows audiences' research to go beyond interpretive opacity.

News repertoires are an approach that is gaining ground, not least because of the way people navigate the media ecology nowadays, using a variety of media for information and entertainment [4]. By definition, these repertoires should "focus attention not only on traditional journalistic outlets but also on the broader concourse of possible information sources in the digital media landscape, which can be drawn upon to aid sensemaking in everyday life" [4].

In this context, Q-methodology is considered well-suited for analysing media reception and use [17]. Schrøder [3] argues that it allows researchers to capture individuals' subjective perceptions of an area of experience and aggregate these perceptions through a factor analysis. Since participants must reflect on their choices during the process, Q-methodology has a dialogical and reflective potential. "When informants have completed the card placing process, accompanied by dialogical negotiation, they have self-analysed their subjective news consumption universe, whose internal architecture is moreover relational", argues Schrøder [3].

In a traditional approach, Q-methodology provides both qualitative and quantitative findings, creating a typological pattern of differences and similarities between the participants' perceptions [3]. Q-methodology is applied in a card-sorting activity with a think-out-loud protocol structured based on the research questions. Participants have to place and rank these cards in a pyramid according to their daily use or importance in their lives. On each card is a statement or the particular sociocultural phenomenon being investigated (Schrøder, 2012), usually defined in a previous research stage.

In a pilot study with people aged between 20 and 30 years, Hasenbrik and Domeyer [5] added visual methods to facilitate speaking about media, a complex and often unconscious process. In this case, participants received blank cards to complete with the main elements of their media repertoires, and in a four-step activity, they had to position the cards in a circle with "me" in the centre. The main data for analysis were verbal comments, and visual data was not used as data on its own [5].

Aiming to facilitate the participatory process and obtain precise and thought-provoking answers within the YouNDigital project a bottom-up approach was implemented in our Q-Methodology. Participants were given eight blank cards to complete and three cards with suggestions (War, Digital Influencer, and Television Journalist) they could accept or decline. In the following section, we describe in detail the research design.

5   Research Design

Aiming to understand young people's perceptions, experiences and understandings of news and digital citizenship, the Youth, News and Digital Citizenship (YouNDigital) project (PTDC/COM-OUT/0243/2021) is structured around a mixed research design. In the first stage of the research, a representative online survey focused on media habits and citizenship was applied to 1362 young people living in Portugal. In the second stage, 42 semi-structured interviews were conducted with young people aged between 15 and 24. The interviews were carried out using card-sorting exercises with a think-aloud protocol focused on the consumption and socialisation of news in the context of a digitalised society. At the end, participants were asked to nominate a person they considered to be an influencer in terms of their news consumption habits - their news influencers.

This paper focuses on the interviews with the nominated news influencers. This group consisted of 12 people, aged between 14 and 60 years old, identified as parents, friends, siblings, or professionals/adults working in institutions attended by the young participants. The interviews were conducted between July and October 2023, via Zoom video call platform, and lasted between 45 and 120 min.

The semi-structured interview took into account two axes: 1) Influencers and Socialisation; and 2) Datafication and Algorithms. The two axes are followed from the perspective of a biographical approach, seeking to understand previous versus current information consumption habits. This paper focuses specifically on the first axe, where interviewees assembled the Q-Sort pyramid on the Jamboard platform as Fig. 1 depicts. There were eight blank cards to be filled in and three suggestions that could be accepted or declined: War, Television Journalist, and Digital Influencer. Using the Q-Sort methodological approach [3, 4] with a think-aloud protocol, the news influencers were asked to identify and classify people, themes and subjects that played a role in their information routine, rating them as very important, indifferent and not very important.

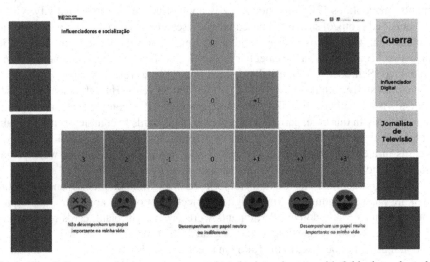

Fig. 1. The Q-Sort pyramid that was presented to the interviewees with 9 blank cards and 3 suggestions (War, Digital Influencer, and Television Journalist) that were not mandatory.

Among the questions asked to the interviewees to promote reflection on the resulting pyramid, two centred on the biographical approach: "Do you think this pyramid could have been different, for example, before or during the pandemic or the war? Or another personal context of yours?".

By assembling the pyramid and clarifying their choices, the interviewees were encouraged to compare their current information consumption with their habits from other moments in their lives. The aim was to have a more retrospective logic, allowing us to capture a biographical approach, with the essence and involvement of media consumption throughout life and, consequently, the changes in that consumption. Two questions served as the basis for this reflection: "Do you think your news consumption has always been like this?" and "Has it been different at other times in your life?". This exercise aimed to prompt reflections about how they experienced news consumption in different periods of their lives and to identify their perceptions about it. As it was a qualitative reflexive exercise, this option allowed us to uncover their in-depth experiences, narrated in the first person [18], through the interviewee's personal sharing.

In the next section, we present a methodological reflection focused on our experience of interviewing people of different ages (14–60) by using Q-sort and a biographical approach.

6 Unlocking Biographical Insights: Asking Questions at the Right Time and Giving Them Space to Speak

The interview script was assembled to ensure the collection of data and subsequent portrait of media biographies. To facilitate the process, we followed Schrøder [3] and Davis and Michelle [17], who propose that Q-methodology is well-suited for capturing media reception and use as it allows for apprehending individuals' subjective perceptions.

The interview was divided into three parts. In the first part, as an icebreaker, the interviewees presented a piece of news that caught their attention in the previous week. Those who didn't bring any were invited to talk about a topic of their choice. In the second stage, the interviewees assembled their Q-Sort pyramid, as previously detailed in Fig. 1. The last section of the interview was dedicated to exercises focused on algorithms and datafication.

The script was structured so that the interviewers could ask distinct follow-up questions to map the news consumption of the interviewees. Within this logic, two questions of biographical approach were included: "Do you think your news consumption has always been like this?" and "Has it been different at other times in your life?". These questions could be asked at any time during the interview.

It was interesting to note that some interviewees, especially the older ones, already linked their news consumption to other moments in their lives, from the beginning. For some of them, talking about their own lives and routines seemed to be easier than for others. Those who spontaneously addressed their routine often ended up forgetting that the focus was on news consumption. They talked about significant events in their lives, and the interviewers deliberately sought to exploit the possible connection with news consumption. For example, Ricardo, 53 years old, talked spontaneously about his resignation and reintegration into the job market. Following this, he was asked if he discussed the news with his coworkers:

You share something, a song, a piece of news about a band, a soccer post, or a joke. I don't have in-depth relationships or discussions with my colleagues... They are not people whom I feel the desire or even the need to influence. (Ricardo, 53 years old).

Then interviewers questioned if this was different from his previous job. Ricardo answered, by exploring connections to his life trajectory: "In my previous job, it was different, firstly because I'd been there for many, many years, I'd been there for 15 years". In this case, Ricardo triggers his memory and differentiates it from his current experience. He considers that he influenced his former colleagues because he had a closer relationship with them. Considering the logic that memory presupposes forgetting [12], Ricardo does not provide an example of how news socialisation was with his colleagues from the previous company.

Similarly, Helena, 18, spontaneously indicated a milestone in her life related to news consumption. After taking part in activities such as the Youth Parliament and the European Youth Parliament, she began to realise the importance of being aware of her surroundings:

From the moment I started taking part in the projects, I began to realise the importance of watching the news, reading the news and knowing what's going on, and from then on I began to consume more of this part. (Helena, 18 years old).

Although the structured questions were direct, some interviewees had difficulty answering them. In this regard, inserting the two biographical questions in moments when the interviewees were already describing their routines or interests seemed to be more feasible.

For example, Tainá, 23 years old, explained that she tends to have a topic she's interested in and read a lot about it for a certain period. When she feels she has delved into the subject enough, she loses interest and seeks another topic. "When it's over, I go back to consuming my normal content until something else catches my interest." The question was asked after she mentioned that she no longer followed news about a particular subject, namely fashion news.

Another strategy used was to pay attention to moments when the interviewees indicated a change in their media consumption. Francisco, 30 years old, mentioned that he stopped watching television with his mother, and then he answered follow-up questions about how his media habits changed over the years:

Yes, yes, yes. It's changed a lot. The television that used to bring people together, sitting on the sofa watching television, I think nowadays... It used to be able to unite, but since everyone already has their own television in their own corner of the house, it's no longer one that can unite. (Francisco, 30 years old).

When asked about the type of content he no longer watches, Francisco mentioned soap operas and gave details about his family routine. "My mother is watching, we're having dinner and she's watching. Since I'm the youngest member of the family, I always have my back on the television.". In this case, the questions brought details about the family's interaction from an intergenerational perspective. Francisco has no interest in soap operas, but his mother watches them nonetheless. However, even if he wanted to watch such or any other media content, he was positioned with his back on the screen because he was the youngest in the household.

Once they finished assembling the Q-sort pyramid, the interviewees also answered some questions outlined in the script. Two questions were centred on the biographical approach: "Do you think this pyramid could have been different, for example, before or during the pandemic or the war? Or another personal context of yours?".

Our experience showed that the word "pandemic" stood out. Most interviewees related it to their experience during the pandemic, many of which were negative. Younger interviewees emphasised pandemic restrictions and their impact on their socialisation and favourite media themes:

Before the pandemic, I used to talk more with people who placed more importance on political TV shows and sports, so all these things related to that would be something that would interest me more because they are part of my social circle. (Giovana, 15 years old).

During the pandemic, soccer ended up dying a little, there were no matches, and no training sessions either. There were no wars during the pandemic either. Friends only spoke by mobile phone because we couldn't have physical contact. And family life remained the same. (Henrique, 15 years old).

In other cases, the interviewees tended to focus their answers on the themes they inserted in the pyramid. Their consumption habits didn't change because their areas of interest remained the same. We understand that the proposed question didn't allow the interviewees to consider, for example, formats, routines, and socialisation. That was the case of Valdemar, aged 60:

The themes of my life, yes, were always very much based on these spaces we had here. Maybe, I'm here, we'll go a little deeper into the family issue, which was very important to me, but I didn't contextualise it because I was more contextualised in the professional issue. But not much has changed. (Valdemar, 60 years old).

Answering the same question, Helena, 18 years old, distanced herself from the influence of the pandemic or war on her interests. She indicated that she becomes interested in the news when she understands its relevance to her life and socialisation:

For example, it wouldn't be a war or the pandemic, in my case, even though I know some people started consuming more news because of that, but that wasn't my case. My case was realising that it's something necessary for social interaction in society. (Helena, 18 years old).

Regarding the difficulties related to being aware of media habits [5], our experience indicates that being aware of changing and past media habits is even more complex. Semi-structured interviews with a biographical approach demand interviewer to be attentive to details that may refer to the past. Being aware of memory as a social process that includes forgetting [12], and that operates in a given cultural context [13] can contribute to a more successful process.

7   Final Remarks

The preliminary findings suggest different perception degrees about changes in the individuals' news consumption routines. All the interviewees associated media routines with distinct times in their lives, following Lesage and Natale [2] idea of a biographical understanding of the time. This aspect can draw attention to more nuanced and nostalgic ways to understand media and its influence on one's news consumption habits.

In generational terms, data suggests some differences between older and younger news influencers. On the one hand, older individuals reported deeper changes related to more frequently used formats (newspapers and television, for example), which, according to their perception, have lost ground to mobile phones and apps. On the other hand, the younger influencers mentioned changes in topics that aroused interest and have changed over time. Furthermore, regardless of their age group, interviewees often associated past habits (e.g. television consumption) with family routines and members from other generations, such as parents, uncles and grandparents. This data suggests the influence of intergenerational contexts and dynamics on media consumption habits throughout a person's life, with the identification of older family members with interests and habits nurtured over time.

Based on the results of this research, we understand that adopting the Q-sort approach contributed to participants' thinking and talking about their media habits. Even though we understand that remembering past experiences and sensations is a complex process, through this biographical approach we were able to reveal compelling findings regarding participants of distinct ages and backgrounds.

Acknowledgments. This study was funded by Foundation for Science and Technology (FCT) under the project YouNDigital – Youth, News and Digital Citizenship under the reference PTDC/COM-OUT/0243/2021 (DOI 10.54499/PTDC/COM-OUT/0243/2021).

Disclosure of Interests. The authors have no competing interests to declare that are relevant to the content of this article.

References

1. Swart, J.: Tactics of news literacy: how young people access, evaluate, and engage with news on social media. New Media Soc. **25**, 505–521 (2021). https://doi.org/10.1177/146144482 11011447
2. Lesage, F., Natale, S.: Rethinking the distinctions between old and new media: introduction. Converg. Int. J. Res. New Media Technol. **25**, 575–589 (2019). https://doi.org/10.1177/135 4856519863364
3. Schrøder, K.C.: Methodological pluralism as a vehicle of qualitative generalization. Particip. J. Audience Recept. Stud. **9**, 798–825 (2012)
4. Peters, C., Schrøder, K.C., Lehaff, J., Vulpius, J.: News as they know it: young adults' information repertoires in the digital media landscape. Digit. J. **10**, 62–86 (2022). https://doi.org/10.1080/21670811.2021.1885986
5. Hasebrink, U., Domeyer, H.: Media repertoires as patterns of behaviour and as meaningful practices: a multimethod approach to media use in converging media environments. Particip. J. Audience Recept. Stud. **9**, 757–779 (2012)
6. Swart, J.: Experiencing algorithms: how young people understand, feel about, and engage with algorithmic news selection on social media. Soc. Media Soc. **7**, 1–11 (2021). https://doi.org/10.1177/20563051211008828
7. Galan, L., Osserman, J., Parker, T., Taylor, M.: How young people consume news and the implications for mainstream media. Reuters Institute for the Study of Journalism, Oxford University
8. Newman, N., Fletcher, R., Eddy, K., Robertson, C.T., Nielsen, R.K.: Reuters Institute Digital News Report 2023. Reuters Institute for the Study of Journalism (2023)
9. Brites, M.J., Castro, T.S., Müller, M.S., Sousa, C., Leote de Carvalho, M.J., Maneta, M.: YouNDigital – Relatório Survey – Task 3 (2023)
10. Amaral, I., Flores, A.M., Antunes, E., Brites, M.J.: Intergenerational digitally mediated relationships: how Portuguese young adults interact with family members over 65+. In: Gao, Q., Zhou, J. (eds.) HCII 2022. LNCS, vol. 13331, pp. 335–348. Springer, Cham (2022). https://doi.org/10.1007/978-3-031-05654-3_23
11. Azevedo, C., Ponte, C.: Intergenerational solidarity or intergenerational gap? How elderly people experience ICT within their family context. Obs. OBS. 14 (2020). https://doi.org/10.15847/obsOBS14320201587

12. Erll, A.: Memory in Culture. Palgrave Macmillan, Basingstoke (2011)
13. Cabecinhas, R.: Memórias (des)alinhadas. Representações sociais da história e comunicação intercultural (2018). https://hdl.handle.net/1822/62836
14. Niemeyer, K.: Introduction: media and nostalgia. In: Niemeyer, K. (ed.) Media and Nostalgia: Yearning for the Past, Present and Future, pp. 1–23. Palgrave Macmillan UK, London (2014)
15. Lizardi, R.: Mediated Nostalgia: Individual Memory and Contemporary Mass Media. Lexington Books (2014)
16. Schrøder, K.C.: Audience reception research in a post-broadcasting digital age. Telev. New Media 20, 155–169 (2019). https://doi.org/10.1177/1527476418811114
17. Davis, C.H., Michelle, C.: Q methodology in audience research: bridging the qualitative/quantitative 'divide'? Particip. J. Audience Recept. Stud. 8, 559–593 (2011)
18. Caetano, A., Nico, M.: Forever young: creative responses to challenging issues in biographical research. Contemp. Soc. Sci. 14, 361–378 (2019). https://doi.org/10.1080/21582041.2018.1510134

The Impact of Color in Phone Software Interfaces on the User Experience of the Elderly

Teng Wang[1] , Zhiyuan Ye[1] , Zhijie Xi[1] , Jie Mei[1] , Jinjin Zhu[1] , and Ao Jiang[2]([✉])

[1] Fuzhou University, Fuzhou, China
[2] Nanjing University of Aeronautics and Astronautics, Imperial College London, ILEWG ESA, EuroMoonMarsLondon, UK
aojohn928@gmail.com

Abstract. In recent years, China has entered an aging society [1]. As they age, the elderly experience a continuous decline in vision. The decrease in the transmittance of the elderly lens and the size of the pupil leads to a weakened sensitivity to light [2]. In terms of color recognition, due to the degeneration of the visual nerves and the reduction of cone cells in the retina, the elderly's ability to distinguish colors deteriorates [3]. They become very sensitive to intense brightness, their sensitivity to color discrimination decreases, and as a result, their speed of processing visual information slows down [4]. Moreover, with the increase in age, cognitive abilities also decline, and the elderly will take longer than younger individuals to complete a given task [5]. Psychologically, the elderly often experience negative emotions such as anxiety and depression due to the decline in vision [6]. As of June 2023, the proportion of internet users aged 60 and over was 13% [7], and the number of elderly people using smart products has gradually increased. Therefore, in the digital age, the design of interactive interfaces plays a crucial role for the elderly in using social apps. Phone apps are commonly used social apps for the elderly. According to color psychology theory, colors have a regulatory effect on human functions and emotional changes [8]. However, most of the existing phone app interfaces are relatively monochromatic, relying solely on characters and layout to convey information. The functionality of searching, dialing, and connecting is not clear, leading to relatively difficult information recognition for the elderly and a poorer user experience.

Keywords: Seniors · Communication Software · Color Perception · User Experience

1 Introduction

Statistics from the Pew Research Center (Pew Research Center) show that 53% of people over the age of 65 own a smartphone in 2019.

Aging can lead to lesions in the visual system [9]. In the elderly, the retina slowly decreases in size, the cornea grows in diameter, and the vitreous hardens as we age, leading to vision loss [10, 11]. The colour perception of the eye changes with age.

Eye colour perception changes with age and the ability to distinguish colours decreases significantly [12]. The production of pigmentation from crystals is one of the main causes of diminished colour perception in older adults [4]. In addition to this, colour discrimination is also poor in older adults due to the degeneration of the optic nerve and the reduction of cone cells in the retina [3]. [3] In addition to this, colour recognition is also impaired in the elderly due to degeneration of the optic nerve and reduction of retinal cone cells [3]. In particular, aging decreases pupil function, which reduces sensitivity to light [4]. [4]. In addition, it reduces colour sensitivity in older people, reducing their ability to judge intermediate shades, especially between blue and green [13].

Research has shown that colour influences our lives in different ways. People's reactions to colour are mainly based on physical sensations and psychological experiences [14].

At the same time colour is an important tool for stimulating cognitive motivation and reflexivity levels in older people. Colour increases the legibility of space and helps them to orientate themselves [15]. Finding the desired object even improves their mood and well-being, resulting in a favourable emotional experience. Colour can influence older people's cognitive abilities, which directly affect the way they perceive information, focus their memory, think and understand educational tasks [16].

The use of smartphones by older people has increased and mobile phones have become an important tool for improving the quality of life of older people. Colour combinations make a difference to the discrimination of older people using displays and have been shown to have a significant impact on their daily lives. Therefore, colour is crucial to the design of the screen [17].

Pastoor [18] and Silverstein [19] argue that colour is a major factor in the performance of computer displays and can be effective in increasing the interaction between the user and the computer. Conversely, improper use of colour can also lead to reduced performance [20], and older people may experience difficulty and confusion when viewing colour images on smartphones and tablets. In addition to improving reading performance, research has also found that colour can make user operations less dull, reduce visual fatigue and stress, and even improve visual performance [21]. Today's smartphone application design phase ignores older users and designers do not pay attention to the needs and requirements of older people. Despite the fact that due to the complexity of the interface, older users are willing to adopt technologies that help them to maintain their quality of life, they are unable to take advantage of the benefits of smartphones. Therefore, the causes of different problems are discussed from two different perspectives. Firstly, there are age-related issues, i.e. cognition, physical abilities, memory loss, mental models and sensory functions that make it more difficult for them to interact with new technologies. Then comes soft-ware design; designers do not carefully design applications that address the needs and requirements of older users. In the age of digitalisation, the design of mobile phone interaction interface plays an important role in the use of social software by the elderly. Whereas phone software is a common social software used by the elderly, older people are not familiar with smartphone technology and tend to encounter difficulties when using the device [22].

Therefore, this study takes elderly users as the target group, analyses the effects of different background colours on the attention of the elderly in the telephone software interface, and deeply analyses the perception of different colours on the psychological emotions of the elderly. It reveals the differences in the emotional experience of the elderly with different colours, and provides insights into the design of interface colour schemes that are more suitable for the elderly. It also provides design guidelines for the interface design of telephony software applications from the perspective of the elderly.

2 Method

2.1 Experimental Design

The overall experiment was divided into two phases: the first phase was a colour selection experiment; the second phase was a software interface colour experiment. The second phase consisted of three parts: the first part was a contact finder test; the second part was an interactive interface colour experiment for answering; and the third part was a dialling experiment as well as an interview and questionnaire on colour perception.

The first stage is colour card selection, where warm colours are usually associated with warmth and cold colours are usually associated with coldness and alienation [8]. The colour cards were divided into warm and cold colour cards see Table 1, and the elderly were asked to select one from each of the warm and cold colour cards, and then to select the three most intimate colours from the selected warm colour cards, and the three more distant colours from the cold colour cards. Finally, the number of times each colour was selected was summed up, and the two most selected colours were chosen among the close and distant colours, respectively.

In the second stage, the two close and two distant colours selected in the first stage were arranged in different combinations, and the closer contacts in the interaction software were marked as close colours, and the stranger contacts were marked as distant colours, with a total of four combinations, which were carried out in two sessions, two groups each time, with a 48h interval between the two experiments, and each group of colour combinations was tested for a variety of interactions respectively in each experiment. Each group of experiments was divided into three parts: the first part measured the reaction time to complete the task by formulating a set task, i.e., to search for contacts with different levels of intimacy in the address book; the second part measured the reaction time to complete the task by having the contacts with different levels of intimacy call the older adults with different colours in the incoming call interface, and the older adults answered or hung up the phone call. In the third part, older adults dialed the phone of contacts with different levels of intimacy, and the communication interface presented different colours. Finally, the colour perception of the older adults was collected through interviews and questionnaires, and then the colour perception was visualised through the questionnaire scoring data (on a scale of 1–5, the higher the score in the close colour the closer the person is, and the higher the score in the distant colour the more distant the person is).

2.2 Participants

This experiment was conducted at the Xiamen Campus of Fuzhou University and introduced to the community, senior activity centre and senior university, covering four life

Table 1. Colour specimens from the first phase of the experiment

No.	colour		warm colours					No.	colour		cool colours				
		R	G	B	L	A	B			R	G	B	L	A	B
1		255	0	0	54	81	70	28		0	255	0	88	-79	81
2		255	77	77	60	68	41	29		77	255	77	89	-70	67
3		255	153	153	74	39	17	30		153	255	153	92	-46	39
4		204	0	0	43	68	59	31		0	204	0	72	-67	68
5		204	61	61	48	57	34	32		62	204	62	73	-59	56
6		204	122	122	60	33	14	33		122	204	122	75	-39	33
7		153	0	0	32	55	47	34		0	153	0	55	-54	55
8		153	46	46	36	45	27	35		46	153	46	56	-47	45
9		153	92	92	46	26	11	36		92	153	92	58	-30	26
10		255	126	0	67	46	75	37		0	0	255	30	68	-112
11		255	166	77	76	28	59	38		77	77	255	43	44	-90
12		255	204	153	86	14	33	39		153	153	255	67	19	-51
13		204	102	0	55	38	63	40		0	0	204	23	58	-59
14		204	133	61	62	23	49	41		61	61	204	34	37	-75

(*continued*)

Table 1. (*continued*)

The following values are printed as stacked digits (read top-to-bottom within each column). Each sample has a colour swatch followed by six values (R, G, B, L*, a*, b*); on the right-hand samples the final b* value is negative.

No.	R	G	B	L*	a*	b*
15	204	163	122	70	12	27
16	153	76	0	42	30	51
17	153	99	46	47	19	39
18	153	122	92	54	9	21
19	255	255	0	98	-16	93
20	255	255	77	98	-14	79
21	255	255	153	98	-10	49
22	204	204	0	80	-13	79
23	204	204	62	80	-12	66
24	204	204	122	81	-9	41
25	153	153	21	61	-4	6
26	153	153	16	62	-10	53
27	153	153	92	62	-7	32
42	122	122	204	54	16	-43
43	0	0	153	15	47	-77
44	46	46	153	25	29	-60
45	92	92	153	41	12	-34
46	167	0	255	45	79	-86
47	194	77	255	55	67	-69
48	220	153	255	73	39	-41
49	134	0	204	36	67	-72
50	155	62	204	45	56	-57
51	176	122	204	59	33	-34
52	100	0	153	26	55	-58
53	116	46	153	34	44	-46
54	132	92	153	45	26	-27

scenarios for use by seniors in each scenario, with a total of 40 research samples (20 men and 20 women) seniors over the age of 60 with no visual impairment, no colour weakness or colour blindness, and no cognitive impairment. Among them, 20 (10 men and 10 women) were subjected to the first phase of the colour selection experiment; the remaining 20 (10 men and 10 women) were subjected to the second phase of the software interface colour experiment, and each elderly person was required to complete the experiment for two different periods of time.

2.3 Experimental Materials

According to the HSB standard, red (H = 0), orange (H = 30), yellow (H = 60), green (H = 120), blue (H = 240), violet (H = 300), three kinds of warm colours, three kinds of cold colours, and each colour in accordance with the brightness (100%, 80%, 60%) and saturation (100%, 70%, 40%) to generate a total of 9 colours, a total of 54 kinds of colors, each colour HSB value was converted to RGB and LAB values, and each color RGB and LAB values were labeled in the color specimen, and the color card was made as in Fig. 1. 54 colours, each colour of the HSB value is converted to RGB and LAB values, each colour of the RGB and LAB values are marked in the colour specimen, and make a colour card in Fig. 1. in the suitable aging colour experiments, through the colour card to select the most representative of the indifference of the two cold colours and the most warm of the two warm colours, the four colours, the four random warm and cold with the combination of the four combinations of four combinations of the four combinations of the four combinations of the four combinations of the four combinations of communication as a communications experimental Colour variables. In the communication APP, these colours are reflected in: the icon in front of the person's name in the address book, and the background colour of the incoming call. Figure 2 (colour random configuration) shows the four system communication in the address book self-designed interface legend, saved in PNG format, the ink knife simulation run as a display, the method resolution of 375 * 812px.Fig. 3, Fig. 4 shows the communication in the incoming call of the self-designed interface legend, saved in PNG format, the method resolution of 375 * 812px. Icons are actual shapes designed by the application icon designer and selected in iPhone 13 min. Image processing software was used to adjust the background colour of the four experimental materials.

Fig. 1 Test Colour Card Selection.

Fig. 2 Directory.

Fig. 3 People Friendly Calling Interface.

Fig. 4 Stranger call screen.

2.4 Experimental Equipment

The experimental equipment included a laptop (Lenovo SAVIOR) to create the experimental interface, two tablets (2020 iPad pro, ipad2020) for colour swatch selection, two mobile phones (iPhone 12 Pro, iPhone 12) to operate the interface experiments, and a stopwatch to keep track of the time to display the self-designed communication interface on the mobile phone in equal proportions, 1 to 1. A stopwatch was used to record the time, and the self-designed communication interface was displayed on the mobile phone in 1 to 1 ratio.

2.5 Data Analysis

Phase II, Colour Card Selection. The statistical results of the colour card selection interview are shown in Table 1, after the data comparison, it is concluded that in the cold colour No. 45 Blue and No. 53 Purple have the highest number of choices, and more subjects think that these two colours are more likely to make people feel cold, of which No. 45 Blue number is 7, accounting for the total number of votes of cold colours 11.67%, and No. 53 Purple number of choices is 6, accounting for the total number of votes of cold colours 10.00%, and in the Warm colours No. 2 Red and No. 10 Orange had the highest number of choices and more subjects felt that these two colours were more approachable, with No. 2 Red having 8 people or 13.33% of the total votes for the warm colours, and No. 10 Orange having 5 people or 8.33% of the total votes for the warm colours. Finally, the two warm colours and two cool colours obtained were matched with each other to obtain four combinations: No. 10 Orange * No. 53 Purple, No. 10 Orange * No. 45 Blue, No. 2 Red * No. 53 Purple, and No. 2 Red * No. 45 Blue.

Table 2. Note: Votes in the table is the number of people who chose that colour value, 20 in total,with a total of 60 votes each for cool and warm colours.

No.	colour	vote	No.	colour	vote	No.	colour	vote
1		7	19		4	37		1
2		8	20		4	38		1
3		5	21		4	39		2
4		1	22		1	40		2
5		0	23		1	41		1
6		1	24		1	42		2
7		1	25		0	43		2
8		1	26		0	44		4
9		3	27		0	45		7
10		5	28		3	46		1
11		4	29		3	47		2
12		3	30		3	48		1
13		2	31		1	49		0
14		1	32		1	50		1
15		0	33		0	51		1
16		1	34		0	52		5
17		1	35		2	53		6
18		1	36		2	54		4

Phase II, Part I - Finding Tasks Experiments. The specific time statistics are shown in Table 2, after the experimental operation time data analysis: No. 10 orange and No. 45 blue colour matching under the find task completion time is obviously shorter than the other three colour matching under the task completion time, the total value is 114.3 s.

Table 3. Note: Values are the total number of hours spent on the 20-person search experiment.

colour matching	Find (intimate people)	Find (alienate people)	total time
orange × purple	87.40 s	101.51s	188.91s
orange × blue	63.78 s	55.20s	118.98s
red × purple	59.17 s	52.94s	112.11s
red × blue	82.26 s	69.90s	152.16s

Phase II, Part II - Answering Tasks Experiments. The specific time statistics are shown in Table 3, after the experimental operation time data analysis: No. 10 orange and No. 45 blue colour matching under the answer task completion time is significantly shorter than the other three colour matching under the task completion time.

Table 4. Note: Values are total experimental time for the 20-person answering task.

colour matching	answer(intimate people)	answer(alienate people)	total time
orange × purple	48.36 s	52.43 s	100.79 s
orange × blue	41.21 s	41.17 s	82.38 s
red × purple	43.66 s	43.85 s	87.51 s
red × blue	46.99 s	48.12 s	95.11 s

Phase II, Part I III - Dialling Experiments and the Colour Perception Questionnaire. The specific time statistics are shown in Table 4, the subjects were scored on a questionnaire about colour feelings after the find, answer and dial trials, each subject scored 1–5 for each group, for colour combinations 5 points represented the highest colour recognition and 1 point represented the lowest colour recognition, for cool colours (purple/blue) 5 points represented the strongest feelings of alienation and indifference and 1 point represented the weakest feelings of indifference, for warm colours (For warm colours (orange/red) 5 represents the strongest feelings of intimacy and 1 represents the weakest feelings of closeness (Table 5).

Table 5. Note: The values in the table are the sum of the fractions for which this colour combination/colour value was selected.

colour matching	total score value	colour	total score value
orange × purple	60	orange	81
orange × blue	81	red	51
red × purple	42	purple	69
red × blue	71	blue	77

3   Results

This study analyses the impact of interactive interface colours on older adults' use of telephone communication software. For older adults, appropriate colours in the interface of communication software can improve the efficiency and emotional experience of retrieving the address book. Therefore, this study aims to find appropriate interface colours that can provide a better user experience for older users, reduce their barriers in using telephone software, and enable more equal access to smart communication devices.

From the above analysis, it can be seen that in the first stage of the colour card selection experiment the results showed that among the warm colours, No. 10 Orange and No. 2 Red scored the highest, and among the cool colours, No. 53 Violet and No. 45 Blue scored the highest.

Based on the above experimental data it is stated that warm colours with higher saturation and luminance are the colours that older people feel close to because these colours remind them of warmth and enthusiasm, whereas cool colours with lower saturation and luminance are the colours that older people feel alienated from because these colours remind them of darkness and indifference. Therefore, two cool colours, No. 53 Violet and No. 45 Blue, were used as markers for distant contacts and two warm colours, No. 10 Orange and No. 2 Red, were used as markers for close contacts.

The second phase of the experiment was an interface manipulation experiment with a sample of 20 individual elderly people.

In the first part of the contact finding task, the No. 53 Purple No. 2 Red combination took the shortest time out of the four groups, with the red colour having the fastest reaction time, suggesting that the colour red is very noticeable in the finding task.

In the second part of the connected call test, the No. 45 Blue No. 10 Orange combination takes the shortest time among the four groups. When a call comes in, the colour sensation from the background colour of the caller ID page will help the elderly to make a quicker judgement, and the use of blue and orange to represent close and distant contacts will enable the elderly to identify the proximity of the contact more quickly.

In the third part of the dialing experiment, the questionnaire data shows that most of the elderly people think that No. 10 Orange, as the background colour of the interface of dialing close contacts, can feel more warm and evoke some good memories. On the other hand, No. 45 Blue as the background colour of the interface of dialing distant contacts can feel more strange and distant.

This was also confirmed in the final colour combination questionnaire, where the No. 45 Blue No. 10 Orange combination scored the highest, with more seniors believing that the blue-orange combination is the pair that best represents close and distant contacts in telephony software.

4 Conclusions

Taken together, the results of the experiments in this study show that the colour of the interactive interface of telephone software has a significant impact on the experience of older people. Different colour combinations do affect the reading speed and accuracy of older people. At the same time different colour tones have different feelings and experiences on the emotional experience of the elderly.

The main conclusions of this study are:

1. Although the red-violet combination was more rapid in the look-up experiment, it did not score as well in the longer response time in the answer experiment and in the final questionnaire, because the colour red gives a strong visual stimulus and a feeling of

alertness [15] This is because red colour gives people a strong visual stimulus and alertness [15], so the red-violet combination does not bring a good experience to the elderly, and the reaction time and final score of the four groups are combined to conclude that the blue-orange combination is more suitable for the elderly.

2. Red is the most striking colour when controlling saturation and brightness23, The colour red can be used in interface design to attract the user's attention to specific interface elements and information, and to be more prominent and conspicuous in the use of the interface.

3. No. 10 Orange is the colour that the elderly consider the closest to them, while No. 45 Blue is the most distant. In the interface design, orange is chosen as the mark of close contacts and blue is chosen as the mark of distant contacts, which is more conducive to the recognition of close and distant relationships and improves the operation efficiency of the elderly.

4. The combination of No. 45 Blue and No. 10 Orange significantly improves the attention and concentration of the elderly when they use the telephone software, and the combination of blue and orange creates a balanced and compelling interface atmosphere. In the interactive interface of the telephone software, the use of vibrant orange and stable blue can be considered to optimise the experience of the elderly in using the interface, and to guide the elderly to use the telephone software more conveniently and attentively.

5. In terms of brightness and saturation, warmer colours with higher saturation and brightness will give the elderly a feeling of closeness and comfort, and can stimulate more positive emotions, making the elderly feel closer and creating a warmer and more pleasurable atmosphere for the elderly. Low saturation and brightness of the cool colours will give the elderly strange and distant feelings, triggering a more calm and peaceful emotional experience.

Also this Study has Some Limitations.   Due to financial as well as practical constraints, we only used the Xiamen campus of Fuzhou University as well as nearby communities, senior activity centres, and senior colleges, which made the representativeness of the sample somewhat limited. Future studies need to expand the scope of the survey to include a wider range of older adults and older adults in different regions to obtain more comprehensive findings.

We only used a total of six colour shades of warm and cold tones in our experimental research, and this simplified design may not fully reflect the experience of older adults with different variations of colours in the telephone software interface. Future research could consider introducing more variation conditions to delve into the combined effects of these factors on older adults' user experience.

These limitations are not only present in the research design, but may also have some impact on the generalisation and interpretation of the results. Therefore, in order to gain a more comprehensive and accurate understanding of older adults' user experiences in communication applications, future research should aim to address these limitations by adopting more diverse samples and more complex experimental designs, which will help to improve the scientific validity and practicality of the study.

References

1. Mitchell, E., Walker, R.: Global ageing: successes, challenges and opportunities. Br. J. Hosp. Med. **81**(2), 1–9 (2020)
2. Okajima, K.: Colour perception of the elderly. In: Proceedings AIC 2003 Bangkok, p. 413 (2003)
3. Jiang, A., Foing, B.H., Schlacht, I.L., Yao, X., Cheung, V., Rhodes, P.A.: Colour schemes to reduce stress response in the hygiene area of a space station: a Delphi study. Appl. Ergon. **98**, 103573 (2022)
4. Czaja, S.J., Boot, W.R., Charness, N., et al.: Designing for Older Adults: Principles and Creative Human Factors Approaches. CRC press (2019)
5. Pereira, L., Brandão, D., Martins, N.: Ageing related human factors to be addressed in the design of visual interfaces of digital applications developed for seniors: a literature review. In: Perspectives on Design and Digital Communication II: Research, Innovations and Best Perspectives on Design and Digital Communication II: Research, Innovations and Best Practices, pp. 65–80 (2021)
6. Jiang, A., et al.: The effect of colour environments on visual tracking and visual strain during short-term simulation of three gravity states. Appl. Ergon. **110**, 103994 (2023)
7. China Internet Network Information Center: The 52nd Statistical Report on Internet Development in China
8. Azeemi, S.T.Y., Rafiq, H.M., Ismail, I., Kazmi, S.R., Azeemi, A.: The mechanistic basis of chromotherapy: current knowledge and future perspectives. Complement. Ther. Med. **46**, 217–222 (2019). https://doi.org/10.1016/j.ctim.2019.08.025
9. Guire, F.A., Boyd, R.K., Tedrick, R.T.: Leisure and Age. Sagamore Publishing, Champaign (1996)
10. Jiang, A., et al.: Space Habitat Astronautics: Multicolour Lighting Psychology in a 7-Day Simulated Habitat. Space: Science & Technology (2022)
11. Jiang, A., et al.: Short-term virtual reality simulation of the effects of space station colour and microgravity and lunar gravity on cognitive task performance and emotion. Build. Environ. **227**, 109789 (2023)
12. Inoyatov, A.: Health and healthy lifestyle of the elderly. J. Pharmaceutical Negative Resul. 3253–3261 (2022)
13. Helve, J., Krause, U.: The influence of age on performance in the Pan-D15 colour vision test. Acta Opthalmologica **50**, 896–901 (1972)
14. Jiang, A., Yao, X., Westland, S., Hemingray, C., Foing, B., Lin, J.: The Effect of Correlated Colour Temperature on Physiological, Emotional and Subjective Satisfaction in the Hygiene Area of a Space Station. Int. J. Environ. Res. Public Health **19**(15), 9090 (2022)
15. Jiang, A.O.: Effects of colour environment on spaceflight cognitive abilities during short-term simulations of three gravity states (Doctoral dissertation, University of Leeds) (2022)
16. Jiang, A., Zhu, Y., Yao, X., Foing, B.H., Westland, S., Hemingray, C.: The effect of three body positions on colour preference: an exploration of microgravity and lunar gravity simulations. Acta Astronaut. **204**, 1–10 (2023)
17. Huang, Z., Wang, S., Jiang, A., Hemingray, C., Westland, S.: Gender preference differences in color temperature associated with LED light sources in the autopilot cabin. In: Cabin. In: Krömker, H. (eds.) HCII 2022. LNCS, vol. 13335, pp. 151–0166. Springer, Cham (2022). https://doi.org/10.1007/978-3-031-04987-3_10
18. Jiang, A., Yao, X., Hemingray, C., Westland, S.: Young people's colour preference and the arousal level of small apartments. Color. Res. Appl. **47**(3), 783–795 (2022)
19. Silverstein, L.D.: Human Factors for Color CRT Displays Systems: Concepts, Methods and Research

20. Po-Chan, Y.E.H.: Effects of colour combinations on the discrimination performance of elderly people using a LCD monitor. In: Universal Design 2014: Three Days of Creativity and Diversity: Proceedings of the International Conference on Universal Design, UD 2014 Lund, Sweden, June 16–18, 2014, vol. 35, p. 149. IOS Press. (2014)
21. Hassan, M.F.: Colour enhancement method to improve the colors of the images perceived by the elderly people. Int. J. Image Graphics **21**(01), 2150004 (2021)
22. Awan, M., et al.: Usability barriers for elderly users in smartphone app usage: an analytical hierarchical process-based prioritization. Sci. Program. **2021**, 1–14 (2021)
23. Wilms, L., Oberfeld, D.: Colour and emotion: effects of hue, saturation, and brightness. Psychol. Res. **82**(5), 896–914 (2018)

Exploring Factors Influencing Visual Realism in Augmented Reality User Experience

Xiaokang Wei[1,2] (iD) and Yan Luximon[1,2(✉)] (iD)

[1] School of Design, The Hong Kong Polytechnic University,
Hong Kong, China
`xiaokang.wei@connect.polyu.hk`, `yan.luximon@polyu.edu.hk`
[2] Laboratory for Artificial Intelligence in Design, Hong Kong, China

Abstract. This study investigates the key factors that affect visual realism in Augmented Reality (AR) user experience. Recognizing the importance of visual realism in enhancing user engagement and integrating virtual elements into the real world, we embarked on a comprehensive exploration of these factors. Our study included an extensive literature review, identifying key parameters beyond conventional elements. A structured questionnaire was designed to systematically capture users' perceptions, involving participants from diverse backgrounds engaging with simulated AR scenarios. Our research carefully adjusted variables such as light(type, intensity, color), shadows(intensity, direction), material properties(texture, roughness), depth occlusion, field of view (FoV), gamma correction value, and high dynamic range(HDR), and categorized participants based on their experience with rendering software to ensure a targeted analysis. Our results showed that various rendering variables all played a role in influencing users' perception of visual realism in AR. Notably, among these variables, light source color and shadows direction had a relatively minor impact compared to others, while material texture and roughness had the most pronounced effects on visual realism perception. Furthermore, our results indicated that users' prior experience with rendering software had no significant influence on their judgments of visual realism. The study contributes to the understanding of factors impacting visual realism in AR, providing valuable insights for refining AR application design and development and optimizing user engagement and satisfaction.

Keywords: Augmented Reality · Visual Realism · User Experience

1 Introduction

1.1 Research Background

AR technology has transformed the way we engage with the world around us. Its journey from a mere concept to a transformative technology reflects a rich history of innovation and technological advancements. AR's ability to overlay digital

Q. Gao and J. Zhou (Eds.): HCII 2024, LNCS 14725, pp. 169–182, 2024.
https://doi.org/10.1007/978-3-031-61543-6_13

information onto the real world has found applications across various industries, changing how we perceive and interact with our environment. This technology has significantly impacted sectors like education, healthcare, entertainment, and manufacturing, showing its flexibility and essential part of modern life. The development history of AR technology is crucial to understanding its current capabilities and potential future advancements [1].

Visual realism in AR is crucial for creating an immersive user experience. This concept involves the accurate depiction of virtual objects in a way that they appear seamlessly integrated with the real world. Understanding visual realism in AR requires an exploration of theories of visual perception and how these theories apply to augmented environments. The realism in computer graphics, as discussed in Sutherland's seminal work [2], lays the foundation for how these principles are adapted and evolved in AR. Further, Milgram et al. [3] discussed the adaptation of these principles in AR is critical for achieving a high level of realism.

The factors contributing to visual realism in AR are multifaceted, including light source, material properties, depth occlusion, FoV, and HDR. Each factor plays a crucial role in enhancing the realism of AR experience. The literature offers a wealth of research on these factors. For instance, Bimber et al. [4] studied light source and its impact on realism in AR, providing insights into the complexity of achieving accurate light in augmented environments. Similarly, research on material properties and depth perception, like the studies conducted by Cutting et al. [5]and Wanger et al. [6], offer a deep understanding of how these elements influence the user's perception of AR content. The comprehensive review of these studies is essential to grasp the full spectrum of factors affecting visual realism in AR.

In the growing field of AR, a important yet overlooked aspect lies in the complex interaction of various factors that contribute to visual realism. Despite substantial research, a significant knowledge gap exists in understanding how different elements like light sources, material properties, and depth cues affect the user's perception in dynamic AR environments. This research seeks to investigate these interactions, with a specific emphasis on determining whether rendering-related factors, including light (type, intensity, color), shadows (intensity, direction), material properties (texture, roughness), depth occlusion, FOV, gamma correction value, and HDR, have an impact on users' visual realism perception in AR interactive scenarios. Addressing these gaps is not just an academic pursuit; it's crucial for advancing AR technology toward creating experience that are indistinguishably seamless and deeply immersive. The goal is to decode these intricate connections to significantly enhance the authenticity and effectiveness of AR applications across various domains, paving the way for profound advancements in the field.

1.2   Research Objective

This research aims to profoundly impact the design and development of AR applications by advancing our comprehension of visual realism within augmented reality. Focusing on how elements such as light, material properties, and depth perception contribute to realism, the study seeks to provide insights essential for refining AR experience. These enhancements are anticipated to lead to more advanced and lifelike AR experience, setting new standards in the field. The broader objective is to significantly enhance user engagement and satisfaction across diverse sectors, including education and healthcare. Ultimately, this study aspires to be play a key role in developing more effective AR applications, marking a crucial contribution to the evolving landscape of augmented reality technology. Therefore, we conclude with two assumptions:

Hypothesis 1: In our study, all examined variables-including light (type, intensity, color), shadows (intensity, direction), material properties (texture, roughness), depth occlusion, FOV, gamma correction value, and HDR-effect users' perception of visual realism in AR;

Hypothesis 2: The judgment of visual realism in AR is influenced by the user's experience with rendering software.

2   Related Work

Sutherland et al. [2] introduced the groundbreaking concept of blending virtual and real-world elements. This seminal idea laid the foundation for the entire field of AR. Azuma et al. [1] comprehensive survey thoroughly presents the evolution of AR technology, which introduces the early developments in the field, including head-mounted displays and overlay techniques, and mapping out the progress leading to the versatile applications of AR we see today. These initial steps were critical in setting the stage for the complex AR systems currently in use across various industries, from entertainment to education and beyond [7,8].

Milgram et al. [3] present the concept of the Reality-Virtuality Continuum. This concept has been instrumental in understanding the blend of real and virtual worlds and in guiding the development of AR technologies that aim for seamless integration. Bimber et al. [4] further explore related methods of enhancing visual realism in AR, specifically through advanced projection mapping and a deep understanding of environmental interactions. These techniques have been crucial in creating AR experience that are not only visually compelling but also contextually relevant to the user's environment. Cutting et al. [5] addresses a crucial aspect of AR-depth perception. Their research explores various depth cues, such as occlusion and perspective, which are vital for effectively placing virtual objects within real-world contexts in AR environments. This understanding of depth perception is essential for creating AR experience where virtual and real-world elements coexist in a spatially coherent manner [9]. The science of color perception plays a significant role in achieving realism in AR. Wyszecki et al. [10] discusses the intricacies of color perception, which are critical for color matching in AR. This aspect is crucial for ensuring that virtual objects appear natural and consistent within their real-world surroundings. Accurate motion tracking is essential for enhancing the realism of AR experience. Johansson et al. [11] research on the visual perception of biological motions fundamental in informing the development of AR systems that can accurately track and render user and object movement. This research helps ensure that interactions with virtual elements in AR are smooth and realistic, mirroring real-world physics and movements.

Bimber et al. [4] highlight the complexities of replicating real-world light conditions in AR. The interplay of light with virtual objects is key to achieving a sense of realism. Accurate simulation of light effects, such as shadows and reflections, is essential for the seamless integration of virtual objects into the physical world [12]. Wanger et al. [6] examine how the material attributes of virtual objects, like texture and reflectivity, impact their perception in AR. This research highlights the importance of accurately rendering material properties to enhance the believability of virtual objects in AR scenarios. Cutting et al. [5] have significantly advanced the field by demonstrating how the exploration of depth cues can enhance the realism of virtual objects in augmented reality environments. The impact of FOV and HDR on user immersion in AR is significant. Studies exploring these aspects emphasize the importance of a wide and dynamic visual range to create realistic and engaging AR experience. A broad FoV and enhanced HDR contribute to a more immersive experience, allowing users to interact more naturally with both the virtual and real components of the AR environment [13]. Sazzad et al. [14] explore the impact of gamma correction value on image quality, emphasizing its significance in improving human visual perception and ensuring accurate image representation.

AR technology has been widely applied in various fields, with significant progress in healthcare [15]. It has proven particularly valuable in complex surgical procedures, offering real-time data and visual assistance to surgeons, thereby enhancing precision and efficiency. Yet, this innovative field is not without its challenges. As discussed in comprehensive research by Zhou et al. [16], AR technology faces several obstacles that need to be overcome to realize its full potential. These include concerns related to user comfort, technological constraints, and issues like system latency. Addressing these challenges is essential for the ongoing development and wider adoption of AR technology in healthcare and other sectors [17].

Despite the progress in AR technology, there remain several areas that are underexplored. The complex interaction of factors such as light, material properties, and depth cues in dynamic AR environments presents substantial opportunities for future research [17,18]. These elements' synthesis is key to creating next-generation AR experience that offer enhanced realism and user engagement. Addressing these challenges and exploring new research avenues will be crucial for the continued advancement of AR technology, potentially leading to groundbreaking developments in the field [19].

3   Method

In this study, a quantitative survey was employed to evaluate the factors influencing visual realism in AR user experience. This approach was specifically chosen for its effectiveness in systematically gathering and analyzing user perceptions of various visual elements within AR environments. The survey was meticulously designed to encompass a range of standardized questions aimed at quantitatively uncovering the impact of these elements on user-perceived visual realism. By leveraging this method, the study aspired to yield objective, statistically significant data that would substantiate our hypotheses and conclusions regarding the influence of specific rendering factors on the authenticity of visual experience in AR settings.

3.1 Participants

Participants in this study are categorized into two groups based on their experience with rendering software and have a wide age range from 18 to 60 years, with an even distribution of genders, including both males and females. All participants should not have any visual problems including color blindness, color weakness, etc. Participants were recruited through an online survey, and their voluntary participation was contingent upon informed consent. Throughout the entirety of the research process, stringent measures were implemented to ensure the anonymity and confidentiality of participant identities. All collected data was securely stored and solely utilized for research analysis purposes. Participants did not receive any form of compensation or incentives for their involvement in this study. Before conducting large-scale data collection, we conducted a pilot test with a small group of participants. This pilot test aimed to ensure participants could easily understand and respond to the questions. The feedback from the pilot test allowed us to make necessary adjustments and refinements to the questionnaire to improve its clarity and relevance. This preliminary testing phase ensured the effectiveness of the survey instrument before moving forward with the full-scale data collection.

3.2 Survey Instrument

The survey was structured into several sections, each aimed at dissecting different aspects of visual realism within AR environments. The first section gathered demographic data, ensuring a diverse representation of ages and backgrounds, critical for understanding the varied perceptions of AR realism. Subsequent sections presented participants with a series of images rendered under varying conditions. Each image was associated with specific rendering factors. To facilitate nuanced feedback, the questionnaire combined Likert-scale questions, allowing for a range of responses, with binary options to capture the presence or absence of visual elements. Additionally, an indistinguishable option was included, enabling the identification of rendering factors that did not significantly alter the perceived realism for participants.

In terms of the specific composition of the questionnaire, we designed a questionnaire consisting of six sections to comprehensively explore visual realism in AR experience. These sections include demographic information and visual realism variables. To assess the perceived realism of AR visuals, the study employed the blender renderer to simulate AR scenarios by inserting virtual objects into real-world scenes. This method allowed for the manipulation of various rendering factors to create different image conditions for evaluation. Participants were presented with these images and asked to judge the visual realism of each scene. This approach facilitated a controlled environment where the impact of specific rendering variables could be systematically measured against the respondents' perception of realism in AR. The titles and brief descriptions of each section are as follows:

Demographic Information. The demographic information collected in the survey included gender (59 males and 47 females), age range (18 to 60 years) with an average age of 30, and participants' experience with rendering software, distinguishing between those with experience (47 participants) and those without (59 participants). Gender distribution was balanced, with roughly equal representation of both males and females. Furthermore, participants were asked to identify factors they believed influenced visual realism and to disclose any visual impairments that could affect their perception, such as color blindness, with the provision to discontinue the survey if applicable. These preliminary questions were crucial in segmenting the data for subsequent analysis and in ensuring the validity of the responses related to the perceptual evaluation of AR experience. The division of participants based on their experience with rendering software or AR devices was considered to account for potential variations in the concept of visual realism. It is possible that these variables may have distinct influences on the final judgment and decision-making regarding visual realism. As shown in Table. 1

Table 1. Variables description on demographic information

Variable Name	Type	Description
Gender	Categorical	Male, Female, Other
Age	Continuous	Age range from 18 to 60 years
Experience with Rendering Software	Binary	Whether the participant has experience using rendering software like Blender, Keyshot, etc
Experience with XR products	Binary	Whether the participant has experience with virtual interaction products like XR, etc
Factors Affecting Visual Realism	Open-ended	Participant's Perception of factors that influence visual realism

Visual Realism Variables. As shown in Table. 2. Visual Realism Variables include light, shadows, materials, FOV, gamma correction values, depth occlusion, and HDR effects. In our study, we employed a survey design to investigate the factors influencing users' perception of visual realism in AR. We maintained a consistent AR environment while systematically varying specific variables to assess their impact on users' assessments of visual realism. Each variable was treated as an independent factor, with various values representing different levels. By systematically manipulating these levels within a stable AR environment, we aimed to understand the influence of individual variables on users' perception of visual realism. In designing the testing options for each variable, we included variable parameter values that align with the original scene as the reference ground truth(GT), along with an option indicating no difference. The remaining options were designed to represent varying degrees of change. Our findings provide valuable insights into the factors affecting visual realism judgments in AR, contributing to the field of AR research. For example, the lighting type variable question is shown in Fig. 1. The options for each question are set as follows:

Please select which of the following three images appears the most realistic.

No Difference

A   B   C   D

Fig. 1. Test of the effect of different lighting types on visual realism

Light: In this section, we investigated different aspects of light, including types, intensity, and colors. Light source types include point light, spotlight, and sunlight. we consider the point light as the ground truth option. Light source intensity is set to 10%, 50%, and 90%, where 50% is considered the GT value in this context. Light source colors include white, blue, and green color, where white is considered the GT value.

Shadows: The degree and direction of shadows are significant factors influencing visual realism. The shadows intensity intensity is set to 0%, 50%, and 90%, where 50% is considered the GT value in this context. The angles between the shadow direction and the original direction are set at 0°C, 90°C and 180°C, with 0°C direction considered as the GT value.

Materials: Texture and roughness of materials can significantly affect users' perception of realism. For the material texture test, we configured two different material options: the first one is the original texture, and the second one is the new texture, with the original texture considered as the GT. In the case of the material roughness test, we set up two different material options: the first one is 5% roughness, and the second one is 95% roughness, with 5% roughness considered as the GT.

FOV: Adjustments in FOV can alter users' visual perception in AR scenes. We set the FOV at three different levels, ranging from 10% to 90%. Among these levels, the FOV set at 50% is considered to be aligned with the GT configuration.

Gamma Correction Value: The gamma correction values are set to 1.0, 2.2, and 3.4, where 2.2 is considered the common gamma value, which is regarded as the GT in this context.

Depth Occlusion: In this variable testing, it includes whether Depth Occlusion is enabled, where enabling it is considered to be in alignment with the GT condition.

HDR: In this variable testing, it includes whether HDR is enabled, where enabling it is considered to be in alignment with the GT condition.

Table 2. Variables description on effecting visual realism

Variable Name	Type	Description
Light Source Type	Categorical	Types of light sources include Point Light, Spotlight, Sunlight
Light Source Intensity	Categorical	Levels of light intensity like 10%, 50%, 90%
Light Source Color	Categorical	Colors of light source including White, Blue, Green
Shadows Intensity	Categorical	Degrees of shadows intensity like 0%, 50%, 90%
Shadows Direction	Categorical	Directions of shadows with origin include 0 °C,90°C, and 180 °C
Material Texture	Categorical	Types of textures like Original Mirror Texture, Replaced Texture
Material Roughness	Categorical	Levels of roughness intensity such as 5%, 95%
FOV	Categorical	Angles representing the field of view like 10%, 50%, 90%
Gamma Correction Value	Categorical	Gamma settings like 1.0, 2.2, 3.4
Depth Occlusion	Categorical	Presence or absence of Depth Occlusion
HDR	Categorical	Presence or absence of HDR

3.3 Data Analysis

Frequency Calculation. In this study, we conducted a frequency calculation aimed at delving into several rendering variables related to visual realism and assessing their association with whether participants have experience using rendering software. These rendering variables include a range of factors related to visual realism. We calculate the frequency and percentage for each level or category under each variable, which allows us to understand the distribution of each rendering variable within the sample and the preferences of participants across different levels.

Chi-Square Test Analysis. Our primary objective was to evaluate the association between these rendering variables and participants' experience with rendering software. To achieve this goal, we performed the chi-square test [20]. The chi-square test is a statistical method used to examine the association between two categorical variables.

We calculated the chi-square statistic, p-value, and degrees of freedom to determine the presence of statistically significant associations. Based on the results of the chi-square test, if the p-value is less than the commonly chosen significance level (typically 0.05), we reject the null hypothesis, indicating a statistically significant association between rendering variables and rendering software experience. If the p-value is greater than the significance level, we fail to reject the null hypothesis, suggesting no statistically significant association.

4 Results

4.1 Frequency Calculation Results

Figure 2 presents the frequency calculation results for all variables, showing the distribution of participants' preferences across different intensity levels. In each question's set of options, we include a reference ground truth(GT) option that aligns with the original real-world environmental conditions for participants to consider.

In terms of the variable of light source type, the proportion of individuals who perceive the difference in comparison to no difference is 96% to 4%. Among these respondents, 49% chose an option that is the GT, representing the highest percentage among the four options. Regarding the variable of light source intensity, the proportion of individuals who perceive the difference in comparison to no difference is 97% to 3%. The majority, with 58%, chose the GT option, which was the highest percentage among the four options. For light source color, the proportion of individuals who perceive the difference in comparison to no difference is 88% to 12%. Among these respondents, 63% selected an option that aligned with the GT, demonstrating the highest percentage among the four options.

In terms of the variable of shadows intensity, the proportion of individuals who perceive the difference in comparison to no difference is 97% to 3%. Among these respondents, 77% chose the GT option, representing the highest percentage among the four options. Moving on to shadows intensity, the proportion of individuals who perceive the difference in comparison to no difference is 90% to 10%. Among these respondents, 51% chose the GT option, representing the highest percentage among the four options.

Regarding the variable of material texture, the proportion of individuals who perceive the difference in comparison to no difference is 99% to 1%. Among these respondents, 95% chose the GT option, representing the highest percentage among the three options. Similarly, for material roughness, 99% of participants perceived a difference compared to 1% who did not. Notably, 92% selected the GT option, which held the highest percentage among the three available choices.

In terms of the variable of FOV, the proportion of individuals who perceive the difference in comparison to no difference is 95% to 5%. Among these respondents, 49% chose the option of 10% angle, and 30% chose the GT option.

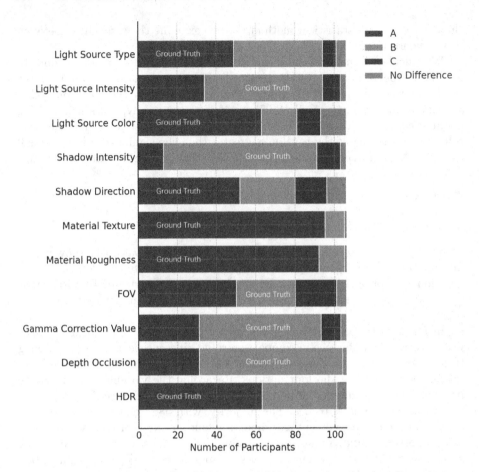

Fig. 2. Frequency results of various variables impacting visual realism.

For the gamma correction value variable, the proportion of individuals who perceive the difference in comparison to no difference is 97% to 3%. Among these respondents, 61% chose the GT option, representing the highest percentage among the four options.

Regarding the depth occlusion variable, the proportion of individuals who perceive the difference in comparison to no difference is 98% to 2%. Among these respondents, 73% chose the GT option, representing the highest percentage among the three options.

Finally, with respect to the HDR variable, 95% of participants perceived a difference compared to 5%. Among these respondents, 63% chose the GT option, representing the highest percentage among the three options (Table 3).

4.2 Chi-Square Test Results

Table 3. Chi-Square Test results on visual realism variables and experience with rendering software

Variable	Chi-Square Statistic	p-value	Degrees of Freedom	Significant
Light Source Type	0.981	0.806	3	No
Light Source Intensity	0.762	0.858	3	No
Light Source Color	7.277	0.064	3	No
Shadows Intensity	2.208	0.530	3	No
Shadows Direction	2.695	0.441	3	No
Material Texture	0.906	0.636	2	No
Material Roughness	2.496	0.287	2	No
FOV	0.530	0.912	3	No
Gamma Correction Value	1.556	0.669	3	No
Depth Occlusion	0.121	0.941	2	No
HDR	0.935	0.627	2	No

In this study, a chi-square test was employed to investigate the association between rendering variables and experience with rendering software. The results indicated that the p-values for all variables exceeded the statistical significance threshold of 0.05, thus Hypothesis 2 is rejected. Notably, although the p-value for the Light Color variable was 0.064, slightly above the significance level, it was not sufficient to demonstrate statistical significance. Hence, despite a marginal trend suggesting that experience with rendering software might affect the perception of light color, this association did not reach statistical significance.

5 Discussion

This study was guided by two central hypotheses: Hypothesis 1 posited that rendering variables affect the perceived visual realism in AR; Hypothesis 2 suggested that the judgment of visual realism in AR is influenced by the user's experience with rendering software.

5.1 Discussion of Hypothesis 1

Based on frequency statistics, we can infer that all the rendering elements included in the hypothesis have an impact on users' perception of visual realism. Among these variables, in the frequency statistics for both light source color and shadows direction, the percentage of participants choosing "no difference" exceeded 10%. Specifically, in the case of light source color, the proportion of participants choosing "no difference" accounted for 12% of the total, making it the highest "no difference" proportion among all the variables. It is noteworthy that relative to the other variables, these two variables are less easily distinguishable, and participants demonstrated a lower sensitivity to changes in these aspects. In the testing of the remaining variables, the "no difference" options were all below 5%. Particularly noteworthy is that for the variables of material texture and roughness, the "no difference" options were even below 1%. This indicates that participants found it quite easy to distinguish between options in the testing of these two variables, suggesting a high level of sensitivity to differences. So we can assume that light source color and shadows direction have a relatively minor impact compared to others, while material texture and roughness have the most pronounced effects on visual realism perception. This conclusion supports our Hypothesis 1 that all tested rendering factors in this study indeed influence users' perception of visual realism.

5.2   Discussion of Hypothesis 2

The chi-square test results did not support a statistically significant association between users' experience with rendering software and their judgment of visual realism. Despite the non-significant overall results, the Light Color variable's p-value approached the threshold of significance, suggesting a potential, albeit weak, correlation that merits further investigation. This outcome indicates that while rendering experience might not broadly influence perceptions of visual realism, there may be specific elements within the rendering process that are subtly affected by such experience. These insights are valuable for AR application developers, as they indicate that a user's technical background may not necessarily limit their ability to discern visual realism in AR-broadening the potential user base for AR applications. The results of the chi-squared test demonstrate that our Hypothesis 2 is not supported, as prior experience with rendering software does not have an impact on users' judgments of visual realism.

5.3   Implications and Future Directions

The results of this study offer a foundation for future research, which should consider larger sample sizes or different methodological approaches, such as mixed methods research that incorporates qualitative data. Further investigation into how nuanced differences in rendering variables impact user perception could lead to more personalized and sophisticated AR experience. Moreover, exploring the intersection of technical expertise and sensory perception could unveil deeper insights into how we interact with and interpret augmented environments.

6   Conclusion

The study primarily aimed to understand the effects of various rendering variables including light (type, intensity, color), shadows (intensity, direction), material properties (texture, roughness), depth occlusion, FOV, gamma correction value, and HDR on the perception of visual realism in AR. It also explores how users' experience with rendering software influences their perception. The research indicates that the variables in our study indeed impact users' perception of visual realism in AR. It should be emphasized that although all variables contribute to the outcome, the impact of light source color and shadows direction is relatively insignificant compared to other variables, whereas the material texture and roughness variables had the most profound effect. Furthermore, this study find that there is no significant relationship between users' prior experience with rendering software and their judgments of visual realism. The findings suggest that while technical accuracy in rendering is crucial, the emphasis should be on those variables that users perceive as most impactful to realism. This nuanced understanding of variable impact could guide the development of more effective and authentic AR experience, focusing on enhancing the aspects most crucial to user perception of realism.

Acknowledgement. This research is funded by the Laboratory for Artificial Intelligence in Design (Project Code: RP1-3), Innovation and Technology Fund, Hong Kong Special Administrative Region, and PolyU project P0046465.

References

1. Azuma, R.T.: A survey of augmented reality. Presence: Teleoperators Virtual Environ. **6**(1), 355–385 (1997)
2. Sutherland, I.E., et al.: The ultimate display. In: Proceedings of the IFIP Congress, vol. 2, pp. 506–508. New York (1965)
3. Milgram, P., Kishino, F.: A taxonomy of mixed reality visual displays. IEICE Trans. Inf. Syst. **77**(3), 1321–1329 (1994)
4. Bimber,O., Raskar, R.: Spatial Augmented Reality: Merging Real and Virtual Worlds. CRC press (2005)
5. Cutting, J.E., Vishton, P.M.: Perceiving layout and knowing distances: the integration, relative potency, and contextual use of different information about depth. In: Perception of space and motion, pp. 69–117. Elsevier (1995)
6. Wanger, L.R., Ferwerda, J.A., Greenberg, D.P., et al.: Perceiving spatial relationships in computer-generated images. IEEE Comput. Graph. Appl. **12**(3), 44–58 (1992)
7. Martins, Valéria Farinazzo., Kirner, Tereza Gonçalves, Kirner, Claudio: Subjective usability evaluation criteria of augmented reality applications. In: Shumaker, Randall, Lackey, Stephanie (eds.) VAMR 2015. LNCS, vol. 9179, pp. 39–48. Springer, Cham (2015). https://doi.org/10.1007/978-3-319-21067-4_5
8. Shirley, P., Ashikhmin, M., Marschner, S.: Fundamentals of Computer Graphics. AK Peters/CRC Press (2009)
9. Lansdown, J.: Visual perception and computer graphics. In: Fundamental Algorithms for Computer Graphics: NATO Advanced Study Institute directed by JE Bresenham, RA Earnshaw, MLV Pitteway, vol. 17, pp. 1005–1026. Springer, Berlin (1985). https://doi.org/10.1007/978-3-642-84574-1_44
10. Wyszecki, G., Stiles, W.S.: Color Science: Concepts and Methods, Quantitative Data and Formulae, vol. 40. Wiley (2000)

11. Johansson, G.: Visual perception of biological motion and a model for its analysis. Percept. psychophys. **14**, 201–211 (1973)

12. McNamara, A.: Visual perception in realistic image synthesis. Comput. Graph. Forum **20**, 211–224 (2001)

13. Lee, C.: Mixed Reality Simulation. University of California, Santa Barbara (2013)

14. Sazzad, T.M.S., Hasan, M.Z., Mohammed, F., Islam, S.: Gamma encoding on image processing considering human visualization, analysis and comparison. Int. J. Comput. Sci. Eng, **4**(12), 1868 (2012)

15. Villagran-Vizcarra, D.C., Luviano-Cruz, D., Pérez-Domínguez, L.A., Méndez-González, L.C., Garcia-Luna, F.: Applications analyses, challenges and development of augmented reality in education, industry, marketing, medicine, and entertainment. Appl. Sci. **13**(5), 2766 (2023)

16. Zhou, F., Been-Lirn Duh, H., Billinghurst, M.: Trends in augmented reality tracking, interaction and display: a review of ten years of ISMAR. 2008 7th IEEE/ACM International Symposium on Mixed and Augmented Reality, pp. 193–202. IEEE (2008)

17. Xiong, J., Hsiang, E.-L., He, Z., Zhan, T., Wu, S.-T.: Augmented reality and virtual reality displays: emerging technologies and future perspectives. Light: Sci. Appl. **10**(1), 216 (2021)

18. Adams, H., Stefanucci, J., Creem-Regehr, S., Bodenheimer, B.: Depth perception in augmented reality: the effects of display, shadow, and position. In: 2022 IEEE Conference on Virtual Reality and 3D User Interfaces (VR), pp. 792–801. IEEE (2022)

19. Grandi, J.G., Cao, Z., Ogren, M., Kopper. R.: Design and simulation of next-generation augmented reality user interfaces in virtual reality. In: 2021 IEEE Conference on Virtual Reality and 3D User Interfaces Abstracts and Workshops (VRW), pp. 23–29. IEEE (2021)

20. Rana, R., Singhal, R.: Chi-square test and its application in hypothesis testing. J. Primary Care Spec. **1**(1), 69–71 (2015)

The Impact of Smartphone Fonts and Text Colors on Visual Recognition of the Elderly

Yulin Zhao[1] and Ding-Bang Luh[2(✉)]

[1] Faculty of Innovation and Design, City University of Macau, Macau 999078, China
[2] School of Art and Design, Guangdong University of Technology, Guangzhou 510090, China
yulinzhao@cityu.edu.mo

Abstract. With the development of mobile communications technology, smart phone has become a necessity in people's life. The aggravation of population aging in China draws the society's more attention to the market of smart phone for the aged. Being convenient, smart phone provides the aged with a brand new reading mode and a flexible reading environment. However, this advantage changes elderly users' habit of using eyes and causes visual fatigue. This research explores the relationship between smart phone screen color combination and visual identification, visual fatigue of the aged. Combining color criterion RGB adopted by most displayers with neutral colors black and white, the author probes into the influence of smart phone screen color combination on visual identification and visual fatigue through experiment. The experiment in this research is about the influence of mobile phone screen color combination on visual identification of the aged. The results showed that the best color sample for male subjects was white on a blue background, while the best color sample for females was green on a blue background.

Keywords: Font · Text color · Visual recognition · Smartphone · Elderly

1 Introduction

Reading as one of the many important daily activities of older persons, not only brings to life more rich experience, at the same time can make older people reduce loneliness and enhance their confidence, slower mental decline. Is now more than 40 years old or more than 30 young people, they have the habit of reading on Smartphones and take it as a hobby, even dependent on demand of Smartphone screens. Among the older people in the future, they have the ability to grasp and learn the smart phone and they has the foundation for Smartphone use.

The aging of the visual function of the elderly will affect their visual senses, resulting in significant differences in visual function. The aging of the visual function of the elderly will affect their visual senses, making their visual function significantly different from that of the general public. In daily life, people receive information from the outside world through the five senses. In daily life, people receive information from the outside world through the five senses, which leads to the generation of senses and behavioral actions, and the formation of thoughts, of which vision is the most important. In fact, as much as 80% of the knowledge acquired by human beings is absorbed through vision.

With the aging of the elderly people's visual and perceptual abilities decline, in the case of surgery and aids cannot be overcome, the only way to solve the inconvenience of the elderly in the use of products is to follow the principle of human factors design "to adapt the object to the person," and people living in this world, it is inevitable that they need to interact with the things around them. Therefore, no matter at home or anywhere, what people do in their daily life is in fact a series of interactions with the surrounding environment.

According to the research on color perception and coordination color mentioned in the study for the stimulation of human impact much larger than the object form, so the excellent color combinations could to help extend the older person operating time and the use of Visual performance and concentration. Therefore, good color vision of consciousness on the Smartphone screen, users can have a better reading experience. This study combines the elderly ocular physiological changes, using smart phone screens, and experiments to investigate the screen color combinations and depending on the relationship of consciousness of the elderly, research helps to guide the design of future products, Visual elements, reference to product design, care of the elderly and so on.

2   Literature Review

The aim of this article is to study the Smartphone screen color combination with the Visual identity of the elderly associated with the Visual fatigue, literature reviews are divided into seniors with vision theory, color theory, Visual recognition, Visual fatigue related literature, Visual performance of five for the collecting and analyzing to extend help in this study.

2.1   Elderly and Visual Theory

For the definition of the elderly, gerontology in China and outside China nation has more than 10 kinds of opinions, one of the more popular are: to define, according to the physiological age to chronological age definition, defined by mental age definition age and society. Daily life in the "old" is usually for people of a certain age, so, in order to facilitate research and understanding, we divided by age method elderly people, according to China's regulations, the elderly citizen aged 60.

According to the United Nations standards, in a country or territory, population over 60 years of 10% or 7% of the population over the age of 65, that is called in this country or region into an aging society. The ageing of the population, is a common problem all over the world.

By the degradation of the organ after the age of 60 have more obvious. Under normal circumstances, people between ages 40 to 45 years old Visual deterioration, sharp decrease to about 65 years old can restore stability, in addition to the deterioration of vision in addition to capture the dynamic effects of fuzzy than before, the light shades of feeling will fade, lower sensitivity to color a lot.

Kline and Scialfa had proposed in 1996 population of light-sensitive, so we cannot adapt to the rapid changes in brightness observed close things begin to weakens; Cerella in 1985, narrows the view of older persons, the width of the field has been weakened.

Delai Men in its studies of cognitive preferences that, based on the cognitive experience of the elderly, the elderly in most cognitive of tonal pleasure when, to order of red, Orange, yellow, blue, green and purple, the preference for the highest purity for purity of color, in the above should be used on the lightness of lightness.

The existence of these problems and widespread in the elderly population, the elderly in the Visual changes will be the Smartphone screen color combinations on the Visual identity of the elderly associated references and theoretical basis.

2.2 Application of Color System

Lin Kunfan mentioned in the color theory, when exposed to sunlight, survive light reflected to the eye as seen in the color of an object, light wave length difference, which produced red, Orange, yellow, green, blue and purple color vision. In the retina, with three types of cone-shaped like the Visual cells can sense that the 380~780 nm light (the range of visible light). Color differences on the formation of color other than purely physical, another level, also have a psychological dimension, which contains subjective factors such as cognition, emotion, affect people of color feel.

R, G, B color model also known as additive color models, color comes from the red, green, and blue base color (RGB) brightness differences between overlapping, it is called additive color model. Model, red, green, and blue three base colours with 256 different values measured, the value from 0 to 255, consists of three different combinations of values, forming a colorful color space. When r is 255, g, b value of 0 is rendered in solid color red when g is 255, r and b values are 0 for solid green; when the b value is 255, r, g is 0, which is solid blue. R, G, B values are all 0 values, to solid black. R, G, B are 255, the colour rendering solid color white. This study sample color schemes, picking colors primary colors R, G, B samples of solid color in design. 1821–1894 hemuhezi made sense three primary colors from the Germans in three types of cone cells in the eye, such as red light mainly dominated by Red cones, use color for a color condition in itself. In addition, the composition monitor screen color mode, tri-color CRT from the screen, which also belongs to the light and shade of gray scale performance and full-color trip (formed by the combination of R, G, B colors). Principles and monitor screens of eyes to distinguish colors, are the three primary colors of light R, G, B color model (Fig. 1).

Legibility, can be called easy reading, debate. Digit refers to can identify with each other which is why property, it affected by stroke, thickness, font, contrast and lighting, digit intervals, distances, influence of surrounding conditions such as white. Color vision of consciousness first depends on brightness difference, followed by color differences. Color combinations based on sample size and comparative view of consciousness is good or bad. Depending on the knowledge of high color, and other samples of the same size, degree of interpretation is the better. In Fig. 2, for example, identification of blue-and-white than yellow background and blue-and-white view of consciousness than the yellow color scheme.

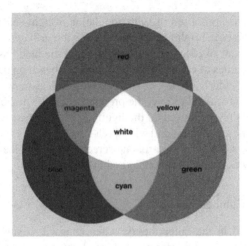

Fig. 1. R, G, B color model.

Ma Shicong (2002), Kaohsiung bus front road sign recognition study mentioned in the different diagrams, color in General is significantly affected, among the blue-and-white color scheme is the best cognitive and yellow background and red on a white background, white, and green knows the difference.

In addition, Ma Shicong (2002), Kaohsiung bus front destination tips mentioned in the cognitive study of P22-23, medium stroke thickness (thick higher than 1:6) digital sample of supposed to know better. Fine stroke thickness (thick higher than 1:8) followed by bold strokes (the rough higher than 1:5) the worst. For font construction also made the following conclusion, structural differences, the greater the font, read better, high similarity of composition, although obviously in design consistency, is likely to cause similar interpretation errors. In addition, Sun j Chambers (2007) digital reading render mode 15–29, found, for example, text size and also affect the interpretation of the form factor, and word-level and 14 for the new reading condition of thin out, the most appropriate.

Lin Qingquan (2000), screen type, ambient lighting, and background color combinations for text terminals Visual task referred to in the study of the impact of Visual performance factors can be divided into three categories: (1) stimulating characteristics, (2) characteristics of the environment, (3) service features. In other words, Visual performance advantages and disadvantages of human external stimuli, human factors and environmental influences. This content contains two low lighting brightness factors such as ambient light and color matching to stimulate. Use of assessment methods in order to determine the advantages and disadvantages of Visual performance, increase the credibility of experimental objective.

3　Experimental Design

There is a close relationship between the factors that affect the vision of the elderly in the life. The ability of color identification provided by the eyes to improve the performance of reading for the elderly. This research will discuss the advantages and disadvantages

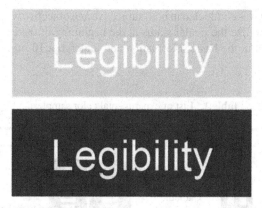

Fig. 2. The difference of visual recognition of color combination.

of the eyes of the elderly for color combination, and the experiment will be based on the combination of color and color combination of the smart phone screen color combination of the elderly visual recognition of the relationship between the two. Due to the popularity of iPhone as well as the user's general praise, this experiment selected Apple's fifth generation mobile phone screen size 4 inches as a benchmark.

1. Font design. Smart phone screen text, usually navigation main title of the font size for the 40 px, the main body size is 32 px, the vice text for the 26 px, small size is 20 px, it will be 40 px, 32 px, 26 px, 20 px as the experimental font size.
2. Color combination design. The design of the experimental samples, color selection color primaries in the R, G and B color and color black and white five color cross match, formation of target and background combinations, and eliminates the color blind patients unable to discern the color combination, for a total of ten groups. For the blue bottom green words, at the end of the green blue words, white background black word, black bottom mispronounced character, white bottom blue words, blue bottom mispronounced character, at the end of the green black characters and black at the end of the green, red bottom mispronounced character, white at the bottom of the scarlet letter, respectively. Influence of object structure, consider the font structure, thickness and for visual knowledge factors and use e character in the history of Nailun e word scale, the strokes of the same thickness, spacing, text structure. And in accordance with the direction of the E word opening, the lower, left and right four groups for change. The 10 groups of color samples were tested, and the targets were 4 groups of 40 groups.
3. The choice of the subject. Choose 20 old people who have the habit of using smart phones, 10 men and 10 women, aged between 65 and 60 years old.

Visual performance based on the error rate of the subjects to answer the color of the sample to determine the relevance of the visual. The higher the error rate, the worse the visual recognition of the sample in the dark environment.

The actual number of Dacuo / actual item number of subjects with *100 = error rate (%).

The experiment was conducted in both subjective and objective ways. In the objective part, in order to stabilize the ocular status at the beginning of the experiment, subjects were required to fill in the basic information and undergo a 10-min dark-conditioning period (Table 1).

Table 1. List of experimental color samples.

4   Results and Discussion

The main purpose of this phase of the experiment was to investigate the factors affecting visual recognition, which were categorized as: gender,

The influencing factors were categorized as: gender, distance, color combination, sample polarity, target orientation, and so on. The results were used to determine the effect of color combination on visual recognition.

The color combinations of the subjects were judged to be good or bad for visual recognition, and then the order of visual recognition among the color combinations was investigated. The results are as follows:

1. To investigate the association between gender and visual identity in darkness.

The results showed that there was no significant difference between gender and visual identity. The results showed that there was no significant difference between the two genders in terms of visual identity. For males, the best sample in terms of visual recognition of color combinations was green on blue background. The worst sample was green letters on a blue background.

For females, the best sample was green letters on a blue background for visual recognition of color combinations. The worst sample was green letters on black background and white letters on black background.

The worst samples were green letters on black background and white letters on black background. The results were consistent. Therefore, there was no difference in the visual recognition of color between the two genders (color figure online).

2. To investigate the relationship between distance and visual recognition under darkness correspondence.

In this experiment, the distance is divided into 300 cm, 250 cm and 200 cm. The number of incorrect answers was taken as a factor in determining the level of visual acuity of the subjects.

The results showed that the color samples had a significant effect on the subjects' performance at distances of 300 cm and 250 cm in a dark environment.

The results showed that there was a significant difference in the performance of the color samples at a distance of 300 cm and 250 cm in a dark environment, while there was no difference at a distance of 200 cm.

There was no difference at a distance of 200 cm. Therefore, a distance of 250 cm or more should be used as a benchmark for judging the visual recognition between color samples.

3. Explore the association of dark-conforming color combinations on visual recognition.

In this experiment, the right and wrong answers of the subjects were regarded as the factors to discriminate the superiority and inferiority of visual literacy, and the results of both sexes in the visual literacy of the color samples, the significance of the right answers was 1.000; the significance of the wrong answers was 0.921, which was greater than 0.05, and there was no significant difference between the two.

In terms of visual discrimination between color combinations, the best color sample for males was green on blue (error rate 4.4%) and the worst color sample was green on black (error rate 16.7); the best color sample for females was green on blue (error rate 2.8); and the worst color sample was green on black/white on black (error rate 15.6%). Thus, the visual legibility of the color samples does not differ by gender (color figure online).

5   Conclusion

In the study of visual recognition, the experimental objective is to explore the factors that affect visual recognition. Divide it into distance, color sample, sample polarity, target orientation, and gender.

The results showed significant differences in visual recognition in terms of distance, color samples, sample polarity, and target orientation. However, there is no significant difference in gender, and color combinations have a greater impact on visual recognition than gender. In addition, this study considers distance as a factor affecting color recognition. In terms of color sample performance, the visual recognition of green characters on a blue background is the best; The black background with green characters performs the worst.

Looking at the sorting of single color samples among different phases, it was found that the color samples with a blue background performed the best in dark environments, followed by the color samples with a white background, followed by the color samples with a green background, and the worst were all the color samples with a black background. It was found that the sample of bright characters with a dark background had poor visual recognition in a dark environment. And infer that sample polarity is a factor affecting visual recognition.

By dividing the sample into two polarities of yin and yang for observation, it can be found that the visual recognition rate of samples with dark background and bright characters (negative presentation) is higher than that of samples with bright background and dark characters (positive presentation). Therefore, in a dark environment, if you want to have good visual recognition, you should avoid a combination of too far line of sight and bright characters on a dark background (presented as negative).

Due to limitations in experimental design specifications and other factors, this study did not achieve completeness and will be reviewed below.

1. Color samples

This study investigates the principle of the cellular composition of the receptor (eye) itself, focusing on the three primary colors R, G, and B, as well as the two colors of colorless black and white, which are interactively made into samples. However, in the field of color, besides the primary colors R, G, and B, there are also possibilities for other color combinations. In this study, it is not possible to fully consider all color combinations, and only the results presented by the combination of three primary colors and black and white interaction can be presented.

2. Experimental posture

This study aims to ensure the fairness of the experiment among participants, limiting their visual range, posture, seat height, etc. But the characteristic of mobile phones is to provide a diverse and mobile way of use, not a single presentation. In this study, it was not possible to fully consider the postures and work forms of all participants, and only the results presented in a sitting position were presented. However, it cannot be ruled out that changes in visual distance, posture, and seat height may also affect the experimental results.

Acknowledgments. The authors gratefully thank all volunteers for their participation in the study.

Disclosure of Interests. The authors have no competing interests to declare that are relevant to the content of this article.

References

1. Long, S., He, X., Yao, C.: Scene text detection and recognition: The deep learning era. Int. J. Comput. Vision **129**, 161–184 (2021)
2. Men, D., Wang, D., Hu, X.: The analysis and research of the smart phone's user interface based on chinese elderly's cognitive character. In: Universal Access in Human-Computer Interaction. Aging and Assistive Environments: 8th International Conference, UAHCI 2014, Held as Part of HCI International 2014, Heraklion, Crete, Greece, June 22–27, 2014, Proceedings, Part III 8, pp. 138-146. Springer International Publishing (2014).https://doi.org/10.1007/978-3-319-07446-7_14
3. Periáñez, J.A., Lubrini, G., García-Gutiérrez, A., Ríos-Lago, M.: Construct validity of the stroop color-word test: influence of speed of visual search, verbal fluency, working memory, cognitive flexibility, and conflict monitoring. Arch. Clin. Neuropsychol. **36**(1), 99–111 (2021)
4. Vatavu, R.D.: Point & click mediated interactions for large home entertainment displays. Multimedia Tools Appl. **59**, 113–128 (2012)
5. Zaslavsky, N., Garvin, K., Kemp, C., Tishby, N., Regier, T.: The evolution of color naming reflects pressure for efficiency: evidence from the recent past. J. Lang. Evolution **7**(2), 184–199 (2022)
6. Bramão, I., Reis, A., Petersson, K.M., Faísca, L.: The role of color information on object recognition: a review and meta-analysis. Acta Physiol (Oxf.) **138**(1), 244–253 (2011)
7. Van De Sande, K., Gevers, T., Snoek, C.: Evaluating color descriptors for object and scene recognition. IEEE Trans. Pattern Anal. Mach. Intell. **32**(9), 1582–1596 (2009)
8. Kuo, J., Wu, F.: The elder's discrimination of icons with color discrimination on the cell phone. Advances in Cognitive Ergonomics, pp. 176–185 (2010)
9. Sha, C., Li, R., Chang, K.: Color affects the usability of smart phone icon for the elderly. In: Duffy, V.G. (ed.) DHM 2017. LNCS, vol. 10287, pp. 173–182. Springer, Cham (2017). https://doi.org/10.1007/978-3-319-58466-9_17
10. Lyu, J., Men, D.: Study on the Product Packaging Color Identification of Elder Men and Elder Women. In: Zhou, J., Salvendy, G. (eds.) ITAP 2017. LNCS, vol. 10297, pp. 284–303. Springer, Cham (2017). https://doi.org/10.1007/978-3-319-58530-7_22
11. Yeh, P.C.: Effects of Color Combinations on the Discrimination Performance of Elderly People Using a LCD Monitor. In: Universal Design 2014: Three Days of Creativity and Diversity, pp. 149–156. IOS Press (2014)
12. Kutas, G., et al.: Luminance contrast and chromaticity contrast preference on the colour display for young and elderly users. Displays **29**(3), 297–307 (2008)

Optimization of Touch Active Area Size Based on Click Position Bias in Older Adults' Touchscreen Interaction

Yanling Zuo, Jingjing Cao, and Jia Zhou[✉]

School of Management Science and Real Estate, Chongqing University, Chongqing, China
jiazhou@cqu.edu.cn

Abstract. Changes in both physiological structure and psychological factors occur in older adults, leading to a decline in fine motor control and inferior performance compared to young adults during touchscreen interactions. It is crucial to understand the behavioral patterns of older adults' touchscreen clicks and subsequently optimize the touch active area size based on click position bias. An experimental prototype was developed using Android Studio, and 25 participants aged 65 and above (9 males, and 16 females) were recruited for touchscreen tasks. Several key findings emerged from the study. Firstly, older adults exhibited significant deviations when clicking targets near the left and right edges of the screen. The leftward deviation was predominantly downward, while the rightward deviation was upward. Secondly, to achieve an 80% accuracy rate for older users, recommended touch active area sizes were determined as follows: 2.3 cm for the left 25% of the screen, 1.1 cm for the central 50%, 1.7 cm for the right 25%, and 2.1 cm for the entire screen. These findings could contribute to enhancing the design of touch interfaces, providing reference parameters for touch active area sizes to achieve optimal click accuracy in different screen areas.

Keywords: Touchscreen · Click Position Bias · Touch Active Area · Parameter Design · Older Adults

1 Introduction

In the current landscape, the primary target demographic for smartphones has been young adults, with a noticeable increase in the proportion of older adults in recent years. The ownership of smartphones among older adults in the United States surged from 18% to 42% in just four years [1], and this trend continues to rise. However, the usage of smartphones poses significant challenges for older adults. The main reasons for these challenges could be outlined as follows: Firstly, older adults exhibit a weaker capacity to embrace novel technologies. Secondly, their cognitive understanding of the interfaces of information products is comparatively lower. Lastly, the operational aspects of smartphones are less suited to the needs and capabilities of older adults. In terms of interactive activities involving touch gestures, older adults commonly suffer significant troubles. On average, individuals spend three hours per day engaged with smartphones [2]. These

Q. Gao and J. Zhou (Eds.): HCII 2024, LNCS 14725, pp. 192–209, 2024.
https://doi.org/10.1007/978-3-031-61543-6_15

users frequently employed touch gestures such as tapping, swiping, and zooming to operate the touchscreens of their mobile devices. According to reports from the research company Dscout, Android smartphone users in the United States touched their phones at an average frequency of over 2617 times per day, with heavy phone users reaching frequencies as high as 5400 touches per day [3]. Improving the touchscreen interaction for older adults and smartphones became a crucial requirement.

More specifically, older adults exhibited poorer performance in touch interactions compared to young adults. For smaller devices such as smartphones, older adults were more prone to click position bias [4]. The average error rate for older users when using smartphones was 32.17%, which is three times higher than that of young adults. Even when using larger-screen devices like iPads, older adults still demonstrated a high click error rate of 16.89% [5]. In comparison to young adults, older adults exhibited lower accuracy in both fine motor skills and finger-pointing abilities [6, 7]. These difficulties in operational tasks might contribute to the challenges faced by older adults in using smartphones, especially when it comes to precise input gestures such as tapping and dragging, as well as multi-finger coordinated touch gestures like zooming and rotating.

In various touchscreen interactions between users and smartphones, such as tapping, swiping, and zooming, tapping is the most frequently used gesture. Concerning tapping gestures, older adults exhibited a higher error rate and longer task completion time compared to young adults. Moreover, their perception of task difficulty was lower than that of young adults [5, 8–10]. Researchers have sought to enhance tapping performance in older adults by increasing the size of smartphone icons. Kobayashi et al. suggested using targets larger than 8mm on 3.5-inch devices [11]. Gao and Sun recommended target dimensions of 15.9 mm × 9 mm on 23-inch devices [9]. However, these recommendations might not be universally applicable to all screens. Simply enlarging the size of interface elements could also compromise information readability.

In addition, to enhance the touch interaction between older adults and smartphones, attention must be directed towards age-related changes in human physiological functions. With advancing age, there is a notable decline in motor control abilities, cognitive capacities, and perceptual abilities. The decline in motor control abilities is primarily manifested in reduced strength control and diminished motor coordination. Older adults, when engaged in touch gestures with smartphones, exhibit increased movement time and decreased movement accuracy [12–14]. The decline in cognitive capacities is evident in prolonged information processing and reaction times among older adults [14, 15]. The diminished perceptual abilities contribute to a weakening of hand-eye coordination in older adults, potentially resulting in greater difficulty in utilizing touch gestures [16].

Therefore, in order to enhance the accuracy of touch interaction for older adults, this study investigated the patterns of click position bias exhibited by older users. Subsequently, based on the findings of these patterns, attempts were made to perform interaction correction.

2 Related Work

2.1 Touchscreens Might Be More Suitable for Older Users

Previous research has indicated that direct interaction with touchscreens requires less cognitive, spatial, or attentional demands from older users [17, 18]. Compared to traditional computer input devices such as mice, touchscreen interaction could reduce movement time and error rates, thereby diminishing age-related performance differences [19]. For users without prior computer experience, touchscreen interaction is also easily learnable, mitigating resistance among older adults toward new technologies [20]. Touchscreen devices are suitable for use anywhere as they do not necessitate intermediary devices. Nowadays, most handheld devices are equipped with touchscreens, and public information kiosks in places like train stations, airports, or bank systems also feature touchscreen devices [21]. Therefore, enhancing the interactive performance of older adults with touchscreen devices is of paramount importance.

2.2 Challenges in Clicking for Older Adults Using Indirect Input Devices

The aging process significantly impacts the motor, cognitive, and sensory abilities related to interactions with computers and handheld devices. Previous research has extensively documented the interaction difficulties faced by older adults when using indirect input devices, particularly mice. Studies indicated that older adults struggle to apply the correct force to the mouse, leading to an increased incidence of selection errors [12, 14]. For older adults, as the target width decreases, the error rate disproportionately increases [22]. The loss of motor function has also been shown to impede mouse control, potentially resulting in cursor loss [23]. Older adults encounter challenges in performing more complex interaction tasks as well, such as double-clicking [24], single-clicking and dragging [25], and turning [8].

2.3 Challenges in Clicking for Older Adults Using Direct Input Devices

Despite not receiving as thorough exploration as indirect input devices, research on age-related interaction difficulties with direct input devices (such as pens and touch) has yielded similar conclusions. Older adults exhibited slower selection times [26–28] and higher error rates [9, 26] compared to their younger counterparts. Additionally, older adults were more likely to encounter difficulties when performing complex tasks, such as dragging [8], turning [8], and sliding [28] through touch input. Direct input devices were considered to provide better support for hand-eye coordination than indirect input devices, which might explain the observed narrowing of performance gaps (in terms of speed and accuracy) between older and younger adults using direct input [29, 30].

3 Materials and Methods

3.1 Experimental Design

The dependent variables recorded in this experiment include click position bias, the success of the click, and finger pressing time. Click position bias refers to the deviation between the actual finger click position and the target position. The value of D is equal to the distance between the touch point when the finger clicks and the center point of the target. This distance is calculated in the two-dimensional coordinate system of the mobile phone screen using the coordinates of these two points, as shown in Fig. 1. The calculation formula is as follows (1). The coordinates of the touch point at the time of the click were obtained through the experimental prototype at the Android system's lower level and were recorded synchronously with the experimental operation. If the click position bias $D \leq 119$px, it is considered a successful click; otherwise, it is considered a failed click. Therefore, the successful click area is a circle with the target center as the center and a radius of approximately 0.9cm. Finger pressing time is the time required to click on each target point, i.e., the time difference Δt between the finger's press-down and lift-up. The calculation formula is given by (2).

$$D = \sqrt{(x_1 - x_0)^2 + (y_1 - y_0)^2} \tag{1}$$

$$\Delta t = t_2 - t_1 \tag{2}$$

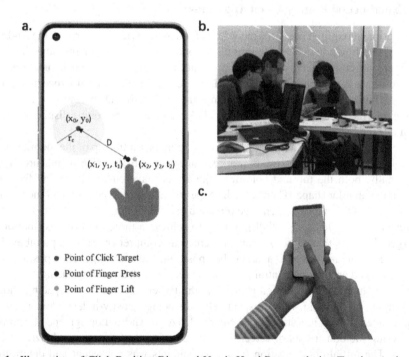

Fig. 1. Illustration of Click Position Bias and User's Hand Posture during Tapping Actions. **a.** Depiction of click position bias. **b.** Third-person perspective of older adults engaging in tapping actions during the experiment. **c.** First-person perspective of users executing tapping actions.

In this experiment, the OPPO Reno8 Pro smartphone was employed for prototype manipulation. The smartphone featured a 6.62-inch display with a resolution of 2400×1080 pixels. The dimensions of the phone were 161 mm in height, 74.2 mm in width, and

7.57 mm in thickness, with a weight of 188 g. In the conducted experiment, participants were instructed to perform a tapping task using both hands, with the left hand holding the mobile device and the right index finger executing the taps, as shown in Fig. 1.

3.2 Participants

Participants were recruited through convenient sampling, voluntary sampling, and snowball sampling. Recruitment messages were disseminated by researchers through social media platforms. A total of 25 older adults (aged 65 and above) and participated in the experiment, including 9 males and 16 females, all of whom were right-handed. Self-reported medical histories indicated that none of the participants had a history of psychological, neurological, or severe cardiac disorders, and Chinese was their native language. The duration of the experiment was approximately 10 min, and all participants were well-informed and provided informed consent before participating. A certain compensation was given to participants after the conclusion of the experiment.

3.3 Experimental Prototype and Apparatus

The experiment required real-time recording of touch behavior data through the Android low-level touch action API, including click coordinates and finger pressing time. As there were no commercially available applications implementing such functionality, a prototype was independently developed and tested for the formal experiment. The prototype, built on the Android 13.0 system using the IntelliJ IDEA compiler, consisted of three interfaces: a welcome interface, a click page, and a prototype display page, as shown in Fig. 2.

Due to the presence of a time information display bar at the top of the mobile phone screen, it was challenging to cover the entire phone page with the experimental prototype. Additionally, both the top and bottom of the screen have curves, deviating from the standard rectangular shape. Therefore, the experimental prototype excluded the top and bottom areas of the phone screen. The remaining rectangular area was divided into 136 squares ($17 \times 8 = $ length $\times$ width), aiming to achieve a more uniform distribution of all target click positions and to cover the screen as comprehensively as possible. The center of each square served as a target click position, and each target click position was evenly arranged around the central point of the screen with a certain spacing.

According to Android design principles, the target size and target spacing should be multiples of 8dp and 48dp, respectively (dp being density-independent pixels, a recommended unit of measurement for control size in Android design specifications). Considering the constraints of screen resolution and size, the target grid size was set to 48dp. The initial click position for all participants was consistent and determined based on the angle and distance of the user's holding position of the smartphone. After participants clicked the starting point, the screen randomly presented one of the preset 135 target points. Upon clicking the presented target point, it disappeared, and the next target appeared randomly. This process continued until participants clicked on all target points, and a notification of task completion appeared at the bottom of the screen. Throughout this procedure, the experimental system automatically recorded user click and operation time data on the smartphone and saved it with the corresponding participant ID.

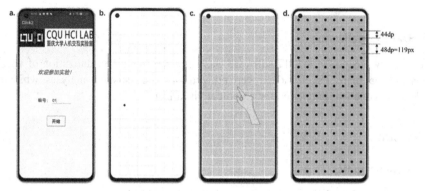

Fig. 2. Experimental Prototype. **a.** Initial interface of the prototype. **b.** Prototype design and target point illustration. **c.** Displayed interface of the prototype. **d.** Dimensions of target point locations.

3.4 Procedure

First, the experimenters introduced the background, purpose, and content of the experiment to the participants. After the introduction, participants were asked to complete an informed consent form. Next, participants were required to fill out a questionnaire regarding personal information, including age, gender, education, and mobile phone usage. Subsequently, experimenters explained the experimental tasks to the participants, leading them into the training and testing phases.

Training Phase. Once the preparatory work for the experiment was completed, the experimenters issued the start command, and participants began practicing clicking on target points. Participants operated with both hands to complete the clicking task— holding the phone with the left hand and using the index finger of the right hand to click on the target points appearing on the screen. During the experiment, participants followed the instructed clicking posture, and the training concluded when the screen displayed the words "Task Completed."

Testing Phase. Participants were instructed to click at their accustomed speed, ensuring minimal movement between the left hand and the phone and maintaining consistent finger positioning, resembling their typical mobile phone usage. The task commenced with participants entering the developed application, and initiating the click task upon reaching the interface. Initially, the screen displayed only a starting point; after participants clicked the starting point, one of the pre-designed 135 targets appeared. Participants then clicked on the target, causing it to disappear while the next target appeared, repeating this process until all target points were clicked. The sequence of target points was entirely random, with each target appearing only once. In each task, participants simultaneously clicked the starting point upon the experimenter's start command. The task concluded when the words "Task Completed" appeared in the center of the screen, and upon returning to the main interface, participants stopped clicking, signifying the end of the task.

3.5 Data Visualization

In this study, RStudio 1.4.1717 software was employed for the visualization of vector fields and heat maps. Psych and car were utilized for basic statistical analyses, while the ggplot2 package was employed for graphical visualization.

4 Results

4.1 Demographics

The characteristics of the participants were shown in Table 1.

Table 1. The characteristics of the participants.

Characteristics	M	SD	N	%
Age (years)	66.4	6.63		
Duration of Smartphone Usage (years)	9.3	4.03		
Time Spent on Smartphone (hours)	5.4	3.63		
Gender				
Male			9	36%
Female			16	64%
Education Level				
Undergraduate and College			3	12%
High School and Vocational			10	40%
Junior High School and Below			12	48%

4.2 Click Behavior

In the conducted experiment, data from 25 participants were collected, comprising a total of 3400 clicks. The mean click position bias for older participants was 210.4 px (SD = 115.12 px, minimum = 3.26 px, maximum = 574.05 px). Initially, the collected click coordinate data underwent organization and outlier detection. Subsequently, deviation values for each participant's every click were computed based on the deviation calculation method mentioned in the research methodology. The results indicated that only 38.74% of the click actions were successful ($D \leq 119$ px), highlighting the necessity to address click interaction gestures for older adults. Finger pressing time serves as a reflection of the sensitivity of click actions for older individuals. The distribution histograms of click position bias and finger pressing time were shown in Fig. 3. The results revealed that the mean finger pressing time for older participants was 76.9 ms (SD = 38.24 ms, minimum = 0 ms, maximum = 301 ms).

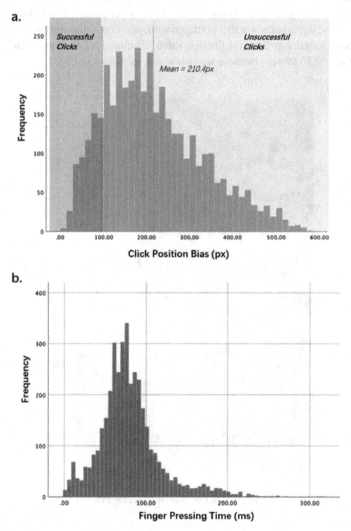

Fig. 3. The Performance of Click Behaviors. **a.** Distribution graph of click position bias; **b.** Distribution graph of finger pressing time.

4.3 Click Position Bias Vector Field

Because click position bias is derived from the behavioral performance of user gestures in the real world, optimization for it is more suitable when described in metric units, specifically in centimeters. In order to explore the distribution pattern of click position bias across the entire screen, a bias vector field was constructed based on click data. Firstly, the offset of each actual click position relative to the target position was calculated using the click position offset formula. Secondly, the average of all participants' click biases at the same target position was taken as the click position bias for that location. Subsequently, starting from the center point of the target point and ending at the touch active area of the participant's actual click position, vectors of bias direction were drawn, with the vector length representing the bias value. Ultimately, a click position bias vector field containing 136 target positions was obtained, as shown in Fig. 4.

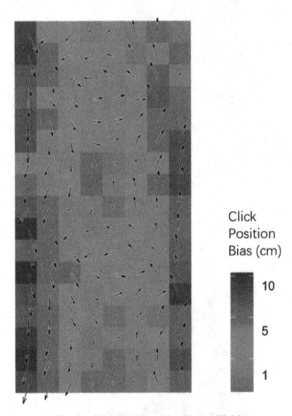

Fig. 4. Click Position Bias Vector Field.

Observing this figure revealed that the bias was greatest near the left edge of the screen, relatively large on the right edge, and minimal in the central area. Moreover, arrows at both ends of the screen were longer, indicating larger biases. The leftward bias mainly shifted downward, while the rightward bias shifted upward, with the leftward bias being greater.

4.4   Optimizing Touch Active Area Size Standards

When performing touch operations on a mobile phone, the target touch area needs to be activated to recognize the touch behavior and trigger corresponding operations or functions. The touch active area size is synonymous with the click position bias threshold. When the click position bias exceeds the threshold, the activation of the target touch area fails. Optimization of the touch active area size for touch clicks centered on older adults is considered from three perspectives: first, based on the click position bias characteristic values of the older adults; second, based on the physiological characteristics of older adults; and third, based on the screen area.

Based on Click Position Bias Characteristic Values. In accordance with the 48dp principle, the quartile range of click position bias (1 cm) was selected to set the size of the touch active area, aiming to assess the applicability of the existing 48 dp principle for older users. The new trend chart of click position bias was depicted on the left of Fig. 5. From the heat map, it was evident that the left and right sides of the smartphone screen exhibited a more pronounced yellow-red hue compared to other areas. This implied that when the touch active area size was set to 1cm, the deviation of older users when targeting the center of the screen was relatively small, while the deviation remained substantial when targeting the sides of the screen. Under this criterion, the click accuracy was 41.55%, indicating that the existing Android system's 48 dp principle was largely inapplicable to older users.

The touch active area size based on the first quartile of click position bias did not significantly improve the click accuracy for older users. Therefore, a larger active area size was set, considering that the mean click position bias (1.5 cm) covered more than 50% of the click biases. Hence, the touch active area size was set to 1.5 cm. The click position bias trend chart after correction was shown on the right of Fig. 5. Under this standard, the click accuracy was 64.66%. Heatmap results indicate that there was almost no bias in the central area of the screen, while there was a small bias in the edge portions on the left and right sides of the screen.

Based on the Physiological Characteristics of Older Adults. The width of the index fingertip of older adults was employed as the parameter for touch active area size. The dimensions of the index fingertip width for adult females and males aged 61 to 70, at the 95th percentile, were referenced from the national standard "Human Dimensions of Chinese Adults (GB/T 10000–2023)." The selected touch active area sizes were 2.1 cm (277 px) and 2.3 cm (304 px). As depicted in the new click position bias trend chart, there was almost no bias on the mobile screen. It was anticipated that older adults could accurately touch the entire screen, achieving an accuracy rate exceeding 80%, as shown in Fig. 6.

By adjusting the touch active area size, different sizes could be simulated to observe their impact on click error and obtain the click accuracy rate. Increasing the touch active area size continuously reduces click bias. However, considering the practicality of the screen, the touch active area could not be infinitely expanded. Combining the optimization results of touch active area size based on click bias characteristic values and the physiological characteristics of older users, it was evident that the click success rate of the 2.1 cm touch active area exceeds 80%, as shown in Fig. 7. Finally, 2.1 cm was

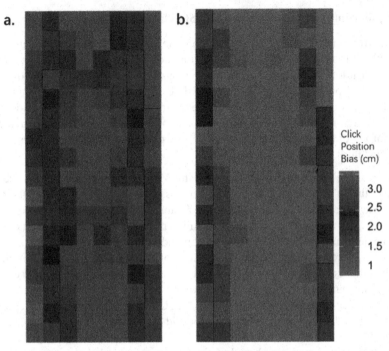

Fig. 5. Click position bias trend charts for setting touch active area size based on click position bias characteristic values. **a.** Click position bias trend chart with the first quartile of click position bias (1cm) as the touch active area size. **b.** Click position bias trend chart with the mean click position bias (1.5cm) as the touch active area size.

selected as the recommended touch active area size for the entire screen (with a screen width of approximately 74.2 mm).

Based on the Screen Area. As depicted in Fig. 4, the comparison of click position bias distribution between the left and right areas of the screen revealed that the click position bias on the left side was greater than that on the right side, necessitating a larger touch active area on the left side compared to the right side. Consequently, the screen was divided into three areas: the left 25%, the middle 50%, and the right 25%, as shown in Fig. 8. Subsequently, different touch active area sizes were assigned to each area to calculate the accuracy of clicks.

Initially, optimization of the touch active area was conducted for the left side of the screen. The touch active area size was set using an equal difference method for leftward correction, with values ranging from 2.1cm to 2.5cm and an equal difference of 0.1 cm. This range was determined considering the physiological characteristics of older adults. Specifically, touch active area sizes were set at 2.1 cm (277.2 px), 2.2 cm (290.4 px), 2.3 cm (303.6 px), 2.4 cm (316.8 px), and 2.5 cm (330 px), as shown in Fig. 8.

Subsequently, optimization of the touch active area size was implemented for the center of the screen. The click position bias in the central area was relatively small, as mentioned earlier. With a selected touch active area size of 1cm, the accuracy of clicks at the center position had already exceeded 70%. Therefore, touch active area sizes ranging

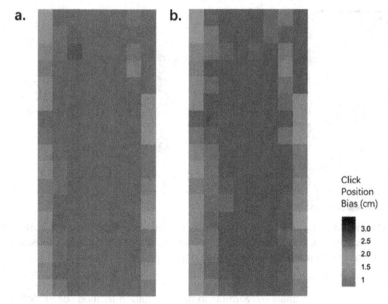

Fig. 6. Click Position Bias Trend Chart Based on Touch Active Area Size Set According to the Physiological Characteristics of Older Adults. **a.** Click position bias trend chart with a touch active area size of the Chinese female index fingertip width (2.1 cm). **b.** Click position bias trend chart with a touch active area size of the Chinese male index fingertip width (2.3 cm).

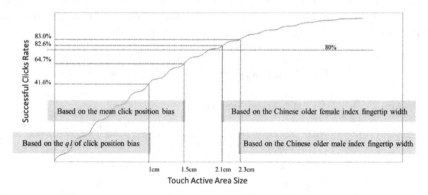

Fig. 7. Correspondence between Touch Active Area Size and Click Accuracy Rate.

from 1 cm to 1.5 cm were analyzed. Similar to the calculation method for the left side of the screen, an equal difference of 0.1 cm was employed.

Finally, touch active area size optimization was carried out for the right side of the screen. Compared to the left side, the click position bias on the right side was smaller. This could be attributed to the ease of accurate clicks on the right side when the device was held in the left hand. Consequently, based on this principle and utilizing the results of touch position bias averaging to optimize touch active area size, a range of 1.5 cm to

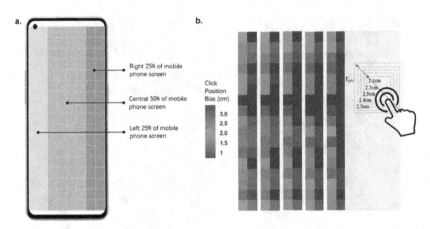

Fig. 8. Optimization of touch active area size for the left area of the screen. **a.** Partitioning of the touch screen area. **b.** Trend chart of click position bias based on screen area for setting touch active area size, using the left 25% area as an example.

2.0 cm was selected for analysis. Similar to the calculation method for the left side, an equal difference of 0.1 cm was applied.

The results of all click accuracy were presented in Table 2. It was observed that, for the left 25% of the screen, a recommended touch active area size of 2.3 cm was appropriate to achieve an 80% click accuracy. For the central 50% of the screen, an optimal touch active area size of 1.1 cm was identified. Regarding the right 25% of the screen, setting the touch active area size to 1.7 cm could effectively address the click position bias caused by the screen boundary, as shown in Fig. 9.

Table 2. Recommended touch active area sizes.

Screen Area	Touch Active Area Size	Click Accuracy
Left 25%	2.1 cm	67.65%
	2.2 cm	76.47%
	2.3 cm	**82.35%**
	2.4 cm	85.29%
Central 50%	**1.1 cm**	**85.29%**
	1.2 cm	86.76%
	1.3 cm	88.23%
	1.4 cm	91.18%
Right 25%	1.6 cm	79.41%
	1.7 cm	**82.35%**
	1.8 cm	85.29%
	1.9 cm	88.23%

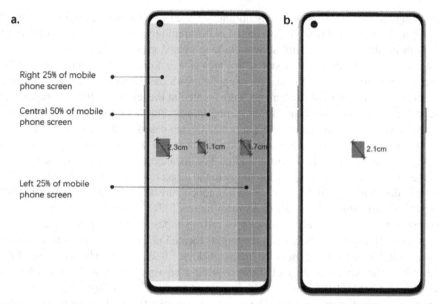

Fig. 9. Recommended touch active area sizes. **a.** Recommended sizes for different screen areas. **b.** Recommended size for the entire screen.

5 Discussion

In this study, after observing the clicking behavior and click position bias vectors of older adults, optimization of the touch active area size was conducted based on the click position bias characteristics of the older age group, their physiological characteristics, and screen regions. Additionally, detailed touch active area size parameters were recommended for the touchscreen based on the observed behavior of older individuals.

It was noteworthy that the target size used in this study was approximately the same as the close button of pop-up advertisements on Android phones. Therefore, the click biases exhibited by participants reflected the practical issue of older users encountering pop-up ads in their daily use but facing difficulties in closing them, potentially leading to unintended interface navigation and the inability to return to the original interface. Previous research on touchscreen clicking behavior often focused on larger target sizes. For example, Sultana and Moffatt used a maximum target width of 9.22 mm and a minimum target width of 4.88 mm (approximately the size of mobile menu icons), but their results indicated no significant relationship between age and click errors [31]. This suggested the need to pay more attention to the clicking behavior of older individuals, especially regarding smaller targets. The difficulty of clicking on small targets on touchscreens was primarily attributed to the "fat finger problem" [32], where the shape and width of the finger, relative to the target size, along with users' misunderstandings of the exact target location, reduced click accuracy and hindered the activation of corresponding functions [33]. Therefore, the most apparent way to reduce errors was simply to enlarge the targets [8]. Previous studies also showed that as the width of the click target increased, click biases significantly decreased. Currently, the most popular smartphone application icon sizes range from 9–10 mm, but many optional elements on the device could be as small as 4 mm. These elements were distributed in different areas of the screen, yet previous research mostly considered full-screen clicking behavior [9, 34, 35]. In the optimization results, the recommended touch active area size (1.1 cm) for the central 50% of the touchscreen aligned well with the sizes of application icons. However, during application interactions, many touchable elements were located in the left and right 25% regions of the screen, especially the close buttons of pop-up ads. For these click targets, this study emphasized the need for touch active area size design based on the screen region.

In the context of improving interaction performance with smaller targets, various strategies were proposed in previous studies. For instance, the "cursor offset" employed a finger-mouse strategy, dragging the finger to the target to avoid missing targets smaller than the finger itself [36]. Similarly, "sliding touch" utilized a similar strategy but with a stylus for selecting very small (1.88 mm) targets [37]. "Zooming" allowed users to successfully select extremely small targets, raising hopes for improved pixel-level click accuracy [38], especially beneficial for targets located at the screen edges and difficult to pinpoint. Other methods included "back-of-device interaction," which leveraged the back of the screen for input and showed success on very small touchscreen devices (diagonal 6.3 cm) [39]. Additionally, "fingerprint tracking" used fingerprints for better detection of selection points [40]. These studies primarily targeted young adults. In this study, older adults were the focus, revealing that when older adults interacted with targets appearing at the left and right boundaries of the screen, a significant bias occurred. The leftward deviation was predominantly downward, while the rightward deviation was upward. Optimization was conducted based on the characteristic values of click position bias in the elderly, the physiological features of older individuals, and the activation area size based on screen regions. This study supplemented the touch gesture parameter design for elderly users in related research, providing potential insights for enhancing the usability of smartphones for the elderly.

This study had three limitations. Firstly, participants were mainly older individuals residing around the campus, often retired teachers with a homogeneous cultural background. Future experiments could include a more diverse group of elderly individuals with varying educational backgrounds and from different regions. Secondly, the fidelity of the experimental prototype was low, and future research might require more realistic touch interaction scenarios to obtain comprehensive design suggestions for click activation areas. Thirdly, there was limited investigation into the characteristics of older individuals, and these characteristics did not show significant correlations with click bias. Future research could focus on exploring more features relevant to older adults.

6   Conclusion

In this study, based on the patterns of click position bias in older users, activation area size optimization was conducted from the perspectives of click position bias features, touchscreen areas, and physiological characteristics of older adults. The results indicated that to achieve an 80% accuracy in clicks for older users, the following activation area parameters were recommended: concerning touchscreen areas, setting the activation area for the left 25% of the screen to 2.3 cm, the middle 50% to 1.1 cm, and the right 25% to

1.7 cm significantly improved the accuracy of older adults' clicks, ensuring an accuracy rate of over 80%. Considering the physiological characteristics of older individuals based on the National Standard "Anthropometric Dimensions of Chinese Adults," setting the activation area size for the entire screen to 2.1 cm resulted in an 80% or higher accuracy in click accuracy for older users.

Acknowledgment. This work was supported by funding from the National Natural Science Foundation of China (Grants No. 72171030), the Second Batch of 2021 MOE of PRC Industry-University Collaborative Education Program (Program No. 202102055009, Kingfar-CES "Human Factors and Ergonomics" Program), and the 2022 Reform in College Elite Curriculum Research Project of Chongqing University, China (CQU-EIE-2022011).

References

1. Pew Research Center: Record shares of Americans now own smartphones, have home broadband. https://www.pewresearch.org/short-reads/2017/01/12/evolution-of-technology/. Accessed 11 June 2023
2. Howarth, J.: Time spent using smartphones (2023 Statistics). https://explodingtopics.com/blog/smartphone-usage-stats. Accessed 11 June 2023
3. Dominic, B.: Opinion | How the smartphone could help us manage our lives far better. https://www.livemint.com/opinion/columns/how-the-smartphone-could-help-us-man age-our-lives-far-better-11580318549883.html. Accessed 11 June 2023
4. Ranganathan, V.K., Siemionow, V., Sahgal, V., Yue, G.H.: Effects of aging on hand function. J. Am. Geriatr. Soc. **49**, 1478–1484 (2001). https://doi.org/10.1046/j.1532-5415.2001.491 1240.x
5. Wulf, L., Garschall, M., Klein, M., Tscheligi, M.: Young vs old – landscape vs portrait: a comparative study of touch gesture performance. J. Assist. Technol. **9**, 136–146 (2015). https://doi.org/10.1108/JAT-10-2014-0029
6. Hwangbo, H., Yoon, S.H., Jin, B.S., Han, Y.S., Ji, Y.G.: A study of pointing performance of elderly users on smartphones. Int. J. Hum.-Comput. Interact. **29**, 604–618 (2013). https://doi.org/10.1080/10447318.2012.729996
7. Olafsdottir, H., Zhang, W., Zatsiorsky, V.M., Latash, M.L.: Age-related changes in multifinger synergies in accurate moment of force production tasks. J. Appl. Physiol. **102**, 1490–1501 (2007). https://doi.org/10.1152/japplphysiol.00966.2006
8. Findlater, L., Froehlich, J.E., Fattal, K., Wobbrock, J.O., Dastyar, T.: Age-related differences in performance with touchscreens compared to traditional mouse input. In: Proceedings of the SIGCHI Conference on Human Factors in Computing Systems, pp. 343–346. ACM, Paris France (2013). https://doi.org/10.1145/2470654.2470703
9. Gao, Q., Sun, Q.: Examining the usability of touch screen gestures for older and younger adults. Hum. Factors **57**, 835–863 (2015). https://doi.org/10.1177/0018720815581293
10. MacKenzie, I.S., Buxton, W.: Extending Fitts' law to two-dimensional tasks. In: Proceedings of the SIGCHI Conference on Human Factors in Computing Systems - CHI 1992. pp. 219–226. ACM Press, Monterey, California, United States (1992). https://doi.org/10.1145/142750.142794
11. Kobayashi, M., Hiyama, A., Miura, T., Asakawa, C., Hirose, M., Ifukube, T.: Elderly User Evaluation of Mobile Touchscreen Interactions. In: Campos, P., Graham, N., Jorge, J., Nunes, N., Palanque, P., Winckler, M. (eds.) INTERACT 2011. LNCS, vol. 6946, pp. 83–99. Springer, Heidelberg (2011). https://doi.org/10.1007/978-3-642-23774-4_9

12. Ketcham, C.J., Stelmach, G.E.: Movement Control in the Older Adult. In: Technology for Adaptive Aging. National Academies Press (US) (2004)

13. Krehbiel, L.M., Kang, N., Cauraugh, J.H.: Age-related differences in bimanual movements: a systematic review and meta-analysis. Exp. Gerontol. **98**, 199–206 (2017). https://doi.org/10.1016/j.exger.2017.09.001

14. Walker, N., Philbin, D.A., Fisk, A.D.: Age-related differences in movement control: adjusting submovement structure to optimize performance. J. Gerontol. Ser. B: Psychol. Sci. Soc. Sci. **52B**, P40–P53 (1997). https://doi.org/10.1093/geronb/52B.1.P40

15. Bashore, T.R., Osman, A., Heffley, E.F.: Mental slowing in elderly persons: a cognitive psychophysiological analysis. Psychol. Aging **4**, 235–244 (1989). https://doi.org/10.1037/0882-7974.4.2.235

16. Charness, N.H., Schaie, K.W. (eds.): Impact of Technology on Successful Aging. Springer Publ, New York (2003)

17. Caprani, N.E.N., Gurri, C.: Touch Screens for the Older User. In: Auat Cheein, F. (ed.) Assistive Technologies. InTech (2012). https://doi.org/10.5772/38302

18. Wood, E., Willoughby, T., Rushing, A., Bechtel, L., Gilbert, J.: Use of computer input devices by older adults. J. Appl. Gerontol. **24**, 419–438 (2005). https://doi.org/10.1177/0733464805278378

19. Schneider, N., Wilkes, J., Grandt, M., Schlick, C.M.: Investigation of input devices for the age-differentiated design of human-computer interaction. In: Proceedings of the Human Factors and Ergonomics Society Annual Meeting. **52**, 144–148 (2008). https://doi.org/10.1177/154193120805200202

20. Umemuro, H.: Lowering elderly Japanese users' resistance towards computers by using touch-screen technology. Univ. Access Inf. Soc. **3**, 276–288 (2004). https://doi.org/10.1007/s10209-004-0098-6

21. Chung, M.K., Kim, D., Na, S., Lee, D.: Usability evaluation of numeric entry tasks on keypad type and age. Int. J. Ind. Ergon. **40**, 97–105 (2010). https://doi.org/10.1016/j.ergon.2009.08.001

22. Keates, S., Trewin, S.: Effect of age and Parkinson's disease on cursor positioning using a mouse. In: Proceedings of the 7th international ACM SIGACCESS conference on Computers and accessibility, pp. 68–75. Association for Computing Machinery, New York, NY, USA (2005). https://doi.org/10.1145/1090785.1090800

23. Paradise, J., Trewin, S., Keates, S.: Using pointing devices: difficulties encountered and strategies employed (2005)

24. Smith, M.W., Sharit, J., Czaja, S.J.: Aging, motor control, and the performance of computer mouse tasks. Hum. Factors **41**, 389–396 (1999). https://doi.org/10.1518/001872099779611102

25. Chaparro, A., Bohan, M., Fernandez, J., Choi, S.D., Kattel, B.: The impact of age on computer input device use: psychophysical and physiological measures. Int. J. Ind. Ergon. **24**, 503–513 (1999). https://doi.org/10.1016/S0169-8141(98)00077-8

26. Hourcade, J.P., Berkel, T.R.: Simple pen interaction performance of young and older adults using handheld computers. Interact. Comput. **20**, 166–183 (2008). https://doi.org/10.1016/j.intcom.2007.10.002

27. Ketcham, C.J., Seidler, R.D., Van Gemmert, A.W.A., Stelmach, G.E.: Age-related kine-matic differences as influenced by task difficulty, target size, and movement amplitude. J. Gerontol. Ser. B. **57**, P54–P64 (2002). https://doi.org/10.1093/geronb/57.1.P54

28. Rogers, W.A., Fisk, A.D., McLaughlin, A.C., Pak, R.: Touch a screen or turn a knob: choosing the best device for the job. Hum. Factors **47**, 271–288 (2005). https://doi.org/10.1518/0018720054679452

29. Murata, A., Iwase, H.: Usability of touch-panel interfaces for older adults. Hum. Factors **47**, 767–776 (2005). https://doi.org/10.1518/001872005775570952

30. Taveira, A.D., Choi, S.D.: Review study of computer input devices and older users. Int. J. Hum.-Comput. Interact. **25**, 455–474 (2009). https://doi.org/10.1080/10447310902865040

31. Sultana, A., Moffatt, K.: Effects of aging on small target selection with touch input. ACM Trans. Access. Comput. **12**, 1:1–1:35 (2019). https://doi.org/10.1145/3300178

32. Vogel, D., Baudisch, P.: Shift: a technique for operating pen-based interfaces using touch. In: Proceedings of the SIGCHI Conference on Human Factors in Computing Systems, pp. 657–666. Association for Computing Machinery, New York, NY, USA (2007). https://doi.org/10.1145/1240624.1240727

33. Holz, C., Baudisch, P.: Understanding touch. In: Proceedings of the SIGCHI Conference on Human Factors in Computing Systems, pp. 2501–2510. Association for Computing Machinery, New York, NY, USA (2011). https://doi.org/10.1145/1978942.1979308

34. Agarwal, A., Zaitsev, I., Wang, X., Li, C., Najork, M., Joachims, T.: Estimating position bias without intrusive interventions. In: Proceedings of the Twelfth ACM International Conference on Web Search and Data Mining, pp. 474–482. Association for Computing Machinery, New York, NY, USA (2019). https://doi.org/10.1145/3289600.3291017

35. Craswell, N., Zoeter, O., Taylor, M., Ramsey, B.: An experimental comparison of click position-bias models. In: Proceedings of the 2008 International Conference on Web Search and Data Mining, pp. 87–94. Association for Computing Machinery, New York, NY, USA (2008). https://doi.org/10.1145/1341531.1341545

36. Potter, R.L., Weldon, L.J., Shneiderman, B.: Improving the accuracy of touch screens: an experimental evaluation of three strategies. In: Proceedings of the SIGCHI Conference on Human Factors in Computing Systems, pp. 27–32. Association for Computing Machinery, New York, NY, USA (1988). https://doi.org/10.1145/57167.57171

37. Ren, X., Moriya, S.: Improving selection performance on pen-based systems: a study of pen-based interaction for selection tasks. ACM Trans. Comput.-Hum. Interact. **7**, 384–416 (2000). https://doi.org/10.1145/355324.355328

38. Albinsson, P.-A., Zhai, S.: High precision touch screen interaction. In: Proceedings of the SIGCHI Conference on Human Factors in Computing Systems, pp. 105–112. Association for Computing Machinery, New York, NY, USA (2003). https://doi.org/10.1145/642611.642631

39. Baudisch, P., Chu, G.: Back-of-device interaction allows creating very small touch devices. In: Proceedings of the SIGCHI Conference on Human Factors in Computing Systems, pp. 1923–1932. Association for Computing Machinery, New York, NY, USA (2009). https://doi.org/10.1145/1518701.1518995

40. Holz, C., Baudisch, P.: The generalized perceived input point model and how to double touch accuracy by extracting fingerprints. In: Proceedings of the SIGCHI Conference on Human Factors in Computing Systems, pp. 581–590. Association for Computing Machinery, New York, NY, USA (2010). https://doi.org/10.1145/1753326.1753413

Older Adults' Digital Competences and User Behavior

Digital Bulgarian Elderly People: Myth or Reality?

Lora Metanova⬤, Neli Velinova⬤, and Lilia Raycheva(⊠) ⬤

The St. Kliment Ohridski Sofia University, Sofia, Bulgaria
lraycheva@yahoo.com

Abstract. The development of ICTs and the increasingly widespread access to the Internet pose significant challenges to mankind in contemporary society. Although high-tech developments bring positives, such as faster access to a variety of information and easier communication, they also pose the challenge of how certain groups of people can be integrated in the new technological realities, because the lack of digital competences actually isolates them socially. Older people seem to be more vulnerable in this regard, and therefore the topic of their adaptation to the digitalized environment is an important part of the discourse on the overall digital media literacy. This study aims to trace trends in the attitudes of the Bulgarian older persons to the transforming usage of media content and communication technologies. The methodology includes comparative analysis of statistical data (2004–2023) and of conducted two empirical surveys (2019/2023). The research has been developed within the framework of the MEDIADELCOM research project of the Horizon 2020 European Commission program.

Keywords: Digital Competences · Digital media literacy · Internet · Elderly · Communication

1 Introduction

The rapid development of high technologies and the Internet in recent years has had a huge impact on social relations in society, as well as on the developments in the information channels. Facilitated communication and quick access to information of all kinds and from anywhere in the world have greatly changed people's lives, imposing the need for new, digital skills and digital literacy standards.

Digital skills and digital literacy have quickly become a prerequisite for full participation in public life. The increasing mobility of people has made new technologies the main means of communication to such an extent that it is difficult for anyone to imagine communication in the modern world without them. However, these changes have created a real danger of social isolation for people who do not or rarely use these technologies or lack digital competences. Many analysts and experts have questioned in their studies the lag behind the elderly in adopting these skills, determined by the fact that they are no longer of an active age and nowadays they fail to adapt to the rapid developments of the technological environment [1]. It is notable that the older people get, the more heterogeneous they become [2]. So, differences in digital media literacy among older persons are also notable [3]. Not all older people are laggards [4]. This raises the issue of the digital culture of the elderly as part of their integration and inclusion in basic activities of daily life, which increasingly require digital skills.

The undertaken study targets the situation in Bulgaria. The conducted research focuses specifically on the digital media literacy of older people and to what extent they use new technologies. The main thesis in the study is that despite the fears of social isolation, the trend is changing and the elderly are gradually starting to adapt to the new realm.

2 Research Methods

The research methodology is based on comparative analysis of official EU and national statistical data, as well as on comparative analysis of the results of two anonymous surveys realized five years apart, the purpose of which is to track the trend in digital culture of the elderly. The first survey was conducted in 2019 among 30 people over the age of 61, who were residents of two large cities – the capital of Sofia and Varna, and representatives of a home for the elderly in the village of Dobrevtsi, Yablanitsa Municipality. The second survey was conducted through face-to-face interviews in 2023 among 50 people over the age of 65 who live in 9 cities of different size, including the capital of Sofia.

The topic is important on one side, from the point of view of concerns about social isolation of the elderly, and from another, from the permanent trend towards the increase of the older population not only in Bulgaria, but also across the EU.

The study raises two main research questions:

1. What are the dynamics in the use of information and communication technologies by the elderly?
2. What are the trends regarding the development of the digital culture of the elderly?

3 Results

According to Eurostat, the average age of the EU population is expected to increase by 5.8 years by 2100, i.e. from 44.4 years in 2022 to 50.2 years in 2100. The increase is projected for both men and women. Average age is projected to increase by +6.2 years for men (from 42.8 years in 2022 to 49.0 years in 2100) and by +5.6 years for women (from 45.9 years in 2022 at 51.5 years in 2100).

The share of the working-age population (15–64 years) in the total EU population is projected to decrease from 63.9% (285.5 mln) at the beginning of 2022 to 54.4% (228.1 mln) in 2100, representing a total decrease of 57.4 mln people. The steepest decline is expected to occur by 2038, reaching 60.0%, followed by a steady moderate decline until the end of the forecast horizon.

At the same time, the proportion of the elderly people (65+) in the total EU population is forecast to rise: from 21.1 per cent (94.3 mln) at the beginning of 2022 to 32.5 per cent (136.1 mln) in 2100, i.e. by +11.4% points, corresponding to an additional 41.8 mln people by 2100. Eurostat data show that as the trend of the total EU population is to decline by 2100, 65+ is the only major demographic age group expected to grow, both in relative and absolute terms [5]. This means that the elderly are a numerous group and their full participation in public and political life is of interest to the whole society. The statistics also show that people aged 55 or over make up a fifth of the total workforce, with their share increasing from 11.9% to 20.2 per cent between 2004 and 2019 (Fig. 1).

Fig. 1. Employment rate, by age class, 2004 and 2019

The number of people employed is growing fastest among people aged 60–64, with the total number of people employed in this age group more than doubling (139 per cent). The number of employed persons aged 65–69 and 55–59 is also growing rapidly, by 99 per cent and 70 per cent, respectively.

Older people who delay retirement earn more money, may accumulate additional pension rights, and may be able to save some of the income or direct it to a private pension plan. Although low, an increasing share of the EU-27 population aged 65–74 continues to work. This trend, although to varying degree, is characteristic of all EU countries, including Bulgaria [6].

3.1   Older People and ICTs in the EU - Trends and Comparative Analysis

General Data on Internet access. According to Eurostat data, a threshold was crossed in 2007 when the majority (53%) of households in the EU now have access to the Internet. This share continues to increase, with statistics exceeding three quarters in 2012, four fifths in 2014 and 90 per cent in 2020. By 2022, the share of EU households with internet access will rise to 93% (Fig. 2).

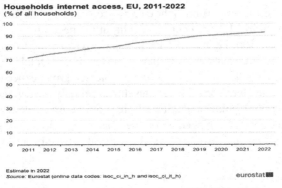

Fig. 2. Households Internet access, EU, 2011–2022

In 2022, the share of households with internet access was 99% in Norway. The Netherlands, Luxembourg and Finland are also among the countries with the highest share of households with internet access at 98 per cent, followed by Spain (96%) and Denmark (95%). Bulgaria (87%), Croatia (86%), and Greece (85%) have the lowest levels of household internet access among EU Member States. While saturation of household internet access is observed among some of the leading Member States, between 2017 and 2022 there is a catch-up with a larger increase in some countries, including Bulgaria (Fig. 3) [7].

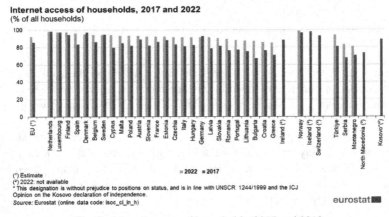

Fig. 3. Internet access of households, 2017 and 2012

Use of High Technologies by the Elderly. More than two-fifths of people aged 65–74 have never used a computer, according to Eurostat data. This share is still significant, but at the same time there has been a tendency in the last few years to decrease it and to shrink the digital gap between generations.

The term "digital divide" describes the gap between those who have access to digital technologies and those who do not; or the gap between those who use digital technologies and those who do not understand in binary terms distinguishing the "haves" from the "havenots" [8].

According to the EU's annual survey of ICT use in households and by individuals, the digital divide is generally narrowing, although older people are relatively slower to adopt new technologies. The data shows that older men are more likely than older women to use digital technology. Analysts explain this data by suggesting that because of their choice of occupation, older men had more access to new technologies in the workplace. Among the younger generations, such a digital gender divide is not observed, almost all young men and women use the Internet daily.

Between 2008 and 2017, the proportion of the EU-27 population aged 55–64 who had never used a computer fell from 47% to 25% (with the decrease recorded for each Member State to a different extent), and this share in the 65–74 age group has decreased from 70% to 44%. In EU Member States, the proportion of people aged 65–74 who have never used a computer before is slightly higher than two-thirds in Italy and Romania and closer to three-quarters in Croatia (73%), Bulgaria (74%) and Greece (78%). At the same time, the proportion of elderly people in 2017 who had never used a computer was lower than among their peers in 2008 (Fig. 4).

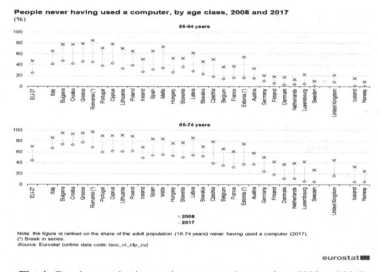

Fig. 4. People never having used a computer, by age class, 2008 and 2017

In 2019, almost a third (31percent) of the 16–74 EU-27 population had above basic digital skills: the shares for older people were much lower, 16% for those aged 55–64 years and 7% for those between 65 and 74 years of age. Statisticians anticipate that older people would use ICT much more widely in the future, given the continuous digitization of society and the increasing number of people with ICT skills entering old age.

In 2019, more than two-fifths (43%) of people in the EU aged between 65 and 74 had not used the internet in the three months preceding the survey. Older people (aged 65–74) were three times more likely not to use the internet compared to the data for people aged 16–74 (14%). In percentage terms, this generation gap is particularly pronounced in the southern, eastern and Baltic EU Member States. For example, in Bulgaria and Greece, the share of elderly people who have not used the Internet is 47% higher than the share in the general data for the entire adult population from 16 to 74 years old. This difference is between 39 and 46% points in Slovakia, Croatia, Poland, Romania, Lithuania, Portugal, Cyprus, Malta and Hungary.

Analysts also note the potential of the Internet to be useful for the elderly. For example, online shopping can free people with mobility problems from trips to the stores that are difficult for them. Similarly, online banking can allow seniors to manage their finances from home. The Internet also provides many ways for the elderly to communicate with family and friends.

The data show that sending/receiving emails is the most common activity among older people in the EU (44 per cent in 2019), while they are less likely to use other forms of communication, such as telephone or video calls over the Internet (24%).

Between 2009 and 2019, the percentage increase in those using the Internet to send and receive email and to look up health information was greater among older adults (Fig. 5) [9].

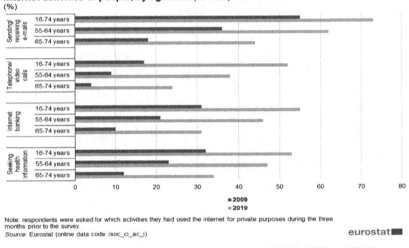

Internet activities of people, by age class, EU-27, 2009 and 2019 (%)

Note: respondents were asked for which activities they had used the internet for private purposes during the three months prior to the survey.
Source: Eurostat (online data code: isoc_ci_ac_i)

eurostat

Fig. 5. Internet activities of people, by age class, EU-27, 2009 and 2019

The Elderly and the Social Networks. According to Eurostat data less than a fifth of people aged 65–74 have used social networks. Overall, older people (65–74 years) in the EU-27 are less likely to use a range of communication activities on the Internet than the general population, defined as the 16–74 age group. In 2019, less than a fifth (18 per cent) of older people participated in social media, compared to an average of 54% for all ages.

In 2021, however, their share is already 21%, according to Eurostat's summary data for 2022 [10]. This share is still lower compared to younger people, but has been on the grow compared to two years ago, and according to the analysis for the last five years it has almost doubled.

In 2021, nearly three-fifths (57%) of the EU population aged 16–74 participated in social networks in the three months before the last survey. The participation rate for 16–29 year olds (83%) is almost four times higher than the corresponding rate for 65–74 year olds (23%). According to the Eurostat's analysis, over the past five-year period, however, there has been a small change in the proportion of youth participating in social networks, as it appears to have reached saturation. On the other hand, the proportion of older people using social networks has almost doubled over the same period.

Seniors and Online Shopping. An increasing proportion of older people use the Internet for online shopping. However, they remain less likely than other age groups to shop online [11]. In 2019, around 28% of the EU-27 population aged 65–74 made at least one online purchase in the 12 months preceding the survey on ICT use. The corresponding share for people aged 55–64 is 45% while the average share for all adults (16–74 years) is 60%.

In 2019, the majority of older people (aged 65–74) in Denmark, the Netherlands and Sweden made online purchases, the highest in Denmark being 65%. There are five EU Member States where fewer than 1 in 10 older adults have made an online purchase, with the lowest in Bulgaria and Romania at 2% and 3% respectively.

3.2   The Elderly and ICT in Bulgaria

General Data on the Use of the Internet in Bulgaria. In Bulgaria, as in all member-state countries, there is a tendency the consumption of the Internet to grow, nevertheless that the older people are increasingly participating in the labor market. In almost all cases using the Internet is via a personal computer either using a dial-up, ADSL or cable broadband access. However, while having Internet at home enables instant connection regardless of geographical distances, it can also disrupt traditional face-to-face interactions. Although text messages, video calls, social media and social networks have become common forms of communication within members of different age in the families, the depth and quality of personal conversations may be affected especially for the elderly.

In 2022, 87.3% of the households in Bulgaria have access to the Internet in their homes, which is 3.8%age points more than the previous year. For comparison, in 2021 83.5% of the households have access to the Internet in their homes, which is 4.6% points more than the previous year, and in 2020 their share is 78.9%, which is again more than the previous year by 3.8% (Fig. 6) [12].

Use of ICT by the Elderly in Bulgaria. The tendency to increase the share of adults who use ICT, including the Internet, is also observed in Bulgaria, although there are still large differences between them and the users in young age groups.

According to National Statistical Institute (NSI) data from 2018, 63.6% of the population between the ages of 16 and 74 use the Internet every day or at least once a week at work, at home or elsewhere. The most active Internet users are the young people between the ages of 16 and 24, with 92.2% of them using the Internet every day or at least once a

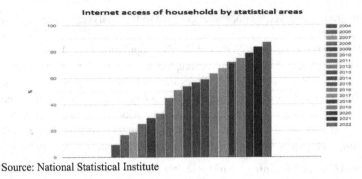

Source: National Statistical Institute

Fig. 6. Internet access of households by statistical areas. Source: National Statistical Institute

week. As age increases, so does the desire and need to be online, with 17.8% of people between the ages of 65 and 74 surfing regularly [13].

In 2021, people between the ages of 55 and 64 who use the Internet once a day or at least once a week have already reached 63.1%, and those between the ages of 65 and 74 who use the Internet at least once a week are 30.8% [14].

According to the data for 2022, the largest share of people using the Internet every day or at least once a week, that is, regularly, are still in the young age group between 16 and 24 years, but the share of regular users of the global network (every day or at least once a week) between the ages of 55 and 64 and 65 and 74 has grown significantly – respectively, they are 71.8% among people between 55 and 64, and 41% among those between 65 and 74 (Fig. 7) [15].

National Statistical Institute data show that the proportion of people aged 65+ are becoming more active internet users, and while they still lag behind younger generations, the increase in this age group of regular users of the global web is greater in percentage

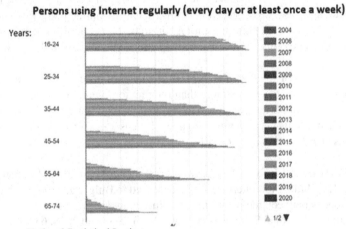

Source: National Statistical Institute

Fig. 7. Persons using the Internet regularly (every day or at least once a week). Source: National Statistical Institute

expression. The same trend is confirmed on an European scale, according to Eurostat data.

In 2017, only 16.3% of people between the ages of 65 and 74 surfed regularly, and 15.7% used a computer in their daily lives. Data show that 98.2% of people in this age group have never shopped online [16]. In 2022, their share decreases to 88.5%.

NSI data shows that the proportion of people aged 65 and over are becoming more active internet users, and while they still lag behind younger generations, the increase in this age group of regular users of the global web is greater in percentage expression. The same trend is confirmed on a European scale, according to Eurostat data.

In 2017, only 16.3% of people between the ages of 65 and 74 surfed regularly, and 15.7% used a computer in their daily lives. According to NSI data, 98.2% of people in this age group have never shopped online. In 2022, their share decreases to 88.5% [15].

3.3 Results of the Conducted Surveys

The aim of the study is to track changes in digital culture of Bulgarian elderly people over the last years, as well as their attitudes towards high technologies and Internet consumption, in particular – online media.

The first survey was conducted in 2019 among 30 Bulgarians over the age of 61 from the capital of Sofia, the city of Varna, and inhabitants of a home for the elderly "Residence Caramel" in the village of Dobrevtsi, Yablanitsa Municipality. The survey consists of 20 questions, some of which have been answered with more than one answer, so the sum does not always add up to 100%.

Within the framework of the present research, in the period 01–31.10.2023 a survey has been conducted among 50 respondents over the age of 65, divided equally into men and women, regardless of their social status, from the cities of Sofia, Varna, Burgas, Stara Zagora, Silistra, Ikhtiman, Kostenetz, Elhovo and Haskovo. The survey consists of 14 questions, some of which have been answered with more than one response, so the total does not always add up to 100% (Fig. 8).

When asked in 2019 what they use the Internet for most often, 63% of the respondents stated that they do not use the Internet at all because they do not have a computer or a smartphone and do not know how to use them.

Survey data in 2023 show that 72% of the respondents over the age of 65 use high-tech devices connected to the Internet.

Six percent in 2019 claimed that they do not use modern devices with Internet access, but through relatives and friends they use for communication the social network Facebook or applications such as Skype and Viber. 17% responded that they use the Internet once a day by logging into a social network, sending emails, or using various communication apps. Seven percent of the respondents used the Internet for communication purposes several times a day, and another 7% used the network for these purposes once a week. Seventeen percent of the respondents said they rarely use the Internet for communication, and 2% answered that they go online once a month to communicate.

Only 24% of the respondents in 2019 used the Internet and, in particular, information sites as the main source of information, with 6% of them stating that they were also interested in trivia, 3% - in information related to their work and the same percentage -

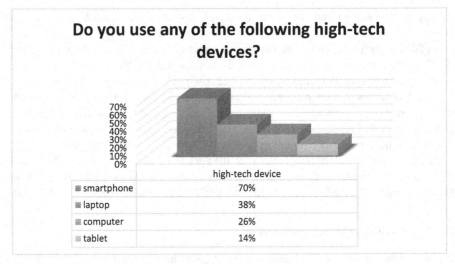

Fig. 8. Do you use any of the following high-tech devices?

from movies. Again, 3% of the respondents answered that they search the Internet for e-books to read and another 3% stated that they make various inquiries on the World Wide Web. The least (2%) say they check the weather forecast on the Internet.In 2023 the most used device for accessing the Internet is the smartphone, with 70% of respondents using it for any type of communication. 80% of the interviewees who use high technology access the Internet every day with smartphone (Fig. 9), while in 2019 17% responded that they use the Internet once a day.

The next most commonly used device in 2023 is a laptop (38%), followed by a computer (26%) and a tablet (14%). Apart from the answers given in the survey, the respondents specify that initially with the introduction of new technologies, they most often used the desktop computer to access the Internet, then it has been replaced by the more convenient and mobile laptop, while finally reaching the mass use of the smartphone. Most often, survey participants use the Internet for communication (97.2%), to find information on topics of interest to them (88.8%), for entertainment (66.6 per cent) and for work (27.7%).

Well over half of the respondents (77.7%) in 2023 who handle modern devices use social networks and have an account on one of them (Facebook, Twitter, Instagram), with 36.1% accessing social networks every day, and 41.6% less often use their profile. Most of the respondents share that they use social networks to communicate with relatives and friends and to obtain additional information. 22.3% claim that do not have profiles on social networks.

Again, the majority of respondents (69%) who use high technology answer that modern devices have brought a positive change in their lives. They share that thanks to access to the Internet, they manage to find the information they are interested in much more easily. Those of them who work (27.7%) state that computers and the Internet greatly facilitate the performance of their official duties. As an advantage, the respondents also consider the easier and more convenient way to communicate with their friends

2023

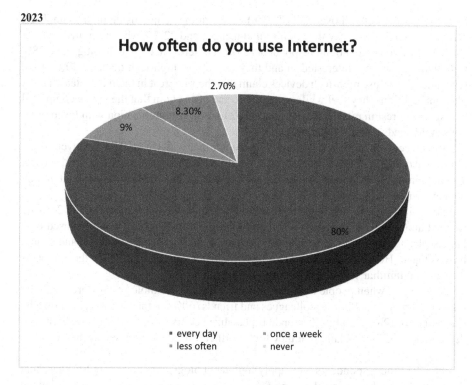

2019

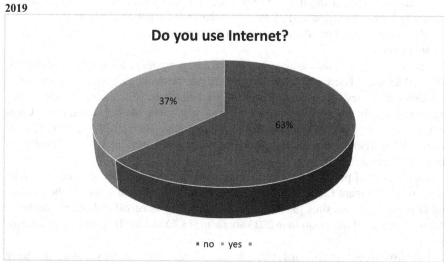

Fig. 9. How often do you use Internet?

and relatives both by phone and via the Internet using applications such as Viber and Messenger, which allow for exchanging messages and video connection. Entertainment like games, movies, cooking recipes and more are also part of the positives reported by the respondents. Well over half (72.3%) state that they enjoy using high technology, compared to 5.5% who say they don't mind using it and 22.2% who are indifferent.

Seventy two percent of all respondents have an interest in high technology, and 28% state that they are not interested in and they do not use high-tech devices. 40% of the respondents who use high-tech devices claim that their interest in them is dictated by the pleasant emotions they feel while using them, and 60% claim that they were compelled to take an interest in modern devices because of work, communication with loved ones, household needs or for other reasons.

The percentage of the respondents who are familiar with ChatGPT is relatively small (14%) and only 2% of them have a registered profile without using artificial intelligence. The remaining 84% admit that they do not know what this application is about and do not have an account in it.

The opinions about the harm or benefit of artificial intelligence are equal – 24% are worried about the consequences whether the artificial intelligence would be used on a large scale, against 24%, according to which artificial intelligence is useful and should be developed. However, the majority of people do not have an opinion on the matter, as they are not familiar with it (52%).

Most often, when people over the age of 65 use new technology, they are taught by their children, grandchildren, colleagues and friends (60%) or they learn on their own by trial and error (28%). Only 4% attended specialized courses for working with high-tech devices. Another 28% claim that they find it difficult to work with new technologies at all.

19.4% of the respondents who apply high technologies in their daily life share that they need help when using them, 55.5% state that they sometimes have to be helped when they have difficulties, and 25.1% claim that they do not need assistance.

28% of the respondents do not use any of the listed devices - computer, tablet, laptop and smartphone.

Survey data shows that women in this age group are more interested in high technology than men. Even when the respondents are husband and wife from the same household, it is very often the woman who handles the new technologies more easily and more often. In comparison, 44% of those surveyed who are not familiar with Chat-GPT are male vs. 40% of females. 40% of smartphone users are female vs. 32% of males. 34% of females use the Internet daily vs. 24% of males, and 18% of men use a push-button phone versus 10% of women.

The number of people in this age group whose main source of information is television is predominant (78%). In second place as an information source is the Internet and in particular news sites (38%), while in 2019 they were 24% of the respondents. The next sources of information in 2023 are radio (18%) and finally printed publications (16%).

Data from a comparative analysis with results from a previous survey show that there is an increase in the proportion of people in this age group who use high-tech devices with access to the Internet.

4 Discussion

The modern world requires continuous acquisition of new skills related to the development of high technologies and their rapid entry into everyday life. Skills that a few years ago were only required for engineers and programmers are now a necessity for participating in everyday activities.

Digital skills and the skills to use new communication devices are necessary even for the usual communication on the telephone. The group of elderly people, most of whom are outside the active labor market, should not be neglected in analyzes of the impact of the new digital reality on social relations. People in this age group have not had to have such skills during their careers, and then, when they are no longer in work, they lag behind the development of technology and are in danger of being isolated from social life. It should be noted that new technologies are increasingly becoming part of the lives of people in this age group. The coronavirus pandemic has undoubtedly forced the need for digital skills due to the isolation and safe remote communication that new technologies offer. The connection with the children and grandchildren, who usually live in other settlements or other countries, also presented to the elderly the need to use new technologies. The fact that some of them work even after retirement also puts them in front of the need to acquire new digital skills.

The diminishing role of print media as a source of communication is also striking, even for people over 65, who until recently have been the main users of print media according to the research.

5 Conclusion, Limitation, Implications for Future Research

A comparative analysis of Eurostat data and comments shows that the share of elderly people in Europe who have never used a computer is decreasing. There is also an increasing trend of older people using social networks for shopping online.

With regard to the first research question: "What are the dynamics in the use of information and communication technologies by the elderly?", the comparative analysis of NSI data shows that the tendency to increase the share of adults who use ICT, including the Internet, is also observed in Bulgaria, although there are still large differences between them and the users in young age groups, as well as in Europe. For the period from 2018 to 2022, the share of people in Bulgaria between the ages of 65 and 74 who regularly access the Internet increased from 17.8% to 41%.

These trends are also confirmed by the surveys conducted among a random sample of seniors over 65 in different cities - one in 2019 and the other in 2023. While in 2019 the majority of respondents answered that they did not use the Internet, because they do not have a device with which to access it, in 2023 more than two thirds said that they use the Internet regularly, have a smartphone or laptop, use social networks. The fact that more than half of the elderly people surveyed in 2023 who use high technology declared that modern devices have brought a positive change in their lives is indicative. They share that thanks to access to the Internet, they manage to find the information they are interested in much more easily. Respondents also consider the easier and more convenient way to communicate with their friends and relatives both by phone and via the

Internet using applications such as Viber and Messenger, which allow writing messages and video connection. Entertainment like games, movies, cooking recipes and more are also part of the positives reported by the respondents. Well over half (72.3%) state that they enjoy using high technology, compared to 5.5% who say they don't mind using it and 22.2% who are indifferent.

Surveys also show that the Internet has displaced print media as a source of information even in this age group, coming in second to television, which still remains the top source of information.

When answering the second research question: "What are the trends regarding the development of the digital culture of the elderly?", the trends outlined by the present study show that, although they remain in the group with the lowest consumption of high technology and the Internet compared to other age groups, people 65 + are gradually adapting to the new realm and are becoming more active in the use of ICT. The proportion of the elderly people who have access to the Internet, possess smartphones and laptops, as well as those who use the global network to inform themselves about topics of interest, for communication and for entertainment, is increasing. More and more of them acquire digital skills, even if they admit that they were rather forced to that out of necessity set by the high-tech society.

Limitations of the study relate to participants in the two survey surveys being randomly selected based on age rather than quota sampling. However, their answers can be an indicator of trends in the use of new technologies.

The results of the research may be of interest to those engaged with the social aspects of new technologies, media consumption and trends in the mediascape.

Acknowledgements. The text has been developed within the international academic research project MEDIADELCOM of the European Union's Horizon 2020 research and innovation programme.

References

1. Hargittai, E., Piper, A.M., Morris, M.R.: From internet access to internet skills: digital inequality among older adults. Univ. Access Inf. Soc. **18**, 881–890 (2019)
2. Stone, M.E., Lin, J., Dannefer, D., Kelley-Moore, J.A.: The continued eclipse of heterogeneity in gerontological research. J. Gerontol. Ser. B: Psychol. Sci. Soc. Sci., **72**(1), 162–167 (2017)
3. Loos, E.F.: Senior citizens: Digital immigrants in their own country?. Observatorio (OBS*) J. **6**, 1–23 (2012)
4. Loos, E., Peine, A., Fernandéz-Ardèvol, M.: Older people as early adopters and their unexpected and innovative use of new technologies: deviating from technology companies' scripts. In: Gao, Q., Zhou, J. (eds.) Human Aspects of IT for the Aged Population. Technology Design and Acceptance: 7th International Conference, ITAP 2021, Held as Part of the 23rd HCI International Conference, HCII 2021, Virtual Event, July 24–29, 2021, Proceedings, Part I, pp. 156–167. Springer International Publishing, Cham (2021). https://doi.org/10.1007/978-3-030-78108-8_12
5. Eurostat Population Projections in the EU (2023). https://ec.europa.eu/eurostat/statistics-explained/index.php?title=Population_projections_in_the_EU#Population_projections

6. Eurostat. Ageing Europe – Statistics on Working into Moving into Retirement (2023). https://ec.europa.eu/eurostat/statistics-explained/index.php?title=Ageing_Europe_-_statis tics_on_working_and_moving_into_retirement#Employment_patterns_among_older_p eople
7. Eurostat. Digital Economy and Society Statistics - Households and Individuals (2022). https://ec.europa.eu/eurostat/statistics-explained/index.php?title=Digital_economy_ and_society_statistics_-_households_and_individuals
8. Hargittai, E.: The digital divide and what to do about it. New Economy Handbook, pp. 821–839 (2003)
9. Eurostat. Internet Activities of People, by Age Class, EU-27 (2009 and 2019). https://ec.eur opa.eu/eurostat/statistics-explained/index.php?title=File:Internet_activities_of_people,_by_ age_class,_EU-27,_2009_and_2019_(%25)_AE2020.png
10. Eurostat. Regional Yearbook (2022) https://www.drugsandalcohol.ie/37936/1/Eurostat_reg ional_yearbook_2022.pdf
11. Eurostat Ageing Europe – Statistics on Social Life and Opinion (2023). https://ec.eur opa.eu/eurostat/statistics-explained/index.php?title=Ageing_Europe_-_statistics_on_social_ life_and_opinions&oldid=449468
12. National Statistical Institute: Households with Internet Access at Home (2023). https://www. nsi.bg/en/content/2808/households-internet-access-home
13. National Statistical Institute Main Results of the Information Society Survey in Households in 2018 (2018). https://www.nsi.bg/sites/default/files/files/pressreleases/ICT_hh2018_KV4 5Z0R.pdf
14. National Statistical Institute: Use of Information and Communication Technologies in House-holds and Persons in 2021 (2021). https://www.nsi.bg/sites/default/files/files/pressreleases/ ICT_hh2021_WB3N3IL.pdf
15. National Statistical Institute (2023). Individuals Regularly Using the Internet. https://www. nsi.bg/en/content/2814/individuals-regularly-using-internet
16. Bulgarian Industrial Association: Main Results of the Survey on the Information Society in Enterprises in 2017 (2017). https://en.bia-bg.com/news/view/23698/

Chatbots as Tools in Parent–Child Relationships

Misato Nihei[1,2,3](✉), Taiga Nohara[1,3], Ikuko Sugawara[2,3], and Takazumi Ono[1,2,3]

[1] The University of Tokyo, Tokyo, Japan
{mnihei,taiganohara}@edu.k.u-tokyo.ac.jp
[2] Institute of Gerontology, The University of Tokyo, Tokyo, Japan
sugawara@iog.u-tokyo.ac.jp
[3] Seibu Bunri University of Hospital, Saitama, Japan

Abstract. We focus on the communication tools (CT) as a means of supporting the psychological well-being of an increasing number of isolated older individuals. We conducted an analysis of the psychological effects of current CT usage using the psychosocial impact of assistive devices scale. Our findings led to the development of the Communication Mediator Bot (CMBot), which was designed to facilitate communication between older individuals and their families. This system, operating on LINE and LLM, includes features to encourage communication and regulate self-disclosure levels. While there is room for improvement in usability, our verification results indicate the potential for enhanced psychological well-being through the control of self-disclosure levels.

Keywords: communication tool · self-disclosure · psychological health · LLM

1 Introduction

In Japan, societal shifts, such as the rise of nuclear families and an increase in single-person households, have emerged alongside rapid economic growth post-war and subsequent lifestyle changes [1]. Particularly in older households, the decline in support and caregiving functions due to nuclearization, coupled with reduced assistance from relatives, has made community mutual aid difficult and challenging. Presently, 29.2% of households with individuals aged 65 and older consist only of spouses, while 24.2% are single-person households [2].

A survey focusing on individuals aged 60 and older, gauging their interaction with neighbors, indicates that single-person households, and males, more than females, experience a decline in social interaction compared with spouse-only household. This contributes to the growing trend of isolated older individuals [1]. The recent impact of COVID-19 has further intensified the issue of isolation due to limited opportunities for face-to-face communication [3]. In these circumstances, older individuals not residing with their children or grandchildren find it challenging to lead emotionally and physically compared with those living with family members [4]. This underscores the importance of communication support to connect people in these challenging times.

© The Author(s), under exclusive license to Springer Nature Switzerland AG 2024
Q. Gao and J. Zhou (Eds.): HCII 2024, LNCS 14725, pp. 228–241, 2024.
https://doi.org/10.1007/978-3-031-61543-6_17

Over the last 2 decades, a notable transformation in communication methods has occurred, driven by the widespread adoption of remote communication via PCs and smartphones [5]. This shift is particularly impactful among the older population, which traditionally had lower internet usage rates. Increased use of non-face-to-face communication tools (CT) has facilitated ongoing interaction with distant relatives and friends [6].

CT, defined as chat applications for transmitting and sharing intentions and information [7], encompasses tools such as email and social networking services (SNS). Recently, CTs have been employed to pilot collaborative systems connecting individuals, families, and caregivers in community comprehensive support systems [8]. Furthermore, the proliferation of CT has complemented face-to-face communication, contributing to the enhancement of psychological health indicators such as life satisfaction and subjective well-being (SWB) [9]. Nevertheless, counterarguments have also been reported.

For instance, Nabi et al. [10] demonstrated a positive correlation between the number of friends on Facebook and a strong perception of social support. This association was linked to stress reduction and subsequent improvement in psychological health, suggesting that having more friends on Facebook is beneficial. In contrast, Bevan et al. [11], in an online survey of 599 individuals aged 18 to 70, reported that increased time spent on SNS and the use of multiple SNS platforms are associated with a decrease in overall quality of life. Consequently, the current understanding of how to use CT to impact psychological health remains ambiguous. Therefore, this study aimed to develop CT functions specifically designed to enhance psychological well-being.

This study focuses on the connection between older adults and their children, with the goal of proposing and evaluating the effectiveness of communication tool functions to improve psychological well-being. To achieve this, this study plans to (i) conduct a survey to extract the psychological effects and issues brought about by existing CT and (ii) propose new functions for enhancing psychological well-being.

2 Psychological Impacts of Each Feature of CT [12]

2.1 Method

To explore the connection between the functionalities of existing CT and psychological health in the older population, an online survey targeted older users. The screening process initially categorized participants based on CT usage frequency (several times per month, several times per week, once or more daily), age groups (60–64 years, 65–69 years, 70–74 years, 75 years and older), and gender (male, female). Subsequently, the main survey was conducted. The survey questionnaire contained basic information such as household income and the highest level of education attained. It also included items related to the frequency of use of various CT functionalities and attitudes toward CT usage. Additionally, to assess psychological effects, psychosocial impact of assistive devices scale (PIADS) [13] was used, comprising 26 items measuring competence, adaptability, and self-esteem.

In this study, we classified existing CT functionalities based on the six functions identified by Richter et al. [14], incorporating features from Twitter, Instagram, LINE, and Facebook. This study identified the following ten commonly used functionalities for interpersonal communication on CT platforms:

Profile: The function to view pages displaying the user's personal information or self-introduction.

Like: The function to express positive reactions, such as pressing the "like" button for posts or replies

Share: The function to forward other users' posts to the place where posts of personal interest are displayed.

Message/Direct Message: The function of engaging in individual communication with specific users

Search: The function to search for specific users or posts.

Block: The function to temporarily restrict or hide the view of specific users.

Notification: The function to receive notifications about newly arrived information relevant to oneself.

Privacy: The function to set preferences for hiding certain information or individual posts that one does not want to be seen.

Tagging: The function to tag or mention other users within posts, notifying or involving them in the conversation.

Emoticon: The function to add emoticons or stickers to express emotions or enhance the text.

We gathered usage frequencies for these 10 features using a five-point scale. Factor analysis was employed to discern usage patterns and understand their impact on psychological well-being. Following this, multiple regression analysis was conducted to validate the psychological effects of these usage patterns. The explanatory variables comprised factor scores, with PIADS scores serving as the dependent variable and age and gender as covariates.

2.2 Results

The survey respondents comprised 359 older individuals with an average age of 69.6 ± 6.3. The total psychological impact score (PIADS score) attributed to CT usage demonstrated improvement in 285 individuals (79%), maintenance in 36 individuals (10%), and decline in 38 individuals (11%). The breakdown of the subscale scores revealed that 281 individuals (78%) showed improvement in competence, 241 individuals (67%) demonstrated improvement in adaptability, and 278 individuals (77%) experienced enhanced self-esteem.

Table 1 displays the outcome of the factor analysis, revealing the extraction of the two factors. To investigate the relationship between these factors and the PIADS score, multiple regression analysis was performed, with the PIADS score as the dependent variable and age and gender as covariates. The analysis revealed that the first factor encompassed features such as profiles, likes, shares, searches, and tagging, while the second factor comprised features such as message/direct message, block, notifications, privacy, and emoticon functionality. Moreover, the regression coefficients (95% confidence intervals) for the first and second factors concerning PIADS scores were 1.63 (−0.62, 3.88) and 3.91 (1.70, 6.11), respectively.

Table 1. Pattern matrix of the regression analysis

Question Items	Factor 1	Factor 2
Profile	0.63*	0.39
Like	0.74*	0.26
Share	0.81*	0.30
Message/Direct Message	0.07	0.81*
Search	0.76*	0.18
Block	0.46	0.63*
Notification	0.39	0.70*
Privacy	0.37	0.66*
Tagging	0.75*	0.37
Emoticon	0.35	0.55*
Proportion of variance explained	52.3	8.93
Cumulative proportion of variance explained up to factor 2	61.2	

$^{*}> 0.5$

2.3 Discussion

The survey results regarding the psychological impact of current CT usage indicate that approximately 80% of individuals perceive an improvement in their psychological well-being, suggesting a positive influence of CT on psychological health. While a small portion experienced a decline and some reported a significant improvement, there is potential for achieving higher effectiveness.

In the results of the factor analysis, the second factor highlighted the potential effectiveness of CT on psychological health. The first factor can be interpreted as functions that involve sharing information with others, such as sharing information, tagging, seeking, and acquiring desired information through search functions. On the other hand, the second factor encompasses functions that actively seek connections with others, such as messaging and notification, which are commonly used during communication. It also includes functions that restrict communication, such as blocking and privacy. Additionally, functions aimed at accurately conveying one's emotions, such as emoticons, were included.

Hence, by incorporating three functions-endeavoring to communicate, endeavoring to restrict communication, and endeavoring to accurately convey one's emotions- individuals can share information and express emotions about themselves to others based on the relationship and situation of the two parties involved in the communication. This dynamic can contribute to the psychological effects during CT usage as needed.

Next, we investigate whether the independent use of specific functions (patterns) has a negative impact on PIADS scores, whether sets of functions that individually influence PIADS scores appear as patterns, or whether the usage patterns of functions affect PIADS scores.

The results of the multiple regression analysis revealed that the five functions constituting the second factor did not negatively impact PIADS scores because of an increase in usage frequency. This suggests that functions forming usage patterns did not independently have negative effects on PIADS scores. Moreover, as some individual functions did not exhibit high regression coefficients, it was found that the collective usage patterns indeed influenced PIADS scores.

Therefore, engaging in communication regarding emotion based on the relationship and situation, along with restricting communication, can prove effective in enhancing psychological well-being.

3   A System to Improve Psychological Well-Being (CMBot)

3.1   Development Concept

The survey identified a development aimed at enhancing the psychological well-being of older individuals, emphasizing the need to tailor communication to the relationship and situation between the two parties and to convey or restrict information and emotions about oneself. The concept of "self-disclosure" was used in this context to express the idea of sharing information and emotions about oneself.

Self-disclosure is defined as the process through which individuals reveal information about themselves to others in interpersonal communication [15], contributing to mutual acceptance and the establishment of trust. Azy Barak et al. [16] focused on the reciprocity of self-disclosure in online communication, examining the interaction between the level of self-disclosure in sent messages and that in responses. The analysis revealed a clear reciprocity in self-disclosure, with a positive correlation between the level of self-disclosure in sent messages and that in response. The level of self-disclosure is defined as the extent to which individuals reveal something about themselves to others.

Building upon the survey results of this study and insights from previous research, the aim was to enhance psychological well-being by introducing functionalities that facilitate the desired level of self-disclosure between the two parties. Consequently, an intervention method was devised to effectively regulate the level of self-disclosure in interactions between older individuals and their children. This led to the creation of the "Communication Mediator Bot (CMBot)" equipped with functions to mediate communication between older individuals and their families. The CMBot facilitates communication while allowing for the adjustment of self-disclosure as needed.

In Particular, the CMBot offers topic suggestions and responses to streamline dialogue between older individuals and their children. The role of the CMBot is similar to that of a facilitator, aiming to improve the quality of communication without disrupting the natural flow or resorting to overt intervention. This enables CMBot to support communication in a seamless and effective manner.

3.2   CMBot

In this study, we introduce a bot named Communication Mediator Bot (CMBot), which was designed to mediate communication between two parties and adjust the level of self-disclosure based on their relationship. Specifically, we develop a function that acts as an intermediary in the communication between the two parties and adjusts the level of self-disclosure as needed. Figure 1 depicts a conceptual AI diagram of the developed system configuration. The system uses LINE [17] as the platform and executes programs within AWS Lambda [18] triggered by notifications through the Amazon API Gateway [19]. Keyword-based message creation is facilitated using data storage in Dynamo DB [20] and ChatGPT 4.0 (LLM (Large Language Models)) [21].

The adjustment of the level of self-disclosure is carried out through the following process:

- Self-disclosure levels:

  The level of self-disclosure is categorized into three levels:

1. Providing only general or everyday information without personal references
2. Providing general information about the interlocutor
3. Disclosing personal information such as physical appearance or behavior related to oneself or someone close to oneself.

This level encompasses the disclosure of personal information, including details about one's physical appearance or the behavior.

- Topic provision:

We supply topics based on the predetermined topics collected in advance using the LLM. The provision of topic occurs regularly between the two parties when there is no ongoing conversation. Topics were derived through a pre-survey on five self-disclosure themes: hobbies, politics/religion, personality, finances, and work. Variations in topics related to these topics are provided using the LLM, utilizing past topic content recorded in the database and introducing other relevant content. This process is facilitated through prompts for topic provision (Fig. 2). The adjustment level of self-disclosure and conversation c prompts initiated by CMBot itself (Fig. 3).

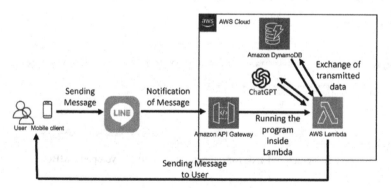

Fig. 1. System diagram of a developed function

Topic Provision Prompt:

- You play a role in livening up the conversation. Please provide a new question that keeps the conversation going on the basis of the following exchange.

- You play a role in answering questions. Provide a question within 20 characters and ending with a question mark (?). The genre of the question is determined by the following probabilities:

- Hobbies/interests: {HobbyRatio}%, Work/academic: {WorkRatio}%, Money/economics: {MoneyRatio}%, Politics/society: {PoliticsRatio}%, Personality: {PersonalityRatio}%.

- Provide a question within 20 characters that is not related to the already mentioned topics and is easy to answer. Example questions: What are your hobbies? What is your favorite food? What is your favorite movie? What is your favorite music? What is your favorite book? What is your favorite sport? Who is your favorite celebrity? Who is your favorite artist?

Fig. 2. Topic Provision Prompt

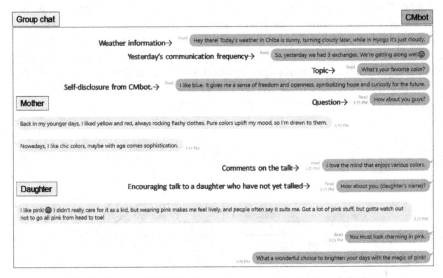

Fig. 3. Screen of LINE for interaction using the developed CMBot

4 Evaluation of a System for Improving Psychological Well-Being (CMBot)

4.1 Evaluation Method

4. Experimental Method:

The effectiveness of the developed CMBot's functions in improving psychological well-being is evaluated through an experimental setup. The participants include older individuals and their family members (children) (e.g., my grandmother and my mother), who are experienced in using LINE. LINE groups are created on devices where LINE is installed, comprising parent, children, and CMBot.

Pre-Intervention: Before the intervention, the participants provided information on the basic attributes, frequency and content of regular communication, ideal communication content, and level of self-disclosure.

Intervention: For the initial 3 days, there was no intervention by CMBot. The CMBot intervention commences on the 4th day.

Post-Intervention: Understand the PIADS, Japanese version of the System Usability Scale, free description.

5. Evaluation Method:

Number of message exchanges: Each continuous exchange of messages by one person is counted as one send/receive event. This metric provides an indication of overall communication engagement.

The number of message exchanges by level of self-disclosure assesses the message exchange categorized by the level of self-disclosure.

4.2 Experiment Result

Attributes of the Participants. The table presents the attributes of the participants, comprising 4 sets of mothers–daughter pairs, 2 sets of mothers–son pairs, and 2 sets of father–daughter pairs. The existing communication frequency ranged from once a week to every three months. In terms of ideal communication frequency, participants expressed preferences ranging from twice a day to once a month, with the common desire for a frequency that was higher or equal to their current frequency (Table 2).

Evaluation of the effectiveness of the developed system.

1. PIADS

Figure 4 shows the results of eight older participants aged 65 years who participated. The total PIADS score improved for all older participants ("0" considered as the baseline when not using CMBot).

Using the CMBot, psychological health improved in all aspects for all participants aged 65 years and above.

Table 2. Attributes of the participants

Group	ID	Role	Age	Frequency of regular communication	Frequency of ideal communication
Group1	1	Mother	68	Once every three days	Once every three days
	2	Daughter	44	Twice a month	Once a week
Group2	3	Mother	71	Once every three months	Once a month
	4	Son	45	Twice a month	Twice a day
Group3	5	Mother	78	Once a month	Once a week
	6	Daughter	56	Twice a month	Once a week
Group4	7	Father	74	Twice a day	Twice a day
	8	Daughter	42	Twice a month	Once every three days
Group5	9	Father	65	Twice a month	Twice a month
	10	Daughter	38	Twice a month	Twice a month
Group6	11	Mother	75	Once a week	Once every three days
	12	Daughter	46	Twice a month	Once a week
Group7	13	Mother	72	Once every three months	Once a month
	14	Son	46	Once every three months	Once a month
Group8	15	Mother	76	Once a week	Once a week
	16	Daughter	52	Once a week	Once a week

2. Level of Self-Disclosure:

Figure 5 illustrates a comparison of the level of self-disclosure. An increase in the number of messages sent at the ideal level of self-disclosure indicates successful control. Among the eight groups, an increase in the number of messages sent at the ideal level of self-disclosure was observed in five groups (Group 2 [ID3–4], 3 [ID5–6], 4 [ID7–8], 5 [ID9–10], and 8 [ID15–16]). In other words, 5 of 8 groups could control the level of self-disclosure.

3. Relationship between the level of self-disclosure and psychological well-being:

The study explored the relationship between the control of the level of self-disclosure and psychological well-being. Comparing the PIADS scores between the group that could control the level of self-disclosure and the group that could not control it, as shown in the results of (ii). Figure 6 depicts the observations. The groups that effectively controlled the level of self-disclosure tended to have higher PIADS scores in total score and all three subscale scores compared with the group that could not.

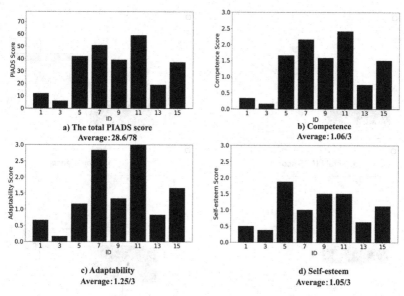

Fig. 4. PIADS scores of participants aged 65 and above

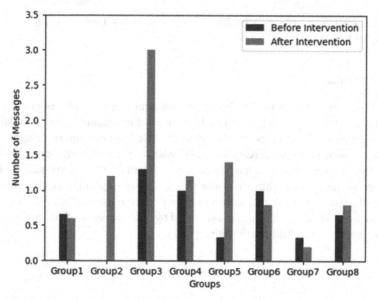

Fig. 5. Number of messages in ideal self-disclosure level before and after intervention

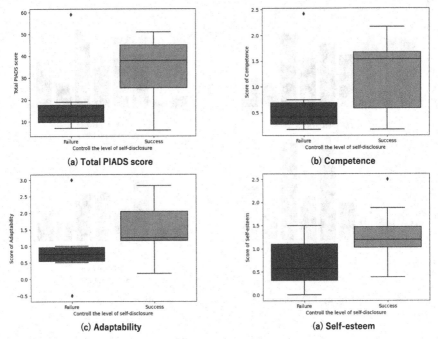

Fig. 6. Relationship between uncontrolling or controlling the level of self-disclosure and psychological well-being

4. Qualitative data

The provision of topics by CMBot yields representative examples of conversations that foster communication between two individuals. For example, in conversation A, there is a demonstration of how previously undisclosed information or thoughts of the other person, such as "music parents listened to when they were young," emerges. Moreover, as illustrated in conversation B, it is possible to learn from the conversation whether parents are indifferent or attentive to health. Conversation C also offers insight into recent living conditions and social interactions (whether they are isolated or not). Thus, using CMBot to promote self-disclosure, as evidenced by qualitative data from conversations, could facilitate parent–child relationships.

Conversation A: Discovering a hidden aspect of the other

CMBot(#g6_50): "You have a wonderful sense of appreciating the diverse charms of movies and selecting one that suits your mood of the day."
Father_11(#g6_51): "Back when I was a student, I used to listen to movie soundtracks a lot."
Father_11(#g6_52): "a delight of movie soundtracks is how they evoke memories of the films when you listen to them."
Daughter_12(#g6_53): "Dad, I didn't know you used to listen to movie soundtracks!"
Daughter_13(#g6_54): "Dad, if you have the DVD of 'Antarctic Chef,' please lend it to me sometime!"

Conversation B: Understanding concerns related to health

CMBot(#g8_75): "Do you have any hobbies you'd recommend?"
CMBot(#g8_75): "I recommend jogging. It's a great way to refresh both your body and mind."
CMBot(#g8_76): "What about everyone else?"
Son_16(#g8_77): "I don't have many hobbies, so I can't really recommend anything, but if I had to say, maybe something involving physical activity."
CMBot(#g8_78): "That sounds like a great hobby."
CMBot(#g8_79): "And what about you, Mother?"
Mother_15(#g8_80): "Good morning. I am 72 years old, and it is certainly difficult for me to recommend anything specific, but as my son mentioned, it would probably involve some form of physical activity. Perhaps for someone of my age, it could be something that involves moving the body and keeping the fingers active daily."

Conversation C Current situation:

CMBot(#g3_138): "What hobbies have you been into late?"
CMBot(#g3_139): "I've been recently trying out a new weight training method."
CMBot(#g3_140): "What about everyone else?"
Mother((#g3_141): "It's a refreshing sunny day! Bright morning♪"
Mother((#g3_142): "I'm all about the smartphone! Reviewing rehab, just trying to get back to my old routine!"
Mother((#g3_143): "Today is a one-coin smartphone class."
CMBot(#g3_144): "I think the smartphone class sounds interesting."
CMBot(#g3_145): "And what about you, Daughter?"
Mother((#g3_146): "My neighbor and I have the same (smartphone) model, so it's convenient!! Smartphones vary depending on the model, so it's tough for the teacher, which affects the pace of learning! That's why it's run by various staff, perhaps tapping into the wisdom of older individuals?"
Daughter(#g3_147): "I'm focusing on ballet conditioning. It's important to strengthen not only the core but also the toes, so I'm producing various ways to do it."

5 Limitation

The study's limitation lies in constraints imposed by experimenters monitoring conversations for evaluation, potentially resulting in participants self-regulating conversations, especially involving personal information.

6 Conclusion

In this study, we introduced a novel feature named CMBot, which is designed to improve the psychological well-being of older adults through a communication tool. To validate its effectiveness, we conducted a trial evaluation. Building on these findings, we proposed CMBot, a tool that tailors communication to the relationship and context between the two parties, enabling the transmission or restriction of self-related information and emotions. Acting as a virtual facilitator, CMBot serves by appropriately adjusting the level of self-disclosure in communication between older adults and their families. Using LINE as the platform, CMBot adjusts the self-disclosure level through LLM. In the trial evaluation involving eight groups of older adults and their children, all older adults experienced psychological benefits from CMBot. Moreover, among the eight groups, those who achieved the desired self-disclosure level (5 out of 8 pairs) showed further improvement in PIADS compared with the groups that did not. Improvements in consistency with previous topics and adjustments in self-disclosure levels are future challenges.

Acknowledgments. We would like to thank the participants of the experiment for their cooperation.

References

1. National Institute of Population and Social Security Research: [National Health Indicators 2022/2023] Kokumin seikatsu no shihyou 2022/2023 69(9):43 (2022). (in Japanese)
2. Cabinet Office: [Annual Report on Aging Society] Koureishakai hakusho (2023). (in Japanese)
3. Heshmat, Y., Neustaedter, C.: Family and friend communication over distance in Canada during the COVID-19 pandemic. In: Designing Interactive Systems Conference 2021, Virtual Event USA, June 2021, pp. 1–14 (2021)
4. Itami, K., Tomari, Y., Asano, M.: [A study on the quality of life of older individuals in "grandparent-grandchild relationships" using the score on emotion (GDS)] Sohubo-Mago kankei ni mita koresha no QOL ni kansuru kenkyu (1) – joucho ni kansuru sukoa(GDS) wo mochiite(in Japanese). J. Jpn. Acad. Nursing Res. **20**(2), 89 (1998)
5. Ministry of Internal Affairs and Communications: White Paper on Information and Communications in Japan 2022 (2022)
6. Goodman-Deane, J., Mieczakowski, A., Johnson, D., Goldhaber, T., Clarkson, P.J.: The impact of communication technologies on life and relationship satisfaction. Comput. Hum. Behav. **57**, 219–229 (2016)
7. Matsumura, K., Nishida, T.: [Development of Communication Tool Evaluation Methodology] Komyunikeshon tu-ru hyoka shuhou no kouchiku. J. Soc. Technol. Res. **2**, 181–190 (2004). (in Japanese)
8. Ministry of Health, Labor and Welfare: [Community-based comprehensive care system] (chiki hokatu kea sisutemu) (in Japanese). https://www.mhlw.go.jp/stf/seisakunitsuite/bunya/hukushi_kaigo/kaigo_koureisha/chiiki-houkatsu/. Accessed 23 Feb 2023
9. Lyubomirsky, S., King, L. Diener, E.: The benefits of frequent positive affect: does happiness lead to success? Psychol. Bull. **131**(6), 803 (2005)
10. Nabi, R.L., Prestin, A., So, J.: Facebook friends with (health) benefits? Exploring social network site use and perceptions of social support, stress, and well-being. Cyberpsychol. Behav. Soc. Netw. **16**(10), 721–727 (2013). https://doi.org/10.1089/cyber.2012.0521

11. Bevan, J.L., Gomez, R., Sparks, L.: Disclosures about important life events on Facebook: relationships with stress and quality of life. Comput. Hum. Behav. **39**, 246–253 (2014)
12. Nohara, T., Ono, T., Sugawara, I., Nihei, M.: [Proposal of Communication Tools Providing Psychologically Positive Effects on older individuals] Koureisha ni shinriteki ni pozitexibu na eikyou wo ataeru komyunikeshon turu no teian. SI2023, pp. 3736–3738 (2023). (in Japanese)
13. Jutai, J., Day, H.: Psychosocial impact of assistive devices scale (PIADS). Technol. Disabil. **14**(3), 107–111 (2002)
14. Richter, A., Koch, M.: Functions of social networking services. In: From CSCW to Web 2.0. European Developments in Collaborative Design: Selected Papers from COOP08 (2008)
15. Derlega, V.J., Metts, S., Petronio, S., Margulis, S.T.: Self Disclosure. Sage Publications Inc., Southern Oaks, CA (1993)
16. Barak, A., Gluck Ofri, O.: Degree and reciprocity of self disclosure in online forums. CyberPsychol. Behav. **10**(3), 407–417 (2007)
17. LINE corporation: Communication Application (in Japanese). https://line.me/ja/. Accessed 23 Feb 2023
18. AWS: AWS Lambda. https://aws.amazon.com/jp/lambda/. Accessed 23 Feb 2023
19. AWS: Amazon APIGateway. https://aws.amazon.com/jp/api-gateway/. Accessed 23 Feb 2023
20. AWS: Amazon DynamoDB. https://aws.amazon.com/jp/dynamodb/. Accessed 23 Feb 2023
21. OpenAI: ChatCompletionsAP. https://platform.openai.com/docs/guides/text-generation/chat-completions-api. Accessed 23 Feb 2023

Game-Based Learning for Fostering Digital Literacy in Older Adults: An Intergenerational Approach

Claudilene Perim(✉) ⓘ, Carla Sousa(✉) ⓘ, and Manuel José Damásio(✉) ⓘ

CICANT, Lusófona University, Lisboa, Portugal

{claudilene.perim,carla.patricia.sousa,mjdamasio}@ulusofona.pt

Abstract. This study explores the intersection of intergenerational dynamics, digital literacy, and game-based learning (GBL) within the context of older adults through a systematic literature review on Scopus, Web of Science, Scopus, B-on and ScienceDirect databases was conducted, employing a combination of keywords and terms, including "game-based learning", "digital literacy", "digital inclusion", "digital divide", "intergenerational", "multigenerational", "cross-generational," "older adults", "seniors", "elderly", and "elderly population". A publication date range of 2010–2023 was applied to ensure relevance. The results indicate a scarcity of research at the intersection of GBL using analogue games and intergenerational interactions aimed at improving the digital literacy of older adults and underscore the significant challenges they encounter in their quest for digital inclusion, personal autonomy, and active social engagement. Analysed studies highlight the potential of incorporating intergenerational interactions and GBL in learning contexts to enhance digital literacy among older adults.

Keywords: Intergenerationality · Game-Based Learning · Digital Literacy · Older People · Systematic Literature Review

1 Introduction

In today's interconnected society, technology has become an integral part of daily life, revolutionizing the way we communicate, work, and access information. Over the past two decades, significant progress has been made in technology and in the availability of tech-enabled services to improve the lives of older people [1]. However, this widespread integration of technology also presents a significant challenge to older populations. Many older adults face challenges in today's digitalised society due to the rapid pace of technological advancement and the increasing importance placed on digital literacy [2, 3]. Although there is empirical evidence regarding their instructional effectiveness, a gap exists in addressing populations with specific needs through analogue Game-Based Learning (GBL), which includes older adults [4]. Moreover, an emphasis on intergenerational interactions within this framework contributes an extra dimension of significance by facilitating reciprocal knowledge exchange and cultivating certain intergenerational

Q. Gao and J. Zhou (Eds.): HCII 2024, LNCS 14725, pp. 242–260, 2024.
https://doi.org/10.1007/978-3-031-61543-6_18

solidarity associated with technologies [5]. The context establishes a foundation for investigating the possibilities of utilising GBL, analogue games, and intergenerational approaches as the fundamental elements in augmenting digital inclusion among older adults.

This study conducts a systematic literature review, adhering to the PRISMA methodology [6] to consolidate existing research on the utilization of GBL as a strategy for the development of digital skills by older adults and to highlight the significance of intergenerational interactions and the use of analogue games in this process, aiming to provide valuable insights into the effectiveness and challenges associated with this approach.

1.1 Research Objectives

This study aims to map three socially and scientifically relevant concepts – intergenerationally, digital literacy, and GBL – considering older people's specificities, contexts, and frameworks. In detail, it focuses on three research objectives:

- O1) Investigate the role of intergenerational approaches in facilitating digital inclusion for older adults.
- O2) Highlight the significance of intergenerational interactions in GBL interventions.
- O3) Provide insights into the efficacy of intergenerational approaches and identify obstacles associated with their implementation.

2 Background

The world is experiencing significant demographic shifts, with populations ageing at an unprecedented rate. This trend is particularly pronounced in the European Union (EU), where the median age is projected to increase from 43.7 years in 2019 to 48.2 years by 2050 [7]. The proportion of older people within the EU is expected to rise dramatically, with a more noticeable increase in the very old population (aged 85 years or more), especially among women [7]. This ageing population trend is not confined to the EU but is a global phenomenon, with the number of people aged 60 years and older expected to double to 2.1 billion by 2050 [8].

World population ageing brings to the forefront the need to improve digital literacy among older adults. As technology becomes increasingly integral to daily life, ensuring that older adults possess the necessary digital skills is essential for their social inclusion, access to services, and continued engagement in community and economic activities. Multilateral organizations such as the OECD have stressed the importance of digital inclusion for older adults, suggesting that ensuring they can access and use technology is a foundation for their active, healthy ageing, and for addressing social isolation [9].

Addressing the challenges and opportunities presented by an ageing global population and the digital divide requires interdisciplinary approaches. Policies and programs need to provide accessible, relevant, and engaging digital literacy training tailored to the needs and learning styles of older people that focus on practical and social applications of technology.

2.1   Gaming and Ageing

Games possess a diverse array of characteristics that contribute to their unique potentialities. These include interactivity and goal orientation [10], motivation through failure, and immediate feedback [11]. Additionally, games often necessitate a systematic response to stimuli, require hand-eye coordination, incorporate reinforcement systems, provide opportunities for peer group attention, and offer approval through competition [12].

Considering these characteristics, digital games have emerged as significant tools in facilitating active ageing, particularly concerning cognitive maintenance [13]. Older adults exhibit a preference for action, adventure, and memory games, recognizing digital gaming environments as avenues for self-expression and exploring interpersonal computer-mediated communication [14].

Specifically, the impact of digital games on cognitive functions such as processing speed, working memory, executive functioning, and verbal memory is noteworthy [15]. Beyond cognition, digital media, with a focus on gaming, has shown potential in promoting healthy and active ageing, fostering participation, social interaction, and psychological well-being. Moreover, digital games contribute significantly to digital literacy through sustained engagement with virtual societal dimensions and the utilization of diverse equipment and hardware [16].

Analogue and board games are underexplored in their role in active ageing. However, Pozzi et al. [17] research highlights their potential to slow global cognitive decline and enhance the quality of life for older individuals. Culturally, analogue games play a central role in older adults' daily lives and socialization, constructing meanings and a sense of belonging [18]. Traditional games like dominoes or chess have been particularly noted for their role in protecting against dementia processes [19].

Given this background, it is crucial to consider the extended potential of games in promoting multiple literacies, specifically media and informational literacy [20–22] and digital literacy [23] as previously studied in other demographics, also among older individuals. Integrating GBL strategies tailored to the preferences and cognitive needs of older adults could yield substantial benefits in enhancing cognitive health, social engagement, and overall well-being in ageing populations.

2.2   Intergenerational Approaches, Lifelong Learning, and Digital Literacy

'Lifelong learning is a concept central to UNESCO's work, particularly concerning the Education 2030 Agenda. It emphasizes the integration of learning and living, covering learning activities for all ages and in various contexts—family, school, community, and workplace. This approach aims to meet a wide range of learning needs and styles through formal, non-formal, and informal approaches [24]. Lifelong learning has become indispensable in today's rapidly changing world, where technological advancements and global interconnectedness demand constant adaptation. It is a means for equipping individuals with the skills and knowledge necessary to navigate the complexities of the 21st century. Beyond economic and professional requirements, lifelong learning is important for personal growth, well-being, and fulfilment. It offers opportunities for individuals to pursue their interests, enhance their quality of life, and engage more fully in their communities.

The current trend of population ageing, combined with rapid societal changes due to ICT development, indeed creates a favourable context for intergenerational learning, as individuals from different generations - with unique experiences, knowledge bases, and learning styles - share the same social spaces. This diversity underscores the importance of lifelong learning, a continuous, self-motivated pursuit of knowledge for both personal and professional reasons.

Intergenerational learning involves people from different generations becoming engaged in learning from each other and learning together [25]. The concept of "generation" encompasses a cohort of individuals born and living around the same time, representing "a particular kind of identity of location, embracing related 'age groups' embedded in a historical-social process" [26].

Intergenerational learning plays a fundamental role in enriching lifelong learning, especially among older adults. Sharing wisdom, experiences, and perspectives fosters a deeper understanding and appreciation among different age groups and enhances social cohesion and mutual respect. For older individuals, engaging in intergenerational learning environments can significantly contribute to their sense of belonging and overall well-being.

The integration of digital literacy into intergenerational learning initiatives is particularly significant for older adults. As the digital divide continues to be a challenge, incorporating digital skills into lifelong learning objectives ensures that older generations are not left behind in our increasingly digital world. Through intergenerational learning, younger individuals can share their digital expertise with older adults, empowering them with the skills needed to navigate digital platforms, access information, benefit from public services and stay connected with their communities and loved ones.

3   Method

3.1 Study Eligibility Criteria

The initial criteria for selecting pertinent studies were based on the core topics of the research questions. The primary objective was to incorporate studies that elucidated the application of GBL within intergenerational contexts to enhance the digital proficiency of older adults. Furthermore, the inclusion criteria for the selection process were defined as the following: (1) empirical and theoretical studies; (2) published in a peer-reviewed journal; (3) published in the English Language; and (4) published from the year 2010 up to the latest search date of December 28th, 2023. Book chapters, book reviews, and systematic reviews were excluded from consideration.

The literature search was systematically conducted across electronic databases, including Web of Science (All Collections), ScienceDirect, Scopus and B-on, and the Online Knowledge Library from the National Foundation for Science and Technology of the Portuguese Government. Content indexed by b-on and made available to Portuguese science and technology research institutions cover, on its standard service, publications from the Association for Computing Machinery, American Chemical Society (limited to some institutions), and American Institute of Physics. Annual Reviews, EBSCO (Academic Source, Business Search, ERIC, eBook University Press, LISTA, Teacher Reference Center), Coimbra University Press, Elsevier, Essential Science Indicators (ISI),

IEEE, Sage Premier, Springer, Taylor & Francis, and Web of Science The search was finalized on December 28, 2023, aiming to gather all pertinent publications up to that date from the selected databases.

3.2 Search Strategy

The Boolean queries utilized in the search process were structured as follows: ("game-based learning" OR "game based learning") AND ("digital learning" OR "digital literacy" OR "digital inclusion" OR "digital exclusion" OR "technology" OR "technological learning") AND ("seniors" OR "older adults" OR "elderly" OR "older population") AND ("intergenerational" OR "multigenerational" OR "across generations" OR "cross-generational" OR "age-spanning" OR "intergenerationally"). Synonyms and equivalent terms for keywords were employed to account for variations in terminology, language, and regional differences, thereby broadening the search's scope and depth. Boolean operators and filters were applied as permitted by each database's search engine, focusing on

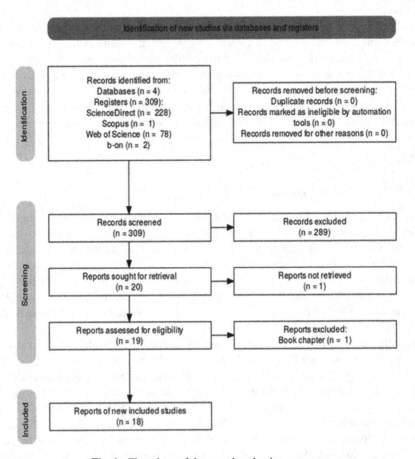

Fig. 1. Flowchart of the sample selection process.

study titles and abstracts. All results from the electronic databases were imported into the RAYYAN Web platform for the subsequent selection process (Fig. 1).

3.3 Study Selection Process

The starting point of the selection process was the use of the RAYYAN platform to identify and eliminate duplicate studies (no duplicates). The next step consisted of screening study titles and abstracts to identify and label the studies as 'included' or 'excluded' in the table according to inclusion and exclusion criteria. This process was conducted by two independent researchers, and differences experienced during the screening were addressed by a joint review session. In summary, the initial screening phase scrutinized 309 studies identified from the database search. Through a consensus-driven process, the researchers agreed to exclude 289 studies and to include 7. Conflicts arose in the evaluation of 13 studies; however, 11 of these were eventually included in the final selection after a joint review session. The final compilation, presented in Table 1, encompasses titles, primary objectives, and an assigned Study ID for each of the 18 selected studies.

Common points among the study´s objectives are centred around themes of intergenerational learning, engagement, and relationships. Several studies explore the dynamics of intergenerational interactions, such as learning between different age groups, the influence of grandparents on grandchildren, and the role of public spaces in fostering intergenerational relationships. Other common themes include the examination of ageing and its representations in various contexts like literature, cinema, and digital games, as well as the application of gamification approaches among older adults. Moving into the second phase of the selection process, the lead investigator conducted a full-text review of the 18 studies preliminarily selected.

Table 1. Summary of selected studies ($n = 18$)

Study ID	Title & Main Objective	
1	Title	"Gamified Money: Exploring the Effectiveness of Gamification in Mobile Payment Adoption among the Silver Generation in China"
	Main Objective	Explore the effectiveness of gamification in promoting mobile payment adoption among older adults in China [27]
2	Title	"Gamification of Digital Literacy for Elder People According to Learning Styles and Polyphasic Activities"
	Main Objective	Enhance digital literacy among older adults through gamified learning approaches [28]
3	Title	"Gerontagogy Toward Intergenerationality: Dialogical Learning Between Children and Elders"

(continued)

Table 1. (*continued*)

Study ID	Title & Main Objective	
	Main Objective	Explore gerontagogy with a focus on intergenerational learning [29]
4	Title	"Constructing a Social Geography of Grandparenthood: A New Focus for Intergenerationality"
	Main Objective	Explore the social geography of grandparenthood in the UK [30]
5	Title	"Intergenerational Language Practices, Linguistic Capital, and Place: The Case of Greek-Cypriot Migrant Families in the UK"
	Main Objective	Examine heritage language practices and transmission across generations in Greek-Cypriot migrant families in the UK [31]
6	Title	"Intergenerationality and Interculturality in Rural Education Experiences"
	Main Objective	Explore intercultural and intergenerational aspects in rural education in Colombia [32]
7	Title	"Aesthetic Social Representations and Concrete Dialogues across Boundaries: Toward Intergenerational CHARACTERization"
	Main Objective	Explore the role of aesthetics in shaping social representations and dialogue across generations [33]
8	Title	"The Potential of Open Public Spaces for Intergenerational Relationships: A Case Study in Santa Cruz de Tenerife, Canary Islands, Spain"
	Main Objective	Investigate the role of public spaces in fostering intergenerational relationships [34]
9	Title	"The View on Aging, Old Age, and Old People that is Conveyed by Children's Books"
	Main Objective	Analyze the representation of ageing in children's literature [35]
10	Title	"Critical reflections from the millennials on the global action against dementia legacy events"
	Main Objective	Offer critical insights and reflections on dementia actions from the perspective of millennials [36]
11	Title	"Cross-generational Companionship: Representations of Ageing in Contemporary French Cinema"
	Main Objective	Analyze representations of ageing and intergenerational relationships in French cinema [37]

(*continued*)

Table 1. (*continued*)

Study ID	Title & Main Objective	
12	Title	"Intergenerational Exchange of Knowledge Skills Values and Practices Between Self-Organized Active Citizens in Maribor, Slovenia"
	Main Objective	Investigate informal intergenerational learning in participatory democracy contexts in Maribor, Slovenia [38]
13	Title	"Transnational Intergenerationalities: Cultural Learning in Polish Migrant Families and Its Implications for Pedagogy"
	Main Objective	Explore the impact of family migration on intergenerational cultural learning among Polish families in Scotland [39]
14	Title	"Grandparents' Resources and Grandchildren's Schooling: Does Grandparental Involvement Moderate the Grandparent Effect?"
	Main Objective	Investigate the influence of grandparents on their grandchildren's educational outcomes and whether grandparental involvement affects this [40]
15	Title	"Growing Pains: Feminisms and Intergenerationality in Digital Games"
	Main Objective	Explore intergenerational and intersectional dynamics in feminist movements within the digital games industry [41]
16	Title	"Keys to the Design of Intergenerational Educational Proposals from an Experience of Physical Activity"
	Main Objective	Examine factors for successful intergenerational engagement through physical activity [42]
17	Title	"Towards a Sustainable Longevity Society: Instrumentalizing Intergenerationality and Human-Centered Design"
	Main Objective	Develop strategies for sustainable societies in the context of increased longevity [43]
18	Title	"Generationality: On Intergenerationality, Transgenerationality, and the 'Generation War'"
	Main Objective	Explore and understand the shifting dynamics of intergenerational relations, particularly in the context of post-Cold War transformations in the economy and society [44]

4   Data Extraction and Analysis

Data were extracted following PRISMA guidelines [6], including study design, sample size, and intervention details – with a particular focus on the contrast between analogue and digital play, research outcomes, and intergenerational elements.

The analysis of the sample was coded to identify the most pertinent analytical categories, including a variety of dimensions, such as the primary objectives of each study, the knowledge field it contributes to, the type of study conducted, the methodological approaches employed, assessment techniques and methods utilized, and demographic information about the subjects, where relevant, with a particular focus on the research outcomes, and on mapping the references to the four critical terms central to this research: GBL, digital literacy, older people, and intergenerationality. Table 2 presents the detailed coding of the 18 papers according to these specific categories. The researchers engaged in a critical discussion of the findings, ensuring a comprehensive understanding and interpretation of the data.

Data analysis reveals that studies in the sample are distributed across seven knowledge areas, with Education and Sociology/Anthropology having the highest representation with four studies (22.2% each). There is a strong focus on qualitative approaches, used in 66.7% ($n = 12$) of studies, with empirical research being the predominant study type with 38.9% ($n = 7$). "Qualitative Interviews and Observations" was the assessment method used in 38.9% ($n = 7$) of the studies. Focus groups and surveys mentioned in one study (5.6%) are among the least frequent methods. The term "Intergenerational" or equivalent terms are highly referenced, appearing in 17 studies (94.4%), while GBL/Gamification or equivalent terms appear in 11.1% of the studies ($n = 2$). Very few studies focus exclusively on a single age group, with "Older Adults" being the least mentioned in one study (5.6%), while multi-generational studies are the most represented in terms of age group classification, with five studies (27.8%). A significant majority of studies do not specify subject gender, or it's not applicable, accounting for 14 studies (77.8%). These highlights suggest a strong focus on qualitative, empirical research with a significant emphasis on intergenerational themes.

Table 2. Characteristics of the studies in the sample.

Category	Classification	$n - \%$
Main Knowledge Area	Education	4–22.2%
	Sociology/Anthropology	4–22.2%
	Media and Cultural Studies	2–11.1%
	Technology and Digital Studies	2–11.1%
	Social Gerontology	3–16.7%
	Global Health	1–5.6%
	Psychology	3–16.7%
Study Type	Empirical	7–38.9%
	Theoretical	5–27.8%
	Descriptive-Exploratory	1–5.6%
	Qualitative	5–27.8%
Methodological Approach	Qualitative	12–66.7%
	Quantitative	2–11.1%
	Mixed	1–5.6%

(*continued*)

Table 2. (*continued*)

Category	Classification	$n - \%$
Techniques/Assessment Methods	Qualitative Interviews and Observations	7–38.9%
	Theoretical Analysis and Model Development	4–22.2%
	Quantitative Techniques	2–11.1%
	Content and Media Analysis	2–11.1%
	Game-based/Gamification Techniques	1–5.6%
	Other Methods	2–11.1%
References to "Game-based Learning" or equivalent terms	Yes	2–11.1%
	No	16–88.9%
References to Digital Literacy or equivalent terms	Yes	2–11.1%
	No	16–88.9%
References to "Intergenerational" or equivalent terms	Yes	17–94.4%
	No	1–5.6%
Subjects - Gender	Male Only	1–5.6%
	Female Only	0–0.0%
	Both Male and Female	3–16.7%
	Not Specified/Not Applicable	14–77.8%
Subjects - Age Group	Older Adults Only	2–11.1%
	Adults	2–11.1%
	Multi-generational (Including Various Age Groups)	5–27.8%
	Children and Parents	1–5.6%
	Not Specified/Not applicable	8–44.4%

5   Results

Detailed results are systematized in Table 3, covering the emerging themes and the diverse contributions of each article, ranging from the impact of gamification on digital adoption among older adults to the broader social and cultural implications of inter-generational learning and engagement. "Contributions" refer to the focus area and the most relevant findings and outcomes for each study. "Emerging themes" depicts each study´s key thematic area (intergenerationality, GBL, digital literacy). Refer to Table 1 for matching Study IDs to the respective study title.

Key aspects covered by the studies include the importance of gamification, project-based learning, cultural and historical integration into learning, geographical and social considerations in learning environments, and the role of family dynamics in educational outcomes. Best practices related to those identified across these studies emphasize adapting learning to participant abilities, leveraging community and cultural knowledge, fostering mutual respect and shared experiences, and the significance of educator roles in facilitating intergenerational interactions.

These insights suggest the need for a multidisciplinary approach to designing effective intergenerational learning programs that are engaging, culturally relevant, and supportive of diverse learning needs.

Table 3. Contribution and emerging themes of the sample of studies.

Study ID	Contribution	Emerging Themes
1	Understanding gamification's role in technology adoption among older adults, highlighting its potential to improve digital inclusion and literacy in an ageing society [27]	GBL Digital Literacy
2	Explores an innovative approach to enhance digital literacy among older adults through gamification. It examines how familiar childhood games can be adapted to teach digital concepts, leveraging the diverse learning styles of older adults [28]	GBL Intergenerationality
3	Explores the importance of dialogical learning between generations, showcasing that such interactions lead to mutual growth and understanding and can enhance educational outcomes and societal cohesion [29]	Intergenerationality
4	Explores the construction of grandparent identities through a geographical lens, emphasizing the relational geographies of age and intergenerationality. Study finds that the identities of grandfathers are not static but are dynamically constructed through interactions within various spaces and relationships [30]	Intergenerationality
5	The research highlights the importance of language as cultural capital and its impact on the sense of belonging and identity among migrant families, emphasizing the need for supportive community and educational practices to facilitate heritage language maintenance and cultural continuity [31]	Intergenerationality
6	The study challenges traditional educational policies by prioritizing internal intercultural strengthening and ensuring that older community members have a central role in educational decision-making. The research emphasizes the importance of incorporating youth as knowledge receivers and active participants in the educational process [32]	Intergenerationality
7	Highlights how representations, especially in intergenerational settings, can bridge subjective and collective experiences, enhancing understanding and empathy across age groups. Findings include the identification of aesthetic and social representations as a powerful tool for enhancing understanding and dialogue between generations [33]	Intergenerationality

(*continued*)

Table 3. (*continued*)

Study ID	Contribution	Emerging Themes
8	Explores how open public spaces can promote intergenerational connections. Results indicate that these spaces hold potential for such interactions, despite of factors like usage patterns, preferences, and generational perceptions. Emphasizes the importance of overcoming stereotypes and nurturing mutual respect and understanding for meaningful intergenerational relationships [34]	Intergenerationality
9	Investigates social representations of ageing in literature and their impact on health education. Identifies two main themes: biological ageing and psychosocial ageing. Emphasizes the role of children's and young adult literature in enhancing educational approaches to ageing positively [35]	Intergenerationality
10	Findings underscore the value of intergenerational collaboration in developing effective strategies against dementia. The paper suggests that engaging younger generations in discussions and research related to dementia can lead to innovative solutions and changes in how dementia is approached. It emphasizes the need for diverse perspectives in the global dialogue on dementia and advocates for the inclusion of younger people to ensure the sustainability of efforts against the disease [36]	Intergenerationality
11	Examines recent French films that portray ageing in a positive light, challenging traditional stereotypes. It focuses on how intergenerational relationships in these films offer a counter-narrative to the societal exclusion of older adults, suggesting that such companionships can lead to empowering and diverse models of ageing identities [37]	Intergenerationality
12	Examines informal learning across age groups, especially among older individuals in self-organized gatherings in Maribor, Slovenia. Results highlight increased intergenerational cooperation, enhancing social awareness and harmony, and emphasizing the role of informal learning in civic engagement [38]	Intergenerationality
13	Investigates cultural learning in Polish migrant families in Scotland, emphasizing intergenerational exchanges and children's cultural identity development. Results show strong intergenerational learning within migrant families, with children often serving as cultural mediators for their parents. Highlights the vital role of children in cultural adaptation, advocating for educational and community efforts to consider these transnational intergenerational interactions in supporting migrant children's integration and learning [39]	Internenerationality

(*continued*)

Table 3. (*continued*)

Study ID	Contribution	Emerging Themes
14	Investigates whether grandparents' involvement moderates their direct effect on grandchildren's educational achievements beyond parental resources. The study finds no direct main effect of grandparents' resources on grandchildren's educational attainment, nor does it observe any moderating effect based on the strength of the grandparent-grandchild tie, challenging the assumption of a significant direct grandparental influence on grandchildren's education [40]	Intergenerationality
15	Explores the challenges and dynamics within feminist movements in the digital gaming industry, particularly focusing on the intergenerational tensions and collaboration among women game designers and community members. It investigates how these interactions reflect broader issues of feminism, intersectionality, and activism within the context of digital games, analysing the impact of generational differences on feminist strategies and objectives within this field [41]	Intergenerationality
16	Focuses on identifying key factors for designing intergenerational educational proposals based on an orienteering sports activity by exploring the resistances and difficulties in intergenerational relationships. Findings emphasize the importance of clear objectives, awareness of educational goals among participants, and the role of educators in facilitating these interactions. The study provides recommendations for designing effective intergenerational educational activities that go beyond superficial engagement [42]	Intergenerationality
17	Focuses on leveraging intergenerational relationships and human-centred design for creating sustainable communities. The study emphasizes the importance of collaboration, respect, reciprocity, and responsibility in fostering sustainable cities and communities, outlining strategies for engaging all generations in contributing to societal development and highlighting the need for inclusive, participatory approaches that value the contributions of both older and younger generations [43]	Intergenerationality
18	Explore and understand the shifting dynamics of intergenerational relations, particularly in the context of post-Cold War transformations in economy and society [44]	Intergenerationality

5.1 GBL with Older Adults

Study ID 1 discusses the use of gamification specifically targeting older adults, referred to as the "Silver Generation," focusing on the effectiveness of gamification in mobile payment adoption among this demographic in China. It explores how gamified cultural practices, like the gifting of red packets, can promote technology acceptance among older adults, integrating digital technology with cultural traditions to encourage the adoption of new technologies by older adults. This indicates a significant interest in applying gamification to engage with intergenerational settings and specifically address the needs and preferences of the older population [27].

The second paper specifically addresses the use of gamification for digital literacy among older adults, based on learning styles and polyphasic activities. It explores a pedagogical methodology developed within the SIG project at MediaLab Prado, which employs gamification of didactic processes closely linked to learning styles. This methodology is founded on project-based activities that incorporate familiar childhood games to help older adults understand new digital processes. The approach aims to achieve gamified literacy without directly using new technologies as educational support, focusing on enhancing digital literacy in older people by adapting learning to their abilities and incorporating gamified elements [28].

5.2 Intergenerationally as an Intervention Path

Each study, with its distinct emphasis and by approaching intergenerational interactions in a variety of contexts, contributes significantly to expanding our comprehension of intergenerational relationships' depth and value, highlighting the necessity for diverse and interdisciplinary methods to leverage their benefits fully. These investigations are categorized based on their approach to intergenerationality as follows:

- Educational and cultural exchanges [29, 31, 32, 39, 42]: Five studies underline the mutual benefits of such interactions, enhancing understanding, identity, and social cohesion. They focus on the educational and cultural exchanges between generations, emphasizing dialogical learning, the importance of heritage language, and the role of grandparents in education.
- Spatial and social dynamics [30, 34, 40]: Three approaches point out the potential of physical spaces and social constructs in enhancing relationships between generations. They examine the spatial and social aspects of intergenerational relationships, including the role of public spaces in fostering intergenerational interactions and the social geography of grandparenthood.
- Media and social representation [33, 35, 37, 41]: Four studies discuss the impact of these representations on societal perceptions of ageing and its potential to foster positive intergenerational dynamics and explore how ageing and intergenerational relationships are portrayed in media, such as children's literature, digital games, and cinema.
- Collaborative approaches to societal challenges [36, 38, 43, 44]: Four other studies advocate for inclusive, participatory approaches that leverage the strengths of both younger and older generations. They highlight the role of intergenerational collaboration in addressing a broad range of societal changes and issues, such as dementia care, sustainability, and other socio-economic challenges.

6 Discussion

Older adults' adoption of technology is influenced by personal and social factors, functional features, and the ease of technology access or acquisition. Challenges include limited technology access, usability concerns, digital skill gaps, lack of social support, and feelings of digital exclusion [45]. Previous studies have shown how intergenerational relationships, particularly with younger family members, can aid older adults in adapting to new technologies and overcoming these obstacles [46]. This emphasizes the importance of intergenerational support in enhancing technology use and benefiting older adults Similarly, and answering O1, the narrative constructed through the systematized review of collected studies underscores the relevance of cross-generational dialogue in fostering understanding, enriching educational practices, and addressing societal challenges. Additionally, the sample points to innovative collaboration strategies that leverage the strengths of different generations to address issues like dementia care [36] and environmental sustainability [43].

From the perspective of O2, the two papers exploring GBL and gamification [27, 28] share a focus on enhancing educational experiences through interactive methods. They both recognize the potential of these strategies to make learning more engaging and enjoyable. The first [27] explores the theoretical foundations and practical applications of game-based learning, while the second [28] explores how familiar games can foster intergenerational interactions through their universal appeal, ease of access, and the integration of elements. This type of game often features competitive elements or collaborative challenges that encourage teamwork and communication across generations.

Within the scope of O3, previous research reports positive outcomes of intergenerational programs, including improved understanding and reduced stereotypes between generations, enhanced social networks, and mutual learning opportunities [47]. It identifies benefits such as improved well-being, cognitive and social engagement for older adults, and adolescent identity formation and skill development [48]. However, it also highlights obstacles such as logistical challenges in coordinating between different age groups, potential resistance from participants or institutions due to preconceived notions, and the need for tailored program designs to meet diverse needs and ensure meaningful engagement [47].

Furthermore, the synthesis of findings underscores the benefits of intergenerational interactions for both individual and social development, the importance of challenging stereotypes, and the potential of such interactions to enhance educational outcomes and social cohesion. The successful implementation of intergenerational methodologies faces multiple challenges, including cultural conventions, linguistic disparities, societal attitudes, and the perpetuation of negative stereotypes that collectively marginalize older people, facilitating age segregation and obstructing meaningful intergenerational exchanges [29, 37–39]. Overcoming these obstacles demands an approach that recognizes that intergenerational learning is more complex than simply bringing together individuals of different ages. Such approaches must leverage intentional design and facilitation to adapt interactions to the needs and interests of all age groups and promote awareness among younger participants about the value of intergenerational cooperation [38].

7 Conclusion

Given the rapid pace of technological advancement and the digitalization of daily activities, the shift of older adults towards a more digital lifestyle necessitates not only the initial acquisition but also the sustained mastery of digital skills, which highlights the indispensable role of the continuous support from the various social stakeholders for the successful adoption and effective utilization of technology by older adults.

The analysed studies emphasize the benefits of intergenerational interactions and GBL for enhancing digital literacy among older people. By leveraging educational and cultural exchanges, spatial and social dynamics, and collaborative approaches, interventions and initiatives related to older adults can foster environments where this population segment feels supported and engaged in learning digital skills. Incorporating game-based elements can make learning more enjoyable and relevant, potentially reducing the technology anxiety often experienced by older generations. Moreover, utilizing intergenerational interactions as a medium for education allows for the transfer of knowledge and skills in a socially enriching and supportive context, capitalizing on the diverse perspectives and experiences of different generations. This approach not only aids in developing digital literacy but also strengthens social bonds and mutual understanding across age groups.

The insights resulting from the investigated studies highlight the potential of incorporating intergenerational interactions and GBL in learning contexts to enhance digital literacy among older adults. However, the specific focus on combining intergenerational interactions with GBL for this purpose remains underexplored. This gap presents a significant opportunity for future research to investigate effective strategies and develop targeted interventions that could significantly benefit digital literacy initiatives for the older population, ultimately contributing to their inclusion in our rapidly digitalizing world.

Acknowledgements. This research was funded by Fundação para a Ciência e a Tecnologia, I.P., under CICANT R&D Unit, grant UIDB/05260/2020 (https://doi.org/https://doi.org/10.54499/UIDB/05260/2020).

Disclosure of Interests.. The authors have no competing interests to declare that are relevant to the content of this article.

References

1. Coughlin, J.F.: The fourth wave of technology and aging: Policy innovation to ensure equity and Inclusion. Public Policy Aging Rep. **30**(4), 138–141 (2020). https://doi.org/10.1093/ppar/praa032
2. Lopez, K.J., Tong, C., Whate, A., Boger, J.: "It's a whole new way of doing things": the digital divide and leisure as resistance in a time of physical distance. World Leisure J. **63**(3), 281–300 (2021). https://doi.org/10.1080/16078055.2021.1973553
3. Schreurs, K., Quan-Haase, A., Martin, K.: Problematizing the digital literacy paradox in the context of older adults' ICT use: aging, media discourse, and self-determination. Can. J. Commun. **42**(2), 359–377 (2017)
4. Sousa, C., et al.: Playing at the school table: systematic literature review of board, tabletop, and other analog game-based learning approaches. Front. Psychol. **14** (2023).https://doi.org/10.3389/fpsyg.2023.1160591

5. Amaral, I., Flores, A.M., Antunes, E., Brites, M.J.: Intergenerational digitally mediated relationships: how portuguese young adults interact with family members over 65+. In: Gao, Q., Zhou, J. (eds.) HCII 2022: Human Aspects of IT for the Aged Population. Technology in Everyday Living, vol. 13331, pp. 335–348. Springer, Cham (2022). https://doi.org/10.1007/978-3-031-05654-3_23

6. Page, M.J., et al.: The PRISMA 2020 statement: An updated guide-line for reporting systematic reviews. British Med. J. **372**, n71 (2021). https://doi.org/10.1136/bmj.n71

7. Eurostat.: Ageing Europe – statistics on population developments. Eurostat - Estatistics Explained. Retrieved January 31, 2024 (2020). https://ec.europa.eu/eurostat/statistics-explained/index.php?title=Ageing_Europe_-_statistics_on_population_developments

8. World Health Organization: Ageing and health. Retrieved January 31, 2024 (2022). https://www.who.int/news-room/fact-sheets/detail/ageing-and-health

9. OECD: Declaration on a Trusted. OECD, Sustainable and Inclusive Digital Future (2023)

10. Costikyan, G.: I have no words & I must design: toward a critical vocabulary for games. In: Mäyrä, F. (Ed.), Proceedings of Computer Games and Digital Cultures Conference, pp. 9–33. Tampere University Press (2002)

11. Boyle, E., et al.: An update to the systematic literature review of empirical evidence of the impacts and outcomes of computer games and serious games. Comput. Educ. **94**, 178–192 (2016). https://doi.org/10.1016/j.compedu.2015.11.003

12. Chandra, S., Sharma, G., Salam, A.A., Jha, D., Mittal, A.P.: Playing action video games a key to cognitive enhancement. Procedia Comput. Sci. **84**, 115–122 (2016). https://doi.org/10.1016/j.procs.2016.04.074

13. Vale Costa, L., Veloso, A.: The gamer's soul never dies: review of digital games for an active ageing. In: 2015 10th Iberian Conference on Information Systems and Technologies (CISTI) (2015). https://doi.org/10.1109/cisti.2015.7170614

14. Vale Costa, L., Veloso, A.I.: Factors influencing the adoption of video games in late adulthood. Int. J. Technol. Human Interact. **12**(1), 35–50 (2016). https://doi.org/10.4018/ijthi.2016010103

15. Bonnechère, B., Langley, C., Sahakian, B.J.: The use of commercial computerised cognitive games in older adults: a meta-analysis. Sci. Rep. **10**(1) (2020). https://doi.org/10.1038/s41598-020-72281-3

16. Regalado, F., Ortet, C.P., Vale Costa, L., Santos, C., Veloso, A.I.: Assessing older adults' perspectives on digital game-related strategies to foster active and healthy ageing. Media Commun. **11**(3), 88–100 (2023). https://doi.org/10.17645/mac.v11i3.6796

17. Pozzi, F.E., Appollonio, I., Ferrarese, C., Tremolizzo, L.: Can traditional board games prevent or slow down cognitive impairment? A systematic review and meta-analysis. J. Alzheimer's Disease **95**(3), 829–845 (2023). https://doi.org/10.3233/jad-230473

18. Hoppes, S., Wilcox, T., Graham, G.: Meanings of play for older adults. Phys. Occupational Therapy Geriatrics **18**(3), 57–68 (2001). https://doi.org/10.1080/j148v18n03_04

19. Lillo-Crespo, M., Forner-Ruiz, M., Riquelme-Galindo, J., Ruiz-Fernández, D., García-Sanjuan, S.: Chess practice as a protective factor in dementia. Int. J. Environ. Res. Public Health **16**(12), 2116 (2019). https://doi.org/10.3390/ijerph16122116

20. Costa, C., Tyner, K., Henriques, S., Sousa, C.: Game creation in youth media and information literacy education. Int. J. Game-Based Learn. **8**(2), 1–13 (2018). https://doi.org/10.4018/ijgbl.2018040101

21. DeJong, S.: Playing with fake news: state of fake news video games. Int. J. Games Soc. Impact **1**(1), 94–111 (2023). https://doi.org/10.24140/ijgsi.v1.n1.05

22. Encheva, M., Tammaro, A.M., Kumanova, A.: Games to improve students information literacy skills. Int. Inform. Lib. Rev. **52**(2), 130–138 (2020). https://doi.org/10.1080/10572317.2020.1746024

23. Costa, C., Sousa, C., Rogado, J., Henriques, S.: Playing digital security. Int. J. Game-Based Learn. **7**(3), 11–25 (2017). https://doi.org/10.4018/ijgbl.2017070102
24. United Nations (2022). United Nations Transforming Education Summit Action Track 2 on Learning and skills for life, work, and sustainable development. Summary key recommendation. United Nations
25. DG Education and Culture (2012). Learning for Active Ageing and Intergenerational Learning: Final Report. European Commission
26. Mannheim, K.: The Problem of Generations. In: Kecskemeti, P. (ed.) Essays on the Sociology of Knowledge: Collected Works, vol. 5, pp. 276–322. Routledge (1952)
27. Wong, D., Liu, H., Meng-Lewis, Y., Sun, Y., Zhang, Y.: Gamified money: exploring the effectiveness of gamification in mobile payment adoption among the silver generation in China. Inf. Technol. People **35**(1), 281–315 (2022). https://doi.org/10.1108/ITP-09-2019-0456
28. Ranilla Rodríguez, M.: Gamificación de la alfabetización digital en mayores según los estilos de aprendizaje y actividades polifásicas. Revista de estilos de aprendizaje = J. Learn. Styles **11**(22), 179–215 (2018)
29. Boulanger, D., Albert, I., Marsico, G.: Gerontagogy toward intergenerationality: dialogical learning between children and elders. Integr. Psychol. Behav. Sci. **54**(2), 269–285 (2020). https://doi.org/10.1007/s12124-020-09522-7
30. Tarrant, A.: Constructing a social geography of grandparenthood: a new focus for inter-generationality. Area **42**(2), 190–197 (2010). https://doi.org/10.1111/j.1475-4762.2009.00920.x
31. Kallis, G., Yarwood, R.: Intergenerational language practices, linguistic capital and place: The case of greek-cypriot migrant families in the UK. Children's Geographies **20**(6), 931–943 (2021). https://doi.org/10.1080/14733285.2021.2003302
32. Posada Escobar, J.J., Carrero Romero, S.A.: Intergenerationality and interculturality in rural education experiences. Praxis Saber **13**(33), 105–120 (2022)
33. Boulanger, D.: Aesthetic social representations and concrete dialogues across boundaries: toward intergenerational CHARACTERization. Cult. Psychol. **26**(4), 778–802 (2020). https://doi.org/10.1177/1354067X19888198
34. Delgado-Acosta, C.R., Calero-Martín, C.G., González-Bencomo, H.: Potencialitat dels espais públics oberts per a les relacions intergeneracionals. Un estudi de cas a la ciutat de Santa Cruz de Tenerife (Canàries, Espanya). Documents d'anàlisi geogràfica, **62**(1), 5–25 (2016)
35. Ferreira, C.P.D.S., et al.: A visão do envelhecimento, da velhice e do idoso veiculada por livros infanto-juvenis. Saúde e Sociedade **24**, 1061–1075 (2015)
36. Newman, K., Booi, L.: Critical reflections from the millennials on the global action against dementia legacy events. Quality Ageing Older Adults **16**(3), 177–182 (2015). https://doi.org/10.1108/QAOA-10-2014-0026
37. Günther, R.: Cross-generational companionship: representations of ageing in contemporary French cinema. Fr. Cult. Stud. **26**(4), 439–447 (2015). https://doi.org/10.1177/0957155815597425
38. Krasovec, S.J., Gregoric, M.: Intergenerational exchange of knowledge, skills, values and practices between self-organized active citizens in Maribor. Slovenia. Aust. J. Adult Learn. **57**(3), 401–420 (2017)
39. Sime, D., Pietka-Nykaza, E.: Transnational intergenerationalities: cultural learning in Polish migrant families and its implications for pedagogy. Lang. Intercultural Commun. **15**(2), 208–223 (2015). https://doi.org/10.1080/14708477.2014.993324
40. Bol, T., Kalmijn, M.: Grandparents' resources and grandchildren's schooling: does grandparental involvement moderate the grandparent effect? Soc. Sci. Res. **55**, 155–170 (2016). https://doi.org/10.1016/j.ssresearch.2015.09.011

41. Harvey, A., Fisher, S.: Growing pains: feminisms and intergenerationality in digital games. Fem. Media Stud. **16**(4), 92–106 (2019). https://doi.org/10.1080/14680777.2016.1193295

42. Becerril-González, R., Bores-Calle, N.: Claves para el diseño de propuestas educativas inter-generacionales a partir de una experiencia de actividad física. Ágora para la Educación Física y el Deporte **21**, 111–124 (2019). https://doi.org/10.24197/aefd.0.2019.111-124

43. Barone, E.: Towards a sustainable longevity society: instrumentalizing intergenerationality and human-centered design. Esic Market Econ. Bus. J. **52**(2), 403–425 (2021). https://doi.org/10.2139/ssrn.3788868

44. Comaroff, J., Comaroff, J.: Generationality: on intergenerationality, transgenerationality, and the 'generation war.' Monist **106**(2), 165–180 (2023). https://doi.org/10.1093/monist/onad005

45. Lee, C., Coughlin, J.F.: PERSPECTIVE: Older adults' adoption of technology: an integrated approach to identifying determinants and barriers. J. Prod. Innov. Manag. **32**(5), 747–759 (2015). https://doi.org/10.1111/jpim.12176

46. Freeman, S., et al.: Intergenerational effects on the impacts of technology use in later life: Insights from an international, multi-site study. Int. J. Environ. Res. Public Health **17**(16), 5711 (2020)

47. Krzeczkowska, A., Spalding, D.M., McGeown, W.J., Gow, A.J., Carlson, M.C., Nicholls, L.A.B.: A systematic review of the impacts of intergenerational engagement on older adults' cognitive, social, and health outcomes. Ageing Res. Rev. **71**, 101400 (2021). https://doi.org/10.1016/j.arr.2021.101400

48. Webster, M., Norwood, K., Waterworth, J., Leavey, G.: Effectiveness of intergenerational exchange programs between adolescents and older adults: a systematic review. J. Intergenerational Relationships (2023). https://doi.org/10.1080/15350770.2023.2267532

Game-Based Solutions for Impacting Digital Competences in Aged Populations: Insights from an Empathetic Workshop

Francisco Regalado(✉) ⬥, Carlos Santos ⬥, and Ana Isabel Veloso ⬥

DigiMedia, Department of Communication and Art, University of Aveiro, Aveiro, Portugal
{fsfregalado,carlossantos,aiv}@ua.pt

Abstract. The growing ubiquity of Information and Communication Technologies and the lack of older adults' digital competences created new challenges and research opportunities. Used to promote the acquisition of knowledge and deeply engage in learning activities, games are a potential medium to be explored. So far, research studies have mainly focused on cybersecurity and younger generations. Tapping into an underexplored research field and leveraging on the DigComp 2.2. framework, this research reports on a two-part workshop with eight experts in the fields of games, digital technologies, digital competences, and ageing. Its aim was to thoroughly delve into this underexplored research field, crafting game mechanics that not only consider the target audience but also directly respond to the areas outlined by DigComp. The results show six new game solutions, such as (i) identifying phishing emails and malware threats, (ii) assessing the authenticity of news items, (iii) acting as hackers to understand and create stronger passwords, (iv) optimizing search queries through interactive story search, (v) interpreting error messages, and (vi) navigating a simulated social media platform with persona-based rewards. Therefore, the range of areas to be explored is expanded, including a wider variety of audiences and new solutions to be implemented. Moreover, the identified game offers practical tools for enhancing digital competences among older populations, and provide a roadmap for future research in designing empathetic digital solutions. Overall, this research highlights the unexplored potential at the intersection of these research fields, paving the way for future developments.

Keywords: Digital Games · Older Adults · Digital Competences · Empathetic Design

1 Introduction

Information and Communication Technologies (ICT) have been assuming an increasingly pervasive role in everyday life [1, 2], propelled by the persistent pace of global digitization [3]. However, this evolution has yet to occur evenly. In fact, despite the numerous advantages and benefits that these technologies may offer [4, 5], older adults are still a demographic group that has not mastered ICT yet [6, 7] and, therefore, lacks digital competences as outlined by the European Commission [8]. The latter, as a way

Q. Gao and J. Zhou (Eds.): HCII 2024, LNCS 14725, pp. 261–274, 2024.
https://doi.org/10.1007/978-3-031-61543-6_19

of addressing the need to understand what digital competences are and to help citizens engage confidently, critically, and safely with digital technologies, created DigComp 2.2 - The Digital Competence Framework for Citizen [9].

In an apparently antagonistic way, digital games are a potential avenue for bridging this gap by facilitating engagement with digital technologies [10]. These games offer opportunities to overcome new challenges [11], interact with other realities, and stimulate learning new knowledge and developing cognitive skills [12, 13]. With their increasing popularity among older audiences [14], these games represent a promising frontier for exploring novel solutions to impact older adults' digital competences.

Nonetheless, current research developments focus highly on cybersecurity [15–18], or younger generations [19, 20], but none of them intersects all the aspects mentioned above. Therefore, a gap in the literature was identified – *i.e.*, research studies that explore digital competences in the context of digital games while targeting older adults.

Therefore, due to the will to start exploring this topic, this research aims to bridge this identified gap and pave the way for the next steps in applied research to build a functional prototype. The workshop method was selected, as it offers a platform to assist researchers in recognizing and delving into pertinent factors within a specific domain, while facilitating comprehension of intricate work and knowledge processes reinforced by technology [21]. Overall, it can be a space where creativity is stimulated, and new ideas are built.

The use of this methodology to build and assess new digital products has been used in various contexts – *e.g.*, (i) augmented-reality (AR) in automotive human-computer interaction (HCI), while tackling issues and practical scenarios of AR in future mobility [22]; (ii) assess a prototype for supporting social interaction between refugees and non-governmental organizations [23]; or (iii) comprehend cross-cultural teams could generate more creative ideas using a design thinking methodology [24]. Moreover, it is recommended to establish an empathetic relationship whenever targeting a product to a specific audience [25, 26].

One of the possible strategies to stimulate empathy is to create personas. In fact, there are several research studies that focus on developing empathetic personas for developing new products [26–28], and some aimed at aged audiences [29–31]. Thus, it is possible to establish the theoretical background that underpins the next chapter describing the construction and application of the workshop. The section that follow describe the results, their discussion, and the main conclusions and takeaways from this study.

2   Methods and Materials

To address the aforementioned objective – i.e., developing digital games to impact older adults' digital competences - a workshop was conducted by three researchers on 24 October 2023. In particular, this workshop was conducted due to the lack of research studies integrating DigComp 2.2 framework into gaming solutions for older audiences. As mentioned in the introductory chapter, the workshop method was selected for its ability to provide researchers with a platform to recognize and delve into pertinent factors within a specific domain, fostering comprehension of complex research subjects and knowledge processes [21].

2.1 Participants' Profile

Firstly, a purposive sample [32] of eight (n = 8) experts were recruited and evenly distributed across two groups (Group 1 – G1, and Group 2 – G2) with three tiers – *i.e.*, Ph.D. students, professors, and technicians – spanning four fields of expertise – *i.e.*, ageing studies, digital competences, game studies, and ICT. For a comprehensive breakdown, please refer to Table 1.

Table 1. Distribution of the three types of participants by fields of expertise and workshop groups (N = 8).

			Ageing studies	Digital Competences	Game studies	ICT
Professor	A	G2	V		V	V
	B	G1	V	V		V
	C	G2		V		V
	D	G1			V	V
Technician	A	G1	V			
	B	G2	V			
Ph.D. Student	A	G2		V		V
	B	G1			V	V

Note: the cells marked in green with a 'V' mean that the participant is a specialist in that field

2.2 Workshop Methodology: Integrating DigComp 2.2 Framework into Gaming Solutions for Older Adults

Upon the selection of the participants and group creation, the two-hour workshop was divided into two main parts. Part 1 centered on empathetically crafting an older adult character, considering four aspects: (i) personality, (ii) foundational life elements, (iii) appearance, and (iv) path and conflicts. While this paper doesn't focus on this initial part, it significantly influenced the ability to create empathetic solutions for this aged audience during the subsequent part. Part 2 involved leveraging the previously created character to brainstorm and conceptualize a game strategy – *cf.*, Fig. 1.

This strategy addressed prompt-based challenges aligned with DigComp 2.2, as outlined in Table 2. The pre-selection of these prompts was based on cross-referencing the observed requirements of older adults [e.g., 33–35] with questions derived from the areas of DigComp 2.2 developed by Lucas and colleagues [36]. It's important to note that each of these prompts was selected randomly by each group, with no opportunity for the same prompt to be chosen twice.

At the end of the workshop, the groups presented their personas and the game solutions they had created, linking them to the selected prompts.

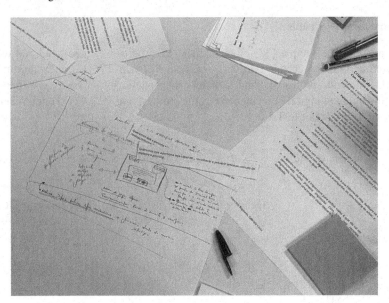

Fig. 1. Example of a brainstorming exercise for a game-based solution.

Table 2. Prompt-based challenges aligned with DigComp 2.2.

Prompts	
We want the character to be able to…	(1)… create a strong and secure password
	(2)… recognize and prevent phishing threats
	(3)… keep software and applications up to date for device security
	(4)… know what types of information can be shared online
	(5)… successfully search for information on search engines
	(6)… discern fake news/information from real news/information
	(7)… identify and report unreliable sources of information on social networks
	(8)… carry out online financial transactions safely, such as bill payments or money transfers
	(9)… engage in productive and respectful discussions on social platforms
	(10)… review and update privacy settings on social media accounts
	(11)… react appropriately to system errors and other pop-up messages

2.3   Data Collection and Analysis Procedures

In both parts of the workshop, data was collected resorting to field notes systematized in an observation table. Participants had the opportunity to organize their ideas in paper form – in particular, during Part 1, they used a toolkit for empathetic character design [37] with targeted questions that allowed them to write down the results of their discussions; and, in Part 2, as illustrated in Fig. 1, white sheets and post-its were distributed, emphasizing brainstorming and the design of low-fi visual solutions.

When analyzing the results, a comprehensive review of the collected field notes and participants' written records was undertaken. This was done by identifying common themes and then interpreting these patterns in the light of the study's goals. The notes were then categorized into two major themes with respective subdivisions: (i) empathetic senior persona; and (ii) game-based solution - divided into presented solutions, game mechanics, and digital skills. Through a careful examination of the findings, commonalities and patterns across various solutions emerged – with particular emphasis on Part 2. The following section describes the results of this research in detail.

3   Results

The following sections present the results of the conducted workshop divided into the two parts mentioned above. However, it is important to emphasize that the detail and depth of Part 1 are not the focus of this article - it only provides context and support for Part 2.

3.1   Phase 1 – Creating an Empathetic Senior Persona

Although it is not the main focus of this paper, creating an empathetic senior persona is important for laying the foundations for the game solutions designed [31, 38, 39]. Thus, each group developed its persona. In particular, group 1 (G1) created a 78-year-old lady called Fernanda – a super organized, productive, energetic, outgoing person who loves philosophical discussions, is a little cold or selfish, and has a sense of superiority. In fact, she finds it difficult to relate with others. Her current companion is her cat, Whiskers. Figure 2 (a) shows the visual representation chosen by Group 1 from their persona's appearance.

Similarly, Group 2 (G2) created a 82-year-old lady called Amélia Maria – a very typical Portuguese name. Amélia's main goal is to be able to live to 100 years old with quality of life. She dreams of continuing to support young actors and creating the status of an actor's career, has difficulty externalizing her emotions, had a hard time while being the daughter of a couple with eight children, has only the fourth grade of education, and likes good wine, music, and books. Similarly, to G1, G2 also visually represented their persona – please refer to Fig. 2 (b).

3.2   Phase 2 – Designing Digital Game-Based Solutions

Upon analyzing the field notes and the participants' written records, it was possible to identify solutions that address some of the prompts outlined in Table 2 – i.e., prompts

(a)   (b)

Fig. 2. Representations of the persona's appearance created by Group 1 - (a), and Group 2 - (b).

1, 2, 5, 6, 10, and 11. The synthesized results revealed recurring themes, indicating that certain strategies were interconnected across multiple prompts. The following is a sum-mary of the solutions presented.

Firstly, cybersecurity-focused solutions emerged, directly related to prompts 1, 2, and 6 – *i.e.*, we want the character to be able to "create a strong and secure password", "recognize and prevent phishing threats", and "discern fake news/information from real news/information", respectively. The first solution (S1 - G1) was branded as 'SPAM' – cf. Fig. 3, which emphasizes the identification of phishing emails and malware threats. Players must engage in an email inbox simulation, distinguishing between legitimate emails and those containing potential threats – i.e., potential phishing situations or containing malware. The player must pay attention to key aspect such as its content, suspicious links, and the sender's email address. Correct identification yields rewards – such as earning a virtual currency –, while mistakes incur in lives being lost.

This first concept can extend to recognizing fake news – where a news item is presented, and the player would have to figure out if it's true or false. Both of these challenges could potentially be initiated with a tutorial emphasizing scrutiny of both emails and news sources. Still on this topic, and in a complementary way, it was also suggested the creation of an interactive challenge to identify phishing-related elements within images (S2 – G2). In particular, players would be shown images where they would have to identify differences related to phishing messages, the presence of suspicious links, or check whether the HTTP protocol is secure or not. Overall, these three game proposals aim to educate users by detecting discrepancies between images, thus enhancing the understanding of potential threats in online communication.

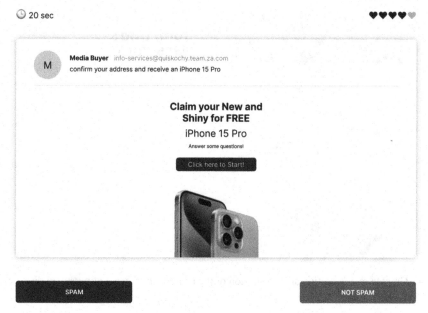

Fig. 3. Graphic and illustrative representation of the SPAM game (S1 – G1).

Moreover, the cybersecurity topic concluded with a proposal to improve the strength of passwords (S3 – G1). This game involves adopting a reverse approach, portraying the persona as a hacker to learn from common password weaknesses – cf. Fig. 4. Here, players are presented with a simulated login page featuring an individual's profile information, like email and details such as birthdate or hometown. As an example, for someone who has an email address of "peter95@gmail.com", having a password that is "peter95" would clearly be bad practice. Thus, the challenge guides players to understand the pitfalls of easily guessable passwords and encourages the creation of stronger ones.

Furthermore, moving on to an area of successful information search on search engines – i.e., prompt number 5 – it was suggested an interactive story search to foster effective practices (S4 – G1). In particular, an example sentence would be given, such as "Whiskers [because Mrs. Fernanda has a cat] has stopped drinking water. You need to find a vet." It would encourage the player to search as optimized as possible, divided into several levels, where the geographical area of the vet or the hours they are open would be asked. Thus, players must optimize their search queries, progressing from basic searches to locating specific information within a given timeframe.

Regarding prompt number 11, i.e., related to reacting appropriately to system errors and pop-up messages, it was suggested the creation of exercises for appropriate system error responses that could involve understanding its anatomy in a simple and concise way and, secondly, have a reverse messaging strategy (S5 – G1) – *cf.* Fig. 5. In other words, if there are Boolean yes or no actions, these would have to be matched with the messages which indicate it in the pop-up itself. Then, with greater difficulty, the players

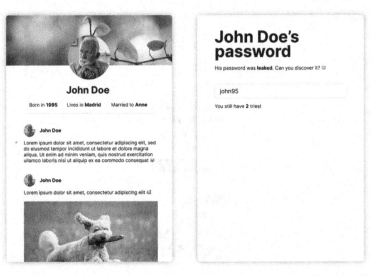

Fig. 4. Graphic representation and illustration of the cybersecurity game of password discovery (S3 – G1).

would have to do the reserve action, i.e., for actions such as "we want the user to save this file", players would have to select the correct option.

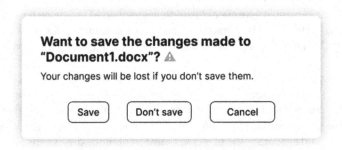

Fig. 5. Graphic representation and illustration of the pop-up message interpretation game (S5 – G1).

Lastly, regarding prompt number 10, related to reviewing and update privacy settings on social media accounts, one of the workshop groups (S6 – G2) suggested creating an interactive interface of a social media platform. Resorting to storytelling from everyday life, this game would consist of various challenges – for example, going to the platform's settings and changing the visibility of posts for a certain group of people, all through a simulation of its user interfaces. Additionally, in order to increase the game challenge, it was suggested that a time variable be added, which, once reset, would require participants to complete a new challenge. If the player managed to successfully complete the challenge throughout the story, they would receive rewards based on the preferences of the defined persona – such as poems, books, or songs.

Table 3 summarizes the various solutions created and their relationship to the prompts on an addressment scale. In a nutshell, the following games were conceived: (i) identification of fishing emails and malware threats in an email inbox simulation, (ii) following the same mechanic, assess the authenticity of presented news items, (iii) acting as hackers, players learn common password weaknesses to create and understand stronger passwords; (iv) optimizing search queries through an interactive story search; (v) understanding error message anatomy and matching Boolean actions with pop-up messages;

Table 3. Distribution of the distributed prompts per solution created and its addressment (X – fully addressed; O – indirectly addressed).

Prompts		Solution	Addressing scale
We want the character to be able to...	(1)... create a strong and secure password	S3 – G1	X
	(2)... recognize and prevent phishing threats	S1 – G1 S2 – G2	X X
	(3)... keep software and applications up to date for device security	Not adressed	
	(4)... know what types of information can be shared online	S3 – G1	O
	(5)... successfully search for information on search engines	S4 – G1	X
	(6)... discern fake news/information from real news/information	S1 – G1 S4 – G1	X O
	(7)... identify and report unreliable sources of information on social networks	S1 – G1	O
	(8)... carry out online financial transactions safely, such as bill payments or money transfers	Not adressed	
	(9)... engage in productive and respectful discussions on social platforms	Not adressed	
	(10)... review and update privacy settings on social media accounts	S6 – G1	X
	(11)... react appropriately to system errors and other pop-up messages	S5 – G1	X

and (vi) navigating a simulated social media platform, with added time variables and persona-based rewards for increased challenge.

4 Discussion

This paper has presented the results of a workshop aimed at developing digital games to impact older adults' digital competences. As previously mentioned, this topic has little to no published information, thus reinforcing the need to conduct exploratory sessions with informed and interested people in the field.

The process of creating the personas, despite not being the focus of this paper nor being something groundbreaking – in fact, several studies explore the creation of personas for ageing audiences [40, 41] –, proves to be important for improving engagement [29] and establishing an empathetic relationship with the audience for whom solutions are being developed [31, 38, 39]. During the second part of the workshop, groups often revisited the persona created. They mentioned them while explaining their created game strategies – thus revealing the attention and empathy created throughout this process, which allowed them to consider the needs, preferences, and particularities of older adults.

Moreover, although the provided prompts were from different areas, the game-based strategies are focused on two of the five digital competences areas defined by DigComp 2.2 – in particular, (i) data literacy and information and (ii) security. Although the field of research and the study of the considered combined variables is innovative, the solutions created follow some good practices that should be considered when developing games for ageing audiences.

As highlighted by Yee and colleagues [42], a comparison between older adults who engage with mobile games, with or without narratives, led to the conclusion that game versions incorporating narratives are not only preferred but also contribute to a heightened and more enjoyable player experience.

Furthermore, other studies [e.g., 43, 44] reinforce the importance of building narratives to ensure greater engagement. In this particular case, it is possible to observe three solutions with this strategy – i.e., (i) the game where one has to discover others' passwords based on their social media profiles, thus embarking on an adventure as a hacker; (ii) the successful browsing on search engines, using familiar narratives to the target audience; and (iii) through the use of everyday situations, the game that would help in the interpretation of social media settings interfaces. Ultimately, the narrative and theme of the games should be meaningful to the players, relating as much as possible to their lives and everyday scenarios [45, 46].

Additionally, analyzing from the perspective of the created games' categories, all of them are within the realm of serious games, with a special focus on the educational genre. From a critical point of view, this was inevitable, given the nature of the challenge posed. Indeed, according to multiple researchers [e.g., 47, 48], older adults' preferred genres tend to be puzzle and strategy, and educational ones.

Furthermore, one of the presented solutions suggested adding the time variable as a way of increasing the game's challenge. However, caution is recommended when implementing time-limited challenges, particularly for older adults, given the potential difficulties they may present [49]. If the integration of a timing mechanism is crucial, designers should explore strategies such as reducing the number of stimuli or limiting the available actions/options [50]. Still on this theme, the presented game proposals rely heavily on using the keyboard, which can be challenging to older adults [33].

Overall, this research shed light on innovative ways to integrate digital competences in games with older target audiences. This will ensure the gradual acquisition of the above-mentioned competences, while promoting a progressive adaptation to an increasingly digital world.

5   Conclusion

This research experiment, in a highly exploratory context, has extended and defined the path for future developments in a field that intersects games, older adults, and digital competences. Through a two-part workshop – i.e., (i) creating an empathetic senior persona and (ii) designing digital game-based solutions – a total of six new solutions emerged, deeply aligned with the preferences, and needs of older adults and DigComp 2.2. Overall, the results have paved the way for our current development, as we are conceiving and designing a game prototype considering them.

Additionally, it is possible to reinforce the methodological framework used to build technological products for a specific audience: (i) recruit a series of experts in the field (at least eight); (ii) organize them by evenly distributed groups; and (iii) conduct a two-part workshop, where the first part consists of creating empathetic personas, and the second one entails creating solutions based on randomly distributed prompts.

Nonetheless, some limitations may be considered for this study. In particular, (i) it is important to emphasize that it was not possible to address all the predefined prompts due to the workshop's time limits; and (ii) some of these solutions fail to have some formal game elements (e.g., clear definition of pre- and post-game states, the outcomes, and rules). Thus, it reinforces the critical and active role of researchers, who must reflect on and adapt the results to their contexts.

Lastly, in future work, it is essential to delve deeper into the proposed themes, thus validating, implementing, and assessing these strategies with older adult audiences.

Acknowledgments. The authors wish to thank not only the participants of this study but also Digi-Media, the Department of Communication and Art at the University of Aveiro. The study reported in this publication was supported by F.C.T. – Foundation for Science and Technology (Fundação para a Ciência e Tecnologia), I.P. nr. 2021.06465. B.D, DigiMedia Research Center, under the project UIDB/05460/2020, and the IC Senior X project funded by DigiMedia (GIP3_2022).

Disclosure of Interests. The authors declare no conflict of interest. Informed consent was obtained from all participants involved in the study.

References

1. PORDATA: Indivíduos com 16 e mais anos que utilizam computador e Internet em % do total de indivíduos: por grupo etário. https://www.pordata.pt/Portugal/Indiv%c3%adduos+com+16+e+mais+anos+que+utilizam+computador+e+Internet+em+percentagem+do+total+de+indiv%c3%adduos+por+grupo+et%c3%a1rio-1139. Accessed 29 May 2022
2. Auxier, B., Anderson, M.: Social Media Use in 2021 (2021)
3. Castells, M.: The Internet Galaxy: Reflexions on the Internet, Business, and Society. Oxford University Press (2002).https://doi.org/10.1093/ACPROF:OSO/9780199255771.001.0001
4. Quan-Haase, A., Wang, H., Wellman, B., Zhang, R.: Weaving family connections on-and offline: the turn to networked individualism. In: Connecting Families?, pp. 59–80 (2018). https://doi.org/10.1332/POLICYPRESS/9781447339946.003.0004
5. Zheng, R.Z., Hill, R.D., Gardner, M.K.: Engaging older adults with modern technology: internet use and information access needs. IGI Global (2012). https://doi.org/10.4018/978-1-4666-1966-1
6. Reneland-Forsman, L.: 'Borrowed access' – the struggle of older persons for digital participation. Int. J. Lifelong Educ. **37**, 333–344 (2018). https://doi.org/10.1080/02601370.2018.1473516
7. Han, S., Nam, S.I.: Creating supportive environments and enhancing personal perception to bridge the digital divide among older adults. Educ. Gerontol. **47**, 339–352 (2021). https://doi.org/10.1080/03601277.2021.1988448
8. Commission, E., Centre, J.R., Pujol Priego, L., Cabrera, M., Kluzer, S., O'Keeffe, W.: DigComp into action, get inspired make it happen: a user guide to the European digital competence framework. publications office (2018). https://doi.org/10.2760/112945
9. Vuorikari, R., Kluzer, S., Punie, Y.: DigComp 2.2 – The Digital Competence Framework for Citizen, Luxembourg (2022). https://doi.org/10.2760/115376
10. Oppl, S., Stary, C.: Game-playing as an effective learning resource for elderly people: encouraging experiential adoption of touchscreen technologies. Univ. Access Inform. Soc. **19**(2), 295–310 (2018). https://doi.org/10.1007/s10209-018-0638-0
11. Isbister, K.: How Games Move us: Emotion by Design. MIT Press (2017)
12. Loos, E.: Exergaming: Meaningful play for older adults? In: Zhou, J., Salvendy, G. (eds.) ITAP 2017. LNCS, vol. 10298, pp. 254–265. Springer, Cham (2017). https://doi.org/10.1007/978-3-319-58536-9_21
13. Costa, L., Veloso, A.: Being (grand) players: review of digital games and their potential to enhance intergenerational interactions. J. Intergener. Relatsh. **14**, 43–59 (2016). https://doi.org/10.1080/15350770.2016.1138273
14. ESA: 2022 Essential facts about the video game industry (2022)
15. Alotaibi, F., Furnell, S., Stengel, I., Papadaki, M.: Enhancing cyber security awareness with mobile games. In: 2017 12th International Conference for Internet Technology and Secured Transactions, ICITST 2017, pp. 129–134 (2018). https://doi.org/10.23919/ICITST.2017.8356361
16. Hartwig, K., Englisch, A., Thomson, J.P., Reuter, C.: Finding Secret Treasure? Improving Memorized Secrets Through Gamification. In: Proceedings of the 2021 European Symposium on Usable Security, pp. 105–117. ACM, New York, NY, USA (2021). https://doi.org/10.1145/3481357.3481509
17. Chellaiah, P., Nair, B., Achuthan, K., Diwakar, S.: Using theme-based narrative construct of images as passwords: implementation and assessment of remembered sequences. Int. J. Online Eng. (iJOE). **13**, 77 (2017). https://doi.org/10.3991/ijoe.v13i11.7774

18. Micallef, N., Arachchilage, N.A.G.: Changing users' security behaviour towards security questions: a game based learning approach. 2017 Military Communications and Information Systems Conference, MilCIS 2017 - Proceedings. 2017-December, pp. 1–6 (2017). https://doi.org/10.1109/MILCIS.2017.8190424
19. Zapušek, M.: A case study of developing educator digital competences with serious game design. Presented at the June 30 (2023). https://doi.org/10.4018/978-1-6684-9166-9.ch004
20. Kreuder, A., Frick, V., Schlittmeier, S.J., Frick, U.: Game jamming as a participatory design approach to foster adolescents' digital competence: game jamming als partizipativer Designansatz zur Förderung der digitalen Kompetenzen Adoleszenter. In: ACM International Conference Proceeding Series, pp. 472–476 (2023). https://doi.org/10.1145/3603555.3608568
21. Ørngreen, R., Levinsen, K.T.: Workshops as a research methodology. Electron. J. E-Learning 15, 70–81 (2017)
22. Riegler, A., Riener, A., Holzmann, C.: Augmented reality for future mobility: insights from a literature review and HCI workshop. i-com 20, 295–318 (2021). https://doi.org/10.1515/icom-2021-0029
23. Almohamed, A., Vyas, D., Zhang, J.: Designing for refugees: insights from design workshop. In: Proceedings of the 30th Australian Conference on Computer-Human Interaction, pp. 92–96. ACM, New York, NY, USA (2018). https://doi.org/10.1145/3292147.3292196
24. Lee, H.-K., Park, J.E.: Digital responsibility insights from a cross-cultural design thinking workshop for creativity. Creativity Stud. 15, 451–466 (2022). https://doi.org/10.3846/cs.2022.14063
25. Kyakulumbye, S., Pather, S., Jantjies, M.: Knowledge creation in a participatory design context: the use of empathetic participatory design. Electron. J. Knowl. Manag. 17, 49–65 (2019)
26. Ferreira, B., Silva, W., Oliveira, E., Conte, T.: Designing personas with empathy map. In: International Conference on Software Engineering and Knowledge Engineering, pp. 501–505 (2015). https://doi.org/10.18293/SEKE2015-152
27. Ferreira, B.M., Barbosa, S.D.J., Conte, T.: PATHY: Using empathy with personas to design applications that meet the users' needs. In: Kurosu, M. (ed.) HCI 2016. LNCS, vol. 9731, pp. 153–165. Springer, Cham (2016). https://doi.org/10.1007/978-3-319-39510-4_15
28. Miaskiewicz, T., Grant, S.J., Kozar, K.A.: A preliminary examination of using personas to enhance user- centered design. In: AMCIS 2009 Proceedings (2009)
29. Hisham, S.: Experimenting with the use of persona in a focus group discussion with older adults in Malaysia. In: Proceedings of the 21st Annual Conference of the Australian Computer-Human Interaction Special Interest Group - Design: Open 24/7, OZCHI 2009, vol. 411, pp. 333–336 (2009). https://doi.org/10.1145/1738826.1738889
30. Wöckl, B., Yildizoglu, U., Buber, I., Diaz, B.A., Kruijff, E., Tscheligi, M.: Basic senior personas: a representative design tool covering the spectrum of European older adults. In: ASSETS 2012 - Proceedings of the 14th International ACM SIGACCESS Conference on Computers and Accessibility, pp. 25–32 (2012). https://doi.org/10.1145/2384916.2384922
31. Varzgani, F., Djamasbi, S., Tulu, B.: Using Persona Development to Design a Smartphone Application for Older and Younger Diabetes Patients – A Methodological Approach for Persona Development. LNCS (including subseries Lecture Notes in Artificial Intelligence and Lecture Notes in Bioinformatics), vol. 14043 LNCS, pp. 214–227 (2023). https://doi.org/10.1007/978-3-031-34917-1_16/COVER
32. Gray, D.E.: Doing Research in the Real World. SAGE Publications, London (2004)
33. Regalado, F., Ortet, C.P., Costa, L.V., Santos, C., Veloso, A.I.: Assessing older adults' perspectives on digital game-related strategies to foster active and healthy ageing. Media Commun. 11, 88–100 (2023). https://doi.org/10.17645/mac.v11i3.6796

34. Desai, S., McGrath, C., McNeil, H., Sveistrup, H., McMurray, J., Astell, A.: Experiential value of technologies: a qualitative study with older adults. Int. J. Environ. Res. Public Health **19**, 2235 (2022). https://doi.org/10.3390/ijerph19042235

35. Colombo-Ruano, L., Gonzalez-Gonzalez, C.S.: Digital competencies in seniors: benefits, opportunities, and limitations. In: 2022 XII International Conference on Virtual Campus (JICV), pp. 1–4. IEEE (2022). https://doi.org/10.1109/JICV56113.2022.9934319

36. Lucas, M., Bem-haja, P., Santos, S., Figueiredo, H., Ferreira Dias, M., Amorim, M.: Digital proficiency: sorting real gaps from myths among higher education students. Br. J. Edu. Technol. **53**, 1885–1914 (2022). https://doi.org/10.1111/BJET.13220

37. Ribeiro, T., Veloso, A.I., Brinson, P.: Creating Empathetic Characters – A Method (2024). https://doi.org/10.7910/DVN/JTZKKQ

38. Siricharoen, W.V.: Using Empathy Mapping in Design Thinking Process for Personas Discovering. In: Vinh, P.C., Rakib, A. (eds.) ICCASA/ICTCC -2020. LNICSSITE, vol. 343, pp. 182–191. Springer, Cham (2021). https://doi.org/10.1007/978-3-030-67101-3_15

39. Dias, I., Costa, E., Mealha, Ó.: Involving older adults in the design process: a human-centric Design Thinking approach. Interact. Des. Architect., 85–110 (2022). https://doi.org/10.55612/S-5002-054-004)

40. Tunc, S., Nijboer, F., Tinga, A.M., Tabak, M.: "Hi, My Name is Robin" – Remotely Co-designing an Embodied Conversational Agent for Empathy with Older Adults. LNCS, vol. 14042 LNCS, pp. 376–391 (2023). https://doi.org/10.1007/978-3-031-34866-2_27

41. Vardoulakis, L.P., Ring, L., Barry, B., Sidner, C.L., Bickmore, T.: Designing relational agents as long term social companions for older adults. In: Nakano, Y., Neff, M., Paiva, A., Walker, M. (eds.) IVA 2012. LNCS (LNAI), vol. 7502, pp. 289–302. Springer, Heidelberg (2012). https://doi.org/10.1007/978-3-642-33197-8_30

42. Chu Yew Yee, S.L., Duh, H.B.L., Quek, F.: Investigating narrative in mobile games for seniors. In: Conference on Human Factors in Computing Systems – Proceedings, vol. 2, pp. 669–672 (2010).https://doi.org/10.1145/1753326.1753424

43. Nieto-Vieites, A., et al.: A narrative video game for adults with subjective and objective cognitive impairment. Design and preliminary results on user-interaction and efficacy. Behav. Inform. Technol. (2023). https://doi.org/10.1080/0144929X.2023.2220042

44. Regalado, F., Ortet, C.P., Veloso, A.I.: "miPlay" as a Transmedia Strategy: Co-designing a Movie-Based Digital Game for Older Adults (2023). https://doi.org/10.1007/978-3-031-34866-2_34

45. De Schutter, B., Abeele, V.: Meaningful play in elderly life. In: 58th Annual Conference of the International Communication Association. Montreal, Canada (2008)

46. Costa, L.V., Veloso, A.I., Loizou, M., Arnab, S.: Games for active ageing, well-being and quality of life: a pilot study. Behav. Inform. Technol. **37**, 842–854 (2018). https://doi.org/10.1080/0144929X.2018.1485744

47. Salmon, J.P., Dolan, S.M., Drake, R.S., Wilson, G.C., Klein, R.M., Eskes, G.A.: A survey of video game preferences in adults: building better games for older adults. Entertain. Comput. **21**, 45–64 (2017). https://doi.org/10.1016/J.ENTCOM.2017.04.006

48. Blocker, K.A., Wright, T.J., Boot, W.R.: Gaming preferences of aging generations. Gerontechnology. **12**, 174 (2014). https://doi.org/10.4017/GT.2014.12.3.008.00

49. Whitlock, L.A., McLaughlin, A.C., Allaire, J.C.: video game design for older adults: usability observations from an intervention study. In: Proceedings of the Human Factors and Ergonomics Society Annual Meeting, vol. 55, pp. 187–191 (2011).https://doi.org/10.1177/1071181311551039

50. Fua, K.C., Gupta, S., Pautler, D., Farber, I.: Designing serious games for elders (2013)

Educational Gerontechnology: Toward a Comprehensive Model for the Education of Digital Technologies for Older Adults

Javiera Rosell[1,2,3]($\boxtimes$) ⓘ, Sofía Sepúlveda-Caro[1] ⓘ, and Felipe Bustamante[4] ⓘ

[1] Centro Estudios de Vejez y Envejecimiento, Pontificia Universidad Católica de Chile, Santiago, Chile
jerosell@uc.cl
[2] Millennium Institute for Care Research (MICARE), Santiago, Chile
[3] Oxford Institute of Population Ageing, Oxford, UK
[4] Escuela de Medicina, Pontificia Universidad Católica de Chile, Santiago, Chile

Abstract. The rapid growth of the aging population and the increasing digitization of processes and services have underscored the necessity for the digital inclusion of older adults. This challenge has evolved into a human rights issue, as it empowers older adults to access opportunities provided by technological advancements and, in turn, exercise their rights. While the disciplines of gerontology and human-computer interaction (HCI) individually address the digital inclusion of older people, they often fail to engage in dialogue. In this context, we propose the concept of educational gerontechnology intending to foster interdisciplinary collaboration between gerontology, HCI, and the human rights approach. We first address each of the three main topics for educational gerontology. Then, we present a comprehensive model for the digital inclusion of older adults, emphasizing that educational gerontechnology encompasses the study and practice of educational initiatives focused on the relationship between technology, old age, and aging. Finally, we discuss future directions in this area.

Keywords: Aging · Digital devices · Digital divide

1 Introduction

The need to digitally include older adults is of utmost importance given the context of a rapidly growing aging population, the rapid digitization of processes and services, and the constant technological advancements. While many older individuals are increasingly interested in and using digital devices, there is a significant gap in usage compared to younger age groups. This situation results in a dual exclusion, both digital and social [1]. To address this disparity, the concept of the digital divide arises, encompassing not only the first level, which focuses on access to digital devices [2], but also the second level, which pertains to digital skills and usage, and the third level, which addresses the benefits or lack thereof resulting from the use of digital technology.

Q. Gao and J. Zhou (Eds.): HCII 2024, LNCS 14725, pp. 275–292, 2024.
https://doi.org/10.1007/978-3-031-61543-6_20

Within this context, understanding the causes of the second level of the digital divide becomes crucial as it allows us to comprehend the heterogeneity within the older adult population regarding digital skills [3, 4]. Several factors contribute to this diversity, encompassing socio-economic status [5], educational level [5–7], gender [8], race [9], social support [10], age [11, 12], health status [13], and self-efficacy [7, 14]. Moreover, 'technology anxiety,' indicating the fear and resistance to using technology, has emerged as a significant barrier for older individuals in adopting and using technologies [15].

Given the unique characteristics of this age group, educators face various challenges, such as the diverse knowledge of the older population, the imperative to address individual needs, and the requirement for a curriculum that comprehensively covers the expansive realm of technology [16]. Therefore, educators stress the importance of receiving methodological and content support to structure educational sessions that meet the expectations of older individuals. Furthermore, addressing mentor anxiety when teaching older adults, influenced by age hierarchy, becomes critical [17].

Moreover, instructors in digital inclusion courses for older adults often comprise volunteers, educators lacking specific knowledge of educational strategies for this population, or professionals with training outside the gerontological or pedagogical field [16, 17]. Thus, not all individuals leading these initiatives possess the necessary knowledge about the use of digital devices, and they are faced with the demand to teach digital skills to this population [17]. This scenario poses the challenge of preparing trainers who require expertise in gerontology and digital devices.

The digital divide among the most excluded has evolved into a human rights issue [18]. In contemporary society, digital inclusion is pivotal for enabling older adults to fully enjoy and exercise their rights, leveraging opportunities brought by technological advances [19, 20]. Furthermore, older individuals lacking digital education may be denying themselves the benefits that come with the use of technologies, such as more efficient access to quality healthcare, increased perception of self-efficacy, social participation, and educational opportunities [19, 21].

Two disciplines, gerontology and human-computer interaction (HCI), address the digital inclusion of older adults. However, these areas often fail to engage in dialogue to develop interventions, research, and public policies on this issue. This context led to the development of socio-gerontechnology as a discipline that promotes dialogue between studies on aging and those on science and technology [22]. Despite its interdisciplinary nature, socio-gerontechnology does not exclusively focus on the educational experience of using technology in old age. Nevertheless, educational opportunities are crucial for digital inclusion, especially considering that education is one of the factors that most significantly influences the digital divide [2].

Our question is how to strengthen an interdisciplinary dialogue that fosters the digital inclusion of older adults. For this reason, we introduce the concept of educational gerontechnology, promoting a dialogue between three essential pillars advocating for the learning and use of digital devices by older individuals: gerontology, HCI, and the human rights approach. Thus, educational gerontechnology encompasses the study and practice of educational initiatives focused on the relationship between technology, old age, and aging.

To better conceptualize educational gerontechnology, we describe the main contributions of each pillar and discuss a comprehensive model for digital inclusion. This section proposes general guidelines for digital inclusion initiatives targeting older individuals. Finally, we outline future directions in this area, recognizing that while this article centers on digital inclusion initiatives for older individuals, educational gerontechnology must expand its scope to encompass the broader world of technologies.

2 Gerontology

Gerontology directs its attention to our population of interest: older persons. Within gerontology, two main topics are particularly relevant to the digital inclusion of this age group:

– Ageism: representing the social representations of old age and aging, while examining their influence on the adoption and use of digital devices.
– Educational gerontology: providing insights into education in old age and aging that can be extrapolated to initiatives addressing digital inclusion.

2.1 Ageism

Ageism is defined as stereotypes and prejudices directed toward individuals based on their age, leading to discriminatory acts [23]. These biases predominantly affect older people, encompassing cognitive, affective, and behavioral components [24]. Common ageist notions include the belief that older people tend to isolate themselves, lack interest in learning, cannot acquire new skills, and experience cognitive impairment [24, 25].

Moreover, a self-fulfilling prophecy occurs, where individuals internalize ageist ideas from an early age and conform to these expectations upon entering old age. Consequently, those with elevated levels of ageism are likely to have shorter lives and experience a diminished quality of life [26]. The costs of ageism manifest in various ways, including higher depressive symptomatology, lower perception of good health, reduced life satisfaction, and lower self-efficacy [26, 27].

The self-fulfilling prophecy and embodiment of ageist ideas have an impact on older people's adoption of digital devices [28–30]. Mariano et al. [29] introduce the concept of stereotype threat, highlighting that those who feel less capable because of their age tend to use digital devices less. Rosell and Vergés [31] observed that greater ageism is associated with a lower perceived self-efficacy concerning Internet use. Therefore, individuals with higher levels of ageism feel less capable of using the Internet and may avoid engaging in online activities beneficial to mental health, such as leisure and entertainment [30, 32]. Ageism thus emerges as a significant barrier to the digital inclusion of older adults, yet it is not always considered in studies and practices aimed at reducing the digital divide.

Digital Ageism. Ageist notions concerning older people and technology have evolved into a concept known as digital ageism, which analyzes ageism in the digital realm. This term focuses on how age is portrayed and encountered in connection with digital technologies [33]. This idea goes beyond older people's access to or use of technology and extends to discrimination created by artificial intelligence algorithms [34] or the design of digital technologies [35, 36].

Regarding artificial intelligence, a scoping review by Chu et al. [34] revealed various degrees of age-related bias in the algorithms and techniques used to analyze data. For example, there is underrepresentation, misrepresentation or omission of groups aged 60 or more in databases, as well as aggregation (such as presenting older people as a homogeneous group).

Furthermore, digital ageism encompasses technology design, with most products or services lacking the participation or involvement of older people [35]. This shortcoming results in the lack of designers' awareness regarding older people's needs (refer to Sect. 3 about HCI).

Other forms of digital ageism may involve negative narratives and images of older people on social networks [37] or the use of surveillance technologies in long-term care facilities without proper consent [38].

2.2 Educational Gerontology

Educational gerontology lays the conceptual foundation for teaching older adults, focusing on educational research and practice involving older individuals, those who teach, and those who work with this age group [39].

Older adults bring a history of learning experiences that influence their educational motivations. Yuni and Urbano [40] developed a typology of learning meanings for older people closely tied to motivations for learning. These meanings should be explored at the outset of any educational intervention to adapt the content and methodology. The typology includes viewing learning as (1) a process of staying up to date, (2) a process of personal development, (3) a challenge for self-improvement, focusing on testing one's skills, (4) an opportunity to acquire coping strategies or resources to face life challenges, and (5) a process of self-understanding, aiming to explore new experiences and establish new goals that lend meaning to the life course.

The typology of learning meanings can be enriched by motivations identified by Xiong and Zuo [41] in older Chinese individuals enrolled in Massive Open Online Courses (MOOCs). They participated in these initiatives for various reasons, including (1) solving problems, (2) acquiring knowledge, (3) improving cognition, (4) seeking fun, (5) benefiting others, and (6) social contact.

These classifications offer valuable insights into the diversity within a group participating in an educational program. It is crucial to recognize that the content and methodologies of an educational initiative must align with these motivations, providing practical significance in participants' daily lives to ensure applicability [42].

A specific area of interest within educational gerontology surrounds the cognitive processes and performance involved in the learning experience. In this context, it is crucial to distinguish between cognitive impairment and normal age-related cognitive changes. The first refers to pathological changes, while the second pertains to non-pathological variations [43].

In non-pathological aging, specific changes in cognitive functions must be considered. For example, processing speed and inhibitory control may decrease with age [43]. This shift does not imply that older individuals cannot learn; instead, it underscores the importance of considering the time required to incorporate new knowledge. Additionally, educational approaches for individuals with cognitive impairment should contemplate the person's cognitive performance. However, this is a topic that merits further research.

As previously mentioned, educational interventions pose challenges as they confront educators with characteristics atypical of education in other age ranges. An example is the asymmetry imposed by age, generally reversed in gerontological education [17]. Unlike other stages of life, it is more common for the educator to be younger than those participating in the activity [44]. This relationship becomes horizontal, necessitating the recognition of the experiences that older people bring to the educational context. Furthermore, this relationship challenges the traditional assumption that older generations educate the younger ones, disrupting the conventional notion of "teaching" and creating a situation where those transmitting knowledge, the older ones, also need to learn [44].

Education becomes a tool for promoting the quality of life of older adults. The educational setting promotes empowerment, self-efficacy, and self-awareness of the skills and knowledge they possess. Additionally, it prevents the decline of cognitive functions and fosters social inclusion by establishing new ties [44].

3 Human-Computer Interaction (HCI)

Human-Computer Interaction (HCI) is interested in the interaction between technology and human action, examining how technology can serve the user [45]. It focuses on the design, implementation, and evaluation of technological systems that are currently in use or will be used by humans. This interdisciplinary field includes computational scientists, engineers, and social scientists, intending to foster a dialogue between these disciplines. The goal is to contribute valuable insights for developing appropriate technological designs for humans and evaluating their social impact. [46].

HCI addresses crucial questions, including the intuitiveness of technological device use, barriers to interaction with the device, factors favoring device adoption, and the development of universal technologies. Research on older adults also explores whether digital devices can benefit their daily lives [47]. The answers to these questions contribute to evaluating technological systems regarding acceptability, usefulness, effectiveness, safety, and usability. Therefore, a product should be easy to use, attractive, effective, and, ideally, deliver a pleasant user experience [48].

However, one criticism of HCI research with older individuals is its failure to encompass the complexity of aging and the diversity within old age [47]. This limitation is influenced by ageist ideas that hinder a comprehensive understanding of the relationship between older people and technological devices [47].

An illustrative example is gerontechnology, a multidisciplinary solution designed to address the challenges of aging with technology [49]. However, sometimes gerontechnology is conceptualized from a welfare-oriented perspective, emphasizing caregiving and dependency. This approach focuses on providing older people with what "they lack" rather than stressing independent living, autonomy, and empowerment [47, 49].

Sayago [47] advocates for an expanded perspective on HCI that goes beyond conventional concerns related to aging, such as decline, health, and isolation. This paradigm shift underscores the importance of adopting a person-centered approach in HCI, considering the characteristics and needs of the user during the design and implementation of technology [45]. An HCI perspective with a gerontological focus becomes the foundation for appropriate product design and development, always considering the needs of older adults. Thus, efforts should be directed toward ensuring that devices are personalized, flexible, and responsive in various contexts and situations [45].

Recognizing older individuals as users involves comprehensively assessing their knowledge, experiences, skills, abilities, needs, demands, and attitudes toward technology [47]. This evaluation must encompass psychological and physical dimensions, acknowledging their variability among individuals and their potential impact on the modes and consequences of technological adoption [50].

In line with the person-centered approach, it is crucial to understand that what seems interesting or easy to use for designers may not necessarily align with the preferences and capabilities of end-users. Thus, usability testing becomes an invaluable tool to identify users' challenges in interacting with devices [48, 51]. However, it is essential to ensure a diverse representation of skills and education levels in usability tests [52].

Additionaly, anxiety is a significant barrier to adopting digital devices, often exacerbated by difficulties handling the device or interface. Such challenges can lead to frustration for older users and those assisting them, potentially resulting in abandoning the learning task [53, 54]. These problems may arise from poorly designed interfaces that hinder usability, leading to time-consuming interactions, mistakes, and demotivation [55].

The evaluation of HCI should consider the activities performed and the contexts in which they occur. Older individuals often perform better in natural contexts than in laboratory settings, and they are more motivated when using tools and applications that have practical relevance in their daily lives [56].

It is crucial to note that technology is constantly evolving. Furthermore, a new generation of older technology users is anticipated, with different attributes, including a life-long familiarity with the digital world. Thus, future directions in HCI should contemplate these changing dynamics [45].

4 Human Rights Approach

As the third pillar of educational gerontechnology, the human rights approach shifts the perception of older individuals from subjects of assistance and charity to being recognized as subjects of rights, which should actively participate in all processes that concern them [57]. This approach underscores the importance of inclusion and participation of older people in society [58], for example, through educational initiatives and digital inclusion.

The rapid pace of digitalization has led to the exclusion of older adults who have not familiarized themselves with digital devices and other technologies [59]. Thus, strategies are needed to support the exercise and enjoyment of the rights of older individuals.

What is more, when considering the human rights perspective, it becomes imperative to delve into ethical considerations. This involves raising questions about the autonomy of older persons' decisions to engage with these technologies, the extent to which their use upholds individual dignity and freedom, whether they foster socialization and companionship, and if the emphasis on improving the quality of life through technology aligns with individual values. [58].

Information and Communication Technologies (ICTs) are identified as powerful tools in achieving Goal 10 of the United Nations' Sustainable Development Goals (SDGs): "Reduced Inequalities" [60]. ICTs promote equality by providing access to information, facilitating active participation, and engaging citizens in the economy [19]. Thus, using ICTs effectively can create more opportunities in areas such as education, training, and employability [19].

Furthermore, recognizing the right to lifelong learning as a fundamental pillar of digital inclusion is crucial. The Inter-American Convention on the Protection of the Human Rights of Older Persons underscores that older individuals have equal rights to education, just as other sectors of the population do [20, 61]. This right encompasses participation in existing educational programs across all levels and the opportunity to share their knowledge and experiences with all generations. Significantly, there is an emphasis on ensuring the accessibility of educational initiatives and adapting them based on the needs of older persons [20]. Within this framework, education is intrinsically valuable and serves as a tool to bridge gaps, foster social inclusion, and promote healthy aging [20, 61].

Lifelong learning encompasses learning activities for individuals of all ages, in all life contexts, and through various modalities [62]. As a human right, efforts should be directed toward designing educational models that recognize and leverage technologies to support education [62]. Access to technology is highlighted by UNESCO [63] as a crucial aspect of lifelong learning. Thus, older individuals with comprehensive knowledge of digital tools are more likely to embark on an autonomous learning journey. This expertise enables them to critically assess and utilize the digital content they access and effectively participate in digitized networks [64].

In sum, the promotion of lifelong learning and digital inclusion has the potential to facilitate the enjoyment and exercise of various human rights, including health, culture, participation, work, independence, autonomy, freedom of expression, access to information, recreation, accessibility, and access to justice, among others [20]. Failing to ensure adequate digital inclusion for the older population hinders the exercise of their rights, constituting age discrimination. The COVID-19 pandemic underscored the importance of Internet access as a fundamental human right, necessitating efforts to provide connectivity and develop the necessary skills to use digital devices [1]. Digital inclusion can amplify the agency of older individuals, enabling them to decide how they want to age and enjoy their lives [65].

5   Toward a Comprehensive Model for the Digital Inclusion of Older Adults

Considering the three pillars of gerontology, HCI, and human rights, educational gerontechnology seeks to promote dialogue between these disciplines to carry out educational efforts for the digital inclusion of older adults. Thus, we define educational gerontechnology as the study and practice of educational endeavors concerning the relationship between technology, old age, and aging. This includes initiatives aimed at the general public, those working with older adults, and older persons.

At this point, it is important to highlight the contributions of socio-gerontechnology in this field, as it is essential for the comprehensive model. Thus, socio-gerontechnology seeks the dialogue between the studies of aging and those related to science and technology. For this reason, this discipline fosters the interdisciplinary work of the first two pillars of gerontology and HCI.

The main principles of socio-gerontechnology lie in the intertwining between aging and technology. This vision rejects the deterministic view that aging is only about biology and corporeality and that technology is only a matter of nuts and bolts. Thus, the focus is on how technology influences the aging process and how older persons' interactions with devices shape technology. In addition, socio-gerontechnology seeks to overcome the assumption that technology will magically solve aging problems and that the focus between aging and technology should not be exclusively on the issue of care [22].

Understanding the significance of socio-gerontechnology contributions, we focus on educating about these topics, given their crucial role in facilitating interaction between older individuals and technology. There is an urgent need to address older adults' digital skills and explore how educational endeavors could promote them.

In this context, it is essential to revisit the levels of the digital divide, as also highlighted by HCI: the first level concerning access, the second level involving skills, and the third level related to outcomes. Although there is less information regarding the third level, an area that should be included in educational gerontechnology, our emphasis will be on the second level since it is the core of educational gerontechnology [2, 47, 66].

To this end, three fundamental aspects for generating educational initiatives for the digital inclusion of older persons are linked to the first level and necessary to work at the second level. The first is the accessibility of digital devices, requiring the co-construction of designs with older persons. This can only be achieved by eliminating ageism at the individual and institutional levels and eradicating digital ageism, for example, the idea that older people are not interested in technology or incapable of learning new things. Second, affordability is crucial, ensuring that digital devices, data plans, and broadband are within reasonable financial reach for older adults. Third, phone signal and internet coverage. Approximately half of the world's population is estimated to have no Internet access [67]. Thus, older people living in rural areas are less likely to use the Internet [68]. In this regard, public policies ensuring accessibility, affordability, and connectivity are required. Educational gerontechnology initiatives will not reach all older adults without advancements in these dimensions.

At the second level, focusing on digital skills, there is a need for more systematic information on the most effective ways to carry out interventions for the digital inclusion of older adults. Three crucial stages—design, implementation, and evaluation—constitute the core of this process (Fig. 1). Notably, these stages are interrelated, and their mutual support signifies a flexible process.

Understanding the demands and needs of older persons involved in the design stage is relevant. Exploring what and why they want to learn, socio-educational trajectories, digital knowledge, experiences, and physical or sensory difficulties are fundamental [69, 70]. Thus, placing older persons at the center of initiative development is imperative [69]. For instance, learning to use YouTube may have different meanings for someone seeking exercise than for someone wanting to entertain their grandchildren. Therefore,

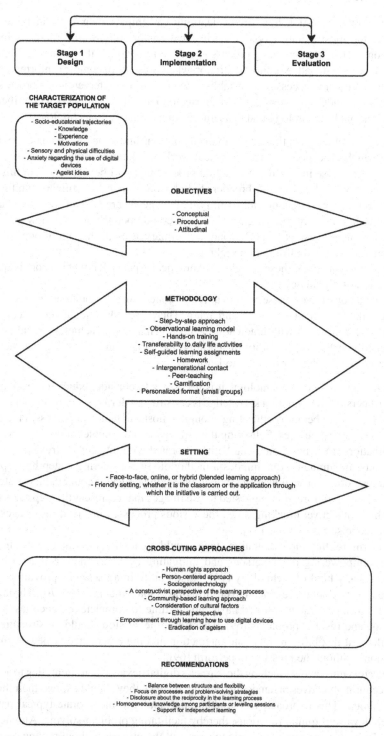

Fig. 1. Overview of the components of a comprehensive model for the digital inclusion of older adults

it is pertinent to question how digital learning can impact their daily activities and determine the most suitable topic, ensuring that content aligns with the participants' motivations [71]. This screening process is crucial to adapting the content's difficulty, promoting learning, and avoiding frustration when presenting complex information.

Additionally, it is necessary to establish the goals of the intervention, a process that should also include older learners [70]. Bermejo García [72] proposes a classification from educational gerontology that is useful in educational gerontechnology:

- Conceptual objectives: these refer to the definitions and concepts. We need to determine which aspects of the technological world are known and necessary to teach, particularly those involved in the digital process that will be addressed. In this context, concepts related to the broader digital world, such as artificial intelligence, cybersecurity, and strategies for identifying fake news, are also relevant for learning [73]. Additionally, introducing new concepts could open the door for new demands, allowing older persons to go beyond the primary uses in this age group, such as communication and information seeking.
- Procedural objectives: these are related to practical aspects. It is when theory is applied to the use of digital devices.
- Attitudinal objectives: these refer to attitudes concerning the topics addressed, in this case, skills for using technology and aging. Therefore, educational gerontechnology should be concerned with eradicating ageism. This can be achieved by addressing beliefs about the impossibility of learning due to age and dispelling the idea that technology is useless or difficult to learn.

For educational gerontechnology, it is necessary to consider education from a constructivist perspective, wherein knowledge is constructed during the educational process [72]. It is crucial to begin by educating about the most fundamental processes related to using technological devices. Following this strategy, more complex processes involving a combination of the basic ones can be incorporated without causing frustration in the participants. In summary, this implies a methodology considering a step-by-step approach and an observational learning model, where the educator could demonstrate how it works [70]. Therefore, it is suggested to use images that represent the steps to achieve the learning objective, breaking down the various processes involved into stages with clear and concise instructions [71].

Furthermore, the implementation stage should create a comfortable and safe environment, empowering older persons and mitigating ageism, which acts as a barrier to adopting any kind of technology [74]. Hands-on training sessions providing a safe space to resolve doubts are crucial to ensuring favorable outcomes [69, 70]. Throughout these sessions, participants should have enough time to complete assigned tasks, pose questions, and resolve problems [69]. Therefore, the session should be structured yet with sufficient flexibility to facilitate interaction and the emergence of new needs and motivations without the pressure to perform [69].

Educators must avoid touching the learner's digital device when attempting to achieve the procedural objectives in hands-on training. Instead, they should express their thought process aloud. This approach will enable older adults to incorporate typical patterns involved in various digital functions, thereby facilitating problem-solving. Another recommendation is to encourage people to carry out the process without relying on notes, which is useful for learning support but may not always be trustworthy due to the constant technological changes that can quickly render notes obsolete. However, by understanding usage patterns and problem-solving strategies, individuals will have a knowledge base to navigate these changes outside the educational setting [69, 70].

Additionally, by applying the principles of transferability to daily life, it becomes possible to reinforce the teaching of different processes through motivation for their practical implementation. Older adults are more likely to learn digital tools if they perceive them as a means to an end [71]: scheduling medical appointments, having fun, feeling included, participating in politics, etc. Once basic and helpful knowledge is acquired, there is a greater likelihood that individuals will continue the path of self-learning using digital tools [64]. Therefore, supporting independent learning and promoting the use of skills in daily routines are essential [69].

The educator must emphasize that learning digital skills is often reciprocal, and both educator and learner can discover new digital processes from the questions that arise. This disclosure is significant because rapid technological development and the constant updating of applications, web pages, and operating systems pose challenges frequently addressed in educational interactions. Therefore, educators should openly admit when they do not know the answer, turning it into an opportunity to showcase different approaches to finding a solution [70]. In this context, self-guided learning assignments and homework could be valuable to reinforce problem-solving strategies [69].

Also, integrating ethical considerations into the model is imperative. Ethical dimensions should address aspects of cybersecurity, which has proven to be a significant factor influencing the reluctance of older individuals to adopt digital devices [75]. Empowering individuals with the opportunity to make informed decisions regarding permissions, such as location tracking, camera access, or microphone usage, ensures that older adults have complete knowledge and agency over the data and functionalities they choose to share, fostering a sense of control.

It is noteworthy that the proposed structure might be understood primarily in a formal educational context. However, in an informal setting, it is equally important to properly assess the requests of older adults to develop an effective method to teaching what is needed (stage 1). This approach can then be applied in a hands-on situation (Stage 2) and the evaluation of the objectives' achievement (Stage 3).

One of the most common informal settings for digital inclusion involves intergenerational interaction, which is also widely used in formal settings. Intergenerational learning is the transfer of knowledge, skills, or values between generations [76]. The benefits of intergenerational learning extend to all participants, as education inherently involves reciprocal learning and support [77]. Moreover, intergenerational settings effectively reduce ageism, as they help break down stereotypes linked to age through interaction among participants [74].

Another methodology used is peer teaching, which is important in collaborative learning and yielded positive results [69, 71, 74]. This strategy can promote social support and a sense of belonging, which is essential for reducing digital inequalities and developing a learning community [69, 78]. Peer support often extends beyond the session, indicating the motivation to share new knowledge and discoveries from the digital world [78].

Moreover, the use of games-based learning has proven to be valuable in this educational context. Participants reported that learning through games is enjoyable and allows exploring different ways to manage digital devices. Furthermore, this approach is effective in promoting the inclusion of individuals with cognitive or physical challenges [79].

All these methodological considerations align with a review of programs designed to teach digital skills, indicating that personalized programs are the most effective [74]. In this context, another systematic review revealed that courses are typically conducted in smaller groups of five to ten people, and the ideal situation is for participants to have similar previous knowledge or to have undergone a preparatory leveling session [69].

Regarding the setting, the physical or virtual environment must support the atmosphere of safety that the educator should transmit. Thus, it is necessary to have a comfortable and friendly setting, such as proper chairs and tables or an easily accessible platform. Additionally, a systematic review revealed that interventions of this kind are not commonly implemented in a remote format. A blended learning approach, incorporating remote exercises and face-to-face sessions, is more effective than 100% online programs, which could be challenging for those with lower digital skills or without technical requirements [69].

At this point, it is important to note that community-based learning opportunities play a pivotal role in fostering the digital inclusion of older adults, especially when considering economic constraints and transportation challenges that this age group may face. Integrating these resources into the community profoundly motivates individuals to actively engage in educational initiatives [69]. Furthermore, the significance of the community context cannot be understated, as cultural factors could play a crucial role in shaping the effectiveness of digital inclusion initiatives.

Finally, the third stage involves the evaluation, which is as important as its development and implementation. This stage provides an opportunity to learn about the experiences of the older participants. Through a systematic evaluation, adaptations can be made to respond to older adults' needs, demands, and interests [72]. Therefore, it is necessary to analyze all aspects, including achieving objectives, methodology, and setting. At this point, one can revisit socio-gerontechnology principles to conduct assessments that consider how the interaction with digital devices impacts aging and how older persons model digital devices [22].

6   Future Directions in Educational Gerontechnology

The field of educational gerontechnology will undoubtedly need to continue developing to address various issues related to the digital inclusion of the older population. This development must align with socio-gerontechnology, considering the reciprocal interaction between technology and older adults. Therefore, the development of these future directions assumes that progress is being made (and will continue to be made) to meet the minimum standards required for the digital inclusion of older individuals, namely: (a) accessibility of digital devices; (b) affordability of digital devices and associated

Internet plans for their operation; and (c) adequate coverage of telephone signal and Internet connection.

Firstly, more studies on the effectiveness of different interventions for the digital inclusion of older individuals are needed. This focus will help us understand which methods and approaches are most successful. These studies should consider group and individual instances and those conducted in person, online, or blended. Additionally, we need more information on the impact of different methodologies used in digital inclusion initiatives for older individuals, and this should be addressed from a gender perspective.

Furthermore, we need more evidence on the best strategies for an older person to adhere to an educational initiative for digital inclusion. As shown by other interventions with older adults, the transfer of knowledge and skills acquired to daily life is fundamental for the adherence and effectiveness of the initiatives. [71]. Therefore, future studies should also include this dimension in their designs.

Similarly, it will be crucial to systematize informal instances of digital inclusion, such as those occurring through intergenerational contacts within the family or those generated among peers. It is essential to develop designs that include randomized control trials and longitudinal approaches to measure the effectiveness of these interventions. Longitudinal studies will allow for tracking usage patterns in old age and aging and identifying factors that promote digital inclusion over time, considering that technology is constantly evolving.

Secondly, detailed information is required on why a person participates in digital inclusion activities, going beyond those presented by educational gerontology and adding those relevant to digital inclusion.

Third, it is vital to acknowledge the right to education and digital inclusion throughout the life course. Therefore, future studies should include comparisons with other age ranges and explore how learning linked to new technological developments is incorporated. It is essential to recognize that future older individuals will be "digital natives," but they will also need to update their knowledge of technological advances constantly.

Fourth, there is a need for further exploration into the impact of digital inclusion interventions and the use of digital devices on the well-being of older adults. This evaluation should encompass psychological and physical aspects, considering both beneficial and detrimental effects, such as problematic Internet use. So far, the focus has primarily been on whether older persons use digital devices rather than the direct impact of digital inclusion interventions.

Fifth, it is crucial to recognize that cultural factors significantly impact older individuals' adoption of digital devices. More cross-cultural evidence should be generated to identify relevant factors influencing the development of digital inclusion initiatives. This will facilitate the creation of culturally adapted interventions, promoting better adherence to them.

Sixth, we need a more in-depth exploration of how ethical considerations and concerns linked to technology may influence the adoption of digital devices and the motivation to participate in digital inclusion initiatives. Issues such as data privacy, cybersecurity, and the potential discrimination that older individuals may face through digital devices are particularly relevant and require attention.

Finally, it is crucial not to overlook the impact of aging, which can bring about sensory, motor, or cognitive changes. In this context, further investigation is necessary to understand how these changes affect the interest in digital inclusion and participation in training on this topic. Similar attention should be given to individuals with health conditions such as dementia.

At this point, it is noteworthy that our focus has primarily been on educational studies and practices related to older adults' use of digital devices. However, the field of educational gerontechnology should also broaden its scope to encompass all types of technologies.

With this comprehensive information, we will be able to inform various governmental and non-governmental institutions interested in the subject and actively develop initiatives for the digital inclusion of older adults. Additionally, educational gerontechnology must serve as the foundation for generating public policies.

7 Conclusion

We aimed to address how to strengthen an interdisciplinary dialogue that promotes the digital inclusion of older adults. Educational gerontechnology is poised to play a pivotal role in meeting this challenge, considering gerontology, HCI, and a human rights approach. Gerontology's significance lies in its consideration of crucial aspects such as ageism and educational gerontology, fostering the development of initiatives free from ageist ideas and focused on the unique aspects of learning in old age. Additionally, HCI needs to invest dedicated efforts in designing technologies that align with the needs and interests of older users, challenging prevailing prejudices, and adopting a person-centered approach. This comprehensive strategy is essential for empowering older individuals to enjoy and exercise their human rights.

The call from educational gerontechnology for interdisciplinary collaboration is not merely conceptual; including the older population in society is imperative. The widening digital gap, which excludes older individuals from the digital world, threatens the complete exercise of their rights. The ongoing digitization of daily processes and services highlights the urgency of recognizing that not everything can be digitized unless all individuals are included in the digital world. While acknowledging people's right to choose not to learn about the use of digital devices, this decision must be made with a comprehensive understanding of the advantages and disadvantages of this choice.

Educational gerontechnology holds implications for the development of public policies. Also, this concept provides a foundation for further research to deepen our understanding and enhance initiatives to foster digital inclusion for older adults.

Acknowledgments. This research was supported by the ANID Millennium Science Initiative Program (ICS2019_024).

Disclosure of Interests. The authors have no competing interests to declare that are relevant to the content of this article.

References

1. Seifert, A., Cotten, S.R., Xie, B.: A Double Burden of exclusion? digital and social exclusion of older adults in times of COVID-19. J. Gerontol. B Psychol. Sci. Soc. Sci. **76**, e99–e103 (2021)
2. Lythreatis, S., Singh, S.K., El-Kassar, A.-N.: The digital divide: a review and future research agenda. Technol. Forecasting Soc, Change **175** (2022)
3. Stone, M.E., Lin, J., Dannefer, D., Kelley-Moore, J.A.: The continued eclipse of heterogeneity in gerontological research. J. Gerontol. B Psychol. Sci. Soc. Sci. **72**, 162–167 (2017)
4. Loos, E.F.: Senior citizens: digital immigrants in their own country? Observatorio (OBS*) **6**, 1–23 (2012)
5. Vassilakopoulou, P., Hustad, E.: Bridging digital divides: a literature review and research agenda for information systems research. Inf. Syst. Front. **25**, 955–969 (2023)
6. Fang, M.L., Canham, S.L., Battersby, L., Sixsmith, J., Wada, M., Sixsmith, A.: Exploring privilege in the digital divide: implications for theory, policy, and practice. Gerontologist **59**, e1–e15 (2019)
7. Augner, C.: Digital divide in elderly: Self-rated computer skills are associated with higher education, better cognitive abilities and increased mental health. Europ. J. Psychiatry **36**, 176–181 (2022)
8. Acilar, A., Sæbø, Ø.: Towards understanding the gender digital divide: a systematic literature review. Global Knowl. Memory Commun. **72**, 233–249 (2021)
9. Tichavakunda, A.A., Tierney, W.G.: The "Wrong" Side of the Divide: Highlighting Race for Equity's Sake. J. Negro Educ. **87** (2018)
10. Cheng, H., Lyu, K., Li, J., Shiu, H.: Bridging the Digital Divide for Rural Older Adults by Family Intergenerational Learning: A Classroom Case in a Rural Primary School in China. Int. J. Environ. Res. Public Health **19** (2021)
11. Friemel, T.N.: The digital divide has grown old: determinants of a digital divide among seniors. New Media Soc. **18**, 313–331 (2014)
12. Jun, W.: A study on cause analysis of digital divide among older people in Korea. Int. J. Environ. Res Public Health **18** (2021)
13. Mubarak, F., Suomi, R.: Elderly forgotten? digital exclusion in the information age and the rising grey digital divide. Inquiry **59**, 469580221096272 (2022)
14. Pejić Bach, M., Ivančić, L., Bosilj Vukšić, V., Stjepić, A.-M., Milanović Glavan, L.: Internet usage among senior citizens: self-efficacy and social influence are more important than social support. J. Theor. Appl. Electron. Commer. Res. **18**, 1463–1483 (2023)
15. Kim, H.-N., Freddolino, P.P., Greenhow, C.: Older adults' technology anxiety as a barrier to digital inclusion: a scoping review. Educ. Gerontol. **49**, 1021–1038 (2023)
16. Tomczyk, L., Mroz, A., Potyrala, K., Wnek-Gozdek, J.: Digital inclusion from the perspective of teachers of older adults - expectations, experiences, challenges and supporting measures. Gerontol. Geriatr. Educ. **43**, 132–147 (2022)
17. Sobral, S.R., Sobral, M.: Computer education and third age universities: a systematic review. Int. J. Environ. Res. Public Health **18** (2021)
18. Sanders, C.K., Scanlon, E.: The Digital divide is a human rights issue: advancing social inclusion through social work advocacy. J. Hum. Rights Soc. Work **6**, 130–143 (2021)
19. Kerras, H., Sánchez-Navarro, J.L., López-Becerra, E.I., de-Miguel Gómez, M.D.: The impact of the gender digital divide on sustainable development: comparative analysis between the European Union and the Maghreb. Sustainability **12** (2020)
20. Orosa, T., Sánchez, L.: La educación como derecho de las personas mayores: avances y desafíos. In: Huenchuan, S. (ed.) Visión multidisciplinaria de los derechos humanos de las personas mayores, Comisión Económica para América Latina y el Caribe, pp. 169–183 (CEPAL) (2022)

21. Arias Lopez, M.D.P., et al.: Digital literacy as a new determinant of health: a scoping review. PLOS Digit Health **2**, e0000279 (2023)
22. Peine, A., Marshall, B., Martin, W., Neven, L.: Socio-gerontechnology: key themes, future agendas. In: Peine, A., Marshall, B., Martin, W., Neven, L. (eds.) Socio-gerontechnology: Interdisciplinary Critical Studies of Ageing and Technology, pp. 1–23. Routledge, London (2021)
23. Butler, R.N.: Ageism: another form of bigotry. Gerontologist **9**, 243–246 (1969)
24. Cuddy, A.J.C., Fiske, S.T.: Doddering but dear: Process, content, and function in stereotyping of older persons. Ageism: stereotyping and prejudice against older persons., pp. 3–26. The MIT Press, Cambridge, MA, USA (2002)
25. Chonody, J.M.: Positive and negative Ageism. Affilia **31**, 207–218 (2015)
26. Levy, B.: Stereotype embodiment: a psychosocial approach to aging. Curr. Dir. Psychol. Sci. **18**, 332–336 (2009)
27. Robertson, G.: Ageing and ageism: the impact of stereotypical attitudes on personal health and well-being outcomes and possible personal compensation strategies. Self & Society **45**, 149–159 (2017)
28. Kottl, H., Cohn-Schwartz, E., Ayalon, L.: Self-perceptions of aging and everyday ICT engagement: A test of reciprocal associations. J. Gerontol. B Psychol. Sci. Soc. Sci. (2020)
29. Mariano, J., Marques, S., Ramos, M.R., Gerardo, F., de Vries, H.: Too old for computers? the longitudinal relationship between stereotype threat and computer use by older adults. Front. Psychol. **11**, 568972 (2020)
30. Rosell, J., Vergés, A., Miranda-Castillo, C., Sepulveda-Caro, S., Gómez, M.: Predictors, types of internet use, and the psychological well-being of older adults: a comprehensive model. J. Gerontol. B Psychol. Sci. Soc. Sci. **77**, 1186–1196 (2022)
31. Rosell, J., Vergés, A.: The Impact of Ageism on the E-Leisure of Older People in Chile. In: Gao, Q., Zhou, J. (eds.) HCII 2021. LNCS, vol. 12786, pp. 228–239. Springer, Cham (2021). https://doi.org/10.1007/978-3-030-78108-8_17
32. Lifshitz, R., Nimrod, G., Bachner, Y.G.: Internet use and well-being in later life: a functional approach. Aging Ment. Health **22**, 85–91 (2018)
33. Rosales, A., Svensson, J., Fernández-Ardèvol, M.: Digital ageism in data societies. Digital Ageism, pp. 1–17. Routledge (2023)
34. Chu, C.H., et al.: Age-related bias and artificial intelligence: a scoping review. Humanities Soc. Sci. Commun. **10** (2023)
35. Mannheim, I., et al.: Inclusion of older adults in the research and design of digital technology. Int. J. Environ. Res. Public Health **16** (2019)
36. Mannheim, I., van Zaalen, Y., Wouters, E.J.: Ageism in applying digital technology in health-care: Implications for adoption and actual use. Digital Transformations in Care for Older People. Taylor & Francis (2022)
37. Lee, S.Y., Hoh, J.W.T.: A critical examination of ageism in memes and the role of meme factories. New Media Soc. **25**, 3477–3499 (2021)
38. Berridge, C., Grigorovich, A.: Algorithmic harms and digital ageism in the use of surveillance technologies in nursing homes. Front. Sociol. **7**, 957246 (2022)
39. Peterson, D.A.: Educational gerontology: the state of the art. Educ. Gerontol. **1**, 61–73 (1975)
40. Yuni, J.A., Urbano, C.: Aportes para una conceptualización de la relación entre aprendizaje y resignificación identitaria en la vejez. Palabras Mayores **6**, 1–21 (2011)
41. Xiong, J., Zuo, M.: Older adults' learning motivations in massive open online courses. Educ. Gerontol. **45**, 82–93 (2019)
42. Zaidman, S., Tinker, A.: Computer classes for older people: motivations and outcomes. Working With Older People **20**, 121–130 (2016)
43. Drag, L.L., Bieliauskas, L.A.: Contemporary review 2009: cognitive aging. J. Geriatr. Psychiatry Neurol. **23**, 75–93 (2010)

44. Yuni, J.A.: Educacion de adultos mayores: teoria, investigacion e intervenciones. Editorial Brujas (2005)
45. Stephanidis, C., et al.: Seven HCI Grand Challenges. Inter. J. Hum.-Comput. Interact. **35**, 1229–1269 (2019)
46. Crawford, K., Calo, R.: There is a blind spot in AI research. Nature **538**, 311–313 (2016)
47. Sayago, S.: Editorial Introduction—Perspectives on HCI Research with Older People. In: Sayago, S. (ed.) Perspectives on Human-Computer Interaction Research with Older People, pp. 3–17. Springer International Publishing, Cham (2019). https://doi.org/10.1007/978-3-030-06076-3
48. Schrepp, M., Thomaschewski, J.: Design and validation of a framework for the creation of user experience questionnaires. Inter. J. Interactive Multimedia Artifi. Intell. **5** (2019)
49. Huang, G., Oteng, S.A.: Gerontechnology for better elderly care and life quality: a systematic literature review. Eur. J. Ageing **20**, 27 (2023)
50. Sims, T., Reed, A.E., Carr, D.C.: Information and communication technology use is related to higher well-being among the oldest-old. J. Gerontol. B Psychol. Sci. Soc. Sci. **72**, 761–770 (2017)
51. Li, Q., Luximon, Y.: Older adults' use of mobile device: usability challenges while navigating various interfaces. Behav. Inform. Technol. **39**, 837–861 (2019)
52. Seifert, A., Charness, N.: Digital transformation of everyday lives of older Swiss adults: use of and attitudes toward current and future digital services. Eur. J. Ageing **19**, 729–739 (2022)
53. Portz, J.D., et al.: "Call a teenager... that's what i do!" - grandchildren help older adults use new technologies: Qualitative Study. JMIR Aging **2**, e13713 (2019)
54. Tyler, M., De George-Walker, L., Simic, V.: Motivation matters: older adults and information communication technologies. Stud. Educ. Adults **52**, 175–194 (2020)
55. McLaughlin, A., Pak, R.: Designing displays for older adults. CRC press (2020)
56. Ten Bruggencate, T., Luijkx, K.G., Sturm, J.: Friends or frenemies? the role of social technology in the lives of older people. Int. J. Environ. Res. Public Health **16** (2019)
57. Huenchuan, S., Rodríguez-Piñero, L.: Envejecimiento y derechos humanos: situación y perspectivas de protección Comisión Económica para América Latina y el Caribe (CEPAL) (2010)
58. Bennett, B.: Technology, ageing and human rights: Challenges for an ageing world. Int. J. Law Psychiatry **66**, 101449 (2019)
59. Doh, M., Schmidt, L.I., Herbolsheimer, F., Jokisch, M., Wahl, H.-W.: Patterns of ICT use among "senior technology experts": the role of demographic variables, subjective beliefs and attitudes. In: Zhou, J., Salvendy, G. (eds) Human Aspects of IT for the Aged Population. Design for Aging. ITAP 2015. LNCS, vol 9193. Springer, Cham (2015). https://doi.org/10.1007/978-3-319-20892-3_18
60. International Telecommunication Union (ITU). United Nations. https://www.itu.int/en/sustainable-world/Pages/goal10.aspx
61. Organización Panamericana de la Salud: La Convención Interamericana sobre la Protección de los Derechos Humanos de las Personas Mayores como herramienta para promover la Década del Envejecimiento Saludable. Organización Panamericana de la Salud (OPS) (2023)
62. United Nations Educational, Scientific and Cultural Organization (UNESCO), https://www.uil.unesco.org/es/unesco-instituto/mandato/aprendizaje-largo-de-vida
63. UNESCO: Embracing a culture of lifelong learning: contribution to the Futures of Education initiative. Report: a transdisciplinary expert consultation. United Nations Educational, Scientific and Cultural Organization (UNESCO) (2020)
64. Sahin, M., Akbasli, S., Yelken, T.Y.: Key competences for lifelong learning: the case of prospective teachers. Educ. Res. Rev. **5**, 545 (2010)

65. 6Rivera, M.: Acceso a la tecnología y a la alfabetización mediática e informacional de las personas mayores. In: Huenchuan, S. (ed.) Visión multidisciplinaria de los derechos humanos de las personas mayores, Comisión Económica para América Latina y el Caribe (CEPAL), pp. 187–195 (2022)
66. Scheerder, A., van Deursen, A., van Dijk, J.: Determinants of Internet skills, uses and outcomes. a systematic review of the second- and third-level digital divide. Telematics and Informatics **34**, 1607–1624 (2017)
67. World Economic Forum. https://www.weforum.org/agenda/2021/10/how-can-we-ensure-digital-inclusion-for-older-adults/
68. Choi, E.Y., Kanthawala, S., Kim, Y.S., Lee, H.Y.: Urban/rural digital divide exists in older adults: does it vary by racial/ethnic groups? J. Appl. Gerontol. **41**, 1348–1356 (2022)
69. Schirmer, M., Dalko, K., Stoevesandt, D., Paulicke, D., Jahn, P.: Educational concepts of digital competence development for older adults-a scoping review. Int. J. Environ. Res. Public Health **20** (2023)
70. Steelman, K., Wallace, C.: Breaking barriers, building understanding. ACM SIGACCESS Accessibility Comput., 9–15 (2017)
71. Hernández Salazar, P.: Inclusión digital de personas adultas mayores. Informatio **28**, 303–330 (2023)
72. Bermejo García, L.: Gerontología educativa : cómo diseñar proyectos educativos con personas mayores. Editorial Médica Panamericana, Buenos Aires (2005)
73. Loos, E., Ivan, L.: Using Media Literacy to Fight Digital Fake News in Later Life: A Mission Impossible? , pp. 233–247. Springer Nature Switzerland, (Year)
74. Gates, J.R., Wilson-Menzfeld, G.: What role does geragogy play in the delivery of digital skills programs for middle and older age adults? a systematic narrative review. J. Appl. Gerontol. **41**, 1971–1980 (2022)
75. Knight, T., Yuan, X., Bennett Gayle, D., Xu, H.: Illuminating Privacy and Security Concerns in Older Adults' Technology Adoption. Work, Aging and Retirement (2022)
76. Berčan, M., Ovsenik, M.: Intergenerational learning: a cornerstone of quality aging. J. Educ. Soc. Res. **9**, 67 (2019)
77. Aemmi, S.Z., Karimi Moonaghi, H.: Intergenerational learning program: a bridge between generations. Int. J. Pediatr. **5**, 6731–6739 (2017)
78. Damodaran, L., Sandhu, J.: The role of a social context for ICT learning and support in reducing digital inequalities for older ICT users. Inter. J. Learn. Technol. **11** (2016)
79. Blazic, A.J., Blazic, B.J.: Digital skills for elderly people: a learning experiment in four European countries. Rev. Eur. Stud. **10**, 74 (2018)

The Impact of Pre-pandemic ICT Use on COVID-19 Vaccination and Recovery Among Oldest-Old in Abbiategrasso

Luca Guido Valla[1], Michele Rossi[1], Alessandra Gaia[2(✉)], Antonio Guaita[1], and Elena Rolandi[1,3]

[1] Fondazione Golgi Cenci, Abbiategrasso, Italy
[2] Centre for Longitudinal Studies, UCL Social Research Institute, University College London, London, UK
`a.gaia@ucl.ac.uk`
[3] Department of Brain and Behavioral Sciences, University of Pavia, 27100 Pavia, Italy

Abstract. The use of Information Communication Technologies (ICT) in old age has been increasing over time. This trend might have been accelerated by the COVID-19 pandemic, which prompted older people to start using digital tools to stay connected with their loved ones and tackle isolation. Similarly, ICT use might have positive effects on vaccination rates and recovery from COVID-19 due to, respectively, access to information on vaccines and e-health services that may accelerate the recovery process. However, while it seems reasonable to assume that the use of ICT may improve access to information regarding the COVID-19 vaccination campaigns and ways to avoid SARS-CoV-2 contagion or access to medical support for a faster recovery, to the best of our knowledge, little is known about the effects of ICT use on the SARS-CoV-2 infection figures, vaccination and recovery rates. To explore these dimensions, we use data from a cohort study of older people aged 82–87 years, residing in Abbiategrasso, a municipality in northern Italy. The data used in this study were collected between 2018 and 2022. While ICT use seems not predictive of fewer infections and higher recovery rates, we found that computer use positively predicted the number of vaccine doses that respondents agreed to undertake. However, Internet use predicted late vaccination. In short, it seems that using the Internet in old age predicts a slowness in vaccinating against COVID-19. The latter result enriches the current knowledge on the side effects of Internet access, which have not been thoroughly assessed in older adults. Moreover, this result stimulates discussion on the possible role of online misinformation and fake news surrounding vaccination campaigns.

Keywords: ICT use · Internet Use · Older Adults · COVID-19 Vaccination · SARS-CoV-2 Infection

1 Introduction

ICT use has soared within the old age population in the last few years [1]. The COVID-19 pandemic might have boosted ICT acceptance by older adults, who started or kept using digital technologies to get in touch with family and friends.

Q. Gao and J. Zhou (Eds.): HCII 2024, LNCS 14725, pp. 293–305, 2024.
https://doi.org/10.1007/978-3-031-61543-6_21

In this regard, scientific research has focused on the effects of ICT use on maintaining or strengthening social connections during the pandemic [2, 3]. Indeed, studies on this topic have mainly considered ICT use to address the pandemic's social consequences, such as isolation.

Conversely, the possible effects of ICT use on limiting the spread of SARS-CoV-2 through the provision of information on how to access vaccination programmes and access to e-health, among the old age population, have been mostly overlooked. Still, some studies that explored not COVID-19-related conditions but other aspects of older adults' health showed that access to e-health is positively related to healthy behaviours [4], communication with healthcare professionals [5] and recovery after surgical operations [6]. This issue is particularly urgent when considering the oldest old population, as this age group proved to be particularly vulnerable to the symptoms originating from SARS-CoV-2 infection [7]. Even more so, this was valid for regions where the mortality rate of the old population following SARS-CoV-2 infection has been remarkably high. This was the case in the region of Lombardy, in northern Italy [8].

The vaccination campaign in Italy started in December 2020, when the vaccine was first administered to social and health workers and people who lived in nursing homes. In Lombardy the vaccination campaign was extended to people aged 80 years or older and fragile patients only in mid-February 2021 (approximately 10 days later than other Italian regions, such as Lazio) [9]. Older people could book their vaccine through the portal AIRA; due to faults in the online booking system the portal was subsequently replaced (in April) with a different portal (run by the national mail service and adopted in the rest of the country). While online reservation remained the most straightforward booking system for most of the population, this method may not have been easy to access to less digitally savvy older people – the challenges associated with accessing online booking by the old age population and the malfunctioning of the ARIA system, generate capacity constraints on other booking methods, such as telephone booking. As a matter of fact, in Lombardy, vaccinations in the age group 80–89 started picking up only around March and peaked in mid-April [10]. In comparison with other countries, in Italy fewer than 1.4 million doses were administered to the population aged 80 + by March 10th 2020, while in the United Kingdom over 2.6 million people over the age of 80 were vaccinated by the same week [11, 12].

Taking into account the above, this study seeks to explore the effects of ICT use on SARS-CoV-2 infections and vaccination and recovery rates from COVID-19 in Abbiategrasso, a suburban municipality of approximately 30,000 inhabitants in the outskirts of Milan, in Lombardy. Particularly, we expected that ICT use would reduce, through information campaigns, the frequency of risky behaviours that, in turn, would increase the chances of getting infected by SARS-CoV-2. Accordingly, we hypothesised that the use of digital technologies would accelerate the administration of vaccine doses against COVID-19. In addition, we assumed that ICT use in older adults may be helpful to accelerate the recovery process by providing those aids that are needed during convalescence.

2   Literature Review

The literature on the effects of ICT use on the readiness to vaccinate against COVID-19 in older adults is somewhat scarce. Previous research on this topic has explored the influence of ICT use on vaccination rates, but disregarded the vaccination timing (i.e. early/late vaccination). Particularly, it seems that older adults who rely on the Internet, social media, and family/friends as the main sources of information express weaker intentions to vaccinate against COVID-19 [13]. Indeed, little is known about the effects of digital technologies on earlier/late vaccination in the general population, not to mention in older age. However, this topic is worth exploring, given the strong increase of ICT use in the oldest population, the importance of earlier vaccination to mitigate the symptoms of COVID-19, and the role of digital technologies during the pandemic.

In this regard, the role of ICT in speeding up the vaccination process or, on the contrary, slowing it down through misinformation should be examined. As a matter of fact, evidence exists on how ICT users can be swayed by online misinformation concerning COVID-19 and underestimate the extent to which they are affected by fake news [14]. Yet, it is still to be confirmed whether such or similar effects hold for the older population. Preliminary evidence showed that older adults seem sceptical about the accuracy of online content regarding COVID-19 prevention and treatment [15]. Nonetheless, such evidence came from research on participants who were, on average, relatively young (mean age equalled 60 years), even if considered "older adults". In light of the above, to the best of our knowledge, this is the first study on the impact of using different digital technologies on the rates of vaccination against COVID-19 in people around and over eighty and late vaccination. Previous research was conducted on interventions via specific modalities, such as dialogue-based interventions (dialogue with people that are vaccine hesitant in order to increase the vaccination administration), to help older people overcome the barriers to vaccinating against COVID-19 [16]. Moreover, existing research explored the gender differences in the readiness to be vaccinated against COVID-19 [17]. Generally, ICT use seems to be associated health practices and higher vaccination rates. However, it is still unclear whether these effects are causal (i.e. whether ICT use fosters virtuous practices).

Another dimension that, to the best of our knowledge, has been unexplored concerns the potential effects of ICT use to reduce SARS-CoV-2 infections. Indeed, also in this case, no quantitative studies to date seem to have explored this specific effect in the general population, not counting older adults. There seems to be only qualitative investigation on this topic [18]. However, measuring the relationship between these two variables can shed light on the benefits of digital technologies in communicating risk-avoiding behaviours related to the spread of the virus. Certainly, previous studies have shown that ICT use in older adults is associated with healthy conduct [19]. Empirical evidence is needed to assess whether ICT use also reduces the chances of risky behaviours related to infectious diseases in old age and, consequently, the chances of getting ill.

Similarly, there is a lack of research on the assessment of the effects of ICT use on the recovery of those suffering from COVID-19. A large part of the existing research has been conducted to explore the use of telehealth as a major issue during the pandemic [20, 21]. Following this stream of research, studying the impact of ICT use on COVID-19 patients' convalescence would enrich the literature on the topic. In fact, studies have started to be published on digital tools that help people with long COVID symptoms to recover [22]. However, as a particularly vulnerable group, more research is needed on short-term effects in older adults.

As a whole, it appears that most of the existing academic efforts have been made to study the use of digital technologies to curb the effects of social isolation during the COVID-19 pandemic. Limited evidence has been provided when considering the impact of ICT use on vaccinating against COVID-19. Nonetheless, it is crucial to assess the influence of ICT use on the health-related behaviours of older adults. Indeed, if proven successful, the use of digital technologies could be further encouraged, and ad hoc protocols could be developed.

3 Hypotheses

Considering the above, this study aims to assess whether higher levels of ICT use are associated with a higher number of COVID-19 vaccine doses. In particular, we expected that access to digital resources fosters healthy behaviours and promotes the adoption of measures to mitigate – through vaccination – the risk of suffering from severe COVID-19 symptoms. Consequently, we hypothesised that ICT use counteracts late vaccination by making older people aware of the importance of vaccinating quickly. In addition, we assumed that ICT use helps reduce the incidence of COVID-19 infections by providing people with information on the critical conditions they might face if they are infected. Lastly, we hypothesised that ICT use promotes better long-term health by aiding people in the recovery process through digital tools.

Accordingly, we considered the following hypotheses:

- (H1) Pre-pandemic ICT use predicts more COVID-19 vaccine doses taken.
- (H2) Pre-pandemic ICT use negatively predicts late vaccination.
- (H3) Pre-pandemic ICT use predicts lower levels of COVID-19 infections.
- (H4) Pre-pandemic ICT use predicts higher recovery rates.

4 Methods

The data were collected as part of a population-based cohort study, InveCe.Ab [Brain ageing in Abbiategrasso] [23], aimed to investigate the effects of ageing on physical and cognitive health. Moreover, it was meant to assess the biological and psychosocial factors associated with the onset of dementia. The eligible population for the InveCe.Ab study consisted of individuals born between 1935 and 1939 and residing in Abbiategrasso on the prevalence day (Nov, 1st 2009) and willing to undergo baseline multidimensional assessment (in 2010). Enrolled participants were then invited to 4 follow-up assessments in 2012, 2014, 2018 and 2022. For the aim of the present study, we considered data collected during the 2018 and 2022 waves. The multidimensional assessment comprised a questionnaire on social and lifestyle variables, a medical visit, a neuropsychological evaluation, and the collection of anthropometric measures and blood samples.

4.1 Participants

One thousand three hundred twenty-one people originally took part in InveCe.Ab baseline assessment [23]. In the present study, we included those who took part in the 2018 and 2022 waves, who did not have a diagnosis of dementia and who completed the full version of the questionnaire on social variables (N = 393). 57.3% of participants were female, with an average age of M = 84.30, SD = 1.36. The level of education equalled 7.41 years, SD = 3.35.

A power analysis was conducted with G*Power, version 3.1.9.7 [24] to assess the minimum sample size for the model used for the analysis. The effect size was set at $f2 = 0.05$, with a significance criterion of $a = 0.05$ and power = 0.80. The minimum sample size was 126. Therefore, our sample size is deemed to be adequate for the purpose of this study.

4.2 Measures

ICT Use. In each evaluation wave, the use of ICT was explored with close-ended questions ("Yes", "No", and "I don't know") during the social and lifestyle questionnaire. Since we were interested in assessing the impact of pre-pandemic ICT use on COVID-19-related variables, we used the information on ICT use collected at baseline in 2018. Participants' use of mobile phones was assessed by asking: "Do you use a mobile phone?". If the participants had responded "Yes" to the question asking whether they used a mobile phone, they were asked, "Is it a smartphone?". The usage of computers was investigated by asking: "Do you use a computer?". Similarly, Internet use was explored with the following question: "Do you use the Internet?". Participants were then asked to state whether they used social media by responding to this question: "Do you use social media sites? (e.g., Facebook)".

COVID-19-Related Variables. In 2022 during the medical visit performed by a geriatrician or by a neurologist, participants were asked whether they had received a diagnosis of COVID-19 infection. The possible responses were "Yes", "No", and "I don't know". Participants were then asked whether they had completely recovered from COVID-19. Response categories were: "Yes", "No", and "I don't know". In addition, data were collected on the number of doses of the COVID-19 vaccine administered to the respondent. A derived variable on late vaccination against COVID-19 was calculated as the difference between the maximum number of doses that a person (in that specific age group) could have received at the moment in time when data were collected and the number of doses actually administered.

Socio-Demographic Variables. Further information included age, gender and education.

5 Statistical Analysis

Analysis was conducted using R [25], RStudio [26], the tidyverse [27], lme4 [28], lmerTest [29], performance [30], ggplot2 [31], sjplot [32], sjmisc [33] and sjlabelled [34] packages.

We ran a series of multiple linear regression models to test our hypotheses. We calculated the Variance Inflation Factor (VIF) to check for multicollinearity. Although no standard cut-off has ever been set, according to previous research, the values ranging from 5 to 10 may legitimately serve as a cut-off reference [35]. All our models showed values well below 5. Therefore, we can conclude that multicollinearity was not a concern in our data.

6 Results

Descriptive statistics of the study sample are reported in Table 1. Age, gender ratio and education were comparable with existing studies on ICT use in older people.

Table 1. Descriptive characteristics of this study's sample (N = 393)

Variables	Study sample N = 393
Sociodemographic Characteristics	
Age	84.30 ± 1.36
Gender, female	225 (57.3%)
Education	7.41 ± 3.35
ICT use	
Mobile phone	341 (86.8%)
Smartphone	104 (26.5 %)
Computer	84 (21.4 %)
Internet	87 (22.1 %)
Social media	36 (9.2 %)
Vaccination against COVID-19	
Vaccine doses (Range 2-5)	3.35 ± 0.56
Late vaccination: 0	118 (30%)
Late vaccination: 1	222 (56.5%)
Late vaccination: 2	38 (9.7%)
Late vaccination: 3	1 (0.3%)
COVID-19-related variables	
Diagnosed with COVID-19	90 (22.9%)
Recovered from COVID-19	70 (17.8%)

Firstly, we considered the number of COVID-19 vaccine doses as the dependent variable. The abovementioned ICT use variables were entered as predictors, and the sociodemographic variables as covariates. The results showed that the predictors explained 5.7% of the variance in COVID-19 vaccine doses, $F(8, 335) = 3.57$, $p < 0.001$. Among all the predictors in this model, computer use significantly predicted the number of COVID-19 vaccine doses. Results are shown in Table 2.

We ran a model with late vaccination as the dependent variable to explore this result further. Computer and Internet use were entered as predictors, and the covariates were the same as in the previous model. The results highlighted that the predictors explained 1.7% of the variance in late vaccination, $F(5, 349) = 2.26$, $p = 0.048$. Internet use significantly predicted late vaccination. Results are presented in Table 3.

Table 2. Linear multiple regression models for COVID-19 vaccine doses

Predictors	Estimates	Std. Error	Std. Beta	Standardised std. Error	CI	Standardised CI	Statistic	p
(Intercept)	11.45	1.85	-0.00	0.05	7.81 – 15.09	-0.10 – 0.10	6.19	**<0.001**
Mobile phone	0.19	0.13	0.08	0.05	-0.06 – 0.45	-0.03 – 0.19	1.50	0.135
Smartphone	-0.00	0.08	-0.00	0.06	-0.16 – 0.15	-0.13 – 0.13	-0.02	0.987
Computer	0.25	0.12	0.19	0.09	0.01 – 0.49	0.01 – 0.37	2.05	**0.041**
Internet	-0.25	0.13	-0.19	0.10	-0.51 – 0.01	-0.39 – 0.01	-1.89	0.060
Social media	-0.12	0.12	-0.06	0.06	-0.35 – 0.11	-0.19 – 0.06	-1.00	0.317
Gender	0.03	0.06	0.02	0.06	-0.09 – 0.15	-0.08 – 0.13	0.44	0.657
Age	-0.10	0.02	-0.24	0.05	-0.14 – -0.06	-0.35 – -0.14	-4.55	**<0.001**
Education	0.00	0.01	0.02	0.06	-0.02 – 0.02	-0.11 – 0.14	0.24	0.813

Observations 344

R^2 / R^2 adjusted 0.079 / 0.057

Table 3. Linear multiple regression model for late vaccination

Predictors	Estimates	Std. Error	Std. Beta	Standardised std. Error	CI	Standardised CI	Statistic	p
(Intercept)	5.58	1.99	-0.00	0.05	1.67 – 9.49	-0.10 – 0.10	2.81	**0.005**
Computer	-0.17	0.13	-0.12	0.09	-0.43 – 0.09	-0.30 – 0.06	-1.29	0.197
Internet	0.26	0.13	0.18	0.09	0.00 – 0.52	0.00 – 0.37	2.00	**0.047**
Gender	0.01	0.07	0.01	0.06	-0.12 – 0.15	-0.10 – 0.12	0.17	0.862
Age	-0.06	0.02	-0.13	0.05	-0.10 – -0.01	-0.23 – -0.02	-2.39	**0.017**
Education	-0.01	0.01	-0.07	0.06	-0.04 – 0.01	-0.19 – 0.05	-1.14	0.256

Observations 355

R^2 / R^2 adjusted 0.031 / 0.017

Crosstabulations were calculated by entering computer and Internet use to check for concurrent or independent use of these two technologies. The results showed that 73 people used both computers and the Internet, 11 people used only computers, 14 used only the Internet, and 272 used neither computers nor the Internet.

A logistic regression model (not shown) was used to assess the effects of ICT use on SARS-CoV-2 infections. All the ICT use variables mentioned above were entered as predictors, and COVID-19 diagnosis as the dependent variable. The covariates were the same as above. Results highlighted the lack of statistical significance of this model, $\chi^2(8) = 12.36, p = 0.136$.

Another logistic regression model (also not shown) was run to explore the effects of ICT use on recovery from COVID-19. Also in this case, all the ICT use variables mentioned above were entered as predictors, and the covariates were the same. Recovery from COVID-19 was entered as the dependent variable. Still, this model proved to be not statistically significant, $\chi^2(8) = 1.90$, p $= 0.984$.

7 Discussion

This work aimed to explore the effects of ICT use on vaccinating against COVID-19, SARS-CoV-2 infections and recovery from COVID-19 in a sample of older adults living in Abbiategrasso, a municipality near Milan, Italy.

We hypothesised that pre-pandemic ICT use would predict higher awareness of the availability of vaccination doses and health-related benefits of vaccination, hence, ultimately a higher number of COVID-19 vaccine doses administered (H1). Indeed, we expected that access to digital technologies would foster behaviours aimed at preserving health, such as vaccinating against COVID-19. Results partially supported this hypothesis. Indeed, we found that computer use predicted a higher number of vaccination doses. This result is in line with the existing evidence on the effects of ICT use on vaccination rates in older adults [36, 37]. The other forms of ICT proved not predictive of more vaccine doses taken.

The abovementioned result was further explored by entering computer and Internet use as predictors in the second model. We expected these dimensions would negatively predict a late vaccination rate (H2). Indeed, we assumed that those who use the computer and the Internet would vaccinate more promptly thanks to higher access to information on the importance of early vaccination. The results did not corroborate this hypothesis. On the contrary, Internet use seemed to predict a delayed vaccination rate. This unexpected result would pave the way for reflection and further research. Indeed, if confirmed by additional evidence, it would suggest a possible role of misinformation and fake news surrounding vaccination campaigns affecting older Internet users' decision to vaccinate. In this regard, previous research demonstrated that Internet users are more at risk of being misled when making decisions on health-related issues [38, 39]. Still, little is known about whether this effect holds for older people's decision to vaccinate against COVID-19. Interestingly, the observed effect was not corroborated by computer use. In fact, as mentioned above, computer use predicted a higher number of vaccine doses. These results seem to go exactly in the opposite direction. It is worth noting that the effects of computer and Internet use were independent and controlled for age, gender and education. Regarding the different uses of computers and the Internet, previous research found that word processing is by far the most common activity of computer users, (and is more frequent than Internet use). Among Internet users, information seeking and e-mail exchange is common [40]. Further research is needed to disentangle the specific impact of online activities on older adults' intention to vaccinate.

This study also sought to elucidate the relationship between ICT use and COVID-19 infections in older adults. Out of the entire sample, 90 people were diagnosed with COVID-19 (22.9%). We expected that ICT use would predict fewer infections (H3). Indeed, we assumed that ICT use would increase older people awareness of the risks they would face if infected, thus contributing to lowering infection rates. This hypothesis was in line with the results in the existing literature on the effects of the use of digital technologies and e-health literacy on health-related behaviour in older adults [41, 42]. However, we found no significant effect of ICT use on COVID-19 infections. This result might be partly due to the reduced mobility of the participants in this study and, consequently, the reduced chances of getting infected. Further research is needed to explore the relationship between ICT use and COVID-19 infections in older adults with a lower mean age.

Lastly, we hypothesised that ICT use would predict higher recovery rates in those older adults who had been infected by SARS-CoV-2 (H4). This effect would reflect the existing evidence on the topic [43], albeit limited. We assumed that those who use ICTs would exploit digital tools to speed up the recovery process (through online access to medical information or access to telemedicine). Even in this case, no statistically significant effect was found. This result might be partly due to the relatively low number of infected people in our sample who, therefore, responded to the question on recovery from COVID-19.

8   Strengths and Limitations

This work has several strengths that ought to be pointed out. Firstly, the study used data from a longitudinal cohort, thus allowing to investigate prospectively the impact of pre-pandemic ICT use on COVID-19 related outcomes. This aspect was crucial to assess the influence of pre-pandemic use of digital technologies (rather than relying on post-pandemic data). In a cross-sectional design, the latter could be biased by the heightened usage of ICT to curb social isolation following the most acute phases of the COVID-19 pandemic.

In addition, the participants in this study belonged to a particular age range: 82–87 years. Therefore, we could be confident enough to exclude the great inter-age group variability that previous research discovered when studying the frequency of ICT use [44]. Similarly, the data were collected from participants residing in a specific geographical area. Hence, we could exclude the influence of inter-regional differences that might impact the frequency of digital tools usage [45].

This study has some limitations as well. First, the specific age bracket mentioned above could be considered a limitation. Indeed, ICT use among people aged 80 years or older is, on average, substantially lower than in other age groups [46]. Hence, the results are hardly generalisable to other age groups.

Another limitation relates to the way ICT use was measured. Indeed, this construct was assessed only with dichotomous variables corresponding to the use/lack of use of five digital tools (i.e., computer, Internet, social media, mobile phone, and smartphone). Therefore, we did not assess dimensions such as frequency of use, digital skills, typologies of usages (e.g. socialisation, purchase of goods, access to services), or conditions under which these technologies were utilised.

Lastly, the research design chosen for this research is not experimental. Consequently, we were not able to draw causal inferences.

9　Conclusions and Future Directions

Overall, the research presented in this paper fits into the literature on the impact of ICT use in older adults' lives. Unlike most of the existing literature on the topic, this study did not focus on the effects of ICT use on social relationships but on COVID-19 infections, vaccinations, and recovery. Unexpectedly, we found that the more older adults used the Internet, the slower they were in vaccinating against COVID-19. This result might stem from the possible role played by misinformation that previous research on Internet users' behaviours highlighted [47].

In light of the results and limitations of this study, more research is needed to disentangle the effects of ICT use on SARS-CoV-2 infections and the decision to vaccinate against COVID-19. Future research may use more refined and extensive measurements of ICT use in older adults that could capture a broader picture on this topic. Furthermore, studying more diverse cohorts could lead to a deeper understanding of this area of investigation. Thus, the intergenerational digital divide that previous research highlighted could be further assessed, though data which includes different cohorts [48]. Lastly, research designs other than longitudinal and cross-sectional may allow researchers to reach firmer conclusions.

As a whole, the results presented in this paper, if confirmed by future investigations, will contribute to understanding the complex relationship between ICT use and health-related behaviours in old age.

Acknowledgments. This work has been supported by Fondazione Cariplo, grant n° 2022–1686.

Disclosure of Interests. The authors have no competing interests to declare that are relevant to the content of this article.

References

1. Räsänen, P., Koiranen, I.: Changing patterns of ICT use in Finland – The senior citizens' perspective. In: human aspects of IT for the aged population. Design for Aging: Second International Conference, ITAP 2016, HCI International 2016, Toronto, ON, Canada, 17–22 July 2016, pp. 226–237. Springer International Publishing (2016). https://doi.org/10.1007/978-3-319-39943-0_22
2. Freedman, V.A., Hu, M., Kasper, J.D.: Changes in older adults' social contact during the COVID-19 pandemic. J. Gerontology: Series B. 77(7), e160–e166 (2022). https://doi.org/10.1093/geronb/gbab166
3. Rolandi, E., et al.: Loneliness and social engagement in older adults based in lombardy during the covid-19 lockdown: the long-term effects of a course on social networking sites use. Int. J. Environ. Res. Public Health 17(21), 7912 (2020). https://doi.org/10.3390/ijerph17217912
4. Buyl, R., et al.: E-Health interventions for healthy aging: a systematic review. Syst. Rev. 9(1), 128 (2020). https://doi.org/10.1186/s13643-020-01385-8
5. Ben Hassen, H., Dghais, W. Hamdi, B.: An E-health system for monitoring elderly health based on Internet of Things and Fog computing. Health Inf. Sci. Syst. 7(1), 24 (2019). https://doi.org/10.1007/s13755-019-0087-z
6. Cook, D.J., et al.: Patient engagement and reported outcomes in surgical recovery: effectiveness of an e-health platform. J. Am. Coll. Surg. 217(4), 648–655 (2013). https://doi.org/10.1016/j.jamcollsurg.2013.05.003

7. Niu, S., et al.: Clinical characteristics of older patients infected with COVID-19: a descriptive study. Arch. Gerontol. Geriatr. **89**, 104058 (2020). https://doi.org/10.1016/j.archger.2020.104058

8. Ferroni, E., et al.: Survival of hospitalized COVID-19 patients in Northern Italy: a population-based cohort study by the ITA-COVID-19 network. Clin. Epidemiol. **12**, 1337–1346 (2020). https://doi.org/10.2147/CLEP.S271763

9. Monaci, S.: Lombardia, azzerati vertici Aria. Tutti i flop: dai vaccini al sistema informatico, *Il Sole 24 Ore* (2021, 21 Mar). https://www.ilsole24ore.com/art/sistema-informatico-tilt-appalti-sotto-inchiesta-escarsa-pianificazione-ecco-perche-la-centrale-acquisti-aria-non-fun ziona-ADEp37RB. Accessed 12 May 2024

10. Vaccini in tempo reale. https://lab24.ilsole24ore.com/numeri-vaccini-italia-mondo/?refresh_ ce=1. Accessed 12 May 2024

11. NHS England. COVID-19 vaccinations archive. https://www.england.nhs.uk/statistics/sta tistical-work-areas/covid-19-vaccinations/covid-19-vaccinations-archive/. Accessed 12 May 2024

12. Task force COVID-19 del Dipartimento Malattie Infettive e Servizio di Informatica, Istituto Superiore di Sanità. Epidemia COVID-19. Istituto Superiore di Sanità (ISS), Rome (2021). https://www.epicentro.iss.it/coronavirus/bollettino/Bollettino-sorveglianza-int egrata-COVID-19_10-marzo-2021.pdf. Accessed 12 May 2024

13. Bhagianadh, D., Arora, K.: COVID-19 vaccine hesitancy among community-dwelling older adults: the role of information sources. J. Appl. Gerontol. **41**(1), 4–11 (2022). https://doi.org/10.1177/07334648211037507

14. Yang, J., Tian, Y.: 'others are more vulnerable to fake news than i am': third-person effect of covid-19 fake news on social media users. Comput. Human Behav. **125**, 106950 (2021). https://doi.org/10.1016/j.chb.2021.106950

15. Choudrie, J., Banerjee, S., Kotecha, K., Walambe, R., Karende, H., Ameta, J.: Machine learning techniques and older adults processing of online information and misinformation: a covid 19 study. Comput. Human Behav. **119**, 106716 (2021). https://doi.org/10.1016/j.chb.2021.106716

16. Desir, M. Cuadot, A., Tang, F.: Addressing Barriers to COVID-19 vaccination among older U.S. Veterans. J. Community Health **47**(4), 616–619 (2022). https://doi.org/10.1007/s10900-022-01087-3

17. Paimre, M., Osula, K.: Gender Differences in ICT Acceptance for health purposes, online health information seeking, and health behaviour among estonian older adults during the Covid-19 Crisis. In: Proceedings of the 8th International Conference on Information and Communication Technologies for Ageing Well and e-Health, pp. 134–143. SCITEPRESS - Science and Technology Publications (2022). https://doi.org/10.5220/0011089400003188

18. Llorente-Barroso, C., Kolotouchkina, O., Mañas-Viniegra, L.: The enabling role of ICT to mitigate the negative effects of emotional and social loneliness of the elderly during COVID-19 pandemic. Int. J. Environ. Res. Public Health **18**(8), 3923 (2021). https://doi.org/10.3390/ijerph18083923

19. Satake, S., Kinoshita, K. Arai, H.: More Active Participation in voluntary exercise of older users of information and communicative technology even during the COVID-19 Pandemic, independent of frailty status.: J. Nutr. Health Aging **25**(4), 516–519 (2021). https://doi.org/10.1007/s12603-021-1598-2

20. Goodman-Casanova, J.M., Dura-Perez, E., Guzman-Parra, J., Cuesta-Vargas, A., Mayoral-Cleries, F.: Telehealth home support during COVID-19 confinement for community-dwelling older adults with mild cognitive impairment or mild dementia: survey study. J. Med. Internet Res. **22**(5), e19434 (2020). https://doi.org/10.2196/19434

21. Li, K.Y., et al.: Perceptions of telehealth among older U.S. adults during the COVID-19 pandemic: a national survey. J. Telemed. Telecare. 1357633X2311660 (2023). https://doi.org/10.1177/1357633X231166031

22. Lloyd-Evans, P.H.I., et al.: Early experiences of the Your COVID Recovery® digital programme for individuals with long COVID. BMJ Open Respir. Res. **9**(1), e001237 (2022). https://doi.org/10.1136/bmjresp-2022-001237

23. Guaita, A. et al.: Brain aging and dementia during the transition from late adulthood to old age: design and methodology of the 'Invece.Ab' population-based study. BMC Geriatr. **13**(1), 98 (2013). https://doi.org/10.1186/1471-2318-13-98

24. Faul, F., Erdfelder, E., Lang, A.-G., Buchner, A.: G*Power 3: a flexible statistical power analysis program for the social, behavioral, and biomedical sciences. Behav. Res. Methods **39**(2), 175–191 (2007). https://doi.org/10.3758/BF03193146

25. R Core Team: R: A Language and Environment for Statistical Computing. R Foundation for Statistical Computing, Vienna, Austria. (2023)

26. Posit team: RStudio: Integrated Development Environment for R. Posit Software, PBC, Boston, MA (2023)

27. Wickham, H., et al.: Welcome to the Tidyverse. J. Open Source Softw. **4**(43), 1686 (2019). https://doi.org/10.21105/joss.01686

28. Bates, D., Mächler, M., Bolker, B., Walker, S.: Fitting linear mixed-effects models using lme4. J. Stat. Softw. **67**(1) (2015). https://doi.org/10.18637/jss.v067.i01

29. Kuznetsova, A., Brockhoff, P.B., Christensen, R.H.B.: lmerTest package: tests in linear mixed effects models. J. Stat. Softw. **82**(13) (2017). https://doi.org/10.18637/jss.v082.i13

30. Lüdecke, D., Ben-Shachar, M, Patil, I., Waggoner, P., Makowski, D.: Performance: an R package for assessment, comparison and testing of statistical models. J. Open Source Softw. **6**(60), 3139 (2021). https://doi.org/10.21105/joss.03139

31. Wickham, H.: ggplot2: Elegant Graphics for Data Analysis. Springer-Verlag, Cham (2016). https://doi.org/10.1007/978-3-319-24277-4

32. Lüdecke, D.: sjPlot: Data Visualization for Statistics in Social Science (2023)

33. Lüdecke, D.: sjmisc: Data and Variable Transformation Functions. J. Open Source Softw. **3**(26), 754 (2018). https://doi.org/10.21105/joss.00754

34. Lüdecke, D.: sjlabelled: Labelled Data Utility Functions (2022)

35. Stine, R.A.: Graphical interpretation of variance inflation factors. Am. Stat. **49**(1), 53–56 (1995). https://doi.org/10.1080/00031305.1995.10476113

36. Ghadieh, A.S., Hamadeh, G.N., Mahmassani, D.M., Lakkis, N.A.: The effect of various types of patients' reminders on the uptake of pneumococcal vaccine in adults: a randomized controlled trial. Vaccine. **33**(43), 5868–5872 (2015). https://doi.org/10.1016/j.vaccine.2015.07.050

37. Minor, D.S., Eubanks, J.T., Butler, K.R., Wofford, M.R., Penman, A.D., Replogle, W.H.: Improving Influenza vaccination rates by targeting individuals not seeking early seasonal vaccination. Am. J. Med. **123**(11), 1031–1035 (2010). https://doi.org/10.1016/j.amjmed.2010.06.017

38. Tan, A.S.L., Lee, C., Chae, J.: Exposure to health (mis)information: lagged effects on young adults' health behaviors and potential pathways. J. Commun. **65**(4), 674–698 (2015). https://doi.org/10.1111/jcom.12163

39. Roozenbeek, J., et al.: Susceptibility to misinformation about COVID-19 around the world. R. Soc. Open Sci. **7**(10), 201199 (2020). https://doi.org/10.1098/rsos.201199

40. Morris, A., Goodman, J., Brading, H.: Internet use and non-use: views of older users. Univers. Access Inf. Soc. **6**(1), 43–57 (2007). https://doi.org/10.1007/s10209-006-0057-5

41. Xie, B.: Older adults, e-health literacy, and collaborative learning: an experimental study. J. Am. Soc. Inform. Sci. Technol. **62**(5), 933–946 (2011). https://doi.org/10.1002/asi.21507

42. Jeong, J.H., Kim, J.S.: Health Literacy, Health Risk Perception and Health Behavior of Elders. J. Korean Acad. Commun. Health Nursing **25**(1), 65 (2014). https://doi.org/10.12799/jkachn.2014.25.1.65

43. Salman, D., et al.: Movement Foundations. The perceived impact of a digital rehabilitation tool for returning to fitness following a period of illness, including COVID-19 infection: a qualitative study. BMJ Open Sport. Exerc. Med. **9**(2), e001557 (2023). https://doi.org/10.1136/bmjsem-2023-001557

44. Näsi, M., Räsänen, P., Sarpila, O.: ICT activity in later life: Internet use and leisure activities amongst senior citizens in Finland. Eur. J. Ageing **9**(2), 169–176 (2012). https://doi.org/10.1007/s10433-011-0210-8

45. Zambianchi, M., Rönnlund, M., Carelli, M.G.: Attitudes towards and use of information and communication technologies (icts) among older adults in italy and sweden: the influence of cultural context, socio-demographic factors, and time perspective. J. Cross Cult. Gerontol. **34**(3), 291–306 (2019). https://doi.org/10.1007/s10823-019-09370-y

46. König, R., Seifert, A., Doh, M.: Internet use among older Europeans: an analysis based on SHARE data. Univers. Access Inf. Soc. **17**(3), 621–633 (2018). https://doi.org/10.1007/s10209-018-0609-5

47. Chia, S.C., Lu, F., Sun, Y.: Tracking the Influence of misinformation on elderly people's perceptions and intention to accept COVID-19 vaccines. Health Commun. **38**(5), 855–865 (2023). https://doi.org/10.1080/10410236.2021.1980251

48. Sala, E., Gaia, A., Cerati, G.: The Gray Digital divide in social networking site use in europe: results from a quantitative study. Soc. Sci. Comput. Rev. **40**(2), 328–345 (2022). https://doi.org/10.1177/0894439320909507

Rethinking Our Approach to Accessibility in the Era of Rapidly Emerging Technologies

Gregg Vanderheiden[1]([⊠]) [iD], Crystal Marte[2] [iD], and Sina Bahram[3] [iD]

[1] University of Maryland, College Park, MD 20742, USA
GreggVan@umd.edu
[2] Raising the Floor, Washington, DC 20002, USA
crystal@raisingthefloor.org
[3] Prime Access Consulting, Cary, NC 27511, USA

Abstract. Accessibility has always played catch-up to the detriment of people with disabilities - and this appears to be exacerbated by the rapid advancements in technology. A key question becomes, can we better predict where technology will be in 10 or 20 years and develop a plan to be better positioned to make these new technologies accessible when they make it to market? To attempt to address this question, a "Future of Interface Workshop" was convened in February 2023, chaired by Vinton Cerf and Gregg Vanderheiden that brought together leading researchers in artificial intelligence, brain-computer interfaces, computer vision, and VR/AR/XR, and disability to both a) identify barriers these new technologies might present and how to address them, and b) how these new technologies might be tapped to address current un- or under-addressed problems and populations. This paper provides an overview of the results of the workshop as well as the current version of the R&D Agenda work that was initiated at the conference. It will also present an alternate approach to accessibility that is being proposed based on the new emerging technologies.

Keywords: Accessibility · Regulations · Policy · Equity

1 Introduction

1.1 Future of Interface Workshop

On Feb 15–16, 2023, a two-day workshop was held by co-chairs Vinton Cerf and Gregg Vanderheiden [1]. The Day 1 panels brought together top experts in their mainstream technology specialization to explore key technologies that will be used to create future interfaces and try to predict where these technologies, and where human interfaces in general, will be in 20 years. Day 2 panels brought together disability and accessibility experts, consumers, assistive technology vendors, and mainstream researchers to identify and explore barriers that these new interface technologies might present, as well as potential ways to address these barriers. The panels explored ways that these new technologies could help to address existing barriers that we are unable to adequately address today. Concluding the workshop was a kickoff to the R&D agenda creation process to lay out research that could/should be undertaken and supported to maximize the accessibility of new technologies as they emerge.

Q. Gao and J. Zhou (Eds.): HCII 2024, LNCS 14725, pp. 306–323, 2024.
https://doi.org/10.1007/978-3-031-61543-6_22

The R&D agenda outlines a forward-thinking approach to accessibility, with a comprehensive framework spanning the next two decades. At its core, the agenda emphasizes capitalizing on emerging technologies to both help integrate accessibility into mainstream technology from the outset, as well as to provide a path to full access to technologies including access by those who are not covered by built-in access. This paradigm combines "born-accessible" for those for whom it is possible, with sure solutions for providing access for all those for whom accessibility is not provided, either because we do not know how to, or because it simply is not done by the manufacturer. Accessibility needs to be embedded into the DNA of emerging and future technologies in a way that does not exclude anyone. Digital technologies have become too integral in our lives today and going forward for them not to be accessibility by all.

Central to the agenda is significant R&D investment in artificial intelligence (AI) and machine learning technologies to create intelligent user agents. These agents would offer nuanced and context-aware assistance, autonomously detecting and adapting to the users' environment, potential dangers, or unfamiliar situations –thereby offering personalized support to users with disabilities.

Direct brain interfaces (DBIs) and extended reality (XR) represent another frontier for accessibility research. The agenda outlines the potential for non-invasive DBIs to enable individuals with severe motor impairments to interact with technology directly through neural signals. With the rapid evolution of XR, including augmented reality (AR) and virtual reality (VR), and integration into society (e.g., Meta Quest, Apple Vision Pro), it becomes essential that these technologies are accessible – and soon. The agenda calls for going beyond addressing visual and auditory experience to a multisensory virtual experience that would include the use of and access to tactile and output. The participants expect that capabilities, digital interactions could be as rich and richer and more complex as those in the physical world. At the same time, they provide an opportunity to provide accessibility options beyond what is possible in the physical world.

In addition to the technical advances, a deeper understanding of the diverse needs, constraints, and abilities of different types, degrees, and combinations of disabilities than we have is also needed so that we can develop more personalized and effective assistive technologies for all types, degrees, and combinations of disability that we do not currently serve.

The draft R&D agenda also includes a need for research on the societal, ethical, and policy implications of technology advancements for people with disabilities, such as data privacy, the economic barriers to access, and the pervasive issue of bias in AI datasets. These technologies pose potential risks and challenges to an already vulnerable population, so there is a need for robust bias, privacy, and security frameworks and measures to ensure these technology environments are safe, appropriate, and effective for all users.

Understanding current and future barriers and opportunities is crucial for creating technologies that are accessible to all and can help remove obstacles that individuals with disabilities face today and might encounter tomorrow. The goal of the workshop and the continuing goal of the R&D Agenda development is to contribute to a collaborative roadmap for researchers, developers, and policymakers, outlining priority areas for investment, development, and policy advocacy; collaboration is of the utmost importance.

One key result was a discussion of whether emerging technologies would allow us to take alternative approaches. In particular, was the concern that current approaches were not resulting in even a substantial percentage of products being accessible, and those that were, were only accessible to some people with some type, degree, and combination of disability. Further, this was not seen as being solvable using existing approaches with new technologies.

2   Is There a Need for a Change in Approach?

2.1   Access to Technology is no Longer an Option - but a Requirement for Daily Living

With the continued integration of computers and digital technologies into all aspects of our lives, including education, employment, health, and social connection, the ability to use digital interfaces has become critical to all aspects of living. Currently, 76% of U.S. hospitals connect with patients and consulting practitioners at a distance through video and other technology [2]. Patients now use online portals to schedule appointments, access medical records, and communicate with doctors. Nearly one in four adults in the US reported using telehealth from April 2021 to August 2022 [3]. When looking at K-12 schools, 75–85% used online textbooks to some extent, according to the National Center for Education Statistics. Additionally, 95% of schools reported that, to some extent, they use technology for classroom activities that would otherwise not be possible [4]. A 2015 Pew Research study found that digital resources were critical to Americans' ability to research and apply for jobs. Specifically, most Americans (54%) went online to look for information about a job, and nearly as many (45%) applied for a job online [5]. In addition to needing access to digital technologies to search, apply for, and acquire a job, there is an overwhelming demand for digital skills when looking at opportunities in the job market, with 92 percent of all job ads requiring digital skills [6].

2.2   Our Current Approach(es) is not Providing Access to Most ICT - and None for Many

To ensure that products with digital interfaces are accessible to people with disabilities, a series of guidelines, standards, and regulations have been developed for computers, websites, telephones, software, medical devices, self-service transaction machines, and consumer products [7–10] Many large companies (e.g., Apple, Google, IBM, Microsoft) have dedicated teams to improve accessibility and have built significant accessibility features directly into their products [11–14] The growing emphasis on accessibility in the industry has given rise to consultants, accessibility evaluation and remediation companies, and programs aimed at developing, training, and certifying accessibility specialists [15–17].

Despite all the progress in accessibility, however, we have barely made a dent in making all of the products that people with disabilities encounter accessible.

Cumulative data on overall product accessibility are sparse, but where we do have data, the results are discouraging. For example, looking at web accessibility, where an entire industry has evolved, with numerous organizations, training courses, specialized consulting firms, and tools (e.g., authoring, evaluation, testing, repairing, etc.), as well as regulations and lawsuits – we still find that the percentage of websites that are accessible is quite low. A 2023 study by WebAIM evaluated website homepages and found that less than 4% achieved full Web Content Accessibility Guidelines 2 Level AA compliance based on automated scanning. And this study only looked at guidelines that could be automatically checked [18].

Furthermore, a 2012 study by the University of York revealed that "only 50.4% of the problems encountered by [blind] users were even covered by Success Criteria in the Web Content Accessibility Guidelines [WCAG] 2.0 [19]. In other words, even pages that do comply with minimum accessibility guidelines like WCAG aren't necessarily accessible and usable by all people with disabilities. The WCAG working group confirms this, as they explicitly state in the introduction of WCAG:

"...even content that conforms at the highest level (AAA) will not be accessible to individuals with all types, degrees, or combinations of disability, particularly in the cognitive, language, and learning areas. Authors are encouraged to consider the full range of techniques, including the advisory techniques in "Making Content Usable for People with Cognitive and Learning Disabilities," as well as to seek relevant advice about current best practices to ensure that Web content is accessible, as far as possible, to this community." [8].

One reason is that it is difficult to establish testable requirements for some groups, such as cognitive, language, and learning disabilities. For example, using plain language is an important recommendation for this group, but there are no reliable measures for plain language, making it hard to set a testable criterion for it. Although there are advisory techniques for CLL disabilities (e.g., the W3C document on "Making Content Usable for People with Cognitive and Learning Disabilities" these are not technical standards and are therefore not able to be used in regulations or other requirements [20].

Mobile apps are similarly not accessible. Yan and Ramachandran used the IBM Mobile Accessibility Checker to analyze the accessibility of 479 Android apps across 23 categories and calculate the degree of violation. They found that 94.8% had violations and 97.5% had potential violations [21]. Ross et al. found that 100% of 100 popular mobile applications had at least one accessibility problem, and 72% had 5 or 6 accessibility problems [22].

Emerging technologies such as virtual and augmented reality are also presenting new challenges. By design, they capitalize on the simultaneous use of sight, hearing, and motor control. These new technologies and their interface techniques can exclude many people with both single and multiple disabilities. Even companies with large accessibility teams struggle to make their cutting-edge technologies, such as VR, accessible, as do many VR researchers and developers [23].

Although corporations like Apple, Google, and Microsoft appear to prioritize accessibility and have accessibility teams that develop products with a range of accessibility features built-in [12–14], they are the exception. Studies have found that many companies do not prioritize accessibility and report a lack of expertise and resources (e.g., staff or tools) that would enable or facilitate the development of accessible products [24–26].

And even products that have *built-in accessibility features* only address some individuals with some disabilities. For example, accessibility features available in smartphones are typically focused on one or another disability type, which doesn't account for people who may have multiple disabilities (and are unable to use many of these techniques). People with multiple disabilities have received less attention compared to research on specific disabilities. In reviewing the accessibility features in phones, some disabilities like cognitive, language, and learning disabilities are noticeably less covered. Furthermore, these built-in features don't consider the spectrum that exists within disability groups and may only be applicable to those who have a more severe limitation or who are more technically adept. Bowman et al. found that people with mild-to-moderate dexterity were not well-accommodated by existing motor assistive technology and suggested that this may be because research and design have typically focused on people with more acute motor needs (e.g., switches and voice input) [27] use the products.

In short, we have come a long way from zero accessibility 40 years ago, but in all this time using our current approaches, we have only managed to provide access to people with some disabilities to a small percentage of the products they encounter – and now need to use to succeed in school, work, social participation, travel, or even independent living.

Moreover, even though only a small percentage of information and communication technologies (ICT) and products with digital interfaces are accessible, progress seems to be slowing rather than accelerating.

3   Current Approach vs. Proposed New Approach

3.1   Current Approach

Our current approach to accessibility has basically been to:

1. **For all products** - require that products be made directly accessible as much as possible/practical
2. **For open products (with accessibility APIs)** - use assistive technologies to cover those who aren't reached with built-in accessibility features
3. **For closed products or functionality (where assistive technology cannot be used)** - build accessibility into the product as you can for key disabilities

   Unfortunately,

- Most companies do not do #1 or #2 above for their products – because the investment of time, expertise, or effort required does not compete within the company against investing in a new feature or other measures that increase marketability or profit. Also, many companies feel they are too small to do this.
- Even for those that do #2, assistive technologies only exist for some disabilities (and even those features often require moderate to higher technical skills).

- For closed products, built-in accessibility features are usually minimal and don't address all disabilities. And for those who are not addressed, nothing else is possible since the products are closed to assistive technologies.

For example, most of the computers, websites, and even smartphones that "are accessible to people who are blind" (e.g., have screen reading built into them) are only usable by individuals who are blind but who also possess a certain level of technical proficiency and fine motor control. There are large numbers of individuals who are blind who are unable to use screen readers or any of the built-in access features in modern smartphones designed for people who are blind. Many find screen readers (including built-in screen readers in mobile devices) too complicated to use or require physical gestures they cannot remember or cannot reliably perform due to physical limitations.

Some of the other big gaps in the current approach are:

1. Most people designing products do not know how to create their products to be usable across disability. Furthermore, training the people involved in the design of every product – across all disabilities – is difficult, even to a basic level. Disability experts, including this paper's authors, find that they need to consult with colleagues whenever they are faced with having to design a product for cross-disability. If this is true for the authors who focus just on this, how can the constantly changing designers in companies be kept up to the challenge?
2. Even when the current design guidelines are met, they are only "minimum accessibility guidelines." Meeting them leaves many individuals with disabilities unable to use the products. In addition, populations like cognitive, language, and learning disabilities are not fully covered in minimum accessibility standards because, as a field we do not know how to make enforceable, testable guidelines to meet their needs. And 'no regulations' means no pressure to include features or characteristics these users need.
3. We are increasingly finding digital interfaces on closed products. Closed products are products where it's not possible to install or attach assistive technologies. These products also often have minimal or no built-in accessibility. Therefore, closed products or products with closed functionality are inaccessible to many, and nothing can be done for those who can't use them as they are designed.
4. Even for the relatively few products that are fairly accessible, users with more severe cognitive disabilities, or multiple disabilities, are usually not addressed. Sometimes, there are features for more severe disabilities (e.g., physical) but not for mild-moderate disabilities [26]

Ultimately, this results in a large portion of the population being unable to use the digital interfaces they find on products all around them. And there is very little chance that companies will or even know how to make all products, both open and closed, accessible to people with all types, degrees, and combinations of disability.

3.2 Proposed Approach

The proposal is to shift the PRIMARY focus of accessibility efforts...
  FROM (currently)

- getting all companies to try to build their products inclusively to meet the needs of all types, degrees, and combinations of disability.
- PLUS (as a safety net for those for whom one is not done) - getting all companies to make their products compatible with all AT for anyone they cannot, or do not accommodate, directly.
- EXCEPT if the product is closed or has closed functionality - in which case there is no safety net.

  TO (proposed)

- Creating an information-robot (Info-bot) functionality that can understand and operate the standard user interface on any product a person encounters – thus requiring no cooperation or action by product manufacturers at all in order to work.
- PLUS - creating Individual User Interface Generators (IUIGs) that are tuned to the specific abilities of each individual person - regardless of types, degrees, and combinations of disability - and can take output from the Info-bot and use it to generate an optimized interface that person for each product that person encounters.
- WHERE - the Info-bot functionality would be open-source and free to use for both companies (for testing and training) and users. And that it runs locally so that there is no data leakage from the user to the cloud from its use or person-specific training or learning.

   This proposed approach would not mean companies should discontinue building accessibility directly into their products. For the people whose needs are fully met by the built-in accessibility, this approach works, it is most convenient, and allows direct access to the products.

   However, for all products where a) built-in accessibility is not provided, b) built-in accessibility does not meet a person's needs, or c) where compatibility with assistive technologies is not provided, this alternate approach would work. It would also work for all those products that have none of the above, or where the manufacturer is unaware or does not make any attempt to make their product accessible (Table 1).

3.3 One Possible Implementation of the General Proposed Approach

This approach would augment our current strategies with a new technology that can interact with digital interfaces without requiring any special APIs and using only the standard interface provided to all mainstream users. That is, it would use computer vision, hearing, and intelligence as input and present the user with an interface tailored specifically to their needs and abilities.

Table 1. A comparison of the two approaches

	Current Approach	Proposed Approach
Primary focus	Built-in direct accessibility	Info-bot + Individual User Interface Generators
Secondary focus	Build in compatibility with assistive technologies PLUS Assuming availability of assistive technologies for each type of disability	Built-in direct accessibility
What safety net is provided if Primary and Secondary focus do not work?	None - for any product where AT compatibility is not provided None - for all closed products	No need for a safety net if IUIGs are available As long as the median user without disabilities can operate the product the Info-bot can, and IUIGs will provide match individuals
Assumptions	all companies will be able to and build in accessibility for all types, degrees, and combinations of disability OR all companies will build open products AND there will be AT that works for all types, degrees, and combinations of disability	An Info-bot can be created that can operate any standard user interface that a median user without disabilities can IUIGs will be designed (or can self-evolve) to match the needs and abilities of people with all types, degrees, and combinations of disability
Percentage of products that are likely to be directly accessible, (meet minimum accessibility standards)	5–10%, perhaps 10–20% with AI assistance	99% (i.e., the percentage of products that have a standard interface useable by median user)
Percentage of types, degrees, and combinations of disability accommodated	3–6% (% of products that are accessible directly or work with assistive technologies)	Limited only by the number and variety of Individual User Interface Generators (IUIGs) created
Probability that the approach would be adopted	100% by the accessibility field (it is the approach today) 6–10% by companies	Probability in short term is not known. Probably it is 100% in 50 years. But sooner? How much sooner?

(continued)

Table 1. (*continued*)

	Current Approach	Proposed Approach
Need to change accessibility policy and regulations	None - continue as now	Potentially large change in accessibility policy required (unless standards / regulations are written as outcomes at the user end and not at product ship or purchase time.)
Need to invest R&D to achieve	Needed for incremental improvement and for new technologies Massive if more than the current small % of coverage is desired	Large amount needed - although much will be done as part of normal AI work Much is also needed to understand what IUIGs need to look like for each type, degree, and combination of disability

Specifically, the two major functions described above could be implemented as follows (see also Fig. 1):

1. **The information robot (Info-bot)** (or information robot functionality) would be a single, open-source intelligent agent – that can be pointed at any interface, and it would be able to understand and operate the interface as well as 50% of the population. It would not be as smart as the best human or even the top 30% of humans. But it would be as smart or as able as the median user of a product at understanding and using the interface on the product.
2. **The individual user interface generators (IUIGs)** would be specific to an individual and take the information from the Info-bot and create an interface for each product a user encounters that would be tailored to that individual's abilities, limitations, knowledge, background, culture, and preferences.

Key to this is that the Info-bot does not require anything or any action on the manufacturer's part for it to work since it works directly off of the standard user interface. Any product that has a standard user interface that can be used by half of the population could be understood and operated by the Info-bot.

1. Manufacturers would not have to understand or make specific provisions for accessibility.
2. They would not have to train their staff.
3. They would not have to implement accessibility standards.
   a. They would not even have to know about disabilities or accessibility standards or guidelines.

And if an IUIG existed for a person - regardless of their type, degree, and combination of disability - any product would be useable by that person.

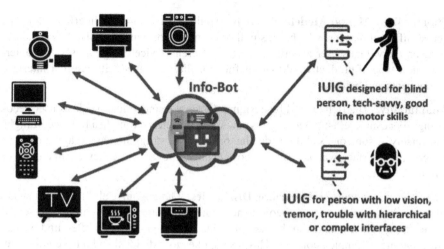

Fig. 1. Diagram showing the relation of devices in the environment, the Info-bot, and Individual User Interface Generators (IUIGs) for two people.

4   Potential Benefits of Such an Approach

4.1   Benefits from a User Perspective

Some potential benefits to users include:

Universally Compatible. Because it would rely only on the standard interface, this strategy does not require any special API to work. Therefore, the system would work on all products everywhere - providing access to essentially 100% of the interfaces a person encounters.

Near Total Accessibility. Because of universal compatibility, the info-bot plus IUIG would provide a major leap forward for accessibility, giving people with disabilities access to **all** the same products in the same places as everyone else.

Unified Interface for Similar Products. Users would only need to learn one interface for products with the same or similar functions. The Info-bot/IUIG could offer a consistent and familiar experience across all similar devices or services. (e.g., all microwaves, all streaming services on TV, thermostats, or any other product – even a new one encountered at a location while traveling would have the same interface presented to the user for the same functionality.)

Control Over [Unsolicited] Changes. The IUIG would generate an interface that remains unchanged for the user, even if the interface of a product undergoes an update or change. The system may prompt users to try out the new interface features, but they would not be forced to use them.

Standardized Mental Model. The IUIG would present familiar interface elements across different devices, whether it's pull-down menus or twisting dials, thus standardizing an individual's user experience across different devices. (e.g., a user encountering a new type of product would see its functionality presented with familiar interface components and behaviors).

Adaptability. The IUIG could be designed to adapt to individual needs as user needs change. For example, as someone gains new skills, the interface might adjust accordingly. Conversely, if someone's abilities decline or if they're struggling due to aging or other factors, the interface would adapt to those changes - even when they change daily or within the same day.

Cognitive, Language, and Learning Disabilities. Our cognitive abilities aren't static. It is a familiar experience for someone to not understand some concept until it is presented more simply, often with a simple example. Once that is grasped, we often find we can grasp the more complex concept. This also applies to individuals who have cognitive, language, and learning disabilities. So, setting a static bar at a low level to allow initial understanding can deny people with intellectual disabilities the opportunity to understand a concept more fully. Instead, the IUIGs could start at a level the user understands and then gradually increase in complexity as a user grasps the concept – allowing every user to engage with technology and content successfully and more fully.

Neurodivergent Users. Neurodivergent users vary widely in their needs. Some require interfaces without flashing. Others need interfaces that are stable and do not change. For others, they need to be able to control how things are presented to them – and to have things done in a consistent way across products from different manufacturers. Some require unique interaction patterns. The proposed approach is ideal for these users in that the interfaces they experience will be tailored for them and be stable over time and across both product types and manufacturers within a product type.

Reducing the Learning Curve. Just as introducing content at a lower level and then raising it, IUIGs could start by using interface paradigms that are simpler or already familiar to the user when they encounter a new device or task. Then, as a person achieves skill and understands the task - more efficient interface elements could be introduced for adoption or rejection by the user.

4.2   Benefits to Industries

Some of the benefits to industry would include:

Decreased Burden. The Info-bot/IUIG would not require anyone to have a deep understanding (or actually any understanding) of disability or accessibility principles in order to ensure wide accessibility coverage for their products. It would also reduce the burden of constantly training staff.

This does not mean that companies should cease developing products that are accessible out of the box for as many people as they can. It does mean, however, that they would be able to reach a much broader range of users - and have a safety net for those who previously were not able to use a company's products (no matter how hard they have tried or how successful they were).

Simplified Design Process. Designers could focus on what they do best rather than trying to learn and design for every type, degree, and combination of disability.

Higher Compliance and Reduced Litigation Risks. The Info-bot and IUIG act as a sort of super-AT to provide an alternate accessible interface to a much wider range of users than is possible by the current strategies. In fact, the range of users that could effectively use a company's products would only be limited by the quality and diversity of IUIGs available to users.

Helps Address the Closed Product or Closed Functionality Problem. Currently, there are an increasing number of products that are "closed" or have 'close functionality' that does not allow the connection or use of assistive technologies. Traditionally, this has led to many people who rely on assistive technologies being unable to use the products. Some products have built-in accessibility features, but those are limited in who they can all reach. However, since the Info-bot doesn't need any API, there are essentially no products that are "closed" to the Info-bot. The problem of closed products and closed functionality would, therefore, not exist at all if this approach were implemented.

Wider Market Reach and Coverage. The Info-bot and IUIG would be able to reach a much wider audience and cover a much wider range of disabilities than current accessibility approaches. The range of users who can use a product would be limited only by the availability of IUIGs for different types of users and the ability of the user to understand the underlying function of the product. Reaching a wider range of users can both increase profits and improve the brand's reputation.

4.3 Benefits to Government and Society

The potential benefits to government and society include:

Fewer Regulations. Accessibility regulations are becoming increasingly complex and difficult to comply with as more and more types of ICT have emerged, and more products are "closed" to assistive technologies. Current guidelines and standards run from 50 to nearly 300 different specific guidelines or requirements. This has both made it difficult for industry and reduced industry's motivation to try to meet them all.

An Info-bot/IUIG approach would remove the need for many new requirements by eliminating the "closed" nature of products. The Info-bot and IUIG can provide an assistive technology-like functionality - whose only "API" is the standard human interface as input. Therefore, there would be no closed products for such an approach. This would make it easier for companies to comply with accessibility standards and would make new technologies accessible to more people.

Fewer Lawsuits. The Info-bot and IUIG could reduce the number of lawsuits around ICT accessibility by making it easier for companies to comply with accessibility standards.

More People Would Be Able to Use New Technologies and Live, Work, and Participate More Independently. An Info-bot/IUIG could make new technologies accessible, more understandable, and operable to people who have trouble or cannot use standard digital interfaces. This would increase the percentage of our population that is able to participate in daily life, work, and society better and more successfully.

Equity would not be a challenge since the Info-bot proposed would be open source and available to everyone free of charge. Thus, it would be available to those with the most and the least resources and available in all countries, languages, and cultures.

5   Questions, Problems, and Issues with the New Approach

The following concerns or potential issues have been identified to date with the proposed approach.

Feasibility. Everything can look easy on paper before it is actually implemented. Many of the capabilities needed to create the Info-bot functionality or Individual User Interface Generators (IUIGs) do not exist today.

Timeline. While all experts consulted had no doubt that everything described could be done someday - it is not clear how soon some of the more difficult aspects, like fully understanding a human interface, will be possible (rather than just successfully recognizing interface elements - which is being done today).

Privacy. The initial implementations are likely to be cloud-based, and this raises the question of data leakage and privacy. To be safe, cloud-based systems would have to be used only for training and generalized learning. A downloadable version that can run locally and that keeps all information learned from the user (and all user training) local and not shared would be required for privacy. This may slow the advancement of the core but is essential for preventing disability information from being exploited.

Funding. If the Info-bot is open-source and free (to companies and users), it will need some source of funding to grow and maintain it. Although its operation would be a fraction of the cost saved by companies and society, this does not mean that companies would invest those savings in the development of the technology. And there would be no savings until it was fully operational - which would come sometime after the initial costs to create it.

Timing of Adoption. A concern expressed by people with disabilities, and one they have previously experienced, is excitement by policymakers and implementers that leads to pressure on consumers to accept a new and unproven (or not yet ready for prime time) solution that causes existing, working solutions to be abandoned or not as well supported. Since new solutions often take much longer than anticipated. This can leave people with disabilities without any good solution while the new one is still in development if support or enforcement of the existing one is diminished or dropped. Until the new approach is mature and proven, it is unlikely that consumers will be anything but wary and concerned.

Cost of IUIGs. While the Info-bot functionality may be a common open-source effort that is free for all to access and use, the Individual User Interface Generators (IUIGs) need to be developed for all the different types, degrees, and combinations of disability. While AI might facilitate or automate this in the future, it is anticipated that this advance will come much later than Info-bot functionality is achieved. This is because there are no large data repositories of interface patterns for each of the very diverse types, degrees, and combinations of disability.

Distributive Justice. If IUIGs are created by the private sector and sold like assistive technologies are today, then there will be a problem with all people with disabilities being able to get the IUIG they need. This may be no worse than with assistive technologies today. But if this approach leads to less accessibility being built-in and more reliance on IUIGs - this could make the problem of distributive justice worse if something is not done to make universal access to IUIGs possible.

Need for Extensive Research on IUIGs for All Types, Degrees, and Combinations of Disability. Although we have extensive guidelines on general strategies for making things more accessible to different disability groups, we are less able to say what the optimum interface for individuals with combinations of disabilities or who have trouble understanding and using technologies, in general, should look like.

Disruption of the Accessibility Market and Industries. "There is nothing more difficult to take in hand, more perilous to conduct, or more uncertain in its success, than to take the lead in the introduction of a new order of things. For the innovator has enemies in all those who profit by the old order, and only lukewarm defenders in all those who would profit by the new order, this lukewarmness arising partly from fear of their adversaries who were favoured by the existing laws, and partly from the incredulity of mankind, who do not truly believe in anything new until they have had actual experience of it".

Niccolò Machiavelli 1513

A significant number of large, successful, and profitable companies now exist whose business model is based on the current accessibility paradigm and helping companies understand and conform. A shift to the approach proposed could present a considerable risk to their business models, which are based on repairing the accessibility of companies' websites or products. Initially, these AI accessibility advancements will make their jobs easier, more efficient, and more effective, leading to higher throughput and profits. But if the shift eventually happens or companies bring these tools in-house, it can lead to a decrease in the need for their services. This will be truer if their business model is based on fear of lawsuit and less so if their business is driven by a desire to have products "born accessible" to more people. Hopefully, those who are based on lawsuit risk will be able to shift to other areas, like all other industries do to accommodate changing technologies and markets. Until then, it is unlikely they will be supporters of such a shift.

Need to rEthink Existing Policy and Regulations. Policy, laws, standards, and regulations are all things that take a long time to create and are hard to change. The rapid pace of technology evolution is already challenging them in so many ways, some because we do not even have good experimental strategies for dealing with the technology, for example VR. This proposed approach may require a complete re-think of accessibility laws and regulations. However, it is possible that, to the extent that current standards and regulations are based on outcomes (what should be true in the end) rather than pre-scriptive (how things should be done), the standards could continue to be applied, with the Info-bot and IUIGs used as a strategy to meet them (when and where it is, in fact, effective at meeting them).

Being Confused With Overlays. Overlays are actually very old and have been around for decades. They provide limited accessibility features to single pages by embedding JavaScript into each page. However, recently, they have been marketed along with some simple auto-repair tools as a means of avoiding accessibility lawsuits. The problems with them include a) they sometimes interfere with users' assistive technologies, b) they only work on a single page/site - leaving the user without access to any other pages - including pages needed to get to the site, c) they do not address all of the accessibility problems that pages have - just ones that are automatically detectable, and d) their repairs are sometimes not very good and aimed more at passing the automated test than actually meeting the full set of accessibility guidelines. The fact that they are marketed as making pages accessible when they do not, that some interfere with users' AT, and that they are sold with language suggesting that they will prevent lawsuits has caused a backlash in the disability and accessibility communities.

The proposed approach is completely different. Some of the ways include: a) it works on all pages and all technologies (as well as all aspects of the product outside of the browser), b) it creates an interface for each individual that is bespoke for that individual, c) it would not interfere with any user AT - because it does not change the original interface in any way, it simply provides a separate custom interface, fit to each user. In addition to not affecting the original interface so it can't interfere with people's existing AT, the premise is that it would not be released until it was acceptable to people with disabilities as an alternate solution.

6 Theme and Variation for the New Approach

Although the approach in its basic form is described as a full post-product-release, user-run-time solution for accessibility, its components can be used at all stages of product development, deployment, and use.

For example:

1. At the development stage to increase the number of products that are "born accessible" to more users
   a. The Info-bot could be used as part of the design process to identify ways to build accessibility in.
   b. The Info-bot could also be used to both review and repair designs prior to release.
2. Creating accessibility at delivery
   a. The Info-bot functionality could be used as an intermediary at the time of delivery. For example, it could be built into web browsers to repair the accessibility of any page encountered.
   b. It could also be combined with some IUIG-like features to give "overlay" like abilities to every page visited.

3. Combining these could provide "built-in" access to some people (sort of like built-in access in smartphones) while repairing any bad pages so they are compatible with AT
4. Born accessible to AT
   a. The Info-bot could create, repair, or populate an accessibility API for AT pre-release.
5. Provide real-time (or pre-stored and buffered) interface socket
   a. The Info-bot could create an interface socket for IUIGs to plug into to access a product.
   b. (this is the basic role described above for the Info-bot)
6. Real-time creation of Individual Interfaces (Info-bot that is also an IUIG)
   a. The Info-bot could be extended to include both Info-bot and IUIG functionality so that it directly creates user-specific interfaces for each product for each user.

For both 4 and 5 (and to some extent all), the Info-bot needs to learn a product's interface only once - unless the interface itself (not the content) changes. This can actually be done at the manufacturer during product testing, or by the first user to use a product. It can then be stored, saving real-time compute cycles and the need to allow the Info-bot to peruse the interface to learn it each time.

7 Conclusion

It is difficult to estimate how easy or hard this will be to do overall or the timeline for it to be feasible. It does appear from industry discussions during and after the Future of Interface Workshop [1] that this would eventually be doable. But that, too, needs further exploration and determination. There are already some underpinnings under development and prototypes of early implementations of the concept in existence [28, 29].

We believe a concerted effort by the field to explore and build the proposed approach will have two key benefits:

1. It will spin up a variety of advances that will have an immediate impact on under-served populations today. These may take the form of new assistive technologies for these populations. It may involve advances that will allow these populations to take advantage of some of the current APIs available for other disability groups, such as individuals who are blind.
2. In the long term, it can provide near-ubiquitous access – i.e., access to essentially all devices and individual encounters in their daily life – for persons with a much, much wider range of types, degrees, and combinations of disabilities than we can dream of today.

However, such an effort could be disruptive at the time of implementation and would need careful study and even more careful implementation to avoid the problems cited above for consumers. It would also be complicated both because of existing markets and interests and due to the number of different stakeholders that would need to be involved.

The best approach would be if an incremental path could be found that keeps enhancing existing approaches until they can evolve into the new approach. Also, key would be if it was possible to continue but satisfy the old requirements with the new approach as an option for automatically meeting many of the requirements.

Acknowledgments. Content from this paper was derived from research funded in part by the National Institute on Disability, Independent Living and Rehabilitation Research at the Administration for Community Living, U.S. Dept. of Health and Human Services (Grant #90REGE0008), and from work funded by the National Science Foundation (Grant #2312370). The opinions herein are those of the authors, not necessarily those of the funding agencies, and no endorsement of the funding agencies should be assumed.

Disclosure of Interests. The authors have no financial interest in this work or the success in implementation of any of it.

References

1. Vanderheiden, G., Marte, C.: About - Future of Interface (2023). https://futureofinterface.org/info-center/about/. (Accessed 14 Dec 2023)
2. Fact Sheet: Telehealth | AHA. https://www.aha.org/factsheet/telehealth. (Accessed 28 Feb 2024)
3. Lee, E.C., Grigorescu, V., Enogieru, I., et al.: Updated National Survey Trends in Telehealth Utilization and Modality (2021–2022). US Department of Health and Human Services (2023)
4. Gray, L., Lewis, L.: x Use of Educational Technology for Instruction in Public Schools: 2019–20. First Look. NCES 2021–017. National Center for Education Statistics (2023)
5. Smith, A.: Searching for Jobs in the Internet Era | Pew Research Center. In: Pew Research (2015). https://www.pewresearch.org/internet/2015/11/19/searching-for-work-in-the-digital-era/. Accessed 23 May 2024
6. Bergson-Shilcock, A., Taylor, R., Hodge, N.: Closing the digital skill divide. Natl Skills Coalit **390**, 8619 (2023)
7. EN 301 549 - V3.2.1 - Accessibility requirements for ICT products and services (2021)
8. Consortium WWW Web content accessibility guidelines (WCAG) 2.0 (2008)
9. Vanderheiden, G.C., Vanderheiden, K.R.: Guidelines for the design of consumer products to increase their accessibility to persons with disabilities. In: RESNA 1991 - Technology for the Nineties. Proceedings of the 14th Annual Conference. RESNA Press, Washington, pp 187–189 (1991)
10. Federal Register: Information and Communication Technology (ICT) Standards and Guidelines. https://www.federalregister.gov/documents/2017/01/18/2017-00395/information-and-communication-technology-ict-standards-and-guidelines. (Accessed 28 Feb 2024)
11. Home – IBM Accessibility. https://www.ibm.com/able/. (Accessed 14 Dec 2023)
12. Accessibility Technology & Tools | Microsoft Accessibility. https://www.microsoft.com/en-us/accessibility. (Accessed 14 Dec 2023)
13. Disability Inclusion in the Workplace and Beyond — Google. https://about.google/intl/ALL_us/belonging/disability-inclusion/product-accessibility/. (Accessed 14 Dec 2023)
14. Accessibility - Apple. https://www.apple.com/accessibility/. (Accessed 14 Dec 2023)
15. Deque Systems: Web Accessibility Software, Services & Training. https://www.deque.com/. (Accessed 28 Feb 2024)
16. IAAP | International Association of Accessibility Professionals. https://www.accessibilityassociation.org/s/. (Accessed 28 Feb 2024)
17. Digital Accessibility as a Service | Level Access. https://www.levelaccess.com/. (Accessed 14 Dec 2023)

18. WebAIM: The WebAIM Million - The 2023 report on the accessibility of the top 1,000,000 home pages. https://webaim.org/projects/million/. (Accessed 14 Dec 2023)
19. Power, C., Freire, A.P., Petrie, H., Swallow, D.: Guidelines are only half of the story: Accessibility problems encountered by blind users on the Web. In: Conference on Human Factors in Computing Systems - Proceedings, pp. 433–442 (2012). https://doi.org/10.1145/2207676.2207736
20. Making Content Usable for People with Cognitive and Learning Disabilities. https://www.w3.org/TR/coga-usable/Overview-mutiple-pages.html. (Accessed 28 Feb 2024)
21. Yan, S., Ramachandran, P.G., Yan, S.: The current status of accessibility in mobile apps. ACM Trans Access Comput 12, 3 (2019). https://doi.org/10.1145/3300176
22. Ross, A.S., Zhang, X., Fogarty, J., Wobbrock, J.O.: Epidemiology as a framework for large-scale mobile application accessibility assessment. In: Proceedings of the 19th International ACM SIGACCESS Conference On Computers and Accessibility, pp 2–11 (2017). https://doi.org/10.1145/3132525.3132547
23. Creed, C., Al-Kalbani, M., Theil, A., et al.: Inclusive AR/VR: accessibility barriers for immersive technologies. Univ. Access. Inf. Soc. 23, 59–73 (2023). https://doi.org/10.1007/s10209-023-00969-0
24. Patel, R., Breton, P., Baker, C.M., et al.: Why software is not accessible: Technology professionals' perspectives and challenges. In: Extended abstracts of the 2020 CHI conference on human factors in computing systems. pp 1–9 (2020). https://doi.org/10.1145/3334480.3383103
25. Xia, X., Grundy, J., Zimmermann, T., et al.: Accessibility in software practice: a practitioner's perspective acm reference format. ACM Trans. Softw. Eng. Methodol. 1,(2022). https://doi.org/10.1145/3503508
26. Miranda, D., Araujo, J.: Studying Industry Practices of Accessibility Requirements in Agile Development, vol. 10 (2022). https://doi.org/10.1145/3477314.3507041
27. Bowman, M., Robinson, J., Kane, S.K., Buehler, E.: "I just thought it was me": how smartphones fail users with mild-to-moderate dexterity differences. In: Proceedings of the 25th International ACM SIGACCESS Conference on Computers and Accessibility. pp. 1–12 (2023). https://doi.org/10.1145/3597638.3608396
28. Liang C, Iravantchi Y, Krolikowski T, et al.: BrushLens: hardware interaction proxies for accessible touchscreen interface actuation. In: Proceedings of the 36th Annual ACM Symposium on User Interface Software and Technology, pp 1–17 (2023). https://doi.org/10.1145/3586183.3606730
29. Li J, Yan Z, Shah A, et al.: Toucha11y: Making inaccessible public touchscreens accessible. In: Proceedings of the 2023 CHI Conference on Human Factors in Computing Systems, pp 1–13 (2023). https://doi.org/10.1145/3544548.3581254

Aging and Social Media

Neighbourhood Natter: A Post-Pandemic Response to Addressing Social Isolation and Connection in a Retirement Village

David M. Frohlich[1]($\boxtimes$), Sarah Campbell[2], Daniel Benn[1], Thomas Booker-Price[2], and Alison Benzimra[3]

[1] University of Surrey, Guildford, UK
d.frohlich@surrey.ac.uk
[2] Playwell for Life, Bristol, UK
[3] United St. Saviours, London, UK

Abstract. Living in retirement communities is often promoted as a solution to problems of loneliness and social isolation which are risk factors for both mortality and poor physical and mental health. However, even there, friendships do not automatically form between neighbours, and it can be difficult for newcomers and those on the margins to engage with existing clubs and groups. In this context, from autumn 2021 to spring 2023, we carried out two studies in a retirement village in Surrey UK to co-design a novel social media system to help address issues of social connection for residents. In this paper we report the requirements, design and evaluation of the resulting system called *Neighbourhood Natter*. This was unusual in not supporting online communication, but rather the facilitation of face-to-face conversations between small groups of neighbours in a community social space. Residents embraced the system and fell into having meaningful conversations with acquaintances or strangers relatively quickly. These led to a significant reduction in reported loneliness levels, positive mood shifts and private plans to meet with conversational partners again.

Keywords: Neighbourhood Natter · conversations · social connection · retirement village

1 Introduction

A key factor for health and wellbeing in later life is the strength of people's social relationships. Those with diverse and supportive relationships with family, friends and local communities report higher levels of happiness than others [1]. Conversely, when people feel that they do not have the quality and quantity of relationships that they desire this can lead to feelings of loneliness which impact negatively on health, wellbeing and quality of life [2]. Indeed, loneliness has been associated with an increased risk of poor mental health [3], dementia [4], cardiovascular disease [5] and mortality [6]. Age UK forecast that by 2025, without intervention, there will be as many as 2m people in England aged over 50 who will often feel lonely, and that this will be most pronounced in those who feel that they have no-one to talk to [7]. There-fore, there is a need to find creative and innovative solutions that could help older adults feel less lonely and more connected to other people.

One potential solution is for older people to live independently in a community with others of a similar age, with access to social facilities, activities and clubs, together with professional care facilities should they need them. This is the philosophy of retirement villages or communities which are very different to other kind of residential options for older people such as care homes, retirement homes or nursing homes. While the latter are based on a medical model of care, the retirement village seeks to promote 'independent living communities' where residents have things in common and can move through different residential options together over time as their needs dictate [8]. As such, retirement village residents are able to 'age well in place' whilst fostering personal independence in a friendly, safe and comfortable environment where a sense of community and solidarity prevail [9–13].

At the University of Surrey we have had a long term relationship with Whiteley Village retirement community run by a charity called the Whiteley Homes Trust. This was funded by the philanthropist William Whiteley after his death in 1907. It opened in 1917 as the first purpose-built retirement village in the UK. Today Whiteley Village is home to around 400 people over 60 years of age, living in over 250 listed almshouse cottages and 50 extra-care flats in a care home block. The village is located on a 225 acre estate near Walton-on-Thames in Surrey, complete with woodlands, gardens, lakes, shop, post office, village hall and clubhouse, allotments, golf course, bowling green and church. Many recreational activities and clubs are available onsite to residents, and local buses run to nearby villages outside the community.

Despite the idyllic setting, prevalence of activities and communal areas for residents to congregate and meet, there are still sources of tension in the community, with instances of loneliness in some residents. Given our prior work on digital storytelling and serious games for emotional wellbeing, we initially partnered with the village on a project called 'Storytelling games for older people', to explore the role of computer mediated communication technology as an intervention to address loneliness. Rather than impose such technology on residents, we adopted a co-design methodology to work with them on understanding problems of community belonging and social isolation from their point of view and designing a solution to improve them together.

In the rest of the paper we report the findings of this study and a follow-on project to develop and test a system called *Neighbourhood Natter* for stimulating and supporting meaningful face-to-face conversations within the community. Our work was carried out over 18 months from September 2021, just after the worst of the Covid-19 pandemic. The pandemic affected Whiteley Village residents deeply, in similar ways to many communities globally, affected by the Covid-19 pandemic. Most residents were confined to their houses or flats for long periods, with severe restrictions on leaving the estate or hosting visitors. Management were able to minimize the number of covid-related deaths in the village, but residents were still affected by the lack of human contact and ongoing bereavement of others. This undoubtedly exacerbated feelings of social isolation in our participants and influenced the technology we eventually co-designed together. However, we believe this was a common experience for many older people in this period and led to a more innovative new media system of relevance to neighbours in any community who wish to get to know each other better. We begin with identifying the requirements and early design concept for the system, before describing its operation and evaluation in a small-scale field trial. The implications of the findings for retirement and other communities will then be discussed.

2 Related Work

There is evidence in the research literature that residents of retirement villages are not immune to feelings of loneliness, social isolation and social exclusion. We review this briefly here, to provide further understanding of the context and subject of our investigation.

Not to be confused with 'being alone', 'aloneness', or 'solitude', which can be experienced positively as the opportunity to enjoy and appreciate one's own company [14], loneliness represents a discrepancy between actual and desired interpersonal relationships on a social and emotional level. It has the potential to occur when one is alone as well as in the company of others [15]. Loneliness is thus centred upon a lack of quality and/or perceived intimacy of relationships [16, 17]. It is used to capture the subjective, emotional experience of this lack of quality relationships.

The above findings are no less prevalent within care homes and retirement villages where residents are living physically close to one another. Indeed, loneliness in retirement villages is linked with a heightened risk of depression, a decreased quality of life, and generally poorer health and well-being, particularly in older adults without partners [11]. Similarly, loneliness is "surprisingly common" in long-term care facilities [18]. They further observe that loneliness in long-term care facilities can be experienced in three ways by residents: (1) *socially,* as a result of a lack of company and peer support; (2) *emotionally,* due to a lack of meaningful others to share their feelings with; and (3) *existentially,* as a feeling of emptiness. With this in mind, it is clear that loneliness and its associated feelings of misery, meaninglessness and emptiness persist within residents living in long-term care facilities despite always have people around them.

Social isolation is an objective measure reflecting the psychological and/or physical distancing of an individual from their network of desired relationships with other people [19]. It captures a quantifiable lack of connections, rather than a feeling state. A separate construct to loneliness which is concerned with subjective experiences of the quality and perceived intimacy of relationships, social isolation emphasises individual-level situations in which a person is involuntarily detached from society. In a similar way to that of loneliness, social isolation is also linked with detrimental effects upon personal health and well-being [20]. These include feelings of loss or marginality from others [21, 22]. Given the restrictions of movement imposed in lockdown during the pandemic, we have all recently experienced forms of social isolation where we are deprived of ordinary levels of human company. These feelings are likely to persist in retirement communities for those unable to get out of their home due to mobility problems, other disabilities such as hearing or memory loss, and forms of social anxiety.

Social exclusion occurs when a person is prevented from participating in society by external means and withdraws from society (voluntarily or otherwise), subsequently experiencing a lack of meaningful or fulfilling social relationships [19, 23]. Although social exclusion can be interpreted positively as a healthy response to, for instance, an overly busy lifestyle where self-care and respite are required [22], it is more commonly employed to emphasise negative social and relational contexts of individual experiences. Conceptually, social exclusion can be understood as having objective and subjective dimensions at societal and individual levels. For instance, an individual who is denied even a limited social network, frequent social interactions, or participation in social activity can be viewed as experiencing 'objective social exclusion', whilst a lack of companionship and accompanying feelings of loneliness are representative of 'subjective social exclusion' [24]. Similarly, on a societal level, inadequate social cohesion, integration or belonging (for example, poverty, material deprivation, and exclusion from health and social services and participation in civic society) are indicative of 'objective social exclusion'. Being unable to build meaningful social relationships and participate in normatively expected social activities would characterise 'subjective social exclusion' [25–27]. Whether subjectively or objectively conceived, social exclusion ultimately centres upon a power imbalance arising from group pressure and other coercive social structures that has, in turn, led to the ostracism and marginalisation of an individual [28, 29].

Within residential care homes or retirement villages, social exclusion is of particular concern as resident compliance with, or deviance from, social norms or acceptable behaviours changes over time as their functional and/or cognitive ability declines [24]. For example, residents may return from a hospital admission with reduced ability to engage in community activities as before. As such, the personal agency of the resident would diminish, resulting in a reduction of meaningful contact with people and society more generally [26, 28]. Without correction, the resident would become increasingly excluded, ultimately experiencing social isolation with potentially dramatic effects upon their physical and mental health.

In summary, although retirement village living is portrayed as having a number of benefits, including enhanced social connection, emotional security and retention of a physical active lifestyle, in practice this may not be the case. Residents can experience confusion, depression and anxiety associated with their transition from, and sense of loss of, their former lives and social networks. This can heighten the risk of social exclusion, isolation and loneliness with potentially serious effects upon the mental health and well-being of residents, particularly if their move is involuntary and associated with declining health or the loss of a partner [9, 10, 28, 30].

3 Requirements and Concept Co-design

3.1 Methods

Working with 25 residents of Whiteley Village, we ran a series of 9 face-to-face workshops to discuss aspects of loneliness, social connection and social exclusion in the village, and then co-design and test a possible solution. All participants were over 60 years of age. The decision to meet face-to-face after the pandemic was a good one, and itself provided an opportunity for residents to get to know each other better and work together towards a common goal. In some ways this was an inspiration for the product concept we developed. This was done in partnership with Play Well For Life: a serious games company specializing in board and mobiles games for emotional intelligence and wellbeing.

Each workshop started with tea and biscuits and lasted about 2 h with a break in the middle. About 18 of the 25 participants turned up to each session which was facilitated by Sarah Campbell and David Frohlich, and we often split the group in two or four smaller groups, when it came to working on design ideas or testing the prototype. Participants did not always agree with each others' comments or ideas, and this often led to lively debate which we treated as part of the insights and findings of the study.

3.2 Requirements

The first four workshops explored issues of community belonging, social connection and reminiscing. An important finding from Workshop 1, introducing the project, was that our initial idea of an augmented reality board game to play remotely with family was not what the community needed. An important finding from Workshop 2 on Community was that neighbourhood community is different from interest group communities such as clubs. In particular it requires respect, tolerance and empathy for people who are not like you. We also found a great desire by residents to meet again face-to-face after the pandemic. A key finding of Workshop 3 on Social Connection was that while family relationships were very important, contact was typically infre-quent or remote. This increased the importance of contact with neighbours in the village, who might be the only people seen on a daily basis. Local friends were greatly valued but also casual interaction with nearby acquaintances and the 'kindness of strangers'. We all had a taste of that in the study workshops were we got to know each other, and listen to different points of view. In Workshop 4 on Reminiscing we found that older people have more time to talk in retirement and to reflect on the meaning of their past life. Several people reported carrying out personal projects to organize their photos, write memoirs or investigate family history and some of them brought these in to show us. Celebrations of people's lives at birthdays or funerals were said to be occasions for storytelling and reminiscing, and there had been a welcome tradition of neighbours celebrating birthdays in the community, but this had died away following the pandemic.

Drawing these findings together in Workshop 5, led us to identify a central requirement to encourage greater face-to-face contact between neighbours through empathic conversations in a communal social space. These should celebrate people's lives and knowledge, and encourage the formation of new or deeper relationships between strangers and acquaintances.

3.3 Co-design

Reflecting on this input, we came up with an initial product concept with the working title of *Face-to-Face Book*. This name draws a contrast with existing social networking systems like Facebook which typically encourage online interaction with existing family and friends, and like-minded people sharing the same values, politics and interest groups. They also encourage speaking ('posting') over listening. In contrast, our participants wanted the opposite: technology to facilitate new forms of neighbourhood community and belonging involving face-to-face interaction. These should encourage respectful, empathic listening and better mutual understanding. They also wanted it to be fun!

Hence, *Face-to-Face Book* used a directory or Book of residents in the village, to encourage face-to-face meetings between strangers. Its three elements were a Profile Builder for creating an entry in the book, some kind of Directory Search to find people to meet, and Facilitated Conversations where those meetings take place safely with others (see Fig. 1).

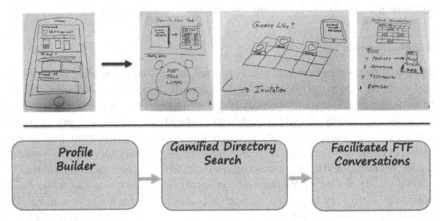

Fig. 1. The initial sketches of the '*Face-to-Face Book*' concept.

In a further three Workshops 6, 7, and 8, we used the Focusgroup + method of co-design, developed at the University of Surrey, to extend and re-design aspects of this concept [31]. A final mock-up of the conversation manager element on a tablet was presented in a final Workshop 9 for group interaction and feedback. This generated questions for discussion in a round. Participants fell enthusiastically into playing the conversation game for real rather than evaluating it systematically. This was a good indication of the attraction of the approach and the feasibility of the system in acting as a conversation facilitator. The findings gave our company partner, Play Well For Life, confidence to develop the mock-up further into a fully working prototype that could be evaluated formally in a field trial. This was done in a follow-up project as described below.

4 Neighbourhood Natter

A working prototype renamed *Neighbourhood Natter* was implemented as an Android app for mobile and tablet devices. Functionality was limited to the conversation manager element of the original *Face-to-Face Book* concept in Fig. 1. This took the form of a tablet 'talking-stick' which generated questions for discussion in a small group, and was passed round to control the floor to answer. A multimodal interface was used to generate textual questions that were read aloud, together with passing instructions and time constraints for each speaker that prevented one person dominating the conversation. The app was developed with the Unity game engine with scripting in C#. Development was guided by mockups of user interaction flow and user interface elements, used to gain feedback from our older adult steering group, with several subsequent rounds of iteration after initial testing. The design was targeted at small group sizes of between 3 and 6, but in principle could accommodate dyadic or larger group sizes.

There were three phases to interaction with the device: set-up, topic selection and conversation. In the set-up phase, one member of the group was prompted to state the group size and time available, before entering initials or nicknames for each 'player'. They were then prompted to select a topic for discussion from three groups under the headings of Practical skills, Hobbies, Serious and Lighthearted (see Fig. 2). For example, there were 6 conversation topics under Lighthearted, including, Music, Theatre, Arts & Crafts, Positive News, Books and Nature. Topics were themselves designed by members of the community and comprised 10 open questions to stimulate discussion under each. Some discussion usually ensued within the group to select a topic of common interest. A conversation began once a topic had been selected, by prompting the first user to spin a virtual wheel on the tablet screen to generate a question.

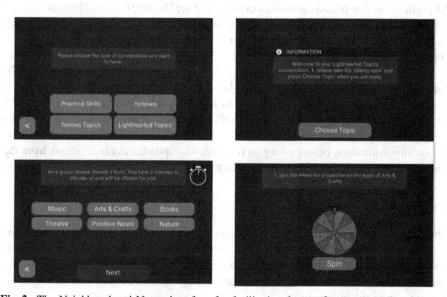

Fig. 2. The Neighbourhood Natter interface for facilitating face-to-face conversations. Here a topic of conversation is being selected.

Users could 'stick' with a selected question or 'twist' once to generate an alternative question on the same topic. Once selected, each user was prompted in turn to answer the question without interruption within a fixed period calculated from the available time (usually between 2 and 4 min). An alarm went off when this time was exceeded to encourage the speaker to stop and pass the tablet to the next speaker. Users could choose to skip the question without answering if they wished. When everyone had responded, users were encouraged to engage in a general discussion for 5 min before selecting the next question. Further question prompts could be selected within this discussion time, but this turned out to be confusing as we shall see below. The conversation ended when the available time elapsed or before this if the users wished.

5 Evaluation

5.1 Methods

27 participants were recruited, (aged 67–92, M = 79.23), with 23 females. Half the group lived independently in the village and half lived in supported housing onsite. Six groups, with around four residents in each group, took part in facilitated face-to-face conversations using the Neighbourhood Natter app. Each group had two 40 mi-nute conversation sessions, one week apart in the village activity centre. Group sizes varied because of the availability of individual members, from 2 to 7, with the medi-an size being 4. This had significant effects on the quality and dynamics of the con-versations.

Participants completed pre and post session questionnaires. Participants took part in focus groups at the end of each session about their experience and impressions of the app. All participants completed a short 6 item version of the De Jong Gierveld loneliness scale before the first session and after the second session [32]. They also rated their current emotional state before and after both sessions. This was done by placing a cross on a graphical diagram of the circumplex model of emotion, with perpendicular axes for level of arousal and positive/negative valence [33]. After each session they completed a 10 item System Usability Scale (SUS) [34]. Questions for the post session semi-structured interview, differed slightly between sessions to ask for more general reflections on the possible use and deployment of the app after the second session. All conversations were audio recorded and auto-transcribed. We begin by summarizing the results from the questionnaire data, before going on to summarise qualitative observations from the conversation recordings and themes emerging from a content analysis of the interviews.

5.2 Quantitative Measures

The questionnaire measures of loneliness, emotion and system usability give some over-all indication of the effect of the system on participants. We acknowledge the small sample size and that measures reflected state changes before and after the conversation, rather than being able to draw any conclusions about general reductions in loneliness over time from the intervention.

Figure 3 shows mean loneliness scores before Session 1 and after Session 2, one week apart. There was a large and highly significant reduction in loneliness across the group, as shown in the graphs and calculated in a repeated measures t-test (t = 15.24, df = 18, p < .001, d = 3.50). In general, the group of 19 participants taking part in both sessions and completing the loneliness scale scored relatively highly on loneliness coming into the trial ($\bar{x}$ = 4.4 out of 6). After the second session this had dropped two points ($\bar{x}$ = 2.0 out of 6). It is likely that rather than showing a large reduction in general loneliness, these data show a reduction in disconnection and state loneliness following coming together with others for a group conversation.

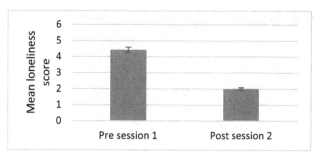

Fig. 3. Mean loneliness scores and error bars showing scores before Session 1 and after Session 2, one week apart.

Emotion is generally defined as a brief, subjective state, compared to loneliness, and was measured before and after each session by asking people to rate how positive and energized ('activated') they were feeling. These questions relate to orthogonal dimensions of emotion on the circumplex model [33] and can be plotted as an x,y position on a scatter graph. Figure 4 shows these emotion ratings for each participant taken before and after Session 1. They show some positive benefit of having conversations through the Neighbourhood Natter system immediately around the event itself. Four additional participants shift their position to the top right quadrant of the graph as a result of the activity (from 13 to 17 people). This quadrant reflects a more positive and energized mood.

Figure 5 shows a similar shift of 5 participants into the top right quadrant across Session 2. Since fewer participants came back for this session (19 compared with 26) this is a higher proportion of the group than before (a 26% rise compared with 19%). Every individual cannot be expected to experience such a positive effect on their mood with a single activity, because of all the other things going on in their lives. But again it is encouraging that, on the whole, the group appears to benefit from the conversational activity.

Finally, the usability of Neighbourhood Natter was measured after both sessions using the System Usability Scale (SUS). The individual scores out of 100 are shown in Fig. 6. These are broadly similar in both sessions, despite a reported learning effect in the post-session interviews reported below, and some improvements in the fluency of the conversation we observed. Hence the group mean scores in usability were 63.8 for Session 1 and 65.1 for Session 1. These are just below the expected average of 68 for most systems and indicate the need to improve its usability further. However, this is a respectable result for this older population which included about three people with dementia from with the supported housing setting.

5.3 Session Conversations

One or two of the authors (Benn & Frohlich) facilitated the questionnaire responses and post-session interviews in each session, and observed the group conversations involving the Neighbourhood Natter tablet app. We tried to position ourselves outside the ring of participants around the table and not engage in the conversation itself, even avoiding eye

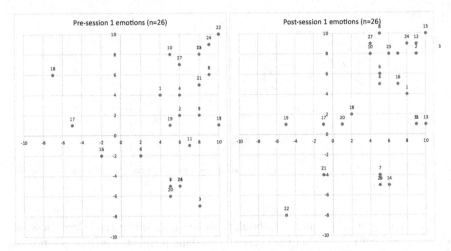

Fig. 4. Emotions of individual participants before and after Session 1. The number above each data point indicates the participant number.

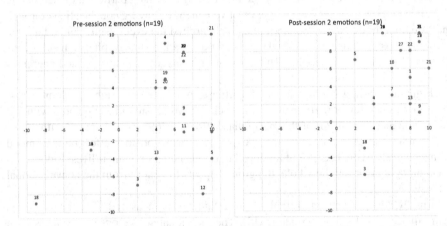

Fig. 5. Emotions of individual participants before and after Session 2. The number above each data point indicates the participant number.

gaze, as participants naturally wanted to include us. In fact, an immediate and compelling finding of these conversations was how authentic they were, in the way participants engaged with each other and tried truthfully to answer the questions generated by the system. Technically the app was a kind of conversational game, but participants treated it from the outset as a kind of conversational manager, and the conversations themselves as real opportunities to chat with each other and get to know their neighbours. Here we report findings from our non-participant observational notes and readings of the transcribed audio recordings, together with our impressions of the tone and character of the talk.

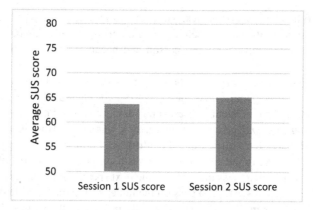

Fig. 6. Mean system usability scale scores after Session 1 (S1) and Session 2 (S2)

To begin with our overall impressions, we found that despite various usability problems with the app and its dialogue rules, participants were generally stimulated and energized by the conversations which often resulted in positive and practical outcomes. For example, participants who were relatively new to the village received practical advice about it from more longstanding residents. This was illustrated most dramatically in Group 3: Session 1 comprised of four seasoned residents and a newcomer who had only been in the village 2 months. The group were extremely welcoming to the newcomer who was quiet at first but talking happily by the end of the session. Unfortunately, she fell and broke her arm shortly after and couldn't join the second session where participants expressed missing her and enquired about her health. In other sessions we observed invitations to join clubs in the village and the exchange of phone numbers to keep in touch afterwards. In general, the groups were actively inclusive of quieter participants, those unfamiliar with technology and a small number of people with dementia who took part from the care home. The advantage of several people taking part was that there was usually sufficient digital literacy in the group to figure out how to use the tablet and app, and to allow some people to listen more than speak if they wanted to. One husband came along with his wife who had dementia, and both shared the speaking slot together when it came to their turn. Participants were always given the chance to talk by the system, but could pass the turn on if they couldn't think of an answer, without judgement from others. This beautifully addressed the user requirement emerging from our earlier study to encourage respectful, empathic listening (see Sect. 3 above).

This is not to say that all conversations ran smoothly or were equally fulfilling. We had one or two system crashes in the earlier sessions, confusion over the language and instructions of the app, difficulties in selecting topics of conversation of interest to everyone, a systematic issue over generating new questions over discussion prompts, failure to pass the tablet along with the turn, and some talking past the timer alarms designed to stop individuals dominating the conversation. These can be explained briefly in relation to the following stages of each conversational session as follows:

1. *Set-up*: after launching the app, the system automatically set the duration of the conversation to 40 min for the trial context but required information about the number

of users and their initials or names. This meant that one participant had to pick up the tablet first and enter this on behalf of the others. Typically this person was often the most technologically confident person and became the informal 'chair' of the conversation.

2. *Topic selection*: the second job of the chair-person was to help the group choose a topic of conversation, from which questions would be generated. This was not always easy as everyone had different interests and sometimes could not agree.

3. *Question generation and answering*: Once a topic was selected the chair-person would spin a virtual wheel for a question and confirm selection, before taking the first turn to answer. This was timed by the system with an alarm going off after the time elapsed, and a prompt to pass the tablet to the next speaker for their turn in the round. Sometimes participants forgot to pass on the tablet sitting on the table or passed it to the 'wrong' speaker in the sequence originally input with the names. Alarm sounds were invariably met with laughter and sometimes ignored to finish a turn. However, on the whole this worked well to stop individuals dominating in the round.

4. *General discussion*: Once a round had finished there was an open discussion period of 5 min in which anyone could comment or extend what had just been said. Individuals were not constrained from dominating in this period and some spoke to the exclusion of others. For example, a quiet woman with two men in Group 1: Session1 was able to speak eloquently during her turn in the round but was not able to speak in the discussion which was dominated by the men.

5. *Discussion prompts*: if the discussion 'dried up' before the 5 min there was a tendency for the group to ask the system for discussion prompts on the same topic to stimulate further open discussion. We found this undermined the control of dominance and selection of another question, as the topic was perceived to be exhausted by the prompts and participants tried to select an entirely new topic at the top level to continue the conversation.

6. *New question or topic selection*: New topics were selected more frequently than we expected because of the issue in 5 above.

7. *Closings*: The group always chose to stop at the end of a conversational cycle, such as the end of a discussion, rather than in the middle of a round or discussion. This could be before the final session alarm at 40 min, but sometimes resulted in the group going beyond that alarm to finish a cycle.

In general, participants became more confident and effective in using the system with learning and experience across the two sessions. This could be seen in the fluency and openness of the talk, the freedom to ask questions of clarification to the speaker in a round, the freedom to move off topic if the conversation got interesting, and the selection of more challenging topics of conversation for discussion. For example, Group 3 comprising 5 participants, chose Practical skills/Gardening in Session 1 but Health and the Afterlife from the Serious topic category in Session 2 as they got to know each other better. We also noticed that the dynamics of the conversation were strongly affected by group size as well as experience. The optimal size was about 4 for the 40 min slot since that allowed everyone to speak for about 2 min on each question, and cover about 3 questions in all. Time allocations increased with smaller groups or decreased with larger ones, and larger groups found it more difficult to agree on topics and open up to each other.

5.4 Post-session Interviews

Of the six groups taking part in this study, all found the app to be a positive experience – particularly during the 2nd session. Indeed, whilst many spoke of some initial trepidation and nervousness about using a 'new' technology, their experience of the conversations being "stilted", the topics and/or questions not being sufficiently meaningful to them, and the app voice sounded like a satnav, all found that familiarity with the system in Session 2 promoted a more successful flow of conversation. For example, in contrast to the 1st session, participants of all groups found the second session to be a more "relaxed and happy experience" (Group 2); the included discussion topics and questions more "interesting" (Group 4), "varied and "challenging" (Group 3); and, the app's structure and flow an efficient way to force everyone to listen to one another's opinions respectfully and not promote gossip. However, for this to occur, three groups identified that a facilitator (whether a staff member or group member) was necessary to keep things moving along. This included taking charge of the app, ensuring that more dominant voices were not taking over the conversation; and helping those who were struggling with the technology and/or conversation to properly engage – especially residents of Huntley House who were more dependent upon others for help and guidance.

While all participants experienced the sessions positively, participants of three groups specifically mentioned how the sessions "got us out of the flat" (Group 3) and "got us motivated to talk" (Group 3). Indeed, a particular point of conversation for Group 5 concerned how much a participant with Alzheimer's contributed to the conversation in Session 2. As opposed to Session 1 where he was largely quiet, during session 2 he was full of information, humour and charm. When asked about this he stated he was "just more relaxed because I really didn't know what to expect last week" and the topics covered in session 2 were "interesting". This ushered in a debate that was echoed across all groups about the role of subject matter as a catalyst for conversation. Many participants felt that conversation topics needed to be more relevant to them in order for them to want to take part more actively. Such topics were identified as 'grandchildren', 'empty-nesters', 'teenage use of technology' and 'public transport', although specialist subject areas were not ruled out if all participants had these interests in common. Conversely, topics concerning politics or religion were deemed too incendiary, particularly for a group of people who didn't know one another very well, if at all. Ultimately, if further sessions were organized around conversations of interest with people they knew or had similar interests to, most participants felt they would join another session in the future.

Although the *Neighbourhood Natter* sessions were generally viewed as beneficial by those taking part in the sessions, many participants saw the potential for further development, putting forward a variety of ideas that were then discussed within the group. Group 1, for example, felt that people may lose interest if the available pre-loaded topics and questions and their depth did not vary, instead suggesting periodic changes in topics and questions and the introduction of beginner/intermediate/advanced 'levels'. They also suggested the introduction of a competitive edge that could progress into a *'Natter League'* which, they felt, could spur wider debate and involvement in relevant topics within the wider Whiteley Village community. Group 2 had a similar idea, suggesting a club or official scheduled '*Natter group*' could promote an interesting option for involvement and interaction between the residents in Huntley House. However, whether the topics and questions varied or the format included a competitive element, all groups recognized the potential of the app to bring people together. The question then, was how to reach more people? Various suggestions were explored of which the most widely supported was the creation '*Natter Ambassadors*' (or those who had benefited from playing the game themselves) who could engage with and encourage their friends and neighbours to give it a try, creating a 'chain of friendship' that could snowball across the Whiteley Village community. Interestingly, this topic extended to the application of the *Neighbourhood Natter* format within other contexts including as a way for long-married husbands and wives to create conversation; a method to promote conversation around a family dinner table (participants rued the fact that family time was being taken over by tech such as mobile phones); a way to hold annual/6-monthly discussions around a specific subject between management and residents at Whiteley Village; and, as an icebreaker for those new to Whiteley Village who don't know anyone. Whilst it was acknowledged here that the format of questions and group discussion may need to change depending upon the use the application was put to, as a means to encourage conversation in differing context, it held much potential.

6 Discussion

We began by considering the problem of loneliness in later life and how it could persist even in retirement communities with many provisions for social interaction. Related issues of social isolation and exclusion were mentioned in the literature, with the former being particularly prevalent in the recent Covid-19 pandemic. We then set out to work with 27 residents of Whiteley Village retirement community in Surrey UK, to explore these issues for them and consider the role of computer mediated communication technology in addressing them. Our early requirements work and later measures of loneliness confirmed the importance of this topic in resident's lives, and identified the need to support greater face-to-face contact and relationships between neighbours. The technological system we co-designed with residents to do this became a kind of tablet talking stick to facilitate small group conversations face-to-face in a community space. What then have we learned about its potential for countering loneliness and social isolation in these kinds of communities, and improving the technology involved?

Although we tried to measure loneliness levels of participants at the beginning and end of the two-session intervention, and found a significant reduction in scores, we recognize that this may have been due to short term effects of taking part in a trial and chatting to other people face-to-face. Indeed, similar effects may have been found without our technology through human facilitation of conversation. These kinds of interventions are common approaches to the alleviation of loneliness by local councils, charities and other social care organisations, but they are limited in scope. This is because they require staff time and facilities to organize and conduct, and do not scale up to address the scale of the problem itself. One way of doing that would be to deploy a system like *Neighbourhood Natter* nationwide, to allow communities themselves to organize conversation sessions using the technology alone. Much more thought needs to go into how this might be done, perhaps on the back of other initiatives to bring people together in community spaces. For example, in Finland, there is notion of a community living room spaces being incorporated into urban 'superblocks' for neighbours to get together in different ways [35]. Facilitated conversations could be one activity for such a space. Closer to home, such conversations could become another kind of 'club' at Whiteley Village that people could run themselves and sign up for. This discussion shows the limitations of any technology for solving social problems in and of itself. It must be embedded in a social context and process for community and user engagement.

Regarding that, while we did find many positive benefits of the system in our trial for helping people to talk respectfully to each other, to listen to multiple perspectives on a topic and to share practical advice and information, the set-up of the groups and topics was rather artificial and unsustainable. Essentially, we allocated people to groups based on availability and they tried somewhat unsuccessfully to select topics of common interest at the beginning of each session. In the original *Face-to- Face Book* concept of Fig. 1 there was a front end to the system which involved some disclosure of a profile of skills and interests by participants, and a discovery mechanism for finding people with matching interests and scheduling conversations. This still seems to be necessary either inside or outside the system boundaries, and would ensure that people sign up to talk about topics of interest to them with people they want to meet. This process should also aim to reach lonely or isolated people who stand to gain most from the system but may be the least inclined to get involved. Longer term, we anticipate a dilemma resulting from the natural way in which people get to know each other and form group bonds. The system could encourage the same people or groups to continue meeting together to deepen their relationships, or it could deliberately encourage them to mix themselves up to continue meeting strangers within the neighbourhood. Both options should be available of course, but they would make a difference to the outcomes for relationship maintenance between both weak and strong tie partners [36].

In terms of improving the technology employed we made many findings on its design and use. The approach in general was unusual, since it supported offline communication and used a conversational agent not as a direct partner or chatbot, but as a facilitator of human-to-human conversation. Furthermore, the dialogue was conducted multimodally through a combination of text display and speech output, making it acccessible to a variety of older users with potential sensory impairments of failing memory, hearing and eyesight. In general, this approach worked very well to keep the focus of the talk on its human recipients, and might be extended to incorporate more intelligence in the dialogue control. Further research is needed to understand how to prevent certain people dominating the conversation in a more sophisticate and human-like way than simply sounding an alarm after fixed speaker durations, and managing topic transitions more elegantly. Social scientists train for many years to facilitate focus groups, so it is not surprising we couldn't match their competence in our simple prototype. As a next step in our own work, the system has now received follow-on funding from UKRI's Healthy Ageing Challenge to be further developed, integrating generative AI to expand the content, and speech recognition to become more conversational. This extended system is being trialled at new sites to identify whether it is appropriate to retirement villages generally.

Beyond this context, there are many other applications of the approach as suggested by our participants, including community consultation and family dinner times.

This involvement of the community in co-researching requirements and co-designing solutions is something we want to recommend further. It was central to our approach in these studies and completely changed our initial assumptions and design ideas which were focused on home-based reminiscing activities. The continuous involvement of Whiteley residents within and between the two studies gave them legitimate roles as community researcher-designers and helped us to get to know them and each other over time, and the everyday concerns of their lives. We believe it optimized the relevance of the technology for them and people like them, and made us more sensitive designers ourselves to the needs of our user population. Such an approach takes time and a dedication to maintain working and personal relationships over the long term, and is a microcosm of the problem we were addressing. Perhaps there is value in the use of *Neighbourhood Natter* in facilitating co-design conversations in diverse groups, as an fitting side effect of this project.

Acknowledgments. The work was carried out across two projects funded separately. The initial Storytelling games for older people project was funded by a grant of £62,475 from the Economic & Social Sciences Research Council (ESRC) Healthy Ageing Catalyst fund. The Neighbourhood Natter project was funded by a grant of £19,972 from the University of Surrey ESRC Impact Acceleration Account (IAA) fund. We thank the staff and residents of Whitely Village retirement community for their generous and sustained participation in both projects over a period of about 18 months from September 2021.

Disclosure of Interests. Sarah Campbell is CEO of Play Well for Life, which was the company partner for this work. Thomas Booker-Price was contracted by Play Well for Life to develop a working prototype of *Neighbourhood Natter* for evaluation.

References

1. Saphire-Bernsteinm S., Taylor, S.E.: Close relationships and happiness. In: Oxford Handbook of Happiness (2013)
2. Cacioppo, J.T., Cacioppo, S.: The growing problem of loneliness. Lancet **391**(10119), 426 (2018)
3. Santini, Z.I., et al.: Social disconnectedness, perceived isolation, and symptoms of depression and anxiety among older Americans (NSHAP): a longitudinal mediation analysis. Lancet Public Health. **5**(1), e62–e70 (2020)
4. Lara, E., et al.: Does loneliness contribute to mild cognitive impairment and dementia? a systematic review and meta-analysis of longitudinal studies. Ageing Res. Rev. **52**, 7–16 (2019)
5. Valtorta, N.K., et al.: Loneliness and social isolation as risk factors for coronary heart disease and stroke: systematic review and meta-analysis of longitudinal observational studies. Heart **102**(13), 1009–1016 (2016)
6. Holt-Lunstad, J., et al.: Loneliness and social isolation as risk factors for mortality: a meta-analytic review. Perspect. Psychol. Sci. **10**(2), 227–237 (2015)
7. Age UK. All the Lonely People: Loneliness in Later Life (2018)
8. Dodds, A.T.: Old age, retirement villages and New Zealand society: a critical narrative analysis of the experiences of retirement village residents [dissertation]. Massey University, Albany, New Zealand (2018)

9. Schwitter, N.: Social capital in retirement villages: a literature review. Ageing Soc. **42**(7), 1560–1588 (2022)

10. Carr, S., Fang, C.: "We are good neighbours, but we are not carers!": lived experiences of conflicting (in)dependence needs in retirement villages across the United Kingdom and Australia. Gerontologist **62**(7), 974–983 (2022)

11. Boyd, M., et al.: Lonely in a crowd: loneliness in New Zealand retirement village residents. Int. Psychogeriatr. **33**(5), 481–493 (2021)

12. Bookman, A.: Innovative models of aging in place: transforming our communities for an aging population. Community Work Fam. **11**(4), 419–438 (2008)

13. Yeung, P., et al.: What matters most to people in retirement villages and their transition to residential aged care. Aotearoa New Zealand Soc Work. **29**(4), 84–96 (2017)

14. Leontiev D. The dialectics of aloneness: Positive vs. negative meaning and differential assessment. Couns. Psychol. Q. **32**(3–4), 548–562 (2019)

15. McHugh Power JE, et al. Exploring the meaning of loneliness among socially isolated older adults in rural Ireland: a qualitative investigation. Qual. Res. Psychol. **14**(4), 394–414 (2017)

16. Cacioppo, S., et al.: Loneliness: Clinical import and interventions. Perspect. Psychol. Sci. **10**(2), 238–249 (2015)

17. Holwerda, T.J., et al.: Impact of loneliness and depression on mortality: results from the Longitudinal Ageing Study Amsterdam. Br. J. Psychiatry **209**(2), 127–134 (2016)

18. Jansson, A.H., Karisto, A., Pitkälä, K.H.: Listening to the voice of older people: dimensions of loneliness in long-term care facilities. Ageing Soc., 1–18 (2022)

19. Nicholson, N.R.: A review of social isolation: an important but understood condition in older adults. J. Prim. Prev. **33**(2–3), 137–152 (2012)

20. Cotterell, N., Buffel, T., Phillipson, C.: Preventing social isolation in older people. Maturitas **113**, 80–84 (2018)

21. Huisman, M., van Tilburg, T.G.: Social exclusion and social isolation in later life. In: Ferraro, K.F., Carr, D. (eds.) Handbook of Aging and the Social Sciences, 9th edn., pp. 99–114. Academic Press, London (2021)

22. Biordi, D.L., Nicholson, N.R.: Social isolation. In: Lubkin, I.M., Larkin, P.D. (eds.) Chronic illness: Impact and intervention, 8th edn., pp. 85–115. Jones and Bartlett Learning, Burlington (2013)

23. Riva, P., Eck, J.: The Many Faces of Social Exclusion. Social Exclusion: Psychological Approaches to Understanding and Reducing Its Impact. Springer International Publishing: ProQuest Ebook Central (2016)

24. Hansen, T., et al.: Exclusion from social relations in later life: micro-and macro-level patterns and correlations in a european perspective. Int. J. Environ. Res. Public Health **18**(23), 12418 (2021)

25. Precupetu, I., Aartsen, M., Vasile, M.: Social exclusion and mental wellbeing in older Romanians. Soc Inclusion. **7**(3), 4–16 (2019)

26. Walsh, K., Scharf, T., Keating, N.: Social exclusion of older persons: a scoping review and conceptual framework. Eur. J. Ageing **14**(1), 81–98 (2017)

27. Silver, H., Miller, S.M.: Social exclusion. Indicators. **2**(2), 5–21 (2003)

28. Nielson, L., Wiles, J., Anderson, A.: Social exclusion and community in an urban retirement village. J Aging Stud. **49**, 25–30 (2019)

29. Reinhard, M.A., et al.: The vicious circle of social exclusion and psychopathology: a systematic review of experimental ostracism research in psychiatric disorders. Eur. Arch. Psychiatry Clin. Neurosci. **270**(5), 521–532 (2020)

30. Jenkins, K., Pienta, A., Horgas, A.: Activity and health-related quality of life in continuing care retirement communities. Res. Aging **24**(1), 124–149 (2002)

31. Frohlich, D.M., Lim, C.S., Ahmed, A.: Keep, lose, change: prompts for the re-design of product concepts in a focus group setting. CoDesign **10**(2), 80–95 (2014)

32. De Jong, G.J., Van Tilburg, T.: The De Jong Gierveld short scales for emotional and social loneliness: tested on data from 7 countries in the UN generations and gender surveys. Eur. J. Ageing **7**, 121–130 (2010)
33. Russell, J.A.: A circumplex model of affect. J. Pers. Soc. Psychol. **39**(6), 1161 (1980)
34. Brooke, J.: SUS: a "quick and dirty' usability scale. Usability evaluation in industry. **189**(3), 189–194 (1996)
35. Makkonen, J., Latikka, R., Kaukonen, L., Laine, M., Väänänen, K.: Advancing residents' use of shared spaces in Nordic superblocks with intelligent technologies. AI & Soc. **38**(3), 1167–1184 (2023)
36. Ogolsky, B.G., Monk, J. (eds.) Relationship maintenance: theory, process, and context. Cambridge University Press (2020)

Understanding the Behavior of Older Adults' Social Media Platform-Swinging in the Philippines

Maureen Olive Gallardo[1,2(✉)], Merlin Teodosia Suarez[2], and Ryan Ebardo[2]

[1] Ateneo de Zamboanga University, Zamboanga, Philippines
billonesmaum@adzu.edu.ph
[2] De La Salle University, Manila, Philippines
{maureen_gallardo,merlin.suarez,ryan.ebardo}@dlsu.edu.ph

Abstract. As older adults embrace social media, their engagement extends across diverse platforms, each offering unique features and benefits. This study investigates platform-swinging among older adults, where they strategically switch between platforms to fulfill specific needs and desires. We interviewed 11 older adults living in the Philippines in November of 2023 who used at least two social media platforms. The platform combination favored by older adults varies based on their context. However, a common combination observed in this study included Facebook, Messenger, and YouTube. Guided by the Uses and Gratification Theory, we applied thematic analysis and revealed four major themes that motivate older adults to practice platform-swinging: managing digital ties, transferring information, uplifting and managing emotions, and optimizing work processes. The respondents' ability to practice platform-swinging is facilitated by adequate internet connectivity and devices, and familiarity with the different platforms.

Keywords: Platform-Swinging · Older Adults · Social Media Platform · Motivation · UGT

1 Introduction

Social media is traditionally associated with the younger population. But older adults are increasingly joining the digital world. Their adoption rate even surpasses that of the younger users [5]. In recent research by the American Association of Retired Persons (AARP), it was revealed that 88% of older adults use one or more social media platforms [21]. In the Philippines, 36% of those aged 50 and older use the internet or report owning a smartphone and 29% use social media according to the survey conducted by Pew Research Center in 2019 [10].

The proliferation of different social media platforms gave more options to users that using more than one platform is inevitable. This phenomenon of routinely rotating among different social media platforms is called "platform-swinging" [38]. The work of Tandoc et al. [38] coined the term platform-swinging and identified the different gratification and gratification opportunities brought by the practice of platform-swinging.

Most social media studies are focused only on a specific platform and comparative works across multiple platforms are limited [7, 38]. Some studies explored gratifications across multiple social media platforms [31, 33] but not in the context of platform-swinging.

The study by Tandoc et al. [38] provided insights into how platform-swinging allowed users to navigate structural, social, and norm barriers to obtain greater gratification opportunities for self-presentation and relationship management. However, despite including older adults in their respondents, the results are not specifically applied to the older adult population. Thus, this study would like to extend and at the same time focus on the concept of platform-swinging to older adults by describing their practice and motivations in using more than one platform.

Several studies used the lens of Uses and Gratifications Theory (UGT) to identify the motivations for using specific social media platforms [1, 6, 13, 39]. Although the motivations can be directed to the use of older adults on specific social media platforms, this study would like to emphasize the motivations for swinging between multiple platforms of older adults in the Philippines, guided by the following research questions:

- RQ1: What are the social media platforms used by older adults in practicing platform-swinging? (Platform Swinging in Older Adults)
- RQ2: How do older adults practice social media platform-swinging? (Behavior of Older Adults and Platform Features)
- RQ3: What are the motivations of older adults in practicing social media platform-swinging? (Older Adults' Motivations in Platform-Swinging)

The subsequent sections present a brief review of social media and usage of older adults, and the uses and gratification theory. The methodology of this study is described in Sect. 4 followed by a discussion of the results in Sect. 5. Lastly, the paper concludes with the limitations and implications of the study in Sect. 6.

2   Social Media Platforms

Social media was initially defined as a system for publishing articles and news and recent definitions shifted the focus to user-generated content, sharing, and connecting people with shared interests [2, 14, 42]. Users actively participate in these platforms, switching between consuming content and creating their own [14]. Popular types of social media platforms include [14]:

- Social Networking Sites (SNS) where individuals may build profiles, connect with other users, and explore connections. Examples are Facebook, X (formerly Twitter), and LinkedIn.
- Blogs are personal websites where individuals share their thoughts about specific topics where other people can comment. With microblogs, people can post short messages with text, audio, video, images, and external links quickly and easily such as on Tumblr.
- Forums are online communities where people with shared interests can discuss topics by posting messages and responding to each other's contributions. Depending on its policy and settings, this platform allows users to post questions anonymously. Examples of forums are Stack Overflow, Quora, and Discourse.

- Sharing Websites used for sharing content are categorized as: Video Sharing Platforms such as YouTube, TikTok, and Vimeo; Photo Sharing Platforms such as Instagram, Flickr, Snapchat, and Pinterest; and Audio Sharing Platforms such as Soundcloud, and Spotify.
- Social Bookmarking allows users to collect, organize, and share web pages for future reference, facilitating research and information sharing. Examples of these platforms are Reddit, Digg, and Newsvine.
- Podcasts are series of episodes featuring audio, images, videos, or PDFs where users can upload and download content from the website. Examples are Podbean and Buzzsprout.
- Wikis are collaboration websites where users can freely modify and share knowledge such as Wikipedia and Fandom.

While no research explicitly categorized instant messaging applications as social media, Hogan and Quan-Haase [17] addressed the question of whether instant messaging applications are considered social media by suggesting that the many-to-many communication in broadcasting availability and status messages are sufficient conditions for it to be a social media. Furthermore, several studies that explore social media included these applications in their analysis [36, 38, 44].

Social media has become an increasingly significant aspect of daily life for people of all ages, including older adults. Research indicates that older adults actively engage with social media and derive diverse gratifications from their use. Compared to younger demographics, older adults display a wider spectrum of motivations for utilizing social media platforms. This includes maintaining existing relationships, fostering social connections, and mitigating loneliness, engaging in lifelong learning, sharing information and establishing community ties, seeking health-related knowledge, and participating in activities that promote fulfillment [35]. Most studies that explored the motivations of older adults in social media are focused on social networking sites [20, 29, 37].

3 Uses and Gratification Theory

Uses and Gratification theory is a communication theory asserting that people seek out and engage with specific media to fulfill their individual needs and desires [22, 33]. By looking at the interplay between the individuals, their needs, and their media choices, UGT provides researchers with the framework to understand the underlying drives and motivations that influence their behavior [33, 41]. UGT is widely used as a valuable perspective for studies seeking to identify the motivations for using social media.

The UGT has been operationalized in studies that involve younger adults' use of social media such as the studies of Falgoust et al. [15] and Ferris et al. [16]. Various studies attempted to identify several gratifications in social media use by older adults such as the study of Kong and Lee [24] and Kim et al. [23]. The general use of social media is compensatory to the decrease in physical social engagements in late life [23].

The increasing number of available social media platforms allowed users to switch to different applications. Using UGT, a recent quantitative study by Sheldon et al. [37] compared the use of Facebook and Instagram among older adults. However, given that gratifications and motivations are influenced by sociocultural backgrounds, research must examine platform-swinging qualitatively [11]. Literature is mostly confined to studies that examine social media's general use and adoption, limited to a single platform, and conducted in the context of developed economies.

4　Methodology

This study investigates the behavior of older adults in social media platform-swinging through semi-structured in-depth interviews. The main guide questions for the interview are presented in Table 1. Before conducting the interviews, a pilot interview with an older adult was conducted to determine the flow of conversation and improve the guide questions [26].

Table 1. Interview questions to answer the research questions.

Research Question	Interview Questions
RQ1: What are the social media platforms used by older adults in practicing platform-swinging?	What are the different social media platforms that you are using?
RQ2: How do older adults practice social media platform-swinging?	How do you use these different social media platforms in terms of • Access • Frequency of Use • Device Used • Platform Functions and Features • Assistance Needed
RQ3: What are the motivations of older adults in practicing social media platform-swinging?	Why do you use these different social media platforms?

In understanding how older adults practice social media platform-swinging for RQ2, this study considered the following aspects: access, frequency of use, device used, platform functions and features, and assistance needed. The frequency of use and platform functions and features were adopted from the questions used by studies [1, 31] while access, device used, and assistance were also considered since these are the common challenges of older adults in social media usage [9, 25].

Through snowball sampling, the study recruited 11 Filipino older adults residing in the Philippines who were at least 60 years old and regularly utilizing at least two social media platforms. While the definition of an older adult varies globally, the United Nations defines it as 60 and above [12]. In the context of the Philippines, this age is also recognized as the start of senior citizenship. Therefore, this study adopted the minimum age of 60 to define older adults.

In-person interviews were conducted for 3 weeks in November of 2023 at the respondents' convenience, adopting a mix of conversational English, Filipino, and Bisaya languages familiar to both the researcher and the respondents. Each interview ranging from

15 to 42 min in length, was audio-recorded with a dedicated device. Before the recording, an orientation explained the study's purpose and procedure emphasizing voluntary participation, collection of personal information, and confidentiality of data. Following this introduction, the respondents signed a consent form, provided demographic information, and listed the social media platforms they were using.

The respondents' ages range from 60 to 76 years old, with nine in their 60s and two in their 70s. The group was predominantly female, with only one male respondent. Marital status varied, with two respondents single, six married, and three widowed. Most of the respondents remained active in their workforce, with six working part-time and four full-time. Only one respondent has never been employed.

Following data collection, 103 pages of interview transcripts were analyzed through thematic analysis [8, 28]. This analysis involved an iterative process of familiarization through repeated listening and reading of the data, followed by open coding of meaningful units of text relevant to the research questions guided by the concept-indicator model in Fig. 1. The codes were then grouped and organized to identify recurring themes. The coding process was conducted by the first author of this study and the themes generated were reviewed and validated by the second and third authors by going through the codes and associated exemplars from the transcribed interview until a consensus agreement is reached.

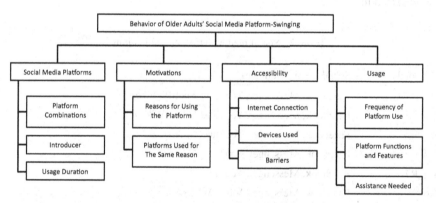

Fig. 1. Behavior of older adults' platform-swinging concept-indicator model

The transcripts of the interviews were used for coding and checking preliminary findings against the raw data to establish credibility. A codebook was created and maintained throughout the analysis to ensure consistent application of the codes for replicability. For each theme generated in the analysis, exemplars were identified to establish traceability. All these were considered to ensure the trustworthiness of the study [30].

5 Discussion of Results

This study investigates the practice of social media platform-swinging among older adults focusing on platform combinations, access, frequency, devices used, platform functions and features, and assistance needed. The motivations for engaging in platform-swinging to fulfill different gratifications are also identified.

5.1 Practice of Social Media Platform-Swinging by Older Adults

Social Media Platform Combinations. RQ1 asked about the social media platforms used by older adults. Based on the list of platforms used by the respondents of this study, the common combination of social media platforms includes Facebook, Messenger, and YouTube. In this study, we considered Messenger as a separate platform from Facebook. The common use of Facebook and YouTube coincides with the findings of AARP where these are the top applications used by older adults [21] In the Philippines, Messenger is one of the top applications second to Facebook [3].

In addition to this common combination, older adult respondents include one or more of these other platforms in their list: Spotify, Viber, Instagram, Wikipedia, WhatsApp, LinkedIn, Telegram, and X. The social media platform combinations of the respondents are presented in Table 2.

Table 2. Social media platform combinations

Respondent	Social Media Platforms
R1	Facebook, Messenger, YouTube, Spotify, Viber
R2	Facebook, Messenger, YouTube, Viber, Wikipedia
R3	Facebook, Messenger, YouTube, Spotify
R4	Facebook, Messenger, YouTube, Viber
R5, R7	Facebook, Messenger, YouTube
R6	Facebook, Messenger, Viber, WhatsApp
R8	Facebook, Messenger, YouTube, Viber, Instagram
R9	Facebook, Messenger, YouTube, Viber, WhatsApp, LinkedIn
R10	Facebook, Messenger, YouTube, Instagram, Telegram, WhatsApp
R11	Facebook, Messenger, YouTube, Instagram, LinkedIn, Twitter, Spotify

Table 2 shows that there are 10 diverse combinations of social media media platforms from the 11 respondents. Furthermore, the degree of social media platform usage varies for every respondent. Some use social media platforms without having an account on YouTube, LinkedIn, and Wikipedia which limits their activities to only consuming information. On other platforms where the respondents had an account, the type of activities they are engaged in also differs. For example, on Facebook, R5 only browsed and liked posts, while R3 searched, joined FB groups, and shared, in addition to browsing and liking.

How older adults practice social media platform-swinging regardless of the difference in combination and degree of usage, is described in terms of access, frequency, devices used, platform functions and features, and assistance needed which answers RQ2. These practices provide valuable insights into the preferences and potential limitations of older adults' platform-swinging practices.

Access. Internet access presents no significant hurdle for the respondents of this study. All respondents have Wi-Fi available at home, allowing seamless social media use. This can be attributed to the increase in internet connections during the pandemic where more than half of the households in the Philippines had internet access in 2020 as reported by the Philippine Statistics Authority [27].

However, outside their residences, not all respondents have connectivity. Like R10, some respondents subscribe to mobile data promos for uninterrupted access specifically on Messenger, their primary communication platform. Others, however, like R7 choose not to procure mobile data to control expenses, limiting their social media engagement while on the go.

"I use Messenger and FB on my mobile phone. But when I am not at home, I am not using it because I don't want to spend on mobile data. I already have an internet connection at home. Besides, most of the time I am at home."(R7).

"We have a Wi-Fi connection at home. My son had it installed. But when I am outside the house, and I have to attend my Arabic class, I will just buy mobile data. For example, if I go to my cousin's place and there's a class, I will excuse myself for a while and I will use my tablet." (R10).

Despite having a Wi-Fi connection at home, a slow or absent internet connection is still identified as the main barrier to social media usage for these participants. On the other hand, others mentioned that they are not able to access social media platforms if they are preoccupied with work.

Frequency. All the respondents are using at least one social media platform daily. However, the specific platform they most frequently use varies depending on their individual needs and activities. Messenger and Facebook emerged as the clear favorites, with most respondents using them daily. The use of Messenger seems to have replaced SMS and cellular calls for daily communication, but they are only used at specific times of the day. For example, R8 only uses Messenger in the morning and the evening.

"I feel like I don't have enough time because like for example, my schedule for looking at my Messenger is in the morning as there might be something important. And I check again in the evening. Then I open Facebook only in the evening because that is my only free time. During the day, it seems like I don't have time to Facebook." (R8).

Moreover, YouTube and Spotify also saw significant daily usage amongst some respondents mostly in the evening while others use it during weekends like R10.

"I use YouTube on Saturday and Sunday. Usually on a Sunday because on a Saturday I have my Arabic class in the morning. Every Sunday we will use YouTube for sing-along and other times, we will just listen." (R10).

Devices Used. Mobile phone is the dominant device for accessing social media platforms among the respondents. Only four of the respondents utilize a variety of devices which include a laptop, tablet, smart TV, and desktop computer (at work) to navigate social media platforms. Like R7, those who are using smart TVs for YouTube opted for the larger screen experience. Moreover, all the devices used by the respondents are personally owned which allows them access to the platforms when needed.

"YouTube is really for relaxation and entertainment because I watch it on a wide screen." (R7).

Platform Functions and Features. While older adults are active social media users, their participation primarily focuses on content consumption rather than extensive social interaction and content creation. On Facebook, the majority browse through feeds, react to posts, leave occasional comments (especially for birthday greetings), and search for information. Posting and sharing content is done by some respondents but seldom. This behavior is consistent with what was observed in previous studies such as that of Waycott et al. [40] where older adults are usually consumers but could embrace different ways to produce content such as posting on their Facebook wall, creating stories, and uploading reels.

- Messenger serves as a vital communication tool for older adults, facilitating the sending/receiving of messages, audio/video calls, and group chats. Older adults also use Messenger in their laptops to be able to send documents as this function is not available when using mobile phones.
- YouTube usage varies significantly. Some older adults do not have an account restricting their access to content discovery through searching and browsing. For those with accounts, engagement involves liking videos and subscribing to channels they like to ensure regular updates in their feed.

Assistance Needed. Most respondents in this study became comfortable using social media platforms after initial guidance from their children or self-exploration. With several years of experience (over 5 or 10 years for most respondents), they can independently perform the tasks they typically engage in.

However, some respondents sought assistance on specific functionalities such as scheduling messages in Messenger (R1), editing photos before sending them (R2), or controlling unwanted video content in their feeds (R6). They primarily attempted to find solutions themselves or sought help from readily available individuals like their children and colleagues.

"I don't need assistance now. The only assistance I sought before was about Messenger -- if it is possible to set a schedule for when to send a message. So far, I have not found anything that allows me to do that with Messenger." (R1).

Interestingly, R4 expressed unwillingness to learn or seek assistance in sharing Facebook posts to Messenger. The respondent preferred to stick with the tasks she already knew. R4 is apprehensive that learning new features might lead to increased time spent using the platform and interfere with her daily tasks.

"I don't know how to share posts on Facebook, unlike my siblings who share posts from Facebook and send them to our group chat. I haven't learned because it seems bothersome and disrupts my time. If I get used to doing these activities on Facebook, I might end up spending too much time online and I won't be able to get my chores done." (R4).

Based on the activities performed on the different social media platforms, older adult respondents of this study mostly consume information and give reactions rather than post content and share information. With the use of their own devices and the availability of an internet connection, it is not hard for them to swing from one platform to another.

5.2 Motivations for Practicing Social Media Platform-Swinging

The result of the thematic analysis identified four themes: maintaining digital ties, transferring information, uplifting and managing emotions, and optimizing the work process. We discuss each of these themes and how the practice of platform-swinging achieves the objectives of older adults.

Maintaining Digital Ties. Communication is vital to older adults as this is the point in their lives when their children are no longer living with them. Some others live in as far as other countries. With the use of social media, digital ties are formed and strengthened through messages, video calls, and seeing what's happening to the lives of their children through social media posts. Messenger is the main communication platform used by the respondents of this study. But to be able to maintain communication with their children, they are compelled to use other applications such as Viber and WhatsApp. This is the case, for example, of R6. Every country has its preference for communication platforms [38]. That is why R6 has to use Viber to communicate with her son and WhatsApp with her other son while using Messenger to communicate with her friends and colleagues.

"Because my first son uses Viber and my other son uses WhatsApp. My other son is using WhatsApp in the U.K. My first son is sometimes in the U.S. but most of the time in Cambodia." (R6).

This digital connection also applies to other relatives, friends, and colleagues. Aside from sending private messages and engaging in audio or video calls, older adults also engage in group chats. The number of group chats can reach as many as more than 28 such as in the case of R2. Aside from having group chats for professional purposes, R2 has group chats with people whom he has common interests with. On the other hand, R8 has friends in other countries who prefer to use Viber for more secure communication. Moreover, R10 is using Telegram and WhatsApp to communicate with her classmates and teachers in other countries for her online Arabic classes.

"Then in Viber, we have a group chat with my classmates in grade school. Most of them are not here [Philippines], so we use Viber because they say that messages are more secure in Viber."

"I have a group of grade school classmates who are trying to link with each other so we can have a reunion. My high school classmates are also doing that, so it's easier for us to look for their FB account and add them to be friends so we can talk to them in Messenger." (R8).

Digital ties are not only maintained through communication platforms such as Messenger, Viber, WhatsApp, and Telegram. This is also sustained by SNS like Facebook and Instagram allowing older adults to be updated with what's happening to their families and friends [20, 29]. Furthermore, posts on Facebook are also used as a reference in Messenger conversations that facilitate in-depth dialogues.

"What you read on Facebook whether it's a piece of informal or formal news or something, can become a topic of conversation among friends. Just like early this morning, because of our connections in social media, we were able to help or ease someone's concerns." (R2).

Transferring Information. Information transfer involves the use of different social media platforms for seeking and sharing information. Certain types of information are accessed only on specific platforms. For example, short videos and varied content are acquired by the respondents from Facebook while long videos and specific content (as a result of searching) are acquired from YouTube. Information seeking is performed by explicitly searching using keywords or discovery by browsing through the feed. Keyword searching is typically done on YouTube, Wikipedia, and Spotify while browsing is on Facebook and Instagram social networking sites. Information that interests older adults includes updates about their family and friends, current events, health-related information, topics of interest (e.g. recipes, gardening, camping), reference materials for work, spiritual and motivational content, and entertainment. For example, R5 joined Facebook Groups for religious content, and R2 for information about motorcycle parts. Moreover, since most of the respondents are employed, searching for reference materials is also common.

"There's a Facebook Group for a certain kind of Honda motorcycle. I think it's Honda Dream. Because I have a Zoomer and it's already phased out. So we share details about difficult-to-find spare parts and just talk about the difficulties and things about motorcycles." (R2).

Most of the respondents are not involved in information sharing. But if they are, they rarely post on Facebook and Instagram. Sharing of information involves the interoperability of platforms where Facebook and YouTube allow older adults to select where to share the information. Most respondents who share information prefer to share it in private messages and group chats in Messenger. Typically, older adults share posts for inspiration (e.g. articles, Bible verses, sayings, reflections, podcasts), knowledge (e.g. science-related topics, recipes), and entertainment (e.g. funny videos).

"I watch videos on Facebook for information and at the same time entertainment. Sometimes when I find it funny and I want others to also laugh, I share the video. Sometimes when there is good information like science-related information, I share the post on Facebook so my students and friends can see it." (R7).

R1 on the other hand does not share information from other social media platforms. She curates the information shared in Messenger group chats. She gathers information from the articles that she has read and phrases it to be incorporated in the photo that she has taken before sending it to her groups.

"I only send reflections in group chats because others appreciate it. I have a friend in college who said thank you. And then if my friend's friends have feedback, she tells me that they liked it because it helps them in their spiritual growth. So, that is my motivation even if sometimes I wonder when can I stop sending. But if I stop or am late in sending reflections, they complain. They would ask what happened to me and why I did not send a reflection." (R1).

With the vast information that older adults encounter every time they use the platform, R7 shares the links that she finds on Facebook to her Messenger account so she can go back to these again.

"For content that I found on Facebook that I don't want to lose, I share it right away to myself in Messenger. Because when I want to go back to it like for example, I liked the food recipe, I share it immediately with myself." (R7).

Uplifting and Managing Emotions. Emotional well-being is one of the important aspects of a better quality of life for older adults. The respondents of this study found different ways to uplift their emotions through entertainment videos and motivational talks from social media platforms. Managing their emotions includes being able to relax and calm themselves through spiritual encouragement and music. Most studies have identified this gratification in SNS [4, 37] while this study presents that this is also achieved in combination with other platforms such as YouTube and Spotify.

Entertainment is usually acquired from Facebook and YouTube. This includes watching movies, Koreanovela, local TV shows, vlogs, and interesting videos (e.g. mukbang, history of things). One respondent said that if she wanted to watch short videos, she would go to Facebook, and for longer videos such as movies and TV series, she would go to YouTube. For example, R5 found micro series videos on Facebook which are on average 2 min long.

"I watch mukbang videos on Facebook. And then that makes me hungry. I am also following The Double Life of My Billionaire Husband which is already ending. It is like a series but with only a few episodes." (R5).

Relaxation involves listening to music, podcasts, religious talks, storytelling videos, and vlogs to start their day, ease their emotional struggle, or make them fall asleep at night. Interestingly, older adults are also using YouTube not for visual purposes but only for listening to music, storytelling, and motivational talks. For example, R4 found a link on Facebook that led her to listen to storytelling videos on YouTube that narrate short stories.

"I use YouTube to listen to vlogs on political topics. Sometimes, also for fantasy stories like Amihan Stories and Ate Jane Stories. It is just there on YouTube."

"I listen only because I intend to sleep. If I watch a video, it will take me long to sleep. I will just put the phone beside me and close my eyes until I fall asleep." (R4).

It was striking that R7 who is single sought more entertainment and R5 who is a widow calms herself with spiritual motivations and music that connects her to her husband. Finding these resources on different social media platforms helps older adults combat loneliness, find solace in their emotional struggles, or just simply lull them to sleep. Moreover, the use of different platforms allowed older adults to access different types of media such as storytelling narration on YouTube, motivational talks both on YouTube and Spotify, and microseries videos on Facebook.

Optimizing Work Processes. Most of the respondents of this study are still employed either part-time or full-time. Some are educators and others are handling administrative functions. The use of social media platforms is extended to support their work-related functions from gathering and disseminating information to communication. For example, R1 is working in the human resource department who uses Facebook to search for profiles of the applicants to assess their character through Facebook posts. On the other hand, R2 uses Facebook to disseminate information about schedules, events, and procedures of the office and to communicate with the different stakeholders.

"Now I already use Facebook as part of background investigation for applicants who already worked somewhere or even new graduates. Because one way of getting to know the person is through the posts that he has on Facebook. For example, there is one applicant who has the same name as another user on Facebook. And I said I didn't like the applicant because of the sexy posts on Facebook. It turned out that they just have the same name, and the applicant is actually a good and family-oriented person who used another name on Facebook. However, that is one way of getting to know the person." (R1).

"We post a lot of notices for the Alumni Homecoming, activities for the office, admissions exams, schedules, procedures, and announcements. Everything related to the university that is connected to the office, I post it." (R2).

"I have 28 group chats (GC) for my Entre class. 10 GCs for small groups. Of course, each group will have their unique concerns. But if the concern affects the entire class, I will address it in the GC for the class. If I have an announcement, I send it in the GC for the class." (R9).

Other work-related functions supported by social media platforms include sending files through Messenger, answering queries through Facebook Page, and accessing reference materials from YouTube. Using social media platforms for work-related functions extended their reach beyond the physical confines of their offices and institutions.

"The person who frequently uses YouTube is my husband. When I saw that the video was nice, he said that he got it from YouTube. There are PPTs and procedures on YouTube. However, I also check if the content of the video follows the standard or is credible. There are lots of lessons on YouTube that are simplified." (R11).

All these themes can be achieved with the common combinations of social media platforms: Facebook, Messenger, and YouTube. However, with the differences in context and needed gratifications of older adults, the common combination is added to include other social media platforms. By swinging between different social media platforms, the practice provided older adults with access to a variety of information, types of media, and fulfillment of different gratifications.

At the start of using these platforms, they might need assistance but eventually, constantly performing the activities based on their needs makes them more comfortable using the platforms.

6 Conclusions, Limitations, and Implications

This study serves as one of the early explorations of platform-swinging among older adults, providing preliminary insights into this behavior by answering the research questions.

Platform Swinging in Older Adults. This study confirms that Filipino older adults practice social media platform-swinging facilitated by the availability of resources such as reliable internet connections and devices. The social media platforms used by older adults practicing platform swinging depend on the context of older adults. However, common combinations include Facebook, Messenger, and YouTube. Other platforms include Spotify, Viber, Instagram, Wikipedia, WhatsApp, LinkedIn, Telegram, and X.

Behavior of Older Adults and Platform Features. How older adults practice platform-swinging is described in terms of accessibility, devices used, frequency of use, platform functions and features, and assistance needed. The social media platforms are accessible to the older adult respondents as they all have a Wi-Fi connection at home. Some others extend their access even outside their home by subscribing to mobile data promos. However, despite having the necessary connection, access to social media platforms is still dependent on the quality of connection provided by the internet service provider (ISP) in the area. Having at least personally owned mobile phones allows older adults to access different social media platforms whenever they want. Some respondents have more options where to access such as on their laptop, tablet, smart TV, or desktop computer. Because smart TVs have a wider screen, some respondents prefer to access YouTube on this device. Because of the availability of internet connections and devices for accessing social media platforms, older adults are using at least one social media platform daily. Messenger and Facebook emerged to be used every day by most respondents. This is followed by YouTube and Spotify which is used by some respondents mostly in the evening or during weekends. The most frequently used social media platform among the combinations for platform-swinging depends on the individual needs and activities of older adults. While older adults are active social media users, their use of these platforms is mainly as consumers of information. Thus, the platform functions and features utilized by older adults are mostly on giving reactions to posts and videos, subscribing to channels and groups, leaving occasional comments, searching, and browsing. Although some respondents go beyond by creating and sharing content. Generally, older adults can independently perform the tasks they are engaged in on the different social media platforms as they have been using these for a long period.

Older Adults' Motivations in Practicing Platform-Swinging. Guided by the uses and gratifications perspective, this study identified 4 themes that motivate older adults to practice platform-swinging. With the different social media platforms to swing to and from, older adults have the advantage of access to specific types and quality of content and wider social connection for managing digital ties, transferring information, uplifting and managing emotions, and optimizing their work process. With the use of Messenger, Telegram, WhatsApp, Viber, Facebook, and Instagram, older adults can maintain communication with different social groups such as their family, friends, and colleagues depending on the preferred platforms used by these social groups. The use of different social media platforms such as Facebook, YouTube, Wikipedia, Spotify, and Messenger for seeking and sharing information allows access to different types and quality of information and content. One of the prominent uses of social media platform content is for uplifting and managing the emotions of older adults through entertainment videos, motivational talks, and relaxing music. Lastly, with most of the respondents being members of the workforce, the use of social media platforms goes beyond their personal needs and extends to optimizing work processes. Older adults use different social media platforms to communicate with colleagues, connect with different stakeholders, disseminate information, and seek information and reference materials related to their tasks and functions. Social media platform-swinging allows older adults to fulfill different needs and gratifications.

However, this study is not without limitations. The limited sample size and potential bias towards female and employed respondents necessitate further research for broader conclusions. Future research investigating factors such as respondent demographics, socio-economic factors, social media platform affordances, and other potential influences could offer deeper insights into the platform-swinging behavior among older adults.

Being able to understand the motivations and how older adults navigate through different social media platforms has implications in gerontology, healthcare, workplaces, and social media. This study contributes to the gerontology knowledge of the social media usage of older adults specifically on how they navigate through different social media platforms. Studies show that the use of social media by this demographic can keep them mentally active and engaged, possibly delaying cognitive decline [34] and improving well-being [18, 19]. Future research can explore the specific cognitive abilities that are exercised in platform-swinging and develop programs that leverage those activities. In healthcare, the dissemination of targeted health-related information by health institutions and professionals that can easily be transferred to different platforms can help address misinformation and disinformation among older adults. While older adults also seek health-related information on social media [43] and practice platform-swinging, verification of health information across platforms can be facilitated. As the use of social media platforms can be integrated into work processes conducted by older adults, training and upskilling of older workers including how to navigate through these different platforms safely should be provided and included in the design of organizations' training programs. Lastly, the results of this study can inform the designers of social media to develop features and interfaces that are more accessible and user-friendly to them to entice more engagement. Aside from the personal preferences of older adults to limit their activities on online platforms, they do not use some features because they are unaware of it, or do not know how it works. Because results have shown that older adults have a strong preference for the use of social media platforms, it is important to consider more interoperability of different social media platforms for seamless information transfer and other functionalities. Furthermore, improving built-in AI-driven personalization and user protection can help older adults enjoy content discovery and do further exploration on the use of social media platforms without fear of online scams and phishing.

References

1. Abril, E., Tyson, K., Morefield, K.: SnapChat this, instagram that: the interplay of motives and privacy affordances in college students' sharing of food porn. Telematics Inform. **74**(6), 101889 (2022). https://doi.org/10.1016/j.tele.2022.101889
2. Aichner, T., Grunfelder, M., Maurer, O., Jegeni, D.: Twenty-five years of social media: a review of social media applications and definitions from 1994 to 2019. Cyberpsychol. Behav. Soc. Netw. **24**(4), 215–222 (2021). https://doi.org/10.1089/cyber.2020.0134
3. Amurthalingam, S.: What are the most used social media platforms in the Philippines 2024?. Meltwater (2023). http://tinyurl.com/u9csedmr. (Accessed 19 Dec 2023)
4. Ancu, M.: Older adults on facebook: a survey examination of motives and use of social networking by people 50 and older. Florida Commun. J. **40**(2), 1–12 (2012)
5. Berkowsky, R.W., Czaja, S.J.: Challenges associated with online health information seeking among older adults. In: Aging, Technology and Health, pp. 31–48. Elsevier Academic Press (2018). https://doi.org/10.1016/B978-0-12-811272-4.00002-6
6. Bowden-Green, T., Hinds, J., Joinson, A.: Personality and motives for social media use when physically distanced: a uses and gratifications approach. Front. Psychol. **12**, 607948 (2021). https://doi.org/10.3389/fpsyg.2021.607948
7. Boyle, S., Baez, S., Trager, B.M., Labrie, J.: Systematic bias in self-reported social media use in the age of platform swinging: implications for studying social media use in relation to adolescent health behavior. Int. J. Environ. Res. Public Health **19**(16), 9847 (2022). https://doi.org/10.3390/ijerph19169847
8. Braun, V., Clarke, V.: Using thematic analysis in psychology. Qual. Res. Psychol. **3**(2), 77–101 (2006). https://doi.org/10.1191/1478088706qp063oa
9. Chan, C., Suarez, M.T.: Social Media as Enabler for ICT Inclusion to Achieve Active Ageing. In: Proceedings of 21st Pacific Asia Conference on Information Systems, Langkawi (2017). http://aisel.aisnet.org/pacis2017/185
10. Schumacher, C., Kent, N.: 8 Charts on Internet Use Around the World as Countries Grapple with COVID-19. Pew Research Center (2020). https://pewrsr.ch/2wOyAYy. Accessed 5 Jan 2024
11. Cho, S.E., Park, H.W.: A qualitative analysis of cross-cultural new media research: SNS use in Asia and the West. Qual. Quant. **47**(4), 2319–2330 (2013). https://doi.org/10.1007/s11135-011-9658-z

12. Coto, M., Lizano, F., Mora, S., Fuentes, J.: Social media and elderly people: Research trends. In: Meiselwitz, G. (eds) Social Computing and Social Media, Applications and Analytics, LNCS, vol. 10283, pp. 65–81. Springer, Cham (2017). https://doi.org/10.1007/978-3-319-58562-8_6

13. Dias, P., Duarte, A.: TikTok practices among Teenagers in Portugal: a uses & gratifications approach. Journalism Media. 3(4), 615–632 (2022). https://doi.org/10.3390/journalmedia3040041

14. Duong, C.T.P.: Social media. a literature review. J. Media Res. 13(3), 112–126 (2020). https://doi.org/10.24193/jmr.38.7

15. Falgoust, G., Winterlind, E., Moon, P., Parker, A.: Applying the uses and gratifications theory to identify motivational factors behind young adult's participation in viral social media challenges on TikTok. Human Factors Healthcare 2(2) (2022). https://doi.org/10.1016/j.hfh.2022.100014

16. Ferris, A., Hollenbaugh, E., Sommer, P.: Applying the uses and gratifications model to examine consequences of social media addiction. Social Media + Soc. 7(2) (2021). https://doi.org/10.1177/20563051211019003

17. Hogan, B., Quan-Haase, A.: Persistence and change in social media. Bull. Sci. Technol. Soc. 30(5), 309–315 (2010). https://doi.org/10.1177/0270467610380012

18. Hunsaker, A., Hargittai, E.: A review of Internet use among older adults. New Media & Soc. 20(10) (2018). https://doi.org/10.1177/1461444818787348

19. Hutto, C.J., Bell, C., Farmer, S., Fausset, C.: Social media gerontology: understanding social media usage among older adults. Web Intell. Agent Syst. 13(1), 69–87 (2015). https://doi.org/10.3233/WEB-150310

20. Jung, E.H., Walden, J., Johnson, A.C., Sundar, S.S.: Social networking in the aging context: why older adults use or avoid Facebook. Telematics Inform. 34(7), 1071–1080 (2017). https://doi.org/10.1016/j.tele.2017.04.015

21. Kakulla, B.: 2023 Tech Trends and the 50-Plus. Washington, DC: AARP Research (2023). https://doi.org/10.26419/res.00584.001

22. Katz, E., Blumler, J.G., Gurevitch, M.: Utilization of Mass Communication by the Individuals. The Uses of Mass Communication. Sage Publications, Beverly Hills (1974)

23. Kim, M.J., Contractor, N.: Seniors' usage of mobile social network sites: applying theories of innovation diffusion and uses and gratifications. Comput. Hum. Behav. 90, 60–73 (2019). https://doi.org/10.1016/j.chb.2018.08.046

24. Kong, J.F.Y., Lee, G.: Elderly's uses and gratifications of social media: key to improving social compensation and social pressure. International Journal of Cyber Behavior, Psychology and Learning. 7(3), 23–36 (2017). https://doi.org/10.4018/IJCBPL.2017070103

25. Lakhan, R., Sharma, B., Sharma, M.: Social media use among older adults and their challenges. In: Effective Use of Social Media in Public Health. pp. 99–124. Elsevier (2023). https://doi.org/10.1016/B978-0-323-95630-7.00012-3

26. Majid, M.A.A., Othman, M., Mohamad, S.F., Lim, S.: Piloting for interviews in qualitative research: operationalization and lessons learnt. International Journal of Academic Research in Business and Social Sciences. 7(4), 1073–1080 (2017). https://doi.org/10.6007/ijarbss/v7-i4/2916

27. Mapa, C.D.: Special Release: More than 50 million have Access to the Internet (2020 Census of Population and Housing). Philippine Statistics Authority (2023). http://tinyurl.com/2p987m85. Accessed 19 Dec 2023

28. Naeem, M., Ozuem, W., Howell., K., Ranfagni, S.: A Step-by-Step Process of Thematic Analysis to Develop a Conceptual Model in Qualitative Research. International Journal of Qualitative Methods. 22(11), (2023). https://doi.org/10.1177/16094069231205789

29. Newman, L., Stoner, C., Spector, A.: Social networking sites and the experience of older adult users: a systematic review. Ageing Soc. **41**(2), 1–26 (2019). https://doi.org/10.1017/S01446 86X19001144

30. Nowell, L., Norris, J.M., White, D., Moules, N.: Thematic Analysis: Striving to Meet the Trustworthiness Criteria. International Journal of Qualitative Methods. 16(1), (2017). https://doi.org/10.1177/1609406917733847

31. Pelletier, M., Krallman, A., Adams, F., Hancock, T.: One size doesn't fit all: a uses and gratifications analysis of social media platforms. J. Res. Interact. Mark. **14**(2), 269–284 (2020). https://doi.org/10.1108/JRIM-10-2019-0159

32. Phua, J., Jin, S.V., Kim, J.: Uses and gratifications of social networking sites for bridging and bonding social capital: A comparison of Facebook, Twitter, Instagram, and Snapchat. Comput. Hum. Behav. **72**, 115–122 (2017). https://doi.org/10.1016/j.chb.2017.02.041

33. Quan-Haase, A., Young, A.L.: Uses and gratifications of social media: a comparison of facebook and instant messaging. Bull. Sci. Technol. Soc. **30**(5), 350–361 (2010). https://doi.org/10.1177/0270467610380009

34. Quinn, K.: Cognitive Effects of Social Media Use: A Case of Older Adults. Social Media and Society. 4(3), (2018). https://doi.org/10.1177/2056305118787203

35. Ractham, P., Techatassanasoontorn, A., Kaewkitipong, L.: Old But Not Out: Social Media Use and Older Adults' Life Satisfaction. Australiasian Journal of Information Systems 26, (2022). https://doi.org/10.3127/ajis.v26i0.3269

36. Rashid, A.A., Devaraj, N.K., Xuan, L.Z., Selvanesan, K., Noorazalan, A.A.: Social Media Use and Hypertension Knowledge among Undergraduate Students during the COVID-19 Pandemic in Faculty of Medicine and Health Sciences, Universiti Putra Malaysia. Malaysian Journal of Medicine and Health Sciences. 18, 1–9 (2022). https://doi.org/10.47836/mjmhs18.s14.1

37. Sheldon, P., Antony, M.G., Ware, L.J.: Baby Boomers' use of Facebook and Instagram: uses and gratifications theory and contextual age indicators. Heliyon. 7(4), (2021). https://doi.org/10.1016/j.heliyon.2021.e06670

38. Tandoc, E., Lou, C., Min, V.L.H.: Platform-swinging in a poly-social-media context: How and why users navigate multiple social media platforms. J. Comput.-Mediat. Commun. **24**(1), 21–35 (2019). https://doi.org/10.1093/jcmc/zmy022

39. Vaterlaus, J.M., Winter, M.: TikTok: an exploratory study of young adults' uses and gratifications. The Social Science Journal. 1–20 (2021). https://doi.org/10.1080/03623319.2021.196 9882

40. Waycott, J., Vetere, F., Pedell, S., Kulik, L.: Older adults as digital content producers. In: Proceedings of the SIGCHI Conference on Human Factors in Computing Systems, pp. 39–48. Paris, France (2013). https://doi.org/10.1145/2470654.2470662

41. Yaqub, M.Z., Al-Sabban, A.S.: Knowledge Sharing through Social Media Platforms in the Silicon Age. Sustainability. **15**(8), 6765 (2023). https://doi.org/10.3390/su15086765

42. Zhao, Y., Liu, J., Tang, J., Zhu, Q.: Conceptualizing perceived affordances in social media interaction design. Aslib Proceedings: New Information Perspectives. **65**(3), 289–303 (2013). https://doi.org/10.1108/00012531311330656

43. Zhao, Y., Zhao, M., Song, S.: Online Health Information Seeking Behaviors Among Older Adults: Systematic Scoping Review. Journal of Medical Internet Research. 24(2), (2022). https://doi.org/10.2196/34790

44. Zheng, H., Chen, X., Jiang, S., Sun, L.: How does health information seeking from different online sources trigger cyberchondria? The roles of online information overload and information trust. Inf. Process. Manage. **60**(4), 103364 (2023). https://doi.org/10.1016/j.ipm.2023.103364

Exploring Reasons for Short Videos Engagement Behaviors of Senior Users

Zhaoyi Ma[1](✉) and Qin Gao[2]

[1] School of Design Arts and Media, Nanjing University of Science and Technology, Nanjing, People's Republic of China
mazhaoyi@njust.edu.cn
[2] Department of Industrial Engineering, Tsinghua University, Beijing, People's Republic of China
gaoqin@tsinghua.edu.cn

Abstract. The surge in popularity of short videos among the elderly has attracted attention, yet the motivations driving their usage remain unclear. This study delves into the factors influencing senior individuals' engagement behaviors, encompassing consumption, participation, and production. Through two focus groups with 10 participants aged over 55, the study revealed that utilitarian and hedonic needs motivated seniors' consumption behaviors, while social needs facilitated participation and production. Additionally, apprehensions about potential social conflicts emerged as a deterrent to the proactive use of short videos by senior individuals. These findings carry theoretical and practical implications for the utilization of social media among the elderly.

Keywords: senior population · short video applications · engagement behaviors

1 Introduction

Short-video applications, such as TikTok, Douyin, and Kuaishou have proliferated fast globally. In China, the top short video application, Douyin, reached 743 million monthly active users in 2022 (Statista, 2022). Short videos usually last no more than a few minutes, with music or some special effects. Compared with other social media like Weibo and WeChat, short video platforms enable users to create content in an effortless way, by providing a series of technical support, such as easy clipping and adding effects (Meng & Leung, 2021). At the same time, short video platforms utilize artificial intelligence technology to provide personal recommendations to users, making the content engage users' interests accurately, and making content creators get traffic more easily(Zhang et al. 2019). Nowadays, short video applications gradually become important information sources as well as mainstream platforms that allow users to create and exchange user-generated content.

As user-generated content platforms, short video applications afford various user behaviors, encompassing viewing, sharing, liking, commenting, and content creation. Some users only browse but do not post any messages in online communities, while

Q. Gao and J. Zhou (Eds.): HCII 2024, LNCS 14725, pp. 362–373, 2024.
https://doi.org/10.1007/978-3-031-61543-6_25

some engage in virtual community building, including commenting, liking, or even producing videos themselves. To conceptualize individuals' utilization of social media, Shao (2009) posited a three-tiered framework, comprising consumption (i.e., browsing and viewing), participation (i.e., liking, sharing, and commenting), and production (i.e., generating personal content). Progressing from consumption to production, users exhibit heightened effort and creativity and are more likely to gain more interactions with other users. Research considering these distinctions has established that motivations differ in level and impact across various engagement behaviors (Bossen & Christina 2020; Omar & Dequan 2020).

Short videos seem to be particularly popular in senior groups. It was reported that older Douyin users have posted over 600 million videos (Douyin & Center for Population and Development Studies at Renmin University of China, 2021), indicating that the senior population is an important part of short video users. Short videos have embedded in the daily lives of many older adults and have an effect on the way senior people get, disseminate, and generate information. Considering the growth of older groups in proportion and size of the total population in China, it is important to gain an understanding of the reasons behind senior groups' participation in short video applications. Due to the gap in lifestyle, psychological, and social environment between retired people and working people (Barnay 2016), this study regards seniors as the retired population whose age is over 55.

However, most current studies about the underlying reasons for short video users' engagement behaviors are based on the young population (Falgoust et al. 2022; Meng & Leung 2021; Omar & Dequan 2020), while little is known about the senior population. Since the substantial differences between young and senior groups in lifestyles, values, and socio-technical environments, studies targeting senior groups may provide specific insights for platform managers to understand and engage these users. Furthermore, since the favorable impact of social media usage on mental well-being and quality of life among older people (Nam 2021), promoting the engagement of short videos among senior groups' may be beneficial for their psychological health and quality of life. Therefore, this study aims to focus on senior groups, investigating the underlying reasons for their short video engagement behaviors. By doing so, this study could extend the current literature on short video engagement behavior and offer practical implications to platform designers.

2 Literature Review

2.1 Motivations for Short Video Use

To understand the reasons that bring users to short videos, a growing number of studies have investigated the effect of different gratifications on users' behaviors. Considering the general behaviors, the most cited motivations were related to social and entertainment needs. Studies have found that social attachment and social presence were positively associated with users' intentions to adopt or continued use of TikTok (W. Wang et al. 2020).

Some studies further take the different engagement levels into account. Meng & Leung (2021) considered three types of engagement behaviors, i.e. contribution, enhancement, and creation, and identified that personal factors and users' needs regarding social seeking, navigability, modality, and interactivity were important predictors for users' engagement behaviors. Other studies mostly applied a three-factor framework, which summarizes that users deal with social media in three ways, involving consuming, participating, and producing (Shao 2009). Omar & Dequan (2020) collected a survey involving 385 participants and found that personality traits had no significant influence on TikTok usage behaviors, while the roles of motivations were critical but differed in levels and influence. Bossen & Kottasz (2020) reported that the gratification of entertainment was the primary driver behind all three behaviors, yet the wish to expand one's social networks became the major motivation for contributory behaviors. These findings showed that the motivations behind different engagement behaviors were somewhat similar, yet differ in many aspects. Thus, it is necessary to consider the different engagement behaviors when investigating the underlying reasons. Furthermore, all the above studies were based on general young people, while little is known about what motivates the use of another important population, i.e. senior groups.

2.2 Influencing Factors of Senior People's Use of Social Media

Since the penetration of the Internet among older adults, there have emerged many empirical studies focusing on senior people to investigate their intentions and user behaviors of social media. It was found that social motivations were the most frequently reported factors that influence senior users' adoption decisions. Yang et al. (2019) found that social motivation as well as perceived interactive richness strongly affected elderly users' intention to adopt ubiquitous mobile social services. Other factors such as perceived enjoyment and perceived ease of use were also mentioned as motivations for social media use for senior people (Ramírez-Correa et al., 2019).

A couple of studies examined the contributing factors of different use behaviors. Zhang et al. (2021) focused on active engagement behaviors (e.g. posting, liking, sharing, or commenting) on WeChat. They combined interviews and questionnaires and identified that the critical roles of social support and information needs. A stream of studies Regarding sharing behavior, Liu et al. (2020) found that senior people's motivations to share information on social media included social interaction, knowledge sharing, and information exchange. Wang et al. (2020) found that senior people with more online health information experience who valued relationship and family were more likely to share health information on WeChat. Recently, Wang et al. (2023) paid attention to producing behavior and found that the need to be needed was positively related to senior users' intention to create short videos.

3 Methodology

Since there were scarce studies on the short video engagement behavior of senior people, focus groups were chosen to elicit participants' opinions, behaviors, and motivations. Another reason for using focus groups was that they could build a natural environment for multiple participants, making them more likely to share their comments and experiences.

3.1 Participants

Since we need to involve senior people with different short video engagements, a snowball sampling method was used because the target population was not easy to access. We first contacted an older person who worked for the Nanjing University of Science and Technology for many years. He was familiar with many retired employees and then helped us contact the other participants who used short videos. Particularly, we asked him to invite some persons who created short videos, with an aim to involve participants with the different engagement levels of short videos.

Finally, a total of ten participants were recruited and two focus groups with 5 participants each were carried out. Among the participants, 4 were female and 6 were male, aged from 55 to 66 (M = 59.7, SD = 4.62). All of them were married and retired.

3.2 Procedure

Each focus group was conducted in a quiet room. After introducing the study's purpose to the participants, the moderator asked questions about their demographic information and use experiences of short videos. Then participants were guided to discuss the following topics:

- Their use behaviors in short video applications (including applications used, use frequency, context for using short video applications, contents of viewed videos, liking, commenting, sharing, and creating behaviors, etc.)
- The motivations for their engagement behaviors (i.e. viewing, liking, commenting, sharing, and creating short videos).
- The reasons for not participating in some activities in short video applications (e.g. liking, commenting, sharing, or creating short videos).
- Overall attitude about short videos posted by others, the number of their acquaintances or friends in the short video applications, support or hindrance received from their family or friends, and anything else related to short videos.

3.3 Data Analysis

All interviews were audio-recorded and transcribed for analysis. A content analysis strategy was used to code the data by integrating both top-down and bottom-up perspectives. By reviewing the literature, a set of initial category themes was established, and undiscovered or unmentioned themes were also allowed to verify and supplement the predetermined themes. To organize motivations, we applied the three dimensions of perceived value, namely utilitarian, hedonic, and social, as delineated by Rintamäki et al. (2006). In this framework, utilitarian value summarizes benefits related to instrumental and functional benefits from product use, hedonic value refers to non-functional and enjoyable feelings acquired from usage, and social value summarizes benefits from building relationships with others. By integrating the framework, the diverse facets of benefits that participants sought through their engagement with short videos could be summarized. Following the framework and initial themes, two students of Human-Computer Interaction at Nanjing University of Science and Technology dependently coded the text. Any inconsistent codes were discussed together. The final code themes with their definitions and examples are shown in Table 1.

Table 1. Coding scheme for interview results analysis

Theme	Aspect	Definition	Example
Motivations			
Seeking information in an effective way	Utilitarian	Older adults' attribution of engaging in short videos to watch news	*Every time I want to know what is going on, I open my short video application. It is much more effective than watching television because short videos push information at any moment*
Learning useful skills for daily use	Utilitarian	Older adults' attribution of engaging in short videos to help them improve their life skills	*I learned a lot of cooking skills from the short videos. This kind of content was very useful for me*
Navigating to other content	Utilitarian	Older adults' attribution of engaging in short videos to lead them to find more and deeper content	*One day I was pushed a scrap of a TV series, I found it very interesting and suited my taste, and then I searched for the TV series*
Passing time	Hedonic	Older adults' attribution of engaging in short videos to pass time, thereby obtaining entertainment value	*When I was free, I would lie on the sofa and view short videos to kill time*
Being able to watch others doing things	Hedonic	Older adults' attribution of engaging in short videos to enable them to view people doing things that they interested	*I like watching people play chess. Some people in short videos played chess very well. I love watching it*
Peeking what other people doing	Social	Older adults' attribution of engaging in short videos to enable them to see what the neighbors were doing, without letting them know	*Some people around me posted videos. Their videos were pushed to me, and I will discuss that with my wife*

(continued)

Table 1. (*continued*)

Theme	Aspect	Definition	Example
Access the videos easily later	Utilitarian	Older adults' attribution of engaging in short videos to find videos effortless	*I added the video to my collections because I want to see it conveniently when I use it*
Keeping connections with friends in real-life	Social	Older adults' attribution of engaging in short videos to interact with their friends or acquaintance	*I often comment on the videos of my friends and relatives, to connect with them*
Express opinions immediately	Social	Older adults' attribution of engaging in short videos to post their feelings at once	*I comment on others' videos because I want to express my recognition to the content or the producers*
Archiving	Utilitarian	Older adults' attribution of engaging in short videos to record automatically	*I could easily view the videos on my profile in the future*
Hobby driving	Hedonic	Older adults' attribution of engaging in short videos to their hobbies	*I like photography, thus I often post my videos in Douyin*
Entertain themselves	Hedonic	Older adults' attribution of engaging in short videos to enjoy themselves	*You know after retirement I have a lot of free time, and doing such things makes me happy*
Capturing memorable moments with family and friends	Social	Older adults' attribution of engaging in short videos to record memorable moments in life	*When I travel or play with friends, I post videos to record these moments*
Appraisals from family and friends	Social	Older adults' attribution of engaging in short videos to obtain recognition	*My family and friends support me in posting videos. They praised me a lot*

(*continued*)

Table 1. (*continued*)

Theme	Aspect	Definition	Example
Barriers			
Excess information		Older adults' expressions that the redundant content provided by short video applications makes them frustrated	*The content of Douyin is endless. I think it's too much and sometimes I feel tired seeing it*
Irrelevant recommendations		Older adults' expressions that the information provided by short video platforms is not their concern	*Sometimes the application did not push any relevant content to me, which made me unhappy*
Avoid conflicts		Older adults' concerns about eliciting arguments with others on short video platforms	*I never give any negative comments to others. This may cause a fight!*
Fear of negative evaluations		Older adults' concerns about being negatively evaluated	*I never post videos because people may judge me. I don't like that*
Introverted personality		Older adults' expressions that their shy and introverted trait prevent them from posting videos	*I am quiet and introverted, and I don't like to put myself out, like people who are keen to show off*

4   Result

4.1   Use Behavior

All participants had used short video applications for over 1.5 years, ranging from 1.5 to 3 years. All participants reported they watched short videos every day, with seven of them using Douyin and the others using other applications such as Kuaishou and Xigua Video. Regarding the video content, participants said that they mainly viewed videos about 1) current news; 2) habit-related content (e.g. playing chess, music, dance, etc.); 3) daily skills (e.g. cooking, vehicle maintenance, etc.); 4) health-related knowledge (e.g. physical activity, health exercise); 5) tourism; 6) clips from movies or TV series. Most of them mentioned that watching short videos plays a major role in their entertainment life.

Although all participants watched short videos daily, they hardly shared short videos with others, and their frequency of commenting or adding to collections was also limited. Four participants reported that they never commented on others' videos, three participants only commented on their friends or acquaintances, and three participants commented on others. The majority of the total participants (N = 8) reported that they usually gave likes to videos. Among these participants, five created short videos on their own, covering traveling, landscapes, festivals, etc.

4.2 Motivations and Barriers of Engagement Behaviors

To conceptualize people's usage of social media content, we adopted the framework from Shao et al. (2009), which involves three levels of usage, including consuming, participating, and producing. From consuming to producing, the effort and creativity of users increased. The motivations and barriers of these different engagement behaviors are summarized in Table 2.

Table 2. Motivations and barriers of short video engagement behaviors of senior users.

	Consuming	Participating	Producing
Motives			
Utilitarian benefits	• Seeking information in an effective way (N = 8) • Learning useful skills for daily use (N = 4) • Navigating to other content (N = 4)	• Access the videos easily later (N = 2)	• Archiving (N = 3)
Hedonic benefits	• Passing time (N = 5) • Being able to watch others doing interesting things (N = 5)		• Hobby driving (N = 2) • Entertain themselves (N = 2)
Social benefits	• Peeking what people are doing nearby (N = 3)	• Keeping connections with friends in real life (N = 5) • Express opinions (mainly recognitions) immediately (N = 5)	• Capturing memorable moments with family and friends (N = 5) • Appraisals from family and friends (N = 4)
Barriers			
	• Excess information (N = 3) • Irrelevant recommendations (N = 2)	• Avoid conflicts (N = 6)	• Fear of negative evaluations (N = 4) • Introverted personality (N = 2)

In terms of consuming behavior, 10 participants together identified 3 utilitarian benefits. The most cited motivation was information seeking. The majority of participants (N = 8) agreed that using short videos to know what was happening in the world and around them was an essential motive to view short videos. The timeliness and richness of the information pushed by short video applications were appreciated by our participants, especially compared to the traditional information acquisition channels (e.g. televisions and newspapers). All of our participants have regarded short videos as important information sources. Other two utilitarian values brought by consuming short videos were skills learning (N = 4) and content navigating (N = 4): Senior participants mentioned the short videos helped them to improve their life skills, since a large number of people sharing their skills and tips in various fields through short videos; The less use of television made them rely on the slices on short video platforms to understand TV shows.

The two hedonic benefits of consuming short videos included passing time (N = 5) and watching others doing interesting things (N = 5): the rich and sometimes humorous content offered by short video applications made short videos become senior participants' first choice in their leisure time, and the wide and numerous video producers make short videos a convenient way to observe people who good at doing something do the things. Interestingly, 3 participants reported liking peeking their acquaintance on short videos motivated them to view short videos. The AI algorithm recommends people and things nearby to users whereby enables senior people to observe others. Despite these benefits, our participants reported the excessive and irrelevant information on short video applications made them feel tired and annoyed, thereby inhibiting their consuming behaviors.

Regarding participating behaviors, 8 participants mentioned 3 motivations, including 1 utilitarian benefit and 2 social benefits. The only utilitarian benefit was reported by 2 participants who added videos to their collections for later easy access to the videos. Other benefits were related to commenting and liking behaviors. Half of the participants said they commented or gave "likes" for articulating their immediate feelings about the videos viewed. Moreover, participants supplemented that they mainly posted positive comments, because negative content may make others feel bad and bring trouble. Another reason for commenting or giving "likes" to others' videos was to keep social ties because many of the senior people's acquaintances also used short videos. Such existence of offline social networks on short video platforms led to participants' activities on short video applications being regulated by social rules in real life. For example, some participants thought they needed to give all their friends "likes" to maintain their friendships, regardless of the quality of their videos, while some participants chose not to give any likes to friends to avoid the embarrassment and misunderstanding brought by unfair "likes" (i.e. giving "likes" to some friends yet not others). Such concerns about possible social conflicts were mentioned as a major barrier to giving "likes" or comments to others (N = 6).

A total of 5 participants identified 2 social benefits, 2 hedonic benefits, and 1 utilitarian benefit related to producing behaviors. The benefits associated with socializing were mentioned by most people. All of them said they created short videos to capture memorable moments with family and friends, and many of them (N = 3) appreciated the archiving function of short videos because they wanted to see the videos easily in the future. Another important motivation for creating short videos was recognition from family or friends. They said they were encouraged and supported by these appraisals and felt happy in producing short videos. Hedonic motivations were also mentioned: Two participants mentioned they were fond of taking photos and posting them on social media platforms; Two participants also reported that they deemed posting videos as a way to entertain themselves. These participants appreciated the easy editing functions of short video applications that enabled them to create videos conveniently. In terms of barriers to producing behaviors, most (N = 6) of those who did not produce any videos explained that they were afraid of being negatively evaluated if they disclosed themselves on the Internet, and two mentioned that they were too shy and introverted to express themselves in public.

5 Discussion

This study identified that senior people's different engagement behaviors were motivated by a variety of utilitarian, hedonic, and social benefits. We found that in terms of consuming behavior, utilitarian and hedonic benefits were most cited, while social benefits were most frequently related to participating or consuming behaviors. In addition, we also found senior people's consuming behaviors were inhibited due to the appropriate content feature, while they refused to participate or produce short videos because of social concerns.

Different from prior empirical studies based on young adults, we found the consuming behavior of senior people was predominantly driven by their utilitarian needs, while younger people were more motivated by hedonic needs. One possible reason of this discrepancy may arise from the relatively restricted media and resource access of older individuals compared to their younger counterparts. Young generations have the ability to use a variety of technology for various needs. For example, they may obtain news about current events via Weibo, learn academic skills on bilibili.com, and seek social interactions on Little Redbook (Chen et al., 2021; Gao & Feng, 2016). Senior people, however, have limited access to online sources (Hayes et al., 2015). Thus, they may tend to achieve their needs with fewer technologies. This finding implies that platform managers should promote and advertise the practical value of their platforms to attract and satisfy senior users.

In terms of more engaging behaviors (i.e. participating and producing behaviors), social needs, encompassing the maintenance of connections with friends and the capturing of moments with family and friends, emerged as primary motivators. This aligns with prior research focused on young adults, signifying that the pursuit of sociality was the predominant incentive for individuals to invest greater effort in short videos (Meng & Leung, 2021; Omar & Dequan, 2020; Shao, 2009). In particular, in contrast to young individuals who seek to both sustain existing relationships and establish new connections, senior individuals predominantly engage with their genuine friends and family. This suggests that while younger people perceive short video platforms as venues for both original and extended offline social interactions, seniors primarily utilize these platforms to complement their offline social activities. One plausible explanation is that older individuals may encounter challenges in text input, rendering it more difficult for them to form new friendships through written communication. This discovery underscores the importance for platform managers to take initiatives, such as implementing voice input technology, to simplify input for older individuals and enhance their ease of social interaction.

Notably, our findings revealed that senior individuals exhibited a notable fear of conflict, acting as a deterrent to their engagement behaviors. They tended to express positive emotions, such as liking and praising others, rather than posting comments that might evoke unhappiness in others. Additionally, they adopted strategies like giving likes to all or none of their friends to ensure perceived fairness and avoided posting videos to circumvent potential negative evaluations. This apprehension could be attributed to the presence of a genuine social network on short video platforms. Many acquaintances of older individuals were also users of these platforms, and the location-based recommendation algorithms increased the likelihood of videos being pushed to people in close proximity. Consequently, online activities became disclosed to the offline world, and adverse outcomes online had the potential to impact real-life interactions. Furthermore, cultural factors may contribute to this phenomenon. Given that China is a harmonious collectivist society, Chinese individuals have a proclivity for a peaceful environment and an aversion to conflict (Hook et al., 2009). This inclination to avoid conflicts may be heightened for older individuals who have been more exposed to such a cultural environment. Concerns about potential social conflicts significantly curtailed the proactive use of short videos among senior people. Recognizing the advantages associated with active engagement in social media, platform developers could design features that enable senior individuals to establish a community where they can interact with close friends or family without apprehensions.

6 Conclusion

This study seeks to elucidate the motivations behind senior individuals' consumption, participation, or production of short videos. Through two focus groups comprising 10 participants, a range of motivations for various engagement behaviors was identified. The results revealed that seniors consume short videos primarily for utilitarian and hedonic benefits, participate with a focus on social goals, and engage in production for both hedonic and social value. These findings contribute to an enhanced comprehension of social media utilization among the elderly, offering practical insights for platform designers.

References

Barnay, T.: Health, work and working conditions: a review of the European economic literature. European J. Health Econ. 17(6) (2016)

Bossen, B., Christina, K.: Uses and gratifications sought by pre-adolescent and adolescent TikTok consumers. Young Consumers 21(4), 1–33 (2020). https://doi.org/10.1108/YC-07-2020-1186

Chen, X., Liu, Z., Wei, S., Liu, Y.: Understanding the role of affordances in promoting social commerce engagement. Int. J. Electron. Commer. 25(3), 287–312 (2021)

Douyin & Center for Population and Development Studies at Renmin University of China. Survey Report on the Use of Short Videos among Middle-aged and Elderly People in China (2021)

Falgoust, G., Winterlind, E., Moon, P., Parker, A., Zinzow, H., Madathil, K.C.: Applying the uses and gratifications theory to identify motivational factors behind young adult's participation in viral social media challenges on TikTok. Human Fact. Healthcare **2**, 100014 (2022)

Gao, Q., Feng, C.: Branding with social media: User gratifications, usage patterns, and brand message content strategies. Comput. Hum. Behav. **63**, 868–890 (2016)

Hayes, M., van Stolk-Cooke, K., Muench, F.: Understanding Facebook use and the psychological affects of use across generations. Comput. Hum. Behav. **49**, 507–511 (2015)

Hook, J.N., Worthington, Jr., E.L., Utsey, S.O.: Collectivism, Forgiveness, and Social Harmony. Counseling Psychol. **37**(6), 821–847 (2009). https://doi.org/10.1177/0011000008326546

Liu, C., Wu, T.Y., Chang, W.: Does authenticity really matter? Exploring the middle-aged and elderly users' motivations to share information on social media. Library Philos. Practice (e-Journal), 3996 (2020)

Meng, K., Leung, L.: Factors influencing TikTok engagement behaviors in China: an examination of gratifications sought, narcissism, and the Big Five personality traits. Telecommunications Policy **45**, 102172 (2021)

Nam, S.J.: Mediating effect of social support on the relationship between older adults' use of social media and their quality-of-life. Curr. Psychol. **40**(9), 4590–4598 (2021)

Omar, B., Dequan, W.: Watch, Share or Create: The influence of personality traits and user motivation on TikTok mobile video usage. Inter. J. Interactive Mobile Technol. (IJIM) **14**(4), 121 (2020). https://doi.org/10.3991/ijim.v14i04.12429

Ramírez-Correa, P., Grandón, E.E., Ramírez-Santana, M., Belmar Órdenes, L.: Explaining the use of social network sites as seen by older adults: the enjoyment component of a hedonic information system. Int. J. Environ. Res. Public Health **16**(10), 1673 (2019)

Rintamäki, T., Kanto, A., Kuusela, H., Spence, M.T.: Decomposing the value of department store shopping into utilitarian, hedonic and social dimensions: evidence from Finland. Inter. J. Retail & Distribut. Manag, **34**(1), 6–24 (2006)

Shao, G.: Understanding the appeal of user-generated media: a uses and gratification perspective. Internet Res. **19**(1), 7–25 (2009)

Statista. Number of monthly active users of Douyin in China from November 2021 to December 2022 (2022). https://www.statista.com/statistics/1361354/china-monthly-active-users-of-dou yin-chinese-tiktok/

Tambellini, E.: Exploring the relationship between working history, retirement transition and women's life satisfaction. Ageing Soc., 1–30 (2021).

Wang, C., Yan, J., Zhang, Y., Huang, L.: Investigating determinants of middle-aged and elderly users' video-creating intention on short-video platforms from a lifespan development perspective. Aslib J. Inform. Manag. ahead-of-print (2023)

Wang, W., Zhuang, X., Shao, P.: Exploring health information sharing behavior of Chinese elderly adults on WeChat. Healthcare **8**(3), 207 (2020)

Yang, H.L., Lin, S.L.: The reasons why elderly mobile users adopt ubiquitous mobile social service. Comput. Hum. Behav. **93**, 62–75 (2019)

Yu, R.P., Mccammon, R.J., Ellison, N.B., Langa, K.M.: The relationships that matter: Social network site use and social wellbeing among older adults in the United States of America. Ageing Soc. **36**(9), 1826–1852 (2016)

Zhang, X., Wu, Y., Liu, S.: Exploring short-form video application addiction: Socio-technical and attachment perspectives. Telematics Inform. **42**, 101243 (2019)

Zhang, X., Xu, X., Cheng, J.: WeChatting for health: What motivates older adult engagement with health information. Healthcare **9**(6), 751 (2021)

"'It's Fake.' 'No, It's not.' 'How is It Fake?'. It Happened to Me and My Grandparents Several Times": Portuguese Generations' Dialogues on Fake News

Margarida Maneta(✉) and Maria José Brites

Lusófona University, CICANT, Porto, Portugal
margarida.maneta@ulusofona.pt

Abstract. Information disorders have introduced additional challenges for democratic participation and citizenship in societies. On this phenomenon, which has received significant attention in recent times, media literacies are pointed to as a solution. Despite this, it can be said that media literacies have mostly centered on children and young people, there is an increasing research interest and discussion on older people [1, 2]. We used a qualitative approach, to better understand the relationship between older people and disinformation in Portugal. We rely on their perspectives and on the views of younger people. The data relies on two projects. Firstly, it refers to the results of a set of workshops held between March and April 2023 in the district of Porto with people aged between 61 and 77 years old. This action research project highlighted their voices, anxieties, and experiences regarding disinformation, with special emphasis on themes, practical cases, and tools. A second project focused on youth and news (YouNDigital - Youth, News and Digital Citizenship - PTDC/COM-OUT/0243/2021) shed light on how and why, in the context of datafication and algorithms, youth aged between 15 and 24 living in Portugal associate older people with episodes of disinformation. The preliminary results point to the fragility of the older in the face of these phenomena, largely justified by a lack of confidence in their abilities, as well as the frequent reference to young people as those who help them.

Keywords: Information Disorders · Older People · Young People

1 Introduction

Vulnerability to disinformation is usually seen from the perspective of young people [2] and media literacy programmes tend to focus mainly on the school context. This article seeks to fill a theoretical gap by focusing on older generations. The older people are the age group with the greatest growth in access to digital technologies in recent years in Portugal. The context of this article is therefore a generation with an increasingly digital life, marked by easy and instant access to information, but also by the growing circulation of disinformation.

Q. Gao and J. Zhou (Eds.): HCII 2024, LNCS 14725, pp. 374–382, 2024.
https://doi.org/10.1007/978-3-031-61543-6_26

The daily experience of older people with disinformation has made relationships with other generations more prominent. If family and friendship relationships were once indispensable in obtaining and sharing information about what is going on around them and in the world [3], they are now strong drivers of the adoption of digital practices and tend to stimulate critical thinking online and intergenerationality. For this reason, this article is based, firstly, on the results of an action research project, which aims to map the knowledge and experiences of a group of older people with disinformation, helping them to acquire tools to combat it; secondly, crossed with another Portuguese project, YouNDigital - Youth, News and Digital Citizenship (PTDC/COM-OUT/0243/2021), we try to understand how the younger generations, strongly referred to on both sides as essential intermediaries in these experiences, perceive the digital competences of older people in the face of disinformation and empower them (or not).

Using the perspectives of older and young people, this article aims to understand whether disinformation is a phenomenon foreign to older generations and how important intergenerational relations are in this context. It is structured in three parts: The literature review will rely on the discussion on facets of disinformation and intergenerational dialogues, namely between children/youth and older people. Below is the methodological approach, explaining the steps followed during the fieldwork in the two projects and how the data will be cross-referenced. This is followed by a presentation and discussion of the results, with some final reflections and pointers for the future.

2 Literature Review

Disinformation is a "current and reinvigorated problem that [continuously] needs special attention" [4]. Various conceptualisations of the phenomenon have been produced, particularly since the 2016 US elections, when scientific production on the subject grew. According to the definition by Claire Wardle and Hossein Derakhshan, disinformation is "Information that is false and deliberately created to harm a person, social group, organization or country" [5]. Disinformation is just one side of a cube that experts have called information disorder, which is also made up of misinformation - false information, but without the intention of causing harm - and malinformation - reality-based information used in a way that causes harm [5].

Disinformation acts through the rapid and uncontrollable dissemination of information within the framework of digital dynamics. The current context of digital instantaneity has given audiences new powers between access to and production of information and content, without intermediaries or gatekeepers, which has - at the same time - fuelled the spread of disinformation. Although this debate is closely linked to technology, the focus is on how it is used and how decisive this use is for the exercise of full citizenship. The media ecosystem has opened doors to new forms of communication, sharing and dissemination of information, including the (re)production of distorted and manipulated messages in response to commercial, emotional, or ideological logics [2]. This duality requires extra attention if we consider that, in this perspective of digital dynamics, the boundaries between empowerment and threat are blurred, placing us between the best informed and the most ignorant [6].

Media and citizenship are correlated and cannot be perceived separately [7]. The spread of disinformation polarises society, causing discredit in institutions and episodes of radicalisation [8]. That's why the challenge for democracy is to "find ways to preserve the freedoms that come with more access to information, while protecting against the threats that come with it" [9].

Given the previous discussion, disinformation is a "multifaceted problem, which has neither a single cause nor a single solution" [10]. The literature has pointed to industry regulation, fact-checking projects and, in particular, media education as answers to the problem [11]. Citizens of different ages are seen in an ambivalent light, as part of the problem and part of the solution [2] - if, on the one hand, they can be seen as amplifiers of the phenomenon, through uncontrolled sharing and poor verification of sources, on the other, their active role, with the right tools, can be the key to combating it. The popularisation of disinformation has emphasised how essential it is to emancipate and raise the awareness of audiences through literacies, stimulating their critical thinking and informed participation.

The inversion of the age pyramid, driven by low birth rates and rising average life expectancy, has redesigned ageing societies. Although compared to the younger age groups they have lower indicators, the older people are the age group whose online presence is growing. For example, it can be noted that in Portugal, over the last ten years, access to the internet by the older population (aged between 65 and 74) has grown by 34.8 per cent, in line with the growth also seen at the European level [12]. However, media literacy is "often considered from the perspective of young people's projects", despite the need to look at it through the lens of other generations [13, 14]. In Portugal, studies on literacy and media rarely focus on older audiences, making research in this area practically non-existent. At the European level, policies to combat disinformation do not specifically target older people [2].

This environment is particularly difficult for older people. However, as already pointed out, the current digital Era brought an opportunity for bringing younger and older generations together. In the literature, they are often described as separate and contrasting groups, especially if we revisit the definitions of digital natives and immigrants, according to Prensky [15]. This concept is now widely contested [16], even if the idea is deeply rooted in social thoughts about generations and technology knowledge. In addition to idiosyncrasies such as age, schooling, and lifestyle, which characterise the heterogeneity of older generations [17], family and social relationships are also decisive in the adoption of digital practices by older people, within co-learning processes and (mutual) moments of support and encouragement. Contact with sons and daughters, nephews, and grandchildren, in the logic of extending their social life [18], older people adopt digital practices while finding bridges to break the isolation and loneliness that are more common at this stage of life. Rasi and colleagues [19] showed that the availability of family members influences the adoption of digital practices by the older people, particularly by clarifying any doubts that arise, strengthening intergenerational relationships.

In turn, this environment reveals the ambiguity of intergenerational relations. If, on the one hand, they stimulate digital inclusion, within the framework of new consumption and digital convergence, on the other, they can weaken it. When generations reflect on their digital practices, they tend to do so in comparison with the others, in a dualistic logic between self- and hetero-evaluation. And there, among the diversity of correlated vectors that (re)configure the relationship with technology, the literature describes episodes of disinterest or giving up, motivated by considering themselves too old to acquire digital skills, fuelled by anxiety, fear, insecurity and low self-esteem [20].

3   Methodological Approach

Recognising that most studies have focused on children and young people [13, 14], with comparably little research and discussion on older people, this article seeks to take a closer look at this scenario, especially as it considers that 1) It prevents preconceived ideas about this generation and their relationship with and consumption of digital media; 2) Promoting media and digital literacy and the acquisition of skills boosts the participation and exercise of citizenship of the age group in question; and 3) Knowing the experience of older adults with the phenomenon of disinformation allows for the adaptation of localised and contextualised public policies, which so far have not been seen in this landscape [2].

Different methods have guided media literacy practices with audiences: intergenerational approaches, time-limited courses, and online learning [1, 21]. This article concerns an option for thematic workshops, one of which is dedicated to disinformation. A workshop was chosen because its dynamic nature allowed for the active participation of all involved, providing a space for learning and, above all, dialogue. This structure has often been successful with groups of "citizens who are not often invited to share their ideas", such as older people [22]. The participants in the session were students from the Academia Sénior de Gaia (in English Gaia Senior Academy), located in Porto district, in the north of Portugal, in the scope of an exploratory project on Media and Digital Literacy that was taking place between March and April 2023. This session was part of that project and aimed to understand older adults' perceptions of their digital competences in the fight against disinformation. A total of nine people were involved: a researcher and eight students (two men and six women).

The Digital Competence Framework for Citizens (DigComp 2.2.) [23] guided the workshop, considering the knowledge, skills and attitudes expected for the full exercise of citizenship. In particular, the "Information and Data Literacy" dimension was considered, emphasising the importance of assessing the credibility and reliability of information sources. Furthermore, in the context of digital dynamics, the need to research different sources, the ability to denounce disinformation and to check the date, authorship and factuality of images were underlined. In a broader sense, it could be said that these topics refer to stimulating people's critical thinking about what they see on the internet, recalling the ideological, emotional, and commercial strategies behind the messages.

The session was designed to last an hour and a half, divided between a moment of contextualisation, exposition and explanation of the phenomenon of disinformation, which included the presentation of real examples at national and international levels, under which the older people were challenged to confirm the veracity of the information, giving them a set of tools they could use outside the session; and, after that, a moment of joint reflection, giving the floor to the participants to share their stories, anxieties and doubts. As this was a very heterogeneous group, with different levels of education, professional activities, and lifestyles, it was possible to bring together different points of view on the same subject, promoting intragenerational sharing and closeness.

This article cross-references data from another Portuguese project - YouNDigital, which focuses on young people, news, and digital citizenship (PTDC/COM-OUT/0243/2021). This project aims to understand the younger generation's links with news, while also considering the role of adults in these young people's news habits and news socialisation processes. In this context, semi-structured interviews were conducted between May and September 2023, with 42 young people, aged between 15 and 24, living in Portugal. The interview had a section dedicated to algorithms and datafication, where the young people were encouraged to comment on a cartoon with references to disinformation and post-truth. Several young people answered this question with concrete examples of situations that had happened to their grandparents, uncles, and parents.

4 Results

Firstly, during the thematic workshop, the participants shared similar thoughts about the phenomenon of disinformation. Analysing these answers allows us to understand their experiences with disinformation and family relationships, particularly with younger generations. Secondly, crossing with the answers given by the young people in the interviews, we realised how the digital competences of older people are constructed in the imagination of young people and, lastly, how they impact older people's perception of their digital skills. These answers and thoughts were divided into three subtopics, which we present and analyse below.

4.1 Definitions of Disinformation

All the participants in the session had social networks (predominantly Facebook and WhatsApp) and everyone had heard the word disinformation. We tried to understand, in their own words, how they defined it or what characteristics they highlighted about the phenomenon.

[Disinformation] It's like knitting… It never ends, it just grows… (Male, 69 years old, Degree).

False information is like rumours in the villages… (Female, 66, Degree).

On Covid, it was non-stop disinformation… And the war [Ukraine-Russia conflict]. (Female, 77, Degree).

Among the responses, the following stand out: 1) despite the heterogeneity of the group, mirrored in the different levels of education of the people, they all had references on the topic; 2) the scale of the phenomenon, which is difficult to reverse once it spreads; 3) the immediate relationship with other historical times, by referring to rumours in which these digital reconfigurations had not yet taken place; and 4) more recent events, such as the pandemic or the war between Ukraine and Russia, which have aroused the population's attention, interest and alertness to disinformation.

4.2 The Age Factor and the (Inter)generational Relationships

When asked about their digital dynamics, the older people perceive it as something that wasn't made for their generation:

Young people have it easier, they do everything online... (Female, 61 years old, Degree). *It's as if they've already been taught to do this.* (Female, 77 years old, Degree). This idea that young people's digital skills are innate and that older people are required to make an unnatural effort to develop these skills, even if not with the same proficiency, has been argued in the literature [15] and reflected in society, despite the deterministic view of this idea. The young people interviewed by the YouNDigital project emphasise, in the same logic, that disinformation affects the older sections of society more, with only chronological age as an explanatory factor:

It's clear that there's a higher incidence in older people. (Male, 23 years old, Degree). *My mum is an example of the situation of old people believing everything they see on Facebook, you know.* (Female, 18 years old, High School).

This says a lot about today. For example, older people aren't used to the internet. Because they're not used to it, it didn't exist in their childhood... They must be used to believing everything they see on the internet. (Male, 15 years old, Middle School).

These perceptions inhibit the full utilisation of digital technologies by the older people, since social imaginary, by themselves and others, sees them as outsiders. These attitudes perpetuate feelings of insecurity, fear, and anxiety, which have already been reviewed in the literature [20]. Furthermore, the idea that all older adults will have the same digital proficiency and skills is reductive. The older generation has been described as the most heterogeneous group, considering the influence of sociodemographic data such as education level and life cycle, as well as age and profession [17].

Despite the stigmatising perspectives in their speeches, young people play an important role in helping to combat disinformation of older people, especially as they are the ones to whom the older people turn for explanations and advice.

[when asked about dialogues with his grandmother about the information she sees online] "It's false." "It's not, it's not fake, how is it fake? Who edited it?" "Yes, grandma, it's a fake." "No, it's not fake." And so on... (Male, 23 years old, Degree).

My grandmother created Whatsapp late, but in the meantime she did and so did people her age. It's a whirlwind of disinformation, and sometimes it's a bit of work to go and find things like "No, grandma, it's not like that". (Male, 23 years old, Master).

My grandmother asks for help or just forwards it to me. It's strange for her generation because they're very suspicious of what's on the internet, but at the same time, because it's on the internet it's true. It's a strange mix. (Male, 23 years old, Master).

Young people therefore play an ambivalent role in this context: if, on the one hand, they can discourage older people when comparisons are made between generations, on the other hand, their help influences the detection of disinformation by older people. Given that in growing contexts all over Europe, and particularly in Portugal, older generations are characterised by isolation and loneliness, it's curious to realise that social relationships have an immeasurable value in their perceptions and digital skills. It could be added that intergenerational relationships are strengthened, proving to be a powerful weapon for bringing generations together in the fight against disinformation.

4.3 Deconstructing the Phenomena

The examples most mentioned by the older people group are related to scams and phishing: offers, promotional items and requests for money. Not only because they're more recurrent, but also because they're easier for older people to identify.

[when asked if they've ever seen something on the internet and immediately thought it was fake] Yes, for example when they put up an advert offering something... if they're going to offer it to everyone, we immediately see that it's fake. (Female, 76 years old, Primary School).

In Portugal, scams carried out in the name of family members have been frequent over the last year. The episodes reported are made by unknown numbers who identify themselves as sons and daughters and request bank transfers from the parents. When one of the participants told us that she had been a victim of this scam, the class was encouraged to stop and think about how they could report it.

You only must ask how many rooms the house has, and they can't answer... (Female, 66 years old, Degree).

Calling the daughter to ask is a good option. (Female, 65 years old, High School).

They appeal to our feelings... They affect us in every way. (Female, 77 years old, Degree).

From these examples, the emotional side was worked on, helping to deconstruct disinformation, one of their objectives (in this case, monetary) and their persuasion strategies. In addition to the credibility suggested by family members, the misuse of public figures' images is also frequent in disinformation.

I clicked on a post by Filomena Cautela [a Portuguese public figure and television presenter]. It said to click on it and see what happened to it... This was a different way I fell for it, and it was a virus. (Male, 69 years old, Degree).

Could it be that [the disinformation campaigns] have psychologists behind them? (Female, 66 years old, Degree).

Also, in the logic of disinformation perpetuated by commercial and monetary logic, the examples in which the participants were the lucky winners were commented on.

I said [on Facebook] that someone had invested and had already won thousands of euros... a few hours later someone asked me what I was sharing, and I didn't even know... I had clicked and it launched a virus. (Male, 69 years old, Degree).

5   Conclusions, Limitations and Future Perspectives

In developing this article, we sought to understand whether disinformation is a phenomenon foreign to older generations and how important intergenerational relationships were in this context. The conclusions drawn from this work relate to a relatively small sample, situated in a short period of time and with only one workshop dedicated to the subject so it is urgent to point out the need to develop studies that are more extended in time, in different contexts, to better capture the diversity of the older people, as well as the relevance of their relationships with others in their digital and information trajectories. Although the results cannot be generalised to the Portuguese older population, as they only concern students who attend the Academia Sénior de Gaia, they indicate i) that digital skills are crucial in combating disinformation, in order to ensure safer and more effective participation; ii) relationships with other generations are a key factor in this process; iii) knowledge of the phenomenon often comes from personal experience in scamming or phishing situations, where young people are called upon to help; iv) older people's perceptions of their digital skills in combating disinformation are formulated from: their understandings of other people from their generation; but also, how young people see them; v) young people tend to associate the spread of disinformation with older generations, being the first to offer to help their relatives in these episodes.

The persistent and erroneous idea that in this context only the older generation has anything to gain ends up being very misleading, even from the point of view of the public policies that can be drawn up [2]. This entrenched view also contributes to a self-stigmatisation that can be pernicious and ignores the multiple social dimensions that are present when we talk about generations.

Organising a themed workshop with older people enabled progress in terms of understanding and awareness of the disinformation, the ability to develop tools to assess the veracity of information circulating online and older adults' self-esteem and confidence in their digital practices, not being belittled for their age. The confluence of these results emphasises the need to promote and strengthen intergenerational practices to bring the generations into contact, learning together and deconstructing stereotypes.

Acknowledgments. This study was funded by Foundation for Science and Technology (FCT) under the project YouNDigital – Youth, News and Digital Citizenship under the reference PTDC/COM-OUT/0243/2021 (https://doi.org/10.54499/PTDC/COM-OUT/0243/2021).

References

1. Rasi, P., Vuojärvi, H., Ruokamo, H.: Media Literacy for All Ages. J. Media Lit. Educ. 11, 1–19 (2019). https://doi.org/10.23860/JMLE-2019-11-2-1
2. Brites, M.J., Amaral, I., Simões, R.B., Santos, S.J.: Generational Perspectives on EU Documents Tackling Disinformation. In: Gao, Q. and Zhou, J. (eds.) Human Aspects of IT for the Aged Population. Technology Design and Acceptance. pp. 349–360. Springer International Publishing, Cham (2021). https://doi.org/10.1007/978-3-030-78108-8_26
3. Loos, E., Nijenhuis, J.: Consuming fake news: a matter of age? the perception of political fake news stories in facebook ads. In: Gao, Q. and Zhou, J. (eds.) Human Aspects of IT for the Aged Population. Technology and Society. pp. 69–88. Springer International Publishing, Cham (2020). https://doi.org/10.1007/978-3-030-50232-4_6
4. Brites, M.J., Amaral, I., Catarino, F.: A era das "fake news": o digital storytelling como promotor do pensamento crítico. J. Digital Media & Interaction. J. Digit. Media Interact. 1, 85–98 (2018). https://doi.org/10.34624/jdmi.v1i1.928
5. Wardle, C., Derakhshan, H.: Information disorder: Toward an interdisciplinary framework for research and policy making. Council of Europe (2017)
6. Kellner, D., Share, J.: The critical media literacy guide: engaging media and transforming education. In: The Critical Media Literacy Guide, Brill (2019)
7. Brites, M.J.: Jovens e culturas cívicas: por entre formas de consumo noticioso e de participação. Livros Labcom (2015)
8. Frau-Meigs, D.: Information disorders: risks and opportunities for digital media and information literacy? Medijske Stud. 10, 10–28 (2019). https://doi.org/10.20901/ms.10.19.1

9. Jolls, T., Johnsen, M.: Media literacy: a foundational skill for democracy in the 21st century. Hastings Law J. **69** (2018)
10. European Commission, Directorate-General for Communications Networks, C. and T.: A multi-dimensional approach to disinformation – Report of the independent High level Group on fake news and online disinformation. Publications Office (2018)
11. Frau-Meigs, D.: Notícias falsas e desordens informativas. In: Literacias cívicas e críticas: refletir e praticar, CECS-Centro de Estudos de Comunicação e Sociedade, pp. 77–79 (2019)
12. Pordata: Indivíduos que acederam à Internet, em média, pelos menos uma vez por semana, em % do total de indivíduos: por grupo etário. https://www.pordata.pt/europa/individuos+que+acederam+a+internet++em+media++pelos+menos+uma+vez+por+semana++em+per centagem+do+total+de+individuos+por+grupo+etario-1486
13. Rasi, P.: On the margins of digitalization (2021)
14. Amaral, I., Brites, M.J.: Trends On the Digital Uses and Generations. In: Inted2019 Proc, pp. 5109–5115 (2019). https://doi.org/10.21125/inted.2019.1272
15. Prensky, M.: Digital natives, digital immigrants. Horiz **9** (2001)
16. Helsper, E.J., Eynon, R.: Digital natives: where is the evidence? Br. Educ. Res. J. **36**, 503–520 (2010). https://doi.org/10.1080/01411920902989227
17. Loos, E.: Senior citizens: digital immigrants in their own country? Observatorio. **6**, 1–23 (2012)
18. Lüders, M., Gjevjon, E.R.: Being old in an always-on culture: older people's perceptions and experiences of online communication. Inf. Soc. **33**, 64–75 (2017). https://doi.org/10.1080/01972243.2016.1271070
19. Rasi, P., Vuojärvi, H., Rivinen, S.: Promoting media literacy among older people: a systematic review. Adult Educ. Q. **71**, 37–54 (2021). https://doi.org/10.1177/0741713620923755
20. Carenzio, A., Ferrari, S., Rasi, P.: Older people's media repertoires, digital competences and media literacies: a case study from Italy. Educ. Sci. **11**, 584 (2021). https://doi.org/10.3390/educsci11100584
21. Brites, M.J., Castro, T.S., Oliveira, A.F., Amaral, I.: Contribution participatory methodologies and generational research. In: Gao, Q. and Zhou, J. (eds.) Human Aspects of IT for the Aged Population. Design, Interaction and Technology Acceptance. pp. 3–11. Springer International Publishing, Cham (2022). https://doi.org/10.1007/978-3-031-05581-2_1
22. Brites, M.J., Oliveira, A.F., Cerqueira, C.: Intergenerational approaches to disinformation and clickbait: participatory workshops as co-learning-based spaces. In: Fowler-Watt, K., McDougall, J. (eds.) The Palgrave Handbook of Media Misinformation, pp. 343–356. Springer International Publishing, Cham (2023). https://doi.org/10.1007/978-3-031-11976-7_23
23. Vuorikari, R., Kluzer, S., Punie, Y.: DigComp 2.2: The digital competence framework for citizens - with new examples of knowledge, skills and attitudes. Publications Office of the European Union, Luxembourg (Luxembourg) (2022)

Enhancing Older Adults' Motivation for Social Interaction: Exploring Design Principles of Social Media Mobile Applications Through a Self-Determination Theory (SDT) Approach

Jie Meng[✉]

University of New South Wales, Kensington, NSW 2033, Australia
jie.meng1@unsw.edu.au

Abstract. This study, grounded in Self-Determination Theory (SDT) [7, 15, 16], aimed to examine the barriers and challenges faced by older adults when using social media mobile applications, focusing on autonomy, competence, and relatedness. Using a mixed-methods approach, the study incorporated observations (n = 33), surveys (n = 33), and semi-structured interviews (n = 4) to assess three popular social media applications in the Chinese market: WeChat, QQ, and Douyin. These applications were evaluated across five features: "Senior" or "Easy" mode, sending text messages, sending voice messages, initiating voice calls, and initiating video calls. By integrating Self-Determination Theory (SDT) principles with research findings, seven primary design principles have been proposed for social media mobile applications tailored to older adults, aiming to enhance their social engagement and motivation.

Keywords: older adults · social media mobile applications · Self-Determination Theory (SDT)

1 Introduction

The global population is experiencing rapid aging. According to data from the World Health Organization (WHO), it is estimated that by 2050, the global population aged 60 and above will reach 2.1 billion, double the number in 2022 [25]. The proportion of the global elderly population is expected to increase from less than 10% to around 17% between 2021 and 2050, as estimated by the United Nations [21, 22].

In China, individuals aged 60 and above are considered older adults, according to the "Law on the Protection of the Rights and Interests of the Elderly" [18]. As of 2021, data from the seventh national population census conducted by the National Bureau of Statistics of China revealed that the elderly population aged 60 and above in China reached 264.02 million, accounting for 18.70% of the total population, an increase of 5.44% compared to 2010 [11]. According to the 49th edition of the Statistical Report on Internet Development in China, as of December 2021, the total number of internet users in China reached 1.032 billion [6]. Among them, the number of internet users aged 60

Q. Gao and J. Zhou (Eds.): HCII 2024, LNCS 14725, pp. 383–397, 2024.
https://doi.org/10.1007/978-3-031-61543-6_27

and above reached 119 million, indicating the potential for social interaction among the elderly population through the internet [6].

Numerous studies have shown that active social interaction is highly significant for successful ageing and for older people's well-being and quality of life [3, 13]. With global aging on the rise, older individuals (who are 60 and over) are increasingly becoming potential internet users in China, especially in the realm of social media mobile applications [4, 24]. Social media mobile applications have become a significant avenue for many older individuals to socialize [4, 26]. The observed increase in internet use among older people can be attributed to the prevalence of COVID-19 over the past few years [1]. However, numerous social media mobile applications available in the market currently fail to stimulate older people's enthusiasm and motivation fully, presenting various design flaws and limitations in terms of user experience, with issues such as complex interaction logic and inappropriate visual design deterring many older individuals [4, 9, 10, 14, 19, 23, 26]. This results in a decreased willingness among many older adults to use social media mobile applications [21, 22, 27]. On April 13, 2021, the Ministry of Industry and Information Technology (MIIT) issued the Universal Design Specifications for Age-Friendly Mobile Applications, which requires major websites and apps to complete accessibility renovations for the corresponding interfaces according to the design specifications [5]. This marks the beginning of the process of age-friendly renovations on social media mobile applications. Therefore, it is crucial to gain an in-depth understanding of the interaction experience issues faced by older adults with social media mobile applications and what stops them using such applications.

Self-Determination Theory (SDT) examines the motivations behind people's choices and the degree of self-motivation and self-determination in individual behavior [7, 15], and it has been widely recognized, extensively researched and applied in different fields and populations such as business, education, welfare, and health. Additionally, it recently finds application in user experience design and digital media [2, 8, 12, 27]. According to the Self-Determination Theory (SDT), individuals are more likely to experience happiness and a sense of achievement if they fulfill three basic human needs: autonomy, competence, and relatedness. Autonomy in user experience design emphasizes providing users with control over their interactions and choices within a system [20, 29]. Competence involves designing interfaces that support users' ability to effectively navigate and accomplish tasks, fostering a sense of mastery [15–17]. Relatedness focuses on creating opportunities for users to connect with others, fostering a sense of community and belonging within the user interface [16, 24].

To improve the social environment for older adults, this study was based on Self-Determination Theory (SDT). The research aimed to optimize and enhance social media mobile applications for older adults, stimulate their initiative to use social mobile applications, and increase their social motivation and willingness. The primary research question of this study was: How can the user experience design of social media mobile applications be improved for older adults to enhance their motivation in using them? To answer this question, the study formulates the following two objectives:

- To investigate the issues that hinder older adults from effectively using social media mobile applications by examining five sections of social functions in three mainstream social media mobile applications used in the Chinese market.

- To identify design principles that can improve the user experience of social media mobile applications for older adults and enhance their motivation for usage.

2 Methods

2.1 Study Design

This study utilized a combination of observational methods, questionnaire surveys, and semi-structured interviews to conduct user research. Initially, participants were invited to complete a survey questionnaire regarding their experiences with social media usage. They were asked to describe their feelings and choices throughout the process. Simultaneously, the researchers acted as observers, documenting the participants' words and actions. With the participants' consent, video, audio, and screen recordings of the entire process were conducted and later transcribed into text records.

The questionnaire design was based on Self-Determination Theory (SDT) [7, 15–17], measuring the degree of autonomy, competence, and relatedness experienced by the participants in relation to social media mobile applications.

The questionnaire depicted the usage process of five social sections from three social media applications. The questions covered the experiences, perspectives, and emotions of participants when using the applications from Self-Determination Theory (SDT). Participants were instructed to watch instructional videos on how to use each of these apps, which included activating "Easy" or "Senior" mode, sending text messages, sending voice messages, initiating voice calls, and initiating video calls from three selected social applications (see 2.2 Research Materials and Fig. 1). For each of the three social media applications, participants were asked for their level of agreement with each of the following five statements (see Table 1) and perceptions (see Table 2):

Table 1. Five statements of five social sections from three social media applications.

Self-Determination Theory (SDT)	Statements
Autonomy	*"I am confident in using this function."*
	"I can use this function freely."
Competence	*"I can easily understand and master how to use this function."*
Relatedness	*"I think this function is relevant to me."*
Motivation	*"I will use this function frequently in the future."*

To further comprehend and supplement the questionnaire and research content, in-depth interviews were conducted with four individuals aged 60 and above. They were asked about the challenges encountered when using social media applications, as well as their expectations and needs regarding these platforms. By integrating the results of the questionnaire surveys and interviews, more comprehensive conclusions were drawn.

Table 2. Perceptions of three social media applications.

Self-Determination Theory (SDT)	Perceptions
Autonomy	Confident
	Autonomous
	Controlled
Competence	Competent
	Independent
Relatedness	Connected to others

2.2 Research Materials

This study selected five sections of social functions from three popular social apps for older users in the Chinese market: WeChat, QQ, and Douyin (see Fig. 1). Here's information on the three social mobile apps selected for the study:

WeChat is a globally popular instant messaging application that has gained popularity among older users in China, particularly in urban and developed areas. It offers various features such as text messaging, voice messaging, voice calls, video calls, Moments (a social feed), and payment services.

QQ, developed and operated by Tencent, is one of the most popular and influential instant messaging applications in China. It provides various communication methods, including text, voice, and video calls. Users can communicate with friends via QQ and join groups for group chats.

Douyin is a popular short video social mobile application where users can record, edit, and share short videos ranging from 15 s to 1 min. Users can explore creative content and interact with users worldwide. Additionally, users can follow their favorite creators, browse popular videos, participate in challenge activities, and engage in social interactions with other users.

The five sections of social functions that were investigated included activating "Senior" or "Easy" mode, sending text messages, sending voice messages, initiating voice calls, and initiating video calls. The selection of these functions has also considered the social needs and skill levels of older users to ensure that they meet the majority of their social needs.

2.3 Participants

In this study, we recruited 33 Chinese participants aged 60 and above through online recruitment advertisements and social media platforms.[1] Among them, there were 15 male participants and 18 female participants. 4 participants underwent semi-structured

---

[1] Ethics: in terms of ethics and privacy, all participants confirmed their participation information and signed an ethical declaration before participating. All video recordings, audio recordings, filming, and screen recordings were conducted with consent.

1. WeChat [1]: From left to right, it displays the "Easy" mode page, the "Me" page, and the "Chat" page with the selected contact.

2. QQ [2]: From left to right, it displays the "Easy" mode page, the "Contacts" page, and the "Chat" page with the selected contact.

3. Douyin [3]: From left to right, it displays the "Senior" mode page, the "Contacts" page, and the "Chat" page with the selected contact.

Fig. 1. Screenshots showing the test interfaces of three selected social media mobile applications. Participants were instructed to watch instructional videos on how to use these apps, which included activating "Easy" or "Senior" mode, sending text messages, sending voice messages, initiating voice calls, and initiating video calls. Participants were then required to answer questions and provide explanations for their answers.

interviews lasting approximately 40 min. To understand the social motivations of the participants, the study also investigated their living arrangements.

The survey results showed that out of older adult's participants in the study, 26 lived with their partners and 8 lived with their children. Regarding the usage of applications, 93.94% (n = 31) of the survey sample had used WeChat, while only 6.06% (n = 2) had not. Additionally, 66.67% (n = 22) had used QQ applications, while 33.33% (n = 11) had not. Moreover, 66.67% (n = 22) had used Douyin applications, while 33.33% (n = 11) had not.

3   Results

Regarding the presentation of the research results, the following representations were used: "a" represents "I am confident in using this function," "b" represents "I can easily understand and master how to use this function," "c" represents "I can use this function freely," "d" represents "I think this function is relevant to me," and "e" represents "I will use this function frequently in the future."

3.1   Basic Psychological Needs of Older Adults in Social Media Mobile Applications

Autonomy. In the realm of digital experiences, autonomy denotes the technology and design's capacity to accommodate and respect users' independent behaviors, encompassing factors like controllability, clear guidance, user empowerment, and expandability.

In this study, the WeChat app scored highest in both confidence in utilizing the "Easy" mode (a) and the freedom to employ this feature (c). Specifically, this encompasses activating the "Easy" mode (a, 4.36; c, 4.21), sending text and voice messages (a, 4.24; c, 4.21), and initiating voice and video calls (a, 4.48; c, 4.36). Particularly, regarding WeChat's voice and video call functions, respondents noted, "*I find WeChat's video and voice call features offer considerable freedom. Once I locate the chat partner's page, I can initiate video or voice calls. Alternatively, there are buttons to initiate video calls when I click to view their detailed information.*" WeChat's "Easy" mode resonates well with participants' usage habits, as one participant commented, "*The font size of WeChat's 'Easy' mode is large, and it also allows me to listen to text messages, which enhances my user experience.*"

Conversely, the functionality of sending text and voice messages in the Douyin app received the lowest scores for descriptions a and c, both scoring 3.85. The absence of a chat list impedes participants from directly locating contacts, undermining their confidence in its usage: "*Douyin lacks a friends' contact list, and I frequently struggle to find the person I wish to contact.*" On the chat page, the excessive auxiliary features in Douyin disrupt participants' usage: "*The chat page has an excessive number of additional buttons, such as 'say hello' and 'Tickle Tickle.' I am uncertain about their purpose, and I am hesitant to click on the wrong one.*" Moreover, the "Send Message" button offers the options of "send" and "view once," which may cater well to the diverse preferences of young users but leave participants feeling perplexed: "*I am uncertain about the meaning of this button. Suddenly, a dialog box appears, prompting me to attempt a long press.*"

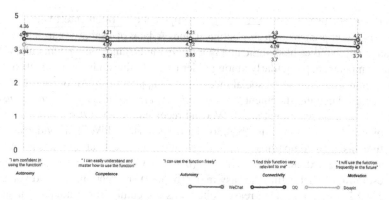

1. The average matrix scale scores of participants' descriptions and ratings for the "Easy Mode" feature of WeChat, QQ, and Douyin.

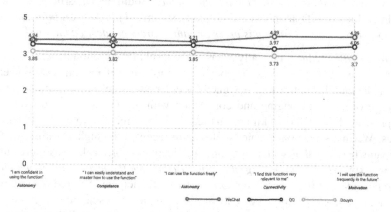

2. The average matrix scale scores of participants' descriptions and ratings for the text and voice messaging features of WeChat, QQ, and Douyin.

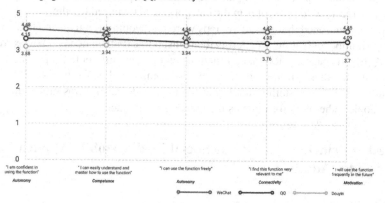

3. The average matrix scale scores of participants' descriptions and ratings for the voice and video calling features of WeChat, QQ, and Douyin.

Fig. 2. Sub-Figs. 1, 2, 3 display a matrix scale showing the average scores of participants' descriptions and ratings for activating the "Easy" or "Senior" mode, sending text messages, sending voice messages, initiating voice calls, and initiating video calls in WeChat, QQ, and Douyin.

Competence. In user experience design, competence is often intertwined with the usability and comprehensibility of actual usage. A lack of usability can lead users to feel inadequate. Studies have indicated that easily understandable content enhances the sense of competence, particularly among older users. In the study, participants assessed their proficiency in using three social media mobile applications. Among them, descriptor "b" encapsulated the statement *"I can easily understand and master how to use this feature."* Across all functional areas, WeChat received the highest ratings, particularly for its voice and video call feature (b, 4.36). Participants found WeChat's video and voice call feature easier to comprehend and utilize compared to activating the easy mode (b, 4.21) and sending text and voice messages (b, 4.27). Conversely, participants assigned the lowest ratings to activating the easy mode (b, 3.82) and sending text and voice messages (b, 3.82) in Douyin. One reason cited was the cumbersome interaction steps in Douyin, which made participants feel uneasy. For instance, *"Activating the easy mode requires restarting the app, which I find troublesome."* Additionally, participants encountered difficulties with Douyin's visual UI icons, stating, *"I find the edit information bar at the bottom too small. I often mis press or cannot press the desired button."*

Relatedness. Relatedness typically refers to the level of connection between users and products or services, as well as the social affiliation and interaction among users. In social media mobile applications designed for older adults, relatedness often manifests as a sense of social belonging and connection with others. In this study, descriptor "d" represents the statement "I think this feature is very relevant to me." Among these features, WeChat's video and voice call feature received the highest rating (d, 4.49). Participants believed that socializing through video and voice calls was more suitable for them, expressing, *"I'm getting older, and I can't see the text on my phone clearly, so I prefer video calls. I don't have to read text."* Participants favored conversational interactions such as calls or video chats over sending text or using other methods.

Conversely, QQ and Douyin received the lowest scores among all the features when it came to the descriptor "d" compared to other descriptors. As shown in Fig. 3, QQ and Douyin received lower scores in the category of "Connected to others" (7.33; 6.91). Participants mentioned that these two apps were too "youth-oriented" and had an overwhelming number of features, rendering them unsuitable for their needs. They expressed, "The QQ friends page has too many functions, with many different groups, and I'm not clear about what these groups mean." They also commented on Douyin's colorful page with numerous buttons, stating that it gave them a headache and was more suitable for young people rather than for them as they were getting older.

4   Design Principles of Mobile Social Media Mobile Applications for Older Adults

4.1   Autonomy

Extensibility. When designing social media mobile applications for older mobile phones, it's essential to consider the principle of extensibility. Extensibility refers to the flexibility and adaptability of the design, allowing users to customize and adjust the application according to their needs and preferences. Special attention should be given

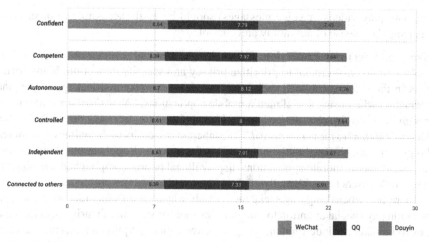

Fig. 3. The figure shows the average scores for the comprehensive ratings of WeChat, QQ, and Douyin by the participants. The ratings were measured using a matrix scale with a maximum score of 10.

to extensibility in the design of social media mobile applications for older adults to accommodate their diverse needs and abilities.

First, the information architecture of the social mobile application should be user-friendly, enabling older users to easily find desired functions and information. A concise and clear interface layout, along with clear navigation paths, can help older users quickly understand the structure and functions of the application, reducing confusion during use. Additionally, the application should provide options for personalized settings, allowing users to adjust the interface layout and function display according to their preferences, thereby improving usability and satisfaction.

Second, the functional design of the social mobile application should be flexible and adaptable to the different communication needs and skill levels of older users. For example, the application can offer multiple communication methods, such as text, voice, and video calls, allowing users to choose the most suitable method based on their preferences. Consideration should also be given to the physical and cognitive limitations that older users may have, by designing simple and easy-to-understand functions that enhance communication efficiency and user experience.

Ownership. The design of social media mobile applications should provide older users with sufficient ownership and control, allowing them to use the application freely according to their preferences. This means considering the need for personalized settings, such as enabling or disabling specific functions or modes. For instance, older users may prefer a simplified mode, commonly known as "Senior" or "Easy" mode, to reduce complexity and difficulty in use. However, according to this study, many older users are not aware that the application they are using have a " Senior "or "Easy" version, partly because these features are buried deep in the hierarchical structure and are not easily discoverable. Therefore, in the design, options for personalized settings (e.g., font size, color themes, notification frequency) and the choice to enable or disable specific functions (e.g., auto-play videos or voice messages) should be easily accessible to older users, enhancing their sense of autonomy and control.

Privacy and Security Protection. When designing social media mobile applications for older adults, it is crucial to prioritize privacy and security protection. Many participants in the study mentioned their concerns about the potential leakage of personal information when using social media mobile applications. *"Now there are many scammers and various fraud schemes, how do I know if they are deceiving me while chatting with me? This makes me very worried."* The inherent insecurity of the online environment adds pressure and diminishes their enthusiasm for using such applications. Furthermore, some social media mobile applications display illegal or non-compliant advertisements, leading older users to accidentally click on them and encounter problems.

Therefore, when designing social media mobile applications for older adults, designers should pay special attention to safeguarding their privacy and security. Specific measures to be taken include implementing effective data encryption and security authentication, providing user privacy settings options, allowing users to control the scope and permissions of personal information sharing, and promptly addressing user security issues and feedback. By implementing these measures, trust in social media mobile applications among older adults can be enhanced, thereby increasing their sense of security and comfort, and promoting their active participation in social interactions.

4.2 Competence

Usability, Understandability, and Availability. The design of social media mobile applications interfaces for older adults should prioritize simplicity, clear operation flow, and reduced learning cost. Use intuitive icons and large buttons, minimize text instructions and textual sections to help older adults quickly understand and use the interface. For instance, design intuitive icons for voice messaging and video calls, place them in easily accessible locations, minimize the number of steps, and enhance user convenience.

Ensure that functions and operations are simple and easy to understand, allowing older adults to fully grasp and enjoy the various features. Provide clear guidance and prompts in the design to help users quickly understand the application's functionality. Avoid using specialized terms and complex technical vocabulary.

Emphasize user experience to ensure that older adults can easily navigate through different functions and find the desired information. The application should be responsive and stable, avoiding lagging and crashing. Provide diverse input methods such as voice input and handwriting input to accommodate the different needs and habits of older adults.

Encouraging Feedback. The design should encourage active participation and exploration of the application's features. Implement feedback mechanisms such as reward systems and achievement badges to stimulate the interest and engagement of older adults. For example, when an older adult successfully sends a voice message or completes a video call for the first time, provide timely positive feedback such as short praise statements or cute animation effects to enhance user satisfaction and enjoyment.

Interaction feedback should be friendly, natural, and easy to understand. Consider the psychological and emotional needs of older adults, avoiding the use of overly formal or serious language and icons. For voice messages, provide clear recording prompts such as waveform graphs or voice volume indicators to inform users about their recording status and quality. In video calls, provide clear connection prompts and call status displays to ensure that older adults can easily make calls and understand the call status.

4.3 Relatedness

Social Connectivity. The design of social media mobile applications should encourage and facilitate connections and interactions among older adults to enhance their social connectedness. For example, design simple and user-friendly group chats, community forums, and sharing functions, allowing older adults to engage in real-time communication and sharing with friends, family, or other users. Support multi-person calls and group chats in voice messaging and video call functions, enabling older adults to communicate more easily with multiple people. This design helps older adults feel like they are an important part of the social community, enhancing their sense of social belonging and self-esteem.

Emotional Connection. When designing social media mobile applications, it is important to consider the emotional needs of older adults to establish closer emotional connections. Social media mobile applications should not only serve as a tool for communication and sharing information, but also as a platform for older adults to express emotions and share joys and sorrows. Focus on channels and methods of emotional expression in voice messaging and video call functions. Design emoticons, stickers, sound effects, and other elements that facilitate emotional expression and are easier for older adults to use. This way, older adults can convey their emotions and feelings more intuitively.

5 Discussion

The study found that many social media mobile applications in the Chinese market have specifically targeted older adults and made some modifications to cater to their needs. However, most of these "Senior" or "Easy" modes of social media applications only make superficial changes to the font and colors, without significant improvements in functionality and user experience. As a result, older users have become less motivated to use these social media applications, and they face numerous challenges and difficulties when using them.

The design of these "Senior" or "Easy" versions does not fully consider the usage habits and needs of the older adult population. Older adults generally have lower technological acceptance when it comes to smartphones and applications. Designers should prioritize simplicity, usability, and user-friendly experiences when creating social media applications for older adults. However, current social applications lack clear guidance and prompts, making it difficult for older adults to quickly understand the various functions. Moreover, complex interface layouts and cumbersome operation processes cause confusion and inconvenience for older users.

Furthermore, a significant number of social media mobile applications do not offer comprehensive and detailed tutorials specifically designed for older users. The official websites and other channels of the three selected samples in this study do not provide relevant tutorials for older adults to learn from. This lack of guidance and support often leads older users to feel confused and uncertain when using these applications. In a technologically advanced country like China, it is important for older adults to be able to enjoy the convenience and enjoyment brought by technology. Therefore, providing detailed tutorials is crucial to help older adults effectively utilize these applications.

To address these issues, future research should focus on designing social media mobile applications that comprehensively consider the usage habits and needs of older adults. The interface design and interaction should be simpler and more intuitive, allowing older adults to adapt and use the applications more easily. Additionally, comprehensive and detailed tutorials should be provided to help older adults learn how to use these applications and overcome any problems or difficulties they encounter.

In conclusion, older adults are an important user group for social media applications and should receive adequate attention. By understanding the needs of older adults and designing and improving applications accordingly, we can enhance the motivation and experience of older users in using social media applications, allowing them to fully enjoy the convenience and fun brought by technology.

5.1 Limitations and Future Plan

The study has several limitations, including the following aspects:

First, there is a limitation in sample size. The study only involves a small sample of older users (n = 33). Due to this limited sample size, the generalizability and representativeness of the research results may be affected. It becomes difficult to provide a comprehensive and accurate description of the overall characteristics of the older population.

Second, the study focuses mainly on specific functions of social media mobile applications, such as voice text messages and video calls. However, social media mobile applications typically offer a wider range of functions and features, including moments, group chats, and news updates. The exclusion of these functions limits the scope of the study.

Third, the study utilizes methods such as observation, questionnaire surveys, and semi-structured interviews for data collection and analysis. However, these methods may not fully capture the true feelings and experiences of older adults when using social media mobile applications. Observational methods may not fully capture participants' feelings and thoughts, and questionnaire surveys and interviews may be influenced by recall bias and subjective evaluations.

Lastly, the study primarily focuses on older users in the Chinese market. The user experience of social media mobile applications is influenced by various external factors, such as network environment, cultural background, and social habits. Therefore, the research results may not be universally applicable and should be cautiously generalized to other regions and populations.

In summary, while this study has yielded certain discoveries and results, there are limitations in terms of sample size, limited research functions, and research methods. Future studies aim to address these limitations by expanding the sample size, broadening the scope of research functions, and improving research methods (such as expert interviews and experimental comparisons) to obtain more comprehensive and accurate research conclusions.

6 Conclusion

This study explored the challenges encountered by older adults when using social media mobile applications, with a particular focus on the Chinese market, examining them through the lenses of autonomy, competence, and relatedness from Self-Determination Theory (SDT). Utilizing various methods, including observation, surveys, and semi-structured interviews, the research evaluated three prominent social media applications in China: WeChat, QQ, and Douyin. Having assessed these mobile applications across five key features – "Senior" or "Easy" mode, text messaging, voice messaging, voice calling, and video calling - the study identified deficiencies in current social media mobile applications. By amalgamating principles derived from the Self-Determination Theory (SDT) with research findings, the study proposed seven primary design principles tailored for older adults in social media mobile applications, aimed at enhancing their social engagement and motivation. Implementing these design principles is expected to alleviate the challenges encountered by older adults when using social media apps, offering them an improved user experience, and fostering active participation in social interactions. Although the study's focus and market context were centered on China, its insights may hold significant value for the development and application of similar solutions in other countries.

References

1. Abbaspur-Behbahani, S., Monaghesh, E., Hajizadeh, A., Fehresti, S.: Application of mobile health to support the elderly during the COVID-19 outbreak: a systematic review. Health Policy Technol. 11(1), 100595 (2022). https://doi.org/10.1016/j.hlpt.2022.100595
2. Ballou, N., et al.: Self-determination theory in HCI: shaping a research agenda. In: CHI Conference on Human Factors in Computing Systems Extended Abstracts, pp. 1–6 (2022) https://doi.org/10.1145/3491101.3503702
3. Chang, P.-J., Wray, L., Lin, Y.: Social relationships, leisure activity, and health in older adults. Health Psychol. 33(6), 516–523 (2012). https://doi.org/10.1037/hea0000051
4. Coto, M., Lizano, F., Mora, S., Fuentes, J.: Social media and elderly people: research trends. In G. Meiselwitz (ed.) Social Computing and Social Media. Applications and Analytics, pp. 65–81. Springer International Publishing (2017) https://doi.org/10.1007/978-3-319-585 62-8_6
5. China Ministry of Industry and Information Technology (MIIT).: Special Action Program for Ageing and Accessibility Adaptation of Internet Applications (2020). https://www.gov. cn/zhengce/zhengceku/2020-12/26/content_5573472.htm
6. China Internet Network Information Center.: The 49th Statistical Report on China' Internet Develo ment. http://www.cnnic.net.cn/hlwfzyj/hlwxzbg/hlwtjbg/202202/t20220225_71727. htm, (Accessed 2 Feb 2024)
7. Deci, E.L., Ryan, R.M.: Self-determination theory: a macrotheory of human motivation, development, and health. Canadian Psychology / Psychologie Canadienne 49(3), 182–185 (2008). https://doi.org/10.1037/a0012801

8. Fu, H.N.C., Wyman, J.F., Peden-McAlpine, C.J., Draucker, C.B., Schleyer, T., Adam, T.J.: App design features important for diabetes self-management as determined by the self-determination theory on motivation: content analysis of survey responses from adults requiring insulin therapy. JMIR Diabetes **8**, e38592 (2023). https://doi.org/10.2196/38592

9. Gao, C., Zhou, L., Liu, Z., Wang, H., Bowers, B.: Mobile application for diabetes self-management in China: do they fit for older adults? Int. J. Med. Inform. **101**, 68–74 (2017). https://doi.org/10.1016/j.ijmedinf.2017.02.005

10. Leist, A.K.: Social media use of older adults: a mini-review. Gerontology **59**(4), 378–384 (2013). https://doi.org/10.1159/000346818

11. Liu, H.: Development trends of aging populations in the world and China. Res. Aging Sci. **12**, 1–16 (2021)

12. Lushnikova, A., Morse, C., Doublet, S., Koenig, V., Bongard-Blanchy, K.: Self-determination theory applied to museum website experiences: fulfill visitor needs, increase motivation, and promote engagement. In: Proceedings of the European Conference on Cognitive Ergonomics 2023, pp. 1–7 (2023). https://doi.org/10.1145/3605655.3605658

13. Macdonald, B., Luo, M., Hülür, G.: Daily social interactions and well-being in older adults: the role of interaction modality. J. Soc. Pers. Relat. **38**(12), 3566–3589 (2021). https://doi.org/10.1177/02654075211052536

14. Navabi, N., Ghaffari, F., Jannat-Alipoor, Z.: Older adults' attitudes and barriers toward the use of mobile phones. Clin. Interv. Aging **11**, 1371–1378 (2016). https://doi.org/10.2147/CIA.S112893

15. Ryan, R.M., Deci, E.L.: Intrinsic and extrinsic motivations: classic definitions and new directions. Contemp. Educ. Psychol. **25**(1), 54–67 (2000). https://doi.org/10.1006/ceps.1999.1020

16. Ryan, R.M., Deci, E.L.: Self-determination theory: Basic psychological needs in motivation, development, and wellness. Guilford Press (2017). https://doi.org/10.1521/978.14625/28806

17. Ryan, R.M., Curren, R.R., Deci, E.L.: What humans need: Flourishing in Aristotelian philosophy and self-determination theory, pp. 57–75. American Psychological Association (2017) https://doi.org/10.1037/14092-004

18. People's Republic of China, State Council.: Law of the People's Republic of China on the Protection of the Rights and Interests of the Elderly, Rule Number 2 (2018). https://flk.npc.gov.cn/detail2.html?ZmY4MDgwODE2ZjEzNWY0NjAxNmYyMGY0YmY4NTE3NDY%3D

19. Peral-Peral, B., Villarejo-Ramos, A.F., Arenas-Gaitán, J.: Selfefficacy and anxiety as determinants of older adults' use of Internet Banking Services. Universal Access Inform. Soc. **19**(4), 825–840 (2020) https://doi.org/10.1007/s10209-019-00691-w

20. Peters, D., Calvo, R.A., Ryan, R.M.: Designing for motivation, engagement and wellbeing in digital experience. Front. Psychol. **9**, 797 (2018). https://doi.org/10.3389/fpsyg.2018.00797

21. United Nations Homepage, Fulfilling the Promises of the Universal Declaration of Human Rights for Older Persons: Across Generations. https://www.un.org/en/observances/older-persons-day, (Accessed 2 Feb 2024)

22. United Nations, Department of Economic and Social Affairs, Population Division: World population prospects 2019 (2019)

23. Wilson, G., Gates, J.R., Vijaykumar, S., Morgan, D.J.: Understanding older adults' use of social technology and the factors influencing use. Ageing Soc. **43**(1), 222–245 (2023). https://doi.org/10.1017/S0144686X21000490

24. Waycott, J., Vetere, F., Ozanne, E.: Building social connections: a framework for enriching older adults' social connectedness through information and communication technologies. Ageing Digital Technol., 65–82 (2019) https://doi.org/10.1007/978-98113-3693-5_5

25. World Health Organization Homepage, Ageing and health. https://www.who.int/news-room/fact-sheets/detail/ageing-and-health, (Accessed 2 Feb 2024)

26. Xie, B., Watkins, I., Golbeck, J., Huang, M.: Understanding and changing older adults' perceptions and learning of social media. Educ. Gerontol. **38**(4), 282–296 (2012). https://doi.org/10.1080/03601277.2010.544580

27. Zhang, L., Zhang, L., Jin, C., Tang, Z., Wu, J., Zhang, L.: Elderly-oriented improvement of mobile applications based on self-determination theory. Inter. J. Hum.–Comput. Interact., 1–16 (2022) https://doi.org/10.1080/10447318.2022.2131264

28. Zhao, S., Kinshuk, Yao, Y., Ya, N.: Adoption of mobile social media for learning among Chinese older adults in senior citizen colleges. Educ. Technol. Res. Developm. **69**(6), 3413–3435 (2021) https://doi.org/10.1007/s11423-021-10048-x

29. Zhao, L., Lu, Y., Wang, B., Huang, W.: What makes them happy and curious online? An empirical study on high school students' Internet use from a self-determination theory perspective. Comp. Educ. **56**, 346–356 (2011). https://doi.org/10.1016/j.compedu.2010.08.006

30. Zuo, S., Wang, Y.: Research on the design of functional requirements for elderly online social platforms—based on 2018 CHARLS data. Operat. Res. Fuzziology **13**, 593 (2023)

Decoding News Avoidance: An Immersive Dialogical Method for Inter-generational Studies

Manuel Pita(✉)

Universidade Lusófona, CICANT, Campo Grande 388, Lisbon 1700-097, Portugal
manuel.pita@ulusofona.pt

Abstract. Understanding the patterns and mechanisms behind news consumption and avoidance is crucial for fostering democratic participation and informed societies. This methodological paper introduces an approach designed to study news avoidance, addressing the limitations and biases associated with traditional self-report surveys and digital-trace data collection. We propose an intelligent, dialogical news delivery application that simulates a real-world news consumption environment. This application segments content to provide nuanced interaction data while controlling for self-report response biases. Thus, the proposed method allows for the integration of behavioural and self-report data, leveraging the strengths of these divergent data types to offer a more comprehensive understanding of news engagement dynamics. By enabling controlled yet naturalistic interactions with news content, our approach seeks to unveil the multifaceted reasons behind news avoidance across different demographics, with a particular focus on understanding inter-generational dynamics. This paper underscores the importance of developing robust methodological tools in media studies to derive scientifically valid and replicable inferences that explain news consumption behaviours.

Keywords: news avoidance · research methods · self-report data · digital-trace data

1 Introduction

The digital revolution has precipitated an unprecedented shift in the ways people consume, disseminate, and interact with news. Concurrently, news avoidance has emerged as a phenomenon of growing concern, with significant implications for democratic engagement and public discourse. In this paper we analyse the current methodologies employed by media researchers to study news consumption behaviours, particularly emphasizing the types of data collected and the validity of conclusions drawn from such data. Following this critique, we introduce a method that integrates artificial intelligence (AI) and human-computer interaction (HCI) principles to address the identified shortcomings in data collection

CICANT—https://doi.org/10.54499/UIDB/05260/2020.

and analysis processes relevant to news consumption studies. This approach aims to enhance the accuracy and depth of our understanding in this area, opening new pathways for more effective and nuanced media research.

In the remaining of this section, §1.1 highlights issues with the current definition of news avoidance that influence its research scope; §1.2 surveys the basics algorithmic media exposure through recommendation systems; and §1.3 analyses the limitations of, and errors induced by, the types of data typically collected to study news avoidance. The paper subsequently proposes a methodological approach to decipher the intricate relationships between user behaviour, algorithmic mediation, and news consumption in §2; explores possible applications in §3, and closes with a discussion in §4, highlighting the advantages and potential caveats of the proposed method.

1.1 News Avoidance

In their 2020 paper, Skovsgaard and Andersen [54], noted the lack of a shared definition of news avoidance in the growing literature on the subject. The paper argues that the essence of news avoidance lies in the individual choice to consume or avoid. However, it also acknowledges the ontological commitments resulting from this binary perspective—warning that "there is a fine line between intentional news avoidance because of news overload, where the individual actively averts the news, and unintentional news avoidance based on a plethora of content on display that leads an individual to opt for entertainment rather than news. In this situation, we need to know the exact constellation of preferences to determine whether the news avoidance is intentional or unintentional" [54, p.470]. This warning brings our attention to a second critical element for defining news avoidance: the multi-factorial complexity of media ecosystems in connection with the wide spectrum of reasons people intentionally, or unintentionally, avoid news.

Such complexity-driving factors in news avoidance phenomena include high-choice environments [14,32], selective exposure [4,6,33], algorithmic mediation [6,31,36], selection cues e.g. news source and social endorsement [41,62] and the fact that there are two levels to news consumption: (a) the interplay between human attention and the different forms of navigation in media ecosystems and (b) what happens when a news article is 'clicked' [45]. News avoidance has been linked to negative collective social behaviours including radicalization and extremism, dissemination of fake news and conspiracy theories, increasing inability to consider diverse perspectives and points of view—all of which affect civic participation in democratic systems [55,59]. Out of these factors, the least understood is *algorithmic mediation*, particularly the mechanisms through which they drive collective social phenomena.

1.2 Algorithms Everywhere

The notion of an algorithm has come a long way since its origin in Al-Khwarizmi's arithmetic operation methods [23,57], Ada Lovelace's visions of machines could one day create art and music [21] and the seminal publication of the Turing

Machine in 1936. Today, algorithms are everywhere. We use them to perform all sorts of different tasks. Indeed, algorithms have become so common that most of us no longer question how they work. Algorithms have also become information filters and social actors in the media ecosystem. Thus, it is now useful to have separate definitions of algorithm [63]. A contemporary 'technical' definition includes the revolution of data-driven Machine Learning (ML) [36]. A second, more 'social' definition [23,42] acknowledges algorithm's institutional nature as a regulator of cognition and behaviour in the complex interplay between media and their audiences in media ecosystems [59].

Indeed, socio-technological ecosystems are constantly reshaped by a flux of interactions on a massive scale. Thus, researchers must consider the effects of hyper-connectivity carefully for situating and understanding recent and future forms of emergent social phenomena that affect how people approach news. Some examples include the emergence of resilient community identities online [11,48], cyber-conflict [16], and the radical transformation of the news media environment, including the recent generative AI revolution [8,61].

Hyper-connectivity has a key role in the context of the present work because (a) it enables almost anyone to access almost any news content available to the entire world; (b) consequently, it blurs previously existing distinctions between global and local spheres—impinging on whether, and how, people transform the information they choose to consume into (adaptive) behaviours; (c) it creates the substrate for the production of massive datasets algorithms can exploit to optimize for corporate and platform goals that are often not transparent to their customers and users. Indeed, the coupling of large datasets on human interaction and opaque algorithmic mediation can create social actors with unprecedented power to shape collective human behaviour in unpredictable ways [see e.g. 6,31].

The complex interactions between hyper-connectivity, availability of massive human-interaction datasets and algorithms raise important questions about what explicit and subtle influences to human behaviour exist in the media ecosystem. For example, what are the consequences of people with low algorithmic literacy accepting and trusting algorithmic mediation [12]? Similarly, how does our limited algorithmic literacy constrain how we interpret news and other content [53]? And, if algorithms 'impose' different ontological constraints on different audiences, how might this affect the flow of information between generations? We know, for example, that older people tend to consume—often unintentionally—significantly more fake news than their children and grandchildren [38]. Does this mean that older people become a channel for younger generations to be exposed to misinformation? Or conversely, do such socio-demographic differences lie at the core of how algorithms fragment society [9]?

In what concerns news avoidance, Thurman et al. [59] note that it is indeed common for people to 'offload' the decision of what to consume to algorithms [59]. But algorithm over-reliance is not limited to news consumption—it also influences how journalists write and disseminate news content [13]. Since such algorithmic reliance can have significant social impacts on civic participation and democracy, Lewis and Westlund [37] agree that researchers must study these phenomena in a new kind of socio-technological (complex) system. Several scholars have emphasized some areas requiring deeper understanding and even regulation, including transparency and accountability [17–19] and the ethical uses of algorithms and AI [3, 20, 27, 46]

Recommendation Systems (RS). While there are many algorithms to filter search results, recommend items, and sort people's newsfeeds in social networking and other media platforms, the focus of this section is on one of the most widely used and foundational approaches: recommendation systems based on collaborative filtering [25, 28]. This approach starts by considering an input matrix, $R = r[u, i]$, where rows correspond to users and columns to items. A matrix element, $R_{u,i}$, contains the rating given by user, u, to item, i. Such a matrix contains *implicit* (binary) rating information if there is no more information beyond knowing a user consumed an item. In other words, we do not have an explicit rating provided by the user. Conversely, the matrix is *explicit* if users provide ratings on some scale (e.g. 1 to 10). In simplified terms, the recommendation problem then becomes estimating the missing ratings in R, which is challenging in real-world scenarios because rating matrices are typically sparse (most elements are zero). Nearest-neighbour approaches or trained Machine Learning models can compute such estimates based on similarity measures like majority votes, correlations, or the angle between pairs of user rating vectors [2].

Consider the dummy example of the collaborative filtering approach depicted in Fig. 1. The matrix, R, represented in panel (A), contains implicit data describing what a set of six users have rated in the past. Given some (new) target user, u, the first step to make a recommendation is to find the users most similar to, u, in, R. In the example, similarity is computed in terms of the items users have rated in common. That is, the user in, R, that shares most rated items with the target user, u, has the highest similarity score. Then, the algorithm ranks the set of items *not* rated by u, but rated by the k nearest neighbours, based on a 'majority vote' (k is a parameter of the model).

There are two key limitations to this approach to recommendation. First, consider that real user-item matrices are usually very large—think for example, about the number of items available for sale on Amazon. Since most users consume a minute fraction of the available items (and explicitly rate even fewer) these matrices are extremely sparse. This makes the computation of accurate similarity measures between users very challenging. While there are methods to overcome sparsity problem, such as using dimensionality reduction [2, 39, 64], each solution often comes with its own trade-offs, e.g. computational complexity or the inability to interpret low-dimensional models. Second, the so-called 'cold-start' problem affects how new items, initially represented as empty columns in R, get to be recommended. An alternative approach to collaborative filtering, called content-based filtering, is useful for overcoming this problem because it leverages item descriptive information, and not only who has rated the item [64]. A standard approach to make recommendations based on content is to use topic modelling algorithms that transform textual item descriptions into category labels [see 1, for a recent review]. This means that the 'cold' new item becomes recommendable based on other items in the same semantic categories.

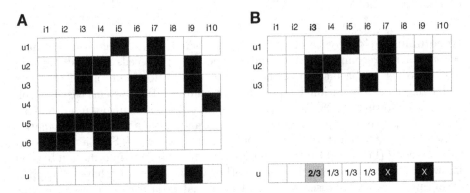

Fig. 1. Illustrative example of the collaborative filtering method for recommendation based on the nearest-neighbourhood approach. (A) toy example of an implicit user-item rating matrix, R, along with a separate target user, u. White (black) matrix elements are zero (one) implicit ratings. The first step in the method is to compute similarity between, u, and the users represented in the rows of, R. Let us assume, for simplicity, a similarity measure based on the number of commonly rated items. Notice that, u, has at least one item rated in common with users $[u1, u2, u3]$, and that the most similar user is $u2$. (B) Considering these three users as the nearest neighbours, disregard items $i7$ and $i9$ (marked with an 'X') because we know that, u, has rated these. Compute the proportion of users that have rated the remaining items (i.e. those, u, has not yet rated). The computation reveals that most of the considered neighbours (two out of three) have rated item $i3$, and one of the three neighbours has rated items $[i4, i5, i6]$. The standard collaborative filtering method would thus recommend $i3$ to u.

Understanding the principles of recommendation systems is useful to investigate the possible mechanisms through which algorithmic mediation influences human behaviour in the media ecosystem. For instance, should a recommendation policy be predicated solely upon the closest neighbours, it is reasonable to infer that the diversity of content made available to users will diminish progressively, thereby conditioning the user to eschew content that deviates from the constricted viewpoint created by the algorithm. A simple approach to mitigate this problem is to tune the recommendation algorithm to optimize for an objective function that balances both relevance and *diversity* when recommending items [see, e.g. 24, for a study in the domain of music recommendation]. A recommendation system that prioritizes relevance alone is markedly distinct from one that integrates a degree of diversity, particularly in terms of their effects as 'institutions' within the media ecosystem. However, the lack of transparency in how algorithms work within the media ecosystem makes it very difficult for regular users to notice these differences when it comes to recommended content.

1.3   Measuring News Consumption

Self-report data—collected mostly through individual surveys—has been the most widely used approach to study audience behaviour in media exposure [see e.g. 14]. Recent work concluded based on extensive empirical evidence that self-report data do not provide accurate information that correlates with logged media interactions, where correlations are even weaker in problematic news consumption scenarios [47]

Indeed, the production of valid self-report observation units requires that subjects can recall past behaviours accurately, and that the researcher can triangulate the collected data with error-correcting units or theoretical models. Psychological constructs created from self-report data rarely undergo the rigorous measurement validity tests that ensure replicability and confidence that inferences derived from the collected data are accurate [22,29]. It is well-established that recall is unreliable or highly inconsistent across different subjects [7,49,51,52]. In addition, several cognitive biases affect self report, including the acquiescence [35] and social desirability biases [43]. Of particular relevance for this methodological paper, Vraga and Tully [60] found that news consumption audience profiles built from self report and logged behavioural data are likely to be very different. The main differentiating factor found in this study was that people tend to over-report news consumption in surveys—particularly young people.

Self-report data has thus been widely criticized in the last few years, with several researchers favouring the use of digital-trace data for studying news consumption phenomena [34]. The term 'digital trace', however, refers to a range of quite different human online behaviours. Some digital-trace data include time-stamped access counts to a site—such as the BBC news or Reddit; the time visitors spent on the accessed page; the act of reposting of some content publicly on a social networking platform, like e.g. X (formerly Twitter), or the keywords used in Google search.

Taneja, Wu, and Edgerly [56] compared the use of digital-trace data obtained commercially with survey data and concluded that, although it leads to more robust empirical results, commercial digital-trace data has its own limitations. Perhaps the most important limitation is that commercial data is aggregated, rather than granular at the individual level. The data collection process is aimed at optimizing the data owner goals, typically for marketing.

Data collected from social networking platforms, such as X (formerly Twitter) or TikTok would allow researchers to get granular data on individual behaviours, but with uncertainties about how the data was collected [44]. Critically, most major platforms have closed their public APIs and only authorize the use of data samples produced by undisclosed sampling processes, and to those who can afford to buy the data. Platform rules typically forbid the public sharing of the collected datasets, making replicability often impossible. Another option to get behaviour data is installing trackers in subjects' computers and/or mobile devices. While such computer programs could provide extremely valuable data, most people are unwilling to install them, mostly because of privacy concerns [see e.g. 50, for data on Spanish users]. Recent research in using such self-report data has led to important insights into the range of errors they produce, and, importantly, on how to mitigate them [e.g. 15, 26]. On the other hand, researchers are only beginning to understand errors associated with the use of digital-trace data to study phenomena like news avoidance—a challenge compounded by the diversity of observation units, data collection methods, data ownership, biased sampling, aggregation and so on.

The issues identified with self-report and digital trace data suggest that research aimed at understanding media ecosystem dynamics might struggle to produce accurate, replicable results. This paper argues that combining self-report with digital behavioural data to create valid observational units is not only possible but beneficial. This approach can lead to stronger models for explaining and predicting behaviours like news avoidance, and enable more reliable statistical analyses across different social-demographic groups. The following section will explore the key requirements for successful integration of these data types.

Observation Units for Studying News Avoidance. The main goal of this paper is to propose a new methodological framework to collect behavioural and self-report data together to gain insights into media exposure and consumption phenomena. Specifically, such integration emphasizes the importance of allowing robust statistical behaviour comparisons across different audiences, such as inter-generational comparisons. As discussed in the preceding sections, survey data and digital-trace data do not allow to extract valid observation units on their own. This section elaborates on four essential factors, the consideration of which can inform the design of a novel data collection method: (a) individual data-point granularity; (b) controlling surface cues; (c) parametrizing algorithmic mediation, and (d) going beyond measuring media exposure to measure interaction.

To truly grasp how individuals select and consume online content, it is essential to monitor their activities with a sufficient degree of nuance. As described earlier, this is a challenging endeavour, as users are unwilling to install tracker software on their devices, and existing platforms do not provide the individual-level interaction data required to capture the full spectrum of user behaviour. This complexity arises from the diverse ways people interact with content, which can range from passive browsing to active engagement. Understanding these patterns requires a sophisticated approach to data collection and analysis that goes beyond simple metrics like clicks or view time. Without these nuanced insights, our comprehension of online content consumption remains superficial.

Secondly, it is also crucial to control, or at least characterize, the surface-level cues in the content that individuals are exposed to during behavioural recording. This includes elements such as headlines, the source of content, and social endorsement. Researchers should also be mindful of layout variations in the spaces where the content is displayed. Content can appear in various formats, such as a newsfeed, a conversational platform like WhatsApp, or the layout of a news channel's front page where it competes with other content.

Thirdly, when content exposure is mediated by an algorithm, it becomes crucial to, at least, understand how that algorithm operates, and ideally, control its parameters. However, as explained earlier, most platform algorithms are not transparent, meaning that the companies behind them do not share how they work. One way to get around this is by observing how the algorithm behaves under different controlled starting conditions. This could involve setting up new user accounts in various locations and with different demographic details, then tracking what kind of content the platform shows to each account. To add depth to the analysis, these accounts could interact with the content to see whether the algorithm offers a variety of material or tends to stick to similar types of content based on past interactions. The key factor to assess here is what kind of content people end up seeing and how varied it is due to the algorithm's influence.

Finally, employing detailed measures of how individuals engage with content can help researchers find more detailed explanations and make more precise predictions. Take, for example, a study aimed at evaluating the impact of 'nudging' strategies designed to increase engagement with local political news. In this context, an algorithmic recommendation system could significantly improve its effectiveness if it had detailed data on a user's past interactions with political content, rather than simply knowing the user was exposed to such content before. The advantage of this approach lies in the detailed interaction history, which provides a richer dataset for the algorithm to base its nudging strategies on, potentially leading to more tailored and effective recommendations. If we focus on observing a sequence of specific content interactions, rather than just whether exposure happened (a binary variable) or measuring the time between clicks, then the inferred user ratings will more closely align with explicit feedback rather than the implicit feedback typically used in recommendation systems, as described in Sect. 1.2.

2   The Proposed Method

2.1   A Purposely Curated Media Environment: Threads and Snippets

The method proposed in this paper is based on a purposefully designed media ecosystem that contains standalone content pieces on a range of topics chosen by the researcher, including, e.g. politics, environment, health, science, technology, culture and others. While most such pieces come from existing news sources, the method allows for other types of public content, as well as artificial content crafted for specific use cases. All contents undergo preprocessing and curation to turn them into 'threads', similar to the now common multi-part posts on social media platforms like, X [see, e.g. 5].

The production of threads from an original public content involves breaking it down into a sequence of snippets—each equivalent to an utterance in a mediated conversation on a chat platform like e.g., WhatsApp. While most snippets are text, some can be short videos or images. Each thread is further processed to turn it into a standalone micro story that users can consume on its own. The number of snippets in a thread is a variable that depends on the complexity of the original content piece. This variable is controlled in the preprocessing and curation stages to, e.g. avoid cognitive overload. This means the method may divide larger and more complex contents into separate independent threads.

Each thread is further annotated with meta-data containing information about how long it would take, on average, for its content to be consumed. For text snippets, the method uses reading speed (238 words per minute) [10]; for images it uses the average time to consume the content known to be about 150ms [58]. When a snippet is a video, its consumption time is simply measured by its duration in seconds and milliseconds. Threads also contain meta-data about the content's source, topic, type of content (news, non-news), style (e.g. formal/informal), sentiment (happy/sad), and tone. Thread meta-data is flexible, thus it can be extended to include further annotations.

During the preprocessing and curation stages, another task is to define what reply options are available for each snippet. The next section describes that the interaction between users and threads is mediated by a *closed* chatbot app. In a closed chatbot replies are options presented to the user. In other words, the chatbot displays a snippet and then a set of possible reply options the user can choose from to continue to the next part of a thread, share a reaction or finish the interaction. Most snippets have three constant default reply options:

1. ask for the next snippet in the thread
2. change to a different thread (the mechanism is explained later)
3. finish the interaction.

Further reply options can be added to create more specific and context dependent interactions with a snippet. These may include self-report reply options create rapport with the user and collect data on the user's emotional or cognitive states. For example, a snippet within a thread may be a yes/no question, for which two extra reply options—a thumbs up and a thumbs down emoji—are included in the snippet interaction repertoire. In any case, when a snippet contains such extra reply options, these are always presented to the user before the default options that allow the user to leave the snippet.

Table 1 depicts an example of a thread automatically generated from a piece published in Dazed & Confused [40] about using tarot readings in TikTok to get over heartbreak. The original text contains 1286 words. The proposed method used the chatGPT API (gpt-4-turbo-preview) to summarize the original text, and then to produce break the summary down into snippets that capture the content for delivery through a chatbot. Below is the summary produced by the chatGPT API (containing 224 words):

TikTok Tarot: A New Age Solution for Heartbreak

In the digital era, young people are increasingly turning to TikTok tarot readings for comfort and direction, especially in matters of the heart. With over 85 billion views on #tarot, these videos offer hyper-specific predictions that resonate deeply with viewers. Many, like 25-year-old Nicholas, find solace and guidance in these readings, crediting them for providing clarity post-breakup.

The surge in online psychic readings reflects a broader trend of young people seeking spiritual experiences outside traditional religious frameworks. According to Linda Woodhead from King's College London, interest in fortune-telling has remained steady since the 1950s, but the focus has shifted from contacting the deceased to seeking personal guidance. This shift coincides with a decline in traditional religious beliefs among Gen Z, many of whom are drawn to tarot for its lack of discriminatory connotations.

TikTok's algorithm plays a mysterious yet pivotal role in delivering these readings, with many users and readers believing that the videos find their way to those who need them most. This belief in destiny, coupled with the platform's opaque algorithm, creates a unique space for spiritual exploration and connection. Despite scepticism, the positive impact of these readings on viewers' lives cannot be denied, offering a blend of optimism and communal belonging in an increasingly isolated world.

Table 1. Example thread: Tarot readings in TikTok

No.	Snippet
1	Ever wondered if the universe has a message just for you? Well, TikTok tarot might be your answer!
2	Imagine scrolling and finding a tarot reading that speaks directly to your situation. That's what's happening to millions, with #tarot views sky rocketing to 85 billion!
3	People like Nicholas found clarity in love through these videos. They're not just random; they're seen as signs meant to guide you
4	But why are so many young folks turning to TikTok for spiritual advice? It's not just about the stars aligning; it's about finding a path that respects all aspects of who they are
5	With Gen Z being the least religious generation in Britain, tarot fills a gap, offering guidance without judgement
6	Behind these mystical messages are young psychics using TikTok's enigmatic algorithm to reach those in need
7	Some believe it's fate that guides the algorithm, connecting videos to viewers for a reason. Do you think there's truth to that?
8	Despite the mystery, these readings often encourage positive action, like reaching out for closure or practicing self-love
9	Critics exist, but can't deny the comfort and optimism these readings bring to many, especially in a world that can feel lonely
10	So, whether you're seeking advice, closure, or just a bit of hope, maybe your next sign is waiting in your TikTok feed
11	Remember, whether it's the stars, the cards, or the algorithm speaking, the message that finds you might just be the guidance you need
12	Why not explore and see if the universe has something to tell you? You're not alone in this cosmic journey

The thread meta-data for this example is the following (also derived using the chatGPT 4.0 API with appropriate prompts):

source: Dazed & Confused Magazine
Expected time to consume: 1.2 min
Type: non-news magazine feature article
Sentiment valence: high, positive
Sentiment arousal: neutral-towards-low, calming
Style: informal
Tone: supportive, inspirational

Notice that most of the snippets generated by chatGPT for the example piece are a form of question or hypothetical situation followed by a suggested answer. For all utterances except U7 (a yes/no question) and U12 (the last snippet) there would be a 'Tell me more' reply option to move deeper in the thread, and another 'Something else?' to switch to a different thread. U7 is an example of a snippet that would require extra reply options before those that allow the user to finish consuming the snippet. In this specific case the thumbs-up and thumbs-down emoji would be a suitable set of intermediate reply options that would provide data similar to the data collected through a survey, but contextualized in the content consumption behaviour.

This crafted media environment allows researchers to collect user behaviour data through a dialogical chatbot interface that is still controlled at the level of the reply options available to the snippets that constitute a thread. Thread experiences are naturally designed to measure behaviour, but snippets can also contain prompts to get reflexive self-report data on how users perceive themselves throughout the interactions with the chatbot, as well as proxies to explicit rating, allowing for useful triangulation and subsequent inferences and comparisons.

2.2   User-Content Interaction: The AIDIAL Brief

Interactions with the media ecosystem take place only through a mobile phone app called AIDIAL. During registration, users fill in a short questionnaire that contains socio-demographic questions, as well as questions about attitudes and media consumption habits. Users also decide how often they want to receive notifications about the readiness of a new session, which depends on the availability of new content to be consumed. These interactive sessions are henceforth referred to as 'briefs'. The options range from individual updates throughout the day to a brief every morning, or a brief once per week. In addition, users can select specific content preferences by toggling the topics they want to get news on in the app's settings panel. Finally, in the same settings panel, there is a snooze option that to pause all notifications for a defined period.

Once registered, users can start a brief session with AIDIAL. At the start of a session, AIDIAL uses a classical recommendation system to decide what thread to show. The algorithmic content selection involves choosing a topic and a thread within that topic. AIDIAL informs cold-start recommendations using the topics selected during registration and the answers provided in the registration questionnaire. As users interact with the different threads, the system stores (a) the reply options selected by the user at the snippet level, and (b) computes the duration of the period between selections as seconds a milliseconds. A brief session is limited to a number of threads. This number is a parameter of the system, e.g. it can be a random number between five and nine, informed by empirical research on cognitive overload, or it can be experimentally controlled. Switching to a new thread occurs when a user chooses a reply of the form 'Something else?' in an unfinished thread (signalling lack of interest in the current thread) or when a thread interaction has been completed. If the number of threads consumed is less than the defined maximum for a brief, the system will rely again on algorithmic recommendation to select the next unvisited thread, and mark the current one as visited by the user, with status complete or incomplete.

The snippets in every thread have variables that are used to collect data about their interactions with users. Such snippet-level data structure contains:

1. user ID
2. thread ID
3. brief number
4. thread number in brief
5. number of visits to this thread (social endorsement)
6. start-of-interaction time stamp
7. end-of-interaction time stamp
8. selected reply options (including their time stamp)
9. exit status (thread completed, or incomplete)
10. recommendation system explanation
11. estimated explicit rating

In this collection of variables, the combination of user ID and thread ID identifies an interaction with a specific thread. Further contextual information includes the brief number and the thread number in the brief (e.g. third thread during the tenth brief session) along with how many times the thread has been visited (when not marked previously as completed). A key variable, the value of which is computed during a brief, is the estimated rating given by the user to the thread. To estimate explicit rating, the method uses the time stamps for the start and end of the interaction with the thread, including all time stamps for chosen reply options and the selections themselves, as well as how the thread interaction ended.

The method gauges the interest elicited by a thread during a session by integrating two information sources. The first is how many snippets were consumed, i.e. how many times the user chose the option to advance to the next snippet. The more snippets visited, the higher the rating. The second is the distribution of periods between selection of reply options The system processes these pieces of information to generate a quantitative (explicit) thread user rating on a 1–10 scale. For new threads with a few or no interactions, the method compares the overall distribution of periods between replies with the theoretically expected consumption time. However, as statistically sufficient data is collected, the method compares this distribution with the population of users that have consumed the thread instead. Distributions that are close to the theoretical or empirical central tendencies will receive the highest rating values. Therefore, as waiting times between replies, and overall thread consumption duration deviate (below or above) the central tendencies, the estimated ratings will be lower. The method does not ask users to rate threads explicitly before they leave them to control for evaluative conditioning (EC) [see e.g. 30]. However, it is possible to introduce reply options that can provide further indirect support for the raw rating estimations computed from the number of in-thread interactions and the inter-reply period distributions.

2.3 Units of Observation and Analysis

The aim of the AIDIAL media ecosystem is to provide a comprehensive repository of diverse content, encompassing both news and non-news, spanning various topics of interest for different generational audiences. Importantly, this media environment is designed to capture user attention by gauging interactions with snippets of information delivered conversationally. The method utilizes attention measures based on the threads and snippets visited by users, as well as the time elapsed between users selecting reply options. This is used as a proxy to infer interest and quantify it as an estimated rating.

Expanding the scope of analysis, the methodology facilitates the comparison of engagement patterns across demographic groups, leveraging statistical tools to elucidate potential disparities in news consumption behaviours. This aspect of the research is particularly valuable for understanding how demographic variables (such as age, gender, educational background, and political orientation) influence the reception and perception of news content. Through such analysis, it becomes possible to identify demographic segments that are more prone to news avoidance, as well as to pinpoint the types of content that resonate with diverse audiences. Furthermore, the snippet-level analyses may reveal useful information about the context and contents that may be most suitable for introducing interventions such as nudging.

The proposed method can, not only help researchers understand the mechanisms that drive news consumption and avoidance, but also inform the development of more effective strategies for news presentation and dissemination. By identifying the factors that drive user engagement and avoidance, media outlets and content creators can tailor their approaches to meet the needs and preferences of their target audiences, fostering a more informed and engaged public sphere.

3 Possible Applications

The methodology delineated in this study offers a versatile framework for researchers aiming to unravel the complex mechanisms that drive news avoidance. By integrating manipulations of headline sources and social endorsements within the experimental design, this approach facilitates a nuanced examination of the interplay between news presentation and user engagement. Such an investigation is pivotal for understanding how variations in news dissemination affect readers' propensity to either avoid or engage with news content. This is especially relevant in an era where digital platforms dominate news consumption, presenting a unique set of challenges and opportunities for news dissemination.

Moreover, this methodological approach enables the exploration of differential impacts across various demographic groups, thereby shedding light on the socio-cultural dimensions of news avoidance. Through targeted experimental manipulations, researchers can assess the influence of factors such as source credibility, social validation cues, and algorithmic recommendations on news consumption patterns. This, in turn, provides valuable insights into the mechanisms driving selective exposure to, or avoidance of, news articles, thereby contributing to a more comprehensive understanding of contemporary news consumption dynamics.

In addition, the application of this methodology extends beyond academic inquiry, offering practical implications for media practitioners and policymakers. By elucidating the factors that drive news engagement or avoidance, the findings from such studies can inform strategies aimed at enhancing news literacy, fostering a more informed citizenry, and mitigating the effects of misinformation. Consequently, this research not only advances our theoretical understanding of news avoidance but also serves as a cornerstone for developing interventions designed to promote a healthier, more robust public discourse in the digital age.

4   Discussion

The investigation into news avoidance through the lens of the proposed dialogical method illuminates the intricate interplay between user interaction patterns and algorithmic mediation to study news avoidance. The paper relies on conceptual framing of news avoidance by Skovsgaard and Andersen [54] as a foundation, enabling a nuanced exploration of user intentional engagement with news snippets in online threads. The method's granularity in capturing user interactions offers a fresh perspective on the dynamics of news consumption, echoing Andersen et al. [4] observations on selective exposure and temporality.

Moreover, the algorithmic underpinnings of our media environment, designed to mimic real-world content navigation, find resonance with Thurman et al. [59] examination of algorithms, automation, and news—particularly as conversational content delivery has become mainstream. This alignment underscores the pivotal role of algorithmic curation in shaping news avoidance behaviours, highlighting the necessity of a multifaceted approach to understand the complexities of digital news consumption.

The proposed method's focus on nuanced interaction patterns within threads, coupled with its capacity for detailed demographic analysis, opens avenues for unprecedented insights into the factors driving news avoidance. Recording actual behaviours, and strategically incorporating self-report variables during media consumption episodes, allow researchers to better understand introspective variables along with contextual variables connected with the intentionality driving news avoidance. The proposed method not only responds to the call for robust methodological frameworks capable of dissecting the multifactorial nature of news avoidance [54,59] but also sets a new benchmark for future inquiries in the realm of digital news consumption research.

Future work will scrutinize one of the potentially most significant drawbacks of the proposed method—its ecological validity. Recruiting participants to engage with a novel news app, which diverges from those currently available in the media ecosystem, may introduce its own biases. Furthermore, future research will empirically investigate the degree to which the artificial media ecosystem succeeds in motivating users to consume news based solely on available content, without any social endorsement. This will be compared against scenarios where social endorsement is controlled in various ways.

Acknowledgements. This work was funded by the ILIND seed funding program (Universidade Lusófona, CICANT) awarded to the author for the project *AIDIAL: an intelligent chatbot to explore new literacies in the age of algorithms and AI*

Disclosure of Interests. The author declares no conflict of interest.

References

1. Abdelrazek, A., Eid, Y., Gawish, E., Medhat, W., Hassan, A.: Topic modeling algorithms and applications: a survey. Inf. Syst. **112**, 102131 (2023)
2. Aggarwal, C.C.: Recommender Systems. Springer, Cham (2016). https://doi.org/10.1007/978-3-319-29659-3
3. Ananny, M.: Toward an ethics of algorithms: convening, observation, probability, and timeliness. Sci. Technol. Human Values **41**(1), 93–117 (2016). ISSN 0162-2439, 1552-8251, https://doi.org/10.1177/0162243915606523
4. Andersen, K., Shehata, A., Skovsgaard, M., Strömbäck, J.: Selective news avoidance: consistency and temporality. Commun. Res., 1552–3810 (2024). ISSN 0093-6502, https://doi.org/10.1177/00936502231221689
5. Aragón, P., Gómez, V., Kaltenbrunner, A.: To thread or not to thread: the impact of conversation threading on online discussion. In: Proceedings of the International AAAI Conference on Web and Social Media, vol. 11, pp. 12–21 (2017)
6. Bakshy, E., Messing, S., Adamic, L.A.: Exposure to ideologically diverse news and opinion on Facebook. Science **348**(6239), 1130–1132 (2015). ISSN 0036-8075, 1095-9203, https://doi.org/10.1126/science.aaa1160
7. Baumeister, R.F., Vohs, K.D., Funder, D.C.: Psychology as the science of self-reports and finger movements: whatever happened to actual behavior? Perspect. Psychol. Sci. **2**(4), 396–403 (2007). https://doi.org/10.1111/j.1745-6916.2007.00051.x
8. Bengtsson, S., Johansson, S.: A phenomenology of news: understanding news in digital culture. Journalism **22**(11), 2873–2889 (2021). ISSN 1464-8849, 1741-3001, https://doi.org/10.1177/1464884919901194
9. Bennett, W.L., Iyengar, S.: A new era of minimal effects? the changing foundations of political communication. J. Commun. **58**(4), 707–731 (2008), ISSN 00219916,14602466. https://doi.org/10.1111/j.1460-2466.2008.00410.x

10. Brysbaert, M.: How many words do we read per minute? a review and meta-analysis of reading rate. J. Mem. Lang. **109**, 104047 (2019)
11. Chiu, C.M., Huang, H.Y., Cheng, H.L., Sun, P.C.: Understanding online community citizenship behaviors through social support and social identity. Int. J. Inf. Manage. **35**(4), 504–519 (2015)
12. Choung, H., David, P., Ross, A.: Trust in AI and its role in the acceptance of AI technologies. Int. J. Human–Comput. Interact. **39**(9), 1727–1739 (2023). ISSN 1044-7318, 1532-7590, https://doi.org/10.1080/10447318.2022.2050543
13. Coddington, M.: Clarifying journalism's quantitative turn: a typology for evaluating data journalism, computational journalism, and computer-assisted reporting. Digit. J. **3**(3), 331–348 (2015). ISSN 2167-0811, 2167-082X, https://doi.org/10.1080/21670811.2014.976400
14. De Vreese, C.H., Neijens, P.: Measuring media exposure in a changing communications environment. Commun. Methods Measures **10**(2-3), 69–80 (2016). ISSN 1931-2458, 1931–2466, https://doi.org/10.1080/19312458.2016.1150441
15. DeCastellarnau, A.: A classification of response scale characteristics that affect data quality: a literature review. Qual. Quant. **52**(4), 1523–1559 (2018). ISSN 0033-5177, 1573-7845, https://doi.org/10.1007/s11135-017-0533-4
16. Denning, D.E.: Cyber conflict as an emergent social phenomenon. In: Corporate Hacking and Technology-driven Crime: Social Dynamics and Implications, pp. 170–186, IGI Global (2011)
17. Descampe, A., Massart, C., Poelman, S., Standaert, F.X., Standaert, O.: Automated news recommendation in front of adversarial examples and the technical limits of transparency in algorithmic accountability. AI Soc. **37**(1), 67–80 (2022). ISSN 0951-5666, 1435–5655, https://doi.org/10.1007/s00146-021-01159-3
18. Diakopoulos, N.: Algorithmic accountability: journalistic investigation of computational power structures. Digit. J. **3**(3), 398–415 (2015). ISSN 2167-0811, 2167-082X, https://doi.org/10.1080/21670811.2014.976411
19. Diakopoulos, N., Koliska, M.: Algorithmic transparency in the news media. Digit. J. **5**(7), 809–828 (2017). ISSN 2167-0811, 2167-082X, https://doi.org/10.1080/21670811.2016.1208053
20. Dörr, K.N., Hollnbuchner, K.: Ethical challenges of algorithmic journalism. Digit. J. **5**(4), 404–419 (2017). ISSN 2167-0811, 2167-082X, https://doi.org/10.1080/21670811.2016.1167612
21. Essinger, J.: Ada's algorithm: how lord Byron's daughter Ada Lovelace launched the digital age. Melville House (2014)
22. Flake, J.K., Pek, J., Hehman, E.: Construct validation in social and personality research: current practice and recommendations. Soc. Psychol. Pers. Sci. **8**(4), 370–378 (2017). ISSN 1948-5506, 1948–5514, https://doi.org/10.1177/1948550617693063
23. Gillespie, T.: Algorithm digital keywords: a vocabulary of information society and culture **8**, 18–30 (2016)
24. Godinot, A., Tarissan, F.: Measuring the effect of collaborative filtering on the diversity of users' attention. Appl. Network Sci. **8**(1), 9 (2023)
25. Goldberg, D., Nichols, D., Oki, B.M., Terry, D.: Using collaborative filtering to weave an information tapestry. Commun. ACM **35**(12), 61–70 (1992)
26. Groves, R.M., Lyberg, L.: Total survey error: past, present, and future. Public Opin. Q. **74**(5), 849–879 (2010)
27. Helberger, N., Diakopoulos, N.: The European AI act and how it matters for research into AI in media and journalism. Digit.J. **11**(9), 1751–1760 (Oct 2023). ISSN 2167-0811, 2167-082X, https://doi.org/10.1080/21670811.2022.2082505

28. Herlocker, J.L., Konstan, J.A., Riedl, J.: Explaining collaborative filtering recommendations. In: Proceedings of the 2000 ACM Conference on Computer Supported Cooperative Work, pp. 241–250 (2000)

29. Hussey, I., Hughes, S.: Hidden invalidity among 15 commonly used measures in social and personality psychology. Adv. Methods Practices Psychol. Sci. **3**(2), 166–184 (Jun 2020). ISSN 2515-2459, 2515-2467, https://doi.org/10.1177/2515245919882903

30. Jones, C.R., Olson, M.A., Fazio, R.H.: Evaluative conditioning: The "how" question. In: Advances in experimental social psychology, vol. 43, pp. 205–255, Elsevier (2010)

31. Kaiser, J., Keller, T.R., Kleinen-von Königslöw, K.: Incidental news exposure on facebook as a social experience: the influence of recommender and media cues on news selection. Commun. Res. **48**(1), 77–99 (Feb 2021). ISSN 0093-6502, 1552-3810, https://doi.org/10.1177/0093650218803529

32. Karlsen, R., Beyer, A., Steen-Johnsen, K.: Do high-choice media environments facilitate news avoidance? a longitudinal study 1997–2016. J. Broadcast. Electron. Media **64**(5), 794–814 (Dec 2020). ISSN 0883-8151, 1550-6878, https://doi.org/10.1080/08838151.2020.1835428

33. Knobloch-Westerwick, S., Westerwick, A., Johnson, B.K.: Selective Exposure in the Communication Technology Context. In: Sundar, S.S. (ed.) The Handbook of the Psychology of Communication Technology, pp. 405–424, Wiley, 1 edn. (Jan 2015). ISBN 978-1-118-41336-4 978-1-118-42645-6, https://doi.org/10.1002/9781118426456.ch18

34. Konitzer, T., et al.: Comparing estimates of news consumption from survey and passively collected behavioral data. Public Opin. Q. **85**(S1), 347–370 (2021)

35. Kuru, O., Pasek, J.: Improving social media measurement in surveys: avoiding acquiescence bias in Facebook research. Comput. Human Behav. **57**, 82–92 (Apr 2016). ISSN 07475632, https://doi.org/10.1016/j.chb.2015.12.008

36. Latzer, M., Hollnbuchner, K., Just, N., Saurwein, F.: 19. The economics of algorithmic selection on the internet. Handbook on the Economics of the Internet, p. 395 (2016)

37. Lewis, S.C., Westlund, O.: Big data and journalism: epistemology, expertise, economics, and ethics. digital j. **3**(3), 447–466 (may 2015). ISSSN: 2167-0811, 2167-082x, https://doi.org/10.1080/21670811.2014.976418

38. Loos, E., Nijenhuis, J.: Consuming fake news: a matter of age? the perception of political fake news stories in facebook ads. In: Gao, Q., Zhou, J. (eds.) HCII 2020. LNCS, vol. 12209, pp. 69–88. Springer, Cham (2020). https://doi.org/10.1007/978-3-030-50232-4_6

39. Luo, X., Zhou, M., Li, S., You, Z., Xia, Y., Zhu, Q.: A nonnegative latent factor model for large-scale sparse matrices in recommender systems via alternating direction method. IEEE Trans. Neural Netw. Learni. Syst. **27**(3), 579–592 (2015)

40. Molloy, L.: Could tiktok tarot fix your broken heart? (January 2024), URL Could TikTok tarot fix your broken heart?

41. Mukerjee, S., Yang, T.: Choosing to avoid? a conjoint experimental study to understand selective exposure and avoidance on social media. Political Commun. **38**(3), 222–240 (May 2021). ISSN 1058-4609, 1091-7675, https://doi.org/10.1080/10584609.2020.1763531

42. Napoli, P.M.: Automated media: an institutional theory perspective on algorithmic media production and consumption: automated media. Commun. Theory **24**(3), 340–360 (Aug 2014). ISSN 10503293, https://doi.org/10.1111/comt.12039

43. Nederhof, A.J.: Methods of coping with social desirability bias: a review. Europ. J. Social Psycholo. **15**(3), 263–280 (Jul 1985). ISSN 0046-2772, 1099-0992, https://doi.org/10.1002/ejsp.2420150303

44. Ohme, J., et al.: Digital Trace Data Collection for Social Media Effects Research: APIs, Data Donation, and (Screen) Tracking. Commun. Methods Measur. 1–18 (Feb 2023). ISSN 1931-2458, 1931-2466, https://doi.org/10.1080/19312458.2023.2181319

45. Ohme, J., Mothes, C.: What affects first- and second-level selective exposure to journalistic news? a social media online experiment. J. Stud. **21**(9), 1220–1242 (Jul 2020). ISSN 1461-670X, 1469-9699, https://doi.org/10.1080/1461670X.2020.1735490

46. Ouchchy, L., Coin, A., Dubljević, V.: AI in the headlines: The portrayal of the ethical issues of artificial intelligence in the media. AI Society **35**(4), 927–936 (Dec 2020). ISSN 0951-5666, 1435-5655, https://doi.org/10.1007/s00146-020-00965-5

47. Parry, D.A., Davidson, B.I., Sewall, C.J.R., Fisher, J.T., Mieczkowski, H., Quintana, D.S.: A systematic review and meta-analysis of discrepancies between logged and self-reported digital media use. Nature Human Behav. **5**(11), 1535–1547 (May 2021). ISSN 2397-3374, https://doi.org/10.1038/s41562-021-01117-5

48. Pita, M., Ehn, K., dos Santos, T.: Community identities under perturbation: Covid-19 and the r/digitalnomad subreddit. First Monday (2022)

49. Prior, M.: Improving media effects research through better measurement of news exposure. J. Politics **71**(3), 893–908 (Jul 2009). ISSN 0022-3816, 1468-2508, https://doi.org/10.1017/S0022381609090781

50. Revilla, M., Couper, M.P., Ochoa, C.: Willingness of online panelists to perform additional tasks. Methods, data, analyses: a journal for quantitative methods and survey methodology (mda) **13**(2), 223–252 (2019)

51. Revilla, M., Ochoa, C., Loewe, G.: Using passive data from a meter to complement survey data in order to study online behavior. Social Sci. Comput. Rev. **35**(4), 521–536 (Aug 2017). ISSN 0894-4393, 1552-8286, https://doi.org/10.1177/0894439316638457

52. Schwarz, N., Oyserman, D.: Asking Questions About Behavior: Cognition, Communication, and Questionnaire Construction. American Journal of Evaluation (2001)

53. Shin, D.: Embodying algorithms, enactive artificial intelligence and the extended cognition: You can see as much as you know about algorithm. J. Inform. Sci. **49**(1), 18–31 (Feb 2023). ISSN 0165-5515, 1741-6485, https://doi.org/10.1177/0165551520985495

54. Skovsgaard, M., Andersen, K.: Conceptualizing news avoidance: towards a shared understanding of different causes and potential solutions. J. Stud. **21**(4), 459–476 (2020)

55. Stromback, J., Djerf-Pierre, M., Shehata, A.: The dynamics of political interest and news media consumption: a longitudinal perspective. Int. J. Public Opinion Res. **25**(4), 414–435 (Dec 2013). ISSN 0954-2892, 1471-6909, https://doi.org/10.1093/ijpor/eds018

56. Taneja, H., Wu, A.X., Edgerly, S.: Rethinking the generational gap in online news use: An infrastructural perspective. New Media Society **20**(5), 1792–1812 (May 2018). ISSN 1461-4448, 1461-7315, https://doi.org/10.1177/1461444817707348

57. Thomas, W.: Algorithms: from Al-khwarizmi to turing and beyond. In: Sommaruga, G., Strahm, T. (eds.) Turing's Revolution, pp. 29–42. Springer, Cham (2015). https://doi.org/10.1007/978-3-319-22156-4_2

58. Thorpe, S., Fize, D., Marlot, C.: Speed of processing in the human visual system. Nature **381**(6582), 520–522 (1996)

59. Thurman, N., Lewis, S.C., Kunert, J.: Algorithms, Automation, and News. Digital J. **7**(8), 980–992 (Sep 2019). ISSN 2167-0811, 2167-082X, https://doi.org/10.1080/21670811.2019.1685395

60. Vraga, E.K., Tully, M.: Who Is Exposed to News? It Depends on how you measure: examining self-reported versus behavioral news exposure measures. Social Science Computer Review **38**(5), 550–566 (Oct 2020). ISSN 0894-4393, 1552-8286, https://doi.org/10.1177/0894439318812050

61. Wach, K., et al.: The dark side of generative artificial intelligence: a critical analysis of controversies and risks of ChatGPT. Entrepreneurial Business Econom. Rev. **11**(2), 7–30 (2023). ISSN 23538821, https://doi.org/10.15678/EBER.2023.110201

62. Winter, S., Metzger, M.J., Flanagin, A.J.: Selective use of news cues: a multiple-motive perspective on information selection in social media environments: selective use of news cues. J. Commun. **66**(4), 669–693 (Aug 2016). ISSN 00219916, https://doi.org/10.1111/jcom.12241

63. Zamith, R.: Algorithms and journalism. In: Oxford Research Encyclopedia of Communication (2019)

64. Zhang, Q., Lu, J., Jin, Y.: Artificial intelligence in recommender systems. Complex Intell. Syst. **7**, 439–457 (2021)

Benchmarking the User eXperience and Usability of Online Social Networks: Proposal of an Evaluation Framework

Francisco Regalado(✉) ⓘ, Óscar Mealha ⓘ, Carlos Santos ⓘ, and Ana Isabel Veloso ⓘ

DigiMedia, Department of Communication and Art, University of Aveiro, Aveiro, Australia

{fsfregalado,oem,carlossantos,aiv}@ua.pt

Abstract. The ubiquity of Information and Communication Technologies (ICT) presents challenges in designing experiences and interfaces. Hence, it becomes crucial to have solutions that facilitate the comparison of various products, discerning their relative strengths and weaknesses. Therefore, this paper presents a proposal of an Evaluation Framework for Benchmarking the user eXperience and Usability of Online Social Networks. Its goal is to provide a holistic perspective of user eXperience and satisfaction, checked in conformance with a detailed heuristic analysis. This Framework is divided into three parts, comprising (i) the selection of experts, and products to benchmark; (ii) the evaluation of UX Satisfaction of each product with Emocards, and (iii) test the User eXperience within a Usability Heuristic Evaluation for each product. By applying the specific study case of seven senior online social networks and resorting to 14 experts in the field of ICT, it was possible to build a holistic Benchmarking Evaluation Framework. In particular, this Framework introduces new perspectives on (i) the priority sequence for UX and satisfaction, followed by heuristic detail; (ii) the seamless incorporation of feedback obtained during the think-aloud process into the analysis and data representation; (iii) the creation of a normalized score for each heuristic of every product, thus allowing for a direct comparison between products; and (iv) the creation of integrated representations of the two dimensions under study – i.e., UX satisfaction and Usability Heuristic Evaluation. Overall, we hope that this proposed Framework can serve as a simple yet effective approach to represent and compare evaluation results between products.

Keywords: Online Social Networks · User eXperience (UX) · Usability · Benchmarking · Evaluation Framework

1 Introduction

Information and Communication Technologies (ICT) have been assuming a ubiquitous role in today's society [1–3]. Spread across various sectors, such as gaming, social media, or e-commerce, ICT plays a fundamental role in fulfilling different jobs and establishing the proper functioning of global institutions. Online social networks have seen exponential growth in all age groups [4], with special attention to senior citizens who have experienced above-average growth [5]. However, the solutions and products developed don't always consider their contexts, needs, and preferences [6].

© The Author(s), under exclusive license to Springer Nature Switzerland AG 2024
Q. Gao and J. Zhou (Eds.): HCII 2024, LNCS 14725, pp. 417–431, 2024.
https://doi.org/10.1007/978-3-031-61543-6_29

As well established by multiple authors [7–11], technology design should consistently prioritize the needs, capabilities, and preferences of its users, ensuring it is intuitive, user-friendly, and accessible to individuals with diverse backgrounds and competences. In today's market, ensuring good user eXperience (UX) and usability can dictate the product's success. By using these indicators, comparing the solutions available on the market can be crucial to understanding whether a particular product is better or worse than the competition [12].

On the one hand, following the principles of User-Centred Design [13], UX can be defined as "user's perceptions and responses that result from the use and/or anticipated use of a system, product or service" [14]. Thus, not only does such a process evaluate the usefulness, efficiency, and usability of these systems, but it also captures the essence of one's interaction [15]. On the other hand, and complementary to the User eXperience, the usability of a product should also be considered. The term usability can be defined as the attribute that determines the ease of use of a given product and may influence the design process [16].

Several research studies have been conducted on UX evaluations and/or usability testing using multiple instruments. As an example, Saavedra and colleagues [17] developed a set of heuristics tailored to UX in social networks, applicable to both mobile devices and website versions. The authors aim to combine UX and usability uniquely, but the representation of the results and the detail provided by the experts is not foreseen. Additionally, other recent studies in the field of UX [18] and usability [19] have also been conducted, implementing different evaluation strategies. However, they do not directly compare various products and the crossing of the two major areas under analysis - i.e., UX and usability.

Meanwhile, two other research studies [20, 21] combine a usability heuristic evaluation with a user experience one. However, there is no integration or direct analysis between the two dimensions. Lastly, Schrepp and colleagues [22] constructed a benchmarking framework for the User eXperience Questionnaire. Despite its relevance, it does not provide the crucial detail fostered by a usability evaluation.

Overall, this research landscape highlights the need to develop a framework that can resolve a technical-emotional perspective – highly focused on user eXperience – alongside a more detailed usability evaluation.

Resorting to seven senior online social networks, specifically developed with the needs, preferences, and contexts of older adults in mind; and 14 ICT specialists, this paper's goals are twofold: (i) propose the construction and implementation of an evaluation framework for benchmarking online social networks; and (ii) define and represent strategies for the integrated presentation of results. This benchmarking framework helps to interpret and compare results, being especially important and helpful in identifying a product's specific problems.

2   Proposal of an Evaluation Framework for Benchmarking Online Social Networks

As previously mentioned, the evaluation of users' interaction with digital technology can take on various perspectives, and this framework is supported by two crucial approaches to evaluate it: user eXperience (UX) and usability.

Building on the foundations of UX and usability, this chapter presents a benchmarking framework to evaluate these two fundamental aspects of online social networks. Its goal is to provide a holistic perspective of user eXperience and satisfaction, checked in conformance with a detailed heuristic analysis. Overall, this framework is divided into three main parts, as shown in Fig. 1: (i) Part 1 – Selection of a purposive sample of experts, products to benchmark and perform on each product a list of pre-specified tasks (activities); (ii) Part 2 – Evaluate UX Satisfaction of each product with Emocards; and (iii) Part 3 – Test User eXperience within a Usability Heuristic Evaluation for each product.

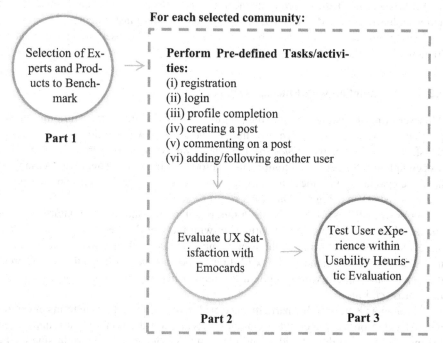

Fig. 1. Schematic illustration of the three-part framework for benchmarking senior online social networks.

2.1 Selection of Purposive Sample and Products to Benchmark (Part 1)

Before evaluating the chosen products for benchmarking, specifically online social networks, it is crucial to address two key aspects. Firstly, select a set of experts in the field of research, ensuring their suitability for the project's goals and tasks (activities). Since this is a highly focused evaluation in a specific area, with detailed features, the selected sample should be purposive and constituted of experts (elite subjects), highlighting the particularity of the evaluators' knowledge. Secondly, the amount of products to be benchmarked and evaluated must be selected. The number of products can vary in number – ultimately, the framework can even be applied to only one product – and the evaluation procedures may focus on its particularities and output important insights to improve the product's characteristics.

Furthermore, given the social nature of the media under evaluation, it is crucial to ensure the availability of key actions associated with sociability. Thus, for the purpose of this study and explanation of the framework's application, the following set of pre-defined tasks/activities was defined: (i) registration, (ii) login, (iii) profile completion, (iv) creating a post, (v) commenting on a post, and (vi) adding/following another user. Each of these activities must be performed before proceeding with the individual assessment for each of the online communities selected. While conducting the evaluation actions, it is important to encourage the "think aloud" of decisions and critical opinions on what has been experienced, thus reinforcing the triangulation between what has been observed and what has been reported through the provided evaluation instruments.

The following sections describe the instruments to be used in this evaluation framework, and the rationale behind their selection.

2.2 UX Satisfaction with Emocards (Part 2)

After selecting the expert sample, the products to benchmark, and performing the six pre-defined tasks/activities, Part 2 of the evaluation framework follows – i.e., Overall Satisfaction evaluation with *Emocards* [23] in the context of each expert's experience and task completion for each community. Thus, before delving into the detail that a usability heuristic evaluation provides, this second part aims to register the user experience and overall satisfaction using the *Emocards semantic scale*.

As previously discussed, UX has a purely subjective and emotive nature – which characterizes and reflects one's relationship with the world. Therefore, it is important to develop products that match the user's emotions due to their wishes, interests, and needs. In this vein, Desmet and Tax [23] developed a tool that helps users to express their emotions without words, while using human-like representations of it – entitled *Emocards* (*cf.* Fig. 2).

Through an 8-item circle, participants can classify their emotions in terms of excitement (located on the upper side), calmness (located on the bottom side), unpleasant feelings (located on the left side), and pleasant ones (located on the right side of the circle) [23]. Thus, in each of the selected products/online social networks, and making use of the eight-element *Emocards* scale, the experts will be able to evaluate their interaction with the various products/online social networks by choosing one of the scale's elements as a score of a holistic perception of the emotions felt.

2.3 User eXperience and Usability Evaluation with Heuristics (Part 3)

After completing the Emocard UX satisfaction evaluation, and in complementarity, a user eXperience test, within a usability heuristic evaluation, is also performed.

As previously mentioned, there is a vast array of possible ways to evaluate an interface. Thus, for the purpose of this framework, a heuristic evaluation was conducted. In addition to the multiple advantages that it presents – *e.g.,* reduced costs, little planning required [24], and its ability to be applied at any stage of product development

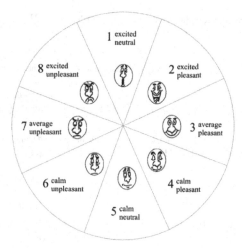

Fig. 2. Emocards. Adapted from *Designing Products with Added Emotional Value: Development and Application of an Approach for Research Through Design* [23].

[25] – Desurvire and Wixon [26] emphasize that this type of usability evaluation technique makes explicit what cannot be easily communicated due to being purely intuitive. Despite these advantages, Nielsen and Molich (1990) warn of a possible disadvantage related to this type of evaluation – *i.e.,* once the usability problems are identified, heuristics do not necessarily provide solution suggestions.

As a way of capturing the user eXperience, and understanding participants' feedback, each heuristic analysis is performed with think-aloud comments where each expert, enlightened by their eXperience, will have the opportunity to elaborate critically on the problems encountered.

A set of 10 evaluation statements derived from the usability heuristics for interface design developed by Nielsen [27] were created to evaluate the main aspects of a user interface in an online social network – *cf.* Table 1. These heuristics have been refined over the years, with its last update in January 2024, thus ensuring greater suitability to the current context of technological development.

It is important to note that, although separated in this table, both the ES and heuristics naturally have a common basis. Therefore, the ES should be used for the evaluation by the participants, and the heuristics for referencing during the analysis and discussion of results.

After applying this Evaluation Framework for each of the selected products/ online social networks, the data collected is analysed. The following sections describe the application of the framework to a set of Senior Online Social Networks, including the corresponding analysis and discussion of the results.

Table 1. Evaluation statements centered on Nielsen's Heuristics [27].

Evaluation Statement (ES)	Nielsen's Heuristic	Heuristic's Description
ES1. I was able to follow the progress of the online social network interface while carrying out the proposed activities	H1 – Visibility of system status	The system should always provide rapid feedback regarding the system's status, allowing users to plan their next steps
ES2. The language and terminology used were familiar and understandable	H2 – Match between system and the real world	The information should be presented in the most natural and logical way possible. In addition, language, images, icons, and concepts should be similar to those used by users
ES3. I felt able to control the online social network interface while carrying out the activities, navigating freely through the various pages	H3 – User control and freedom	When users take an action by mistake, they should be given a clear exit while stimulating their sense of freedom and confidence, and avoiding potential feelings of frustration
ES4. Similar types of information were presented uniformly on the different online social network pages	H4 – Consistency and standards	Industry standards should be followed, providing ease of understanding and navigation
ES5. There were clear instructions or validations to avoid mistakes when interacting with the online social network	H5 – Error prevention	Although it is important to notify with good error messages, it is even more important to prevent errors. Error-prone situations should be eliminated, or present a confirmation option before taking a potentially wrong action
ES6. All the information was easily visible whenever needed, so I didn't have to remember additional information while browsing	H6 – Recognition rather than recall	It should not be necessary for the user to remember information while navigating the platform. All information should be available and visible when needed
ES7. There was the possibility of using or creating shortcuts to carry out actions in the online social network	H7 – Flexibility and efficiency of use	Experienced users should be allowed to create and use shortcuts, making it easier to perform repeated actions
ES8. The online social network did not present superfluous information that competed with what was important	H8 – Aesthetic and minimalist design	Superfluous information competes with important information. Therefore, only the information strictly necessary for the proper platform's functioning should be displayed

(continued)

Table 1. (*continued*)

Evaluation Statement (ES)	Nielsen's Heuristic	Heuristic's Description
ES9. Error messages are clear, concise and provide a well-defined way to solve the problem	H9 – Help users recognize, diagnose, and recover from errors	Error messages should be clear, concise, and provide a well-defined way of solving the problem
ES10. The online social network provides additional information with informative icons or contextual support	H10 – Help and documentation	In an ideal scenario, the system does not need documentation. However, it may be necessary to provide it to help one understand how to perform particular actions

3 Application of the Framework

3.1 Selection of the Senior Online Social Networks

Resorting to the previously presented evaluation framework, a set of seven (n = 7) senior online social networks was selected. In particular, *Buzz50*[1], *Early Retirement*[2], *Gransnet*[3], *miOne*[4], *Older is wiser*[5], *Silversufers*[6], and *Stitch*[7] were the chosen online social networks according to the following criteria: (i) popularity among the target audience [28]; (ii) having the characteristics of a online social networks [29]; and (iii) the possibility of allowing the tasks/activities suggested by the proposed framework – i.e., (i) registration, (ii) login, (iii) profile completion, (iv) creating a post, (v) commenting on a post, and (vi) adding/following another user.

3.2 Recruiting the Purposive Expert Sample

To implement and assess the proposed framework, a purposive universe of subjects specialists in the area of Information and Communication Technologies was selected. Invitations were sent via email, with a three week deadline to complete the required evaluation activities. In the end, a total sample of 14 experts in the field was obtained. This sample integrates PhD students, PhD researchers, and university professors, all with expertise and competences in the specified domains.

---

[1] Available at: https://www.buzz50.com/ (Access date: 12–12-2023).

[2] Available at: https://www.early-retirement.org (Access date: 12–12-2023).

[3] Available at: https://www.gransnet.com/ (Access date: 12–12-2023).

[4] Available at: https://mione.altice.pt (Access date: 12–12-2023).

[5] Available at: https://www.olderiswiser.com/ (Access date: 12–12-2023).

[6] Available at: https://www.silversurfers.com/community/ (Access date: 12–12-2023).

[7] Available at: https://www.stitch.net/ (Access date: 12–12-2023).

3.3 Framework Application

The entire process of contacting and recruiting the experts and application of the framework was done online. As previously mentioned, the experts were invited by email. To expedite data collection and afford participants greater flexibility in undertaking the proposed tasks, the expert's inquiry was adapted into an online form.

Thus, data was collected using an online survey hosted on the FormsUA[8] platform. The questionnaire comprised seven sections, each corresponding to a distinct online social network. In each section, a series of standardized questions and designated areas for input were provided. Specifically, each section was structured into five key areas: (i) an introduction to the online social network, accompanied by a link for direct access; (ii) check boxes where experts could indicate which of the six activities were completed; (iii) select an *Emocard* element that represents their overall satisfaction after completing the activities, along with an optional area for additional comments; (iv) selection of the evaluation statements based on the heuristics they consider to be fulfilled in the online social network, with the opportunity to provide additional comment for each statement; and (v) upload images related to the online social network under analysis to highlight specific issues, with the option to include comments for each image.

3.4 Representation and Analysis of Results

As a consequence of the framework application and ensuring the proper response to all proposed activities, it is possible to proceed with the representation and analysis of the collected data. This is also a pertinent instrument of a benchmarking framework, allowing one to quickly visualize the design and interaction problem areas of a product. This section describes in detail the possible representation and analysis procedures recommended for this benchmarking framework.

Following the previously described data collection sequence, the analysis will start by presenting the UX satisfaction with *Emocards*. As previously mentioned, participants were asked to score the emotion felt after completing the six proposed activities for each online social network. Due to potential challenges in interpreting raw data on a radar chart for each online social network, an alternative indicator was calculated. Consequently, using the assigned numbering of each *Emocard* (1 to 8), the median, first quartile, and third quartile were calculated – cf. Table 2.

The radar in Fig. 3 represents an overlaid perspective of the variation in the different emotions per senior online social network. Specifically, each axis represents the various senior online social networks evaluated, varying their medians, and first and third quartiles. It should be noted that the lower the median value, the closer the overall evaluation of the online social network is to more pleasant emotions.

---

[8] Available at: http://forms.ua.pt/ (Accessed date: 12–12-2023). A service offered by the University of Aveiro using the LimeSurvey software – https://www.limesurvey.org/pt/ (Accessed date: 12–12-2023).

Thus, from a quick view of Fig. 3, it becomes evident that miOne and Stitch predominantly evoke an "average pleasant" emotion. In contrast, Gransnet is characterized by a prevailing "calm pleasant" emotion, while Buzz50 is notably marked by "calm unpleasant."

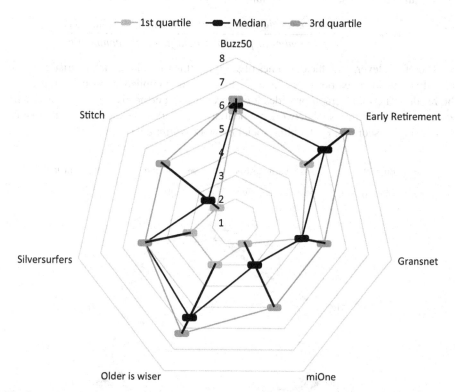

Fig. 3. Radar graph representing the distribution of emotions felt by senior online social network.

The second part of the data collection was to validate the conformity of the various evaluation statements based on the pre-defined heuristics (cf. Table 1) and the participants' comments provided for each of them. Since this is a user eXperience and usability evaluation based on heuristics, in which the participant's opinion and detail are requested after contacting with the evaluation statements, an integrated calculation was adopted. This analysis aims to focus more on the participants' perspectives and experiences, and obtain a normalized score. Therefore, to systematize the information collected, the following formula was created for each senior online social network and each evaluation statement (ES) based on the heuristics:

$$score = \frac{number\ of\ different\ problems\ identified\ (in\ that\ ES)}{total\ number\ of\ problems\ identified\ in\ the\ community}$$

As previously stated, the goal of this formula is to derive a normalized score for each ES within each senior online social network. To achieve this, the number of problems identified in participants' comments for each ES (numerator) is divided by the total number of issues identified in participants' comments for the entire online social network (denominator). The result is a value between 0 and 1, tailored to the characteristics of each online social network. However, to highlight the negative impact of identified issues, the formula has been adjusted to the unit value (1) subtracted from the score:

$$score = 1 - \frac{number\ of\ different\ problems\ identified\ (in\ that\ ES)}{total\ number\ of\ problems\ identified\ in\ the\ community}$$

Therefore, leveraging the outcomes of applying this formula to each heuristic across all online social networks – cf. Table 2, Fig. 4 was compiled to visually represent the results. The radar graph provides a comprehensive perspective on the diversity in scores for each online social network per heuristic. Each axis corresponds to a heuristic, showcasing its score for each online social network within the range of 0 to 1.

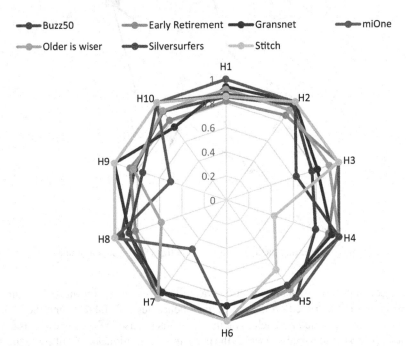

Fig. 4. Radar graph representing the variation in the normalized score of the heuristics in each online social network.

It is essential to recognize that a higher score signifies fewer identified problems. A quick look at Fig. 4 shows that Heuristics 1 and 2 are the most compliant, and that miOne and Stitch, despite being more uniform, display a few identified errors that assume significant proportions.

Finally, and based on the results previously observed, it is important to establish a macro indicator (MI) for the heuristics that would allow a direct comparison with the *Emocards* and, therefore, to understand if there is any relationship between the two. Thus,

Table 2. Results of the calculations made for the *Emocards* and the Heuristic evaluation score per senior online social network.

		Buzz50	Early Retirement	Gransnet	miOne	Older is wiser	Silversurfers	Stitch
		Senior Online Social Networks						
Emocards	1st quartile	5,75	5	4	2	3	3	2
	Median	6	6	4	3	5,5	5	2,5
	3rd quartile	6,25	7,25	5	5	6,25	5	5
Heuristics/Evaluation Statements	H1	0,85	0,82	0,94	1	0,92	0,88	0,86
	H2	0,97	0,86	1	1	0,92	1	1
	H3	0,76	1	0,81	1	0,92	0,63	1
	H4	0,79	0,91	0,94	1	1	1	0,43
	H5	1	0,91	0,88	1	0,92	0,88	0,71
	H6	1	1	0,88	1	1	1	1
	H7	0,94	1	0,94	0,5	1	1	1
	H8	0,94	0,82	0,88	1	0,58	0,88	1
	H9	0,82	0,86	1	0,5	0,83	0,75	1
	H10	0,91	0,82	0,75	1	0,92	1	1

a formula was developed to be applied to each online social network, which is characterized by the following: proportion of problems identified (i.e., the number of problems identified in the analysed senior online social network, divided by the maximum number of benchmarking problems that occurred in a product/online social network) multiplied by the total number of heuristics affected in that online social network. This formula is shown below.

$$MI = \frac{no.\ of\ problems\ identified\ for\ each\ product\ max\ no.\ of\ problems\ detected\ in\ a\ product}{\times} \times no.\ of\ heuristics\ affected$$

Leveraging the outcomes of applying this formula to each heuristic across all analysed products – cf. Table 3, Fig. 5 was compiled to represent the results visually. Based on what was already shown in Fig. 3, the new Macro indicator calculated was added. The radar graph provides an overview of the diversity of scores per online social network. As can be observed, each axis corresponds to a senior online social network, showing variations in the *Emocards'* median, first and third quartiles; and in the Heuristics macro indicator.

By observing Fig. 5, the following analysis can be done: (i) Sitch has the best score on the *Emocards*, but it has some heuristic problems; (ii) Gransnet has positive expectations, but it turns out to have a lot of heuristic problems; and (iii) miOne doesn't get the best score on the *Emocards*, but after a detailed analysis reveals that it is almost heuristically perfect.

In particular, both miOne and Stitch have very close medians and more dispersed first and third-quartile values – thus, their exchange of places in the rankings of the two

Table 3. Upward comparison of the Emocards' median and the Macro indicator calculated per senior online social network.

	Emocards median		Macro indicator
Stitch	2,5	**miOne**	0,12
miOne	3	**Stitch**	0,62
Gransnet	4	**Silversurfers**	1,18
Silversurfers	5	**Older is wiser**	2,47
Older is wiser	5,5	**Gransnet**	3,76
Buzz50	6	**Early Retirement**	4,53
Early Retirement	6	**Buzz50**	8

evaluations is not very critical or noteworthy. Nonetheless, Gransnet moves from third place in the evaluation with *Emocards* to fifth place in the heuristic evaluation, which is highly reinforced by its solid position in the median and respective quartiles analyzed.

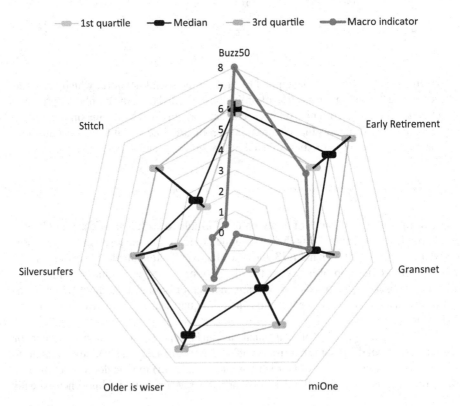

Fig. 5. Radar graph representing the comparison between *Emocards* median and Heuristics macro indicator in each online social network.

4 Conclusions and Future Work

In this paper, we considered the problem of comparing the UX and Usability of online social networks and representing the differences among them. We resorted to the particularities of analysing senior online social networks as a study case, in a panorama that reveals the high importance of developing a more universal design.

Through a framework divided into three fundamental parts, this benchmarking instrument provides a holistic overview of the UX satisfaction, and the User eXperience within a Usability Heuristics Evaluation. The sequence in which the evaluation is performed is different from the industry norm, but it is justified: it captures the general emotion of the participants towards the products initially, and to allow them, after the particularities have been analysed through the heuristics, to express the detail of their analysis. This ensures that the detailed perspective on the product doesn't influence the overall impression, thus providing more authentic results.

Following this vein, the think-aloud method introduced and its direct representation in the results, provides a very specific and detailed view of each heuristic and each product under evaluation and analysis.

The analysis and representation of results play a crucial role in constructing a benchmarking framework. On one hand, generating a normalized score for each heuristic of every product facilitates a direct comparison among the various products under analysis. On the other hand, the use of radar graphs – a standard in this form of data representation—enables a comprehensive overview of the comparison under analysis, while preserving every detail.

Moreover, the demo application of this Benchmarking Framework with a set of serve senior online social networks does not invalidate its application in other products. The instruments utilized are well-known, highly proven to be efficient, and easily generalizable. Thus, this proposed framework only addressed the analysis, representation, and visualization of data.

Ultimately, our goal was to achieve a straightforward yet effective way of representing and comparing results, with the added objective of understanding the key insights on the most impacted design fields.

In the future work, we believe that it would be important to understand the interaction and interface design recommendations that can be directly derived from this Framework through the think-aloud registration process. Additionally, a synthesis of these recommendations could be associated with the satisfaction indicators collected. Lastly, we also believe it would be important to apply this Benchmarking Framework to other online social networks and products, thus ensuring greater robustness and prediction of data representation scenarios.

Acknowledgments. The authors wish to thank not only the participants of this study but also Digi-Media, the Department of Communication and Art at the University of Aveiro. The study reported in this publication was supported by F.C.T. – Foundation for Science and Technology (Fundação para a Ciência e Tecnologia), I.P. nr. 2021.06465. B.D, DigiMedia Research Center, under the project UIDB/05460/2020, and the IC Senior X project funded by DigiMedia (GIP3_2022).

Disclosure of Interests. The authors declare no conflict of interest. Informed consent was obtained from all participants involved in the study.

References

1. Castells, M.: The internet galaxy: reflexions on the internet, business, and society. Oxford University Press (2002). https://doi.org/10.1093/ACPROF:OSO/9780199255771.001.0001
2. PORDATA: Indivíduos com 16 e mais anos que utilizam computador e Internet em % do total de indivíduos: por grupo etário. https://www.pordata.pt/Portugal/Indiv%c3%adduos+com+16+e+mais+anos+que+utilizam+computador+e+Internet+em+percentagem+do+total+de+indiv%c3%adduos+por+grupo+et%c3%a1rio-1139, (Accessed 29 May 2022)
3. Faverio, M.: Share of those 65 and older who are tech users has grown in the past decade - Pew Research Center (2022)
4. Pew Research Center: Use of online platforms, apps varies – sometimes widely – by demographic group, https://www.pewresearch.org/internet/2021/04/07/social-media-use-in-2021/pi_2021-04-07_social-media_0-03/, (Accessed 01 June 2022)
5. Pew Research Center: Social Media Fact Sheet. https://www.pewresearch.org/internet/fact-sheet/social-media/, (Accessed 01 June 2022)
6. Villani, D., Serino, S., Triberti, S., Riva, G.: Ageing positively with digital games. LNICST, pp. 148–155. Springer Verlag (2017). https://doi.org/10.1007/978-3-319-49655-9_20
7. Lee, H.R., Riek, L.D.: Reframing assistive robots to promote successful aging. ACM Trans. Human-Robot Interact. (THRI) 7 (2018). https://doi.org/10.1145/3203303
8. Langley, J., Wheeler, G., Partridge, R., Bec, R., Wolstenholme, D., Sproson, L.: Designing with and for older people. Intell. Syst. Reference Library. 167, 3–19 (2020). https://doi.org/10.1007/978-3-030-26292-1_1/COVER
9. Vandekerckhove, P., De Mul, Ma., Bramer, W.M., De Bont, A.A.: Generative participatory design methodology to develop electronic health interventions: systematic literature review. J Med Internet Res. 22 (2020). https://doi.org/10.2196/13780
10. Sumner, J., Chong, L.S., Bundele, A., Wei Lim, Y.: Co-designing technology for aging in place: a systematic review. Gerontologist 61, E395–E409 (2021). https://doi.org/10.1093/GERONT/GNAA064
11. Cole, A.C., Adapa, K., Khasawneh, A., Richardson, D.R., Mazur, L.: Codesign approaches involving older adults in the development of electronic healthcare tools: a systematic review. BMJ Open 12 (2022). https://doi.org/10.1136/BMJOPEN-2021-058390
12. Schrepp, M., Hinderks, A., Thomaschewski, J.: Applying the user experience questionnaire (UEQ) in different evaluation scenarios. In: Marcus, A. (eds.) Design, User Experience, and Usability. Theories, Methods, and Tools for Designing the User Experience. DUXU 2014. LNCS, vol. 8517. Springer, Cham (2014). https://doi.org/10.1007/978-3-319-07668-3_37
13. Chammas, A., Quaresma, M., Mont'Alvão, C.: A closer look on the user centred design. Proc. Manuf. 3, 5397–5404 (2015). https://doi.org/10.1016/j.promfg.2015.07.656
14. ISO: ISO 9241–210:2019 - Ergonomics of human-system interaction — Part 210: Human-centred design for interactive systems, https://www.iso.org/standard/77520.html, (Accessed 07 Feb 2024)
15. Boy, G.: The Handbook of Human-Machine Interaction. CRC Press (2017). https://doi.org/10.1201/9781315557380/HANDBOOK-HUMAN-MACHINE-INTERACTION-GUY-BOY
16. Nielsen, J.: Usability 101: Introduction to Usability, https://www.nngroup.com/articles/usability-101-introduction-to-usability/, (Accessed 19 Jan 2022)
17. Saavedra, M.-J., Rusu, C., Quiñones, D., Roncagliolo, S.: A set of usability and user experience heuristics for social networks. Presented at the (2019). https://doi.org/10.1007/978-3-030-21902-4_10
18. Saleh, A.M., Abuaddous, H.Y., Enaizan, O., Ghabban, F.: User experience assessment of a COVID-19 tracking mobile application (AMAN) in Jordan. Indonesian J. Elect. Eng. Comput. Sci. 23, 1120 (2021). https://doi.org/10.11591/ijeecs.v23.i2.pp1120-1127

19. Larbi, D., Denecke, K., Gabarron, E.: Usability testing of a social media chatbot for increasing physical activity behavior. J Pers Med. **12**, 828 (2022). https://doi.org/10.3390/jpm12050828
20. Faradina, H.R., Wahyuningrum, T., Prasetyo, N.A.AI.K.: User Experience analysis on e-wallet using a combination of heuristic evaluation and UMUX. In: 2022 IEEE International Conference on Cybernetics and Computational Intelligence (CyberneticsCom), pp. 46–51. IEEE (2022). https://doi.org/10.1109/CyberneticsCom55287.2022.9865427
21. Halim, I., Saptari, A., A.Perumal, P., Abdullah, Z., Abdullah, S., Muhammad, M.N.: A review on usability and user experience of assistive social robots for older persons. Intern. J. Integrated Eng. **14** (2022). https://doi.org/10.30880/ijie.2022.14.06.010
22. Schrepp, M., Hinderks, A., Thomaschewski, J.: Construction of a benchmark for the user experience questionnaire (UEQ). Inter. J. Interact. Multimedia Artifi. Intell. **4**, 40 (2017). https://doi.org/10.9781/ijimai.2017.445
23. Desmet, P., Overbeeke, K., Tax, S.: Designing products with added emotional value: development and application of an approach for research through design. Des. J. **4**, 32–47 (2001). https://doi.org/10.2752/146069201789378496
24. Nielsen, J., Molich, R.: Heuristic evaluation of user interfaces. In: Proceedings of the SIGCHI Conference on Human Factors in Computing Systems Empowering People - CHI 1990, pp. 249–256. ACM Press, New York (1990). https://doi.org/10.1145/97243.97281
25. Nielsen, J., Mack, R.L.: Usability inspection methods. Wiley (1994)
26. Desurvire, H., Wixon, D.: Game principles: change, choice & creation: making better games. In: CHI 2013 Extended Abstracts on Human Factors in Computing Systems on - CHI EA 2013, p. 1065. ACM Press, New York (2013). https://doi.org/10.1145/2468356.2468547
27. Nielsen, J.: 10 Usability Heuristics for User Interface Design. https://www.nngroup.com/articles/ten-usability-heuristics/, (Accessed 13 Jan 2022)
28. Nimrod, G.: The fun culture in seniors' online communities. Gerontologist **51**, 226–237 (2011). https://doi.org/10.1093/geront/gnq084
29. Wolf, M., Sims, J., Yang, H.: Social media? what social media? In: UK Academy for Information Systems Conference Proceedings 2018 (2018)

Author Index

© The Editor(s) (if applicable) and The Author(s), under exclusive license
to Springer Nature Switzerland AG 2024
Q. Gao and J. Zhou (Eds.): HCII 2024, LNCS 14725, pp. 433–435, 2024.
https://doi.org/10.1007/978-3-031-61543-6

Printed in the United States
by Baker & Taylor Publisher Services